ITALIAN CONFRATERN
IN THE SIXTEENTH CEN

The Madonna and Brothers of the Confraternity of S. Maria della Morte, Bologna, Miniature from the frontispiece for the 1562 Statutes (see pp. 82, 108, 219). [The brothers in the foreground wear full processional robes; some show hoods pulled over to preserve anonymity; some show the painted boards used when escorting the condemned to execution. The background illustrates a confraternity procession with Cross, outside Bologna, with its tell-tale leaning tower.] Reproduced courtesy of the Library of L'Archiginnasio, Bologna.

ITALIAN CONFRATERNITIES IN THE SIXTEENTH CENTURY

CHRISTOPHER F. BLACK
Department of Modern History
University of Glasgow

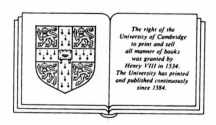

The right of the
University of Cambridge
to print and sell
all manner of books
was granted by
Henry VIII in 1534.
The University has printed
and published continuously
since 1584.

CAMBRIDGE UNIVERSITY PRESS

CAMBRIDGE

NEW YORK · NEW ROCHELLE · MELBOURNE · SYDNEY

PUBLISHED BY THE PRESS SYNDICATE OF THE UNIVERSITY OF CAMBRIDGE
The Pitt Building, Trumpington Street, Cambridge, United Kingdom

CAMBRIDGE UNIVERSITY PRESS
The Edinburgh Building, Cambridge CB2 2RU, UK
40 West 20th Street, New York NY 10011–4211, USA
477 Williamstown Road, Port Melbourne, VIC 3207, Australia
Ruiz de Alarcón 13, 28014 Madrid, Spain
Dock House, The Waterfront, Cape Town 8001, South Africa

http://www.cambridge.org

First published 1989
First paperback edition 2003

A catalogue record for this book is available from the British Library

Library of Congress cataloguing in publication data

Black, Christopher F.
Italian confraternities in the sixteenth century/Christopher F. Black.
p.   cm.
Bibliography.
Includes index.
ISBN 0 521 36487 6 hardback
1. Confraternities–Italy–History–16th century.   2. Italy–
Church history–16th century.   I. Title.
BX808.5.18B53   1989
267′.18245–dc 19   88–27456   CIP

ISBN 0 521 36487 6 hardback
ISBN 0 521 53113 6 paperback

Transferred to digital printing 2003

CONTENTS

ILLUSTRATIONS

Acknowledgements Plates 4–5 courtesy of the Foto Soprintendenza di Beni Ambientali Artistici Architettonici e Storici dell'Umbria, Perugia, plates 1–3 and 6–10 courtesy of Osvaldo Böhm Fotografo, Venice.

PREFACE AND ACKNOWLEDGEMENTS

A study of confraternities or religious brotherhoods in the early modern period should not be a narrow exercise in ecclesiastical history, but a wide-ranging social history. Though these largely voluntary associations were designed primarily to prepare members for the afterlife, they were fully involved in the social, political and cultural life of the community. Potentially, they could affect all men and women, as members, as the recipients of charity or as the subjects of ecclesiastical and social control. Confraternities organised Sunday schools and funerals, hospitals and orphanages, were patrons of art and music, harboured and pursued heretics, provided dowries and escorted condemned men to the scaffold. In studying these fraternal organisations in sixteenth-century Italy, this book deals with a key transitional period, when they expanded in numbers and diversified their activities in response to religious and socio-economic crises. Confraternities have attracted the attention of a variety of scholars with different specialisms—ecclesiastical historians and social anthropologists, art historians and students of guilds, musicologists and folklorists. Most of the literature on Italian confraternities has had a narrow focus. A few medievalists have attempted a broader survey across the peninsula. This book is however the first attempt to cover a range of confraternities throughout Italy during the early modern period, and to look at them from many different angles and perspectives.

My study combines archival research in Perugia, Bologna and Venice with a survey of the work of many kinds of historians who have covered, between them, a considerable area of Italy. It should have something to offer anybody who has an interest in early modern Italy. Those who have encountered confraternities in a limited context may appreciate having a wider view of their pervasiveness and roles. For non-Italianists as well as Italianists this book is also intended as a contribution to the study of Catholic Reform and Counter-Reformation, and to the discussion of philanthropy in early modern Europe.

While this book is intended to be comprehensive—in its span of geography and topics—I am only too aware of the gaps, of the archives, books and articles not consulted, (or consulted at the wrong moment without the opportunity to return to them in the light of other reading), the questions that have not been answered. It is hoped that by digesting, or at least indicating the existence of, a considerable amount of material, by raising a large number of issues while suggesting rather fewer solutions, this book will stimulate others who can spend longer in Italian archives and libraries, to proceed with further research.

As this book is aimed at those who do not read Italian as well as those who do, I have given most quotations cited in the text in translation (mine or others'). If the original Italian or Latin text is not readily accessible, or the phraseology is considered important for a specialist, this is given in the notes. Where the meaning is obvious, or where an English translation would not be very meaningful, the Italian has been retained. Quotations in the notes, primarily designed for the more specialist readers, are normally in the original, without a translation. Titles of confraternities and other institutions are not translated and churches, saints and personal names are given in their Italian form (e.g. S. Rocco, Carlo Borromeo), except in obvious cases where the anglicised version is very well known (e.g. St Peter's). Names of famous places appear in their English form.

My road towards this study has been long and twisted; many people have contributed to it. For some years I was preparing a book on the post-tridentine Church in Italy; my colleague Bruce Collins suggested that my discussion of confraternities merited a separate short study of them on its own. This book, later than anticipated and with many more ingredients, is the outcome.

The production of a first book, unlike an article or conference paper, allows the author to thank many people, and repay many debts of gratitude. A model history teacher, R.W. Harris, first showed me the delights of Italian culture, classical and Renaissance. Through the good offices of Erna Low, a stimulating guide, mentor and generous friend to many young people, I studied at the foreign students' university in Perugia; so began a love-hate relationship with that enigmatic city. I owe much to the encouraging supervision of Peter Partner, and to Roberto Abbondanza, the then director of the Archivio di Stato in Perugia, who made it a welcome and efficient place to study in the 1960s for my postgraduate research on Renaissance Perugia.

During a sabbatical year in 1975–6 I was able to undertake major researches on the post-tridentine Italian Church. Generous grants from the British Academy and the Carnegie Trust enabled me both to study in Perugian archives and to travel throughout Italy looking at churches, oratories and paintings from Milan to Naples and Lecce. The Carnegie Trust and the Court of Glasgow University have generously funded subsequent visits to archives and libraries in Perugia, Bologna, Rome and Venice, as well as excursions to ecclesiastical buildings and works of art in other cities. Stimulated by Brian Pullan's studies of Venetian confraternities, particularly the *Scuole Grandi*, I took a particular interest in Perugian confraternities as part of a broader study of post-tridentine church and society. I am grateful to the officials of the Sodalizio Braccio Fortebraccio for permission in 1975 to consult their private archive housing (it must be admitted rather inadequately because of their limited resources) the records of Perugia's three most important confraternities to which the Sodalizio is heir.

Having decided to publish first on confraternities I was able to use a sabbatical term in 1983 to write the first draft of this study. Since then the critical comments and encouragement of several Readers for Cambridge University Press have caused new dimensions to be added, more forthright conclusions to be drawn, and the text to be expanded. Some advice so offered was mutually irreconcilable in one book, but I trust all Readers will feel that what I have accepted and acted upon has produced an improved study that at least partly justifies their painstaking efforts. To them, and my supervising editor Richard Fisher, I am profoundly grateful. The rewriting process since 1983 has enabled me to add archival material from Bologna and Venice, and examples from early printed books—especially on attitudes to poverty—which have contributed to a more rounded study.

In producing this book I have incurred a number of other debts great and small. In Perugia—besides those already mentioned—I am appreciative of the help and encouragement of Mario Roncetti, Director of the Biblioteca Augusta, and his staff, and grateful to Giovanni Antonelli and Paola Pimpinelli, Director and Secretary of the Deputazione di Storia Patria per l'Umbria, to Don Costanzo Tabarelli, archivist of the Archivio di San Pietro, and to Professor Ugolino Nicolini. Hospitality and encouragement shown years ago to a lonely research student by Contessa Elisabetta Oddi-Baglioni (who also helped me gain access to a private family archive), and the Principessa Barberini are still fondly remembered. I am grateful to Francesco Santi and the photographic staff of the Pinacoteca for supplying illustrations of the works of Perugino and Alunno (5 and 4). In Bologna I have been most grateful for the Istituto per le Scienze Religiose—a specialist library which is an efficient and pleasant place to work—and to its staff. There I have benefited from suggestions from Professors Daniele Menozzi and Giancarlo Angelozzi. At the library of the L'Archiginnasio the deficiencies of its facilities are more than compensated for by the cooperation and friendliness of the staff at all levels that I have encountered. I am also grateful for permission to use an illustration from one of their archival volumes (frontispiece).

In Venice I am indebted to all those connected with the Fondazione Giorgio Cini at S. Giorgio Maggiore for inviting me to a Seminario in April 1984, where I could air my views on Italian confraternities, meet others similarly involved (in an atmosphere of generous hospitality), and reawaken my tastes and sensibilities when I felt most jaded. The international fraternity of Venetian scholars have collectively and severally provided much help and encouragement, particularly Alex Cowan, Nick Davidson, Giuseppina De Sandre Gasparini, Richard Mackenney, Paola Pavanini, Brian Pullan, and Bill Wurthmann. Richard Mackenney and Nick Davidson introduced me to the Venetian Archivio di Stato, and saved me much time by guiding me through its resources. I am particularly indebted to Brian Pullan, not only for the initial stimulus —reflected in the notes and bibliography below—of his *Rich and Poor in Renaissance Venice* and other published work, but also for his comments on an earlier draft, for securing an invitation to Venice, and for general encouragement and advice.

To Roberto Rusconi I am likewise heavily indebted both for access at a crucial moment to his own study of confraternities prior to publication, and for advice and stimulating companionship.

In Glasgow my colleague Thomas Munck has valiantly wrestled with various drafts, providing valuable suggestions and emendations. I am grateful to several generations of tolerant Honours students taking courses on the Counter-Reformation and on Poverty in early modern Europe, on whom I have inflicted various ideas, puzzling examples and unspellable names. Some have been stimulated to read and write about confraternities, and provided valuable feedback. Pat Ferguson made a valuable contribution in typing and improving the first version of this book. I am particularly appreciative of the services of the Inter-Library Loan organisation across the globe.

For permission to consult unpublished theses I thank Oliver Logan, Anthony Wright, Richard Mackenney and Bill Wurthmann. Unpublished material given in lectures and seminars by the last two has also proved valuable, as acknowledged in appropriate places in the notes. Michael Bury, besides helpful advice on religious art some years ago, has recently contributed some points about Umbrian confraternity banners in advance of his book on the subject. Maria Calace Torre kindly sent an unpublished paper on Bari confraternities.

It is argued below that confraternities could be in life and in death a more helpful community than the family. When it comes to writing books the family is hard to bypass, or finds it difficult to escape involvement–for good or ill. My parents generously supported me through student and research days, though sometimes doubting the wisdom of my historical pursuits. I hope they will accept this as in some way a return on their investment of faith and charity in my work over many years. The book has in various ways been affected by the adoption of foundling twins from Colombia, and chapter 9 perhaps reflects academic interests they aroused. As so often, there is also a suffering spouse to whom one owes most. Elizabeth's medieval and theological interests have saved me from various errors and misconceptions; her more recent experience in supervising postgraduate students of stylistics and linguistics has been applied in valiant efforts to loosen my contorted syntax and overcrowded paragraphs. Neither she, nor others who have been so helpful, are responsible for the sins of omission and commission remaining in this text. Finally, in place of fraternity assistance we have had by adoption and grace the support of Jessie Gardner, as a sorority on her own helping the family, making it easier to pursue my researches, and quietly encouraging this enterprise through its long gestation.

Christopher F. Black
Glasgow, June 1988

ABBREVIATIONS

AA.VV.	Various Authors (Autori Varii)
AEM	*Acta Ecclesiae Mediolanensis*
ASP	Archivio di Stato, Perugia
ASPietro	Archivio di San Pietro, Perugia
ASVen	Archivio di Stato, Venice
BCB	Biblioteca Comunale, Bologna. (L'Archiginnasio)
BCP	Biblioteca Comunale, Perugia. (Biblioteca Augusta)
Bibl. Vat.	Biblioteca Vaticana
Bol. Ist	Istituto per le Scienze Religiose, Bologna
Bol. Ist. BAB	Istituto per le Scienze Religiose. Biblioteca Archivescovile di Bologna. (The section now housed in the Institute)
BSPU	*Bollettino della Deputazione di Storia Patria per l'Umbria*
COD	*Concilium Oecumenicorum Decreta*
CT	*Concilium Tridentinum*
EHR	*English Historical Review*
F.O.	Fondo Ospedale [in BCB]
J. Ecc. H.	*Journal of Ecclesiastical History*
RSCI	*Rivista di Storia della Chiesa in Italia*
RSI	*Rivista Storica Italiana*
RSLR	*Rivista di Storia e Letteratura Religiosa*
RSRR	*Ricerche per la Storia Religiosa di Roma*
S.	San, Santo, Santa [Saint]
SBF	Archive of the Sodalizio Braccio Fortebraccio, Perugia
SS.	Santissimo, Santissima, Santissimi (Most Saintly, Most Holy); or Santi (Saints)
TLS	*The Times Literary Supplement*

Map of Italy

SETTING THE SCENE

IMAGES OF LAY CONFRATERNITIES, AND THE BOOK'S FOCUS

A confraternity, for present purposes, will be taken to mean a voluntary association of people who come together under the guidance of certain rules to promote their religious life in common. Normally this is a group or brotherhood of laymen, and is administered by the laity. There were some exclusively clerical confraternities, but this study is predominantly concerned with lay confraternities. Such brotherhoods could, however, involve clerics—and also women and children. Membership was not always voluntary, especially when the confraternity overlapped with some other social grouping, such as a trade guild. The complexities will emerge as we proceed. As largely voluntary lay associations, confraternities have played an important, if not well publicised, part in the religious life of Catholics, and have provided 'vital forms of social insurance in life and in death'.[1] Confraternities still exist in Italy and elsewhere, though much more discreetly than in the early modern period.

The term 'confraternity' is likely to conjure up varied images. Where Protestant or agnostic influences have prevailed the images will be coloured by tones of ridicule or unseemly barbarity. Luther attacked such brotherhoods in Germany as centres of immorality:

If there were a brotherhood which raised money to feed the poor or to help the needy, that would be a good idea. It would find its indulgence and its merits in heaven. But today nothing comes of these groups except gluttony and drunkenness . . . [They] should be snuffed out and brought to an end.[2]

Some readers will recall processions of men dressed in black, white or coloured robes with their faces hooded—possibly reminiscent of the American Ku Klux Klan; processions following a Crucifix and sometimes banners, with some brothers carrying smaller

---

[1] R.F.E. Weissman, *Ritual Brotherhood in Renaissance Florence* (New York and London, 1982), p. ix.

[2] 'To the Christian nobility of the German nation concerning the reform of the Christian state' in *Luther's Works*, eds. J. Pelikan and H.T. Lehman (55 vols., Saint-Louis and Philadelphia, 1955–75), vol. 44, p. 193; and cf. 'The Blessed Sacrament of the Holy and True Body of Christ, and the brotherhoods', vol. 35, pp. 67–9, on 'the evil practices of the brotherhoods... it's a swinish way of life. It would be far better to have no brotherhoods in the world at all than to countenance such misconduct.'; cf. R. Mackenney, *Tradesmen and Traders. The World of the Guilds in Venice and Europe, c. 1250–c. 1650* (London and Sydney, 1987), pp. 166–7, and pp. 67–8, 72 on Nuremberg confraternities as drinking clubs, and civic nuisances. Also on Luther's attitude, B.S. Pullan, 'Catholics and the poor in early modern Europe', *Royal Historical Society Transactions*, 26 (1976), 30.

crucifixes or candles, others flagellating themselves—in earnest with barbed ropes, or symbolically with silken cords. In modern times such processions have been associated with Spain, but recently from Italy there has been a colourful photograph of a Holy Thursday, Corpus Christi procession at Chieti, showing brethren in black gowns and golden copes.[3] Books about Venice reproduce a seventeenth-century print showing long snaking processions of confraternities in and around St Mark's square, as part of the Republic's major festivals.[4] The confraternities' contribution to Venetian pageantry is shown in Gentile Bellini's famous painting *Procession in Piazza San Marco;* now in the Accademia gallery in Venice, it once decorated the rooms of a leading confraternity, the Scuola Grande di San Giovanni Evangelista.[5] This gallery itself incorporates the former building of another confraternity, the Scuola della Carità. One of the most prestigious and powerful Venetian confraternities, the Scuola Grande di San Rocco, remains a major tourist attraction, displaying its large halls filled with Tintoretto's vast canvases depicting the lives of the Virgin and Christ, and his extensive panorama of the raising of the three crosses for the Crucifixion, [illustration 3.].[6]

The English diarist and gardener John Evelyn recalled his visit to St Peter's in Rome on Good Friday 1645 to see the major relics on show to a devout crowd, but the later developments were less admirable in his eyes:

and the night a procession of several people that most lamentably whipped themselves till all the blood stained their clothes, for some had shirts, others upon the bare back, with vizors and masks on their faces, at every 3 or 4 steps, dashing the knotted and ravelled whipcord over their shoulders as hard as they could lay it on, whilst some of the religious orders and fraternities sung in a dismal tone, the lights and Crosses going before, which shewed very horrible, and indeed a heathenish pomp;[7]

More darkly there may be images of hooded figures hovering like crows around the gallows, encouraging contrition and offering comfort to the condemned, ready to whisk the body away for seemly burial afterwards. When the essayist Montaigne visited Rome in 1580-1 he (or his secretary) gave an excellent description of work of the brothers of the archconfraternity of S. Giovanni Decollato as they accompanied a notorious criminal to his end:

They carry in front of the criminal a big Crucifix with a black curtain, and on foot go a large

---

[3] *Conoscere l'Italia,* (Novara), vol. 21: *Abruzzi-Molise* (1983), p. 70.

[4] B.S. Pullan, *Rich and Poor in Renaissance Venice. The Social Institutions of a Catholic State, to 1620* (Oxford, 1971), plate facing p. 135; E. Muir, *Civic Ritual in Renaissance Venice* (Princeton, 1981), p. 228, Giacomo Franco's *The Procession of Corpus Christi.*

[5] S.M. Marconi, *Gallerie dell'Accademia di Venezia. Opere d'Arte dei secoli XIV e XV* (Rome, 1955), no. 62, pp. 61–3; inscribed with his name, and dated 1496; it commemorated an event in 1444 when a Brescian merchant, seeing the Scuola di S. Giovanni Evangelista parading a relic of the Holy Cross, implored its assistance in healing his son, who then recovered. The painting has often been reproduced to illustrate discussions of Venice; see. e.g. M. Girouard, *Cities and People. A Social and Architectural History* (New Haven and London, 1985), Fig. 85 (colour); D.S. Chambers, *The Imperial Age of Venice 1380–1580* (London, 1970) ill. 5 (poor quality colour of part); F. C. Lane, *Venice. A Maritime Republic* (Baltimore and London, 1973), Fig. 16 (black and white); R. Rosand, *Painting in Cinquecento Venice. Titian, Veronese, Tintoretto* (New Haven and London, 1982), ill. 59 (black and white), and see pp. 89–90.

[6] Tintoretto and his work for the Scuola are discussed in chapter 11 below. 'Scuola' is the normal word in Venice, and some other places, for confraternity; it should not of course in this context be translated as 'school', as sometimes happens.

[7] J. Bowle (ed.), *The Diary of John Evelyn,* (Oxford, 1983), p. 97, (spelling modernised).

number of men dressed and masked in linen. There is a brotherhood of them, who, they say, are gentlemen and other prominent people of Rome who devote themselves to this service of accompanying criminals led to execution and the bodies of the dead. There are two of these, or monks dressed in the same way, who attend the criminal on the cart and preach to him; and one of them continually holds before his face a picture on which is the portrait of Our Lord, and has him kiss it incessantly; this makes it impossible to see the criminal's face from the street. At the gallows, which is a beam between the two supports, they still kept this picture against his face until he was launched ...[8]

Such pictures held before the condemned by the confraternity brethren still survive.

A complex pictorial reminder of the wide range of confraternity activity comes from Caravaggio's *The Seven Acts of Mercy*, which received wide publicity at the Royal Academy's 1982 exhibition of Neapolitan art. Hitherto, since its installation and until the oratory was damaged by earthquake, this painting was jealously guarded there by the noble confraternity that originally commissioned it and—unlike the patrons or clients of some other Caravaggio paintings—was pleased by his interpretation. The picture illustrates the acts of charity that confraternity members undertook when following the Gospel text, Matthew 25: 35–40; caring for the hungry, thirsty, strangers, the naked, sick and imprisoned. This text was an important guide to the practice of charity.[9]

Some confraternities are still active in Italy. This has come as a surprise to various historians and even knowledgeable Italian citizens, who thought they petered out after the middle ages, or during the period of the French Revolution. Most were closed in this latter period, but some survived unnoticed, while others were revived or were created after the Restoration, and then weathered the antagonisms of united Italy's early liberal governments. Visitors to Venice's Scuola di San Rocco may still be guided by a brother. Accident victims in Florence may be helped by brothers from the ancient Misericordia confraternity, based near the Cathedral and Baptistery, who maintain their tradition of helping the sick, by acting as part-time ambulancemen. Less obviously Naples' greatest confraternity, the Compagnia dei Bianchi dello Spirito Santo, is still active—even if its numbers and functions have diminished since the seventeenth century. The Santo Spirito bank, started by the confraternity, has long been divorced from it. There are apparently a number of confraternities in Bari, though my citizen informant suggests that the main reason for belonging is to ensure a fitting burial plot that might not otherwise be available.[10]

[8] D.M. Frame (ed.) *The Complete Works of Montaigne* (n.p., 1958), pp. 941–2; *Montaigne: Travel Journal*, trans. with introduction by D.M. Frame (San Francisco, 1983), p. 77; discussed by S.Y. Edgerton, 'A little-known "Purpose of Art" in the Italian Renaissance', *Art History*, 2, no. 1 (March 1979), 45–61, along with surviving paintings in Florence and Rome. The confraternities' services to criminals are discussed below, chapter 10.2.

[9] *Painting in Naples 1606–1705 from Caravaggio to Giordano*, eds. C. Whitfield and J. Martineau (London, 1982), pp. 125–8 and plates on pp. 65–7. See below chapter 11.3 on Caravaggio. A seventh act of mercy, burying the dead was added to the gospel list in the middle ages; these philanthropic acts as practised by confraternities are discussed in chapters 9 and 10. Cf. M.M. Flynn, 'Charitable ritual in late medieval and early modern Spain', *The Sixteenth Century Journal*, 16, no. 3 (1985), 336, 338–9, where she argues that the Seven Acts guided confraternities in 'creating a welfare program for society'.

[10] M. Miele, 'L'assistenza sociale a Napoli nel Cinquecento e i programmi della compagnia dei Bianchi dello Spirito Santo', *Xenia Medii Aevi Historiam Illustrantia Oblata Thomae Kaeppeli O.P.*, eds. R. Creytans and P. Kunzle (Rome, 1978), vol. 2, pp. 833–62; for comments on Bari I am grateful to A. Torre, visiting Glasgow as a political scientist, whose wife, M. Calace, is an expert on Bari confraternities during the Counter-Reformation period.

Historical writing in English has recently given greater prominence to confraternities in various countries in the early modern period, and their importance is better understood than when I first became interested in them. J. Scarisbrick has emphasised the vitality of English fraternities on the eve of the Reformation, though they disappeared quickly. For J. Bossy they were part of the fraternal, communal Christianity of the medieval world that lamentably gave way to the individuality of modern Christianity. L. Martz has indicated the strengths and limitations of confraternal philanthropy in sixteenth-century Toledo, P. Hoffman the parochial roles of brotherhoods in the diocese of Lyon. For Italy, B.S. Pullan, in his pioneering *Rich and Poor in Renaissance Venice*, had already highlighted (among other things) socio-economic functions of the top group of that city's confraternities; more recently R. Trexler and R. Weissman have pursued an anthropological approach and have stressed the socio-religious importance of these corporate bodies in a Florence that supposedly exemplified Renaissance 'individualism'.[11] A number of articles from British and American art historians have contributed much by wide-ranging or unusual approaches to confraternity art (such as S.Y. Edgerton's). My own book has benefited from this recent work for general approaches, as well as for cited details. All these works are restricted in their coverage of confraternities, concentrating on a comparatively narrow area, or on selected aspects of confraternity life and activity.

The Italian literature that deals directly or indirectly with confraternities is vast and unwieldy. Individual studies discuss limited geographical areas and/or restricted aspects. Much of the work has been poorly presented and argued, though it may contain useful nuggets of information; but in the last few years more important and stimulating work has appeared as scholars appreciate the importance of the confraternities in the early modern period. My survey draws on this extensive literature to indicate the different approaches that have been used in interpreting the importance of confraternities, and to depict the variety of experiences and developments through the Italian peninsula. The one contribution which comes closest to indicating the variety and variability of confraternity history as I have tried to approach it is the chapter on confraternites by R. Rusconi, which has now appeared in the Einaudi *Storia d'Italia*.[12] As will be made clear later, besides surveying and interpreting secondary literature I have added examples from archival research in Perugia and, to a lesser extent, Bologna and Venice.

The aim of this book is to present in English a study that covers a broad and diverse geographical area from densely populated urban centres to rugged rural regions, and to discuss the great variety of confraternities and their manifold roles in Italy.

The focus of this book is on lay confraternities in Italy, particularly in the sixteenth century. It is primarily designed to stress the wide range of activities of the societies, whether these took place internally within the brotherhood, or were conducted in the outside world. The book is not intended to present one particular thesis or single point of view other than to argue that confraternities had a key role—often neglected by historians—in the religious, social, political and cultural lives of a large number of Italians

---

[11] See Bibliography B, under these authors for the obvious works.
[12] *Storia d'Italia*, Giulio Einaudi editore, (Turin, 1972-), supplementary *Annali*, vol. 9 pp. 469–506. I am most grateful to Roberto Rusconi for giving me a copy of his typescript ahead of publication so that I could opportunely revise my own text, and for his friendly help and encouragement generally.

in the period, with implications for the later evolution of Italian society. However, my exemplification of the activities and policies of confraternities should contribute to debates on two broad themes in Italian (and European) history in the early modern period: (1) the nature and extent of Catholic Reform, and (2) 'the poverty problem' and the evolution of philanthropy in theory and practice. It might help the reader if I comment on some of my assumptions, and on the ways in which my evidence on confraternities links with these broader themes.

2 CATHOLIC REFORM, COUNTER-REFORMATION, AND CONFRATERNITIES

It is now generally recognised that western Christendom experienced a number of reform movements before the Lutheran Reformation, and that Italians contributed to such movements.[13] It can be argued that there was by the later fifteenth century a wide-ranging Christian reform movement, or series of movements, the antecedents of which can be traced back to the Devotio Moderna in fourteenth-century Netherlands. In this atmosphere there was a greater stress on the role of Christ as Man and Mediator, greater weight was attached to lay participation in religious experience and religious activity in the world, with the use of the vernacular rather than Latin as the means of instruction. There was an increasing emphasis on the individual's religious role, his personal contemplation and meditation (aided by instructional writings and mystical works), and correspondingly less emphasis on the role of the Church's institutions and the clergy. Deep piety and virulent anticlericalism could be combined. The 'Reformations' emerge from this background, though the resulting new established churches

---

[13] The discussion here has been influenced in particular by the following, most of which have extensive bibliographies: H.O. Evennett, *The Spirit of the Counter-Reformation* (ed. with a postscript by J. Bossy, Cambridge, 1968), esp. chapter 1 'Towards a new definition'; L. Febvre, *The Problem of Unbelief in the Sixteenth Century. The Religion of Rabelais*, trans. B. Gottleib (Cambridge, Mass., and London, 1983); *idem*, 'The origins of the French Reformation: a badly put question?', *A New Kind of History from the Writings of Febvre*, ed. P. Burke (London, 1973), pp. 44–107, but for a criticism of Febvre's views see also A.G. Dickens and J. Tonkin, *The Reformation in Historical Thought* (Oxford, 1985), pp. 287–9; J. Delumeau, *Catholicism between Luther and Voltaire: A New View of the Counter-Reformation* (with an introduction by J. Bossy, London, 1977), esp. chapter 1 and Bossy's comments; D. Fenlon, *Heresy and Obedience in Tridentine Italy. Cardinal Pole and the Counter Reformation* (Cambridge, 1972); A.D. Wright, *The Counter-Reformation. Catholic Europe and the Non-Christian World* (London, 1982), esp. chapters 1 and 6, which postulates an Augustinian age from the mid-fifteenth century that cuts across Catholic–Protestant divisions; H. Jedin and J. Dolan (eds.), *History of the Church*, vol. 5: *Reformation and Counter Reformation* (London, 1980), notable for its bibliography, but see pp. 431–2 for Jedin's brief comments on terminology in this context; J.W. O'Malley, 'Catholic Reform', *Reformation Europe. A guide to research*, ed. S. Ozment (St Louis, 1982), pp. 297–319, esp. 301–5 on Delumeau, Jedin, Evennett and on terminology; P. Prodi, 'Riforma Cattolica e Controriforma', *Nuove Questioni di Storia Moderna* (Milan), vol. 1 (1968), pp. 357–418; G. Zarri, 'Aspetti dello sviluppo degli ordini religiosi in Italia tra Quattrocento e Cinquecento'. *Strutture ecclesiastiche in Italia e in Germania prima della Riforma*, eds. P. Prodi and P. Johanek (Bologna, 1984); R. Rusconi, 'Dal pulpito alla confessione. Modelli di comportamento religioso in Italia tra 1470 circa e 1520 circa', *ibid.* pp. 259–315; M. Marcocchi, *La Riforma Cattolica. Documenti e Testimonianze* (2 vols., Brescia, 1967–70), for its introduction, plus brief notes about, and extracts from the writings of some reformers mentioned below. For a strong view largely dismissing Catholic Reform, and pre-Lutheran 'Reform' see R. De Maio, 'Riforme e Controriforma' in his *Riforme e miti nella Chiesa del Cinquecento* (Naples, 1973), pp. 11–29. For an impassioned lament against the failure of true 'reform' in Italy, P.M.J. McNair, 'The Reformation of the sixteenth century in Renaissance Italy', *Religion and Humanism* ed. K. Robbins, (Studies in Church History, vol. 17, Oxford, 1981), pp. 149–66.

on all sides were in many ways a contradiction, or betrayal, of the earlier spirit of reform.[14]

The term 'Catholic Reform' can designate those movements or developments which took place in areas ultimately remaining loyal to the Roman apostolic succession either before Luther's challenge, or contemporaneously with Protestant movements, but independent of them. 'Catholic Reform' after the schisms may also be applied to reform movements and attitudes which belong to the broader Christian reform movement, and were not primarily counter-attacking the northern reformations. This distinguishes certain attitudes and policies that cannot strictly be called 'Counter-Reformation'. The latter term applies to those reforms and activities that were fairly specifically designed to oppose and frustrate the Protestants, and to assert the traditional teaching and power of the Roman church. Counter-reformation attitudes increasingly tended to predominate after the ratification and promulgation in 1564 of the decrees of the Council of Trent, which had met intermittently from 1545 to 1563, but aspects of Catholic Reform attitudes remained powerful.

In Italy in the fifteenth and early sixteenth centuries there were some notable reformers, calling for conventional or innovatory reforms—the most famous being St Bernardino of Siena, Archbishop Antonino of Florence and fra Girolamo Savonarola. Among the lesser known were Ludovico Barbo who reformed the Benedictines, and Bernardino da Feltre who was one of the advocates of the Monti di Pietà, 'Christian' pawn-broking institutions designed to save the poor from the clutches of professional money-lenders, especially the Jews. (The support of confraternities for these institutions will be discussed later, in chapters 5.2 and 10.4.)[15] In 1497 Ettore Vernazza founded the Compagnia del Divino Amore in Genoa, the first of many companies of Divine Love for clerics and laity in many parts of Italy. They stressed the importance of an ascetic moral life, discipline, regular confession and communion, and charitable activities. Many other lay confraternities and clerical societies derived from them—most notably what became the new Theatine Order. These societies allowed spiritual renewal while the central church authorities remained deaf to calls for change.[16]

The companies or confraternities of Divine Love, representing the spirit of Catholic Reform, made an important contribution towards revitalising confraternities, and to what I detect as a move to a more outward-looking philanthropy in the work of such societies (see chapter 2.1).[17] Increasingly in the first half of the sixteenth century Catholic

---

[14] J. Bossy, contrary to many historiographical trends, sees the emphasis on the individual's own path to salvation as detrimental, when it replaced the vitality of the corporate popular Christianity of old: *Christianity in the West* 1400–1700 (Oxford, 1985), with the review by B. Bradshaw in TLS, 2 May 1986, p. 480, 'Utopia lost'.

[15] The Monti di Pietà spread from Umbria in the 1460s; see S. Majarelli and U. Nicolini, *Il Monte dei Poveri di Perugia* (Perugia, 1962); V. Meneghin, *Bernardino da Feltre e i Monti di Pietà* (Vicenza, 1974); Pullan, *Rich and Poor*, Part III.

[16] Marcocchi, *Riforma Cattolica*, vol. 1, pp. 137–40, 187–91, 254–9, 347–54. On the origins of the Companies of Divine Love: Pullan, *Rich and Poor*, pp. 231–4; P. Paschini, 'Le Compagnie del Divino Amore' in his *Tre ricerche sulla storia della Chiesa nel Cinquecento* (Rome, 1945); M. Bendiscioli and M. Marcocchi (eds.), *Riforma Cattolica. Antologia di Documenti* (Rome, 1963), pp. 9–15 for early companies, and the rules of the Genoese confraternity. Pullan, *Rich and Poor*, pp. 232–8, 257–8. See G. Alberigo's comments in his contribution to a *tavola rotonda* discussion, printed in *RSRR*, 5 (1984), p. 33.

[17] For general points about confraternity revitalisation from the later fifteenth century G. Angelozzi *Le confraternite laicali. Un'esperienza cristiana tra medioevo e età moderna* (Brescia, 1978).

reformers were challenged to respond with assistance for the less fortunate. The invasion of Italy by the French in 1494 made the peninsula a centre of international conflict on a much greater scale.[18] Armies were larger, the destruction by cannon greater, the imposition of taxes to pay for them heavier than in the past. Diseases, especially syphilis, spread rapidly. Many years in the 1520s to 1540s brought dearth and famine conditions throughout Italy, caused by armies, the elements and epidemics. The Sack of Rome by imperial troops in 1527 destroyed much in the city, and scattered many people throughout Italy to influence others. It was a major shock to end the complacency—religious or political—of a significant number of Italians.[19] Seeing the casualty lists of wounded, the orphaned, the sick lying in the streets, or unburied bodies rotting there, provoked the new religious orders and confraternities into action. (The impact of these conditions on the need for assistance will be discussed more fully in chapter 8.1). A Venetian nobleman, Girolamo Miani (or Emiliani) responded to the disasters of war in northern Italy by (among other charitable and religious acts) founding a company, Dei Servi dei Poveri (1534), to organise orphanages in various cities like Brescia, Como and Pavia (see chapter 9.5). This company or confraternity was later (1568) to become a full religious order, the Regular Clerks of Somasca, or the Somaschi, who became notable as educators of the urban poor.[20] The sack of Brescia in 1512 and the ravishings by soldiers led Countess Laura Gambara to found a refuge for the protection of vulnerable girls, the Conservatorio delle Convertite Della Carità; this stimulated the creation of many institutions to protect females at risk (see chapter 9.6).[21] The dislocations of war challenged religious reformers to take a philanthropic path to salvation.

In the later fifteenth and early sixteenth centuries the numerical growth of confraternities, and the diversity of their philanthropic activities were affected by Catholic Reform spirituality in conjunction with perceived increases in the need for assistance for the less fortunate. From the 1560s confraternities were likely to be affected by the Counter-Reformation mood, and became potential agents for reform under clerical supervision. The Council of Trent and post-tridentine reformers sought to ensure that

[18] There is no adequate modern study in English of Italian history in the sixteenth—seventeenth centuries, though much is hoped from the relevant volumes in the Longman series (especially that due from the late E. Cochrane which seems to have been almost complete before his untimely death). Beginners may derive help from P. Laven, *Renaissance Italy 1464–1534* (London, 1966) for background to the early period; from essays in E. Cochrane (ed.), *The Late Italian Renaissance 1525–1630* (London, 1970); readers of French can use J. Delumeau, *L'Italie de Botticelli à Bonaparte* (Paris, 1974). There is no short but suitable modern study in Italian. At great length there is the multi-volume *Storia d'Italia*, published by the Einaudi press; despite its cumbersome structure, its initial socio-economic and antipolitical biases (in part compensated for in the later supplementary volumes of *Annali*), it is invaluable. The extensive footnotes attached to most chapters make it a key bibliographical guide. Much valuable background knowledge can still be derived from L. Von Pastor's *History of the Popes*; K.M. Setton, *The Papacy and the Levant* (1204–1571) (vols. 3–4, Philadelphia, 1984) is a very detailed narrative that covers the international scene on a grand scale, and goes far beyond the topic implied by its title. (See my review in *History*, 71 (1986), 145–6.) On warfare; J.R. Hale, *War and Society in Renaissance Europe 1450–1620* (London, 1985).

[19] A. Chastel, *The Sack of Rome, 1527* (Princeton, 1983), esp. pp. 22 and 244 n. 3, where he quotes laments about 'Misera Italia', and 'Italia, afflitta, nuda e miseranda'.

[20] C. Pellegrini, 'San Girolamo Miani, I Somaschi e la cura degli orfani nel sec. XVI', AA. VV. *San Girolamo Miani a Venezia* (Venice, 1986), pp. 9–38; P. Lopez, 'Le confraternite laicali in Italia e la Riforma Cattolica', *Rivista di studi salernitani*, 2 (1969), p. 178; Marcocchi, *La Riforma Cattolica*, vol. 1, pp. 268–71; Pullan, *Rich and Poor*, pp. 259–62, 271, 278–9; idem. 'Le Scuole Grandi e la loro opera nel quadro della Controriforma', *Studi Veneziani*, 14 (1972), 103; AA.VV. *Storia di Brescia* (n.p.), vol. 2 (1961), pp. 453–4.

[21] AA.VV. *Storia di Brescia*, vol. 2, p. 451; see below chapter 9.4, on vulnerable females.

all confraternities—and any dependent institutions such as their hospitals or Monti di Pietà—were supervised by bishops (see chapter 3.1).[22] It can be said, with some reservations, that by the end of the sixteenth century the Counter-Reformation atmosphere resulted in increased dominance of lay confraternities by clerical authorities.

Various historians dealing with the Counter-Reformation, as with the Protestant Reformations, stress the growth of 'social control' over the populace by church and state authorities. The parish priests and parochial organisations were the key to this control.[23] Confraternities can be seen as part of the control system, as and when they were based in the parish church, operating from a chapel or altar there. The negative side was a loss of lay initiative. But the interconnections between parish and confraternity did have positive benefits and many parish-based confraternities, devoted to the Virgin Mary or to the Eucharist, were expressions of popular devotion (see especially chapter 3.4). The Counter-Reformation policy was not however all-embracing. Some lay confraternities escaped clerical domination and social control; this was most evident where the societies continued to have their own separate premises, or obtained new ones (as will be discussed in more detail in chapter 11.1). In these chapels or oratories one might detect the persistence of various strands of Catholic Reform. But a different form of social control is found when the social and political elite dominated the lesser orders within a confraternity (see chapter 2.2).

The nature and activity of confraternities in the early sixteenth century were affected by adverse social conditions. From the late sixteenth century confraternities were also challenged (but affected more adversely) by social troubles, and by the 'decline' of Italy. The 1590s in particular saw years of serious dearth, unemployment and brigandage (chapter 8.1)[24] The inadequacies of public and private assistance were revealed; attitudes towards the poor, and potentially dangerous elements, hardened. Yet it was clear, as in Rome, that state confinement policies were not the answer; philanthropic individuals and confraternities were needed (chapter 10.1).

There has been much debate on the nature, extent and timing of an economic decline in Italy that would supposedly have increased social problems and poverty, and so increased the need for confraternities and hospitals, while also possibly reducing the funds available for effective philanthropy. It now seems to be agreed that serious 'decline' did not occur until the 1620s and 1630s.[25] Up until then there were likely to

---

[22] The literature on the Council is considerable; concise summary and ample bibliography in Jedin and Dolan; see also my 'Perugia and post-tridentine church reform', *Journal of Ecclesiastical History*, 35 (1984), esp. 429–31.

[23] On arguments about social control see K. von Greyerz (ed.) *Religion and society in Early Modern Europe 1500–1800* (London, 1984), esp. the essays by R. Muchembled, J. Wirth, B. Lenman, M. Fulbrook, M. Ingram and J.-P. Gutton; all have full references concerning the debate; and see my review in *English Historical Review*, 101 (1986), 437–40. For the relationship of confraternities to such debates see e.g. N. Z. Davis, 'Some tasks and themes in the study of popular religion' and A.N. Galpern, 'The legacy of late medieval religion in sixteenth century Champagne', *The Pursuit of Holiness in Late Medieval and Renaissance Religion*, eds. C. Trinkaus with H.A. Oberman, (Leiden, 1974), pp. 307–36, 141–76.

[24] P. Clark (ed.), *The European Crisis of the 1590s* (London, 1985).

[25] See note 18 above for general books; see also F. Braudel, *The Mediterranean and the Mediterranean World in the Age of Philip II* (English trans. of 2nd edn, 2 vols., London and New York, 1972–3), esp. pp. 226–30, 295, 432–8, 594–606, 628–42: in rewriting this classic work, originally published in 1949, he postponed the 'decline' of the Italian and Mediterranean economy from the earlier sixteenth century to after 1600; idem, *Civilisation and Capitalism 15th–18th Century* (English trans., 3 vols., London, 1985), esp. vol. 3, p. 79 'the long age of prosperity of the "extended" sixteenth century was (after an Indian summer between

have been resources to support the ostentatious building and decoration of confraternity premises, religious display, and charitable work for the poor. Italy initially recovered from the adverse impact of the discovery of the Americas, the creation of the Portuguese and Spanish empires, the expansion of the Ottoman Turkish empire in the eastern Mediterranean and along the north African coast. If Venetian patricians retreated from long-distance trade, they were partly replaced by traders of lower status; investments were shifted to retailing, or to industries based on the dependent cities and rural areas of the mainland (Terraferma) like Vicenza and Padua, or to agricultural developments that were initially productive. Other parts of Italy may have gained, for a while, from the Spanish connection—by supplying troops and material for the Spanish armies attempting to retain or reconquer parts of the Netherlands, from the 1560s. Spanish Lombardy and the Genoese Republic (pro-Spanish out of necessity rather than admiration) were launch areas for Netherland ventures. It was probably not till the 1620s that the tax bills, especially in the Viceroyalty of Naples, became seriously damaging. Then Italian problems did increase. What became known as the Thirty Years War got under way, causing bank failures and crises in Italy in 1618–19. There followed indirect effects of the Germanic war on Italian trade, then the incursion of war into northern Italy, with the fight over the succession to the Dukedom of Mantua. There were devastating plagues in 1629–33 and again, especially for Naples, in 1656.

It could be argued that the mounting difficulties from about 1630, while they increased social problems and the number of needy poor, also reduced the ability and confidence of governments or philanthropists to provide solutions or palliatives. There is some evidence to suggest that enthusiasm for religious reform and philanthropy decreased or remained static in the face of these challenges—though we shall note some exceptions.

In the light of the above comments about Catholic Reform, the Counter-Reformation and the timing of the 'decline of Italy', it should be clear that while my main focus is on the sixteenth century, I am often treating it as 'the long sixteenth century' of F. Braudel and some followers—from the mid-fifteenth to mid-seventeenth centuries. The fifteenth century saw a new wave of confraternity enthusiasm, built upon some solid foundations of medieval corporate Christianity; then came the crucial problem of adapting to the new challenges of reformed theology, church organisation, and 'the new poverty'. It is not clear until well into the seventeenth century how the Italian church generally, the confraternities and their institutions more particularly, had responded to the conflicting challenges. Sometimes where it helps form a judgement about the effectiveness or otherwise of confraternity activity in our period, reference will be made to evidence and judgements up to the late eighteenth century.[26]

1600 and 1630–1650) drawing to a close . . . The Mediterranean system had already collapsed with Spain, Italy . . . and now the Atlantic economy was breaking down,' leading to the triumph of Amsterdam; R. Romano, 'Italy in the crisis of the seventeenth century', P. Earle (ed.) Essays in European Economic History 1500–1800 (Oxford, 1974), pp. 185–98, with comments on earlier debates; B.S. Pullan, (ed.), Crisis and Change in the Venetian Economy in the Sixteenth and Seventeenth Centuries (London, 1968); D. Sella, Crisis and Continuity. The Economy of Spanish Lombardy in the Seventeenth Century (Cambridge, Mass., and London, 1979); R. Villari, La rivolta antispagnola a Napoli. Le origini (1585–1647) (Rome, 1976).

[26] O. Chadwick, The Popes and European Revolution (Oxford, 1981) provides an excellent opportunity to take stock of the long-term impact of the Tridentine and other reforms of the church; he is particularly strong on the Italian scene.

3 ATTITUDES TO SALVATION AND 'GOOD WORKS'

The second debate on early modern European history to which some of my discussion of confraternities should contribute concerns 'the poverty problem': the extent to which there was an increase in poverty during the sixteenth century, and a change in attitude to how 'the poor' should be defined and treated.[27] My later discussion will demonstrate that confraternities reflected different attitudes towards the poor, and that a fair number of them made important contributions in assisting those deemed needy, and worthy of help. I have considered it desirable to explain at some length, in chapter 7, general attitudes to poverty; both modern ones that can affect our judgement of past contributions to the poor, and early modern attitudes that directly or indirectly may have affected confraternity activities. Italian confraternities shared the sixteenth-century view that some poor were more 'deserving' than others. They were 'discriminating' in their distribution of physical welfare benefits. (See especially chapters 7.3. and 9.1 and 2.) Medieval confraternities to some extent had rendered physical as well as spiritual assistance to their members, and to relatives, especially female. Certain early modern confraternities contributed also to the welfare of those outside their membership (chapters 9 and 10). Some confraternity philanthropy can be interpreted as a clear expression of a humane spirit of Catholic Reform. However, other activities reflected a 'social control' attitude that various types of poor should be disciplined and confined while their basic needs might be satisfied (see chapter 10.1).

Before embarking on my main discussion of the confraternities it would be as well to warn readers against certain possible misconceptions, especially as a preliminary look at the contents list might suggest that there were neat divisions between the internal and the external life of confraternities, between the spiritual and the physical, between brotherly self-centredness and outward-looking philanthropy. For ease of discussion and comprehension I have imposed divisions where these did not exist in the minds of confraternity brothers and where indeed there were complex interactions.

Misconceptions can arise, and false judgements be made of confraternities, from a failure to appreciate some contemporary attitudes to salvation and 'good works'. Firstly, 'good works', which—in the eyes of Catholics—could be a cause of justification and salvation, meant more than physical activity and 'alms-giving'. Secondly, in discussing the pursuit of salvation we are considering the salvation of both the donor and the recipient, and their inter-relationship. Our judgements on the efficacy of philanthropy and the role of confraternities have to acknowledge the priority usually given to the donor's salvation. Thus, thirdly, in dealing with philanthropic activities and institutions we should not be seeing this as the origins of a modern welfare state or society, which—presumably—is most concerned with the needs of the recipient. However, these activities and institutions did condition the eventual formation of modern social welfare. It might help some readers understand attitudes and activities both within and outside the confraternity if I elaborate on these points here.

The Reformation arguments about salvation by faith alone and salvation through

---

[27] For a preliminary consideration see Pullan, 'Catholics and the poor'; S.J. Woolf, *The Poor in Western Europe in the Eighteenth and Nineteenth Centuries* (London and New York, 1986), esp. chapter 1 on the background early modern developments. More studies of the problems of poverty and assistance will be cited in chapter 7.

works were likely to affect confraternities and their philanthropy. Yet in practice there were no major discrepancies between Catholic and Protestant areas in philanthropy and the treatment of the poor, and there were variations within each confessional area.[28] The Council of Trent in 1547 condemned by anathema the view that good works were merely fruits and signs of justification, not causes of its increase.[29] Catholics might deduce from this that good works not only *could* increase justification, but almost certainly *would*. This could have enhanced Catholic charitable action. Catholics also were ready to argue that Protestant attacks on the causal role of good works in receiving salvation would lead to selfish inwardness, immorality and the abandonment of charity. In reality this did not happen because, among other considerations, Protestants argued that–in the words of the Anglican Thirty-Nine Articles of 1553–while good works are 'the fruit of faith and follow after justification' and 'cannot put away sin', they are 'pleasing to God in Christ, and do necessarily spring out of a true and lively faith, insomuch that by them a lively faith may be as evidently known as a tree discerned by the fruit'. It was common ground that the fruit should be visible. Protestants attacked what they saw as the inefficient, indiscriminate and sometimes immoral charity, especially monastic, of the old church. As W.K. Jordan argued for England this possibly encouraged philanthropists to concentrate more on educational philanthropy and on the discriminating distribution of assistance. In Italy while there was an incentive to defend and build on old institutions such as the confraternities and ancient hospitals, awareness of the criticisms also made philanthropists more circumspect and ready to find new outlets; this will be indicated later in the context of confraternity philanthropy (chapters 9 and 10).[30]

The incentives to undertake 'good works' came from both a physical awareness of the need for practical help, and from theoretical ideas on the salvation of donor and recipient. The city of Brescia was at various stages in the sixteenth century host to a number of influential reformers and philanthropists, and created some model institutions. It has already been noted above that the physical impact of the 1512 sack of the city stimulated influential philanthropists. The citizens at the close of another crisis period in the 1530s were the beneficiaries of a moving oration from Isidoro Chiari, urging them to renew themselves in Christ and help the poor. Chiari was a leading member of the Cassinese Congregation of Benedictines; he was interested in Protestant theology, without succumbing to Protestant interpretations of St Paul and St Augustine. Part of his oration can be seen as a traditional homily against greed and in favour of charity, but some of the argument exemplifies the ideas of Catholic Reformers. He

---

[28] Pullan, 'Catholics and the poor', is a key preliminary study of Catholic–Protestant attitudes. Attitudes to poverty are further discussed below, chapter 7.

[29] G. Alberigo et al., (eds.), *Concilium Oecumenicorum Decreta* (3rd edn, Bologna, 1973) [hereafter *COD*] p. 680, chapter 24; *Canons and Decrees of the Council of Trent*, trans. H.J. Schroeder (Rockford, Ill., 1978), p. 45; *Concilium Tridentinum: diariorum, actorum, epistolarum, tractatum nova collectio* (13 vols., Freiburg, 1901–38) [hereafter *CT*], vol. 5, pp. 790–820; for general arguments about faith alone and salvation through works: B.M.G. Reardon, *Religious Thought in the Reformation* (London and New York, 1981), pp. 56, 102, 195–6, 249–50, 271–2, 311.

[30] Article XII of The Thirty-Nine Articles, 'Of Good Works'; Reardon, *Religious Thought*, pp. 270–1; see W.K. Jordan, *Philanthropy in England 1480–1660* (London, 1959), pp. 151–79, with Thomas Becon's attack on Roman perversions of charity (pp. 163–4), pp. 229–30, 235–6, with opposition to Rome being seen by some English as an incentive for Protestant philanthropy.

exhorted the citizens to recognise the majesty and *beneficentia* of Christ crucified, to remodel their lives to be nearer that of the Saviour; sinfulness would be cured by the Cross, and through a total response to the Gospel. All life would be affected by this renewal through Christ and the Gospel, and the new man so created would then help his brothers by avoiding anger, sharing his goods and giving to the poor. B. Collett in a recent study argues that there is a particular Cassinese doctrine, derived from St Paul and the Greek Fathers of the Church, stressing Sin, the Cross and a new life based on the Gospel. Chiari was here adapting it for lay consumption. The renewal of the donor through Christ would benefit him, and the poor of Brescia.[31]

Collett also sees this doctrine as an ingredient (mixed with the ideas of Juan de Valdés and of Calvin) in one of the most famous Italian religious works of the sixteenth century, the *Beneficio di Cristo*. One of its authors, Benedetto da Mantova, was affected by the Cassinese teaching. This spiritual manual, after selling thousands of copies and being recommended by leading reform bishops like G.M. Giberti of Verona, was condemned as heretical for supporting the argument that faith alone justifies. But parts of the book stressed the social responsibility of good works and that they could not be divorced from faith. The inquisitors seem to have succeeded in eradicating all copies from Italy. The fate of the manual may have curtailed the Benedictine theological contribution to Catholic Reform, but one suspects that the social teaching of the Benedictines had already had some impact, at least in northern Italy.[32]

An appreciation of confraternity philanthropy is complicated by the realisation that good works, *opere pie*, and *elemosina* (often translated as alms-giving), have wider and more complicated meanings than normally appreciated by Protestants past and present. *Elemosina* could cover all the Seven Acts of Mercy. When Cesare Ripa produced his major handbook on iconography at the end of the sixteenth century he commented on how *Elemosina* should be personified—though in his most influential edition of 1603 which was illustrated with woodcuts he did not include a picture of her. She was described as a woman of beautiful aspect, but veiled because though the giver of alms should see the recipient, the receiver should not know from whom or where it comes. Hidden hands give money to two children; to follow biblical precepts, 'nesciat sinistra tua quid faciat dextera' and 'ut sit Eleemosina tua in abscondito, & pater tuus, qui videt in abscondito reddat tibi' (Matthew 6.3–4: '[But when thou doest alms] let not thy left hand know what thy right hand doeth', 'That thy alms may be in secret: and thy Father which seeth in secret himself shall reward thee openly.'). Ripa then adds: 'Elemosina is a charitable work with which man succours the poor person by housing, feeding, clothing, visiting, redeeming and burying him'. A lighted garland around her head is to indicate one light lighting others, and that God will fulfil the promise of rewarding a gift a hundredfold. While Ripa is important for some influences on artistic formu-

[31] B. Collett, *Italian Benedictine Scholars and the Reformation. The Congregation of Santa Giustina of Padua* (Oxford, 1985), esp. pp. 140–3 on Chiari.

[32] Collett, pp. 172–82 on the *Beneficio*. The controversial literature on the latter is considerable, as modern scholars argue about the authorship, and the relative influences of Valdesianism from Naples or Calvinism from the north. Collett provides an up-to-date summary, and demonstrates the eclectic and muddled nature of the surviving text. English translation consulted: 'The Beneficio di Cristo', translated and introduced by R. Prelowski, *Italian Reformation Studies*, ed. J.A. Tedeschi (Florence, 1965), pp. 21–102. Cf. D. Fenlon, *Heresy and Obedience*, pp. 73–88, 91–6, 227 on reactions to the *Beneficio*.

lations, he can also be seen as codifying, in his interpretative comments on images, the views of fellow academicians in northern and central Italy.[33]

Good works and *elemosina* did not just mean this physical and monetary assistance, but also prayer, frequent confession and communion, and spiritual help for one's neighbour. When Michelangelo's *Last Judgement* painting in the Sistine Chapel came under attack not only for unseemly nudity in a papal chapel, but also for doctrinal offenses, it was defended from the latter charge by Gilio da Fabriano (who, however, was otherwise critical of Michelangelo's work). He exonerated Michelangelo from a charge of believing in salvation by faith alone, and said it was permissible to depict angels pulling saved souls upwards: 'for by this Michelangelo means to show the diversity of ways by which man can be saved; the rosary denotes that prayers are a means for salvation, other than faith, for without prayers and other good works it is impossible to be saved.'[34]

Good works included the spiritual *elemosina* of praying for the sick and dying, then for souls in Purgatory. Tulio Crispoldo, preacher and writer, published a collection of prayers for saying with confession and communion, and prayers for the period of death and for the souls of the dead. In one of his interlarded comments he argued that some of these prayers should be read and meditated on daily, because every day and every hour all over the world people were dying, who could not be personally helped. But we could contribute a spiritual *elemosina* for them, by saying prayers usually said in church, and in this way the Church helps us. Help for the dying, whether present or far away, known or unknown, was a major contribution from the charitable individual; it could help the dying face the agony of death, as Christ faced his agony. It could appeal to the mercy of the Lord to reduce that agony for one's neighbour or the friendless. Subsequently prayers for the souls of the departed could reduce the time spent in Purgatory and bring forward the soul's progress to Paradise. Praying for the living and the dead was one of the seven spiritual works of mercy—along with converting sinners, instructing the ignorant, counselling the doubtful, comforting the sorrowful or afflicted, bearing wrongs patiently, and forgiving injuries. In Italy, unlike Portugal, the seven spiritual works do not appear to get the same prominence collectively as the seven acts as a programme for 'good works'.[35]

[33] C. Ripa, *Iconologia, overo descrittione di diverse imagine cavate dall'antichità, e di propria inventione* (Hildesheim and New York, 1970; a photocopy of the Rome, 1603 edition, with an introduction by E. Mandowsky), p. 120. The first edition appeared in 1593; but the third in 1603 with woodcuts had the main impact, and spawned other editions. The personifications of *Elemosina* and of *Misericordia* (pp. 328–9), and *Povertà* (in three versions (pp. 408–10)), are female for grammatical reasons, rather than because it was necessarily expected that the donor and recipient of assistance would be female. See M. Warner, *Monuments and Maidens. The Allegory of the Female Form* (London, 1987 paperback edn), esp. pp. 64–5, 250 on Ripa.

[34] C. Dempsey, 'Mythic inventions in Counter-Reformation painting', in *Rome in the Renaissance. The City and the Myth*, ed. P.A. Ramsey (Binghampton, N.Y., 1982), p. 70, citing Gilio da Fabriano, *Due Dialoghi* (Camerino, 1564), p. 101; see R. De Maio, *Michelangelo e la Controriforma* (Rome and Bari, 1978), pp. 32–3, n. 71 and pp. 56–7 on Gilio da Fabriano.

[35] T. Crispoldo, *Orationi volgari per la confessione et Communione, et per lo tempo della morte, & anco per le Anime de Morti* . . . (Brescia, 1566), p. Bvi: 'Appresso sarà bene ogni di leggere, & meditare qualcuna di queste orationi, per che ogni di, & a tutte le hore, per tutto il Mondo moiono di molte persone, le quale non auiteremo, anchor che noi non siamo corporalmente presente alla morte loro, e saremo questa elemosina spirituale per loro, dicendo sopra ogni cosa de Pater nostri, in supplimento di tutto quello doue si mancasse, o altre Orationi consute nella S.R.Chiesa, perche in. ciò haueremo l'aiuto essa Chiesa'. Cf. Flynn, 'Charitable ritual', 342–3, where she notes that the seven spiritual as well as the seven corporal acts were part of the programme of the Portuguese confraternities of the Misericordia, of which 114 were founded between 1498 and 1599.

Confraternities spent much of their time praying for the souls of departed brethren; most had a policy of visiting sick brothers and their families, to provide spiritual comfort through prayer—and sometimes physical assistance as well. Increasingly through the sixteenth century some confraternities undertook to give spiritual and physical *elemosina* to those outside the membership. From the later sixteenth century specialist confraternities were increasingly formed to concentrate on the good work of praying for the release of souls from Purgatory. The Roman archconfraternity of Natività Agonizzanti, in the preface to its 1616 statutes, indicated that this was an important part of the reform programme of the post-tridentine church, with the rekindling of the spirit of the primitive church. By undertaking works of charity those who loved God could most honour Him by helping this society rescue many souls from eternal damnation. Souls were more important than bodies and help at the agonising point of death was the most efficacious.[36] Later in the century the record book of the confraternity Delle Anime del Purgatorio in Chioggia indicated that its members saw *elemosina* exclusively in terms of supporting daily prayers for souls in Purgatory that they might be rapidly released from torment and proceed to heaven and ultimate salvation. Physical good works for the living were not apparently their concern.[37]

Frequent confession and communion, and the encouragement of these in others, were similarly interpreted as 'good works'. The campaign to encourage the laity to confess and take communion frequently was accelerated in the early sixteenth century. One of the most important exponents was a leading lay reformer in Naples, Bonsignore Cacciaguerra, who initially had to convince his priest that frequent communion was not heretical for a layman. Eventually his *Trattato della Communione* (1557) helped revise this attitude. Cacciaguerra was closely associated with Dominicans and their lay protégés—some of them still admirers of the 'heretic' Savonarola, who was burned at the stake, and of his role as a spiritual adviser to Florentines in the late fifteenth century.[38] The Jesuits were, however, probably the leading promoters of frequent communion. Their work contributed much to the increase in confraternities dedicated to the eucharistic Sacrament, as we shall see. It could have meant that many lay brethren felt they had fulfilled the injunctions in favour of good works by promoting reception of and devotion to the eucharist, and were less impelled towards more practical good neighbourliness. However, some reformers stressed the interconnection of the sacraments of confession and eucharist with charity—expecting the ambiguous word *caritas* to be interpreted as practical love of one's neighbour. Fra Giovanbattista da Napoli in 1569 argued that: 'the reason why our times abound in iniquity and the charity of many is frozen, is because the holy sacraments of confession and communion are not frequented . . . Sin separates man from God, confession returns him to God, communion unites him with God'.[39]

---

[36] V. Paglia, 'Le confraternite e i problemi della morte a Roma nel Sei–Settecento', *RSRR*, 5 (1984), 208–11, where he quotes extensively from the Proemio to the manuscript of the 1616 statutes.

[37] ASVen Scuole piccole, Busta 31, 'Libro de Ballottati 1666–1718'.

[38] R. De Maio, *Bonsignore Cacciaguerra un mistico senese nella Napoli del Cinquecento* (Milan and Naples, 1965); M. Rosa, 'Vita religiosa e pietà eucaristica nella Napoli del Cinquecento' in his *Religione e società nel Mezzogiorno tra Cinque e Seicento* (Bari, 1976); Black, 'Perugia and post-tridentine church reform', p. 434 n. 18; copies of Cacciaguerra's correspondence in BCP Ms 135 and Ms 479. On eucharist devotion and the confraternities see below, chapter 4.4 and 4.5.

[39] P. Lopez, 'Le confraternite laicali', 191–2 and n. 104, 185 (quotation), 185–98 (Jesuit attitudes to communion).

Thus good works could be interpreted in many diverse ways; the heightened awareness of their role, through the Reformation controversies, could lead to practical or spiritual help for others, to consolidation of old ways, or the introduction of new.

The pursuit of salvation through philanthropy had two aims: the salvation of the receiver, but also that of the giver. Tulio Crispoldo, in the book of prayers cited above, stressed that charity through prayer might help secure grace for the person praying as well. As the Roman archconfraternity of Orazione e Morte put it: 'He who will have charity will show it with works of piety and mercy done for his neighbour for the love of God. We want the brothers and sisters of this archconfraternity to give abundantly of these fruits, being fruits of eternal life, that with the works of mercy they may reach the Kingdom of Heaven.'[40] The extent to which confraternity members looked beyond their own salvation, and considered the recipient—his physical well-being in this world, and his spiritual salvation hereafter—depended on varied and complex attitudes to the poor and needy. As will be discussed more fully later (chapters 7 and 8.1), there was argument and debate about poverty throughout the period, and a belief that conditions for the poor were deteriorating. Some were shocked by current social conditions, recognised that there were deserving poor—made poor by old age, widowhood, illness, enforced unemployment— and promoted confraternity and/or hospital activity which was designed to provide effective remedies in this world. Others saw poverty largely as the fault of the poor, or treated it as a divine castigation, with no remedy on earth. They concentrated on achieving the salvation of the giver, and possibly that of the recipient. Philanthropy for them was a spiritual affair, any practical results of limited interest.[41]

One of the best expressions of the humanity of Catholic Reform can be found in the statutes (1578) of the Roman archconfraternity of SS. Trinità, which argued that love (carità) towards one's neighbour (il prossimo) derived from love of God; this is learned from the first three precepts of the Ten Commandments which deal with the love of God, while the others concern one's neighbour. Love of God is the principal reason for loving one's neighbour; love of God will inspire love for one's neighbour, and so all the works undertaken for his benefit and help. Furthermore the word prossimo meant each person—whether citizen or foreigner, friend or enemy—who with us can walk in eternal blessedness. This confraternity was already widely renowned for its help and loving care towards pilgrims to Rome (notably during the Holy Jubilee of 1575), and towards the convalescent sick of the holy city.[42]

[40] Paglia, 'Le confraternite', p. 208: 'Chi haverà dunque carità lo mostrerà con l'opere di pietà e misericordia fatte al prossimo per l'amor di Dio. Di questi frutti desideriamo che abbondino li fratelli e sorelle di questa archiconfraternita essendo frutti di vita eterna, perciocche con l'opere di misercordia s'acquista il Regno di Cielo'.

[41] L. Fiorani, 'Religione e Povertà. Il dibattito sul pauperismo a Roma tra cinque e seicento', RSRR, 3 (1979), 43–131; B. Geremek, 'Il pauperismo nell'età preindustriale (sec. XIV–XVIII)' in Storia d'Italia, vol. 5 (1): I Documenti, 669–98; B.S. Pullan, 'Poveri, mendicanti e vagabondi (secoli XIV–XVII)', Storia d'Italia, Annali, vol. 1, pp. 981–1047; V. Paglia, 'La Pietà dei Carcerati': Confraternita e Società a Roma nei secoli XVI–XVIII (Rome, 1980), pp. 46–71.

[42] L. Fiorani, 'L'esperienza religiosa nelle confraternite romane tra cinque e seicento', RSRR, 5 (1984), 191: 'Quale sia questa vera carità verso il prossimo si può imparare dalli tre primi precetti del decalogo che hanno per subietto e materia Dio, et gli altri il prossimo et però bisogna che la carità verso il prossimo sia in noi dalla carità verso Dio, et quindi sequirà che entrando noi a fare quest'opere di carità, le faremo principalissamente per amor di dio, del quale accesi et infiammati produrrà in noi l'amor verso il prossimo, et consequente tutte l'opere, che potremmo a beneficio et a sovventione di lui. Et è da sapersi che questo vocabolo prossimo significa al presente ciascuno che insieme con noi può camminare nella eterna beatitudine, sia cittadino, forestiero, amico o nemico, il che si trahe dalla dottrina di Cristo'.

The 1563 statutes of the Roman confraternity Madonna della Pietà della Casa, which offered hospital services, indicated that its work arose from a direct reaction to current misery:

Some desirous of fulfilling the law and of serving Our Lord, and often finding certain poor wretches [*meschini*] lying in the streets and dying of cold, were moved by compassion for their misery and thought to provide a bed or two in a small house where they could succour these poor; so they began, and as charity grew in them they began to increase the number of beds, and so their mercy [*misericordia*] grew and their hospitality, not only towards these poor but also to strangers who found themselves with nowhere to stay.[43]

The Roman archconfraternity Pietà dei Carcerati (which, as we shall see later, became responsible for many prisoners) showed a more complex attitude. The brotherhood's aim was 'to exercise themselves in works of piety generally, but primarily towards poor prisoners'; this was not a pursuit of pure philanthropy or glory 'but primarily to procure the salvation of the soul and only secondly that of the body'. Works of piety were to be undertaken 'without regard to anything but the glory of God and the benefit of one's neighbour [*il prossimo*]'. The dedication to the salvation of those poorer than oneself was a condition of seeking one's own salvation; the prize consisted 'in being made worthy of hearing Our Lord Jesus Christ's voice 'in carcere eram et venistis' (I was in prison and you came to me).[44]

The Pietà confraternity was sponsored by the Jesuits and was particularly influenced by A. Possevino, who helped compose the first edition of the rules, and by G. Loarte, whose books of spiritual advice were provided by the confraternity for Roman prisoners. These Jesuit writers and preachers, and subsequently Roberto Bellarmino, had a major impact on attitudes to the poor, and to philanthropy.[45] Possevino told a Naples confraternity that nothing was more useful for a spiritual life than carrying out works of piety; but such works were as much spiritual as corporal. Charity was necessary for salvation, and Matthew 25: 35–40 was an excellent text for confraternity action. In his influential booklet on the art of dying well Cardinal Bellarmino, the leading Jesuit controversialist at the end of the sixteenth century, turned his attention to the rich man: he might legitimately gain riches, but must render account of his administration, since he was not master (*padrone*) of his wealth. In particular he should consider the poor about him. There is no doubt, he argued, that the rich man should give *elemosina*, as Matthew 25: 45–6 showed. Not to give was a kind of theft. But the fruits and benefits of *elemosina* are copious: freedom from eternal death; satisfaction; a way of disposing grace. Performed by a just man with true charity it merits eternal life; like baptism as St Cyprian, St Ambrose and St John Chrysostom argued, it cancels sin; it increases trust in God and produces spiritual happiness; it acquires the benevolence of many; it disposes one towards sanctifying grace (Proverbs 15: 27); it might even increase temporal goods, as suggested by the miracle of the loaves and fishes. But the method and attitude must be right: to please God, not to acquire popularity; *elemosina* must be given quickly and spontaneously, not grudgingly after much pleading; given as widely and generously as

---

[43] Fiorani, 'Religione e povertà', p. 105.
[44] Paglia, '*La Pietà dei Carcerati*', pp. 129–33, esp. p. 130; the reference is to Matthew 25: 36; see M. Rosa et al. 'Poveri ed emarginati. Un problema religioso', *RSRR*, 3 (1979), 11–41, discussion.
[45] On Possevino and Loarte: Paglia, '*La Pietà dei Carcerati*', pp. 114, 131–6, 176–7; on Bellarmino: Fiorani, 'Religione e Povertà', pp. 54–61.

possible after due consideration of what is surplus to the donor's requirements, and charity should be given to the poor. The kind of giving from superfluity can vary: some may legitimately be spent on a church or cemetery, on paying dowries for poor girls to marry, helping the multitudes of sick people in hospital, or the mendicants in the squares, or releasing slaves. Bellarmino here was concentrating on the dying rich man, and had no discussion on the effects on the poor.[46] Elsewhere he argued that the poor should live poorly, and not expect too much help, and he reflected the resentment, current in Rome at least at the end of the century, against the begging poor, the criminal and undeserving, who took advantage of generous donors.[47]

A little later P. De Angelis, a Sicilian priest who came to study theology in Rome, argued in another notable treatise that poverty was an irreversible castigation, but that it provided a valuable opportunity to have some influence in the Final Judgement. Material alms-giving was necessary in this life, but even more so for the future. Again he was concerned with saving the rich man's soul; what he loses here, he gains, and more, in heaven:

Such is the debt of charity, the more a man gives, the more he becomes a creditor; whatever you give in alms here on earth, you deposit in heaven, and whatever you give to your brother, you keep for yourself, so it is with alms, by answering to the needs of another, you yourself acquire merit, and by helping others you yourself profit.[48]

In one of his crisper passages he argues that: '*Limosina* cleans, frees, redeems, protects, requests, entreats, perfects, blesses, justifies, and saves the soul of the sinner, purges it so that it is rendered capable of receiving grace and mercy from our Lord God'. He concludes, after a lengthy discourse on the Acts of Mercy, that 'the justice of he who distributes and gives to the poor lasts for eternity'.[49]

Such attitudes, expressed sometimes by those who also sponsored and advised confraternities, or who provided manuals well enough known to have influenced sponsors or brethren, were likely to foster confraternity philanthropy. But this background exemplification of attitudes is designed to warn the unwary. Concepts of salvation, of good works, were complicated. The spiritual dimensions were as important as the physical. There were complex relationships between the donor and the recipient of philanthropy. The donor's soul might be seen as having a higher priority than the soul or body of the recipient. These factors must affect how we judge the intentions and effectiveness of confraternities. The interconnection of the spiritual and the physical should also be remembered later, when—for convenience of description and analysis—aspects of a confraternity's spiritual and philanthropic life are treated separately.

4 THE PROBLEM OF SOURCES

To explain why some assessments can, or cannot, be made at present about the roles of confraternities in early modern society it is necessary to understand what sources have

[46] R. Bellarmino, *L'arte di ben morire* was first published in 1619. I have used *Dell'Arte di Ben Morire* (Florence, 1927), translated from the Latin edn, and have summarised Bk 1, chapter 9, the ninth precept on *L'elemosina*, pp. 64–75, and Book 2 chapter 5, pp. 169–70.
[47] Paglia, 'La Pietà dei Carcerati', pp. 153–6; Fiorani, 'Religione e Povertà'; see below chapter 2.
[48] Fiorani, 'Religione e povertà', pp. 61–6, quoting p. 63.
[49] P. De Angelis, *Della limosina overo opere che si assicurano nel giorno del final giuditio* (Rome, 1615 edn), pp. 59, 66, 415.

been available, and the strengths or limitations of the different types of evidence. There are major discrepancies between what is available for the larger urban areas of north and central Italy, and for the rest of the peninsula. But there are also contrasts between the formal material that tells us what should have happened, and other evidene about what did take place.

Much of confraternity history has been written on the evidence of formal confraternity statutes. These sometimes survive in manuscript, but many were printed after the mid-sixteenth century, especially once bishops asserted their claims, after the Council of Trent, to supervise the confraternities (chapter 3.1). Many books, theses and articles reproduce the old statutes, and comment on such theoretical material. These sources present a clear view of what confraternity officials, episcopal authorities or spiritual advisers wanted to happen formally and are sometimes an excellent guide to underlying mentalities and spirituality. The statutes are eloquent on officials, elections, and sometimes on moral behaviour (see especially chapter 4.1 and 2.2(e)). They are much less revealing, even theoretically, on religious practices or charitable activities, though they can guide us on attitudes about who should be assisted (chapter 9.1–2).

The next major sources of information have been the visitation records. These are of two major types: the extensive reports of bishops or apostolic visitors after official tours of parishes, and the shorter *visitationes ad limina*. After Trent episcopal visitations became more frequent and thorough. If bishops were negligent, or if the local bishop felt he lacked the power and resources to conduct his own visitation effectively, the pope could appoint an apostolic visitor (often an experienced diocesan bishop from elsewhere) to investigate. He was granted supplementary authority to deal with religious Orders, or lay institutions like confraternities and hospitals that might claim exemption from the ordinary bishop's visitation. Some extensive reports from these visitations survive, and have been studied and published, but many are largely inaccessible in poorly organised and underfunded episcopal archives. The reports are often extremely cumbersome and difficult to analyse. They are valuable in indicating where confraternities existed, and may give some evidence on financial resources, on numbers involved, or the state of buildings. The visitors seldom got involved in detailed questioning of lay members and their activities, but we can sometimes use them for value judgements on the vitality or otherwise of confraternities.[50]

For the period from the 1590s onwards historians can also use the reports of *visitationes ad limina*. In 1585 Sixtus V, to improve papal control over diocesan reform, ordered all bishops to come to Rome at stated intervals to report on their dioceses and be instructed. In the case of Italy, Dalmatia and nearby islands this was to happen every three years. The bishop was to deposit a report on the state of his diocese; if he was

---

[50] U. Mazzone and A. Turchini (eds.) *Le visite pastorali. Analisi di una fonte* (Bologna, 1985), esp. for Italy, A. Turchini, 'Studio, inventario, regesto, edizione degli atti delle visite pastorali: esperienze italiane e problemi aperti', pp. 97–148, and 'Tesi di laurea relative a visite pastorali italiane (dal 1958 al 1984)', pp. 207–70, including a list of 608 theses; C. Russo, *Chiesa e comunità nella diocesi di Napoli tra Cinque e Settecento* (Naples, 1984) is an example of an extensive use of visitation material, not always well digested or helpfully presented; M. Grosso and M.F. Mellano, *La Controriforma nella Arcidiocesi di Torino (1558–1610)* (3 vols., Vatican City, n.d. [c. 1957]) was based on visitation records; cf. briefer studies, G. Casagrande, 'Ricerche sulle confraternite delle diocesi di Spoleto e Perugia da "visitationes" cinquecentesche', *BSPU*, 75 (1978), 31–61'; L. Proietti Pedetta, 'Le visite apostoliche e pastorali nelle diocesi di Foligno, Assisi ed Orvieto', AA.VV. *Orientamenti di una regione attraverso i secoli*. (Perugia, 1978), pp. 543–65.

unable to do so, the report was to be lodged by a deputy. The reports do contain valuable information. For confraternities and hospitals they record rough numbers of institutions, and sometimes their names, indicating their type. They are of little value for membership numbers or the extent and efficiency of activities undertaken. They have been shown to under-record when the bishop only counted confraternities he had officially sanctioned and modernised. Figures, if given, are often rounded approximates. Reports may have been distorted by the bishop's wish to emphasise to Rome what he had achieved, or the problems he had courageously tackled—or the impossibility of his task.[51]

The *ad limina* reports, which survive in large numbers in the Vatican, were to have been the major source for the ecclesiastical maps and assessments in the great historical Atlas of Italy projected a few years ago. The Atlas has been hit by financial crises, but some interim by-products have emerged and have been particularly used in this book for parts of southern Italy. The limitations of the Atlas evidence, and of the visitations records have affected what can be achieved in quantifying the confraternities and allied institutions (see chapter 2.3).[52]

The third category of sources that can be used are the archival documents generated by the confraternities themselves. Confraternity archives have been inadequately studied, especially outside the major cities like Venice and Florence. Given the fate of confraternities in the later eighteenth and nineteenth centuries the survival rate for materials has been poor; what does exist is scattered amongst state and ecclesiastical archives, and a few surviving private archives (such as that of the Sodalizio Braccio Fortebraccio, Perugia which I have used). Much of the confraternity documentation was haphazard and ill-written in the first place. Past and present deficiencies mean that it is very difficult to find reasonably long-running series—whether of minute books or accounts—to provide systematic analyses of long-term developments. That said, much can be learned from looking at different examples of the confraternities' in-house records.

Most revealing of the confraternity records can be the minute books of official meetings. These indicate what preoccupied the active members, how they arrived at decisions, what priorities they had for activities or expenditure, and how thorough or not they were about supervising the membership. In conjunction with these records there may be evidence about petitions for assistance, or testimonial letters. I have quoted at length from such records which I found in Perugia, Venice and Bologna to elucidate the inner workings of confraternity organisation. Membership records are fairly rare,

---

[51] Jedin and Dolan, p. 506; M. Spedicato, 'Episcopato, instituzioni ecclesiastiche e vita religiosa a Bitonto nel XVII secolo attraverso le "Relationes ad limina"', *Cultura e Società a Bitonto nel sec. XVII*, ed. V. Garafalo (Bitonto, 1980), pp. 62–94), with warnings about the limitations of this source material.

[52] L. Donvito and B. Pellegrino, 'L'organisation ecclésiasticae au lendemain du Concile de Trente en deux régions du royaume de Naples', *Miscellanea Historiae Ecclesiasticae*, 5 (Louvain, 1974) 'Colloque de Varsovie', pp. 213–18; *eidem*, *L'organizzazione ecclesiastica degli Abruzzi e Molise e della Basilicata nell'età Postridentina* (Florence, 1973); M. Rosa, 'Geografia e storia religiosa per l' "Atlante Storico Italiano"', *Nuova Rivista Storica*, 53 (1969), 1–43; *idem*, (ed.) *Problemi e ricerche per le Carte Ecclesiastiche dell'Atlante Storico Italiano dell'età moderna* (Florence, 1972). For further examples of the profitable use of *ad limina* reports on areas that are otherwise poorly documented: P. Sposato, *Aspetti e figure della Riforma Cattolico-Tridentina in Calabria* (Naples, n.d. [*c.* 1965]); F. Russo, *Storia dell'Archidiocesi di Reggio Calabria*, vol. 2 (Naples, 1963); A. De Girolamo, *Catanzaro e la Riforma Tridentina. Nicolo Orazi (1582–1609)* (Reggio Calabria, 1975).

and not easy to use. Typically they are alphabetical lists (under Christian names) compiled over some years without indicating when members joined, or when they died or left (see chapter 2.3). Financial records are also disappointing; the confraternities, or subsequent archivists, have not been intent on keeping account books, though some confraternities were better at preserving documents showing entitlement to properties and income. It is very difficult to assess the overall funding of confraternities, developments over any lengthy period, or reactions to crises. We can obtain some idea of priorities for expenditure over a short period. A few valuable examples of what can be done with financial records will, however, be discussed in chapter 6. Other confraternity records which are few in number, but revealing in content, are reports on great events in confraternity life: the major processions or pilgrimages (see chapter 5).

Another form of evidence of value for understanding confraternities is the visual. A reasonable number of confraternity oratories and chapels survive, even if altered in purpose. Their form and decoration can provide insights into the life and activity of the brotherhoods, especially when linked with surviving archival materials. Paintings visually instructed the brethren; they also assist the historian's understanding of attitudes to philanthropy or to the afterlife (see chapter 11 in particular).

It is necessary to establish what is lacking or in too short supply in the evidence. We have found virtually no personal testimony, in letters or diaries, from confraternity members indicating their personal feelings about such societies. We have an inkling of the enthusiasm and dedication of a Christian Doctrine teacher from the diary of Giambattista Casale in Milan (chapter 10, note 36), but little else. The study of wills is not well favoured in Italy, though there is a vast supply of notarial records that could be utilised. The mountains of volumes, and the difficulties of sifting through them, are daunting as I know from a brief foray (for a different purpose some years ago) into the densely packed ex-convent hall in the Perugian state archive. It is work for a long-time resident. Though the dominance of the Italian notary and his formulae may render the wills less revealing than those in Britain, a study of testamentary dispositions should indicate more about attitudes of testators towards confraternities, as well as about finances (briefly discussed in chapter 6). We have some idea of the attitudes of individual outsiders towards the public activities of confraternities; I have already quoted some foreign observers. Direct evidence on the reactions of Italians as outsiders, in a private or official capacity, is somewhat meagre. The limitations of visitation reports have been noted already. The rare evidence from Inquisition records is revealing, as for Perugia (chapter 3.1), or Venice (chapter 3.4), but one suspects that more might eventually be unearthed. Reports from state officials are rare. Venetian authorities like the Council of Ten who had a watching brief over confraternities (see chapter 3.1), are more informative about their disturbances of public order than about their regular practices.

There is disappointingly little evidence so far about confraternity hospitals, and the precise role of confraternity brothers and sisters. Even if one discovers documentation about the sponsoring brotherhood, as in Perugia and Bologna, it may say little about the actual hospital, which had a separate organisational system (if any) (see chapter 9.4). Hospital records have probably suffered more from losses and archival reorganisations than even the main confraternity documents. However some of my discoveries for dependent institutions, such as the Perugian houses for girls in danger (chapter 9.6), suggest that more might be revealed through assiduous archival searches in other cities.

From the above general comments on sources it should be clear that historians can achieve a reasonable idea of the general nature of confraternities and their theoretical organisation. From a limited number of archival records, which are however fairly diverse, we can obtain insights into how some confraternities worked in practice, what their religious and social attitudes and priorities were. From a few case studies we have to deduce the general picture. Given the nature of the records we are unlikely to obtain anything like an accurate idea of the numbers of confraternities in existence, or the numbers of persons involved. Documentary limitations make it impossible to assess the financial contributions of confraternities to social welfare generally. But as some evidence does make clear the physical dimension of philanthropy was not the highest priority. We can obtain some insights into confraternity motivation, even if personal records are few. Since it is difficult to assess why confraternity officials arrived at certain priorities, whether they were influenced by the sight of street squalor or by Jesuit tracts on saving their souls, I have spent some time commenting on the wider climate of opinion about poverty, the poor and the rich (as in chapter 7). It is unlikely that confraternity officials of leading institutions, at least in great cities like Rome, Naples or Venice, were ignorant of the current debates. Only rarely can one point to a confraternity member specifically contributing to the public debate, like Giulio Folco on alms-giving (chapter 9.2). Given the sources used by other historians, and those that I have used directly, there are opportunities for informed generalisations and deductions, but few cases of quantifiable 'proof'.

Why are the confraternities important in the sixteenth century? It is the contention of this book that Italian confraternities developed and changed in vital ways during the early modern period. They were not outmoded medieval forms of social religious organisation that should have died away (as they did in England), or been abolished as Luther wanted. Catholic reformers could be as critical of confraternity immorality as he was. Lay confraternities could have been vulnerable in Catholic lands as potentially subversive of episcopal and parochial authority. But they took on new leases of life, adapted to changing circumstances from the later fifteenth century, and again from the mid-sixteenth. They remained a major part of Italian society until the eighteenth century. Many Italians were involved in them: either as members or as recipients of their ministrations. Confraternities appealed to some of the religiously committed who stopped short of taking full vows in an Order or congregation. They are a key to the religious spirit of the age, as the arenas for lay piety, or 'religiosity' in a non-pejorative sense. Their social and religious rituals remained important in defining and patterning social relationships. For large urban centres like Florence and Venice, the confraternities were at the heart of changing social relationships and tensions; they could be agents of elitist social control, or promoters of more harmonious social relations. Confraternity activity could be a compensation for lost political influence. The confraternities played a significant role in various cultural ways (chapters 11 and 12). They offered answers to some philanthropic problems, an approach to largely anonymous 'associated philanthropy' that can be contrasted with the English solutions, described in famous works by W.K. Jordan and David Owen, of charitable trusts running schools, alms-houses and hospitals.[53] The English systems involved more secularisation of charity than the Italian. In the end the British state took over much social welfare, the Italian much less. The contrast may be attributed to different attitudes to family responsibilities, but some explanation comes from the roles played by the confraternities in the early modern period, which reduced the pressure on governments within Italy to take action. In the nineteenth century, when there again appeared to be a need for interventionist action in social welfare, and there were few endowed confraternities to accept the challenge, it was rather similar secularised organisations that responded: Mutual Aid societies, Cooperatives, Chambers of Labour and even Trade Unions.[54] The confraternities, though now largely defunct, have left their mark. This book is designed to illustrate a major period of challenge and adaptation in their long history.

[53] Jordan, *Philanthropy in England*; D.E. Owen, *English Philanthropy 1660–1969* (London and Cambridge, Mass., 1965).

[54] M.F. Neufeld, *Italy: School for Awakening Countries* (Ithaca, 1961), pp. 60, 172–89, 319–23; C. Seton-Watson, *Italy from Liberalism to Fascism* (London, 1967), pp. 88, 228–9, 302–5; G.B.R. Magaglio describes the legal position of confraternities in modern Italy in AA.VV. *La Liguria delle Casacce. Devozione, arte, storia delle confraternite Liguri* (2 vols., Genoa, 1982), vol. 1, 97–114; for the historiography of Italian assistance, and the tardy development of the Italian welfare state, see E. Bressan, *L"Hospitale' e i poveri.* (Milan, 1982), esp. pp. 42–3.

2

CONFRATERNITIES: WHAT, WHERE, FOR WHOM?

An idea of the variety of confraternal organisations and their preoccupations should already have emerged from chapter 1. This chapter will elaborate on the various kinds of associations that can be called 'confraternities'; it will outline the background history of different types of confraternities to show the wide range of such brotherhoods that existed in Italy by the later fifteenth century. With some knowledge of this medieval medley we can understand the changes—and continuities—in the early modern period as confraternities responded to the challenges of Catholic Reform, Counter-Reformation and the poverty problem. In the second part of the chapter I shall establish more clearly who belonged to the confraternities. While it is comparatively easy to establish the different kinds of membership, by sex or social composition, it is much more difficult to make an accurate assessment of the numbers of confraternities in existence throughout Italy, and the size of the membership.

I TYPES OF CONFRATERNITIES AND THEIR HISTORICAL EVOLUTION

By the close of the sixteenth century confraternities in some form were established all over Italy, involving all sorts and conditions of men, women, and sometimes children or juveniles; lay and clerical, noble women and merchants, guild apprentices and village peasants, even licensed beggars. The first chapter outlined a variety of 'confraternities' to suggest different types of visible activity. No attempt was made to define a confraternity closely. In practice I am using the word to cover an assortment of societies and associations for which contemporaries and historians have used a number of names. Generally we mean groups of people who come together in conformity with certain rules to promote their religious life in common. These people stop short of taking full religious vows within some canonically recognised Order, and most of the time they are part of the secular world.

In my discussion I shall use the words confraternities, fraternities, sodalities, brotherhoods, and companies interchangeably, without implying categorical differences, unless specifically stated. The commonest Italian words in the recognised titles of confraternities were and are *confraternita* and *compagnia*; though I shall frequently omit them when naming the institutions. Numerous other names have been used in Italian and Latin, reflecting different historical backgrounds, or regional peculiarities. In Venice, as already noted, the confraternities were usually called *scuole*, but this name was also fairly common in Lombardy. In Genoa the particular word for a flagellant confraternity was *casacca*.[1]

I have not found it helpful to follow certain historians, or the old canon law, in making distinctions between 'fraternities' and 'confraternities', *pie unioni, sodalizi* and *confraternite*.[2] In the historical context—with some exceptions—those involved were not concerned with the niceties of strict categorisation. In many cases we do not have enough information to codify the societies precisely. However, it can be noted that sixteenth-century Jesuits could stress a distinction between a confraternity and a rather similar congregation: the congregation Della Buona Morte in the Jesuit church of Il Gesù in Rome was deemed not to be a confraternity because it did not have a specific gown (*sacco*) or standard, did not have its own chapel, and did not accompany the dead to burial. Members were concerned to achieve a good death and Paradise through pious acts. But it is clear from the wording of its constitutions that the point about its nature and title had to be made—because it was not well understood. On the continent there is not a distinction found apparently in pre-Reformation London where 'fraternity' meant a guild or parish group which was a spontaneous and self-motivated association, and 'confraternity' signified a group linked to a larger association—such as lay appendage to a religious house.[3] It seems more convenient here to follow past Italian usage and the broad scope of the term 'confraternity' (except in a few particular discussions).

There can be confusion between confraternities and two other types of social groupings, the Tertiaries and the guilds. The Third Order organisations, or Tertiaries, were affiliated to the Mendicant Orders. Tertiary brothers and sisters, at least until the Tridentine period, remained part of the secular world, but made stricter vows and were—theoretically—more tightly ruled by the Religious than were confraternity members. Third Order implied a fuller 'professional religious' commitment.[4]

---

[1] Some of the other Italian and Latin names used: *confraternitas, fraternitas, fraterna, confratia, agape, caritas, consortia, consorzio, devotio, fraglia, casa, societas, sodalitas, collegium*. G.G. Meersseman, *Ordo Fraternitatis. Confraternite e Pietà dei laici nel Medioevo* (3 vols., Rome, 1977), esp. vol. 1. pp. 3–87; Angelozzi, pp. 7–11; G. Le Bras, 'Les confréries chrétiennes' in his *Etudes de sociologie religieuse*, vol. 2 (Paris, 1956), p. 423; A. Noto, *Gli amici dei poveri di Milano. Sei secoli di lasciati e donativi cronologicamente esposti* (Milan, 1953), e.g. pp. 157–8 for mixed terminology in legacies.

[2] The old canon law distinguished pious unions (associations established for some work of piety and charity), sodalities (such institutions which were constituted as organic bodies), and confraternities (such institutions established for the increase of public worship). The recently revised canon law talks more simply of 'associations', *consociationes*. Angelozzi, p. 7 commenting on the old Canon 707; see now Canons 298–329, *Code of Canon Law, Latin–English Edition* (Canon Law Society of America, Washington DC, 1983), pp. 104–17; Le Bras, p. 459.

[3] Meersseman, *Ordo Fraternitatis*, pp. 8–17; V. Paglia, 'Vita religiosa nella Confraternita della Pietà dei Carcerati (sec. XVI–XVII)', *RSRR*, 2 (1978), 55, n. 10: according to the constitutions: 'Si hanno da persuadere che la congregazione della Buona Morte non è confraternita, e percio non veste di sacco, non tiene né porta stendardi . . . non accompagna morti alla sepoltura, non ha oratorio proprio . . . la congregazione è dunque una divota adunaza di uomini e donne pie, che cerca di tenersi il più che può presente il pensiero della morte il quale gli serva di stimolo ad allontanarsi dai vizi e praticare opere pie, e ad assicurarsi una morte buona e con essa il Paradiso'; Paglia, '*La Pietà dei Carcerati*', p. 98, n. 67. The SS. Crocefisso per gli Agonizzanti founded in Rome in 1637 and similarly preoccupied with achieving a good death also refused to accept full confraternity status or obligations, Paglia, 'Le confraternite', pp. 206–7. Cf. C.M. Barron, 'The parish fraternities of medieval London', *The Church in Pre-Reformation society* eds. C.M. Barron and C.Harper-Bill (Woodbridge, Suffolk and Dover, New Hampshire, 1985), p. 17.

[4] D. Hay, *The Church in Italy in the Fifteenth Century* (Cambridge, 1977), pp. 66–7, 78–80; *idem* 'The Church in Italy', *Historical Studies* 9 (1974), 110–11; F.L. Cross (ed.), *The Oxford Dictionary of the Christian Church* (Oxford, 1963 edn), 'Tertiary' and 'Third Orders'.

With the guilds there is more confusion, and genuine overlap. Flagellant confraternities and economic guild organisations both developed strongly in Italian towns during the thirteenth century, and probably mutually influenced each other in organisation. Some guilds created confraternities as offshoots of their trade activities. In Venice most trade guilds, *arti*, created fraternities, *scuole*, to cater for the religious and social welfare interests of their members. These *arti* and *scuole* usually shared some officials. A member of the guild was often compelled to join the related *scuola*, unless he was already a member of another guild-linked *scuola*; a craftsman or trader could be a member of two guilds, but of only one *scuola delle arti* (possibly to prevent double welfare claims). He could also be a member of a devotional *scuola*. Confusion is compounded when documents also use *scuola* loosely to refer to the trade-guild side of the organisation. Few other Italian cities had such a close connection between guilds and confraternities, though some interesting examples will be cited later. There are some closer parallels in medieval London where, however, there may have been a clearer tendency for a guild to emerge out of a neighbourhood fraternity. We will return to the Venetian complexities later.[5]

This study is concerned with *lay* confraternities: associations that primarily involved the laity and were designed for the laity, though they might have clerical membership or be dominated by spiritual advisers from Religious Orders.[6] There were, however, confraternities or companies exclusively for secular clergy, and a few designed for the clergy but with which some laymen might be associated. Occasionally in the records it is difficult to disentangle these clerical confraternities from the lay fraternities which are our prime concern here. Reforming bishops, like Cardinals Carlo Borromeo in Milan and Gabriele Paleotti in Bologna, encouraged—or forced—parish priests and chaplains to form confraternity-type societies, in attempts to improve control over parishes and dioceses. Through these societies the clerics were to coordinate parochial life, to advise and encourage each other in their pastoral activities, and to promote their own spiritual development. While these are clearly distinguishable from lay confraternities, there are some borderline examples, such as the clerical confraternity for the *pievania* of S. Pietro in Mercato in the Val d'Elsa (Tuscany).[7] In this particular Tuscan

---

[5] J. Larner, *Italy in the Age of Dante and Petrarch 1216–1380* (London and New York, 1980), p. 196; R. Mackenney, 'Trade Guilds and devotional confraternities in the state and society of Venice to 1620', (PhD, Cambridge, 1981); much of this crucial work on the Venetian situation has now been incorporated in his *Tradesmen and Traders*, with chapters 2 'Guilds and Christian brotherhood, c. 1350–c. 1520', and 5 'Guildsmen and the Counter-Reformation, c. 1550–c 1600', being particularly relevant here; for guild-fraternity confusion or overlap in medieval England see R.H. Hilton, *The English Peasantry in the Middle Ages* (Oxford, 1975), pp. 91–4; Barron, 'The parish fraternities', pp. 14–17, 20–1; S. Brigden, 'Religion and social obligation in early sixteenth-century London', *Past and Present*, no. 103 (May 1984), 94–102.

[6] R. Rusconi, 'Confraternite, compagne e devozioni', in *Storia d'Italia. Annali*, vol. 9 (1986), pp. 473–5 and n: 12; D. Zardin, 'Confraternite e comunità nelle campagne milanesi fra Cinque e Seicento', *La Scuola Cattolica*, 112 (1984), 704; A. Samaritani, 'Il "conventus" e le congregazioni chiericali di Ferrara tra analoghe istituzioni ecclesiastiche nel secoli x-xv', *Ravennatensia*, vol. 7 (1979), 159–202.

[7] The term *pievania* refers to a system of parochial organisation in which one church, the *pieve*, provided the full range of pastoral care, and maintained the only baptismal font in the area. Dependent churches, fulfilling only part of the care, made up the *pievania*. In some cases the priests of the *pievania* would live as a collegiate society, reside at the centre and travel to dependent churches as required. Hay, *The Church*, pp. 20–25; *idem*, 'The Church in Italy', pp. 107–9; A. Vezza, 'Evoluzione socio-religiosa della parrocchia e dei benefici parrocchiali di Pescantina (Verona)', *Sociologia religiosa*, 8 (1964), 61–5; A. Mastalli, 'Parrocchie e chiese della Pieve di Lecco, ai primordi del 1600', *Memorie storiche della Diocesi di Milano*, 2 (1955), 72–125.

pieve the fourteen parish priests formed themselves into a clerical confraternity for their spiritual life, but they ruled that other priests, and lay men and women, could join them for some spiritual purposes. The meetings were to be preceded by the celebration of mass by the prior, there would be a lunch, with simple food specified (to avoid it being a banquet), eaten in silence or with limited conversation, or with prayers and a reading with commentary by the prior. Afterwards members would recite the office of the dead, and discuss problems. The rules, approved by Cardinal Archbishop Alessandro de'Medici of Florence in 1587, do not show how much associated lay members participated. But their role was clearly inferior; it was different from being in one of the lay confraternities which had powerful clerical advisers as members.[8]

The variety, and confusion, of the lay confraternities by the sixteenth century derives from the long, muddled history of such societies.[9] Arguably there were precedents for lay confraternities from the fourth century (though probably the societies recorded were all clerical), but they developed from the ninth and tenth centuries. A society of men and women in Modena, entitled S. Geminiano, in the tenth century, was responsible for providing candles and lamps for the Cathedral. Early organisations appear to have had a strong clerical element, as in the mixed-sex *societas* in Ivrea, active in about 947. These may well have been extensions of sacerdotal confraternities (distinct from strict monasticism) fostered in England, Germany, France and then Italy by St Boniface (680–754) and his followers.[10] The main concern was prayer for the living and the salvation of souls. By the twelfth century there were more lay confraternities in towns and some villages. From then date the early hospital confraternities, at Viterbo in the early twelfth century, and Orvieto in the later part of the century, which undertook to assist the sick poor and travellers.[11]

From the thirteenth century there was a major expansion of the lay confraternities, led initially by the Dominicans. Such brotherhoods, attached to their monasteries, were designed to ensure the salvation of souls, and also to undertake works of charity. One of St Dominic's leading disciples, St Peter Martyr, was the inspiration behind new Congregations of the Virgin, in Milan in 1232 and Florence in 1245. These associations were more polemical and anti-heretical than other Marian confraternities that had already emerged primarily to maintain churches. In 1232 Peter Martyr also launched a lay society specifically to combat heresy. This was to spawn many societies which used his name or were called Crocesignati. Some of these survived into the sixteenth century, and a few (as we shall see later) revived the anti-heretical, crusading enthusiasm of their distant predecessors.[12]

A notable feature of the epoch was the penitential movement led by the Franciscans,

[8] A. D'Addario, *Aspetti della Controriforma a Firenze* (Rome, 1972), pp. 443–6.

[9] For the early history of confraternities: Angelozzi; Meersseman, *Ordo Fraternitatis*; Le Bras; G.M. Monti, *Le confraternite medievali dell'alta e media Italia* (2 vols., Venice, 1927), a pioneer work that has received detailed correction and glossing from medieval historians, notably from Meersseman; Bossy, *Christianity*, pp. 57–63, though not particularly concerned with Italy.

[10] Angelozzi, pp. 13–14 (Ivrea and Modena), 14–15 (St Boniface); Meersseman, *Ordo Fraternitatis*, vol. 1, pp. 25–9.

[11] *Ibid.* vol. 1. pp. 144–9.

[12] Rusconi, 'Confraternite', pp. 471–2; N.J. Housley, 'Politics and heresy in Italy: Anti-heretical crusades, orders and confraternities, 1200–1500,' *J. Eccl. Hist.*, 33 (1982), 193–208; on Dominicans and confraternities generally, Meersseman, *Ordo Fraternitatis*, vols. 2–3, pp. 578–1270, more particularly pp. 578ff, 754, 921ff; Angelozzi, p. 25; D. Zardin, 'Le confraternite in Italia settentrionale nell'età moderna e contemporanea' (forthcoming).

with its high point the Great Devotion of flagellants launched by the lay preacher Raniero Fasani in 1260. Huge processions of people flagellating their bare backs and chanting for divine mercy took to the streets and roads, first in Perugia, then south to Rome, and north to Bologna and Parma. The background to this was both the warfare between the Papacy and the German Empire, and the struggles against Cathar heretics that had inspired Peter Martyr's confraternity work. The habit of public and private flagellation as a penitential activity had been growing during the earlier part of the century. The Franciscan St Antony of Padua's procession of flagellants in 1230 was a precedent for the 1260 mania. The Flagellant Movement, in its broader manifestations, did not last long; the amorphous, unorganised processions were dangerous to public order, and disruptive of economic life. But flagellation became part of the popular religion of Italy, and the phenomenon gave rise eventually to a large number of confraternities whose chief concern was to express penitence through corporal penance, whether privately in confraternity rooms, or publicly in organised processions. Many older confraternities adopted flagellation as part of their penitential life, or sections of the brotherhood specialised in it. In Florence the Mendicant Orders had in the thirteenth century sponsored *Laudesi* companies, with processional singing of religious songs in praise of God, or *Misericordia* fraternities of devotion and hospitality; by the fourteenth century they were more inclined to support flagellant confraternities.[13]

During the fourteenth century confraternities developed both through some dramatic episodes, and more mundane organisation. Some evidence suggests that in rural areas confraternities were promoted to help parish priests in their work, which can be seen as precedents for a much more developed parochial confraternity system in the sixteenth century. However, elsewhere confraternities had been established because of the lack of adequate resident parish priests. A detailed study of the pre-1400 confraternities in the Val d'Elsa rural communities in Tuscany shows that most were attached to parish churches, not to those of the Mendicants, and had a Marian orientation.[14] A more dramatic revival or expansion of confraternities followed from the Great Plague of 1348, again involving much flagellation. There was further mass religious enthusiasm in 1399, with the movement of the *Bianchi* or Whites, when white-robed penitents from countryside and town indulged in a great peace-keeping movement with processions and singing. The enthusiasm led to the foundation of new confraternities or reorientation of old ones.[15]

---

[13] Angelozzi, pp. 20–30; Monti, *Le confraternite*, vol. 1, pp. 197–285; J. Henderson, 'The flagellant movement and flagellant confraternities in central Italy, 1260–1400', *Religious Motivation*, ed. D. Baker (Oxford, 1978), pp. 147–60; M. Papi, 'Confraternite ed ordini mendicanti a Firenze. Aspetti di una ricerca quantitativa', *Mélanges de l'Ecole Francaise de Rome. Temps modernes*, 89 (1977), 723–32; C. De la Roncière, 'Les confréries en Toscane aux XIV et XV siècles d'après les travaux récents', *RSRR*, 5 (1984), 50–64.

[14] G. Cherubini, 'Parroco, parrocchiale e popolo nelle campagne dell'Italia centro-settentrionale alla fine del Medioevo', *Pievi e Parrocchie in Italia nel basso medioevo (sec. XIII–XV). Atti del VI Convegno di Storia della Chiesa in Italia. (Firenze 21–25 Settembre 1981)* (2 vols., Rome, 1984), vol. 1, pp. 351–414, esp. pp. 381–2; Z. Zafarana, 'Cura pastorale, predicazione, aspetti devozionali nella parrocchia del basso medioevo', *ibid.*, vol. 1, pp. 493–539, esp. pp. 535–6.

[15] Angelozzi, p. 35; Monti, *Le confraternite*, vol. 1. pp. 289–99; Bossy, *Christianity*, p. 60; D.M. Webb, 'Penitence and peace-making in city and contado: the "Bianchi" of 1399', *The Church in Town and Countryside*, ed. D. Baker (Oxford, 1979), pp. 243–56; P. Lucertini, 'La compagnia dei SS. Antonino e Jacopo di Anghiari,' *BSPU*, 70, II (1973), 235–64; C.M. De la Roncière, 'La place des confréries dans l'encadrement religieux du contado Florentin: l'example de la Val d'Elsa', *Mélanges de l'Ecole Française de Rome (Moyen Age–Temps modernes)*, 85 (1973), 31–77, 633–71.

The supposition that religious enthusiasm and confraternity vitality diminished in the fifteenth century, before a revival at its close, is increasingly being contested. This Renaissance period is no longer seen as thoroughly irreligious or pagan. Evidence is increasingly produced to show confraternity activity through the fifteenth century, though it should be stressed that much of this evidence is in fact from sixteenth-century sources, particularly revised statutes which give some historical information—or myths. The two cities most studied in the Renaissance period, Florence and Venice, do demonstrate religious piety (sometimes accompanied by anticlericalism), and lively confraternity activity. For the rest of Italy it might be safest to judge the situation as patchy—with some areas of vitality and others of neglect.[16] At least in terms of numbers of confraternities a positive reading can be recorded for large cities like Genoa, Bologna and Milan, lesser northern cities such as Belluno, Biella, Ferrara, Novara, Padua or Saronno, and in some rural areas of Lombardy and Piedmont. In terms of confraternities, there was in the fifteenth century an increase in the number of 'national' confraternities; brotherhoods that held together the aliens (non-Italians or from distant Italian regions) in cities like Rome, Florence, Venice and Palermo. There was an increase in guild or work-based confraternities, for example in Piedmont. There also Spirito Santo confraternities seem to have been active, as they do in neighbouring France, at least in celebrating Pentecost with feasts and banquets. Towards the end of the century Italy witnessed an increase in the cult of the Madonna della Misericordia, or dei Poveri, especially in areas around Milan and Bergamo, in Piedmont and in Paduan rural districts, some of this encouraged by dedicated confraternities. The Franciscans' advocacy of the doctrine of the Immaculate Conception in the 1470s—against Dominican opposition—led to the foundation of various Conception confraternities, particularly in Lucca and in S. Francesco Grande, Milan, for which Leonardo da Vinci painted the first *Virgin of the Rocks* (Louvre).[17]

The positive development of confraternities in this period was assisted by a few reforming bishops, such as Niccolo Albergati, bishop of Bologna, 1417–43;[18] and by the intercommunication of confraternities. Across large parts of Italy they exchanged rules, ideas and symbols—and so prefigured some post-tridentine developments. In looking at the relationship between confraternity and parish we again find varying experiences. In the Veneto area discipline fraternities have been seen as creating parochial cohesion, but (since they usually had their own separate buildings) undermining the parish church and its priest in the process. On the other hand in the Campania region confraternities were mostly based on the parish church, and harmonious relationships between parish and confraternity organisation apparently persisted at least until the seventeenth century.[19]

---

[16] On the fifteenth century see particularly Rusconi, 'Confraternite' and Zardin, 'Le confraternite in Italia settentrionale' on which most of what follows is based.

[17] See, besides Rusconi and Zardin, A. Serra, 'Funzioni e finanze delle confraternite romane tra il 1624 e il 1797', *RSRR*, 5 (1984), p. 269, n. 25; see below on 'national confraternities', chapter 2.2 (d). For the Franciscans and Conception confraternities, H. Glasser, *Artists' Contracts of the Early Renaissance* (New York and London, 1977), pp. 68–70, 109–11.

[18] On Albergati and confraternities, M. Fanti, *L'Ospedale e la Chiesa di S. Maria della Carità* (Bologna, 1981), p. 37.

[19] A. Rigon, 'Organizzazione ecclesiastica e cura d'anime nelle Venezie. Ricerche in corso e problemi da risolvere', AA.VV. *Pieve e parrocchie*, vol. 2, pp. 704–24, esp. pp. 721–4; G. Vitolo, 'Pieve, parrocchie e chiese ricettizie in Campania', *ibid.*, vol. 2, pp. 1095–1107, esp. p. 1106.

Localised events can also explain the ebb and flow of confraternity development, as in the case of Florence. From 1376–8 Florence was put under Interdict by Pope Gregory XI, as a result of typically complex political conflicts in central Italy and attempts to consolidate the Papal State. With the resulting ban on public worship and the popular exposition of the Host, there was a revival of confraternity activity, which allowed for private religious expression. Briefly in 1376–7 there were also public processions, involving both the singing of Lauds and flagellation, in an attempt both to express Florentine penitence for the sins which caused their troubles, and to pray for the end of papal stubbornness. Florentine authorities feared such public demonstrations as potentially uncontrollable, and suspected some private confraternity meetings were breeding grounds for sedition. Despite curbs, confraternities seem to have thrived, with new ones being spawned. R. Weissman's major study of Florentine confraternities stresses social and political as well as religious reasons for this vitality. Periodic bans on meetings, when the regime feared political opposition, did not long deter them. However, the fall of the Medici family and the dominance of fra Girolamo Savonarola in the 1490s, and the subsequent struggles between republicans and the Medici, saw an apparent decline in confraternities until the mid-sixteenth century, when they took on vital but revised forms under Counter-Reformation influences and Medicean ducal absolutism. Confraternities became reinforcements of parochial religious-social life; those representing wider neighbourhood or occupational groups were largely superseded.[20]

Florence has been used to illustrate the development of confraternities into the main period of our concern. Before turning to more specific aspects of the confraternities it might be worth stressing the prominent features of Italian confraternity development through the long sixteenth century. The importance of the Companies of Divine Love has already been mentioned in the context of Catholic Reform (chapter 1.2). The Compagnia del Divino Amore founded by Ettore Vernazza in Genoa in 1497 was the pioneer. Earlier fraternities in place like Parma and Brescia that encouraged a new spirit of philanthropy and devotion set some precedents, but the Companies of Divine Love in Genoa, Rome and Venice are probably rightly credited with the major impact on the philanthropic confraternity movement of the sixteenth century.[21]

At the same time another development was under way, that of the Corpus Christi or Sacrament confraternity, whose purpose was to encourage frequent communion and devotion to the sacraments by the laity. With these the emphasis shifts to parish-based societies, under strong clerical and diocesan leadership. This type of confraternity that

---

[20] R.C. Trexler, *The Spiritual Power. Republican Florence under Interdict* (Leiden, 1974), pp. 126–32; Weissman, *Ritual Brotherhood*; see below chapter 3.4; see now J. Henderson, 'Confraternities and the church in late medieval Florence', *Voluntary Religion* eds. W.J. Sheils and D. Wood (Oxford, 1986), pp. 69–83.

[21] See above chapter 1, n. 20; Angelozzi, pp. 172–83, with statutes of the Genoa company; Monti, *Le confraternite*, pp. 300–3; Zardin, 'Le confraternite in Italia settentrionale'; M. Fanti, *La chiesa e la compagnia dei Poveri in Bologna* (Bologna, 1977), pp. 77–8; V. Meneghin, 'Due compagnie sul modello di quelle del "Divino Amore" fondate da Francescani a Feltre e a Verona (1499, 1503)', *Archivum Franciscanum Historicum*, 62 (1969), 518–64, with pp. 519–21 on the precedents; R. Savelli, 'Dalle confraternite allo stato: il sistema assistenziale genovese nel Cinquecento', *Atti della Società Ligure di Storia Patria*, n.s. 24 (1984), 178–80; E. Peverada, 'Note sulle confraternite e luoghi pii a Ferrara dal 1574 al 1611', *Ravennatensia*, 4 (1974), pp. 325–6, for S. Giobbe, Ferrara founded in the late fifteenth century under the Company's inspiration, to help the incurably sick.

specially adored the Host probably dates from the twelfth century, and adoration of the Host was part of popular piety (as R.C. Trexler noted when dealing with the Florentine Interdict of 1376–8) but the major impetus for confraternity foundation began at the close of the fifteenth century. In 1535 A. Zanetti, suffragan bishop in Bologna, exhorted all parish priests to start one; in 1542 Bishop G.M.Giberti of Verona ordered a Corpus Christi confraternity to be founded in each parish. Paul III's approval of the Roman Sacrament company in S. Maria sopra Minerva in 1539 made this a model for such societies. Subsequently there was a tendency for new Sacrament societies to absorb older ones, whether they were lively or poorly supported, and so bring about stricter supervision of members. During the sixteenth century Capuchins, Benedictines and then Duke Cosimo I of Florence, with his architect Giorgio Vasari, made it easier for the populace to watch the celebration of the Eucharist and adore the elevated Host by clearing church naves of monuments, tombs and screens. Sacrament confraternities were created to assist this process of adoration and the seemly presentation of the Host.[22]

Another expanding type of confraternity in the sixteenth century was the Marian. Marian confraternities had arisen in the thirteenth century to invoke the help of the Virgin as protector of the faithful against heretics, and to encourage corporal penance. Such societies declined, but revived when the Dominicans started to promote the Rosary in 1480, in S. Domenico di Castello, Venice—after the practice was well established in France and Germany. Further expansion came from its systematic promotion by the Jesuits from 1563. The most popular Marian devotion, that of the Rosary, received a major boost after 1571 when Pius V associated the Holy League's naval victory over the Turks at the battle of Lepanto with the Virgin's intercession, encouraged by prayers and meditations on the Rosary.[23]

The proliferation of the Sacrament and Rosary confraternities helped increase parochial control over much confraternity life through the sixteenth century. Other developments to be briefly noted—and which will be discussed further in appropriate sections—are the greater involvement in education, in helping the poor outside the confraternities, in assisting prisoners and the condemned, in improving the moral standards of society as well as of members of confraternities. Finally one can detect a greater preoccupation with making a good death, and with souls in Purgatory generally (as opposed to a long-standing concern for the souls of brethren and their immediate families). This attention to the host of souls is, in Italy, a rather late development, and

[22] Angelozzi, p. 42; Lopez, 'Le confraternite laicali', pp. 161, 185–6; M. Fanti, San Procolo. Una parrocchia di Bologna ([Bologna], 1983) pp. 211–12; D. Zardin, Confraternite e vita di pietà nelle campagne lombarde tra Cinquecento e Seicento. La pieve di Parabiago-Legnano (Milan, 1981), pp. 26–7; Trexler, The Spiritual Power, pp. 126–7; Weissman, Ritual Brotherhood, pp. 206, 215; M.B. Hall, Renovation and Counter-Reformation. Vasari and Duke Cosimo in Sta Maria Novella and Sta Croce 1565–1577 (Oxford, 1979), and see below chapter 11.1, on other effects of this church clearance policy. Corpus Christi confraternities might of course survive from an earlier period, but be devoted to processions on that feast-day (instituted in 1264 by Urban IV), and to prayers for the dead, rather than particularly to the Eucharist; cf. M. Rubin, 'Corpus Christi fraternities and late medieval piety', Voluntary Religion, eds. Sheils and Wood, pp. 97–109.

[23] Angelozzi, pp. 42–3; Meersseman, Ordo Fraternitatis, pp. 1144–1232; M. Sensi, 'Raccomandati di Maria e disciplinati a Spello nel secolo XIV', BSPU 70 (1973), 223–33; M. Rosa, 'Pietà mariana e devozione del Rosario nell'Italia del Cinque e Seicento,' in his Religione e società, pp. 217–43; Pastor, History of the Popes, vol. 18, pp. 444–9, and Storia dei Papi, vol. 8, pp. 561–2; E.H. Gombrich, 'Celebrations in Venice of the Holy League and of the Victory of Lepanto', Studies in Renaissance and Baroque Art ed. J. Coutauld (London, 1967), pp. 62–8.

not a prominent factor until well into the seventeenth century. By the eighteenth century confraternity preoccupations with death, the afterlife, and various associated devotions, such as those linked to the Holy Sepulchre or the 'transit' of the Virgin, seem more noteworthy than confraternity interest in philanthropy.[24]

The above survey indicates that for the sixteenth century we are dealing with a whole medley of confraternities, and with apparently contradictory developments, as old interests wax and wane, new dimensions are added, and external influences are brought to bear upon them. Attempts have been made, in various methodological or morphological approaches to classify and categorise certain types of confraternities. It has been suggested that there should be a division between the flagellant or 'discipline' confraternities and others, based on the view that the former represent the medieval confraternities, and embody the true spirit of these lay organisations. It is further supposed that at the close of the fifteenth century most confraternities were flagellant—in name if not in regular practice. But while the flagellant movement was certainly influential, this is only part of the picture as outlined above. Many flagellant societies diversified their interests by, or during, the sixteenth century. Many retained the nomenclature without (as far as evidence suggests) maintaining the practice. Other confraternities, founded for other purposes did encourage discipline as a devotion. While flagellation was an important practice for some sixteenth-century brotherhoods it seems misleading to use it as the focal point of research, a pointless flail for the historian himself.[25]

R. Rusconi has provided an alternative kind of classification for confraternities in the fifteenth century, dividing them into four broad categories: (1) *Laudesi*, (2) *Disciplinati*, (3) eucharist societies based on the Cathedral, and (4) devotional confraternities allied to religious Orders and their churches. This 'locational' classification has the merit of stressing the difference between those, (1) and (2), that were to some extent independent in their own oratories and rooms, and the other two groups which were under closer clerical supervision or influence.[26] The sixteenth century in particular added other categories, notably those with a strong link with the parish church, and those preeminently concerned with philanthropic institutions.

Narrow or inflexible categorisation will obscure the developing picture which shows that from the later fifteenth or early sixteenth century there was a proliferation of various societies within many areas, and that more individual confraternities diversified their activities and devotions, even if the majority remained specialist. The composite

---

[24] Brief outlines of later seventeenth- and eighteenth-century developments will be found in Rusconi, 'Confraternite' and Zardin, 'Le confraternite in Italia settentrionale', sections 4–5, both with full bibliographical information. Concern with the afterlife is discussed below, chapter 4.8.

[25] P.L. Meloni, 'Topografia, diffusione e aspetti delle confraternite dei Disciplinati', extract from AA.VV. *Risultate e Prospettive della Ricerca sul Movimento dei Disciplinati* (Perugia, 1972); this was the main report on the initial work of the Centro di Documentazione sul Movimento dei Disciplinati in Perugia, whose research has unfortunately been hampered by financial shortages; it has led to the publication of various individual studies of confraternities, especially in articles in the *BSPU*. Cf. review by E. Ardu, 'Risultate e prospettive della recerca sul movimento dei disciplinati', *RSLR*, 5 (1969), 765–8; for a more complex approach to categorisation, in one city, E. Grendi, 'Morfologia e dinamica della vita associativa urbana. Le confraternite a Genova fra i secoli XVI e XVIII,' *Atti della Società Ligure di Storia Patria*, 79 (1965), 239–311, which will be used below.

[26] Rusconi, 'Confraternite', pp. 474–5; Zardin, 'Confraternite e comunità', p. 721; below chapter 4.6.

attitude to confraternity aims and ambitions was succinctly expressed in the preamble to the rules, *capitoli*, drawn up in 1571 for the company of the SS. Sacramento in the church of S. Felicità, Florence:

> The first aim is the contemplative life, which consists in raising the mind to God in prayer and meditation. The second aim is the active life, which consists in helping, with the purest of intentions, one's neighbour in his needs; the third is the moral life, which consists in leading an honest, virtuous life full of holy converse.[27]

The separation in some subsequent chapters of this book between religious life and social activity (or between dimensions within either of those divisions) should not obscure the view that many brothers and sisters in such confraternities saw the contemplative and active lives as part of an overall programme, or, as I have already indicated, saw philanthropy as a path to personal salvation and an expression of devotion.

2 MEMBERSHIP OF THE CONFRATERNITIES

It is time to clarify who joined confraternities—and who might be excluded. Confraternities were predominantly for adult laymen. These brothers had mixed feeling about the admittance of clergy, women and youths. If admitted they were likely to be accorded inferior or limited roles and privileges. Many confraternities were for an exclusive group of males, but some were designed to mix individuals from a range of social groups or classes. Some of these fraternities became agents of social control when members of an elite dominated within the company, others are better seen as promoters of communal harmony, replacing secular tensions by a brotherly association.

(a) The clergy

While the priestly involvement in some confraternities was large, in others laymen were intent on asserting their autonomy. At one extreme confraternities would hire a priest for minimal services as and when required—paid as it were on a piece-time rate, and not allow him membership. The apostolic visitor to Assisi in 1573 indicated that Regulars, especially Franciscans, usually celebrated in such circumstances.[28] Many other fraternities would simply use the parish priest of the church where they had a chapel. Some confraternities had an associated chaplain on a more formal contract: the Sacrament company of S. Felicità, Florence hired a chaplain for a year at a time to confess the sick when summoned, to say mass when the company met, but not to act as spiritual advisor. By the late sixteenth century Florentine sacramental confraternities were obliged to have their parish priest as chaplain.[29] In 1578 the Venetian Scuola di S. Cristoforo (or

---

[27] D'Addario, *Aspetti*, p. 432.
[28] L. Proietti Pedetta, 'Alcune note sulla situazione delle confraternite nel Assisi nel periodo post-tridentino (secc. XVI–XVII)', *Chiesa e Società dal secolo IV ai Nostri Giorni. Studi storici in onore del P. Ilarino da Milano* (Rome, 1979), vol. 2, pp. 457–73.
[29] D'Addario, *Aspetti*, p. 433; Weissman, *Ritual Brotherhood*, p. 212; Henderson, 'Confraternities', pp. 74–9, stresses the importance of friars as spiritual guides and correctors of Florentine *Laudesi* companies from the thirteenth century; and argues that archbishops A. Corsini and St Antoninus in the early fifteenth century started a move towards greater control by parish priests.

S. Cristofalo) dei Mercanti contracted with the canons of S. Maria dell'Orto to conduct their major celebrations.[30]

Those societies that were promoted by the Orders, especially the Capuchins and Jesuits, could expect close relations with a spiritual director from the Order, who might be a member, and be present for business affairs. When the Jesuit B. Realino founded, the S. Annunziazione della Beata Vergine in Lecce, in 1581, the rules specified a Jesuit as spiritual director; this also applied to the Jesuit foundation of the Pietà dei Carcerati, responsible for Roman prisons.[31] In Venice the Scuola of S. Orsola in the sixteenth century employed the friars from the neighbouring grand church of SS. Giovanni e Paolo. But relations were clearly not always harmonious, with disputes over who celebrated when, over processions or the collection of alms. This confraternity had a chaplain for normal occasions, and resisted the claims of the friars to control his election (e.g. in 1629), until they were forced by a legal decision in 1672 to surrender their independent chaplain and accept a friar. Under such circumstances the clergy were not full members of the confraternity, and the fraternal spirit between laity and clerics was weak.[32]

Some confraternities, however, were happier with clergy as full or partial members. In Rome S. Girolamo della Carità, which was connected with leading Catholic reformers like Filippo Neri and Cacciaguerra, enrolled a large number of clergy, but seems to have rigorously preserved lay control. The Venetian Scuole Grandi had a clerical membership of 5–6 per cent, but the clergy did not take part in the wider, philanthropic, activities of the confraternities.[33] In Perugia the confederation of three confraternities of S. Agostino, S. Domenico and S. Francesco (which will be discussed later as notable defenders of their lay independence from ecclesiastical control) allowed priests to join—but as if they were laymen. The records, though quite full, do not state who celebrated mass for the brothers, whether one of these clerical brothers or an outside priest; they did not have a permanent chaplain.[34] Perugia had other confraternities . showing different approaches to clerical membership. The company of S. Tommaso D'Aquino linked Dominicans (the original promoters), Franciscans and Canons Regular of S. Salvatore with leading lay patricians. From 1539 they jointly promoted an institution to look after abandoned or vulnerable girls (derelitte). Later in the century one of its leading members, Don Giovio Valentino, can be cited as an

[30] ASVen Scuole piccole, Busta 413, 1 December 1578, notarial agreement. Cf. Mackenney, Traders and Tradesmen, p. 50 on the spiritual dedication of this confraternity, and its earlier concern with the monastery and church.

[31] Paglia, 'La Pietà dei Carcerati', pp. 114, 133–9; Lopez, 'Le confraternite laicali', p. 211 (rule 9).

[32] ASVen Scuole piccole, Busta 599, no. 33: folder 'sec. XV–XVI, 1501–', copy of undated pact; folder dated 1665; docs. dated 10 November 1555, 18 October 1629, 5 November 1672. For the location of the oratory of S. Orsola at the side of the great church of SS. Giovanni e Paolo see the old map reproduced in N-E. Vanzan Marchini (ed.), La Memoria della Salute. Venezia e il suo ospedale dal XV al XVI secolo (Venice, 1985), p. 17.

[33] L. Fiorani, 'L'esperienza religiosa', p. 175; B.S. Pullan, 'Le Scuole Grandi', p. 87.

[34] SBF S. Francesco. Pluteo IV, no. 509, 'Verbali' 1628; witnesses claimed there was no permanent chaplain, that they made private arrangements, and changed their priests frequently; see below chapter 3.1; R. Guèze, 'Confraternite di S. Agostino, S. Francesco e S. Domenico a Perugia' in AA.VV. Il Movimento dei Disciplinati nel Settimo Centenario dal suo inizio (Perugia–1260) (Perugia, 1962), pp. 597–623.

exemplary reformed, and reforming, parish priest.[35] Similarly the company of S. Girolamo linked laymen and Franciscans in caring for needy and abandoned girls in the Pia Casa della Carità from about 1561–3. The confraternity that fostered the main Perugian general hospital of S. Maria della Misericordia had parish priests as *ex officio* members, but these were heavily outnumbered by lay officials, often powerful patricians. In Florence the Misericordia confraternity, of nursing fame, specified a ratio of 42 laymen to 30 clerics. It seems clear that these lay confraternities insisted on the lay management of their affairs.[36]

(b) Female members

The confraternities were primarily male societies, but not wholly so. The early mixed-sex society at Ivrea has already been mentioned, and this duality was maintained in many later groups. There were also female-only confraternities. Attitudes towards female members varied considerably. That male officials succumbed to pressure to admit women is shown in the Florence Interdict crisis of 1376–8. The company of S. Zanobi redrafted its constitutions in 1376 and admitted women: 'These women, seeing this company making the several and devout processions, begged with every pure affection to be received and allowed to participate in the blessings and merits of our spiritual company'.[37] But a thoroughly antagonistic attitude can be found in the 1569 statutes of S. Giovanni Decollato, Faenza—which peremptorily excluded females from the houses of the confraternity and put them along with beasts in an exclusion clause. The male prejudice against females as gossips was shown in 1573 by the Corpus Domini company attached to S. Frediano, Florence; women could attend company meetings (for business) only once a year:

It is prohibited and forbidden, not only to our sisters, but to every other woman, under penalty of expulsion, to enter our oratory in any manner, except for the Sunday of the octave of Corpus Domini and not at any other time, so that the opportunity to expose or slander us will be removed and this is done for the salvation of the souls of each of our sisters.[38]

Whether the existence of women-only confraternities resulted from male prejudice and exclusiveness, or more positively from the women's desire to be independent, and run affairs themselves is debatable.

Until recently the best known female-only confraternities were the Neapolitan Devote di Gesù (from at least 1554, for noble women), dedicated to the sacraments and helping their neighbours; and the Roman S. Anna per le Donne (from 1640), through which good, especially noble, women could organise the spiritual and physical welfare

[35] O. Marinelli, *La Compagnia di San Tommaso d'Aquino di Perugia* (Rome, 1960), pp. 18–19; For Giovio as a 'model' parish priest see my 'Perugia and post-tridentine church reform', pp. 423–4; ASP Sodalizio di S. Martino, 'Libro I delle Congregationi', fols. 8v–11r, 17v, 25r, shows him active in another important confraternity.

[36] E. Valeri, *La Fraternita dell'Ospedale di S. Maria Della Misericordia in Perugia nei secoli XIII–XVII* (Perugia, 1972); S. Nessi, 'La Confraternita di S. Girolamo in Perugia', *Miscellanea Francescana*, 67 (1967), 78–115; D'Addario, *Aspetti*, pp. 434–8.

[37] Trexler, *The Spiritual Power*, p. 131.

[38] L. Scaramucci, 'Considerazioni sui statuti e matricoli di Confraternite dei Disciplinati' in AA.VV. *Risultati e Prospettive*, p. 150; Weissman, *Ritual Brotherhood*, pp. 212–13.

of the less good and less fortunate.[39] But research is revealing more female societies–for all social classes. A recent study, using visitation records, has revealed eleven women-only confraternities in the Perugian diocese, eight in the Spoletan, none of them in the episcopal cities. But other evidence–of varying quality and allusiveness–suggests that Perugia city had three or four such sororities in the sixteenth and early seventeenth centuries: the ancient Spedaliere, the Madonna del Soccorso (which commisioned its own standard in 1570), and the Madonna di Monte Cardello, which, however, united with a mixed-sex company in 1580. Details on membership and activity remain obscure, though one Perugian *contado* sorority had twenty-four members and the names of societies suggest devotion to Mary and the Rosary. Some sororities were primarily responsible for a particular altar.[40] Elsewhere in Italy there were confraternities of S. Orsola, primarily for women of marriageable age, and of S. Anna for widows. Cardinal Carlo Borromeo was particularly enthusiastic about such societies in the Lombard archdiocese, seeing them as encouraging women to live an innocent life of Christian piety and to study *caritas*. But some of the S. Orsola societies were very small; that in Canegrate in 1583 had only four sisters, that of Legnano about twenty in c. 1590. D. Zardin argues that there was a strong claustral attitude behind such sororities, and that in the seventeenth century some turned into convents. In the area around Naples some of the Rosary confraternities were for women only–and were sometimes short-lived. One suspects that fuller research will reveal a fair number of women–only confraternities, even if their activity was minimal. Certain Rosary sororities may have had no corporate life at all but were a matter of gaining indulgences through inscription and distance learning or prayer.[41]

Mixed confraternities were common, but the degree of female participation and the extent of their welcome was very variable. Shifting attitudes to women members were shown by the Scuola di S. Rocco, Mestre. In the fifteenth century this *scuola* was open to men and women alike, by the end of the sixteenth it welcomed only wives of *confratelli*, who could remain in the society as widows, but the dangerous abuse of admitting *unmarried* women was stopped. In 1669 the *scuola* again was open to women in their own right.[42] Various confraternities made clear that women were only partial or inferior members. In Perugia's Annunziata, according to the 1587 revised statutes, women were excluded from office and from general assemblies (business meetings), but they could share in other activities, probably including processions and the care of formerly 'dishonest' women in hostels. When the Sacrament company in the church of S. Lorenzo, Ponte a Greve (downriver from Florence) revised its statutes in 1564, it devoted one chapter to female membership: as God created woman to help man, Adam,

[39] Lopez, 'Le confraternite laicali', p. 198; M. Maroni Lumbroso and A. Martini, *Le confraternite romane nelle loro chiese* (Rome, 1963), pp. 45–6.

[40] Casagrande, 'Ricerche', 38–47, 57–61; O. Marinelli, *Le confraternite di Perugia dalle origini al sec. XIX. Bibliografia delle opere a stampa* (Perugia, 1965; with later index vol., n.d.), pp. 608–9, 641–2, 658, 1026, with the bibliographical sources.

[41] Zardin, 'Confraternite e comunità', pp. 709–10; *idem, Confraternite e vita di pietà*, pp. 45–7, 73; *idem*, 'Le confraternite in Italia settentrionale';*Acta Ecclesiae Mediolanensis ab eius initiis usque ad nostram aetatem*, ed. A. Ratti, vol. 2 (Milan, 1890) [hereafter *AEM*], cols. 493–4, 4th Provincial Council; Russo, *Chiesa e comunità*, p. 306; the Bologna company of S. Marco turns out to be a female-only one in 1631, Scaramucci, 'Considerazioni sui statuti', p. 164. On Rosary confraternities see also below, chapter 4.7.

[42] L. Sbriziolo, *Le confraternite veneziane di divozione* (Rome, 1968), pp. 15–20, 26–8.

so the society should admit women–if honest, and ready to pay fees; they could share in indulgences, graces, spiritual privileges and suffrages enjoyed by the men, but they could not hold office, or attend general meetings except on the feast of Corpus Domini. The records for the Venetian Scuola di SS. Trinità show the women members receiving charitable benefits, but do not indicate that they attended business meetings, and their names were kept in separate registers.[43] In the constitution for the *disciplinati* of Domodossola an appendix deals with women members, stating how they should dress, recite prayers at canonical hours, abstain and fast, visit the sick and imprisoned. They had their own prioress, but it was emphasised that she was subject to the prior and male counsellors. It was not indicated whether the women flagellated.[44]

Flagellation may have influenced a confraternity's approach to female membership, though they were not excluded from discipline societies. It might have appeared unseemly for women to witness the men flagellating their bare backs, let alone share in this. Some Lombard statutes banned women from meeting rooms during feast-day prayers, probably so they would not witness flagellation. Many societies would not have had the room to provide for segregated activities. G.G. Meersseman records that, before 1260 and the growth of the major penitential processions, women did flagellate in private. Women joined the confraternities of discipline in the fourteenth century, but then seem to have been excluded from flagellation practices. Discipline societies in later centuries still record female members. The episcopal visitor to the Umbrian village of Oro di Piegaro in 1577 noted that women were members of the Madonna society, which was identified as a discipline (*frustra*) confraternity. Their preoccupation may have been with Marian devotions, including the Rosary, rather than corporal penance. Discipline confraternities might admit women, or increase their numbers, when they branched out into other activities, as with Ferrara's S. Maria Annunziata. In the fourteenth century it was a discipline brotherhood of artisans, by the sixteenth century it combined all classes, enrolled bishops and members of the ruling D'Este family, and from 1536–45 listed 254 *sorelle*.[45]

More positive and egalitarian attitudes to women in mixed confraternities are found in Lombardy and Rome, where attempts were made to form family-based societies. The Barnabites, at least initially, were enthusiastic about married couples joining together. Other confraternities in Lombardy and Piedmont allowed women autonomous and co-equal roles; in the Varese area they could take part in processions featuring dramatic recitations or tableaux.[46] That women might help overall recruitment and add to confraternity funds was made explicit in one of Venice's lesser Scuole, S. Agnese, which in 1457 admitted women after the male society had come to nothing ('è vegnuda a niente'). Later, if not then, this confraternity ran a small orphanage for children of

[43] C. Pizzoni, 'La Confraternita dell'Annunziata in Perugia' in AA.VV. *Movimento dei Disciplinati*, pp. 146–55; D'Addario, *Aspetti*, p. 442; cf. Meersseman, *Ordo Fraternitatis*, vol. 1, pp. 498–504; ASVen Scuole piccole, Busta 706, 'Notariato Libro primo' (1531–59), 'Libro Secondo' (1560–76), *passim*, and I fol. 7v for note about separate registers, which have not survived.

[44] Scaramucci, 'Considerazioni sui statuti', p. 157.

[45] Zardin, 'Confraternite e comunità, p. 725, n. 39; Scaramucci, 'Considerazioni sui statuti', *passim*, esp. pp. 165–6 on Ferrara.

[46] Zardin, 'Confraternite e comunità', p. 719, n. 31; *idem*, 'Le confraternite in Italia settentrionale'; Paglia, '*Pietà dei Carcerati*', pp. 89–93.

deceased members, until by 1525 this was taken over by the Procurators of St Mark's. Women would have had a philanthropic role here. The role of women in confraternities is often obscure, until illuminated by a statute sanctioning or recommending some activity, which implies that this was not normal. In the diocese of Naples the *sorelle* of S. Sebastiano in Resina acted as visitors of the sick, while those of the Rosary confraternity of S. Giovanni a Teduccio were specifically allowed to participate in members' funerals. According to Archbishop Paleotti the Bologna Sacrament confraternity had its women members looking after the chapel, equipping it with furnishings and other necessities; the men processed with torches and candles every third Sunday of the month, organised the major Corpus Christi procession, and the Forty-Hour (*Quarantore*) prayer and celebrations of the eucharist.[47]

Some confraternities happily allowed women to become prioresses and take on other official posts, as well as administering outside activities. In Rome the Crocefisso di S. Marcello had women *infermieri* organising hospital work, and the Corpus Christi company in S. Maria sopra Minerva had women organising processions. When women were admitted to the Pietà dei Carcerati they were given an active but subordinate position. They could not aspire to the leading offices, or be fully involved in prison work. They had their own officials and a separate congregation to run their affairs, they elected their own *signora baronessa* as protector for life and their principal task was to provide officials to help collect alms in the thirteen districts (*rioni*) of Rome. Most women members seem to have been wives of *fratelli*, joining after their husbands.[48]

Documentation is not very helpful on the extent of female membership. In the above-mentioned Roman Pietà confraternity there was a major *Quarantore* celebration (13 January 1583) soon after women were admitted; 40 brothers and 54 sisters participated.[49] For Perugia's largest confraternity in the seventeenth century, the Nome di Dio, there is a partial and poorly organised membership list from 1602–3; it recorded 402 male and 422 female names by 1613. The women had their own officials, including a female sacristan. Friars were included, and so were *suore*, the word implies nuns or Tertiaries, rather than lay sisters (usually called *sorelle*); some, but not all, are entitled Suor Tertiara. Given the Tridentine rules about the proper enclosure of nuns and attempts to end female Third Orders by banning new recruits, it would be interesting to know more about the role and status of these *Suore* within an essentially lay organisation. The confraternity was primarily designed to stamp out blasphemy, but like other Nome di Dio companies it might have been involved in social pacification and arbitration.[50]

[47] L. Sbriziolo, 'Per la storia delle confraternite veneziane; dalle deliberazioni miste (1310–1476) del Consiglio dei Dieci. Scolae communes, artigiane e nazionali', *Atti dell'Istituto Veneto di Scienze, Lettere ed Arti*, vol. 126 (classe di scienze morali, lettere ed arti), (Venice 1968), pp. 405–42, at p. 438, n. 75; Pullan, *Rich and Poor*, p. 260; Russo, *Chiesa e comunità*, p. 306; but cf. the ban on the women of a Florentine company attending funerals, Weissman, *Ritual Brotherhood*, p. 213; P. Prodi, 'Lineamenti dell'organizzazione diocesana in Bologna durante l'episcopato del card. G. Paleotti (1566–1597)', AA.VV. *Problemi di vita religiosa in Italia. Convegno di Storia della Chiesa in Italia* (Padua, 1960), pp. 348–9.

[48] *Statuti et Ordini della Venerabile Arcicompagnia dell' Santiss. Crocefisso in santo Marcello di Roma* (Rome, 1565); *Capitula Statuta et Ordinationes, Piae ac Venerabilis Confraternitatis, sacratissimi Corporis Christi in Ecclesia Minervae Alma Urbis Romae* (Rome 1561); Paglia, '*Pietà dei Carcerati*', pp. 123–5.

[49] *Ibid.* pp. 105–6; unfortunately he does not provide further figures for subsequent developments.

[50] ASP S. Domenico Misc. 77. These are minimum figures; this list confusingly repeats some, but not all, names that appeared on another notice of officials for a couple of years earlier; discrepancies do not seem explicable by death; on Nome di Dio societies see Prodi, 'Lineamenti', p. 359.

This high proportion of female members was certainly unusual—except possibly among Rosary devotional confraternities, which might be seen as essentially feminine societies. In rural Lombardy for example, the Rosary confraternity of Parabiago between 1576 and 1596 recruited 2,952 women, and only 1,224 men, and it had female officials. In 1589 that at Legnano had 561 women out of 723 members.[51] Generally the proportion of female members would have been lower—and their exact number harder to calculate—than for men. For example in the diocese of Assisi the 1573 visitation covered eleven confraternities in the city (and four remained unvisited). It has been estimated that 25 per cent of the population, or 35 per cent of communicants, were members of confraternities. Women were registered as belonging to four of the eleven, totalling 155. The highest proportion was in S. Maria Assunta del Vescovato, with 60 women to 93 men. For two nominally discipline societies the figures are suspiciously rounded: 50: 100 and 25: 100. For the twenty-eight confraternities visited in the Assisi *contado* membership figures were given for only four, without indicating whether women were involved. Quantifying female membership is even harder than counting the brothers.[52]

In general female relatives of confraternity brethren could derive spiritual and philanthropic advantages from these societies, by sharing in indulgences, joining pilgrimages, by receiving assistance if they fell on hard times, for dowries, for widowhood, and burial. Actual membership of a confraternity, even if the roles were restricted, did provide some functions within the society, and sometimes outside it. Post-tridentine clerical control, where effective, may have helped to increase female involvement in confraternities, since it should have made the society morally safer than it might have been when dominated by autonomous laymen. Most importantly, confraternities provided a social grouping and participation beyond the family. For many women in the sixteenth century this was a rare opportunity.[53]

(c) Social diversity and 'class' domination

Confraternities represented virtually all levels of society, from peasants and artisans to merchants and noble ladies, though there would seem to have been an obvious bias in favour of urban established orders—skilled artisans upwards. Opinion was divided on whether individual confraternities should be limited to an occupational group, a particular level of society, or a well-defined territorial sector of a city, or should be socially mixed, linking the high-and low-born, rich and poor. There is some debate about the significance of the patterns and the developments between inclusive and exclusive confraternities. The sixteenth century, while witnessing the formation of all

[51] Zardin, *Confraternite e vita di pietà*, pp. 75–8; see below, chapter 4.7, Rosary confraternities.
[52] Proietti Pedetta, 'Alcune note', pp. 457–73, esp. Table A, p. 461.
[53] Weissman, *Ritual Brotherhood*, pp. 212–3 on women as spiritual members; Rusconi, 'Confraternite', pp. 495–6; cf. Hoffman, *Church and Community in the Diocese of Lyon*, (New Haven and London, 1984), pp. 114, 126–7, 145; Brigden, 'Religion and social obligation', pp. 98–9 where it is argued that a fraternity in London was the one association where women were accorded nearly equal rights. In seventeenth-century France women seeking autonomy in their own sororities, or near-equality with men in joint fraternities possibly had a considerable struggle against male domination and suspicion: K. Norberg, 'Women, the family, and the Counter-Reformation: women's confraternities in the 17th century', *Proceedings of the Annual Meeting of the Western Society for French Historians*, 6 (1978) [1979], 55–63.

types, possibly saw a tendency towards mixed fraternities, whether the object was philanthropy, or parish devotions, while by the end of the seventeenth century discrimination and exclusiveness may have increased. The uncertainty arises because for most confraternities that can be named or numbered there are no surviving membership lists for analysis.

Medieval confraternities were probably predominantly artisan in membership, but from the fifteenth century their social composition widened, they became more 'respectable' and acquired members from the upper ranks of society. Efforts were also made to encompass more of rural or small-town society.

The possible confusion between confraternity and trade guild has already been noted. Trade guilds might have a religious confraternal element in addition to their economic and legal operations, while a confraternity formed for devotional purposes might recruit almost exclusively from a particular group of craftsmen or traders. The religious element of a trade guild might be deemed inadequate and lead members to form or join a devotional fraternity.[54]

The Venetian guilds, *arti*, usually had (as already indicated) related *scuole*, confraternities, to carry out their religious and social welfare activities. Members of the *arti* were obliged to join the related confraternity (where it existed) unless members of another *arte* and its *scuola*. But the *scuola* could also admit people not part of the guild. The compulsory element in the membership obviously affects judgements about religious and philanthropic dedication. R. Mackenney argues that the *scuole* tended to break down the solidarity of the *arti* as economic groups, and to encourage solidarity as Christians and Venetians. The Venetian guilds were, socially, broadly based—especially in comparison with the Florentine—since they comprised employers (*maestri*), and many levels of employees, rich and poor alike. Even if status divisions remained within the fraternity co-membership was likely to erode class tensions through cooperation in joint enterprises and worship. There were other *scuole piccole* not attached to the guilds, membership of which was voluntary, and similarly cut across social categories. It would be hard to distinguish absolutely between voluntary confessional *scuole piccole* and the compulsory *scuole delle arti* which might also include voluntary brothers. Venice is unique, in Italy, for the number and important characteristics of these guild confraternities, though medieval London provides some parallels.[55]

By the sixteenth century the proportion of artisan-guild confraternities in Italy declined, partly because the secular role of the guild system, with a powerful stake in the communal politics of certain cities, became attenuated. Venice was again exceptional in having strong guilds by the early seventeenth century capable of resisting—as R. Mackenney has argued—the republican government's 'absolutist' tendencies, and of promoting economic change and development to postpone overall decline.[56] Exclusive

---

[54] Brigden, pp. 96–7; A.J.R. Russell–Wood, *Fidalgos and Philanthropists. The Santa Casa da Misericòrdia of Bahia, 1550–1755* (London, 1968), pp. 2–3, argued that a true confraternity was defined as such when a corporation ceased to be drawn from one class in society, but this seems unduly restrictive; though primarily dealing with Brazil he initially discusses confraternities in a wide context.

[55] Mackenney, 'Trade Guilds', esp. pp. 5–6, 16–17, 121–4; *idem* 'Guilds and guildsmen in sixteenth-century Venice', *Bulletin of the Society of Renaissance Studies*, 2, no. 2 (October 1984), 7–12; *idem, Tradesmen and Traders*, chapter 2. On London, Brigden, pp. 94–7; Barron, 'The parish Fraternities'.

[56] Mackenney, 'Trade Guilds', esp. chapter 6 and pp. 374–5; *idem, Tradesmen and Traders*, pp. 232–7.

guild-based or occupational confraternities still existed in Milan, Rome and Genoa, but in the sixteenth century few new ones were created. There were some late foundations in Genoa: in 1600 a confraternity for inn-keepers, one for tailors in about 1623, and for music teachers sometime during the seventeenth century. In Florence there was an increase in the number of craft confraternities in the late sixteenth century, with the Medici Grand Dukes compelling workers (*sottoposti*) in certain trades to join. This was both a way of controlling the behaviour of workers–notably keeping them out of taverns–and an attempt to forestall discontent by ensuring that workers had some protection against adversity and help in old age through the welfare benefits of confraternity membership. Compulsion may have been a perversion of the confraternity spirit, but this is an interesting reflection on the state's view of the efficacy of confraternity provisions.[57]

Rome had both compulsory and voluntary occupation-based fraternities. All those working under master tailors were instructed to join the S. Croce dei Sarti founded in 1616, though the motivation and circumstances which led to this regulation are unclear. The S. Maria dell'Orto was a voluntary association for various guilds active in the poor Trastevere district. It provided a hospital for the brothers, and fostered the cult of the Madonna associated with the church. For painters, engravers, goldbeaters (*battilori*), and similar artisans there was the guild-confraternity of S. Luca; for sculptors, carvers and similar craftsmen the *università* (guild) di Marmorari, also called the company of SS. Quattro Coronate. From about 1539–40 more prestigious artists, sculptors and architects allied themselves instead to the devotional S. Giuseppe di Terrasanta company (or Virtuosi al Pantheon). This last confraternity and that of S. Luca evolved into the Academy and confraternity of S. Luca which operated effectively from 1593. The Academy is famous for its professional role, and its indication of artistic status, but for some artists it was an important religious and charitable fraternity.[58]

A relative decline in occupation-linked confraternities in some areas was due to government suspicions of their possible political and economic activity, and to a more charitable attitude that neighbours of different social standing should work with, as well as for, each other. The Florentine establishment's fears of subversion by confraternities has already been recorded for both the fourteenth and sixteenth centuries. In the fifteenth century there was also reason for apprehension. New artisan–neighbourhood or occupation-based societies emerged, as *sottoposti* confraternities, among the wool-beaters and scissors makers. They derived from highly secular festive societies and carnival organisations which had been notable in Florence. In some cases the motivation might still have been more festive than pious, as indicated by the statutes of the company of the Resurrection sent for episcopal approval in 1486. Alms raised for an ecclesiastically sanctioned confraternity, supposedly to celebrate Easter, might be used to finance subversive carnival activities and traditional inversion-of-the-world plays, mocking the hierarchical structures of society and satirising normal social relationships. New economic roles could also be added. The wool trimmers, (*cimatori*), were allowed to create a confraternity in 1494. The brothers soon used this for economic organisation,

---

[57] Grendi, 'Morfologia', esp. Table II, pp. 309–11; Weissman, *Ritual Brotherhood*, pp. 202–5.
[58] Maroni Lumbroso and Martini, pp. 103–4, 223–4, 261–71; A. Blunt, *Guide to Baroque Rome* (London, 1982) pp. 102–3; S. Rossi, 'La compagnia di San Luca nel Cinquecento e la sua evoluzione in Accademia', *RSRR*, 5 (1984), 367–94.

and by 1508 were allegedly conspiring to fix prices and strike. The society was allowed to reconvene in 1510, after the wool guild (masters) had asserted their authority, and had guaranteed that the workers and apprentices would be controlled. The involvement in politics of the plebeian neighbourhood and artisan confraternities, as well as the youth companies—especially during the crisis years for the Republic 1494–1512 and 1527–30—would have encouraged the upper ranks to develop confraternities that were more socially mixed, and more susceptible to control. Florence may have had more political problems with its confraternities than did other cities, but it has also been argued that Neapolitan artisan confraternities were fashioned as 'class' organisations from the later sixteenth century and that, besides fulfilling religious needs, they sought to use corporate solidarity to fix minimum wages. Such non-religious activities occasioned episcopal fulminations.[59]

A different 'class' argument has come from V. Paglia in his study of the Roman Pietà dei Carcerati, where he argues that confraternities developed in the later sixteenth century as part of the evolution of the new middle classes under capitalist development. He, like G. Le Bras for France, depicts the confraternity as the cradle of the bourgeois. He sees the Pietà and other Roman confraternities as dominated by northern Italian immigrants, bringing entrepreneurial and artisan skills. Unable fully to expand economically in Rome because of the clericalisation of the Papal State and because of the imbalance of consumption over productive industry, these people sought a role in the confraternity world—which gave them space to be active. The birth of the capitalistic society, and especially the breakdown of traditional agricultural organisation (despite papal attempts to curb excessive pasturing) increased poverty, and so the new confraternity members had an object for their activity and philanthropy. This interesting argument remains insecure at least until there is clearer evidence on the social composition of the Roman confraternities. Paglia has not been able to provide detailed information on the Pietà's membership. His citations suggest a wide social spread, when he names members entering in the early 1580s. Among the lower middle classes there was a barber from the Via Giulia, a wine-storeman, a joiner and a turner, a shoemaker and a painter from the piazza di S. Marta (Giovanni Venusta from Como); there was a chaplain from S. Girolamo di Ripetta, a physician and an advocate, a bookseller at the Chiesa Nuova (Angelo Marchiano from Savona), and the *maestro di casa* for the Rusticucci nobles; at the highest social level there were the bishops of Florence and of Alisso, and Signora Abalante from the family of the Counts of Corbara. This social spread would seem too broad to suit any meaningful concept of 'class'. Given the fluidity of the Roman population the confraternities were bound to enrol many not born in Rome. Paglia also suggests that members of the Roman tribunals were encouraged to join to provide links between the official structure of the city and the assistance systems.[60]

---

[59] R.C. Trexler, *Public Life in Renaissance Florence* (New York and London, 1980), pp. 407, 411–14; Villari, *La rivolta antispagnola* pp. 53–4; cf. L. Martz, *Poverty and Welfare in Habsburg Spain*(Cambridge, 1983), p. 165: Luis Hurtado wanted guild-linked confraternities abolished: 'Instead of meeting to dedicate themselves to pious works, they meet to conspire against the common good of the republic'; but note Hurtado's basic prejudice against confraternities (p. 166).

[60] Paglia, '*La Pietà dei Carcerati*', pp. xi, 46, 87, 151, and for names of members pp. 106–9; cf. on Rome's mobile population, Delumeau, *Vie économique et sociale de Rome dans la seconde moitié du XVIe siècle* (2 vols., Paris, 1957–9) vol. 1, 135–220.

Unlike Paglia, various historians stress the social diversity of important confraternities in key Italian cities, with membership including artisans, merchants, clerics and nobles. In Naples this may have helped lessen class prejudice and foster some social harmony (even if there were some very prominent and exclusive noble societies as well). In Genoa there was apparently a preference among the nobles—through to the eighteenth century—for joining socially mixed societies rather than confining themselves to exclusive noble ones, though new ones of the latter type were still founded. Social control may have been involved, but so was a charitable instinct. Around 1557 a Jesuit, D'Ottono, wrote of Genoa: 'There you will see some of these nobles and rich persons teaching the poor with very great humility and charity, which is a matter for praising God.'[61]

If confraternities were socially mixed, there was a likelihood that leading nobles or professionals would dominate the offices and administration, as seems to have happened in Genoa, in Rome's Pietà and SS. Trinità dei Pellegrini, or in the *pieve* of Parabiago-Legnano (Lombardy). In the last case D. Zardin argues that the parochial aristocracy dominated the offices of the different kinds of confraternity, and that it was rare for a brother of lower rank to play a leading role. The Rosary confraternities may have been more popular in organisation, but then it was a matter of the male minority ruling the female majority.[62] The Perugian hospital confraternity of S. Maria della Misericordia was certainly dominated by the patrician members, but in other Perugian mixed fraternities, like the confederated group of S. Agostino, S. Francesco and S. Domenico, affairs were (in our period) run by officials with varied backgrounds. The officials of the S. Tommaso d'Aquino company were interestingly mixed. Some came from leading aristocratic families like the Baglioni, Della Corgna and Della Staffa; the clergy provided Bishop Vincenzo Ercolani—a Dominican scholar, preacher and Savonarola-inspired pastoral leader—and the model parish priest Giovio Valentino; the lawyers were represented by Marco Torelli, a notary who worked for various confraternities and monasteries, and Marcantonio Eugenii, academic lawyer and city ambassador. There were also artisans like the goldsmith Antonio di Francesco and the poulterer Perniola Fibbieta; they were leading collectors of alms for, and helpers of, the abandoned or vulnerable girls, *derelitte*, who were the confraternity's chief philanthropic target.[63]

The domination of office-holding by the upper strata in a socially mixed fraternity was a matter of social control. It also had the advantage that such persons were in a stronger position to deal with bishops or local government, and to raise money. There could be resentments; there seems to have been a class conflict over offices in Vicenza's Crocefisso confraternity, which led to a resolution in 1603 that offices should be equally distributed and not dominated by the nobility. The Milanese confraternity of S. Croce e della Pietà dei Carcerati was dominated by an elite group, which provided most of the officials and was largely preoccupied with helping prisoners, to the annoyance of the

---

[61] A Fiori, 'L'archivio dell'Arciconfraternita della Dottrina Cristiana presso l'Archivio Storico del Vicariato. Inventario', *RSRR*, 2 (1978), 365–8, for a socially mixed Roman archconfraternity; Lopez, 'Le confraternite laicali', pp. 195–6, 198; Grendi, 'Morfologia'; F. Garofalo, *L'ospedale della SS. Trinita dei Pellegrini e dei Convalescenti* (Rome, 1950), pp. 28–31.

[62] Zardin, *Confraternite e vita di pietà*, pp. 145–73, 201–21, 229–30.

[63] Marinelli, *La Compagnia*, esp. pp. 73–97, 119, n. 243; Black, 'Perugia and post-tridentine church reform', pp. 433–4, 443–4; on the house of the *Derelitte* see below chapter 9.6.

majority of members who argued that their religious devotions, and particularly processions were neglected.[64] In Florence the Medici Grand Dukes wanted the prestigious city-wide confraternities (as opposed to parochial and craft ones) to be ruled by officials approved by them—almost inevitably patrician courtiers. But besides a policy of political control R. Weissman detects the attitude that socially respectable persons should perform key roles as courtiers of God, lending dignity to eucharistic devotions and processions.[65]

The top category of Venetian confraternities, the *Scuole Grandi*—officially approved and separated from the others for administrative and public policy purposes by the powerful Council of Ten—were socially mixed, but divisions developed between the rich and the poor through the sixteenth century: the rich directed affairs while the poor were passive recipients. However, individuals could readily change from one status to another as family fortunes waned, or more occasionally waxed. Prestigious families feeling, or being, 'poor' were seldom reluctant to accept confraternity charity. These *scuole* were not dominated by the patrician families, but were largely controlled by the middle-ranking *cittadini*. The latter, excluded from central political power, could play a significant role through the confraternities, especially as these had wide-ranging activities, as will become clearer later. For a lower social level similar points can be made about the *scuole delle arti* and *scuole piccole*, where the middling *maestri*—notably members of the mercers' guild (*marzari*)—could play a dominant, but not domineering role. The comparatively rich and expanding mercers' guild and confraternity could still have poor masters, and numbers of poor journeymen and apprentices, to be helped directly or indirectly. There was a social mix, encouraged by this guild's flexible policy on new admissions, which allowed people to flee from declining crafts into retailing. There were some divisions, possibly increasing in the early seventeenth century, between rich and poor members, but also mobility between these categories, when, for example, plume sellers prospered and stringers or sellers of needle and thread failed.[66]

(d) 'National' confraternities

The larger cities in the fifteenth century and later had confraternities exclusively, or at least predominantly, for foreigners or alien 'nations': for Germans, Flemings, French, or Albanians, but also for Lombards, Florentines or Bolognesi resident in or visiting another part of Italy. They catered for merchants and migrant artisans, non-Italian clerics in Rome, and also for students (where there could be overlap and confusion with the university Nations which were sometimes the basis of student organisation, for example in Perugia). While some foreigners were long resident in a city, and formed the core of the confraternity, such societies had a particularly transitory membership. The matriculation lists can be misleading since they might register those passing through

[64] G. Mantese, *Memorie Storiche della Chiesa Vicentina. Volume Quarto. (Dal 1563 al 1700)* (2 vols., Vicenza, 1974), vol. 1, pp. 567–8; M. Olivieri Baldissarri, *I 'poveri prigioni'. La confraternita della Santa Croce e della Pietà dei Carcerati a Milano nei secoli XVI–XVII* (Milan, 1985), pp. 144–8, with Appendix II (pp. 262–98) identifying many of the elite office-holders. See my review in *Cristianesimo nella Storia*. 9 (1988), 200–2.
[65] Weissman, *Ritual Brotherhood*, pp. 233–5.
[66] Pullan, *Rich and Poor*, pp. 75, 91–4; idem, 'Le Scuole Grandi', pp. 83–109; Mackenney, 'Trade Guilds', 237–43, 263–91, 299–302; idem. *Tradesmen and Traders*, pp. 94–6, 101–7.

very briefly as pilgrims or merchants, and might include (notably in Rome) names of people who never visited, but who wanted to be registered to benefit from the indulgences and privileges awarded to the confraternity, its church or chapel.[67] While these confraternities had a religious function, they clearly played a vital role socially, providing cohesion in a potentially hostile, xenophobic environment, or establishing lines of communication and introduction for newcomers. They also offered philanthropic help for poor nationals in transit as job-hunters, pilgrims and students, or for the sick. Rome probably had the fullest range of national confraternities, about nine existed at the end of the fifteenth century, twelve were added in the sixteenth and six in the seventeenth. In addition it should be recognised that some famous confraternities were founded by a foreign group, especially the Florentines, but later broadened their membership—such as S. Giovanni Decollato.[68]

In the course of the sixteenth century non-Italian 'national' confraternities were under threat and in decline, as the Reformation, Ottoman imperialism and economic shifts took their toll. In the 1560s the famous Venetian Scuola di S. Giorgio dei Schiavoni finding itself short of Slav nationals sought permission to enrol Italians. In the 1570s S. Nicolo dei Greci similarly broadened its membership, but it continued to fulfil a wide-ranging concept of philanthropy, derived from the Byzantine tradition, which was made available to outsiders as well as the Greek community within Venice.[69] Perugia had a confraternity Degli Oltramontani, for the religious and social needs of all non-Italians who might be in Perugia for a long or short period. A surviving record book (of accounts for 1579–1615) fails to clarify some of the problems of relations between the confraternity and the French and German student Nations within the University (which provided the priors of the confraternity), but it does demonstrate that the German contingent increasingly dominated the confraternity—not without friction with the less numerous, declining and poorer French and Flemish groups. 'German' included Hungarians and Bohemians from the Austrian Habsburg Empire. Leading scholars, clerics, nobles and merchants are found among the priors.[70] The society had

---

[67] C.W. Maas, *The German Community in Renaissance Rome, 1378–1523*, ed. P. Herde (Freiburg, 1981), esp. chapter 4, analysed the membership of the main German confraternities at S. Spirito, the Campo Santo and S. Maria dell'Anima and their links with churches and hospitals, and revealed the extent of long-distance membership; he partially corrected the otherwise still useful pioneering work of M. Vaes, 'Les fondations hospitalières Flamades à Rome du XV au XVII siècles', *Bulletin de l'Institut historique belge de Rome*, 1 (1919), 161–371, which also discussed S. Maria dell'Anima and S. Maria a Campo Santo. On Maas see review by M. Lowry in *English Historical Review*, 100 (1985), 657–9.

[68] Serra, 'Funzione e finanze', p. 269, n. 25: 15th century: 4 Italian (Senesi, Lombardi, and 2 Florentini), and 5 non-Italian (Belgi, Teutonici-Fiammenghi, Francesi, Catalani; and the Transalpini of Quattro Nazioni for Francesi, Lorenesi, Borgognoni and Savoiardi); 16th century: 7 Italian (Bergamaschi, Genovesi, Bresciani, Bolognesi, Napoletani, Siciliani, Piedmontini-Savoiardi-Nizzardi), and 5 non-Italian (Tedeschi, Lorenesi, Bretoni, Portoghesi, Spagnoli); 17th century: 5 Italian (Norcini, Lucchesi, Casciani, Marchigiani and Camerinesi [separating the Marchigiani]), and only one non-Italian (Borgognoni). S. Di Mattia Spirito, 'Assistenza e carità ai poveri in alcuni statuti di confraternita nei secoli XV–XVI' *RSRR*, 5 (1984), 137–54, on S. Giovanni Battista della Pietà dei Fiorentini, and S. Giovanni Battista dei Genovesi. On S. Giovanni Decollato see below chapter 10.5 and chapter 11.1 for its oratory.

[69] J. Ball, contribution to VI Seminario Internazionale di ricerche di Storia Veneta, Fondazione Giorgio Cini, Venice. April 1984; J. Ball, 'Poverty, charity and the Greek community', *Studi Veneziani*, 6 (1982), 129–45; Mackenney, *Tradesmen and Traders*, p. 48.

[70] BCP Ms 1186 fols. 7v, 22v, 30v; the Priors included Pietro Wlazek, Baron of 'Hulezen et Buonfando', protonotary apostolic and canon of Ulmutz (1582); Joannes Count of Hohenzollern (1594); Hieronimus Fugger (1598); cf. F. Weigle, *Die Matrikel der Deutschen Nation in Perugia (1579–1727)* (Tübingen, 1956), pp. 26, 35, 39.

limited funds but it did contribute alms for foreign students, priests, pilgrims, and unidentified poor from various parts of Europe, or provided funerals and burials for those dying in Perugia. How far the foreigners of lesser social standing participated in the confraternity, remains unclear.[71]

The archconfraternity for the Bologna nation erected in Rome in 1576 might be taken as a representative sixteenth-century national confraternity. According to the 1636 edition of its statutes it was presided over by a Bolognese prelate as Governor. It celebrated major festivals, held the Forty-Hour eucharistic devotion with lights and 'apparatus', organised visits to the sick Bolognesi (with separate visitors for nobles and for the others), provided dowries for girls born in Bologna or of Bolognese parents but resident in Rome. It had the privilege of releasing a condemned prisoner each year. As an archconfraternity it could aggregate other companies provided they took up the dedication to St Petronio, the patron saint of Bologna. The devotional and philanthropic aspects are typical of many sixteenth-century confraternities, but in this case there is a national bias in dedication, membership and persons assisted.[72]

National confraternities were likely to be viewed with suspicion by the authorities, especially in the uneasy mood of the Counter-Reformation. We shall return to cases where the Venetian Inquisition investigated a confraternity of Florentines at the Frari church, and the fraternity of German cobblers and shoemakers (chapter 3.1). The latter was a particularly narrow group, exclusive on occupational and well as national grounds. Most national societies would, however, have involved a reasonably broad social spread in the membership, with the defence of their suspect foreign identity and interests being more important than the maintenance of a social pecking order. S. Giovanni Battista della Pietà dei Fiorentini made clear in its 1544 statutes that it was ready to accept nobles, non-nobles, rich, poor, men, women, young, old, and in fact anybody–if Florentine. It had a strong charitable impulse towards its poor brethren.[73]

(e) Social and moral exclusiveness

The above discussion has stressed the extent of social integration in some, largely urban, confraternities. But confraternal exclusiveness did not disappear. Though there was a larger chance of nobles and particians being incorporated into confraternities than in the fourteenth century, a number of them preferred their own exclusive companies. This conformed to the general tendency in the sixteenth century to accentuate noble status, to emphasise titles and the formality of social intercourse. R. Rusconi has detected among discipline confraternities a change from social mediation in the fourteenth century to aristocratisation. It has been argued that even Sacrament confraternites became increasingly oligarchic in the seventeenth century, though not exclusively

---

[71.] BCP Ms 1186, e.g. fols. 5v: in 1581 two French priests given 22 bolognini, 6v: in 1582 a poor French scholar given 18.2 bol., 11v: in 1585 'on pisano malato in presensio del toto la capania' given alms of 10 bol., [the written Italian in this book is often heavily contaminated by first languages], 33v: 6 paoli for a poor German priest in 1600, 58r: May 1606 donations to 3 Flemings, a poor soldier from Hungary and two poor pilgrims from Franconia–the prior was then a Bohemian, Solenico Wytha (cf. Weigle, p. 47, no. 464 and p. 51).

[72.] Statuti dell'Arciconfraternita di S. Gio. Evangelista della Natione di Bologna eretta in Roma l'anno MDLXXVI (Bologna, 1636). See below, chapter 4.5, on Forty–Hour devotions.

[73.] Di Mattia Spirito, pp. 140–4, esp. p. 142: 'vogliamo che si possa accettare nella nostra compagnia nobili, ignobili, ricchi, poveri, uomini, donne, giovani, vecchi et finalmente ogni ragion di persone'.

'gentlemanly', but more evidence from matriculation lists is needed to test these impressions.[74]

Naples—attracting feudal barons from all over the South—provides key examples of exclusive confraternities; as with the Devote di Gesù of 1554 for noble women only, and the Jesuit-founded Venerazione del SS. Sacramento for noblemen. The latter, after a series of debilitating quarrels, was revitalised by Father Corcione in 1612. Thereafter the nobles fostered mission work in Naples and overseas, and established hospices for converted prostitutes and abandoned girls. This attitude of *noblesse oblige* or *richesse oblige*—that an exclusive noble society should actively work for the less fortunate, and not just leave money at death—may be likened to English merchant attitudes to philanthropy. The Oratory of Divine Love, and subsequently the Theatines and Oratorians, encouraged active charitable work by nobles. Filippo Neri tested the dedication of young nobles wishing to join his Oratory and allied institutions by at once sending them to clean wounds and sores in hospitals.[75]

Though this ran counter to the general trend in Genoa, exclusive confraternities were still being founded, most notably two noble Della Morte companies were created to ensure the decent burial of the poor. In Perugia Bishop Bossio in 1565, when Governor of the city, founded the Annunziata (or Delle Vergine) confraternity exclusively for nobles, and encouraged the brothers to spend their money on dowries for poor girls. Bossio, himself a Milanese nobleman, joined the company.[76] Though the Jesuits had some 'democratic' ideas that allowed an intermingling of social classes within the Order, when it came to starting lay confraternities they were inclined to create segregated companies. In Perugia they formed separate fraternities for nobles, for artisans and for *contadini*, with separate oratories under their church of Il Gesù. In Lecce the Jesuits organised five different confraternities—for nobles, students, scholars, youths and artisans. Peasants had their own confraternity of S. Egidio, but apparently unconnected with the Jesuits.[77]

A different kind of exclusiveness was based on moral criteria. The confraternities' statutes unsurprisingly banned heretics, usurers, adulterers, sodomites and so on. But they could also list as undesirable the frequenters of taverns, gamblers and card players—thus excluding particularly those lacking the means to relax at home.[78] Two

---

[74] Rusconi, 'Confraternite', pp. 478, 495–6' Zardin, 'Le confraternite in Italia settentrionale'; *idem*, 'Confraternite e comunità', pp. 728–30.

[75] Lopez, 'Le confraternite laicali', p. 198; *idem*, *Riforma Cattolica e Vita Religiosa e Culturale a Napoli* (Naples and Rome, n.d. [c. 1965]), pp. 81–9; cf. Jordan, *Philanthropy in England*, p. 153; L. Ponnelle and L. Bordet, *St. Philip Neri and the Roman Society of His Times*, trans. and introduction R.F. Kerr (London, 1979 reprint edn), pp. 154–6, 218–20; M. Trevor, *Apostle of Rome. A Life of Philip Neri 1515–1595* (London, 1966), pp. 95, 112; G.B. Del Tufo, *Historia Della Religione de'Padri Chierici Regolari* (Rome, 1609), pp. 125–7.

[76] Grendi, 'Morfologia'; BCP Ms 1221, R. Sotii, 'Annali, Memorie et Ricordi', fol. 42; Black, 'Perugia and papal absolutism in the sixteenth century', *EHR*, 85 (1970), p. 535.

[77] C. Crispolti, *Perugia Augusta* (Perugia, 1648), pp. 156–63; S. Siepi, *Descrizione Topologico–Istorica della Citta di Perugia* (3 vols., Perugia, 1822), p. 523; Rosa, 'Geografia', pp. 36–9.

[78] BCB F.O.42, the 1562 statutes of S. Maria della Morte, Bologna, chapter 25 (pp. 44–6) excluded 'scandalosa, usuraria, concubinaria, et di mala condittione, et fama'. The 1479 statutes of the Bologna company of Corpo di S. Procolo had more fully excluded: 'Heretici, publici usuaii o secreti, sodomiti, concubinari publici, adulteri, biastemaduri di Iddio e di sancti, giugaduri, tavernari, publici partesani, o che facesse arte prohibita, o chi conversasse in dishonesti luoghi o con disoneste persone, o chi fusse ladro, o chi facesse incanti o maliè o desse fede e semel cose al postuto', printed in Fanti, *San Procolo*, p. 164.

Florentine societies also considered that certain jobs rendered people unfit to be brothers. The Sacrament company in S. Felicità, already noted for its attitudes to the active and contemplative life, excluded lesser bureaucratic officials–those serving the Otto di Guardia, the guilds or the Grand Duke's Palace as spies, messengers or waiters. The archconfraternity Della Misericordia, for nobles and artisans, excluded anybody serving in the *famiglia* of any government office or magistracy. It explained its attitude at breathless length:

The reason for this is, although Jesus Christ was not an excluder of persons, but was very often with publicans and sinners, he did this to give salvation [*salute*] to all miserable sinners, and so that the flock, that is our lost soul, should be found again. Nevertheless, not to contradict the action and example of our Redeemer Jesus Christ, but because order cannot exist without reason, where there is no order there is confusion, and just as in the eternal life there is order and distinction amongst the ministers of God, so in church the recipient of the first tonsure should not sit next to the bishop to whom superiority and reverence should be granted [:] so that in pious places such as this company order should not be absent, after we had elected good secular persons noble and of good habits, leaders and rulers of our city of Florence, and as at the time of the council they are called by name to sustain our company where there may be need of their patronage before magistrates and offices to maintain this pious work of mercy, it appeared to us an opportune and reasonable matter that such familiars or servants, as stated above, should not enter our company, because if such men were present, it might happen that they [the leaders] might sit with such familiars at our company's table, and that we brethren would have it in our mind to murmur or think that perhaps it would be well to say: friend, descend below, to whom then it would not be honour but very great dishonour; and to remove any doubt from the mind of our brethren, we again wish and order that if any of our company should enter as servant or familiar to such offices, he cannot as such exercise any office in our company.[79]

Such exclusions combined social snobbery, fear of moral contamination, and probably fear of informers passing on information to the Grand Duke and his increasingly absolutist-minded government, though in the case of the Misericordia the leading officials of the confraternity came to be nominees of the Grand Duke serving for life.

(f) Youths

It was mentioned above that in Lecce there was a confraternity especially for youths. Here and elsewhere the Jesuits were increasing the numbers of special youth confraternities, but very little is known about them.[80] Attention has recently been paid to fifteenth-century boys' confraternities in Florence. These seem to have developed from about 1410 when a goldsmith started the company of the Archangel Raphael for *fanciulli*–also known as the Natività del Signore. Before 1427 the Vangelista (or S. Giovanni Evangelista) confraternity was founded for youths aged between twelve and twenty-four. Ambrogio Traversari positively recommended such societies for young persons to Pope Eugenius IV (who subjected them to papal control in 1442) for their recitation of psalms, singing of hymns and worthwhile covoquies. Confraternity singing may well be what is recorded in Luca Della Robbia's sculptures on his *cantoria* for the Duomo (now in the Opera del Duomo museum). These societies filled many needs,

---

[79] D'Addario, *Aspetti*, pp. 432–8, translating from p. 437; Weissman, *Ritual Brotherhood*, p. 201.
[80] Zardin, 'Le confraternite in Italia settentrionale'.

social and religious, in the preparation of members for adulthood. (But it should be remembered that 'youth' could last until about thirty.) The juvenile confraternities provided religious and secular education, organised entertainments such as ball games, and dramatic productions. They may have been designed to protect youths from sodomitic attacks by their elders, or restrain their own inclination, since Florence in particular was judged to have a major homosexual problem from the early fifteenth century. These youth societies became involved in politics, most notably at the end of the century in the struggles between supporters and opponents of fra Savonarola and his republicanism. It is supposed that such confraternities died out under subsequent regimes, discouraged by both religious and political authorities, until they were partially replaced by youth confraternities for Christian Doctrine.[81]

Segregated youth confraternities were too similar to the secular Youth Abbeys which certainly existed in Piedmont as well as in France. They mocked adult institutions in ceremonies, and discomfited certain people, such as those marrying for a second time, or marrying somebody outside their village or parish. Bishops, who attacked such practices in synodal legislation, were unlikely to encourage youth confraternities that might imitate such practices. Adult confraternities could admit new members when very young—or have youths attached as supervised novices, as in Bologna's S. Maria della Morte or S. Maria della Vita.[82]

However, several special youth confraternities, besides the Lecce one, existed in the new climate of the Counter-Reformation. A survey of Umbrian dioceses in the 1570s reveals two, in Cascia and Norcia, but they are names only.[83] We know something about one Florentine youth confraternity for Christian Doctrine in the later sixteenth century—S. Salvatore for boys aged six to fifteen. It was established by the adult Sacrament confraternity in the church of Ognissanti, according to its 1579 statutes:

to keep the youths [giovani] in this very holy purity, to praise and magnify God in behaviour and in divine lauds; therefore they will have white garments, to denote the innocence and purity they have to maintain, wearing on their left shoulder the sign of the holiest Saviour, and this sign will be on the standard when they go out in processions. But none will be received into our company unless of good reputation, so that no vicious person shall corrupt the others by his bad example.

[81] Weissman, *Ritual Brotherhood*, pp. 102, 116, 189–90, 213, 230; Trexler, *Public Life*, pp. 368–99; *idem*, 'Ritual in Florence: adolescence and salvation in the Renaissance', *The Pursuit of Holiness in Late Medieval and Renaissance Religion*, ed. C. Trinkaus with H.A. Oberman (Leiden, 1974), pp. 247–64; W.J. Bouwsma challenged (*ibid*, pp. 270–1), the stereotype of Florentine homosexuality, to which Trexler replied that it was perceived as a problem, even if it was not objectively so; R.L. Mode, 'Adolescent *Confratelli* and the *Cantoria* of Luca della Robbia', *The Art Bulletin*, 68 no. 1 (March 1986), 67–71, who dates the Alleluia side panels to c. 1434, before the foundation of the school of chant and grammar, and the introduction of polyphonic chant under G. Dufay and A. Squarcialupi, with which the *cantoria* has usually been associated.

[82] Cf. N.Z. Davis, 'The reason of misrule: youth groups and charivaris in sixteenth-century France', *Past and Present*, 50 (February 1971), 41–75; *eadem*, 'Some tasks and themes', pp. 318–26 on youth confraternities and other youth groups, with comments on Trexler's work on Florence; Weissman, *Ritual Brotherhood*, p. 64, n. 72 on the young in adult companies; BCB F.O.6, e.g. fols. 61r (1427+), 75r (1457+) novice members in S. Maria della Vita; BCB F.O.42, S. Maria della Morte, statutes caps. 4 and 11, pp. 8, 19–20. Jewish communities also had youth confraternities, see E. Horowitz, 'A Jewish youth confraternity in seventeenth-century Italy', *Italia. Studi e ricerche sulla storia, la cultura e la letteratura degli ebrei d'Italia*, 5 nos. 1–2 (Jerusalem, 1985), 36–74, primarily dealing with the foundation of one in Asti in 1619, but also referring to one in Verona, which was absorbed into an adult confraternity in 1586. I am grateful to the author for sending me a copy of this study.

[83] Casagrande, 'Ricerche', p. 38.

And it is not possible to receive anyone without knowing his father or mother, or else others who would have care of him.

The boys were supervised by a guardian, elected from members of the adult Sacrament company and confirmed by the Archbishop, who vetted admissions. They were to be educated by masters of the novitiates, according to the precepts of St Paul and St Timothy. The boys had special officials (called *festaioli*) to organise processions and outdoor displays: 'everything should be done with moderation, always in a spirit of devotion, and this will be observed even when a triumphal display is erected for the procession of San Giovanni or during some devout representation at carnival time, which will be useful in keeping the boys busy at such dissolute times'.

This company maintained some characteristics of fifteenth-century confraternities, but greater control was imposed, and membership was probably less fun. The parish processions for Corpus Christi provided important opportunities for fathers (in red) and sons (in white) from the adult and youth Sacrament companies to parade together, and for youths to be presented as a well-educated and well-governed generation.[84] Cogent reasons for having separate youth confraternities were removed in various areas by the late sixteenth century. Christian Doctrine schools (chapter 10.3) and Jesuit schools and colleges could provide a fuller religious education, and a better training for the priesthood than old-style youth confraternities.

This section has highlighted the involvement of priests, women, and youths in the confraternity networks which were intended mainly for laymen. It has also shown that socially among the men there might be societies primarily for a restricted sector—nobles, artisans, particular alien nationals. However, other important confraternities sought to commingle the classes, orders and sexes in the pursuit of social harmony, or social control. Having established who was involved, we need to obtain some idea of how many were concerned.

3 COUNTING CONFRATERNITIES AND THEIR MEMBERS

Problems with source materials, as indicated in chapter 1.4, make it very difficult to produce accurate assessments of the numbers of confraternities and their geographical distribution or of the number of Italians associated with confraternities, even in one city. The projected historical Atlas for Italy would have provided some foundation for assessing the geographical distribution of confraternities and allied institutions, but this has only produced minimal results so far. The *visitationes ad limina* reports, as the main accessible record for a study diocese by diocese are daunting and, as already indicated, the figures they provide can be suspect. It should be recalled that Italy had about 290 dioceses, the exact figure depending on the definition of 'Italy', which islands or parts of the Dalmatian coast in conflict between Venice and Turkey are included at any given point, or which dioceses had been newly created or suppressed. This was a higher ratio of dioceses than in any other European area, but many Italian dioceses were little more than parishes. Montepeloso and Lavello were virtually one-city bishoprics of about 800

---

[84] D'Addario, *Aspetti*, pp. 438–40 from which I have translated; Weissman, *Ritual Brotherhood*, pp. 213–14 on Sacrament and Christian Doctrine companies for youths. For Christian Doctrine confraternities of adult teachers see below, chapter 10.3.

and 500 households respectively. Nicotera was composed of a 'city' of fifty families and a few villages. But such dioceses presented *ad limina* reports that have been or could be studied.[85]

What follows is a comment on some assessments that have been made and some specific local studies that will move us closer to a numerical analysis. These studies are based on figures from the reports of the *visitationes ad limina*, some episcopal and apostolic visitations and records for individual confraternities. My own experience of reports which cite numbers has inclined me towards scepticism. Bishops might not count all the confraternities, because they had not been officially sanctioned, or they might record societies that were essentially defunct. In assessing the number of people involved we can find major discrepancies between the numbers enrolled or claimed by an outside evaluater, and those who appear to be 'active' brothers and sisters. But an individual's activity level might fluctuate considerably over the years. In the end we can as yet rarely move beyond impressionistic guesses, even when we appear to have solid figures.

It might be agreed that by the later sixteenth century nearly every sizable village and parish throughout Italy had at least one confraternity. This was an expansion, and Italy may by then have rivalled parts of Spain in the number of fraternities. It is difficult to believe P. Lopez' contention that this coverage in Italy had been achieved by the late fifteenth century. He seems to have been following J. Duhr, who was generalising from the supposed French situation, which again is open to doubt.[86] This is not to deny that the major urban centres in the fifteenth century had a high density of confraternities: at the end of the century Florence had over 100 fraternities—and that despite periodic suppressions and suspensions. What is in doubt is the density in smaller towns and villages. In noting an increase through the sixteenth century we might be deceived by the relative abundance of evidence after the Council of Trent, because of its pressures for recording evidence. But reformers in the later sixteenth century were themselves under the impression that they were both adding to the stock of confraternities, and revitalising older institutions that were more or less moribund. Such reformers, especially Jesuits, Capuchins and Somaschi, when conducting 'missions' into remoter rural areas and the more destitute urban parishes of some cities like Genoa and Naples, argued that they were bringing religious activity, or Christianity generally, into places where it had been almost totally lacking. This would imply the absence of confraternities as well as active parish priests and chaplains. The reformers then promoted confraternities as remedies against irreligion and immorality.[87]

[85] Jedin and Dolan, vol. 5, p. 506; Black, 'Perugia and post-tridentine church reform', p. 431; Donvito and Pellegrino, *L'Organizzazione Ecclesiastica*, pp. 50–1, 101; P. Sposato, *Aspetti e figure*, p. 177; Spedicato, pp. 62–94, with warnings about the limitations of this source.

[86] Lopez, 'Le confraternite laicali', p. 166; J. Duhr, 'La confrèrie dans la vie de l'Eglise', *Revue d'Histoire Ecclesiastique*, 35 (1939), 437–78; cf. Le Bras, pp. 433–4; cf. Henderson, 'Confraternities', p. 70, based on detailed work for his London PhD thesis. For the claim that Spain heads the league-table of confraternities, see Flynn, 'Charitable ritual', 337–8; her forthcoming book will presumably substantiate this claim more fully.

[87] Paglia, *'La Pietà dei Carcerati'*, pp. 164–5; Donvito and Pellegrino, *L'Organizzazione Ecclesiastica*, pp. 57–8. Useful on missions generally and where they were conducted, C. Faralli, 'Le missioni dei Gesuiti in Italia (sec. XVI–XVII): problemi di una ricerca in corso', *Bollettino della Società di Studi Valdesi*, 138 (1975), 97–116; E. Novi Chavarria, 'L'attività missionaria dei Gesuiti', *Per la Storia Sociale e Religiosa*, eds. G. Galasso and C. Russo, vol. 2 (Naples, 1982), pp. 159–85; J. Coste, 'Missioni nell'Agro Romano nella primavera del 1703', *RSRR*, 2 (1978), 165–223, esp. pp. 173–6 on earlier missions.

An expansion towards one confraternity per parish or village came from the increase in devotionally oriented societies, notably associated with the Eucharist and the Rosary. The spread of these, and some philanthropic groups, especially those involving the burial of the dead, was fostered by offering enticing arrays of indulgences; Carlo Borromeo's promotion of Sacrament confraternities all over Lombardy exemplifies this.[88] By the late sixteenth century visitation records are reporting Sacrament or Rosary societies in poor southern dioceses. The 1609 *ad limina* report on Cosenza claimed a Sacrament confraternity in virtually every parish; the smaller, poorer see of Nicotera claimed a number of Rosary and Sacrament societies. In comparison other types, such as hospital or Christian Doctrine fraternities, remained rare in the south. The total of confraternities in north and central Italy increased with the additional proliferation of other kinds of confraternities, especially those connected with the teaching of Christian Doctrine, or supervising hospitals/hospices and other philanthropic institutions. In the south, instead of having a separate institution, the philanthropic work might be undertaken by a devotional company. This is known to have happened outside Naples, where, for example, the Rosary confraternity of Boscotrecase also looked after prisoners and generally observed the Seven Acts of Mercy, and that at S. Sebastiano, Resina, assisted the non-resident poor and sick.[89]

The geographical variation is explained by the relative differences in economic prosperity, as well as discrepancies in enthusiasm for reform. However, one should still be wary of numbers. There are warnings in studies of both rural Lombardy and Naples that devotional societies could flounder soon after foundation, especially as many were established under episcopal command rather than local enthusiasm, and did not necess- arily take root. Bishops elsewhere might well have been recording confraternities that were moribund and excluding others that were thriving but operated without full canonical approval.[90]

Numbers within confraternities varied considerably. We have already noted that a Lombard Rosary society had only four women. Numerous fraternities must have had between ten and twenty enrolled at any given time. But at the other end of the scale some confraternities had hundreds of members—however inactive they might be. One of the largest Italian confraternities in the sixteenth century was the Neapolitan Compagnia dello Spirito Santo (or Santo Spirito), also known as the Compagnia dei Bianchi, from the white robe worn by at least some of its members. According to its own statutes by November 1562, ten years after foundation, the company had 6,000 members; the papal Bull *Super gregem* granting final approval in April 1563 put the number at 7,000. At least one writer has put these large figures down to a boastful exaggeration typical of the city. Given a city population of 220,000 the figure is feasible. It has been considered as the centre of Neapolitan piety; it undertook numerous activities and was supported by the most prestigious families. It led the campaign to encourage the laity to take communion frequently; it helped widows, homeless, abandoned girls, and the daughters of prostitutes. According to a contemporary

[88] Zardin, 'Confraternite e comunità', pp. 712–13, 732.

[89] Sposato, p. 198; Russo, *Chiese e comunità*, pp. 311–2.

[90] *Ibid.*, pp. 300–4, 393–4, Table XVII, pp. 332–6, Tables XIII–XIV; Zardin, *Confraternite e vita di pietà*, pp. 19–22, 81 n.1: within one *pieve* the Sacrament confraternity at Canegrate was soon thriving, that at nearby Cantalupo was not, as in this case the visitor in 1596 admitted.

historian, the institution (*conservatorio*) for this last group housed 400 girls in 1587. Such undertakings—which may have proved too ambitious and diversified—would have required many activists, though not thousands. An equally famous and active Neapolitan confraternity, the Compagnia dei Bianchi della Giustizia, limited itself to 100 members. Few other cities would have had a confraternity with more than a thousand brethren. In Genoa the Sodalizio della Vergine del Rosario grew to about 1,200 members after an intense preaching mission by the Jesuits among the triremes, so many would have been irregular attenders. The Perugian Nome di Dio had a minimum of 824 brothers and sisters, and could have come close to a thousand. In all these cases there is the problem of what proportion of a large number are active participants. Many have registered merely to obtain indulgences or a decent burial and subsequent prayers. Members of some Rosary confraternities may never have met as a corporate group.[91]

To obtain an impression of the extent of membership of confraternities we can look at a selection of areas that have received some detailed investigation, giving an idea of the number of confraternities, their types, and their density.

Venice had several large confraternities. In the early sixteenth century there was a top group of five *Scuole Grandi*: S. Marco, S. Rocco, Della Misericordia, Della Carità, and S. Giovanni Evangelista; a sixth was elevated to this status in 1552, S. Teodoro. The Council of Ten limited their numbers officially to 500–600 members each, but these limits were exceeded in the fifteenth and sixteenth centuries. B.S Pullan estimates that before the great plague of 1575–6 these six societies totalled between five and six thousand brothers, or 10 per cent of the adult male population. The city had many lesser *scuole* of various kinds and sizes, about 120 in the early sixteenth century rising to 357 in the eighteenth. Only a limited number have been studied in detail. Many of the later sixteenth-century foundations were parochial Sacrament confraternities, membership of which could easily be combined with others. Many of those active in cloth production and retailing and in their related *scuole delle arti* seem also to have been members of the *Scuole Grandi*. This makes it hard to assess how many Venetians might have been involved in confraternities, but one might suggest that between a third and a half of households were linked to at least one fraternity. For some, membership was compulsory, as we have noted above.[92]

According to visitation reports on some central Italian dioceses in the 1570s confraternities were widespread. In the Spoleto diocese there were at least 210, and the bigger cities had many: Norcia 14, Spello 13, Spoleto 12, and 92 smaller places had at least one confraternity, most often a Sacramental one, and twenty places had at least two companies. The Visitor ordered that the thirty-five places visited which mentioned no confraternity should create one immediately. Assisi with a diocesan population of about 14,000, was served by eleven city confraternities, and twenty-eight in the surrounding villages; the Visitor criticised their running of hospices and noted other deficiencies. In

[91] Zardin, *Confraternite e vita di pietà*, p. 73; Miele, 'L'assistenza sociale', pp. 834–7, 858; E. Pontieri, 'Sulle origini della Compagnia dei Bianchi della Giustizia in Napoli e su suoi Statuti del 1525', *Campania Sacra*, 3 (1972), 1–60; R. De Maio, 'L'Ospedale dell'Annunziata' in his *Riforme e miti*, pp. 245–53; Grendi, 'Morfologia'; for Perugia's Nome di Dio see above n. 50; for a very large confraternity in Verona, see below chapter 10.4.

[92] Pullan, *Rich and Poor*, pp. 33–4, 86–98; *idem*, 'Le Scuole Grandi'; information in unpublished papers given by R. Mackenney and W.B. Wurthmann in Edinburgh and Glasgow.

the Perugian diocese there were 138 fraternities in 88 places other than Perugia itself.[93] My own studies of Perugian urban confraternities indicate that over forty existed by the early seventeenth century. An exact tally is not possible; contemporary archival material or statutes exist for only a few, and for many the information comes from later sources which do not clarify when certain societies petered out, or when, in the seventeenth century, others started.[94] Membership ranged from over 800 in the Nome di Dio to a dozen or so in some parish companies. Membership of S. Maria della Misericordia was fixed by statute at a little over 300: there were to be fifty lay members from each of the five districts (*Porte*) of the city, and in addition the forty or so parish priests, the city's judges and doctors were automatically members. Many of these *ex officio* members must have been inactive in the confraternity.[95]

Record books of the confraternities, where they survive, can help establish the size of the active membership. The city's three old societies of S. Agostino, S. Domenico and S. Francesco were confederated, in that they shared common rules, and sometimes met together for major constitutional and business purposes. Their records show that joint meetings were attended by eighty to a hundred brothers in the post-tridentine period, though they had mustered 115 for the June 1565 Corpus Christi assembly. Normally each of these confraternities met in its own oratory. In S. Francesco twenty to thirty attended meetings in the later sixteenth century; the peak seems to have been thirty-six for Christmas 1575, when special indulgences in connection with the Church's Jubilee were available. With that number the oratory would have been well filled— assuming the main rooms were the same size as now, since the early seventeenth-century redecoration did not apparently involve restructuring. No full membership list has been discovered for S. Francesco. The above figures come from votes at general meetings held on major feast days, so they suggest a maximum number of active members. When the S. Domenico confraternity scrutinised its membership in 1566 it counted 54 names, and the voting figures recorded at meetings in the 1560s and 1570s vary from 24 to 38. A sample in the 1490s suggests active membership was then in the twenties. There was, surprisingly, an overlap of membership between the three linked confraternities, though in the absence of proper matriculation lists the extent of this is unclear. In the 1560s Emilio Alfani, from a leading patrician banking family, attended both S. Domenico and S. Francesco. When for Christmas 1564 the officials of S. Domenico drew up a list of those defaulting on their Christmas communion, they noted that one had taken communion at S. Agostino and another at S. Francesco, and that Ieronimo di Euliste Baglioni was absent because he was prior of the fraternity of Corpus Christi in the cathedral of S. Lorenzo.[96]

Ieronimo Baglioni's case raises the question of how many individuals were members of, and active in, more than one fraternity. Some statutes banned brothers from being members of another brotherhood, but there is evidence—as here, and from the above

[93] Casagrande, 'Ricerche', pp. 34–5, 38–9; Proietti Pedetta, 'Alcune note', pp. 457–73.
[94] Since my 'Perugia and post-tridentine church reform', p. 445 (where I suggested 30 plus city confraternities), I have found more indications.
[95] Valeri. His study has little on the actual operation of the confraternity.
[96] SBF records (see Bibliography A), esp. S. Domenico vol. 427, Adunanze 1488–1514; vol. 430, Adunanze 1564–1607, with fols. 5v, 7r, 13r–v for examples of joint membership; S. Francesco vol. 457, Libro dei Verbali 1566–90.

discussion of Venice—of multi-membership for some persons. The lack of contemporaneous membership lists for a group of confraternities in any given city makes it impossible to judge the scale of the overlap.

A lesser Perugian confraternity, that of S. Pietro Martire for the artisans of one district, recorded between sixteen and twenty-five attending general meetings between the years 1548 and 1601. The participation rate in this humble society was probably higher than in the more prestigious confederated group, where some patricians in particular might have joined for honour rather than pious dedication, or might have been frequently absent because of other commitments. At a later date, in 1653, the confraternity of SS. Rocco e Sebastiano, of no great social prestige, seems to have had sixty to sixty-five members when it opened a new book of decisions (*partiti*), but at the general meetings of that year there were between eighteen and thirty-four present to vote on major propositions.[97]

Using what figures are available, and deducing the probable size of types of confraternities that are merely named, one could (very tentatively) suggest that the city of Perugia had a confraternity membership at the end of the sixteenth century of a little over 2,000, when the population was about 19,000. This is a somewhat lower proportion than the estimate for neighbouring Assisi of 25 per cent of the population or 35 per cent of communicants; I suspect this Assisi evaluation involves exaggerated, rounded figures. The numbers of active confraternity brothers and sisters would be considerably less at any given moment, judging from internal voting figures. At various points in the text and notes below I shall give votes recorded for decisions taken, to alert the reader to the number of activists involved. However, again there are qualifications to make. At the end of the century the Venetian Convicinato Scuola di S. Marcilian recorded thirty to forty members attending the major council meetings, yet when the widow of a late *confratello* appealed for a dowry grant for one of her daughters the decision to award her 25 *scudi* was made by 68 to 14 votes. While general council meetings, usually held on a day when the confraternity was celebrating a feast devotionally, are expected to reveal the active membership, here we have evidence of a much higher participation for a philanthropic matter.[98]

Further caution over figures and their meaning comes from R. Weissman's exemplary study of the membership of the Florentine confraternity of S. Paolo in the fifteenth century. People could be members of a fraternity for a long period, but their participation might fluctuate according to age and family commitments—with peaks of involvement as novices and in maturity as office-holders. Weissman needs a lengthy chapter to draw sensible conclusions from the figures for one society. Given the great numbers of recorded confraternities but the paucity of evidence on most, and the problems of interpreting those figures we do have, the historian must be shy of making numerical assessments about confraternity coverage.[99]

---

[97] ASP Ex Congregatione di Carita, no. 30, Confraternita di S. Pietro Martire, vol. 1, Adunanze e ricordi vari, 1548–1601; BCP Ms 1301 'Libro dei partiti . . . SS. Rocco e Sebastiano di Perugia', 1653–1743, fols. 1r–7r; on Assisi above at n. 93.

[98] ASVen Scuole piccole Busta 296, nos. 24 (1599–1603 miscellaneous sheets), and 13: 31 December 1603 petition of Chiara Galletti, with the vote of approval recorded on it.

[99] Weissman, *Ritual Brotherhood*, chapter 3, pp. 107–61. Other points from this analysis will appear below in later chapters.

For Genoa we have a good study of the number of confraternities in existence. E. Grendi identified 134 associations founded or existing in the period 1480–1582, of which at least seventy still survived in 1700, and from 1582 until the suppression of confraternities in 1811 a further 124 were launched. He detected a tendency for the discipline confraternities to abandon the custom of meeting at a public place, especially when celebrating Corpus Christi, and to move into private oratories, or chapels within churches. The civic authorities had distrusted and discouraged the public devotions. Sixteenth-century foundations showed a predilection for Sacrament and Rosary devotions; sixteen and five, respectively, were founded between about 1500 and the major visitation of Bishop F. Bossio in 1582; two more Rosary confraternities were added by 1630. The number of discipline confraternities remained static. The other new creations showed the variety of spiritual and philanthropic concerns expected from a major city in the Counter-Reformation period. Grendi suggests that the proliferation of Sacrament confraternities indicated a social broadening of the confraternity movement, and a lay assertiveness in liturgical affairs that, judging from Bishop Bossio's report, led to considerable conflict with parish priests. He sees the Jesuits as the leading force behind missionary work, among the seamen in the galleys from 1558, and later in the countryside above the city, as well as behind confraternal philanthropic work for the sick, 'ashamed poor' (*poveri vergognosi*), prisoners and repentant prostitutes. Confraternity membership figures are not available before the late seventeenth century, but Grendi notes that the new aristocratic Della Morte company of S. Salvatore expanded its membership from 54 to 140 between 1594 and 1604, thus rapidly breaking its own rule about limiting membership to one hundred.[100]

Rome witnessed a major expansion of the number and type of confraternities through the sixteenth century and after, as befitted the expansion of the city and its revival as a spiritual leader. Camillo Fanucci in his 1601 guide to the city's *Opere Pie* enumerated 52 'universal' confraternities, including 17 with a Sacrament title, 49 confraternities based on guilds or on 'national' groups of foreign residents, and 11 confraternity-hospital associations. Modern studies do not entirely agree on the numbers, but possibly 27 were founded before 1500, between 74 and 85 in the sixteenth century, and 34 in the seventeenth. Calculations are not helped by the complicated processes of amalgamation, or splitting, of confraternities—as earlier exemplified with the societies for artists and craftsmen in Rome. Further discrepancies arise from trying to establish the identity of Sacrament societies based on a single church; this category may be underestimated, though some individual Sacrament fraternities may have had few members. Rome provided examples of all the specialist types of confraternity, and more will be said about them in subsequent chapters.[101]

The situation in remoter areas can be exemplified from the small diocese of Comacchio, suffragan of Ravenna, then noted as being poor and insalubrious. The 1574 apostolic visitation revealed three confraternities in the city of 5,000 persons: the Rosary and Corpus Christi with about sixty members each, and a newly founded Nome di Dio.

[100] Grendi, 'Morfologia'.

[101] C. Fanucci, *Trattato di tutte le opere pie dell'alma citta di Roma* (Rome, 1601), pp. 33–75, 105–316, 317–421; Paglia, '*La Pietà dei Carcerati*', pp. 303–13, Appendix; Maroni Lumbroso and Martini, pp. 441–5; Fiorani, 'Religione e Povertà', p. 97; V. Monachino, (ed.) *La Carità Cristiana in Roma* (Bologna, 1968), p. 191.

Comacchio also had a hospital for the poor, and a school of Christian Doctrine, with some 300 male and female members; apparently neither was based on a constituted confraternity. In the nine other parishes in the diocese there were three fraternities: a Sacrament society in Cadigoro, a Corpus Christi and a Concepton of Mary in Ostellato.[102]

Some indication that Rosary and Sacrament confraternities outside the cities could have sizable memberships is found in D. Zardin's study of the Lombard *pieve* of Parabiago–Legnano. These confraternities were strongly encouraged by archbishop Carlo Borromeo, and later by Federico Borromeo. In 1589 the enrolment figures reported in the visitations were:

Place	Population	Rosary	Sacrament	Discipline
Arluno	820	260	226	—
Parabiago	1,000	117	43	14
Legnano	2,834	723	388	45
Canegrate	682	—	300	—

Zardin estimates that the Canegrate figure for the Sacrament company amounts to 75 per cent of the parish communicants; it also had a S. Giuseppe fraternity with about 200 members, and a S. Orsola for women with only four in 1582, but an unspecified 'reasonable' number by 1596. Legnano's S. Orsola in 1590 had about twenty women. In purely numerical terms this indicates a high level of involvement, but the question remains as to how much was active membership, and what it meant to the participants.[103]

The area in the south (outside Naples itself) to exhibit the greatest variety of confraternity activity was Lecce in Apulia. Lecce today stands as a rich gem in the Mezzogiorno, calm and clean (at least when visited in 1976), with many of its architectural splendours well restored, showing the fascinating sculptural decoration, full of the fruits of the earth as well as odd monsters, that decorate the churches and their rich twisting–columned altars. A profusion of confraternities here made up for the paucity of parochial organisation; there was a long struggle to create an adequate number of parishes for the city, decentralising the cure of souls away from the Cathedral. The *relationes ad limina* at the turn of the century reported that the city, with 10,000 people, had seventeen confraternities, but Infantino, writing about the city in 1634, recorded twenty-seven, possibly counting companies that did not have formal episcopal approval. Most confraternities were connected with the Orders, rather than the Cathedral, or with independent oratories. The Rosary confraternity was under the Dominicans, the Crocefisso (for nobles) and the Anime del Purgatorio (for artisans, *artisti*), under the Theatines. The Jesuits supervised the five societies already mentioned in the context of social segregation, and they probably contributed even more widely to confraternity enthusiasm and devotion. The confraternity of S. Eligio for peasants was apparently independent. The Archconfraternity of S. Trinità administered a major

---

[102] A. Samaritani, 'Catechismo, Eucaristia e Tempio nella Comacchio postridentina', with documentary support in 'Fonti inedite sulla riforma cattolico–tridentina a Comacchio', *Ravennatensia*, vol. 2, 467–501, esp. pp. 492–3.

[103] Zardin, *Confraternite e vita di pietà*, pp. 20, 28, 69–73.

hospital, though the city-controlled hospital of S. Spirito was more important, and promoted Forty-Hour Eucharist celebrations. The noble Gonfalone assisted prisoners and the condemned, and administered the Monti di Pietà, founded in 1569 to provide easy loans to the poor. In the rest of the diocese there were substantial numbers of confraternities, especially in the inland areas. Most towns had a Sacrament and/or a Rosary company, though the two most southerly towns of Roca and Pasule had none. M. Rosa detects a movement from the turn of the sixteenth century away from the Eucharist-based societies of the Tridentine period to confraternities dedicated to the Virgin. The Lecce region provided a rich profusion of confraternities, especially by southern standards. Unfortunately no local historian has yet found evidence on the numbers involved and their detailed practices.[104]

By the sixteenth century there was a variegated profusion of lay associations that can loosely be called confraternities. A short account of the medieval developments has indicated that new enthusiasms or threats added to the variety, without there being a major decline in older institutions. By the late fifteenth century new philanthropic fraternities, inspired by Catholic reformers, were being added to those that had started as discipline fraternities, Marian or *Laudesi* companies. Old companies took on new dimensions, which suggests that it is unwise to produce too rigid a typology of confraternities.

The confraternities could directly involve nearly all in society from young boys to old noblewomen, even if there was a bias in favour of men from the respectable middle classes. Confraternities could be instruments of elitist control, or could attempt to counteract social tensions and class/status divisions. In the absence of a significant number of membership lists it is difficult to judge whether elitism and social control predominated over brotherly egalitarianism.

Overall it is impossible to quantify confraternity membership, again given the state of the documentation available. Precise facts and figures are rare and sometimes misleading when cited by early modern sources. What I have to report above should both warn against an over-reliance on quoted statistics, and encourage other researchers to pursue a variety of sources for a more accurate assessment of select institutions or sample communities. Available evidence, however, suggests that by the end of our period we should assume that every reasonable-sized village, and most urban parishes, would have had a confraternity to which parishioners could belong, though the level of activity might be low. Judging from Perugia or Assisi it may be said that up to a quarter, or even a third, of the adult population might have had a family member enrolled in a confraternity, which they would have seen as bringing some spiritual benefit to the family. Through philanthropic activities, or through organising public processions, confraternities could touch the lives—however intermittently—of many others, as later chapters will show. Given their significant numbers it is not surprising that both secular and clerical authorities were anxious to control and direct such fraternal organisations. Such patronage and supervision, which affected what was available to whom and where, are the subject of the next chapter.

---

[104] Rosa, 'Geografia', pp. 28–30, 36–74; *idem, Religione e società*, pp. 53–6. M. Paone, *Chiese di Lecce* (2 vols., Lecce, 1978–9) well demonstrates the architectural and decorative richness of the city and its churches.

3

CONTROL AND SPONSORSHIP

The nature and numbers of confraternities were affected by the competition both to control and to sponsor such brotherhoods. Both secular and ecclesiastical authorities had ambivalent attitudes towards confraternities and dependent institutions such as their hospitals. There were grounds for curbing confraternities—or even abolishing them—as secret centres of political or religious dissent. There were good reasons for closing some confraternity hospitals as inefficient organisations. But if properly controlled, confraternities could be used positively for propagating orthodox religious ideas and practices, for consolidating a revitalised parochial organisation, or for ensuring the subordination of the lower orders to the established government and the social elites. The evidence below shows that attempts to impose social control or discipline on confraternity members were made, and that they partially changed the nature of lay confraternities and their activities. Against the loss of lay initiatives and vitality could be balanced some gains in efficiency to the benefit of both the spiritual and the physical life of members, and of some outsiders. However, control was resisted. Both authoritarian control and potentially stultifying standardisation were undermined by a lively competition to sponsor new confraternities. Some confraternities were also in a position to pressurise governments or sectors of the clerical establishment, and to weave between the competing jurisdictional claims so they could secure their own policies. The story in the sixteenth century is not a simple one of growing Counter-Reformation centralisation and absolutist state control.[1]

I STATE AND EPISCOPAL INVOLVEMENT

It has already been noted that the ruling bodies in cities like Genoa and Florence were afraid that confraternities, by nature secret for at least part of their activities, could be centres of political opposition, or that public processions would threaten social order. The hooded uniform enabled people to parade anonymously. In Florence, during the 1376–8 Interdict, civic authorities first encouraged confraternity activity as conducive to city morals, then from 1377 curbed it, apparently fearing opposition to state policies or a breakdown in public order. During the fifteenth century political leaders saw the confraternities as helping certain moral causes or controlling such sectors of society as 'youths', but fraternities were also accused of supporting rival factions or a different type

[1] For arguments about the limitations of 'absolutism' in practice, especially in the Papal State, see my 'Perugia and papal absolutism', 509–39.

of government, and of plotting to manipulate tax assessments (in 1426, when the famous
Catasto tax register was being planned). Also as philanthropic activity developed in
Florence during the century, so civic leaders wanted to exert greater control over
benefactions to prevent fraud.[2] Government control and intervention remained active
through the sixteenth century under the Dukes and Grand Dukes. In 1542 Cosimo I
launched a major reorganisation of the hospital system, and secured a Bull from Pope
Paul III in 1543 to allow substantial reallocations of bequests for this purpose. Dual
intervention, from the Senate or the Archbishop, threatened philanthropic institutions.
Cosimo and his successors also ensured that their own courtiers officiated in the more
powerful confraternities.[3]

In Venice civic control over confraternities developed from the fourteenth century.
From 1312 the recently established special security committee, the Council of Ten,
issued supervision orders, banning night meetings and controlling public processions.
By the sixteenth century the Republic had various institutions and systems for supervising and manipulating the confraternities and their hospitals. Under Venetian law the
Scuole Grandi were lay institutions and not 'pious places', and so subject to the Council
of Ten's particular authority. This obtained until 1622–7 when two special magistracies
were established to supervise the various *scuole*. The Ten controlled the membership
numbers and public activities of the *Scuole Grandi*. These were effectively manipulated
to perform charitable functions for the general benefit of the city rather than solely for
their members, and they were used to support the navy, by helping to push poor
unemployed men into the ships. Because they were not pious places in the eyes of the
State, these confraternities escaped the 1536 Senate law prohibiting pious institutions
from investing in real estate in the city, and thereby augmented their charitable funds,
with effects that will be discussed later. Ecclesiastical authorities did little to challenge
this lay control over the city's *scuole*.[4]

The lesser confraternities in Venice were subject to other government institutions in
addition to the Ten, particularly the Provveditori di Comun. These Provveditori
periodically issued general rules for the *scuole piccole*, as well as orders in particular cases.
They provided the basic rules for what officials the confraternities should have, how
they should be elected and conduct business. They issued licences for the major meetings
of the Banca and Zonta committees that ran the confraternities, and stipulated when a
quorum rule could be evaded. They ratified the important financial decisions of these
committees, and tried to ensure that proper records were kept and handed over to
subsequent office holders.[5] These confraternities might also have to deal with other

[2] Trexler, *The Spiritual Power*; cf. Le Bras, pp. 459–61 on civic fears of confraternities; R. Hatfield, 'The
Compagnia de' Magi', *Journal of the Warburg and Courtauld Institutes*, 33 (1970), 107–61, esp. p. 110; M.B.
Becker, 'Aspects of lay piety in early Renaissance Florence', *The Pursuit of Holiness in Late Medieval and
Renaissance Religion*, eds. Trinkaus with Oberman, pp. 180–1, 189; Weissman, *Ritual Brotherhood*, pp.
163–73. Information on the early activity of the Ten comes from W.B. Wurthmann in unpublished papers
delivered at Strathclyde and Glasgow Universities.
[3] Weissman, *Ritual Brotherhood*, pp. 173–94; D'Addario, *Aspetti*, pp. 67–82, 89–97.
[4] Pullan, *Rich and Poor*, esp. pp. 61, 86, 108–9, 125, 132–56; cf. on Church attitudes, Le Bras, pp. 454–9;
Mackenney, 'Trade Guilds', chapter 4, pp. 315–66, and *Tradesmen and Traders*, pp. 219–32 on guild
confraternities and galleys.
[5] ASVen Provveditore del Comun, Busta 47: Leggi, Testimonianze 1508–1764; cf. Pullan, *Rich and Poor*,
pp. 45–6; *idem*, 'Natura e carattere delle Scuole' *Le Scuole di Venezia*, ed. T. Pignatti (Milan, 1981), p. 24.

government bodies, such as the Giustizia Vecchia, the Milizia da Mar (especially if they were *scuole delle arti* and contributing sailors to the navy), and the Provveditori sopra gli Ospedali e Luoghi Pii when hospitals, hospices and legacies were involved.[6] In 1555 when the Scuola di S. Orsola was in conflict with the friars of SS. Giovanni e Paolo there were arguments about who should have jurisdiction; the Provveditori di Comun took out an inhibition against the Giustizia Vecchia to prevent the latter's involvement, and the *scuola* officials voted for the Provveditori to handle the case. In Venice bureaucratic control was everywhere; confraternities could not escape this, though they could play officials off against each other. State control or presure on the *scuole delle arti* grew more burdensome through the sixteenth century, as they were increasingly treated as tax units and providers of galleymen. The guild confraternity officials often argued in the early 1600s that the government policy was detrimental to their limited resources. Eventually protests were effective, and after 1639 the guilds no longer had to ballot members to provide oarsmen. While they still paid levies, they no longer dispatched breadwinners to the boats, leaving women and children to be succoured by confraternal charity.[7]

Confraternity involvement in politics was suspected, or actually took place in other cities, and occasioned intervention. In Bologna in the 1490s the dominant Bentivoglio family suspected that the Company of Lombardi harboured too many opponents of the regime and supporters of the *Popolo*, or middle classes. So in 1494 it was amalgamated with the hospital confraternity of S. Procolo to form the Compagnia di S. Maria degli Angeli dei Lombardi, where presumably loyal brothers could control the disaffected. Meetings were not be held in the old Lombardi premises. The fall of the Bentivoglio led to the reestablishment of the Lombardi as a separate confraternity in 1509, with 108 members from thirty-eight families, few of whom had been Bentivoglio supporters.[8]

In Siena during the 1530s various confraternities were centres of both political intrigue and enthusiasm for some Reformation ideas; the invitation to Bernardino Ochino to preach in the city came from confraternity members who knew perfectly well that he was crossing the theological border into heresy. Soon after he fled Italy.[9] This kind of activity encouraged both the Spanish authorities and later the Tuscan Dukes to keep strict control over confraternities — with some justification. In 1543 heresy again appeared in a Sienese confraternity. Pietro Antonio, son of a goldsmith, in the confraternity of the Trinity (largely for lower-class artisans) attacked the role of the saints and their powers to intercede; saints were to be imitated, but they were not there for veneration or adoration. When presented with a text from St Augustine against his views, he riposted that the Church Fathers could err. Though his confraternity members dared not challenge him initially, he was expelled before news of his discourse reached the archbishop's vicar general. Pietro Antonio was sentenced to retract

[6] ASVen Scuole piccole: e.g. S. Orsola, Busta 599 no. 101 8 July 1553; SS. Trinita, Busta 709, Libro primo, fols. 40v, 43r–v, Secondo Libro fol. 126v (1575/6). Cf. E. Favaro, *L'arte dei pittori in Venezia e i suoi statuti* (Florence, 1975), pp. 96–8 on intervention in the affairs of the *scuola d'arte* by officials of the Provveditori sopra la Giustizia Vecchia, Provveditori di Comun, and Cinque Savi alla Mercanzia.

[7] ASVen Scuole piccole, S. Orsola, Busta 599, 10 November 1555; Pullan, *Rich and Poor*, p. 645; Mackenney, 'Trade Guilds', pp. 9–10, 86–7, 315–66; *idem, Tradesmen and Traders*, pp. 229–31.

[8] Fanti, *San Procolo*, pp. 171–83. Despite its name the company dei Lombardi was not a 'national' fraternity, but one of native Bolognesi.

[9] Information from the late Judith Hook in reply to questions after a paper given at Strathclyde University, reflecting a study then in progress in Siena; and see her 'The search for an ideology in sixteenth-century Siena', *The Italianist*, 4 (1984), 73–92.

his sermon before the same confraternity, to fast on bread and water for two years, and to appear before the Archbishop once a month to attest his faith. A similar attack on the cult of saints had been revealed in the Bologna confraternity of S. Maria della Vita in 1543. A *droghiere* Girolamo Rainaldi had argued that the brothers should not invoke the saints or the Virgin, but have recourse to Christ alone. He soon retracted his views.[10]

It is not surprising that in the suspicious age of the Counter-Reformation 'national' confraternities faced official investigation, especially in Venice with its numerous contacts with Protestant lands. The Venetian Inquisition tribunal had lay inquisitors appointed by the Republic as well as ecclesiastical inquisitors; both sides were intent on preserving orthodoxy and order.[11] In May 1588 the Venetian Inquisition started enquiries about the Scuola dei Calegheri e Zavattoni Todeschi (shoemakers and cobblers). Though of long standing, and governed in a good Catholic manner ('cattolicamente') in obedience to the Holy Mother Church's rules, it was seen to be now under Lutheran influence. Recent immigrants from Lutheran lands were forced to join the *scuola* if they wished to stay in business and had changed the character of the *scuola*. So alleged two delators, who had been tried for heresy in another context. They claimed that Venice had many Lutherans. The main complaint was that certain confraternity members lived in a Lutheran manner ('luteranicamente') with their families, by eating meat on Fridays and Saturdays and avoiding the Mass. The investigators and witnesses also raised issues about working on feast-days, the removal of the Cross from the *scuola*, and words spoken against the Pope. The inquisitors concentrated on *messer* Martino Todesco — largely because he was the leading official (*gastaldo*) of the Scuola — and mildly punished him for illegal meat-eating and, in a sense, for lies and evasions under questioning. It can be noted that one of the documents in the case, designed to favour him, was a testimonial (*fede*) from the parish priest of S. Samuele attesting Martino's membership of the Sacrament confraternity of that church, where he confessed and took communion; and there was another from the *scrivano* of the Scuola della Madonna in S. Samuele declaring that he was a devoted member of that confraternity and had helped to decorate it and was generous with alms at Easter. Membership of a devotional confraternity was a sign of orthodoxy. It is doubtful whether the inquisitors were happy that an alien with dubious connections and background could so combine membership of national and local devotional confraternities and demonstrate such integration into Venetian society.[12]

---

[10] A. Prosperi, 'Intellettuali e Chiesa all'inizio dell'età moderna', *Storia d'Italia. Annali* 4 (1986), p. 186; V. Marchetti, *Gruppi ereticali senesi del Cinquecento* (Florence, 1975), pp. 51–67; A. Rotondò, 'Per la storia dell'eresia a Bologna nel secolo XVI', *Rinascimento*, 13 (1962), 137ff.

[11] N.S. Davidson, 'The Inquisition and the Italian Jews', *Inquisition and Society in Early Modern Europe*, ed. S. Haliczer (London and Sydney, 1987), pp. 19–46; *idem*, 'Il Sant'Ufficio e la tutela del culto a Venezia nel '500', *Studi Veneziani*, 6 (1982), 87–101, esp. pp. 89–90 on the common interest of church and state in containing heresy. His forthcoming major study on the Venetian Inquisition will stress the cooperation between lay and clerical, Venetian and Roman inquisitors; J. Martin, 'Popular culture and the shaping of popular heresy in Renaissance Venice', *Inquisition and Society in Early Modern Europe*, ed. S. Haliczer, pp. 115–28; B.S. Pullan, *The Jews of Europe and the Inquisition of Venice, 1550–1670* (Oxford, 1983).

[12] ASVen Santo Uffizio, Processi Busta 61, folder 'Verseman Giovanni e compagni'; in fact G. Verseman (or Vorsemano), maker of women's capes, was not the main subject of the investigation, though he admitted killing a pig in the hospital courtyard to make an untimely feast (fol. 24v). Martin was judged to be a formal heretic but, having confessed sacramentally, was merely sentenced to abstain from meat additionally on Wednesdays for 6 months, confess three times a year, and say a rosary to the Virgin on Fridays and Saturdays. Cf. Mackenney, *Tradesmen and Traders*, p. 207 n. 22. Venetian cobblers apparently were especially addicted to arguing about Scripture: Martin, 'Popular culture', p. 121. Cf. below chapter 12 which starts with the case of Gaspar Ribeiro, a converted Jew who was a prominent confraternity member.

In May 1590 the Venetian inquisitors received a denunciation from Bernardino de Ferris, *rassarius* at the sign of the Lion, against the Scuola of S. Giovanni at the Frari church, a confraternity for Florentines. He alleged that they met at night, and after the sermon they extinguished the lights, flagellated themselves, and took it in turns to proclaim the Gospel in the dark ('dichiara l'evangelio al scuro'). Reports reached the delator at his own *scuola* which was guided by a Jesuit, who was scandalised by these reports. He named a *scuola* at S. Polo, headed by a Florentine, which also met at night, without a priest, like that at the Frari. In contrast master Bernardino's confraternity had a priest as prior; Capuchins, Jesuits and Tolentini also participated. The inquisitors appear not to have followed up the case, presumably deciding that there was nothing heretical in the Gospel recitation by laymen. It is unclear whether the complainant, a layman from a clerically dominated devotional fraternity, was motivated by his concept of what was inappropriate for a religious organisation—laymen reading and commenting on the Gospel, and not using a priest, or by hostility towards aliens who may have been economic rivals.[13]

Other evidence of establishment fears of confraternities comes from correspondence between Philip II of Spain and the Governor of Milan in 1573–4. They were concerned that Milanese confraternities were causing trouble, with secret meetings, and with unruly public funerals which often involved inter-family disputes and the undesirable participation of women. The Spanish authorities were determined to assert their jurisdiction and supervision over confraternities. In the 1580s Philip II ordered the exclusion of the laity from the Neapolitan confraternity of the Bianchi della Giustizia— which then specialised in helping prisoners and the condemned—because he feared plots by its socially powerful members against the Crown. It would be safer as a clerical confraternity.[14]

Ecclesiastical involvement in confraternity affairs was likely to be more widespread than civic, especially after Tridentine reforms were implemented. Church leaders were concerned with all types of confraternities: with their moral behaviour, with possibly heretical discussions, with the efficient implementation of wills and legacies, with their support for, or opposition to, parochial church life. The clerical attitude was inevitably ambivalent. Expansion and renewal of confraternities bore witness to the Catholic church's revival; it would be unwise to curtail new spirituality and social involvement in good works. But lay initiatives could be suspect, as could those of the religious Orders in the eyes of bishops. There were fears that parishioners would be distracted from their parish church, and the authority of parish priest and bishop be lessened, as archbishops of Florence complained in the fifteenth century. The partial answer was to encourage confraternities but under much stricter episcopal supervision; to foster devotional societies in the parish church, and discourage those in independent oratories. By 1540 Bishop G.M. Giberti of Verona offered precedents and guidelines (as so often in the

---

[13] ASVen Santo Uffizio, Processi Busta 66. folder 'S. Giovanni, (Confraternite)', 8 May and 14 June 1590. Mackenney, *Tradesmen and Traders*, pp. 186–7 and n. 67, for this and a similar case of artisans interpreting the vernacular Bible. According to N.S. Davidson (who kindly suggested looking at this and the previous case), the inquisitors frequently filed denunciations and recorded no further action.

[14] R. Bottoni cited this correspondence in his contribution to the VI Seminario Internazionale di Ricerche di Storia Veneta, Fondazione Giorgio Cini, Venice, April 1984; G. Mascia, *La Confraternita dei Bianchi della Giustizia a Napoli "S. Maria Succurre Miseris"* (Naples, 1972), pp. 14, 74.

pre-tridentine scene) by seeking uniformity in confraternity practice—outlined in his *Capitoli ordinati*—by imposing supervision through parish priests, and by promoting eucharistic devotion through the parish-based Societas Corporis Christi. Carlo Borromeo built on these precedents in his Lombard reforms.[15]

In the middle ages there had been no canon law control over confraternities, and there was much confusion over what was required to establish such a society. Many societies initiated by laymen clearly sought, long after the original foundation, a canonical creation or *erectio*, with episcopal approval as a guarantee of stability, and as a path to certain immunities and indulgences. In contrast various confraternities like the *Scuole Grandi* considered themselves entirely lay, and requested no links with the bishop. The Council of Trent, in Session XXII in 1562, claimed control over most confraternities, hospitals and other pious places:

Canon VIII: The bishops, also as delegates of the Apostolic see, shall in the cases conceded by law be executors of all pious dispositions, whether made by last will or among the living; they shall have the right to visit hospitals and all colleges and confraternities of laymen, even those that are called *scholae* or are known by some other name (not, however, those that are under the immediate protection of kings, except with their permission); also eleemosynary institutions known as loan or charity foundations, and all pious places by whatever name designated, even though the care of the aforesaid institutions be in the hands of laymen and the said pious places protected by the privilege of exemption; by virtue of their office they shall, moreover, take cognisance of and execute in accordance with the ordinances of the sacred canons all things that have been instituted for the worship of God or for the salvation of souls or for the support of the poor; any custom, even though immemorial, privilege or statute whatsoever to the contrary notwithstanding.

Canon IX: Administration, whether ecclesiastical or lay, of the revenues of any church, also of cathedrals, hospitals, confraternities, eleemosynary institutions known as loan foundations (*mons pietatis*), and of all pious places, shall be bound to render to the ordinary each year an account of their administration, all customs and privileges to the contrary being set aside, unless perchance it be expressly provided otherwise in the institution and regulation of such a church or fund. But if by reason of custom, privilege or some local regulation their account shall also be employed conjointly with them, and releases made otherwise it shall be of no avail to the said administrators.[16]

Further papal rulings in the 1570s ordered bishops to control new creations so that there would not be a multiplicity of similar confraternities in a small area. Clement VIII's Bull *Quaecumque*, 7 December 1604, was the fullest expression of the claim for episcopal control; it all but excluded lay initiatives for new creations, and confined this role to religious organisations. All new foundations were clearly meant to be under diocesan control and discipline. In addition no existing confraternity could be aggregated to an archconfraternity unless it had been previously erected under apostolic or ordinary authority. The importance of the archconfraternity will be discussed below (section 3), but this ruling meant that old lay organisations had to submit specifically to episcopal supervision before establishing beneficial links with a broader network of

[15] Rusconi, 'Confraternite', pp. 483–5; Zardin, 'Confraternite e comunità', pp. 714–15; Henderson, 'Confraternities', pp. 80–3; A. Prosperi, *Tra evangelismo e controriforma: G.M. Giberti (1495–1543)* (Rome, 1969), p. 272.

[16] COD, p. 740; cf. Duhr, 'La confrérie', pp. 437–78 on the background.

confraternities — and their indulgences. This still left contested areas between ecclesiastical authorities and lay administrators, in cases of ancient societies which insisted on
their completely lay status and had no wish to aggregate.[17]

Meanwhile archbishops and bishops had supplemented the Council's rulings,
through their own claims to visit confraternities and hospitals, and through detailed
rules promulgated in provincial councils and diocesan synods. The major legislation
came in provincial councils like those of Ravenna in 1568 and Milan in 1569, both of
which influenced later legislation. In the 1569 council Carlo Borromeo was adamant
that visitations of confraternities should not be resisted by the laity, and that statutes had
to be inspected and rectified. In subsequent councils and synods he kept up the pressure
for control over confraternities while simultaneously encouraging new foundations.[18]
Similarly his friend Gabriele Paleotti in Bologna legislated to ensure both control and
sponsorship, being particularly concerned that bishops and clergy should check on
Christian Doctrine and Nome di Dio (anti-blasphemy) societies.[19] It was sometimes
admitted that ordinary diocesan visitations did not have full jurisdiction over lay
hospitals and their annexed churches and confraternities. For Perugia in 1601 an
apostolic visitor was authorised under papal brief to visit the hospitals and their chapels,
run by various trade guilds; this visitor's rights were not to be contested, but the brief
accepted that oratories and hospitals of the *arti* could not be visited by the present, or
any future, bishop of the diocese, without special faculty presented under papal brief.[20]

The general principle that episcopal permission was needed to start a confraternity
was asserted by the Theatine bishop of Mileto, Marcantonio del Tufo, in 1587, but he
also issued forty-two rules concerning their foundation. He banned the lay brothers
from performing anything that pertained to the offices of the clergy. They were not to
dress, bless or preach like them, nor give the peace by kissing each other, they had to
leave their weapons outside the chapel or church, and they were banned from feasting
at the confraternity entrances. Brothers should know at least the Pater Noster, Ave
Maria and Credo, and be expelled if they did not learn them within three months. Parish
priests were strongly urged to introduce confraternities where they did not yet exist,
especially those dedicated to the Sacrament, the Rosary, teaching Christian Doctrine,
and societies of Nome di Dio.[21] Such legislation and recommendations went further
than the Tridentine rules in claiming the right and duty to interfere in the daily affairs
of confraternities, and impose restrictions. It was more than a matter of vetting funds
and general administrative structures.

Decrees from the archbishop of Milan in 1595–6 banned the Sacrament confraternities from electing their own officials, who were instead to be chosen by the *vicario*

[17] Lopez, 'Le confraternite laicali', p. 166; Meloni, 'Topografia', pp. 17–18; Le Bras, pp. 448–9, 457.

[18] J.D. Mansi, *Sacrorum Conciliorum Nova et Amplissima Collectio* (reprinted Paris and Leipzig, vols. 0–47 [sic],
1901–13), vol. 35, cols. 594, 597, 620, 639–41 (for Ravenna), vol. 34, col. 129 (Milan); AEM, vol. 2, cols.
200–1 (1569 Council), 278–9 (1573), 432, 486–94, (1576). See G.D. Gordini, 'Sinodi diocesani emiliani dal
1563 al 1648 ed il Concilio provinciale di Ravenna del 1568', *Ravennatensia*, 2, pp. 247–8, 265.

[19] G. Paleotti, *Archiepiscopale Bononiense, sive De Bononiensis Ecclesiae administratione* . . . (Rome, 1594), pp.
7–23, 77–81 (promoting and checking on Christian Doctrine and Nome di Dio fraternities), 215–16,
244–5, 396–404 (roles of Visitors), 215 (Sacrament confraternities).

[20] BCP Ms 3121, 'Visite dei Spedali e delle Chiese delle Arti', eighteenth century copy; Brief dated 18 June
1601, and report on hospitals and chapels; fols. 11v–12v for the jurisdictional admissions.

[21] Sposato, pp. 59–63.

foraneo; parish priests were to underwrite the lists compiled for the distribution of alms. There is at least some evidence that such supervision was practised. Much legislation was negative, to eradicate abuses, or limit areas of action. The 1568 Ravenna council, for example, subjected sacred representations or plays performed by confraternities to episcopal permit — and so probably to veto — on the grounds that they led to laughter and scandal, not piety. But the council more positively ordered the establishment of Nome di Dio confraternities to help eradicate swearing.[22]

Control and stimulation of confraternities and hospitals came through the visitation system; following particular investigations the more energetic visitors attempted reform and restructuring (not then a euphemism for closure). For example in 1574 monsignor G.B. Maremonti visited the poor diocese of Comacchio. In the course of it he met the sixty-odd brothers of the Rosary confraternity in S. Maria in aula regia. He ordered their rules to be renewed and confirmed by the ordinary within three months; he accepted their right to celebrate on Christmas night in their own chapel within the Cathedral, without prejudice to the parish, but he banned them from singing in Italian during processions, and ordered Latin hymns and canticles instead. Visitors seem seldom to have questioned lay individuals and their conduct, but they might scrutinise clerical officials attached to confraternities. Domenico Bollani of Brescia during his episcopal visitation of 1565–6 did investigate some priests in Corpus Christi and Rosary societies. At Malapaga di Calvisano he found the priests of the Scuola Corpus Christi, who celebrated three times a week, able to answer his questions satisfactorily. But the priest of a similar society in Verola Nuova, celebrating daily, knew virtually nothing: 'Examinatur nihil aut parvum scit'. This was to be remedied and he would be reexamined. At Pontevico one of the lay officials of the Corpus Christi confraternity complained that the curate of S. Andrea — presumably the fraternity's priest — was not good, was ignorant like other priests of the area, and too litigious. What Bollani did about these deficiencies is unclear.[23]

Episcopal interventions did not pass unnoticed. Some confraternities claimed they were lay organisations, by foundation and operation, and so not subject to ecclesiastical jurisdiction of any kind. Much resistance was token, as when the confraternity of S. Agnese, Ferrara opposed the episcopal visitation with the claim that it was a lay organisation — but they let the bishop come. When Pietro Camaiani, during his visitations of the Umbrian dioceses in the 1570s, tried to confront the S. Antonio confraternity of Bastia, its fifty-two members deserted the oratory and refused to meet him. Other societies relied on civic support for their resistance. The Scuola dei battuti of Mestre in 1554 opposed the delegate from the bishop of Treviso, and the brethren called on secular authorities to obtain the revocation of the subsequent interdict imposed on them by the bishop. The latter diplomatically withdrew the sanction, though apparently securing some marginal acceptance of control.[24] In 1587 a discipline confraternity of Redonesco — in the diocese of Brescia, but under the Duke of Mantua's

[22] Zardin, *Confraternite e vita di pietà*, pp. 50–3; Mansi, vol. 35 (as above note 18).
[23] A. Samaritani, 'Fonti inedite sulla riforma cattolico-tridentina a Comacchio', *Ravennatensia*, 2 pp. 492–3; P. Guerrini, *Atti della visita pastorale del vescovo Domenico Bollani alla Diocesi di Brescia* (3 vols: 1, Brescia, 1915; 2, Toscolano, 1936; 3, Brescia, 1940), 2, 64, 73–5 and 3, 117–19; C. Cairns, *Domenico Bollani. Bishop of Brescia* (Nieuwkoop, 1976), pp. 175–7, 198 n. 217, 285.
[24] Meloni, 'Topografia', pp. 24–5, 28.

territorial power, not Venice's — defended its lay autonomy, and appealed to the Duke. With or without his request the Rectors (Venetian) of Brescia city issued a printed sheet (*grida*) forbidding the clergy from interfering in the workings of the 'Fraglie over Discipline di Brescia e suo distretto'; in other words, it claimed immunity for all discipline confraternities of the region. It is unclear how long this resistance lasted; there were further protests in 1597 and 1615. Yet it should be stressed that for Bollani's visitation in 1566 the discipline confraternities had accepted his investigation.[25]

Previous acceptance of a visit, even if reluctant, could tell against later opposition, as happened in Crema. In 1579 the discipline confraternity of S. Maria Elisabetta of Porta Rivolta opposed the apostolic visitation of the experienced Borromean bishop of Rimini, G.B. Castelli. Castelli summoned the officials, and argued that they were liable to his jurisdiction despite previous documents — including the Venetian Republic's claim in 1566 that the discipline fraternities were subject to lay burdens of taxation and so exempt from ecclesiastical tithes. When the confraternity refused to open its rooms and church for the visitation, Castelli excommunicated the brothers. He then secured witnesses to show that the confraternity had accepted the 1566 visitation, albeit under protest. This helped him deal with the Doge of Venice's intervention requesting the revocation of the excommunication. A compromise was reached; the confraternity paid a contribution to the bishop's episcopal income (*mensa*), which was probably at the root of the dispute — but at a reduced rate. This meant accepting episcopal rights.[26]

Adamant reformers, or skilled diplomatic bishops, could overcome much opposition; many confraternities capitulated under protest, and church authorities usually avoided recognition of lay independence. The struggles involved could not have been conducive to speedy investigation and reform. Archbishop Federico Borromeo in his 1597 Relation could still complain about confraternities resisting visitations, with the encouragement of secular authorities. This was despite years of persistent efforts to control and reform them by his predecessors, Carlo Borromeo and Gaspare Visconti. Many lesser visitors may have been deterred from challenging powerful confraternities, or being more than cursory scrutinisers. It was not difficult for confraternities to ignore orders and general legislation, to forget to incorporate new rules and recommendations into their statutes. Despite the Bull of 1604, in remoter dioceses like Bitonto, new confraternities (such as the Purgatorio, the Del Carmine and the Spirito Santo), were founded in the seventeenth century without proper episcopal authorisation or vetting of statutes, and so remained essentially independent.[27]

There is one case where the claim for lay independence was finally recognised by the Papacy: the inquisitorial investigation of the claim reveals some interesting attitudes to lay confraternities. The case concerned the Perugian confederation of the three confraternities of S. Agostino, S. Francesco and S. Domenico. The long struggle opened in 1564 when Cardinal Fulvio Della Corgna, newly inspired by Trent to resume active

[25] *Ibid.* p. 24.
[26] G. Cecchini, 'La vertenza fra una Confraternita di Disciplinati a Crema e il visitatore apostolico', *BSPU*, 67 (1970), 115–78.
[27] A.D. Wright, 'Post-tridentine reform in the archdiocese of Milan under the successors of Saint Charles Borromeo, 1584–1631' (Oxford, DPhil thesis, 1974), chapter 6, p. 36 (for Federico Borromeo), chapter 2, pp. 11–12, 44–5, chapter 3, pp. 52–4 (for his predecessors' visitations of confraternities, their mixed findings and successes); Zardin, 'Le confraternite in Italia settentrionale'; *idem* 'Confraternite e comunità', p. 711; Rusconi, 'Confraternite', pp. 485–6; Spedicato, pp. 83–4.

pastoral cares, launched a visitation of his Perugian diocese. The confraternities opposed his jurisdiction, but he succeeded in visiting — possibly under the additional powers of an apostolic delegate. He was then somewhat critical of the conduct of the hospitals run by these three confraternities and their inactivity. In 1567 Della Corgna ordered all hospitals to prepare themselves for another visitation, and issued copies of a papal order of 8 April 1566 that no exceptions to such visits were to be allowed. S. Francesco preserved a copy of the order — officially endorsed by command of Paul V in 1610. Confraternity resistance was maintained against later bishops, notably against Napoleone Comitoli (1591–1624) and Cosimo De Torres (1624–34). It was the especial intransigence of the latter (in the view of the confraternity's indexer), which led to the 1628 enquiry under Inquisitor Giuseppe Alessi. He heard a number of witnesses on the life and background of the confraternities. They were hazy about the historical antecedents of both the confraternities and their hospices for the poor, but were agreed that bishops had not been involved in their institution. Witnesses conflicted or were vague on other matters; whether or not the brothers actively participated when masses were celebrated in the oratories, or only said the Office of the Madonna and prayers; whether the oratories were open to the public or not; whether members enjoyed ecclesiastical immunity.

The arguments for full lay status, as openly claimed or implied by witnesses were that: no bishop had been involved in the foundation of the confraternities or their hospices; they had no full-time chaplains but employed a private priest as needed; their oratories had no facades or bell-towers, and did not look like churches; there were no sung masses; they paid for their own hospices and appointed officials without reference to bishops; they made no claims for ecclesiastical immunities and nobody sought refuge there from civil jurisdictions. The most prestigious of the witnesses, Carlo di Galeotto Baglioni, held the old-fashioned view that all that was necessary to make a confraternity was for laymen to gather themselves together under certain regulations and orders, and they did not need anybody else's licence to meet. Roman authorities would not have accepted his argument, but they were clearly prepared to countenance some of the more precise points made by other witnesses, and possibly some more legalistic arguments presented in costly suits before the Congregation of the Council (the body that interpreted the Trent decrees on behalf of the Pope) in 1617–18. Finally a document recognising the lay status of this confederation, and its immunity from ecclesiastical jurisdiction, was granted on 11 August 1632. The precise legal grounds for the decision are unclear to me. The document appeared to be missing or misplaced when I secured access to the confraternity archive. As important as the technical reasons may have been the political weight of the patrician witnesses ready to support the confraternities against the bishops and secure curial backing in Rome. But it was certainly unusual — if not unique — for Rome to retreat from its Tridentine control by sanctioning lay independence in an official ruling.[28]

---

[28] Meloni, 'Topografia', p. 25; Guèze, pp. 597–623; SBF S. Francesco no. 509 gives documents of the 1628 enquiry with the testimony of witnesses; and copies of the 1564 visitation report, the 1567/1610 order. Previous historians have variously reported the 1632 document as a Bull or a Brief; it should have been housed as Pergamena no. 209 in section D II/i in the Sodalizio's archive (according to the typed index by U. Barberi), but it could not be found when I obtained access to the ill-lit and cold archival room in November 1975; no. 510(a) includes accounts in connection with cases pending in the Congregation of the Council 1617–18.

It should be stressed that Rome seldom spoke with a single coherent voice on any jurisdictional matter. The College of Cardinals, however much it appeared to bow to papal absolutism by diminishing discussion in consistory, soon dissolved into competing factions, who represented the incompatible interests of rival jurisdictions. Confraternities could join secular princes, city governments from the Papal State, religious Orders, bishops and many others as lobbyists seeking the assistance of monsignors and cardinals based in Rome to pursue a particular cause. In 1596 the Bologna confraternity of S. Maria della Morte decided it needed a Protector in Rome to resist the evil tongues that threatened it with ruin, and to argue its case whenever necessary. They approached two Cardinals, both of whom eventually responded favourably, though one did stress that the authority of the local Vicelegate would normally have to prevail. Such Protectors could fight rumours or legal battles, or help secure indulgences to attract more recruits to a confraternity. Even in major decisions like that over the status of the Perugian confraternities, much depended on the support a confraternity could muster to influence the Pope, his nephews or most powerful advisers. This was not a recipe for coherent policy-making. The extent to which confraternities were effectively controlled or allowed to pursue their own way — conscientiously or immorally — could vary considerably depending on struggles for power and influence both in Rome and in the locality.[29]

2 POSITIVE SPONSORSHIP OF CONFRATERNITIES

When we turn to the positive aspects of promotion and patronage of confraternities we can again detect some changing patterns in the sixteenth century. As in the past most new confraternities were probably the product of individual initiatives under particular local circumstances; the result of some leading preacher's fiery Lenten sermon, the organisational talent of a pastoral bishop, or the reaction of an old soldier to the devastations of war. Major confraternities could arise from a chance occurrence stimulating the devotion of a particular person, as exemplified in the story of the Roman archconfraternity of SS. Crocefisso in S. Marcello. The church of S. Marcello was burned in 1519, but a large wooden cross was left undamaged. When Rome was afflicted by plague in 1522 the titular cardinal of S. Marcello, Guglielmo Raimondo di Vich, used this cross to lead a flagellant, barefoot procession to implore God's mercy. On the disappearance of the plague the Cardinal founded the confraternity to honour the cross. This brotherhood (elevated into an archconfraternity in 1562), besides rebuilding and decorating the chapel for the cross, undertook visiting the sick and prisoners, endowing poor girls, and hosting pilgrims, especially during Holy Years. Members of the Roman aristocracy and artists were notable members, and were to finance a model confraternity meeting hall with narrative frescoes.[30] Other individual and idiosyncratic promotions of confraternities will be recorded in passing.

---

[29] BCB F.O. 43 fols. 42r–v, 44r, 45v; see my 'Perugia and papal absolutism', pp. 524–6, 536 on having powerful protectors and agents in Rome, and resulting inconsistencies in policy.

[30] A. Vannugli, 'L'arciconfraternita del SS. Crocefisso e la sua cappella in San Marcello', *RSRR*, 5 (1984), 429–43; J. Delumeau, 'Une confrérie romaine au xvi siècle "L'arciconfraternita del SS. mo Crocefisso in S. Marcello"', *Mélanges d'archéologie et d'histoire*, 68 (1951), 281–306; J. von Henneberg, *L'Oratorio dell'Arciconfraternita del Santissimo Crocefisso di San Marcello* (Rome, 1974). See below chapter 11 on its artistic importance.

However, in general terms the sixteenth century witnessed increased sponsorship by bishops and by the new religious Orders, particularly the Jesuits. The regulatory functions and procedures of the bishops outlined in the previous section had positive byproducts. Bishops and their assistants noted the absence of confraternities in certain areas, or the lack of particular types, and ordered or recommended new creations. The pastoral concern of model bishops like Carlo Borromeo and Gabriele Paleotti led to numerous Christian Doctrine confraternities in the provinces of Lombardy and Bologna.[31] In the south many of the Rosary and Sacrament societies were the result of episcopal sponsorship, though often in cooperation with the Orders — especially as many of the southern bishops were themselves Franciscans or Theatines. In the Terra di Lavoro region between Rome and Naples the philanthropic confraternities in dioceses like Sessa, Carinola and Calvi owed most to bishops. The rich and active charity in Capuan societies derived much from Bishop Roberto Bellarmino's pastoral concern in the early seventeenth century. On the other hand another diocese in the region, Teano, was more indebted to the monastic Orders for its philanthropic confraternities — and the monks were partly in conflict with their bishops.[32]

The religious Orders continued to play a major part in the promotion and functioning of confraternities. The old Orders like the Dominicans and Franciscans maintained their sponsorship of devotional societies. In the Vicenza area, for example, the renewal of old or the foundation of new confraternities came first, in the 1490s, from fra Bernardino da Feltre (Observant minor), whose promotions included an early Nome di Dio society (1496) and the Oratory of S. Girolamo; he was followed by the Dominicans Battista da Crema and Tommaso Stella, with another Observant minor Antonio Pagani. The Dominicans of Prato, inspired by Savonarola's preaching in 1496, had a major impact on confraternity life in that city through the following century.[33] The Dominicans throughout Italy enhanced their contribution throughout the sixteenth century by promoting numerous Rosary, and several Nome di Dio confraternities. But it is the development of new Orders, or reformed branches of old ones, which enhanced confraternity life in many areas. The Capuchins, as reformed Franciscans, maintained the interest in discipline confraternities, but Capuchin preachers, like Giuseppe da Fermo with his advocacy of the Forty-Hour (Quarantore) celebrations, could also cause a concentration on eucharistic devotion in old and new societies. The Capuchins have the chief credit for revitalising the old Roman hospital confraternity of S. Giacomo degli

---

[31] See above notes 18–19, 21; and below chapter 10.3, on Christian Doctrine confraternities; P. Prodi, Il Cardinale Gabriele Paleotti (1522–1597), (2 vols., Rome, 1959–67), vol. 2, pp. 179–82; G. De Sandre Gasparini, 'La confraternita di S. Giovanni Evangelista della Morte in Padova e una "riforma" ispirata dal vescovo Pietro Barozzi (1502)' in Miscellanea G.-G. Meersseman, vol. 2 (Padua, 1970), pp. 765–815.

[32] See above note 21; K. Eubel et al. (eds.) Hierarchia Catholica (Regensberg), vol. 3 (1910) indicates the Franciscan and Theatine background of many southern bishops; L. Donvito, 'Chiesa e società nelle diocesi di Terra di Lavoro a nord del Volturno in età postridentina (1585–1630)', Archivio Storico di Terra di Lavoro (Caserta), 6 (1978–9) [1979], 137–260, esp. pp. 228–9; A. Fino, 'Chiesa e società nelle diocesi di Terra di Lavoro a sud del Volturno in età postridentina (1585–1630)', RSCI, 35 (1981), 388–449, esp. pp. 428–9. On more widespread conflict between confraternities under Religious sponsorship and those under episcopal and parochial support see Rusconi, 'Confraternite', p. 486 and n. 31; Zardin, Confraternite e vita di pietà, pp. 40–1; and section 4 below.

[33] L. Giacomuzzi, Vita cristiana e pensiero spirituale a Vicenza dal 1400 al 1600 (Rome and Vicenza, 1972), pp. 34, 37–40. On Bernardino da Feltre, see above chapter 1, n. 15. St Gaetano Thiene was a member of S. Girolamo for two years while in Vicenza, with Pagani as his spiritual advisor; he went on to launch what became the Theatine congregation. E. Fasano Guarini (ed.), Prato storia di una città, vol. 2: Un microcosmo in movimento (1494–1815) (Prato, 1986), pp. 515, n. 27, 539–40, 543–5.

Incurabili, which became one of the prize charitable institutions of the century.[34] The Oratorian followers of Filippo Neri were promoters and activists for hospitals and confraternities to help pilgrims in Rome, especially the SS. Trinità dei Pellegrini e dei Convalescenti, and S. Spirito in Sassia, which was revived by Cirillo of Aquila, a close friend of Neri's.[35]

Jesuit activity overshadows that of all other groups. In comparison with members of other Orders, or bishops and cardinals, the Jesuits may have received disproportionate credit for achievements in Catholic Reform, thanks to their own loquacious, sometimes eloquent advocates and historians, who have not been matched by those for their rivals. Nevertheless the Jesuit contribution to confraternities has almost certainly been under-recorded.[36] The Oratorians, and to some extent the Theatines, deliberately confined themselves to certain areas or roles. The Jesuits did not. They appeared everywhere in Italy, and become involved in the greatest variety of devotions and activities. Ignatius Loyola saw the lay confraternities as playing a major role in the reconquest of the world for true catholicism, and was closely involved in the Roman company of the Dodici Apostoli. An early Jesuit preoccupation with devotion to the sacrament was extended — as they developed the roles of teaching generally — into catechismal instruction through confraternities and schools of Christian Doctrine. From about 1563 the Jesuits became systematic promoters of Marian confraternities, following in the wake of the Dominicans. Initially led by the Belgian Jean Leunis the Jesuits aimed their campaign at young Italians, who were primarily to recite the Office of the Madonna and learn the fundamentals of Christian Doctrine. Their first Marian congregation of this type, the Annunziazione di Maria, was founded in 1584, and more were stimulated by a Bull from Sixtus V in 1587 giving Jesuit colleges and other institutions the right to erect such confraternities in their midst. Wider promotion came through the work of L. Pinelli, a prominent teacher of theology and philosophy across Europe and author of a *Libretto di brevi meditazioni* (Naples, 1598), and that of F. Pavone who, in leading missions in Italy, tried to launch a Marian congregation in every town or castle for persons of all ages and conditions. Those Jesuits conducting missions in the Roman Campagna received instructions from Rome to erect confraternities to bolster their crusading work.[37]

---

[34] Meloni, 'Topografia', p. 35; G. Chiaretti, 'Di alcune fraternite laicali di disciplinati dei secoli xv–xvii regolate dalla spiritualita cappuccina', *BSPU*, 65 (1968), 229–60; C. Urbanelli, *Storia dei Cappuccini delle Marche* (3 vols. in 4, Ancona, 1978–84), vol. 2, pp. 528–31, 558–9, 564–7, 570–1 on Capuchin reforms of confraternities in Fossombrone, Montefiore, Tolentino, Fermo, Recanati; documents relating to some of these in vol. 3/I, pp. 214–17, 291–2, 305–6; Padre Arsenio d'Ascoli, *La Predicazione dei Cappuccini nel Cinquecento in Italia* (Loreto [Ancona], 1956), pp. 216–19, 233 on Capuchin inspirers of confraternities in places like Ancona, Chioggia and Trapani, and pp. 271–92 on eucharistic sermons; P. De Angelis, *L'arcispedale di San Giacomo in Augusta* (Rome, 1955).

[35] P. De Angelis, *L'arciconfraternita ospitaliera di Santo Spirito in Saxia* (Rome, 1950); Garofalo, *SS. Trinita*, pp. 12–13.

[36] G. Angelozzi, who is working on Jesuit teaching and influence, especially in the Bologna area, reinforced this verdict during a discussion in March 1986, and argued that a major study of Jesuit confraternities in Italy could and should be undertaken.

[37] Fiorani, 'L'esperienza religiosa', pp. 161–3; Lopez, 'Le confraternite laicali', *passim* on the Jesuits, and pp. 199–203 on Marian aspects; Paglia, '*La Pietà dei Carcerati*', pp. 133–9 on wider Jesuit contributions to confraternities, with n. 101 citing Jesuit instructions; E.A. Barletta (ed.), *Aspetti della Riforma Cattolica e del Concilio di Trento. Mostra Documentaria* (Rome, 1964), pp. 90–1; for the Jesuit foundation of a Rosary confraternity, by T. Rosanova, in rural Lombardy see Zardin, *Confraternite e vita di pietà*, p. 29: the Legnano society founded in 1585 had 723 members by 1589.

Jesuits expected to remain spiritual directors of the confraternities they sponsored, as was made clear in the rules of Lecce's Annunziazione della Beata Vergine, founded by B. Realino in 1582. This society was designed for the spiritual welfare of its members, and to assist the naked poor. Jesuits wanted close supervision of lay confraternities to ensure proper devotion and prevent heresy. G. Loarte provided books suitable for the laity in such societies, on the exercise of a Christian life, or meditations on the Rosary. From the 1550s Lainez and other Jesuit leaders particularly emphasised the value of philanthropic work by lay confraternities — for the elimination of poverty and its concomitant vices. In Genoa Jesuit promotions stressed public confession but private discipline; simplicity of processions, but lavishness of charity; caring for the sick in hospitals, encouraging the repentance of prostitutes and their subsequent protection, helping the ashamed poor (*poveri vergognosi*), aiding and visiting prisoners, and settling disputes, especially in the villages above the city. In Turin the dominant confraternity was that of the company of S. Paolo which, though started by local laymen, came under Jesuit influence from about 1562 and consequently founded a number of philanthropic institutions; a Monti di Pietà, a hospital and several refuges.[38] A French Jesuit, Jean Tellier, was instrumental in founding the Roman Pietà dei Carcerati to help prisoners. Antonio Possevino, secretary to the Jesuit General, was closely linked with Tellier's work, but also used his central position to advise confraternities and sponsor philanthropy more broadly. He stressed the philanthrophic injunctions of Matthew 25 as a basis for confraternity work, and argued that charity was necessary to achieve salvation.[39]

Many Jesuit aims are summarised in the 1626 statues of Milan's congregation of Madonna di Loreto, founded in 1601 by the Spanish Jesuit M. Funes:

The principal purpose of our congregation is to carry out works of piety, and particularly towards the *poveri vergognosi*, helping them with all solicitude, procuring for them with all Christian charity the salvation of their souls, and then that of their bodies, without having any other care than for the glory of God, and the salvation of one's neighbour [*salute del prossimo*].[40]

Popes were more important for their general encouragement of confraternities through their Bulls and letters of ratification, and their grants of indulgences, than for the particular promotion of individual institutions. But Leo X — a Pope more associated with hunting or inertia in the face of challenges from the north than for charity — should be mentioned as the key promoter in 1520 of the institution Delle Convertite, run by the confraternity Della Carità to assist reformed prostitutes, and Pius V was a substantial donor in 1566 to the SS. Annunziata alla Minerva which became a leading provider of dowries for poor girls. More significant among Roman sponsors was Cardinal A.M. Salviati (d. 1604) who might be seen as the hospital cardinal, responsible for founding, reforming or patronising many Roman hospitals and their allied confraternities.[41]

---

[38] Lopez, 'Le confraternite laicali', pp. 209–38, esp. p. 210 on Jesuit spiritual director; Fiorani, 'L'esperienza religiosa', pp. 159, 164–5; Grendi, 'Morfologia', pp. 248–9, 278–9; A. Erba, *La Chiesa Sabauda tra Cinquecento e Seicento* (Rome, 1979), pp. 248–58.

[39] Paglia, 'La Pietà dei Carcerati', pp. 93–102, 131–3.

[40] Lopez, 'Le confraternite laicali', p. 197 n. 117; on the meanings of *poveri vergognosi* see below chapter 7.3.

[41] Barletta, (ed.), *Aspetti della Riforma*, p. 56; Monachino, p. 251; P. Partner, *Renaissance Rome 1500–1559* (Berkeley, Los Angeles and London, 1976), p. 105. On Salviati and the Roman hospital confraternities, see below, chapter 9.4.

One lay ruler deserves mention as a confraternity sponsor: Duke Ercole d'Este of Ferrara, noted for his strong religious piety and a commitment to charitable works. He came from a family famous as soldiers in the fifteenth and sixteenth centuries, but reacted to some of the horrors of war (against Venice), and encouraged a charitable attitude that was to bear some fruit within Ferrara. In particular in 1490 he founded the Scuola di San Martino to aid deserving ashamed poor. Organised in imitation of Christ and his twelve apostles, this confraternity's twelve lay members under one priest were, with the maximum anonymity, to collect funds for distribution to the deserving poor.[42]

As an ideal exemplar of a lay promoter of more than one confraternity we might cite Alessandro Luzzago (1551–1502). He was a Brescian patrician who took doctorates of philosophy and theology at Padua University. He became an admirer and friend of dominant church reformers: Filippo Neri, Roberto Bellarmino, Cesare Baronio and Federico Borromeo, and a close associate of Cardinal G.F. Morosini, bishop of Brescia from 1585 to 1596. From the 1580s Luzzago revived or promoted various confraternities in Brescia, such as the S. Giovanni Battista for aiding prisoners and the condemned, S. Spirito for gentlemen, prepared to help settle disputes in society, S. Caterina for the spiritual welfare of young students. Luzzago backed the Istituzione della Dottrina Cristiana to teach the rudiments of the faith, and finally activated the Casa di Dio hostel for mendicants from 1585. One lay reformer thus had a major impact on Brescia's social and religious institutions.[43]

In the sixteenth century the promotion of new confraternities came more from ecclesiastical leaders, or from a combination of lay and clerical figures working in cooperation, than from independent laymen. Given the increased formality of foundation procedures, and the theoretical measures for regulating them, especially after Trent, ecclesiastical authorities and clerical advisers were likely to play a leading role. But, as we shall see later, lay initiatives and sponsorship were often necessary as well to provide the buildings and the money needed especially for the philanthropic societies.

3 ARCHCONFRATERNITIES

Ecclesiastical control over lay confraternities, and the standardisation of their rules and behaviour was affected by the growth of archconfraternities during the sixteenth century. From the third decade of the century certain important companies — first in Rome, but later elsewhere — were elevated as archconfraternities. They received additional status and prestige from full papal recognition and obtained impressive grants of indulgences. They become the centre of a network as other confraternities of a similar type aggregated, or affiliated, to the central archconfraternity. The latter set the standard for rules and procedures, for particular devotions and dress. An aggregating company had to have its rules checked and amended, thus many older companies were brought under episcopal authority, especially after the Bull *Quaecumque* of 1604. Bishops naturally favoured such aggregation of old societies. The local confraternity in joining the wider network might adopt additional obligations and pious practices, but in

---

[42] W.L. Gundersheimer, *Ferrara. The Style of a Renaissance Despotism* (Princeton, 1973), pp. 186–91.
[43] AA.VV. *Storia di Brescia*, vol. 2 (n.p., 1961), p. 470–3.

particular would share in a wider range of indulgences. Most of the archconfraternities were in Rome, and the growth of the system can be seen as evidence of the increased centralisation of the surviving and reforming Roman Catholic church. While the main emphasis was on standardisation and control, there was also a resulting magnetic attraction to Rome. A number of Roman archconfraternities developed an excellent reputation for hospitality, encouraging distant fraternities to undertake pilgrimages to St Peter's and the ancient basilicas.[44]

A Perugian historian, and member of the city's Crocefisso confraternity, emphasised that his company enjoyed a 'treasury' of indulgences because it had aggregated to the relevant Roman archconfraternity. The city's Della Morte company in 1615 revised its statutes to conform to the 1570 statutes of its Roman archconfraternity. By 1575 Perugia's three confederated confraternities had some links with the Roman Gonfalone archconfraternity, for the primary purpose of helping to release Christian slaves held by the Turks. By 1580 there was apparently a full affiliation, supervised by Cardinal Protector Alessandro Farnese, who sanctioned the allocation of indulgences and spiritual benefits. This was publicised in a printed leaflet, but still did not nullify the case for lay autonomy which we have previously discussed. Again Perugian confraternities did not change their names or dedications. When the brothers of these companies went on a pilgrimage to Rome for the 1575 Jubilee, they took with them a specially commissioned banner to present to the Roman Gonfalone; it seems to have been normal to bring some such gift for the host archconfraternity.[45]

Aggregations to Roman archconfraternities reached considerable proportions. During the sixteenth century the archconfraternity of S. Spirito in Saxia (or Sassia), which supervised a major hospital complex, received about 170 aggregations world-wide, with 76 of them Italian. Most of these affiliations date from the 1580s and 1590s, and there were 164 more in the next century. S. Spirito was unusual in having so many non-Italian affiliations. During the 1625 Jubilee celebrations the Gonfalone archconfraternity was host to eighty-six aggregated confraternities, involving 29,550 men and women. There were eventually to be about 250 aggregations to the Gonfalone. The SS. Trinità, specialising in assisting pilgrims and convalescents, aggregated a hundred companies. The archconfraternities of S. Rocco, S. Crocefisso, the Pietà dei Carcerati, and the Sacre Stimate di S. Francesco all had over thirty companies in their network. But the prize seems to go to the Orazione e Morte with over a thousand affiliated societies by the eighteenth century, probably the result of the lower middle and artisan classes' growing concern for the 'good death'.[46]

[44] Rusconi, 'Confraternite', pp. 489–90; Meloni, 'Topografia', pp. 17–18, 35–6; Paglia, 'La Pietà dei Carcerati', pp. 85–6.

[45] Crispolti, Perugia Augusta, p. 176; Marinelli, Le Confraternite, pp. 29, 349–50, 403, 817; Guèze, p. 599; SBF S. Francesco no. 457, fol. 128r–v. For an example of a smaller Umbrian town pursuing indulgences see: G. Casagrande, 'Inventario-regesto delle pergamene della chiesa parrocchiale di S. Maria Maggiore a Spello (1187–1844)', BSPU, 83 (1986) [1987], 5–66, esp. docs. 42, 45, 55, 56, 72, 74, 80: from this one church between 1565 and 1644 seven confraternities secured indulgences and privileges — with or without a formal aggregation — from their association with archconfraternities in Rome and (in the case of the Cintura di S. Monica in 1644), Bologna.

[46] De Angelis, S. Spirito, Appendix III; Paglia, 'La Pietà dei Carcerati', pp. 85–6; Rusconi, 'Confraternite', p. 499.

There were archconfraternities outside Rome. From 1569 Carlo Borromeo started them for his Milan diocese as part of his own campaign for centralisation and, initially, the standardisation of discipline confraternities. In Bologna in 1586 Sixtus V elevated the company of S. Maria della Morte into an archconfraternity in order to establish an alternative network to the Roman. It affiliated companies from within the same city, as well as those scattered through the province, with SS. Sebastiano e Rocco being one of the first to join. The archconfraternity had an annual right to liberate a condemned prisoner. But the remoter city of Cosenza had five archconfraternities as the centre of a local network by the end of the sixteenth century. The bishops of Bari in the seventeenth century encouraged confraternities to seek aggregation to a Roman arch-confraternity, but by mid-century Bari had its own archconfraternity of S. Antonio da Padova. This company had been founded in 1604, but it did not request proper episcopal ratification and approval of its statutes until 1651, when it specifically wanted additional indulgences. Once episcopally approved it still maintained some autonomy; as one of the confraternities sponsored by the Minor Franciscans it was free from episcopal visitation—but subject to the head of the Franciscan Conventuals, under a concession made by Urban VIII in 1628 (despite the Bull *Quaecumque*). What control was in practice exercised is not clear. Making this company an archconfraternity presumably impeded Roman centralisation.[47]

The archconfraternity system in general led to Roman standardisation and control. When in 1607 Paul V elevated the Congregazione della Dottrina Cristiana into an archconfraternity he probably ensured that Rome would finally replace Milan as the model for the catechism-school system. But the Milanese could resent Roman leadership. After the end of the plague in 1577 Carlo Borromeo encouraged the formation of parish-based confraternities of S. Croce, to thank God for the end of the pestilence, to honour the crucified Christ, and to erect little crosses around Milan for remembrance and devotion. A number of these S. Croce fraternities aggregated with Roman archconfraternities to extend their devotions or activities, and to obtain indulgences. The S. Croce society in S. Babila aggregated with the Pietà dei Carcerati in 1585, and undertook to help Milanese prisoners. In the early years it reported its activities to the Roman archconfraternity, but gradually resentment grew against Roman control, and the imposition of statutes and orders—particularly those concerning the number of offices within the fraternity, and the degree of clerical control over the brothers and sisters. Local pride and resentment against outside domination led the elite leadership in Milan to sever relations with Rome from about 1605. The fraternity may have regretted this later when, having got into trouble locally over building an oratory, it might have benefited from Roman support.[48]

In general however, Roman archconfraternity control must have been seen to offer more benefits than handicaps, judging by the number of aggregations.

[47] M. Calace, 'Vita religiosa e francescanesimo a Bari nel secolo xvii', [typescript of unpublished conference paper]. I am most grateful to Dottoressa Calace, at the University of Bari, for sending me this paper prior to fuller publication in a book; BCB F.O.43 fol. 27r–v; E. Misefari, *Storia sociale della Calabria* (Milan, 1976), pp. 369–70.

[48] M. Turrini, ' "Riformare il mondo a vera vita christiana": le scuole di catechismo nell'Italia del Cinque-cento', *Annali dell'Istituto storico italo-germanico in Trento*, 8 (1982), 412; Olivieri Baldissarri, *I "poveri prigioni"*, pp. 3–5, 74, 86–8, 220–2.

4 CONFRATERNITIES AND PAROCHIAL CONTROL

We have already seen that a number of confraternities were used to enhance parochial control over the laity, to enforce morality, to check on heresy or blasphemy. They were in this context part of a social control mechanism, at least for some areas and regimes, as already noted for Tuscany under the Medici. There has been much debate recently over the extent to which during the early modern period, in both Catholic and Protestant countries, there was a major increase in social control by the ruling classes over the general population, particularly through tighter parish organisation, and church indoctrination—by sermons, confessional procedures, Sunday schools, consistory courts, or increased documentation of births, marriages, communions and deaths, which led to a better knowledge of parish and family life. There is little doubt that in most areas parish life was fuller and more organised, and that church or state authorities were better informed about the populace. More contentious is whether there was a one-way 'acculturation' process whereby the official churches and the dominant elite imposed their religious culture and social control over popular culture and religion. Some of us argue that the two 'cultures' were in fact intermingled, and that official church teaching could be influenced, modified and invigorated by the beliefs and practices of the commonality. Liturgical practices would be imposed from above, but could also adopt or perpetuate popular elements, such as rogation processions.[49]

The relationships between the lay confraternities and parish organisation have some relevance to part of this debate. The relationships are complex and inconsistent. We know very little about normal parish life, and the relationship between the parish priest and his parishioners; the extent to which a priest could frighten or persuade through a superior education, at least where seminaries or Jesuit colleges could provide educated priests, or the extent to which the priest could be controlled through the purse-strings held by powerful families or confraternities who possessed chapels, and could help pay church bills. In Venice, where parish priests were elected by the laity, and where most priests and chaplains came from Venice there was unlikely to be an exaggerated clerical dominance, and we know that confraternities could be important for funding the parish church. In other cities some clergy might have had a much tougher control over parishioners and their institutions.[50]

The increase during the sixteenth century and afterwards of devotional confraternities based in the parish church—particularly devoted to the Eucharist or the Marian cults—was likely to augment the parish priests' control and authority. They usually acted as the officiating priests to the company. They could oversee—if not entirely regulate—access to the confraternity chapel, and it would be difficult for the confraternity to act autonomously as long as the parish priest was resident and active. Bishops increasingly sponsored Sacrament confraternities as a means whereby the parish priest could use a devout elite to control parochial devotion and behaviour. Bishops Giberti of Verona and then Carlo Borromeo of Milan wanted such devotional confraternities to be standardised, and thereby to standardise parochial worship. The Bull *Quaecumque* of 1604 in

---

[49] On arguments about social control see chapter 1, n. 23.

[50] On financial aspects see below, chapter 6; on tension between confraternities and parent churches also chapter 11. On the Venetian situation: N.S. Davidson, 'The clergy of Venice in the sixteenth century', *Bulletin of the Society for Renaissance Studies*, 2, no. 2 (October, 1984), 19–31.

general, and some synodal legislation more specifically, gave parish priests powers to control these confraternities, to curb their autonomy, to elect or at least veto confraternity officials, to scrutinise their accounts, even to license their every meeting.[51]

Such Italian policies are similar to those that have been highlighted in discussions of the French Counter-Reformation. As in France there was resistance to control policies, which were also frustrated by conflicts between confraternities, and between confraternity and parish priest.[52] Even in the authoritarian world of Borromean Lombardy older *scuole* and Marian societies resisted the rivalry of parochial Sacrament confraternities, and opposed episcopal interventions. There were rivalries and conflicts between parish-based confraternities (particularly Marian and Sacrament) and independent fraternities or those sponsored by the Order—which might be discipline societies, but also wish to compete with their own Marian and eucharistic devotions. The Orders sometimes competed with the parish system in promoting their own Rosary fraternities. If a confraternity operated from premises owned by an Order—with a chapel or rooms in the monastic church or cloister—or relied on the Order for preachers and confessors, then it would be under pressure to follow the Order rather than the parish priest. Some confraternities resented being within a parish and, as we shall see in chapter 11, sought escape in their own premises.[53]

The continued existence of confraternities which were specifically meant to curb heresy may be another example of the 'social control' environment. It has been noted already that Peter Martyr had launched or fostered antiheresy companies, often named Crocesignati or S. Croce. Such confraternities, or others that might be understood to be in part agents or assistants of the Inquisition, existed in the later sixteenth and seventeenth centuries — in cities such as Rimini, Imola, Faenza and Modena. In Turin a S. Paolo confraternity in 1562 seems to have been involved in antiheresy campaigning. It is however difficult to know what role these confraternities actually played, though it has been claimed that the S. Pietro Martire company in Milan, and Crocesignati or similar fraternities in Lombard cities like Pavia, Como and Cremona were valuable assistants to the inquisitors. Italians were ready to denounce suspected heretics to the inquisitors, even if they were not quite as enthusiastic as Spaniards or Sicilians.[54]

Archbishop G. Paleotti of Bologna wanted a confraternity created especially to hunt

---

[51] Rusconi, 'Confraternite', pp. 486–92; Zardin, *Confraternite e vita di pietà*, pp. 24–5, 40–1, 84 n. 26, 106 n. 98; *idem* 'Confraternite e comunità', pp. 711–14, 715 n. 29, 731–2; *idem* 'Le confraternite in Italia settentrionale'; L. Allegra, 'Il parrocco: un mediatore tra alta e bassa cultura', *Storia d'Italia. Annali 4* (1981), p. 926, who particularly cites for its strong demands for parochial control: *Sanctiones in Synodo ab . . . Clemente Trotto episcopo Fossani* (Cuneo, 1664), pp. 170–2.

[52] On France see J-P. Gutton, 'Confraternities, *Curés* and Communities in rural areas of the diocese of Lyons under the Ancien Régime', *Religion and Society*, ed. von Greyerz, pp. 202–11; Hoffman, *Church and Community*, pp. 105–6, 109–14, stressing the conflict between old Holy Spirit confraternities and new parochial devotional societies.

[53] 'Confraternite e comunità', pp. 707–8 and n. 15; Rusconi, 'Confraternite', p. 493; Fasano Guarini (ed.), *Prato*, p. 540, new confraternities in Prato from the seventeenth century sought to have their own premises, and avoid parochial or monastic control.

[54] A. Turchini, *Clero e fedeli a Rimini in età post-tridentina* (Rome, 1978), pp. 137–9; A. Biondi, 'Lunga durata e microarticolazione nel territorio di un Ufficio dell'Inquisizione', *Annali dell'Istituto storico italo-germanico in Trento*, 8 (1982), 88; Zardin, 'Le confraternite in Italia settentrionale'; Rusconi, 'Confraternite', p. 491; AA.VV *Storia di Milano* (Treccani degli Alfieri), vol. 10 (1957), pp. 275–6: the confraternities in Milan and Como were or had become exclusively noble.

out heretics; but the direct outcome of his wish is unclear. In the seventeenth century Bologna had a supposedly heretic-hunting company of Santissima Croce. According to its statutes it had been started in 1097 with the promulgation of a crusade, but it clearly had an allegiance to Peter Martyr as well as the Holy Cross. Its members now had to take a vow before the inquisitor or his vicar, in defence of the holiest faith of Christ against heretics and their supporters, and to act instantly at the inquisitor's command. They were obliged to reveal heretics or suspects, their supporters and protectors, to denounce blasphemers, and those who held prohibited books, and to take up arms against heretics if required. They were to demonstrate their role by wearing the symbol of the red cross openly on their shoulder.[55] As yet there is no evidence of the members' actual activities. One suspects that membership, and the wearing of the symbol, was honorific, and that the brothers were not of much practical assistance to the inquisitors.[56] The statutes advocated an intense spiritual and devotional life, and social assistance for members — which they may have regarded as the more important element. The monthly congregational meetings were meant to be in the presence of the local inquisitor or his vicar.

Confraternities were probably more important in combating heresy in an indirect way. Their promotion of the eucharist and other sacraments, their involvement in teaching Christian Doctrine in some areas, their campaigns against blasphemy and swearing, their advocacy of salvation by good works were positive, if indirect, measures to counteract heresy.

The account given so far of the parochial system gaining increasing domination over confraternities and using them to achieve greater social control or religious uniformity has a reverse side. In some areas at least the confraternities could control the parish church and its clergy. They might play a dominant role as financial supporters of the parish church, providing income through the use of a chapel, renting other premises from the parish church, paying for the equipment of altars, and for wax and oil for lamps. If the confraternity chapel was blessed with popular indulgences and privileges the increased flow of worshippers would add to the funds and alms of the whole church and thereby the confraternity's influence on the clergy. We know too little about the finances of both confraternities and parish churches — especially which fraternities received free accommodation and services and which were helping to finance churches through rent and offerings — to make a general judgement on which side was in a better position to play the financial card, and so exert pressure on the other.

A confraternity could act as a vestry committee, with an official role in church organisation, as a study of communities situated north of Naples or near Mount Vesuvius shows for the seventeenth century. The Sacrament confraternity of S. Castrense at Marano (north of Naples) shared the temporal control of the church with

---

[55] Paleotti, *Archiepiscopale Bononiense*, p. 223: 'Laudabile quidem in primis esset, si confraternitatem cuius praecipium munus esset haereticos denuntiare, erigendam curarent, qualem multis in locis magno cum fructu constitutum sumus.' This section derived from his first Provincial synod. (The copy I used, from the former archiepiscopal library, has this passage underlined in what seems an old annotation); *Capitoli che devono osservare li Confratelli della compagnia della Santissima Croce di Bologna* (Bologna, 1637), esp. pp. 6–7, 11.

[56] G. Angelozzi of Bologna University in private conversation gave this as the verdict of Bologna specialists; he had heard of similar societies in Modena and Florence in this period, or later.

the parish priest. At Trocchia the administrators had to be selected from the *Confratelli* of the Sacrament company; at Ponticelli the governors of the Rosary confraternity were also *maestri* of the parish church. By the later seventeenth century the confraternity of Purification had taken over the church at Mugnano. In some other churches the parish priest shared temporal power with confraternity members as *maestri*, but had apparently some say in their selection. Here it should be noted that the parish priest rarely dominated the church in temporal matters; it was common for there to be a *fabbriceria*, or vestry committee, appointed by the village or town government. Confraternities sometimes came to replace these bodies. A similar close involvement of confraternity officials, especially from Sacrament companies, in parish churches as *fabbricerii* has been noted for parts of Lombardy. The degree of harmony or conflict between confraternity and parish clergy, who controlled whom, would have varied, depending on local personalities and situations.[57]

Our comments on the control and sponsorship of confraternities should have indicated that throughout our period, and increasingly so after the Council of Trent, there were more and more attempts to impose clerical control — by bishops, inquisitors, regulars or parish priests — on the lay companies. There was competition from state authorities, especially if hospitals were involved. There was conflict and competition between the different branches of the clerical establishment, and they met opposition from some independently minded confraternity leaders. Uniformity and control was undermined by competition and conflict between different types of confraternities. While there were movements towards central Roman control, there was also some resistance, for instance with the rival networks under archconfraternities elsewhere. There were limits to the control that could be exercised by the parish priest, and he could be pressurised by a powerful confraternity. On the other hand there could be cooperation between laity and clergy in common causes of devotion, of philanthropy, and even of social control. This should become clearer through a close study of what constituted confraternal life.

[57] Russo, *Chiesa e comunità*, pp. 234, n. 54, 237 n. 68, 315; Zardin, *Confraternite e vita di pietà*, pp. 126–9; *idem* 'Confraternite e comunità', pp. 713–14; Olivieri Baldissarri, *I "poveri prigioni"*, Appendix II lists several officials of the confraternity of S. Croce in S. Babila who were involved in the *fabbrica* of that church. These need to be matched by similar detailed studies of parochial control in other areas.

4

INTERNAL ORGANISATION AND RELIGIOUS LIFE

The membership of a confraternity was governed by rules, and by officials appointed or elected to impose them. Active membership centred on official business occasions as much as on devotional practices, and often the two aspects were entwined. This chapter moves from the rule-book to its partial implementation in religious and social activities that primarily concerned the brothers and sisters, and their immediate family. These activities include both corporate events such as feasts, communal singing and elaborate celebrations of the communion, and more private or intimate devotions such as flagellation or praying for departed relatives. Being a member of a confraternity could be a marginal activity or a burdensome commitment; despite the rules, the individual concerned could usually decide which it would be. Once a member, a brother was not, in practice, readily dismissed; he could pick his time to be active, and when to seek benefits from his membership.

I STATUTES AND OFFICIALS

Confraternities were by definition governed by rules. The society was formed by people coming together for religious purposes and agreeing to conduct their social relationships according to certain rules. Whether these rules were of their own making, or were imposed from outside, in theory they formed the basis of the confraternity. It did not follow that the brothers and sisters readily knew those rules, or paid much attention to them after their initial formulation. Formal statutes might not be adopted until long after the group had been established, and in the case of older confraternities–especially those like the Genoese *casacce* that met in public places just for processions–there may never have been a formal written set of rules. But the social contract fiction had to be maintained. When post-tridentine episcopal visitors appeared, armed with their new powers of supervision over confraternities and pious places, it was standard form (if not invariable practice), to demand sight of the society's constitution, to be vetted by bishop or vicar general. The rules were often declared to be 'lost', others were deemed inadequate. Reforming bishops ensured that new, acceptable, constitutions were created and, to enhance the chances of survival and observance, many were printed under episcopal licence.

Such printed constitutions have provided the modern historian with valuable evidence. They indicate formal structures, the numbers of officials, the electoral system and they may give some strictures on correct moral behaviour, but they are often unhelpful about religious practices or procedures concerning philanthropic activity.[1]

The bias of the statutes is, of course, of some significance; the stress on office-holding, on role-playing, suggests that these organisations had an important part in the patterning of society beyond the 'religious' functions. The short duration of office-holding in numerous cases, and the high proportion of offices to general membership, meant that many members could hold a position of responsibility or status if desired. This might be seen as particularly important for people who were excluded from political activity in their community. As the sixteenth century progressed proportionately fewer people were involved in politically or administratively responsible roles (even if there was a growth in bureaucracies). There were fewer little states in Italy and the larger states became more 'absolutist'. In the previous centuries politics in northern and central Italian cities had been lively, if violent. Partly democratic, or broadly oligarchic city councils, often resting on a broader base of guildsmen, vied with 'tyrants' or *signori; signori* quickly vied with each other. Many could play a political role, legally or illegally. By the mid-sixteenth century much of this had changed. Urban politics was probably more peaceful, as major courts and capital cities—whether in the Papal State or Medicean Tuscany—became more dominant, and communal councils and guilds lost power and influence. In this context the exercise of influence and social power through office-holding in confraternities might have been a compensation for many, whether nobles, merchants or artisans. It has recently been argued that Roman confraternities provided social opportunities for immigrant members of the *borghesia* who were excluded from power elsewhere by the clericalisation of the Papal State, and restricted by the limited economic structure of Rome. It has been argued since the sixteenth century that the comparative stability of the Venetian Republic and the apparent lack of resentment against the closed oligarchy which filled the Grand Council owed something to the situation whereby the next ranks of society excluded from the main political system dominated the main confraternities, especially the *Scuole Grandi*. Through these the *cittadini originarii* could play many social roles, and exercise a compensatory power, especially as office-holders deciding who could or could not be assisted. This does not mean that all brothers wanted to hold office; as we shall see, some found it too burdensome.[2]

A good example of lengthy constitution writing is provided by the 1565 revised statutes of the Roman archconfraternity of SS. Crocefisso di S. Marcello: a 134-page printed book with fifty-eight chapters of rules, with some additional material, such as papal Bulls, pertaining to confraternity life. The rules cover the election and duties of the officials. There were twenty-two male officials: three *guardiani*, three *deputati*, a

---

[1] On confraternity constitutions generally see Le Bras, pp. 444–6; Monti, *Le confraternite*, vol. 2, pp. 31–54; Weissman, *Ritual Brotherhood*, pp. 58–63, 198–201. G. De Rosa suggests that one of the marks of a 'modern', as opposed to 'medieval', confraternity is the development of internal government on the basis of much more formal and legal procedures: contribution to a *tavola rotonda*, printed in *RSRR*, 5 (1984), 26–7.

[2] For the change in communal politics cf. my 'The Baglioni as tyrants of Perugia, 1488–1540', *EHR*, 85 (1970), 245–81 with my 'Perugia and papal absolutism'. On the sixteenth-century changes in various states towards a narrower regime: E. Fasano Guarini (ed.), *Potere e società negli stati regionali italiani fra '500 e '600* (Bologna, 1978). On Roman confraternities: Paglia, 'La Pietà dei Carcerati', pp. xi, 46, 79, 212–15, but see above chapter 2.2(c). On Venice see esp. Pullan, *Rich and Poor*, pp. 99–108, where he quotes the contemporary Venetian Gasparo Contarini (pp. 107–8), but some officials proved reluctant to serve, p. 124.

camerlengo (treasurer), two *sindici* (scrutineers) and thirteen *signori*, one for each of the thirteen districts, *rioni*, of Rome; and twenty-eight female officials: two prioresses and twenty-six *infermieri*, two for each district. Duties were specified: to pray; to provide dowries for young girls; to visit sick members in their homes, taking the sacrament in procession to them and sending the company's doctor; to assist widows, orphans and other children connected with confraternity members; to visit prisoners and to exercise the special privilege of releasing a condemned person; and to bury dead members fittingly. The archconfraternity was to honour the feast of the Holy Cross in May, and related feasts such as Easter Day and the September Holy Cross day, then they were to sing hymns before an image of the Crucifixion, prior to setting off in procession. The company could organise torchlit processions for special noble or ambassadorial visitors. Other rules dealt with the appointment for life of two *Signori Illustri* who—with the aid of two gentlemen and two artisans serving for four months at a time—would judge disputes between members and settle feuds. Thus the society showed a hierarchical division though, or because, it had a wide social intake—including reformed prostitutes. The *Illustri* would also supervise the aggregation of other companies to the archconfraternity and select a Reverend Protector from a short list of eight cardinals. The statutes explained the confraternity's foundation after the survival of a wooden cross in a church fire in 1519. The 1565 revised statutes show the constitutional structure of what had become an all-purpose philanthropic society.[3]

The statutes of sodalities can give a cumulative impression of their members attitudes and not all are preoccupied with official organisation. The 1612 revised constitutions of the Perugian Madonna della Consolatione combined detailed discussion of election and balloting procedures, reminiscent of Perugia's complicated communal council electioneering, with a concern for the spiritual welfare of its members through prayer and procession.[4] The 1561 rules of the Corpus Christi society in Rome's S. Maria sopra Minerva strongly emphasised the moral conduct required of members.[5] The statutes of S. Francesco e S. Bernardino, Cavaglia, in 1563, were little interested in organisational structure, but concentrated on sacraments, discipline and prayer, stressing that the basic object was the love of God.[6] Similarly the new rules of 1568 for the Annunziata company attached to the convent of S. Francesco del Borghetto, Florence were most concerned with the religious spirit. They included biblical quotations and particularly advocated the confession of sins, for 'to sin is human, but it is angelic to repent with St Peter'.[7]

Confraternities sometimes took great pride in their statutes, as in other documents such as service books, or membership lists, especially when they were preserved in a unique manuscript copy, written out in a fine hand, decorated with miniatures and bound in elaborately tooled leather. The impact of printing and of outside controls may

[3] *Statuti . . . S. Crocefisso*; see chapter 3.2 above on its origins.
[4] *Constitutioni et Capitoli Della Venerabile Confraternita della Madonna della Consolatione di Perugia P.S.A. Reformati nell'Anno MDCXII* (Perugia, 1613).
[5] *Capitula . . . Corporis Christi . . . Romae*, esp. pp. 30-7.
[6] E. Ardu, 'Lo statuto cinquecentesco dell'Arciconfraternita dei disciplinati di S. Francesco e di S. Bernardino in Cavaglia', Centro di Documentazione sul Movimento dei Disciplinati. *Quaderno 5* (Perugia, 1967), pp. 37-79.
[7] D'Addario, *Aspetti*, p. 429.

have made these volumes rarer in the sixteenth century, but not obsolete. This can be seen in a fine example from Bologna's S. Maria della Morte, produced in 1562. The frontispiece miniature [Frontispiece] shows the Madonna holding out her deep blue cloak to protect the kneeling brethren; the city of Bologna with its leaning towers and the countryside are depicted in the background, in which environment the confraternity is shown leading a public procession. Two of the hooded brethren in the foreground are holding *tavolette*; boards with pictures used to comfort the condemned on their way to execution. Such an illustration encouraged the work and devotion of the company as scheduled in the text. The company claimed to have been founded in 1336, to serve the poor sick (which duty the text of the statutes still outlined), but by now care of the dead and condemned was a greater concern and pride, as reflected in the miniature.[8]

The independent confraternities operating from their own premises were the societies most likely to produce lengthy statutes, to have many officials, and a complex organisation. The parochial devotional societies would have had a more limited corporate life, though they still needed a few organising officials. The more complex confraternities had dominant governing officials, such as priors or prioresses, who were elected for a set period. Perugia's Consolatione had two priors elected for two years; anybody refusing the office was fined, implying that it involved burdens and commitments that some would want to avoid. All members were enjoined to obey their priors, and there were penalties for injuring them. In this fraternity two *visitatori* were required with a dual role: to assist, or substitute for, the priors in correcting the brothers, and to investigate the possessions of the society and of sick members (for an assessment of need).[9]

Confraternities could require a whole range of lesser officials. Most stipulated a sacristan or two to look after church and altar, and be servers at Mass. In the case of the Consolatione they controlled the processional standard. Like this one, many had *festaioli* or similar officials, to adorn the church or chapel for festive occasions, using drapes, silk cloths, paintings and standards. In some companies they were also involved in staging elaborate processions and religious tableaux. Fraternities with property and income needed a financial official who might be called a *camerlengo, depositario,* or *massaro*. The Perugian Consolatione ruled that he must be a member only of this confraternity, presumably to preserve confidentiality and ensure dedicated service. Sometimes such financial officials were salaried employees.[10] The Consolatione like many others required a secretary and messenger (who also carried the Cross in processions). Other confraternities needed hospital officials, as with the Roman S. Crocefisso, or prison visitors, as in the Pietà dei Carcerati. In the larger societies the officials would have been kept busy, with weekly or even daily commitments. It is harder to gauge the involvement demanded of lesser officials in smaller companies. *Festaioli* would have been active only around the major feast or feasts, but visitors to the sick or poor could have been much busier. The Consolatione rules imply that it was time-consuming to be a prior or his assistant. A detailed study of office-holding in

---

[8] BCB F.O.42.; cf. M. Fanti, 'Il "Fondo Ospedali" nella Biblioteca Comunale dell'Archiginnasio. Inventario', *L'Archiginnasio*, 58 (1963), 25 and illustration opposite p. 36. On condemned prisoners and *tavolette* see chapter 10.2 below.

[9] *Constitutioni . . . Consolatione . . . Perugia.*

[10] On financial problems and officials see below chapter 6.

Florence's S. Paolo suggests that it encouraged fuller participation in all the society's activities, including more regular confession and communion.[11]

2 COUNCILS AND GENERAL ASSEMBLIES

Much confraternity activity was controlled by general assemblies of members, convened by the priors and similar administrators, or by smaller councils of officials. In a very large confraternity such as Venice's Scuola di S. Rocco, where membership rose to about a thousand, there was a General Chapter of thirty to fifty members for regular administration. For the Venetian *scuole piccole* the government required committees of Banca and Zonta to rule the society, severally or together according to the business. Meetings of the whole membership then played a limited role.[12] For most confraternities elsewhere the whole membership was expected to assemble for general business meetings. They might take place only once or twice a year, in connection with the confraternity's most important religious feasts, but general meetings could be more frequent. In the 1570s Perugia's S. Francesco was holding them on average once a month. The statutes of this city's S. Annunziata Delle Vergine stipulated a number of general assemblies each year, and ruled that one should be in the presence of the bishop, another in that of the papal governor. The confraternity was under the joint protection of these two personages from its foundation in 1565. Such external supervision would have been unusual. These assemblies controlled the system of office filling, and ratified or revised the society's constitutions and basic rules. They might also sanction major financial decisions, while lesser ones were left to smaller councils or individual officials. It is possible that surviving documents under-record the frequency of general congregations, if they only minute those taking important decisions.[13]

Surviving records from Perugian confraternity councils show considerable variations in content and orderliness, which might be governed by the quality of the scribe or the activity of the fraternity. The records for the general meetings of S. Francesco during the late fifteenth and early sixteenth centuries are meagre; those from the 1570s to the mid-seventeenth, more enlightening. This seems to indicate rising enthusiasm, not just improved administrative efficiency. The general meetings of the small confraternity of S. Pietro Apostolo (with from fourteen to twenty-six persons present) suggest that initially they were only concerned with membership and whether brothers were fulfilling their obligations, or should be expelled. In the late 1570s they became more busily concerned with the building of a new oratory, and so with fund-raising. The seventeenth-century records are fuller, with discussions both about decorations and furnishings, and about processions or the celebration of feast-days. The meetings of the similar-sized S. Pietro Martire dealt more fully with the physical conditions of the oratory, especially its restructuring in the 1570s and the later accumulation of furnishings. However, the minutes also point to discussions on the problems of visiting the sick, or donating bread to those seeking it at the door in times of trouble (as in 1596). In the

[11] Weissman, *Ritual Brotherhood*, pp. 130–9.
[12] Pullan, 'Le Scuole Grandi', pp. 91–2; *idem, Rich and Poor*, pp. 67–72; see above, chapter 3.1, on the councils of the *scuole piccole*.
[13] SBF S. Francesco no. 456 'Libro dei verbali 1438–1510', no. 457 (1566–90), no. 458 (1591–1629); Marinelli, *Le Confraternite*, p. 182. See above, chapter 2.3 at n. 98 on the problem of meetings and attendance.

case of SS. Rocco e Sebastiano, perversely, its surviving 'Libro dei partiti' (from 1653) restricts its entries very largely to matters of membership, and tells little about what took place in the company's life.[14]

The first surviving record book for the Sodalizio di S. Martino is more helpful than most, since it coincides with the effective inauguration of this society which was dominated by leading members of the Perugian oligarchy. Its record to some extent elaborates on procedures, whether over helping the poor, or finding a suitable permanent home. It makes clear that general meetings involved lengthy discussions, but might leave only a minor entry–a decision voted upon. This should be a warning that cryptic record books–if designed only to register votes or constitutional matters–may mislead over the number and vitality of general fraternal meetings.[15]

The minutes of the general congregations of Perugian confraternities such as S. Francesco and S. Domenico show the whole community involved in a wide range of decision-making. The meetings debated general rules and their periodic revision, dealt with office-holding, the employment of chaplains, the holding of processions and ceremonies, and with the problem of contumacious brethren. They discussed regular and irregular payments of dowries to poor girls, donations to disadvantaged members and their relatives, to outside individuals, to nunneries or churches that needed financial assistance or sustenance and, increasingly, there was much consideration of the confraternities' finances, with the buying, selling and renting of land and shops. These two confraternities ran hospices or hospitals, but virtually nothing concerning them is recorded in the general congregation meetings, implying that they were separately administered and not of great concern to the bulk of the membership–hence possibly Bishop Della Corgna's criticisms during his 1564 visitation. The general meetings record very little concerning normal religious practices, though special events such as the pilgrimage to Rome in 1575 or a major city procession were minuted.[16]

3 ENROLMENT, DISCIPLINE AND EXPULSION

One of the tasks of leading officials and then of general meetings was the scrutiny and admission of new members. General rules about who could or could not join were laid out in statutes which ultimately were the responsibility of the corporate body, though outside authorities from church or state might have their say as well. The admission of individuals was supervised by the confraternity's leading officials; in some cases there was also a major role for a general congregation. By statute Perugia's Consolatione operated a double system of scrutiny. Potential brothers were first vetted by the officials and came to the oratory on trial. If six out of eight were in favour, the name was put to the general congregation for a two-thirds vote for acceptance. Supposedly there were checks that the applicant led a good life and was a true Christian, ready to accept the

---

[14] On S. Francesco above note 13; ASP Ex Congregatione di Carità no. 30: Confraternita di S. Pietro Martire, vol. 1, 'Adunanze e ricordi vari. 1548–1601'; ASP Archivio Corporazioni Religiose Soppresse. S. Pietro Apostolo, vol. 20, 'Adunanze 1575–1688'; cf. Marinelli, Le Confraternite, pp. 862–80 (S. Pietro Apostolo), 880–905 (S. Pietro Martire); BCP Ms 1301 'Libro dei partiti 1653–1743'.

[15] ASP Sodalizio di San Martino, Div. II. Cl. IV. Pl. III, no. 1 Verbali: 'Libro I delle Congregazione', for 1576–1643. See below Chapter 9.2, for alms-giving procedures, and chapter 11.1 for the pursuit of an oratory site.

[16] For S. Franceso as in note 13; SBF S. Domenico no. 427 'Adunanze 1488–1514', no. 430 (1564–1607).

rules of the confraternity and obey its officials. Those with major defects would be excluded: the concubinous, usurers, blasphemers, gossips, card and dice players, frequenters of taverns, as well as homicides and the excommunicated.[17]

It is rarely indicated how much serious scrutiny actually took place, though as membership of a confraternity—especially a parochial devotional one—was taken as testimony against a charge of heresy, outside authorities must have assumed effective scrutinising occurred. In Venice's S. Maria dei Mercanti the names of applicants were put by officials to the whole congregation which balloted them for acceptance or rejection. However, as on occasions up to a hundred new places were on offer (because money was needed from entrance fees), doubt has to be cast on the extent of serious scrutiny.[18] As already indicated (when dealing with youth membership) some confraternities operated a novitiate system, which might also involve full adult applicants. In Florence's S. Paolo and S. Girolamo companies the novitiate could last a year and many were rejected during this time. Once found acceptable the new brother could be received ceremonially. That some people disliked this procedure was indicated by Bologna's S. Maria della Morte: applicants who were nobles or the sons of gentlemen could be excused the ceremonial entry, and be quietly matriculated on the simple orders of the rector, prior and *massaro*.[19]

Some confraternities had an entrance fee and subsequent membership payments, but it is not clear how common this was, because of the limited evidence. In Venice the lesser *scuole* usually had fixed entrance fees and annual payments (as *luminaria*), while the *Scuole Grandi* switched between fixed fees and those graduated according to the means of the applicant. The Scuola di S. Maria dei Mercanti in 1543 indicated that there was an annual fee, *luminaria*, of one ducat; if it was not paid by the end of November there was a fine of 20 *soldi* and the culprit was debarred from voting or receiving candles until the *luminaria* was paid.[20] For the Roman SS. Crocefisso di S. Marcello the entrance fee was 35 *baiocchi* for men and 20 for women, the annual payments 30 and 15 *baiocchi* respectively. The Perugian S. Pietro Martire required a 20 *soldi* entrance subvention, but otherwise the requirements in this city's confraternities are unclear. Bologna's S. Maria della Morte required monthly payments of alms—for masses for the dead—though with the alternative of saying twelve Ave Marias and ten Pater Nosters.[21] There will be further discussion of financial issues (in chapter 6), but here it can be stressed that the

[17] *Constitutioni . . . Consolatione . . . Perugia*, esp. chapters 1 and 2; cf. D'Addario, *Aspetti*, p. 443 on S. Lorenzo at Ponte a Greve; Pullan, *Rich and Poor*, p. 50; Weissman, *Ritual Brotherhood*, pp. 77–8; cf. also Angelozzi, *Le confraternite laicali*, pp. 178–9 on Genoa's confraternity of Divine Love.

[18] ASVen Scuole piccole, Busta 420 S. Maria dei Mercanti, e.g. fols 22v (7 elected), 27r (23 elected), 25r (35 elected in Jan. 1542, overturning a vote of December 1540 not to have an increase in membership), 30r–v (99 new members in November 1543), 40v–1r (100 new members out of 180 orginally submitted for balloting), 45r (1546, specifically saying that 100 new members should be chosen to help pay for building operations; but not clear when these materialised), 61v (39 new members accepted in 1550); for a Perugian example of a slower, possibly more thorough, procedure for accepting two or three members at a time, ASP Conservatorio della Carità, Adunanze I (1615–26).

[19] On novitiates see above, Chapter 2.2 at n. 82; Weissman, *Ritual Brotherhood*, pp. 139–41; BCB F.O. 42, chapter 25 p. 45.

[20] Pullan, *Rich and Poor*, pp. 89–90, 158; ASVen Scuole piccole, Busta 420 S. Maria dei Mercanti, fol. 27v; *Statuti . . . S. Crocefisso*, Rome, chapter 1; cf. Favaro, pp. 79–80 on payment of *luminarie* in the Venetiar, painters' *scuola dell'arte*, with fines and suspensions for non-payment.

[21] BCP Ms 3139 'Regola et Constitutioni de la devota Compagnia del corpo de Christo et de Sancto Pietro Martyre', Ms rules of 1531, with additions, cap. I fol. 3r; BCB F.O.42, cap. 25 p. 40.

scrutiny of applicants, and of the continuing good behaviour of members, was likely to be influenced by financial considerations. We know that Venice's Scuola di S. Maria dei Mercanti (cited above) and the *Scuole Grandi* had overt campaigns to extend membership lists precisely in order to pay off debts.[22]

The scrutiny of members' conduct was meant to maintain high moral and religious standards, and regular attendance. Statutes made clear that people should be expelled or punished in some way if they lapsed from good behaviour. Evidence concerning the reality of such scrutiny reveals various problems. In Florence's S. Paolo in the fifteenth century scrutinies and suspensions were common; most were expelled for irregular attendance, and some after revealing secrets; few were specifically accused of moral turpitude. More positively others were struck off the register because they had joined other confraternities or become priests.[23] The minutes of Perugian confraternities in a later period suggest more haphazard efforts to control conduct. S. Pietro Apostolo often voted on whether members should be dismissed, but usually without stating the offence. In 1621 a shoemaker was expelled after various warnings for failing to attend rogation processions. Earlier there had been the case of a mason, Simone di Giovanni; in 1580 he had asked to join the company when working on their oratory, but was dismissed in 1591—whether because he had lost interest, or because he had moved away is not clear. At S. Pietro Martire one member was dismissed for not attending communion at Christmas; the society had a set fine for failure to attend monthly celebrations.[24] The records of S. Francesco and S. Domenico mention reprimands and unspecified punishments for not attending communion or meetings; presumably it meant imposing the fines laid down in the rules. Many lapses were needed before a brother could be expelled.[25]

Expulsion was clearly undertaken reluctantly in most societies, and was difficult to carry out. In 1584 the Prior of Perugia's S. Martino indicated that many brothers were disobedient, so that the collecton of alms was very inadequate. He proposed a scrutiny of the membership; this was postponed at least twice and finally held in March 1585. Fifty-one brothers attended, nobody was voted out, and the absentees were confirmed as members 'in the name of God'. The reluctance to expel may have been affected by the imminent move to an independent oratory.[26] In SS. Trinità, Venice when the Banca e Zonta officials voted (by 19–3) to discipline a brother who as a former office-holder had misused the fees, by banning him from further offices, the subsequent general meeting reversed this verdict (by 3–31).[27] In April 1584 the Bologna company of S.

[22] Pullan, *Rich and Poor*, pp. 96–9; and see below chapter 6.

[23] On the theory of scrutiny see e.g. Perugia's Consolatione (note 17 above), or Florence's S. Sacramento in S. Felicita: D'Addario, *Aspetti*, pp. 433–4; Weissman, *Ritual Brotherhood*, pp. 120–9.

[24] ASP S. Pietro Apostolo, vol.20, e.g. fols. 5v, 6r–7r, 8v–9r for scrutinies that led to no dismissals, fols. 11r, 18v, 23r, 30r where brothers were dismissed, and fol. 29r notes that there was no scrutiny of the membership from 1628–31; S. Pietro Martire, vol. 1, fols. 31r, 43r, 44v for fines and dismissals; BCP Ms 3139, cap 1.

[25] SBF S. Francesco, vol. 457 fols. 106v, 113r–14r, revising the rules on contumacy in 1573–5; for first offence, e.g. of not attending a meeting, 5 Paters and 5 Aves before the altar and pay a *grosso*; six months suspension if fail to comply; on second offence some prayers in the middle of the oratory and pay one *giulio*, and a year's suspension. Only on continuing contumacy was expulsion the penalty.

[26] ASP Sodalizio di S. Martino, 'Libro I delle congregazioni', fols. 37r–9r.

[27] ASVen Scuole piccole, S. Trinita Busta 706, Libro Primo fols. 16r–v, 19v, 24 September & 3 December 1536.

Maria della Vita voted to expel Francesco di Fabri for disobedience, after three years of difficulties over speaking in the congregation, for his refusal to carry a torch at a woman's funeral when ordered by the Prior, for threatening words against the Prior, and other infractions. However, in August the spiritual father of the company proposed Francesco's reinstatement in the society when the culprit showed a willingness to accept correction by the said father; the company unanimously accepted this. Later Alessandro 'dalla rosa' was expelled for unexplained reasons. In 1563 two former brothers, expelled because of some great scandal (which was not recorded in the surviving account), petitioned for readmission; one was accepted, the other not.[28] Sometimes a suspension for a period was preferred as a penalty, as shown by another Bologna confraternity, S. Maria della Carità, in the 1580s; for example, G.F. Guiani was suspended until he left his friend, a prostitute, and F. Bonfiglioli was suspended for ten years for continually frequenting hostelries and similar debauchery.[29]

The problems of scrutinising confraternity morality and dedication are well exemplified in Perugia's confraternity of S. Girolamo, which ran the Conservatorio della Carità for vulnerable girls. In the period 1616–18 there were four scrutiny meetings. It is notable how few attended the general assembly to vote on the membership roll: 17 scrutinised 65 names in July 1616, 16 voted on 66 in January 1617, 22 on 71 in the following January, and 20 scrutinised 69 in July 1618. While no adverse, black, votes were recorded in the 1617 session, a fair number were registered at the others, and this included black-beaning members present. After the January 1618 meeting four brothers (who had received 13 to 11 black beans) were reported to Bishop Comitoli as dismissed. He ordered their reinstatement, provided they asked pardon. Three of them had protested to the bishop that they saw no demerit in their conduct warranting dismissal, and claimed that the scrutiny was illegitimate, because all had not been properly notified of the meeting. On the evening of Good Friday they asked pardon of the company, and were readmitted. At the next scrutiny two of the three received one black vote, the other four. The fourth of the original offenders no longer features, and presumably his dismissal had become effective. Such a protracted procedure hardly encouraged even conscientious officials to attempt to discipline ordinary members.[30]

In the rules of many societies, and as indicated by one of the above cases, taverngoing was treated as a punishable offence for a confraternity member. But it was not seen as incompatible with a serious religious life by all brethren. Faithful members of the discipline confraternity of Brianza (Lombardy) in about 1578 were happy to recite their offices, celebrate religious feasts and practise flagellation and still play traditional

[28] BCB F.O.14 fols. 1v, 5r–6v, 19r: 2 February 1561 Alessandro's expulsion 'per le ragioni e cause che moueno gli animi', was accepted by votes of 22–7 and 23–6; fol. 26v: 21 March 1563 after their 'demandando perdono dal gran scandolo dato per loro' and after 'fatto assai longo discurso sopra di questo negotio' Francesco di Ferrari was rejected by 5–14, and Giovanni di Anselmi accepted by 36–3.

[29] Fanti, Ospedale . . . Carità, pp. 37–40, 44–6: Bonfiglioli was expelled 'per il suo continuo andare alle osterie e simille altre porcherie'.

[30] ASP Conservatorio della Carità, Andunanze I fols. 6v–7v, 11r–v, 12r, 14v–15r. The supplication to the bishop contained this interesting phrasing: '. . . supplicano V.S.R. ma si degni o per se stessa decidere questa causa et differenza overo commettere al suo S. Vicario che informatosi della verità del fatto con ogni sommarietà et senza strepito ed figura di giuditio debbi dichiarare dicto scrutinio nullo. ed mantenere le detti oratori nel lor quasi possesso di dicta fraternita . . .' [my emphasis] (memorial interleaved between fols. 12 and 13).

games in public or frequent taverns. There is also evidence of other groups of brothers holding meetings in taverns–albeit not their formal assemblies.[31]

A breach of secrecy was another offence warranting expulsion. Perugia's Consolatione ordered that the affairs of the company should not be discussed outside–for fear of scandal. The famous Divino Amore of Genoa also required secrecy: 'everyone is obliged to keep secret the brethren, the works and the ways of the fraternity', or risk expulsion. Partly it was designed to avoid any boasting of penitential behaviour or charitable work, but Archbishop Paleotti also recognised that secrecy was justified to avoid ridicule and abuse from outsiders. The secrecy could, however, lead other authorities in church and state to be suspicious of confraternities and their activities. There is little evidence as to whether many people were expelled for breaching secrecy rules, but twelve brothers in S. Paolo, Florence, were expelled between 1434 and 1493 for revealing secrets. Florentines may then have had a lot to hide in a politically volatile environment.[32]

Some confraternities had internal divisions. As already noted, there could be a division between an office-holding upper group and other socially inferior members for political and social reasons, or there could be a division between rich and poor as in the Venetian *Scuole Grandi*. In a slightly different way Bologna in particular had an officially recognised difference between a *stretta*, inner group, and the *larga*, wider membership, based on religious commitment; this could help resolve some of the problems raised above over scrutinising the dedication of brothers. N. Albergati, a reforming bishop of Bologna from 1417 to 1443, seems to have fostered this *stretta–larga* division in attempting to revitalise confraternities. Enrolment in the *stretta* section involved both deeper spiritual and devotional dedication and more involvement in practical work for hospitals, orphanages and the poor. In the S. Maria della Misericordia (or della Carità), according to the 1518 rules, those who belonged to the *stretta* group were committed to more frequent confession and communion, disciplined themselves every feast-day morning on which there was an obligation to attend the oratory, were more obligated to a strict moral code, and had to visit the sick regularly. They had extra meetings under their own secretly elected officials, and they were expected to avoid the company of women. Women were part of the *larga* section, but not the elite group. This company was for artisans and the *piccolo borghese*, not merchants of the upper rank or nobles. In other cases the division may have involved social 'aristocratisation', especially (later in the period) in the Compagnia dei Poveri. The inner group may not have guaranteed higher moral or devotional standards, but the division did allow for a decision about the degree of commitment to confraternity life and activity, and it might have constituted an overt recognition that the need for many confraternity brethren to work consistently hard to earn a living inhibited participation in too many processions, devotions and acts of charity.[33] The division could also indicate the difference between

[31] Zardin, 'Le confraternite in Italia settentrionale'.

[32] Zardin, *Confraternite e vita di pietà*, pp. 74, 111, n. 229; Paleotti, *Archiepiscopale bononiense*, pp. 39–41. See above chapter 3.1, on Florentine suspicions of confraternities; Weissman, *Ritual Brotherhood*, pp. 128–9, and generally on secrecy, pp. 30–5, 82, 94–5.

[33] Fanti, *La chiesa dei Poveri*, pp. 85–95; *idem*, *San Procolo*, p. 184 where he suggests that S. Maria degli Angeli had an intensely religious *stretta* section. Cf. generally Rusconi, 'Le Confraternite' pp. 478, 482.

flagellant and non-flagellant members; this separation can also be noted in some Venetian *scuole*.

While Bologna is most noted for a formal *stretta–larga* subdivision, there are signs of it in urban Genoa or extra-urban Neapolitan confraternities. Without any formal arrangement there seems to have been a division—ultimately debilitating—within the Milanese confraternity of S. Croce e della Pietà dei Carcerati. This company was in essence an amalgamation between a parish-based devotional confraternity (S. Croce), devoted to Christ Crucified, and a society responsible for prisoners. An inner group emerged, which was based on a social elite of nobles, professional lawyers and doctors, and notaries, who monopolised the confraternity offices, and who concentrated on prison philanthropy. This preoccupation annoyed the wider membership, which complained that the confraternity's devotional practices, and the pomp of funerals for deceased members were neglected. This division highlighted the problem of moving from parish-based devotions to wider philanthropic activities.[34]

Most societies theoretically expected all members to maintain the same standards and level of commitment, except when office-holding imposed more duties. In practice there were major differences between active and passive brothers and sisters, and the evidence suggests that it was considered difficult and even undesirable to expel backsliders.

4 FEAST–DAYS AND PRIVATE CONFRATERNITY DEVOTION

The religious practices of fraternities varied according to the society, the nature of its physical environment, and the enthusiasm of its members. Only a few records report what occurred, as opposed to what the rule-books stipulated. Because much was normal and routine, by the day, month or year, it was rarely recorded. The rest of this chapter, using both statutes and internal records, will describe those devotional—and sometimes social—activities that were primarily private. With some events there is no neat division between private and public; outsiders might attend confraternity Forty-Hour devotions, processions could move from the oratory to the public streets. But this chapter will concentrate on ceremonies, events and devotions that primarily concerned the confraternity members themselves. Chapter 5 will illustrate some of the most overt events like public processions involving propagandist display, plays, and pilgrimages.

The major religious and social occasions were those centred on the feast-day or days associated with the particular confraternity: the feast of St Peter the Apostle or St Peter Martyr, all the major feasts of the Virgin, Corpus Christi and so on. These celebrations could be public as well as private, involve devotions within the chapel or oratory and then a major city procession. On such occasions the *festaioli* or other officials decorated the oratory or chapel with coloured cloths, tapestries, painted banners, and used more than the usual supply of candles. Mass would be said or, in the more prosperous and ambitious societies, sung, with or without the assistance of extra clergy. The statutes of the Bologna confraternity of S. Maria della Morte stipulated many celebrations both in its own hospital chapel and in other city churches, despite the considerable outside

[34] Zardin, 'Le confraternite in Italia settentrionale'; Russo, *Chiesa e comunità*, pp. 307–8, with a division in the Sacrament society of S. Maria d'Ayello at Afragola; Grendi, 'Morfologia', p. 286; Olivieri Baldissarri, *I 'poveri prigioni'*, pp. 103–5, 114–16, 225–6.

activity required in operating its medical hospital or in comforting prisoners. It expected to have money spent on a well-decorated church and music for the feasts of the Madonna and that of S. Rocco. An organist was paid to play at vespers each Sunday. For the feasts of the Assumption and of S. Rocco (or St Roch) in 1595 new 'apparatus'– decorated structures–were ordered, especially with a figure of the saint, the portico was adorned with gilded leather and paintings of St Philip by Agostino and Lodovico Carazzi (i.e. the famous Caracci cousins), and the music was never bettered–according to the Prior's account.[35]

Increasingly through the sixteenth century all members were encouraged to confess and take communion on such major feasts, rather than treat the Mass as a display of the Host to be venerated. The brethren might process around the oratory, or organise a public procession. For some feasts this involved celebrating in the fraternity's own oratory and in some public place. In Perugia the S. Pietro Martire company had its own oratory for private devotions, in the Porta S. Pietro district near the great church and cloisters of S. Domenico, but on its major feast-day of 29 April this confraternity also paraded from the Cathedral in the city centre down the steep hill to S. Domenico, accompanied by officials and clergy in a lighted procession.[36] The celebration of major feasts could involve the recitation of various offices, the singing of hymns and lauds, and flagellation–in the discipline companies and some others.

Some confraternities required substantial clerical contributions to their celebrations as an aid to devotion, to greatly increase 'la divotione et Religione à Laude de la divina Maestà' as it was put when the Venetian Scuola di S. Maria e S. Cristoforo dei Mercanti contracted with the canons of S. Maria dell'Orto in 1578, not previously having had regular contributions from priests. The canons were to celebrate the Virgin's feast on 8 September, and its vigil. Priest, deacon, subdeacon, servitor and acolyte would come to celebrate Prime, Vespers and sung Mass in the oratory. For the second Vespers they would add two assistants 'per maggior honore', and say five low Masses before high Mass. They were also obliged to say three Masses on St Christopher's day, sung Mass on each ordinary third Sunday of the month, on every feast of the Virgin, and when the confraternity held formal meetings of the Banca or of the general chapter. The priest would be accompanied by torches. On All Souls' day the confraternity would provide candles in recognition of the canons' services and it would pay 20 ducats at the feast of the Nativity of the Virgin. This expansion of clerical involvement followed the completion of a new set of buildings next to the church of Madonna dell'Orto, to the design of Andrea Palladio, and the joining of the Scuola di S. Maria e S. Francesco with that of S. Cristoforo dei Mercanti in 1576.[37]

On major occasions a confraternity might hear a sermon or homily from a priest or a lay brother, but the frequency of this occurrence is unclear. The large Neapolitan confraternity of Spirito Santo, was by statute to elect a preacher for a year–from any

[35] BCB F.O.42, caps. 27–33, pp. 48–51; F.O.43 fols. 29v–30r.
[36] Marinelli, Le Confraternite, p. 903; ASP S. Pietro Martire, vol 1.
[37] ASVen Scuole piccole, Busta 413, notarised agreement 1 December 1578, and unnumbered folder of 18 sheets starting 'Fu presentato, letto, porta Parte . . .', 1574–91; AA.VV. Scuole di Arti Mestieri e Devozione a Venezia (Venice, 1981), no. 71, pp. 118–19. The guild of S. Cristoforo (or S. Cristofalo) had built a hospital/hospice in the vicinity also of S. Maria dell'Orto in the 1470s: Mackenney, Traders and Tradesmen, p. 64.

religious Order in the world–to preach regularly throughout the year and to act as confessor, to the great salvation of the brothers' souls. There is some evidence that in Italy as well as France in the medieval period fraternities which were sponsored by Franciscans and Dominicans heard sermons not only from members of the Orders, but also from literate laymen, particularly lawyers.[38] During the fifteenth century humanists joined the ranks of confraternity preachers, at least in Florence. The notable Florentine chancellor Bartolomeo Scala was a member of a flagellant confraternity, where he gave or heard sermons that encouraged asceticism, the rejection of *voluptas* and the body. His recent biographer has argued that this flagellant connection and moral environment might have led to his use of corporal punishment on cowardly soldiers in 1479. More famously the Florentine Compagnia de' Magi heard sermons from leading humanists like Cristoforo Landini, Donato Acciaiuoli, Alamanno Rinuccini–on penitence or on 'the body of Christ', delivered on Holy Thursday. The most striking and literary of the sermons was on Charity, delivered by Giovanni Nesi in 1486 under the influence of the neo-Platonic philosopher Marsilio Ficino. Some of these preachers were, like Landino, trained theologians and the confraternity meetings probably involved interesting controversies. The humanist sermons to Florentine confraternities can be judged as literary contributions to an academy or as stimuli for an elite religious group.[39]

At a less prestigious level it has already been noted that in Siena during the 1540s there were sermons and debates in S. Trinità, one of which–by the youthful Pietro Antonio–involved an attack on the cult of saints.[40] The German community in Rome, at the confraternity of S. Maria dell'Anima, heard sermons on the feast of the Purification–from a priest approved by the president of the fraternity–at least during the fifteenth century. In Perugia in our period the small S. Pietro Martire still expected to hear a monthly exhortation from a Dominican, and Lecce's S. Annunziazione members were to attend sermons in the neighbouring Jesuit College. Carlo Borromeo ordered that confraternities should not have sermons or colloquies dealing with dogmatics, but have topics suitable for lay people on which each bishop should check. This implied it was not uncommon to have special sermons for confraternities. But there was clearly pressure in the Counter-Reformation period for these to be by clergy not lay brethren, and under scrutiny. The fraternities of S. Croce, which Borromeo promoted to give thanks for the ending of the plague, were required to assemble in the Cathedral on Fridays to hear a sermon, and venerate the sacred Nail of the Cross.[41]

Banquets in association with confraternity religious feasts were increasingly criticised by clerical authorities. It is clear that throughout Europe a fraternal meal was considered a key element in the society's life. In France in particular the old Holy Spirit confraternities struggled to maintain their common meals–and the subsequent distribution of food to others–as the authorities, sponsoring parochial confraternities, sought to eradi-

[38] Miele, 'L'assistenza sociale', p. 848; Monti, *Le confraternite*, vol. 2, pp. 108–10; D.L. D'Avray, *The Preaching of the Friars. Sermons diffused from Paris before 1300* (Oxford, 1985), pp. 33–5, where evidence for Brescia, Milan and Imola is cited.

[39] A. Brown, *Bartolomeo Scala 1430–1497. Chancellor of Florence* (Princeton, 1979), pp. 89, 318–21; Hatfield, 'The Compagnia de' Magi', pp. 128–35, and 153–61 (extracts from sermons); Becker, p. 190.

[40] Marchetti, p. 51; see above, chapter 3 at n. 10.

[41] Maas, p. 76; BCP Ms 3139 'Regola et Constitutioni . . . Santo Pietro Martyre', cap. II, fol. 4v; Lopez, 'Le confraternite laicali', p. 224; Olivieri Baldissarri, *I 'Poveri prigioni'*, p. 40.

cate them. The prestigious Santa Caridad of Toledo in the sixteenth century held three confraternity feasts a year, and spent considerable sums of money on them.[42] It is doubtful that Italian societies matched the swinish drunkenness that Luther alleged was characteristic of German beer-swilling brotherhoods, but the accusation may have encouraged them to treat fraternal banqueting as unseemly and a betrayal of the penitential spirit. It might be noted in passing that the civic authorities in Venice disapproved of large-scale feasting in private houses and tried to restrict it. This was partly an aspect of sumptuary legislation, but also in the fifteenth century the Council of Ten thought it might encourage homosexuality. Confraternity feasting could be equally suspect. However it has been suggested that the 'banquets' of Venetian *scuole piccole* and *scuole delle arti* in the fifteenth century in fact had a philanthropic dimension, with the richer brothers paying for the poorer.[43]

Various synods and councils discouraged, or totally banned, feasting and drinking in confraternities, at times–as in the synods of Urbino (1569) and Genoa (c. 1574)–linking such activities with the equally deprecated production of sacred plays. The 1573 Florentine synod banned all confraternal banquets except those associated with Corpus Christi celebrations; the archbishop wanted to replace feasts by eucharistic worship. During his visitation of the Assisi diocese in 1573 P. Camaiani ordered the destruction of kitchens in a number of confraternities, to avoid the abuses of conviviality. In 1591 the Sacred Congregation of the Council approved his attack, though it wanted action by dissuasion rather than direct banning. The Council also expressed a worry about people being members of more than one confraternity, because they would then have more occasions for such meals on key feast-days.[44]

Only a much closer look at internal records of confraternities will reveal to what extent confraternity meals persisted against authoritarian opposition from the mid-sixteenth century. Odd hints suggest circumspect persistence behind closed doors. In Perugia, the office and rules for S. Pietro Martire (after 1545) indicate that a common meal was regular, while for S. Pietro Apostolo the accounts for 1546 record payments for the feast of St Peter, and an inventory for 1574 lists eating-tables. An apparently casual reference in 1586 to lunch before the scrutiny of official appointments in the S. Domenico oratory may indicate a continuing, discreet practice. In May 1598 the confraternity for foreigners, Degli Oltramontani, enjoyed the recreation of wine, courtesy of their leading official, who recorded the event.[45]

[42] A Black, *Guilds and Civil Society in European Political Thought from the twelfth century to the present* (London, 1984), p. 56; J-P. Gutton, 'Confraternities, *Curès* and Communities', pp. 203–6; Hoffman, *Church and Community*, pp. 196–7; Martz, *Poverty and Welfare*, p. 192.

[43] G. Ruggiero, *The Boundaries of Eros. Sex Crime and Sexuality in Renaissance Venice* (New York and Oxford, 1985), p. 139; Mackenney, 'Trade Guilds', pp. 19, 139–40; *idem, Tradesmen and Traders*, pp. 6, 166. Cf. Flynn, 'Charitable ritual', pp. 338–9, where it is indicated that some Spanish confraternities provided food and wine over the graves of the departed, for the benefit of priests and paupers in this world, so that the charity might assist the soul in Purgatory.

[44] Mansi, vol. 35 col. 695, vol.36B col. 601; F. Santucci, 'Gli statuti in volgare trecentesco della confraternita dei Disciplinati di S. Lorenzo in Assisi', *BSPU*, pt. i (1972), pp. 156–7; the Congregation commented:- 'L'abuso di mangnare nelle compagnie sia tolto via non a forza di cinture, ma con persuadere all'offiziale che non è bene continuare'.

[45] BCP 3140 'Officio, regole e matricole della Compagnia del Corpo di Cristo e di San Pietro Martyre di Perugia', fol. 42v; ASP S. Pietro Apostolo, vol. 23 'Miscellanea–Inventario delle robbe', fol. 5r, vol. 6 'Depositario', fols. 44v–7r; SBF S. Francesco, no. 457 fol. 258r; BCP Ms 1186, fol. 29v: 'ho pagato per 14 bocali di uino comprato d'un cittadino Perugino per recreatione delli confrati–pauli 8' (at 10 paoli per ducat.

The frequency of confraternity corporate meetings, other than those on feast-days closely connected with the saintly patron or the particular devotion, is hard to gauge. The statutes sometimes designated those meetings and the general assemblies recorded in the minute books tended to coincide with days of religious festivity. Some confraternity statutes specify a fuller range of devotions. Several Perugian confraternities required a monthly communion to which all members were to come, or pay a fine. Some constitutions ordered only a minimal attendance, but strongly urged a much fuller commitment, as with Perugia's Madonna della Consolatione. On the morning of their own feast-day the brothers were to attend Mass in their oratory and sit in choir to recite or sing the Office of the Madonna, 'warning each to give ear to the choir, so as not to create a dissonance'. Otherwise they were to be ready to attend the oratory as ordered by their priors to participate in processions; usually this would be for Rogation and Ascension, when they were to be dressed in white garments and hood. They were to confess and take communion at Easter in the parish church, and at Christmas in the oratory; and they were urged to do so also for the Virgin's Nativity, her other major feasts, and additional movable feasts. All this implied flexibility for group religious practice, and leadership from the officials. Those failing to respond to the priors' orders to attend were to be fined four *soldi*. Administrative records do not survive to check the degree of compliance.[46]

In addition there were personal devotions. The Consolatione wanted brothers to recite seven Pater Nosters and seven Ave Marias daily. The requirements from the Perugian confederated confraternities were greater: they should say seven penitential psalms, twenty-five Paters and Aves or the Office of the Madonna daily; they had to confess and take communion at Easter in the parish church, and at Christmas in the oratory—or failing that celebrate on certain other feast-days. The 1628 investigation of these confraternities suggests that community religious practices were variable and haphazard, certainly for some of the fraternity's witnesses. Some implied there was no sung Mass, but an inventory for S. Francesco, dated 1573, included a large book for singing Mass, in addition to twenty-six psalm books, twelve books of the Office of the Madonna, three missals and a breviary. There was another note of 142 books, large and small, written by hand—which may have been devotional works or administrative records. The inventory suggests plenty of vessels and vestments for regular corporate worship. The Office printed for these confraternities in 1557 gave the seven penitential psalms, litanies for leading saints, prayers for saying before and after communion, and the office for the dead. It added brief notes (in Italian) on what to do before, during and after Mass, and it noted sixteen mysteries to be contemplated while Mass was being said. The 1617 revised edition of this manual added the Office of the Madonna. Witnesses in 1628 confirmed that many offices were said, and that the confraternities had a good supply of books. For tactical reasons some might well have underplayed the amount of activity in the confraternities, especially of corporate religious worship that would indicate they were too like a church.[47]

[46] *Constitutioni . . . Consolatione . . . Perugia*, chapters 2–3, 6, 23, 25.

[47] *Ibid.* chapter 20; *Costitutioni et Capitoli Generali delle Fraternite de S. Agostino, S. Domenico, et S. Francesco di Perugia* (Perugia, 1565; and reprinted with additional reforms, Perugia, 1621), esp. chapters 24–5; SBF S. Francesco no. 508 (a), no. 1 'Sacrestie Fraternit. S. Franc. i. Inventarij'; no. 509 'Verbali' 1628, fols. 6r, 12r, 28r, and for claims by witnesses A. Massera, aged 67, and G.F. Fazi not to have heard sung Masses, fols. 48v–9r, 56r; on the 1628 investigation, above chapter 3.1.

The statutes of the Jesuit-sponsored confraternity of S. Annunziazione della Beata Vergine in Lecce also set a high level of devotional activity. The rules were drawn up and amended between 1582 and 1598. Each member was enjoined to hear Mass daily, to examine his conscience in the evening, to indulge in mental prayer assisted by some spiritual book, to recite the Office of the Madonna, a third of the Rosary, Paters and Aves. Spiritual books were to be read regularly, on the advice of the Jesuit confessor. A collection of such spiritual works was kept under lock and key by the secretary for use as required by individuals, and to be used for readings at corporate meetings. Confession, to a Jesuit, was to be fortnightly, communion every first Sunday and on all feasts connected with the Virgin and Christ; optionally on other days subject to Jesuit advice. The confraternity was to meet every Saturday evening, except Holy Saturday, and Sunday morning, and on some other feast-days, such as those of the Apostles, All Saints' Day, and the Baptist's Nativity. At Christmas the Forty-Hour devotion was celebrated. By implication all these celebrations could involve music, with two choirs, since the rules also stipulated the saying of Vespers, without music and choirs, on certain days such as the Circumcision, Epiphany, the first day of Easter, Ascension, All Saints, and feasts of the Madonna. The use of the discipline was optional, as were fasts and other austerities. Members were expected to hear morning sermons when given in the Jesuit College. As an unusual devotion, each brother was, on the first Sunday of the month or on a saint's day close to it, to select a saint as his Advocate by picking out a printed card with the saint's picture, as used by the Jesuit College. The saint was to act as guide for the month, and the brother was to offer works appropriate to that saint–though the Jesuit confessor could gently discourage excessive fervour. The following month brothers would be balloted to report on their activities, on the virtues exercised, and to seek penances. The brothers were required to be active in the world helping the poor. All had to have a copy of, and know well, the booklet on Christian Doctrine as a guide to devotion. This Lecce confraternity required much of its devotees; but no records seem to survive to test the degree of compliance.[48]

For personal devotion and the honour of the company, the Bologna confraternity of S. Maria della Vita required each brother, on passing an image of the Virgin or a saint, to kneel and say at least one Pater and Ave Maria. Each day he should say three of each to ward off bad company (and avoid going to dishonest places such as taverns), and before dining say a blessing and at least one Pater and Ave.[49]

The interaction of clergy and laity within a confraternity was obviously variable; sometimes the clergy played a minimal role, present as functionaries soon to be dismissed. But the Lecce example cited above indicates powerful involvement by a confessor. The records of the Venetian Scuola di SS. Trinità suggest a genuine lay appreciation of a clerical employee. The entry for 3 December 1536 has an effusive prelude about bad changing to good, people becoming good and faithful Christians, helped by the precious blood that has redeemed human nature and by a particular devotion to the Trinity. Central to such improvements was the chaplain, whose role was also crucial in all other saintly confraternities ('che in ogni altre confraternite di sancte è principal'). While outlining the chaplain's specific duties for services, this

---

[48] Lopez, 'Le confraternite laicali', pp. 209–38 reproduces most of the statutes.
[49] BCB F.O.42, 1562 statutes, chapters 31–3, pp. 52–3.

confraternity stressed that he should be present every Sunday, and virtually all day, to communicate what devotion he could. He was thus seen as a personal counsellor as well as a functionary. Subsequently the *scuola* elected additional priests to serve it in various ways, as well as for feasts and Lenten vespers.[50]

Certain lay confraternities were in the forefront of the campaign to encourage the laity to respect and adore the Sacrament of the Eucharist, receive the Bread as flesh, and to understand better thereby Christ's sacrifice. Sacrament confraternities had been promoting this from the twelfth century—at least for the veneration of the Host. But, as indicated in chapter 1, the campaign was revitalised and accelerated under Catholic Reform movements, with the addition of stronger arguments that the laity should receive communion more frequently. There were two separate issues: the veneration of the Host, and the reception of the sacrament by the laity, though they were both positively and negatively connected. From the twelfth century the host was elevated at the consecration, for the laity to observe; later a second elevation was advocated, before the Pater Noster. As R. Trexler argues: 'Some Christians were of the opinion that continued staring at the host was equivalent to Communion itself.' In some areas the practice developed of people moving from Mass to Mass just to see the elevation; when the citizens of Florence were deprived of this sight during the 1376–8 Interdict there were signs of trouble and discontent.[51] The public procession of the Host during the Corpus Christi feast became a major feature in various Italian cities; confraternities were often involved in the procession.

Faced with evidence that the Mass was improperly or too casually administered, the Host inadequately respected by clergy or laity, and the Host misused, even for the purposes of black magic, sixteenth-century reformers attempted to ensure due veneration. Legislation from Borromeo and his followers stipulated a proper placing of altars, providing room for the priest to celebrate unencumbered and for the congregation to worship from a respectable distance. The increase in Sacrament confraternities accompanied this; the members' chief tasks were to keep altars properly established and equipped, to maintain the supply of candles and oil, to help display the Host on special occasions, and to participate in Corpus Christi celebrations. They were also to be ready to process with the Host in full honour to the sick at home.[52] But the veneration of the Host in this way led some clergy to argue that it might be a contamination to have too frequent administration of the eucharist to the laity. This attitude explains the adverse reaction of clergy to campaigners for frequent lay communion like B. Cacciaguerra. His *Trattato della Comunione*, first published in 1557, is seen as a major contribution to changing attitudes, though since the later fifteenth-century preachers and confessors had been encouraging more frequent confession and communion. The Council of Trent, in its thirteenth session of 1551, had advocated that the laity should develop firmness of

[50] ASVen Scuole piccole, SS. Trinita, Busta 706, 'Primo Libro' fols. 20v–1v, 40v, 43r–v. The chaplain's official duties were on Sundays to lead processions with the officials, and sing Mass, and sing vespers solemnly on Lenten Sundays. For this he was paid 7 ducats, and up to 20 ducats in expenses.

[51] Trexler, *The Spiritual Power*, pp. 125–7; J. Jungmann, *Missarum Solemnia* (2 vols., Turin, 1953), vol. 1, p. 104; Bossy, *Christianity*, pp. 66–72; *idem*, 'The Mass as a social institution, 1200–1700', *Past and Present*, no. 100 (August 1983), 29–61; Brigden, 'Religion and social obligation', pp. 76–7.

[52] C. Borromeo, *Instructionum Fabricae et Supellectilis Ecclesiasticae libri duo*, 1577, reprinted in P. Barocchi (ed.), *Trattati d'Arte del Cinquecento*, vol. 3 (Bari, 1962), pp. 3–113; Zardin, *Confraternita e vita di pietà*, pp. 114; Rusconi, 'Confraternite', pp. 484–5.

faith 'to receive frequently that substantial bread', but it repeated the church rule that there was only an obligation to receive annually, at Easter. Cacciaguerra, and Jesuits like G. Loarte, L. Pinelli, V. Bruno and A. Possevino (all of whom had an impact on confraternities) were intent on making communion more frequent than once a year.[53] Cacciaguerra argued that confession and frequent communion could change people dramatically; greedy wolves became meek lambs, the most sordid and stinking people, immersed in the sins of the flesh, had become chaste and sweet-smelling, prostitutes had reformed, the avaricious became charitable, the proud humble.[54]

Eucharistic piety was much stimulated from the later fifteenth century by the Roman Sacrament confraternity of S. Giovanni in Laterano, and more especially (from 1501) the one in S. Lorenzo in Damasco alla Cancelleria. The latter parish church was frequented by curial officials. The Catholic reformer Egidio da Viterbo preached on the eucharist there; Julius II asked to be inscribed in its Sacrament confraternity when he ratified it. When members took to escorting the sacrament in the streets to visit the sick, it was viewed as something new and miraculous in Rome.[55] Further official encouragement came with the 1539 Bull *Dominus Noster Jesus Christus* issued to the Sacrament confraternity in S. Maria sopra Minerva, which made available numerous indulgences and privileges for the laity of both sexes who venerated the sacrament and took communion frequently. The chief promoter of this particular papal benefit was a Venetian Dominican Tommaso Stella, who had already made a reputation with the Sacrament confraternity in Vicenza Cathedral from about 1530. Under Stella the Minerva was the largest Sacrament confraternity in Rome, with 271 brothers and sisters by the late 1550s. Stella preached to the 1551 session of the Council of Trent (which had moved to Bologna) and in Venice at SS. Giovanni e Paolo, where he emphasised the important link between eucharistic devotion and help for the poor.[56] Others around Venice who helped promote eucharistic devotion were Gaetano Thiene and Girolamo Stella. By 1581 the apostolic visitor concluding the controversial visitation of the city could eulogise the Sacrament confraternities for fostering eucharistic devotion in the parishes–though he was not free to investigate closely the confraternities themselves. The Sacrament confraternity in S. Giacomo dall'Orto between 1598 and 1604 contributed a new chapel with paintings illustrating Passion scenes to emphasise various aspects of eucharistic devotion and belief. It has been suggested that the iconography closely reflected a book recently published in Venice: N. Laghi's *Miracoli del Santissimo Sacramento* (1598). (Laghi also particularly argued that the sufferings of Christ are

[53] De Maio, *Bonsignore Cacciaguerra*; Black, 'Perugia and post-tridentine church reform', p. 434; Fiorani, 'L'esperienza religiosa', p. 175; Rosa, 'Vita religiosa', pp. 193–216; see above chapter 1, n. 37. On fifteenth-century preachers: R. Rusconi, 'Dal pulpito alla confessione', pp. 276–7.

[54] B. Cacciaguerra, *Trattato della SS. Comunione* (Venice, 1575), p. 3r–v: 'di lupi rapacissimi son diventati agnelli mansuetissimi; molte persone sordissime e puzzolenti, immerse nel peccato della carne, son divenute caste e odorifere . . .'; Fiorani, 'L'esperienza religiosa', p. 178; *Canons and Decrees*, pp. 78–80: Session 13, chapter 8 and canon 9.

[55] The comment about the new and miraculous parade of the Host came in the prologue to the 1512 statutes. Fiorani, 'L'esperienza religiosa', pp. 167–9.

[56] Lopez, 'Le confraternite laicali', p. 185 for the Bull, and generally pp. 187–94; Barletta (ed.), *Aspetti della Riforma*, pp. 42–5; P. Tacchi Venturi, *Storia della Compagnia di Gesù in Italia* (2 vols. in 4, Rome, 1950–1 ed.), 2.i, pp. 222–3; Giacomuzzi, p. 33; Fiorani, 'L'esperienza religiosa', pp. 169–71. See below, chapter 11.3, on Tintoretto's *Last Supper* paintings and charity.

renewed in the act of communion by chewing; his burial by the Host's entry into the stomach).[57]

'Frequent communion' was variably interpreted. Carlo Borromeo recommended, for the laity, communion every first Sunday of the month and on the principal feasts of the year. He was a notable promoter of Sacrament confraternities in Lombardy to encourage this. Roman confraternities such as SS. Trinità dei Pellegrini and the Nome di Dio in S. Maria sopra Minerva considered twelve communions a year sufficiently frequent. The Sacrament fraternity of S. Giovanni in Porta, Naples—when founded in 1568—treated three to six confessions and communions a year as the minimum, but regular Sunday communion as desirable. The Jesuits during their 1617 mission to Genoa introduced monthly general communions in the societies they sponsored.[58] There is little evidence as to how often members followed the prescriptions. As the Catholic laity did not receive the chalice we miss the evidence of hefty wine bills registered by some complaining ministers of the Scottish Kirk as parishioners gulped at their rare communions. One notary in Perugia's S. Francesco showed an unusual interest in communicants, while recording business meetings; on Christmas Day 1586 41 took communion, on the 26 December 40 did so; on 1 January there were five, including Giovanni Taddeo himself; on the 29th he and the sacristan had been present when Mass was celebrated. The fulfilment of the Christmas obligation by so many was facilitated by the concurrence of major business meetings on both 25 and 26 December.[59]

R. Weissman has argued that whereas in the fifteenth century communion was seen in Florence as 'a rite of fraternity and a preparation for confraternal assembly' (and the minimum obligations of confession and communion were, generally, fulfilled only by the office-holders in S. Paolo), in the later sixteenth century 'fraternal rituals prepared the brothers for the now central rite of communion'. This may not have necessarily increased the actual reception of the eucharist in the confraternity; the rituals could be the prelude to parochial reception, or to witnessing a celebration involving a clear display of the Host. It should be remembered that the actual reception of the sacrament required a prior personal confession, which presumably was taken much more seriously—by penitent and confessor—than had been the case for many in recent times. Since it meant actually giving up a concubine, or making peace in an inter-clan feud, some proved reluctant to complete a confession and so take communion in full contrition. Frequent communion could be a troublesome challenge. However, the climate of opinion was changing about the frequency of communion, and confraternities were central to this.[60]

[57] A. Niero, 'Riforma cattolica e concilio di Trento a Venezia', *Cultura e Società*, eds. Branca and Ossola, pp. 90–1; cf. S. Tramontin, 'La visita apostolica del 1581 a Venezia', *Studi Veneziani*, 9 (1967), 453–533, on the contentious visitation; Pullan, *Rich and Poor*, pp. 343–4; A. Niero, *Chiesa di S. Giacomo dall'Orio* (Venice, 1979), pp. 26, 70–8. The paintings were by Tizianello, G. Del Moro and Palma il Giovane, whom Niero sees as particularly influenced by Laghi.

[58] Zardin, *Confraternite e vita di pietà*, pp. 24–5, 84, n. 26, 106, n. 198; *idem*, 'Confraternite e comunità', p. 715, n. 29; J. Duhr, 'Confréries', *Dictionnaire du Spiritualité*, 2 (1953), cols. 1474–5; Grendi, 'Morfologia', p. 278.

[59] SBF S. Francesco no. 457 fols. 264v–6r; cf. I. Cowan, *The Scottish Reformation* (London, 1982), pp. 147–8.

[60] Weissman, *Ritual Brotherhood*, p. 224 (quoted) and pp. 137–9 for S. Paolo's communicants in 1480; Bossy, *Christianity*, pp. 46–8. On the importance of peace-making before mass, in the eyes of Londoners, cf. Brigden, 'Religion and social obligation', pp. 72–4, 77–9.

The honouring of the sacrament was of great importance. The 1564 revised statutes of the Sacrament confraternity in S. Lorenzo, Ponte a Greve (Florence) in its preamble argued:

Considering that among all the Christian exercises the most pious and most useful is that of honouring and revering the holiest Sacrament of the altar, which has been left to us by Our Lord in remembrance of his passion, we are resolved that for the perpetual glory of such a sacrament our company, previously called S. Sebastiano, for the future should be called the company of the Sacrament, so that those devout persons who wish to enter it will always have a keen incentive to acquire those much-favoured virtues faith, hope and charity, and will continually think of the benefits and gifts which the greatest God has given us, which all reveal themselves to us as in the clearest of mirrors in this most worthy sacrament, and especially in the gift of the redemption and sanctification of the world.[61]

From such honouring of the sacrament followed the better keeping of altars in churches and oratories. It led to the greater display of the Host. Many confraternities undertook to escort a priest and the Host to the sick and dying in their houses or hospitals, as depicted for example by Guido Cagnacci in an altarpiece commissioned by the Sacrament confraternity in S. Biagio, Saludecio (near Cattolica, in situ). This painting shows a parade of the Host, clergy and brethren under a canopy, with a passing brother kneeling in reverence in the street. Members of Perugia's Corpus Christi confraternity were enticed into this escorting activity by the offer of forty days' indulgences. The eucharist was seen as an aid to the sick, and as preparation for a good death. The public reverential parade with canopy, banners and lights would enhance veneration, and possibly philanthropy. Eucharistic devotion and charity went together. When Gabriele Paleotti issued norms for the Corpus Domini confraternities in 1567 he declared that they should not only look after the sacrament and its altar, but provide visitors to the poor sick in the parish. Certainly in the large parish of S. Procolo these policies were implemented.[62]

The devout in this period could readily visualise a transposition from symbol or essence to corporeal reality: the near presence of the Host becoming the Risen Christ. There is a striking drawing executed about 1620 by Jacopo Palma the younger (in the Correr Museum, Venice), showing Christ standing in a chalice and supported by angels. This was apparently based on a decoration in the mariegola, rule-book, of the Scuola di S. Corpo di Cristo, in S. Agnese. The elevation and demonstration of chalice and host could make Christ seem very close, and a very present reminder of his life to be imitated.[63]

---

[61] D'Addario, Aspetti, p. 441.

[62] A. Colombi Ferretti, Dipinti d'altare in età di Controriforma in Romagna 1560–1650 (Bologna, 1982), pp. 109–10 and Fig. 36; Constitutioni della Ven. Confraternita del Sacratissimo Corpo di Christo, et di S. Pietro Martire di Perugia P.S. Pietro (Perugia, 1601), chapter 8. Cf. the 1531 Rules in BCP Ms 3139 'Regola et Constitutioni de la devota Compagnia del corpo de Christo et de Sancto Pietro Martyre', fols. 2r–9v, which provided for escorting the sacrament to the sick, but without inducement; Fanti, San Procolo pp. 211–15. Two visitors: 'essamineranno bene il bisogno dei poveri et con charità et discretione specificheranno la quantità et qualità dell'elemosina che gli farà, aggravando in questo la conscientia de detti visitatori quali doveranno molto bene mirare alla possibilità della Compagnia et alla necessità del povero infermo'.

[63] Museo Correr, Venice, Inv. no. 1242, seen when it was exhibited there 1985–6; see catalogue Drawings from Venice. Master works from the Museo Correr, Venice, eds. T. Pignatti and G. Romanelli (New York, 1985), no. 6 p. 52; cf. R. Scribner, Review article 'Religion in early modern Europe', European Studies Review, 13 (1983), p. 95 and n. 10 for prevalence of this sort of illustration in Catholic Europe.

5 FORTY-HOUR DEVOTIONS: 'QUARANTORE'

The Forty-Hour or *Quarantore* devotion was the most elaborate presentation of the Host. It was particularly promoted by Capuchins and Jesuits, in the confraternities sponsored by them. But bishops like Carlo Borromeo were equally enthusiastic. For this devotion the sacrament was displayed prominently for forty hours or so, either continuously, or over three days with the chapel closed overnight. A succession of people were organised to arrive for spells of adoration and prayer, and to hear a sermon or homily. There could be much elaboration on this theme. The rules of Lecce's S. Annunziazione detailed a full version to take place at Christmas. Following an eight-day prelude (presumably of general exhortations and spiritual preparation) there was the three-day full devotion during which the Sacrament was displayed under a baldacchino on a candle-lit altar in the Jesuit College. The confraternity was to organise a continuous succession of people (in this case only men, since it was inside the College), who would watch for a period in the cycle of devotions, and participate in a *Te Deum*. At the end of each day there was to be a culminating torch-lit procession to the church, where there would be singing by two choirs, with lutes, viols, cittern (*cetra*) and small organ, 'which should not impede the singing'. This confraternity also held a *Quarantore* celebration for the last three days of the Lenten Carnival, this time in the church. A celebration could instead involve a continuous cycle through a night, culminating in a high Mass, often celebrated by a leading dignitary.[64]

A *Quarantore* was used to promote eucharistic devotions generally, as when the Capuchin Giuseppe da Fermo preached at such a celebration in Sansepolcro in 1537, and led reformed confraternities to adopt eucharistic devotions.[65] The Perugian Della Morte company (highly prestigious, and probably wealthy by the late sixteenth century) held monthly *Quarantore* displays in its own oratory, but this frequency must have been unusual.[66] A lesser fraternity like S. Pietro Apostolo did not have its own celebration, but could assist at others. In 1630 the brethren were recorded as escorting women of two parishes from their own churches to a major *Quarantore* display in the Cathedral.[67]

Many of these displays involved elaborate decorations of altars, scenic and lighting effects with the use of reflecting mirrors, sumptuous canopies, cloths and monstrances. While the most elaborate spectacles were organised in Cathedrals or churches of the Orders, such as Il Gesù in Rome, individual confraternities could easily compete. The Bologna confraternity of S. Maria della Morte boasted of a sumptuous Forty-Hour celebration on 3 March 1597. The proud Prior inserted a sketch of the altar and its decorations into the prioral record book for posterity. In the alcove behind the altar was a perspective scene with veils and gold; in the ceiling above a blue heaven full of veils and roses of various colours, to stupendous effect. To the right of the altar was a statue of the Madonna, to the left an Annunciating Angel; the balustrade was furnished with angels, candles and lights, which were reflected by mirrors behind. Everywhere there

[64] Tacchi Venturi, *Storia della Compagnia di Gesù*, vol. 1.ii., pp. 229–48; Weissman, *Ritual Brotherhood*, pp. 229–34; on Lecce, Lopez, 'Le confraternite laicali', pp. 233–5. Capuchin and other Franciscan influence on the Forty-Hour devotions have been noted by: F. Russo, *Storia dell'Archidiocesi di Reggio Calabria*, p. 94; Calace, 'Vita religiosa', p. 20 and n. 52.

[65] Meloni, 'Topografia', p. 35.

[66] Crispolti, *Perugia Augusta*, p. 176. The Perugian company may have been influenced by the Roman Morte e Orazione archconfraternity which had taken up the *Quarantore* in 1551, Monachino, pp. 275–6.

[67] Marinelli, *Le Confraternite*, p. 872, and *passim* on other confraternities escorting people to celebrations.

were swags of cloths, veils, gold, roses and colour. A trumpet sounded when the sacrament was elevated for display. Brother Francesco Cavalone designed this–at a cost of forty *scudi*. This celebration was deemed to surpass the 'superbly musical' *Quarantore* held by the confraternity for Easter 1593, which was blessed by Archbishop Alfonso Paleotti.[68]

6 FLAGELLATION

For some confraternities one of the major aspects of religious life was the penitential exercise of flagellation, or the discipline (*disciplina*), though its prevalence in the sixteenth century is more difficult to establish than some might think. As already indicated many confraternities that were designated as flagellant–*della frustra, dei battuti, di disciplina*–took on other devotions and philanthropic activities, and discipline may have disappeared in all but name. Some flagellation was possibly merely symbolic, with silken flails shown as symbols of penitence, but for many the use of the barbed cord or leather strip was a serious mortification of the flesh, whether used in private or in public processions.

In Venice the *Scuole Grandi*, which were *scuole dei battuti*, still had public displays of flagellation. When in 1530 these confraternities processed on Holy Thursday to St Mark's to see the relics, the Scuola di S. Rocco's contingent included ninety flagellants. Later in the century this confraternity was hiring flagellants to take part in such processions–'to preserve the ancient devotion of the flagellants who are accustomed to come and honour our Scuola on the evening of Holy Thursday'. The regular members were no longer prepared to do public penance in this way. However, on the Venetian mainland in Brescia similar *scuole* were committed: weekly over 700 people walked barefoot through the streets following the Cross and beating themselves.[69]

Capuchins particularly promoted public flagellation in the confraternities they sponsored, since it was a regular penitential practice for themselves. The constitutional reforms, inspired by Giovanni da Capistrano, ordered discipline to be exercised thrice weekly, with a fixed ritual based on the psalms *Miserere Mei Deus* and *De Profundis*. The Biblical inspirations were 1 Corinthians 9:27: 'I bruise my own body and make it know its master, for fear that after preaching to others I should find myself rejected'; and Colossians 1:24: 'It is now my happiness to suffer for you. This is my way of helping to complete, in my poor human flesh, the full tale of Christ's afflictions still to be endured, for the sake of this body which is the church.' Two Capuchins, Antonio Corso (d. 1548) and Giuseppe da Leonessa (d. 1612), were leading propagandists for public flagellation in Umbria, the latter often used an iron chain in his own discipline. He inspired the Oratorio del Buon Gesù in Foligno and later the Congregazione del B. Giuseppe at Leonessa. How far lay members went in repeating the 6,666 beatings supposedly received by Christ–in the view of these Capuchins–is unknown.[70]

Some Jesuits in their missions throughout Italy organised penitential discipline.

---

[68] BCB F.O.43 fols. 46–7 for description, 47–8 for sketch: 'fu la piu superba et piu vistosa et ricco apparato che mai sino al di hoggi si sia fatto in Bologna per simile occasione'; fols. 32v-3r for the 'superbissima musica' at Easter 1593.

[69] Pullan, *Rich and Poor*, pp. 51–2, quoting n. 86, and p. 39.

[70] Chiaretti, pp. 229–60.

Corporate discipline was for men only, though women could flail themselves as a private penitential act; they also wept, wailed and begged for God's mercy outside the church while men flagellated inside. Confraternities were often erected thereafter to perpetuate the mission's work, and maintain the discipline along with frequent confession and communion. The Jesuits tended to advise that the discipline should be exercised discreetly and in private (even if as a group), and with moderation.[71]

There were doubts about the suitability of public flagellation as an expression of piety. In the fifteenth century Venetian authorities, whom G. Ruggiero argues were increasingly suspicious of homosexual practices, discouraged flagellation if 'nudity' was to be involved. In one case at least noble flagellants who had appeared 'naked' in S. Maria Zobeniga on Good Friday 1438 to be whipped by others were arrested, gaoled and then banished.[72] In Genoa ecclesiastical authorities discouraged ostentatious disciplining, while the lay powers—for more secular and political motives—had already tried to curb flagellant processions altogether. The 1569 Milan Provincial Council warned that processional flagellation should be for the grace of piety, not for reward. Paying the poor to flagellate for the honour of a confraternity could discredit all. Though Easter processions with flagellation have survived till the present, the policy from the sixteenth century tended to favour individual or corporate discipline in discreet seclusion, usually during Advent and Lent. When the old Florentine company of S. Benedetto 'Bianco' (in existence since 1357) issued revised statutes in 1570, it recommended Advent as suitable for corporal penance through discipline, 'far from the eyes of the world, because God should be the only witness'. In Bari, the mid-seventeenth-century statutes of the Franciscan-sponsored S. Antonio da Padova indicated that the men would have corporate discipline in church on Fridays in March; women could satisfy this penance privately at home. The processions did not involve the discipline.[73] Bishop N. Comitoli, planning an elaborate public celebration of communion in Perugia's Cathedral in November 1614, issued a printed pamphlet inviting members of discipline confraternities such as the S. Girolamo and Della Morte to exercise the discipline as a fitting preparation, in their own oratories.[74]

Evidence on the regularity of flagellation within a confraternity, and by what proportion of the membership, is hard to find. For the Foligno society of S. Girolamo constitutions, apostolic visitations and account books all testify to active flagellation, and in this case we know that the flails were made of cord, covered with paper, with little cords at the end to which were stitched little metal spikes or studs (*piccarelli*). Witnesses in the 1628 investigation into the Perugian confederation indicated that the *opera della disciplina* was weekly within the oratory, but no indication could be found in records about how many participated. Inventories partly help with Perugia's S. Pietro Apostolo, in 1574 eighteen flails were recorded (for an active membership in the twenties), none

---

[71] Novi Chavarria, pp. 172–3, 175–7; Calace, 'Vita religiosa', n. 50 recommends as a guide to Jesuit practice: S. Paolucci, *Missioni de' Padri della Compagnia di Gesù nel Regno di Napoli* (Naples, 1651).

[72] Ruggiero, *The Boundaries of Eros*, pp. 141, 196, nn.137–9. It is not clear how far nudity went; or what background factors were involved in the case. Weissman, *Ritual Brotherhood*, pp. 82–3: the members of the Compagnia del Gesù were told to 'wear the garment [with a slit at the back] in such a manner that one is uncovered modestly, without appearing naked'.

[73] Grendi, 'Morfologia', esp. pp. 278–9; Meloni, 'Topografia', p. 37; Mansi, vol. 34, col. 129, decree 22, 'non mercede conducti, sed pietatis gratia'; D'Addario, *Aspetti*, pp. 429–30.

[74] Marinelli, *Le confraternite*, pp. 454, 822.

was recorded in the 1588 and 1602 lists, but ten counted in 1627. A matter of fluctuating enthusiasm, or merely administrative vagueness?[75] In some cases there was a select flagellant group within a confraternity. In the Sacrament confraternity of S. Magno (Lombardy) in 1589 an elite of thiry-three out of 388 *confratelli* exercised the discipline and recited the Office of the Virgin for major feasts.[76]

There may have been regional variations in the enthusiasm for flagellation. Lombardy in the sixteenth century saw the foundation of over 200 new discipline societies, followed numerically by Piedmont with 87, and Umbria with 81, but there was apparently little enthusiasm in the south — Lucania, Puglia and Calabria having no new foundations, Abruzzi and Sicily only one each. In the seventeenth century Piedmont recorded at least 232 new ones, Lombardy 50; few appeared elsewhere. These figures (in data recorded up to 1969) were based on surviving institutions. They are bound to be distorted by the lower survival rate of archival and printed material in the south, possibly also by the more limited research activity there. However, they very tentatively suggest that fraternal flagellation was more popular in the more phlegmatic north.[77]

A visual reminder and encouragment for brethren to practice flagellation appeared in the miniatures decorating rule-books, or membership books, or on the processional standards (*gonfaloni*) and altarpieces they commisioned. The 1447 *Madonna del Pergolato* altarpiece by Giovanni Boccati (Perugia, Pinacoteca), which used to be in the oratory of the discipline confraternity of S. Domenico, Perugia, shows brothers wearing gowns with oval holes at the back so that the flail would strike bare flesh, with flails made of three knotted strings (without barbs).[78] Dono Doni in 1553 painted the *gonfalone* for the Assisi confraternity of S. Lorenzo. The group of *fratelli* kneeling before the saint are shown in hoods and gowns, again with a hole in the back; a flail is draped over the shoulder.[79]

A detailed description of procedures in the Florentine discipline confraternity of S. Antonio Abbate in 1485 indicates that confraternal corporate discipline could be charged with emotion and significance. Ritualistically members assembled and ratified their cohesion as a group; they cast off their external social status, along with their inhibitions, by donning their hooded robes, open at the back, and created a bond of brotherhood. Within the brotherhood confession preceding penance was public — to

---

[75] M. Sensi, 'Fraternite disciplinate e sacre rappresentazioni a Foligno nel secolo xv', *BSPU*, 71 (1974), esp. pp. 148–9 nn. 36–7 on sixteenth-century developments; SBF S. Francesco no. 509, 'Verbali' 1628, fol. 28r; ASP S. Pietro Apostolo vol. 23 'Miscellanea', fols. 5r, 36r; vol. 6 'Depositario', fols. 44v–7r.

[76] Zardin, *Confraternita e vita di pietà*, p. 42.

[77] Meloni, 'Topografia', p. 10 Table; Zardin's work supports the view that Lombard confraternities had a strong interest in penitential discipline: 'Confraternite e comunità', p. 722 n. 35; *Confraternita e vita di pietà*, pp. 42–5, 54–60; and his 'Le confraternite in Italia settentrionale', n. 78 cites sources indicating an increase in flagellation, even in public, in the later seventeenth and eighteenth centuries.

[78] Perugia, Pinacoteca. Inv. 150–151. Dated 1447. Giovanni di Piermatteo, called Boccati, from Camerino had become a Perugian citizen in 1445; he painted other works for confraternities, but this seems the earliest. Two of the saints were repainted in 1519. F. Santi, *Galleria Nazionale dell'Umbria. Dipinti, Sculturi e Oggetti dei secoli XV–XVI* (Rome, 1985), no. 8 pp. 22–4, colour plate 8a; F. Santi, *La Galleria Nazionale dell'Umbria in Perugia* (Rome, 6th eds, 1974), p.20.

[79] Santucci, p. 157 and Plate III. F. Russell, 'A Gonfalone by Dono Doni', *The Burlington Magazine*, 120 (1978), 190, 193 and Fig. 94; AA.VV. *Pittura in Umbria tra il 1480 e il 1540* (Milan, 1983), p. 117. Doni painted a number of *gonfaloni* and altarpieces for confraternities in Assisi, *ibid.*, pp. 117–18. On other confraternity art and *gonfaloni* see below chapter 11.3.

the whole group. Flagellation began after prayers and hymns in a darkened sanctuary. So purged and humbled they offered prayers for the wider community and for the departed, before cleaning their wounds and retiring to the dormitory for symbolic death through sleep. The following morning the brothers returned to a fully lit sanctuary for open corporate prayer and celebration.[80]

The physical and emotional commitment of such rituals, the attempt to distance self from the secular world and status, confession in front of relatives, neighbours and those of different social backgrounds within the brotherhood could lead to intense fraternity. But when concepts of status were heightened through the sixteenth century, and when some confraternities maintained, or even increased, social mixing, such elaborate disciplinary rituals were likely to be discarded. The full rituals of fraternal discipline were probably preserved best in closely knit, socially exclusive, companies. Rules of secrecy will have hidden the evidence from outside contemporaries, and from historians.

7 ROSARY DEVOTION

If penitential flagellation was primarily a male activity, it can be assumed that the saying of the Rosary and the contemplation of the Mysteries was more predominantly — though certainly not exclusively — a female devotion. As already indicated Rosary confraternities seem to have been both female-centred and popular. They have been described as 'a great universal alliance for prayer' and a 'common devotion at the level of popular piety'.[81] It has been argued that women joined the French Rosary confraternities from the late fifteenth century because they were excluded from most other societies, and because this type did not involve common masses, processions or banquets — merely prayer. In Italy as in France statutes might concentrate on rules that members should recite the Marian psalter each week, and thereby earn indulgences, with little other activity. But there are arguments that Italian Rosary confraternities involved a strong parochial community spirit, as much through looking after chapel and altar as through corporate worship. It might also be noted that a Capuchin preacher could inspire a Rosary confraternity to found a refuge for orphans at Ancona as an act of outward-looking philanthropy.[82]

Some Rosary chapels were well decorated and possessed major paintings on the theme of the Rosary, which suggests a degree of corporate pride and organisation. One of the earliest examples in Italy was the chapel of the Scuola dei Tedeschi in S. Bartolomeo di Rialto, Venice, which originally housed Dürer's *Feast of the Rosegarlands* (1506, now in Prague). This German national confraternity (founded between 1504 and

---

[80] Weissman, *Ritual Brotherhood*, pp. 92–5.
[81] Zardin, 'Le confraternite in Italia settentrionale'; Rusconi, 'Confraternite', pp. 492–3. A few cases investigated by the Venetian Inquisition suggest that devotion to the Rosary by pious Catholic women was bitterly resented by heterodox husbands, and by a group of women with Protestant sympathies: J. Martin, 'Out of the shadow: heretical and Catholic women in Renaissance Venice', *Journal of Family History*, 10 (1985), 21–33, esp. pp. 28, 30.
[82] N.Z. Davis, 'City women and religious change' in her *Society and Culture in Early Modern France* (London, 1975), p. 75 and n. 26 p. 292; Zardin, 'Confraternite e comunità', pp. 717–19; Meersseman, *Ordo Fraternitatis*, pp. 1144–1232, esp. pp. 1215–18 for the 1480 statutes of the Rosary company of S. Domenico di Castello, Venice–each weekly recitation of the psalter earned 57 years and 240 days of indulgences; Arsenio D'Ascoli, *La Predicazione dei Cappuccini*, p. 233: the preacher was a Spaniard, Pietro Trigosa.

1506) and its painting may be seen as important promoters of the Rosary cult in Italy.[83] The emphasis on the benefits of the Rosary devotion for men, women and children, and on corporate involvement in the devotion is illustrated by the painting, *La Madonna del Rosario*, commissioned in 1589 by the Rosary confraternity of Cesena from the then fashionable Giuseppe Cesare, Cavaliere D'Arpino (now in S. Domenico, Cesena). The mixed crowd in a room below pick up roses distributed from the heavenly scene above. In 1534 friar Domenico Baglioni renewed a Marian chapel in the immense Perugian church of S. Domenico, reorganised the old society as a Rosary confraternity, and had the chapel decorated with paintings alluding to Mary and the mysteries. He claimed that by 1548 he had attracted more than five thousand men and women to join the confraternity. It is difficult to believe that this many Perugians shared a meaningful corporate life and I suspect that the inscriptions include non-resident persons enrolling for the benefit of some indulgences. Even at a distance the association with a large praying community, aided by the illustrated Rosary manuals and prints being produced in Italy, could have an impact on the life of individuals.[84]

A Jesuit, Troilo Rosanova, provided the Rosary society in Legnano with its rules in 1585. They required a weekly recitation of the Marian psalter, and 15 Paters and 150 Ave Marias—whether kneeling, walking or sitting. He stressed the value of meditation while saying the Rosary. But the devotions went further: Mass every first Sunday, with procession; every Saturday evening singing the Salve Regina and recitation of litanies; and half an hour of common prayer every feast-day, so that all could understand something about the Passion of Christ and the fifteen mysteries of the Rosary, as elucidated by Jesuit Father Loarte. Rosanova also stressed the need for frequent communion, full attention to death, burial and suffrages. Evidence suggests that past members were well remembered.[85]

8 DEATH AND THE AFTERLIFE

Remembering dead brothers and sisters was a predominant concern amongst all confraternities. The living and the dead were part of one brotherhood. The living prayed to help the departed; the departed once they reached heaven might intercede for the living. Probably the main motivation behind many people joining the confraternities was that the society would help them to die well, provide them with a fitting passage into the afterlife through a decent funeral, and then organise corporate assistance with prayers for relief in and from Purgatory, and for a final favourable Judgement.[86]

Confraternity prayers could possibly be more surely relied on than those of one's surviving family. Confraternity statutes had regulations about brothers taking the sacrament to the sick and dying brothers, sisters and relatives, accompanying the dead

[83] P. Humphrey, 'Dürer's *Feast of the Rosegarlands*: a Venetian Altarpiece', *Bulletin of the Society for Renaissance Studies*, 4, no. 1 (April 1986), 29–39.

[84] Colombi Ferretti, p. 71 and Table 13. Typically D'Arpino took until 1601 to produce this work, and then only after threats of prosecution. On Perugia, Meersseman, *Ordo Fraternitatis*, p. 996 n. 4, 1190–2.

[85] Zardin, 'Confraternite e comunità', pp. 221–33. On Troilo Rosanova see also Olivieri Baldissarri, *I 'poveri prigioni'*, pp. 134–7.

[86] See generally Davis, 'Some tasks and themes', pp. 326–8; cf. R. Scribner, 'Cosmic order and daily life. Sacred and secular in pre-industrial German society', *Religion and Society*, ed. von Greyerz, pp. 17–32, esp. p. 18; P. Ariès, *The Hour of Our Death* (London, 1981), esp. pp. 185–6, 462–6.

to burial, and praying for the repose of the soul. Perugia's Madonna della Consolatione ruled that a dead brother should be accompanied to burial by other brethren, processing with lit candles, saying prayers while the priest sang the usual responses, and intoning litanies and the psalm *De Profundis*. Each brother was to say ten Paters and Ave Marias when they all returned to their oratory, and the following day they were to reassemble to say the Mass for the Dead.[87] The regular religious meetings of most confraternities would have involved remembering the faithful departed of the company.

In the case of parochial confraternities funeral accompaniment was sometimes expanded in the sixteenth century to include outsiders within the parish. Venetian Sacrament companies (which existed in at least a third of the parishes) attended the funerals of all parishioners whose families considered they were of some status. Social prestige became involved, with much honour attached to ensuring a full processional funeral, well attended by colleges of priests and by confraternities. Confraternities from neighbouring parishes might also be recruited. This could involve payment, and caused scandal. In the *Scuole Grandi* poorer members were paid to grace the funerals of others, or, put another way, they might not receive alms if they failed to attend. But, as will be discussed later (chapter 10.5), some confraternities came to specialise in providing suitable funerals for the poor as one of the highest acts of charity. Most concentrated on securing a good funeral as a reward for a companionable brother or sister. This might well have been the most time-consuming obligation for many brethren.[88]

It must have been a common sight to behold hooded brothers escorting a body to the cemetery, with or without a large following. Such scenes sometimes appear discreetly in the background of famous paintings. For example (to take two works in the National Gallery, London), in Filippo Lippi's *Virgin and child with Sts Jerome and Dominic* there is at top right on the hill-side a church scene, where two hooded brothers are bringing a body to church, and in Bronzino's *Madonna and child with St John the Baptist and St Anne [or St Elizabeth]*, at the top is a cemetery wall, with black hooded figures going through the doorway.[89]

Confraternity devotion seems to have shown a growing concern for souls in Purgatory, of former companions, then of specific individuals, and finally of the generality of Souls in Purgatory. For all but a few who escaped Hell there would be a period of greater or lesser torment in Purgatory before they could achieve heavenly bliss; executed prisoners in a state of full contrition, having endured the torments of their gruesome death might achieve Paradise directly, according to some comforters (see chapter 10.5). While many would have earned remission of time in Purgatory through indulgences and contrition while on earth, there would still be a period of purgation. It was believed that this could be moderated and shortened by the prayers of the living petitioning for the intercession of Christ, the Virgin and saints. The souls of departed brethren were to be remembered when the funeral of one was being conducted. In addition, as with the Divino Amore fraternity in Genoa, there might be a special service in the oratory on All Saints' day. Additionally in this company there was another service

---

[87] *Constitutioni . . . Consolatione . . . Perugia*; cf. Weissman, *Ritual Brotherhood*, pp. 49–50 on Florentine *laudesi* companies and their funerals.

[88] Pullan, *Rich and Poor*, pp. 76–7, 79, 137, 189; idem, *The Jews of Europe*, pp. 126–7. Cf. Flynn, 'Charitable ritual', pp. 338–9, on Spanish confraternities burying paupers as well as their own members.

[89] National Gallery, London, Inv. nos. 293 and 5280.

for the dead to be organised in Lent during which the names of all dead brothers were read out. Brothers were enjoined to remember in their individual prayers the souls of the departed.[90]

Gradually there also developed a concern for souls in Purgatory generally, for those who had nobody living ready to pray for their relief and salvation. A number of confraternities were founded as specialists in this charitable activity from the later sixteenth century. In Italy this devotion appears later than in France, and may not have had a major impact until late in the seventeenth century. There was some acceleration when the Theatines inaugurated the devotion in Naples in S. Paolo Maggiore in 1624 and helped spread within the kingdom from there.[91] Visual aids were produced to encourage consideration of souls. The sculptor and designer Alessandro Algardi produced a print showing souls rising from Purgatory, which was probably used by Roman confraternities, and the specialist Compagnia delle Anime del Purgatorio in Bologna in 1643 commissioned Guercino to paint an altarpiece for S. Paolo (*in situ*), which shows souls (as fairly delicate and attractive bodies) being joyfully released from below with the intercession of St Gregory, while God the Father, the Son and the Virgin await them in heaven.[92]

Some attitudes to this devotion, and a specialised refinement of it, find eloquent expression in the preamble to the statutes of the Roman archconfraternity of Natività Agonizzanti in 1616. Members joined not just for their own salvation, but for the spiritual benefits of those who at the extremity of their life find themselves without counsel and help. True lovers of God in undertaking works of charity could save many souls from eternal damnation and torments and make them citizens of heaven, by healing the soul rather than the body. Help was most urgently needed when the soul was passing from this life to the next, the point of true agony when the battle between good and evil was underway. Souls were in greater need then than when in Purgatory, since those souls that arrived there were assured of the mercy of God—though further prayers could shorten the period before which this was granted. The popularity of this particular concern for the agonising soul at the point of transition can be judged by the record of societies from 186 towns and cities, mainly in northern and central Italy, aggregating to the archconfraternity during the seventeenth century.[93]

[90] Angelozzi, p. 178, appendix with statutes, chapter 9.

[91] P. Ariès, *Images of Man and Death*, trans. J. Lloyd, (Cambridge Mass., and London, 1985), pp. 160–70; Zardin, 'Le confraternite in Italia settentrionale', sections 4–5; Paglia, 'Le confraternite'; Russo, *Chiesa e comunità*, pp. 441–2.

[92] J. Montagu, *Alessandro Algardi* (2 vols., London, 1985), pp. 179, 260 and n. 5, fig. 203, pl. 179; on Guercino's altarpiece, E. Mâle, *L'Art religeux après le Concile de Trent* (Paris, 1932), pp. 60–3 and Fig. 29: St Gregory's Dialogue had argued for the efficacy of prayers and masses for the dead. He is here dressed like a seventeenth-century Pope.

[93] Paglia, 'Le confraternite', pp. 208–12: congregate 'non solo per attendere più comodamente alla propria salute, ma per impiegare le forze loro in benefizi spirituali di quelli che, giunti all'estremo del vivere loro, si trovano privi di consiglio e d'aiuto . . . Perciò primieramente ogni divoto spirito a quanta gloria di Dio venga egli a cooperare con questo santo istituto, potendo essere mezzo efficace per cui non una, ma molte anime, scampando dall'eterna damnazione, venghino ad essere fatte cittadine del cielo, con che verrà ad impedire quelle biasteme horrende che esse contra Dio haverebbero vomitate se si fussero perdute in quei tormenti eterni, e sarà cagione che Iddio venga, senza prescrizione di tempo alcuno, eternamente lodato e glorificato . . . Non si medica e si fomenta il corpo, ma l'anima, nobilissimo spirito, bisognoso di molte necessità che non hanno del temporale, ma dell'eterno; ne mai più vi sarà riparo se una volta solo in esse si chiudono gli occhi a questa luce'.

But to return from specialist devotion to general issues, it should be emphasised that people joined confraternities primarily out of concern for their own salvation, and possibly of those closest to them. Membership of the fraternity, devotion and charitable acts in life were preparations for a good death; from there brothers and sisters would honour the body, and help dispatch the soul as quickly as possible through Purgatory to Heaven. Gian Lorenzo Bernini in the latter part of his life joined the specialist confraternity of Bona Mors at Il Gesù, which had been founded in 1648 under the impact of Roberto Bellarmino's book on the art of dying. Bernini attended regularly and sought to prepare well for death. But membership of all kinds of fraternities, the work and prayer there, could be seen as part of the preparation.[94]

The organisers of confraternities showed a considerable concern for a structured organisation governed by officials who would impose elaborate rules; there was an interest in the assignment of rules within the organisation and in respectability. Office-holding in the fraternity may have been some compensation for the absence, or loss, of power in the wider community. Not that all brothers wanted to undertake the burdens that office-holding clearly imposed in some brotherhoods. According to the rule-books much of fraternity life seems clear-cut. Consultation of other documents suggests a more muddled picture. Once somebody was accepted into the fraternity, foibles, laxity and misdemeanours were tolerated. Expulsion was apparently not easily achieved. The range of devotional activity from prayers to corporate whippings, from hymn singing to adoration of the Host, was considerable. Brothers and sisters could participate at different levels of intensity without risking expulsion. Surviving records are coy about the intensity and density of devotional life for most members; but the examples given above suggest that confraternity life in private could be demanding, especially when people were active in the organisational system as well. However, for many, concern for the soul in the next life was paramount. This might not be a private preoccupation within the confines of the fraternity. The salvation of the soul might be more efficaciously pursued through public devotions and public works, as a regular practice, or in a once-in-a-lifetime pilgrimage or great procession.

[94] I. Lavin, 'Bernini's Death', *The Art Bulletin*, 54 (1972), 158–86.

5

EXTERNAL RELIGIOUS DEVOTIONS

The previous chapter discussed some practices that moved between the private and the public sector; flagellation could be in the privacy of the oratory, or out on the processional route; the Forty–Hour devotion might involve many outsiders, or be a fairly restricted occasion; escorting the sacrament to the sick was obviously public, but in most cases it was essentially a domestic relationship between the patient and his fraternal supporters. This chapter will, however, concentrate on the more deliberately outward manifestations of public faith: public processions, pilgrimages, plays and sacred representations.

For individual brothers and sisters some of these public events would have been a rare, but life-enhancing event, while the lavish indulgences so earned held out the hope of early release from Purgatory thereafter. The events could be emotional, and entertaining. For the confraternity as a whole the public devotions, as well as expressing corporate solidarity, might be important for social prestige, recruitment and fund-raising, provided they did not lead to unseemly competion and riot.

Here I have chosen to use lengthy accounts of an exemplary procession with relics, of a procession with sacred representations, and of a spectacular pilgrimage to Rome to illustrate types of external devotions. These should give a full flavour of what could be involved–though obviously most processions and pilgrimages would have been less elaborate.

I PROCESSIONS

Processions remained a major part of popular religious life in sixteenth-century Italy, even if some authorities frowned upon them. A confraternal public procession is shown in the background scene of the frontispiece to the statute book of S. Maria della Morte, Bologna [Frontispiece]. While secondary to its philanthropic work for the condemned, the procession is being emphasised as a contribution to city life and religion. Confraternities could be a small element in a mass popular procession, or they could stage their own confraternity-centred parades. The most popular occasions were those connected with the saint's day at a major sanctuary, with Holy Thursday, or most especially with Corpus Christi. This last (on the Thursday after Trinity Sunday) was the major eucharistic commemoration from the fourteenth century, for which St Thomas Aquinas had established a service and hymns. Michel de Montaigne saw the confraternity parades as a major sign of popular devotion in Rome in 1581. He was much impressed by the

confraternities' contributions–parading, singing, flagellating and showing devotion–
during Lenten and Easter celebrations in St Peter's. The Holy Thursday activities, which
included night-time processions involving 12,000 torches were the highlight.[1] Local
cults of saints could give rise to spectacular parades of a less standard form. Puglia still
has a number of patronal festivals at leading sanctuaries like those of St Michael
Archangel at Monte S. Angelo, and St Nicola at Bari. Here there are popular customs
of distant origin, like the burning of fires and the parading of tree branches. On these
occasions, and for Holy Thursday processions, confraternities were–and are–primarily
responsible for carrying the Cross, and images of the saint concerned and the Madonna.[2]

Throughout Italy in the sixteenth century confraternities were involved in
communal processions, or organised their own. Brothers, and sometimes sisters, of the
company dressed in cloaks, with a colour or insignia denoting their particular society.
Sometimes they were hooded to preserve anonymity. Some, often specific officials,
carried large crosses, banners or paintings, others took smaller crosses or candles, some
were preoccupied with flagellation. Confraternities were not necessarily restricted to
major feasts for such processions. Rome's SS. Crocefisso di S. Marcello in its 1565
statutes suggested several variations: general processions of the Crucifix to the accompaniment of hymn singing; torch-lit parades to welcome illustrious visitors; the escorting, in a parade, of girls awarded dowries by the company for them to marry fittingly;
the thanksgiving procession of a prisoner whom they had been allowed to release from
a death sentence; and quieter, more regular processions of the sacrament to the sick.[3]
The Sacrament confraternity of S. Lorenzo, Ponte a Greve (Florence) had a procession
of the sacrament in church every third Sunday of the month. On 1 May there was an
external procession to the Vergine Maria di Scandicci, and there was an annual
procession to S. Annunziata in Florence. Women were allowed in these celebrations.[4]

Venice was a city where church and state processions played many important and
varied roles. The great ritual occasions, such as the Ascension Day Marriage of the Sea,
linked state and church in a complex mix of propaganda and myth-making for this
everlasting Republic, Catholic but independent of papal control. The confraternities
were expected to contribute impressively to such displays, and their contribution was
recorded for posterity in print and paint, as already indicated in chapter 1. The funerals
of important personages in church and state included the parade of many *scuole*; for
Doge Leonardo Loredan in 1521 there were 119 *scuole* in attendance; for Cardinal
Corner in 1525 there were 111; while Bartolomeo d'Alviano, formerly one of the more
loyal and competent *condottieri* to serve the Republic seems to have had 87 at his funeral
in 1515. Confraternities were also involved in special celebrations, such as those to mark
the peace treaties between France and Spain in 1559 and 1598. When Venice was put
under an Interdict in 1606–7–after the Republic and the irascible Pope Paul V had

---

[1] Rusconi, 'Confraternite', p. 479; F.L. Cross (ed.), *The Oxford Dictionary of the Christian Church*, p. 345
'Corpus Christi, Feast of'; M. Lautrey (ed.) *Montaigne. Journal de voyage* (Paris, 1906), pp. 258–9: 'La plus
noble chose et magnifique que j'aie vue, ny ici ny ailleurs, ce fut il incroiable nombre du peuple espars ce
jour là par la ville aus devotions, et notamment en ces compaignes . . .'; see now *Montaigne: Travel Journal*,
p. 94.
[2] S. La Sorsa, *Religiosità popolare pugliese* (Florence, 1962).
[3] *Statuti . . . S. Crocefisso*, esp. chapters 25–6, 43 and 47.
[4] D'Addario, *Aspetti*, pp. 441–2. Those failing to attend the May procession were fined 3 *soldi*.

quarrelled over various jurisdictional matters, especially the treatment of criminous priests—the confraternities were involved in defiant and morale-boosting processions. The most notable took place for Corpus Christi in May 1606, when the *Scuole Grandi* not only paraded in their finery, but also created various tableaux, some of which ostentatiously supported the Republic's cause against the Pope. The *Scuole Grandi* had numerous processions in more normal times; these were now less concerned with flagellation and more with the ostentatious parade of relics and vessels. Despite government attempts to curb sumptuary extravagance, these processions became more lavish and costlier for the confraternities and individual members. Officials doubtless argued that such costly parading would be offset by increased testamentary, or other, donations, from those impressed by the confraternity's presentation.[5] The lesser *scuole delle arti* were also tempted to spend proportionately more of their income on display; for such as the mercers this might simply be good business, attracting new customers among strangers coming to watch processions and religious displays which included rich textile decorations.[6]

Processions were not always harmonious expressions of brotherly love since, besides competition in the display of candles and banners, there were conflicts over the order of precedence. Decisions on which confraternities participated in a parade or funeral, and in which order, reflected the social prestige or historical antiquity of the companies concerned. In 1537 the Bologna hospital confraternity of S. Maria della Vita obtained a legal settlement against the Buon Gesù, which had claimed precedence in funerals and processions on grounds of earlier foundation. In 1586 S. Maria della Vita was in conflict with S. Maria della Morte, over who should bury a layman from Cesena. The Morte claimed that it had been invited first, and that the brethren of the Vita had come and seized the Morte's *palio* from under the body. Although the prior of the Vita came and apologised, he maintained his right of precedence. It is not clear who actually paraded and buried the body—possibly a less important matter for the record-keeper than that of honourable precedence. Soon after, the companies conflicted over burying Monsignor Aloiso Marscotti, bishop of Stromboli but a Bolognese. In the end a compromise was reached, and 'reason overcomes force'—the force of the Vita. When in 1587 Senator Boncompagno Boncompagni, brother of Pope Gregory XIII, died, the order of precedence for the relevant confraternities was the Vita, the Trinità and then the Morte; but (in compensation?) only the priors of the Morte went into the house. For the next major funeral, that of Cornelia Riario, both the Vita and Morte attended, with the Vita again leading, and its prior going to the house. A notarised accord in 1588 seems to give the victory to the Vita. But in compensation the Morte won its precedence battle against the Buon Gesù, when both were invited to celebrate the funeral of Senator Antonio

---

[5] Mackenney, *Traders and Tradesmen*, p. 140; M. Sanuto, *I Diarii* (58 vols., Venice, 1879–1903), vol. 21, col. 276 on Bartolomeo D'Alviano's funeral: 'Poi principià ussir di la chiescia di San Marco li penelli picoli di le scuole con do dopieri avanti per uno, fono numero 82, ancora che ne mandrò molte che non vanno. Poi vene quattro scuole di batuti, una driedo a l'altra con 24 torzi, una per . . . che la signora se le dete, et a quella di San Marco portava il corpo, numero 50'. After friars, monks and congregations of priests, there were others from the Scuola Grande of S. Marco; there is much in Sanuto's diary on this *condottiere's* activities for Venice; Muir, *Civic Ritual*, pp. 228–30 on the Corpus Christi parade of 1606; Pullan, 'Le Scuole Grandi', pp. 89–90; *idem*, *Rich and Poor*, pp. 52–62, 75, 127–8. See above chapter 1, n. 4, and below chapter 11.3. Cf. the importance of confraternities in eighteenth-century funerals, Chadwick, p. 41.

[6] Mackenney, 'Trade Guilds', pp. 234–5, and *Tradesmen and Traders*, pp. 141–9.

Legnani in 1595; the episcopal vicar forced the Buon Gesù contingent to remain at home when it refused to keep quiet, and Archbishop Alfonso Paleotti then ruled against its claim.[7]

In Venice there were frequent disputes between confraternities over precedence in processions, or over priorities along the narrow, tortuous routes of *calle* and bridges, which the Council of Ten tried to control, as after the jostling between the *Scuole Grandi* in St Mark's Square on Good Friday 1512. When in the 1620s two communities outside Naples were in dispute, with one seeking to be an independent parish, they expressed their feelings through confraternity processions parading rallying standards.[8] Confraternity processional disputes might be unseemly, especially for the family of the deceased, but they reflected intense loyalty and probably generated more when the honour contest was won.

The general public often obviously appreciated confraternity processions and display. People were prepared to buy window space, for two or three *scudi*, to obtain a good view of the procession of the relic of St Carlo Borromeo's heart through Rome on 22 June 1614. The parade involved twenty-five cardinals and their entourages, many prelates, and about 1,500 torches carried for the most part by confraternity members.[9]

Processions could offer the participating public both religious and social satisfactions. When in 1482 the Chapter of the Augustinians met in Perugia, there were various celebrations and parades. The discipline confraternity of S. Domenico played a major role, and organised a public meal after sung masses in front of the Cathedral. The Virgin's wedding ring was then shown in the square; the ring had recently been brought from neighbouring Chiusi by a disgruntled German friar who felt it was being poorly venerated. Perugia soon ensured that it was well honoured.[10]

Over a century later Perugia had a much more spectacular celebration involving confraternities, with mass appeal on similar cultic and entertainment grounds. On 17 May 1609 between 40,000 and 60,000 people allegedly attended a festival organised by Bishop N. Comitoli to celebrate the movement of the relics of three local saints (Bevignate, Abbot Peter and Bishop Ercolano) to better positioned altars. The bishop had conducted an intense publicity campaign beforehand to attract worshippers from all over Umbria and further afield. He ensured through printed descriptions that the celebrations would be well remembered. The various churches involved were decorated, with tapestries and silks, with gold and silver decorations on the main doors. There were three triumphal arches, provided by civic authorities, nobles and clergy, with statues, mottoes, epigrams and poetry; streets were decorated with lesser arches,

---

[7] BCB F.O.6 fols. 27r–8r, copy of notarial document 17 October 1537; F.O.43, 'Memorie . . . S. Maria della Morte', fols. 26v–7r, 28r ('et qui si vede che la ragione vince la forza'), 28v–9r, 34v–5r. The Buon Gesù had formerly been called S. Maria della megga ratta (or media rata).

[8] Mackenney, *Tradesmen and Traders*, pp. 135–6; W.B. Wurthmann's unpublished talks have indicated that the Council of Ten records are full of evidence of such disputes between confraternities; see his forthcoming article 'The Council of Ten and the "Scuole Grandi" in early Renaissance Venice' for *Studi Veneziani*; Russo, *Chiesa e comunità*, pp. 466–7; cf. for eighteenth-century examples in Policastro and Rome, Chadwick, p. 40.

[9] F. Cerasoli, 'Diario di cose romane degli anni 1614, 1615, 1616', *Studi e documenti di storia e diritto*, 15 (1896), 273–4.

[10] Pietro Angelo di Giovanni, 'Cronaca inedita', ed. O. Scalvanti, *BSPU* 9 (1903), 205 and, on the ring, p. 83; E. Ricci, 'La leggenda di S. Mustiola e il furto del Sant'Anello', *BSPU*, 24 (1918), 133–55; G. Bonazzi, *Storia di Perugia dalle origini al 1860* (2 vols., 2nd edn., Città di Castello, 1959–60), vol. I, pp. 542–5.

epigrams and so on, and altars were set up at strategic points along the route. The three confederated confraternities provided one of the four fountains of wine that poured forth for six hours to refresh the participants. The procession was led by the shield of St Michael, captain of the Heavenly Militia, followed by a multitude of angels accompanying various representations devised by the Barnabites: of the saints concerned, and of pilgrims with crowns of Obedience, Chastity and Poverty. Then came the confraternities; seventeen of them in fourteen groups, with about 725 brothers participating (though a few in this total may have been children dressed as angels). The three confederated confraternities led this section with 164 *fratelli*. Some carried a large standard depicting the three saints, others batons; they provided an impressive choir. Other confraternities contributed crucifixes, torches, batons, images or insignia. Later in the procession came the religious, civic officials, civilians and forty-nine abbots from the Benedictine houses that were then holding a General Chapter in Perugia. At the end came a large contingent of women, marshalled by gentlemen from the confraternities and separated from men on the bishops's orders. Various choirs led the lengthy singing, which included specially composed verses. This kind of civic and religious celebration was a major popular event; it was also the fullest extension of the confraternities' processional activity.[11]

We can turn from a printed report of a major celebration to an instructive painting of a lesser, but possibly more common procession: a Rosary procession. The scene was painted by a Venetian artist, Tommaso Dolabella (1560–1650), who moved to the Polish court. While it was probably painted when he was in Cracow, it reflects a Venetian origin. It is a very crowded scene. Christ, the Virgin and entourage are at top left, cherubs below distribute roses to leading figures in the procession, which stretches back into the centre of the painting, and curls downhill to boats in the water. These allude to the battle of Lepanto, the Christian naval victory over the Turks which as associated with the Rosary. As part of the procession there is a group of hooded *confratelli*, with a large banner of the Virgin and Child.[12]

Another kind of confraternity procession was less celebratory. This was the intercessory procession to curtail or ward off disasters, such as the processions in Perugia in June 1587 after a period of heavy rains. The previous year there had been a riot linked to the high prices of grain and bread, occasioned by poor harvests and the requisitions made for Rome; it had led to a change in the papal Governor of the city. Tension was likely to be high. With another harvest threatened, several parades were organised—on whose initiative is not entirely clear—for three days, with prayers for the end of the rains. Though various friars were involved, the main roles were played by confraternities; those of SS. Francesco, Domenico and Agostino (acting separately on different

---

[11] A. Giovio, *Descrittione de sei Apparati et pompe fatte in Perugia* (Perugia, 1610); cf. BCP Ms 3288, Anon., 'Storia di Perugia', pp. 116–53 which contains a version of the account, which could be the original. There was another printed description, which I have not been able to see, G. Panziera, *Relatione dell'apparato, e processione fatta in Perugia* (Perugia, 1609); Marinelli, *Le confraternite*, pp. 47, 873; SBF S. Francesco, no. 151 fols. 58v–62r: the confraternity obtained musicians from Spello, Assisi and Orvieto, paid for wine, a new standard and a new silver cross.

[12] R. Pallucchini, *La pittura veneziana del seicento* (2 vols., Milan, 1981), vol. 2 p. 515 and plate 191 black and white, with pp. 73–4 on Dolabella (c 1560–1650). The painting is in the church of the Canons Regular at Krasnik. Dolabella was a pupil of A. Vassilacchi called L'Aliense, who had worked in Perugia as well as Venice.

occasions), S. Pietro Martire and S. Pietro Apostolo. The processions involved the carrying of banners (*gonfaloni*), torches and crosses, and the saying of prayers in various churches. The company of S. Pietro Martire, according to one of its brothers, adapted its Rogation procession for this irregular importuning of God's mercy.[13] Rather similarly in Bologna in 1589 when heavy rains followed the usual Rogation processions of the company of S. Maria della Morte, it took the holy image of S. Luca on three other processions, with great devotion from the populace who saw the miracle of the Holy Mother liberating the city. A contemporary writer also praised the great processions of priests, confraternities and congregations made at times of distress—and the consequent offerings of gold objects to help the poor. They were some remedy against God's wrath, as well as a public assistance.[14]

2 PLAYS AND SACRED REPRESENTATIONS

Feast-day celebrations and processions were sometimes enhanced by the presentation of plays, pageants, *sacre rappresentazioni*, or tableaux. By the fifteenth century some were very elaborate and famous, especially in Florence. These were the religious equivalent of the secular *palio*, horse-races, jousts, stone-throwing battles, public dances and secular plays that were a significant part of communal life in various Italian cities; several have survived or been revived as tourist attractions. Some religious contributions were full-scale plays, others recitations with a background of elaborate scenic effects, machinery, and people dressed up in suitable costumes. Confraternities might be involved alongside other organisations, as in the Florentine displays for the *Festa di San Giovanni* for the city's patron saint, John the Baptist (23 June). On other occasions a particular confraternity was the chief organiser: the Florentine Compagnia de' Magi provided the main attractions for the celebration of Epiphany.[15] In Rome the Gonfalone produced a theatre of the Mysteries of the Passion on Good Friday, in the Colosseum; the Passion story was recited in front of painted scenery, illuminations and machines to raise Christ and the Virgin to Paradise.[16]

During the fifteenth century the play element, on a static site, seems to have been replaced by the use of extravagant tableaux at various sites which a procession would visit (for example the Palace of Herod in Florence's Piazza San Marco), or erected on carts moving with the procession. Authorities increasingly discouraged the drama

---

[13] ASP S. Pietro Martire, vol. 1, 'Adunanze', fol. 24v; cf. on 1586 riot, Black, 'Perugia and papal absolutism', pp. 533–4.

[14] BCB F.O.43 fol. 29v. G.B. Segni, *Discorso sopra la carestia e fame* (Ferrara, 1591), p. 34; idem, *Trattato sopra la carestia e fame* (Bologna, 1602), p. 89.

[15] Generally, and with exemplification: A. D'Ancona, ed. *Sacre rappresentazioni dei secoli XIV, XV, e XVI* (3 vols., Florence, 1872); V. De Bartholomeis (ed.), *Laude drammatiche e rappresentazioni sacre* (3 vols., Florence, 1943) with many of the lauds cited in vol. 1 coming from Perugia. More specifically for Florence: Hatfield, 'The Compagnia de' Magi', esp. pp. 108–19; Trexler, *Public Life*, esp chapter 8, 'The ritual of celebration', pp. 215–78. Cf. the instructive discussion of how plays were performed on the move in England, with scenic waggons and spectacular effects: W. Tydeman, *English Medieval Theatre 1400–1500* (London, Boston and Henley, 1987), esp. pp. 52–71 on the Croxton *Play of the Sacrament* which is seen as part of the European tradition; pp. 114–36 on the York Passion sequences using scenic waggons, and the problems of staging scenes in different locations; pp. 161–202 on general problems of staging; and p. 175 for mechanical effects in a Florentine staging of the Assumption in 1439, which may have influenced England.

[16] A Cavallaro, 'Antoniazzo Romano e le confraternite del Quattrocento a Roma', *RSRR*, 5 (1984), 356–60.

element; such occasions could get out of hand, as Florentine civic authorities found in the fifteenth century–because of ridiculous or bawdy presentations, or political comments. But there could be effective portrayals of biblical stories and emotional messages from the lives–dramatised or recited in verse–of Mary Magdalene or a leading local saint. But in 1536 plays were banned in Rome, though not in other cities of the Papal State. Post-tridentine provincial councils and synods added their disapprobation: Ravenna and Urbino banned plays altogether, while Florence and Genoa put them under stricter episcopal control.[17]

However confraternity-produced drama was not totally curtailed. In Bologna the S. Maria della Carità organised sacred representations in 1561 and 1640 of which the texts survive.[18] In Rieti until at least the 1590s plays were being produced by five of its nine confraternities, intermittently rather than on an annual basis, it seems. In the case of a 1584 production on the Passion of Christ it was specifically mentioned that the bishop not only permitted but personally funded it. Over the years the topics dramatised included the Passion, Ascension, Resurrection, the stories of Sts Barbara, John the Baptist, Biagio (Blaise) and George. People came from a distance, including deprived Rome, to see these productions. It is not clear whether they were all full dramas, or some were elaborately staged tableaux. Acting talent was available, since tragedies and comedies were performed in the city. In 1589 Pope Sixtus V's sister, Camilla Peretti, was honoured with a tragedy when staying in the bishop's palace on her way back from a pilgrimage to Loreto.[19]

More usual and acceptable in the sixteenth century were sacred representations in *tableaux vivants*, which might be mounted on carts for a procession. The Venetian *scuole* provided lavish examples, linked to their parade of relics. The Scuola di San Rocco was noted for its biblical scenes, though it also mounted more political scenes, as in 1511 to celebrate the formation of a League, when (against a tableau of figures of Venice and St Mark) actors showed a discomfited King of France confronting the Republic, St Mark and the Kings of Spain and England.[20]

An instructive example of such confraternity activity occurred in Todi in 1563. Bishop G.A. Cesi had invited the Capuchin friar Stefano of Faenza to preach the Lenten cycle. This led to the reactivation of the Monte di Pietà pawn-broking institution, with· a new confraternity to help administer it. Two elaborate representations were organised to raise capital to fund the Monte: the Triumph of the Passion on Holy Saturday, and the Triumph of the Resurrection on the Sunday after Easter.[21] About 600 persons participated as actors, or accompanied the carts and horses with tableaux. The organisers were the Monte confraternity, with others resurrected from their torpor and provided with new garments. Streets were decorated with tapestries and cloths, and the public joined the singing as the processions moved about the city. For the Passion, a Mount

[17] A.M. Terruggia, *Attività teatrale a Rieti nei secoli XV e XVI* (Perugia, 1966) [reprinted with index from *BSPU*, 62 (1965), 307–55], pp. 309–11; Meloni, 'Topografia', p. 27; Mansi, vol. 35, col. 695, vol. 36B, col. 601; Trexler, *Public Life*, pp. 254–6.

[18] Fanti, *Ospedale . . . Carità*, p. 64.

[19] Terruggia, pp. 307–55; her evidence, and its presentation, are unhelpful.

[20] Pullan, *Rich and Poor*, pp. 52–4 (for the 1511 celebration and a description of a biblical presentation by the *Scuola* at the festival of the Madonna in 1515), 59–62; cf. Wurthmann, 'The Council of Ten'.

[21] M. Pericoli (ed.), *Il trionfo della passione e resurrezione a Todi nella Pasqua 1563* (Todi, 1963); it reproduces the descriptive text contained in the Archivio Vescovile, Todi: S. Maria di Pietà, Registro delle Congregazioni, 1563–1705, fols. 3–11. On the Monti di Pietà see below chapter 10.4.

of Olives was created outside the Cathedral; the company of S. Giovanni led the other confraternities with the Saviour and his disciples to pray at the Mount. An Angel sang to Jesus to comfort him; Judas and a crowd appeared, and some of the Gospel story was recited. The yellow-robed S. Giovanni brothers then bound Jesus and led him off in procession. Other scenes took place at the Tribunal of Annas and Caiaphas (with Annas ostentatiously dressed); at the Palace of Herod, where a crowd of Jews cried out for Jesus to be crucified; Mount Calvary, with a large scene organised by the green-robed Annuziata company; at the Sepulchre where Christ was carried by brothers of the new Monte fraternity, in black robes with a red cross and Pietà on the front. The public reacted very emotionally, with much weeping; quantities of money and jewellery were donated to fund the Monte as the procession moved through the street.

For the Resurrection procession, after a sermon, the five main confraternities headed the parade in their different coloured robes. They were followed by King David, with a lyre, singing psalms; the Sybils, women with strange hair-styles and coloured habits; Prophets with long hair and books; Abraham, in velvet and brocade, turban and naked scimitar; Isaiah, in white satin with bare legs and a staff, using many fine gestures that moved the crowd to tears; Patriarchs, in green to express the hope of going to heaven, attached by green cords to a cart dressed in green, on which rode Christ dressed for the Resurrection; Death was at the feet of Christ, who had his right hand raised high, his left holding a cross with a standard, 'as one sees painted in many places'; at the corners of the cart were many kneeling angels in white with wings in various colours and gold and also attached to it were seven kings representing the deadly sins, each with a page-boy. Attached to them and to the cart, on a longer chain, came the terrifying Devil, shoeless and with a cross on his shoulder; he held the rudder of a cart painted all in red pulled by his apostles in black velvet; on top of the cart was a beautiful, bejewelled woman in crimson velvet, with her feet on a golden cross, carrying a naked sword in her right hand, and a chalice with the Host in her left; she represented the Catholic church. Prostrate at her right foot was a deformed servant girl, dishevelled in an old dress, representing the Synagogue; she had in her left hand various cards indicating the laws and ceremonies of the Jews, and in her right a rod (bacchetta) signifying rule by fear. This figure acted the part of a person conquered and timid, a servant and payer of tribute. (The Monte di Pietà had been designed to replace the private, mainly Jewish, moneylenders). Also on this cart were Hope and Charity with suitable emblems. Then came other figures representing the Evangelists, the four Doctors of the Church, Sts Stephen, Lawrence, Biagio, Lucy (with silver gilded cup, two eyes in one hand, a dagger in the other), Catherine (a piece of wheel on her back), Barbara (fortress in hand), Vincent (with white lily), Benedict (with silver pastoral) and, then the city's protectors, Sts Fortunato, Callisto and Cassiano, each with a model of Todi. The four kings, from the four parts of the world, followed. Behind all came the company of the Monte di Pietà, in black. After a parade through the streets to the cemetery and back to the main square, there was an enactment of Jesus meeting his Mother (greeting her in Latin). The procession went through other streets to an altar made up to look like Paradise. The Capuchin friar praised the Monte institution; the kings then led the way in taking offerings to the altar, followed by the confraternities, civic officials, and the populace.

These Todi representations and processions show the impact of a preaching friar, leading to the reinvigoration of confraternities and the revival of a philanthropic institution. The public was moved and instructed by the elaborate displays, and provided the funds. In subsequent years at least the Passion mystery play was reenacted. But in 1600 Bishop A. Cesi refused to license it, because 'it is no longer represented with that reverence and devotion that is suitable'. He recalled that once it was recited 'with many sins and unpleasant crimes'. Familiarity had turned to indifference and contempt.

The displays could become very elaborate and expensive; in Genoa confraternities built huge carts to carry giant illustrative figures of saints. By the mid-sixteenth century the expenditure on garments for the accompanying humans was deemed excessive. The most famous example was probably Naples' *Carro di Battaglino*, on Holy Thursday, organised by the noble confraternity of SS. Crocefisso. The confraternity started in 1579 and within ten years it was running a hospice for poor noble girls. In 1616 a leading Spanish noble and government official, P. Battaglino, secured the help of the confraternity in creating a fund to launch a nunnery, the Purità di Maria. The procession was started by him to help with fund-raising; finding himself in difficulties with his projects, he left it to the confraternity to organise them. The procession involved taking a statue of the Madonna on a lavishly decorated cart from the church of Montecalvario to the Royal Palace, accompanied by leading members of the court, halberdiers, Palatine guards, other officials, and confraternity brethren. At some point choirs and instruments were added, and various tableaux: fifteen groups of dummy figures (not actors), dressed to represent episodes in the life of Jesus and Mary. *Confratelli* and others escorted them. The carts were lavishly decorated with statues, flowers, candles and images and leading artists were recruited as designers. By 1653 the Viceroy of Naples, the Count of Onate, could claim this procession to be 'the most grandiose, sumptuous and majestic celebrated in all Italy'. But by then the confraternity could not afford it, and applied—successfully— for a royal subsidy. The *Battaglino* procession had become an integral part of viceregal court life; it came to dominate and control the confraternity in a secular way, ceased to be an instrument of fraternal religious devotion, or an aid to philanthropy.[22]

Some mysteries and displays were taken on pilgrimages to impress. For the 1600 Jubilee in Rome companies from Pisa, San Ginesio and Foligno in particular impressed with their accompanying representations. From Foligno the Compagnia della Misericordia arrived in Rome on 9 May at night; the brothers paraded with torches and carried on carts through the city mysteries representing the passion, death and resurrection of Christ, with children dressed as angels, and the enactment of dramatic episodes. They then met their host confraternity, the SS. Trinità. With such performances in Rome piety was publicly demonstrated.[23]

[22] Grendi, 'Morfologia', p. 293; A. Fiordelisi, 'La processione e il carro di Battaglino' *Napoli Nobilissima*, 13 (1904), 33–7, 54–7, 75–8.
[23] F. Clementi, *Il Carnevale romano nelle cronache contemporanee. 1: Dalle origini al secolo XVIII* (nd rev. edn, Città di Castello, 1939), pp. 360–1; F. Allevi, 'Una processione ginesina per il giubileo del 1600', in AA.VV. *Studi Maceratesi. II: Vita e Cultura del Seicento nella Marca. Atti dell'undecesimo convegno di Studi Maceratesi. Matelica 18–19 ottobre 1975* (Macerata, 1977), pp. 71–132; various confraternities were involved in the community's repeat production of the 'Trionfo di S. Chiesa', which they had previously presented in Rome during the 1575 Jubilee. The orginal production (and choice of topic) may have been to atone for the scandal of producing Lutheran heretics, including nine who were brothers in the confraternity of SS. Tommaso e Barnaba, who had been condemned in 1568. (See also Pastor, *Storia dei Papi*, vol. 8, pp. 209, 605–6).

3 PILGRIMAGES

The organised confraternity pilgrimage was an extension of the more normal processions. Most pilgrims, to sanctuaries or to Rome, would have gone as individuals, journeying in fulfilment of vows, as thanksgiving for graces received, in the hope of cures for ills or problems, as a penance or punishment. Later we will consider the philanthropic help offered them in Rome. Some confraternities however organised corporate pilgrimages; these seem to have increased in the sixteenth century, whether to sanctuaries such as those in Loreto (The Virgin's House, miraculously transported there by angels) and S. Maria degli Angeli, below Assisi, or to Rome. Partly there was greater enthusiasm for pilgrimages, fostered by increased indulgences, but given the recognised dangers of brigandage on some travel routes, especially from the 1570s, the group pilgrimage might appear safer. It could also be more enjoyable and less expensive than an individually organised journey.[24]

In 1600 the small Perugian confraternity of S. Pietro Martire was involved in two pilgrimages; one which it organised itself to S. Maria degli Angeli, at a cost of 2.50 ducats, the other to Rome for the Jubilee in conjunction with the larger and more prestigious company of S. Tommaso d'Aquino; brothers participating in this were subsidised by the whole company with one ducat.[25]

Perugia's three confederated confraternities organised a pilgrimage to Rome in 1575 for that Jubilee. Those going were allocated 3 *scudi* towards expenses; the confraternities also paid 35 *scudi* for a new standard to accompany them on their progress to Rome and around the city. This was later donated to the Gonfalone archconfraternity, which had presumably acted as their host in Rome. Under the impetus of this visit the S. Francesco confraternity officially recorded that certain brethren, notably the doctors and nobles, were lax in their religious duties, and should undertake works of charity and mercy. In 1577 or 1578 (the sources conflict over the date) it was the turn of the Perugian confraternities to host a Roman archconfraternity–the SS. Trinità–on its own pilgrimage tour. It included the composer Palestrina.[26] Music was an important element during pilgrimages and in the ceremonies organised for their reception. When on Ascension Day the Bologna confraternity of S. Maria della Morte received the company of S. Geminiano di Modona which was making a pilgrimage to Loreto, it gathered as many of the nobility as possible, and the group of musicians ('la più grossa musica') that had ever gone forth. The guests were taken in procession from the city gate to the Cathedral of S. Pietro, to the older and more famous church of S. Petronio and then to the confraternity hospital, where they were 'stupefied' by the superb apparatus and honours done them. The forty-five visitors were lodged in the houses of ten Bologna *confratelli*, and given a ceremonial send-off the next day.[27]

[24] On background: J. Sumption, *Pilgrimage. An Image of Medieval Religion* (London, 1975); P. Brezzi, *Storia degli Anni Santi. Da Bonifacio VIII ai giorni nostri* (Milan, 1975 edn.), esp. chapters 6–8 on the 1575, 1600 and 1625 Jubilees, and on Roman hospitality; Zardin, 'Le confraternite in Italia settentrionale', n. 27 for useful bibliography on confraternities and pilgrimages; P.F. Zino, *L'Anno Santo MDLXXV* . . . ([Venice, 1575]).

[25] ASP S. Pietro Martire, vol. 1 fol. 45r.

[26] SBF S. Domenico, vol. 430, fol. 89r; S. Francesco, vol. 457, fols. 121v, 127v–8v; BCP Ms 1221, Soti 'Annali', fol. 153v; A.S. Pietro Div. 38 fols. 121v–2r.

[27] BCB F.O.43 fol. 36r. The record reads 'Modona', a place not known to me; Modena may have been intended.

Significant aspects of confraternity pilgrimages can be exemplified from a long report on that organised by the Perugian Compagnia della Morte for the Jubilee in 1600; the following extensive précis should give some indication of what must have been the high point of fraternity life for most participants, and capture some of the reporter's enthusiasm. The account was written by Marc'Antonio Masci, a Cathedral canon, who had been on a similar pilgrimage to Rome in 1575, and was now lieutenant to the governor of the pilgrimage—and probably the chief organiser.[28] The decision to go was made in a general council meeting in November 1599, when organising officials were selected by ballot. Rules were formulated and put to the company; outsiders were invited to participate as associate members. Before departure, which was delayed by heavy rains, the participants' vestments were blessed by the bishop in the Cathedral; he gave a learned sermon and they then processed with torches and music around Perugia.[29] On the day of departure they either took communion in their oratories or in the Cathedral, assembled for the bishop's blessing, then formed the procession. Singing as they went, keeping strict order in squads behind their Cross, 140 set out; more were to join in Rome.

The procession crossed the river at Ponte Nuovo, escorted by the Della Morte company of Torgiano, which provided a meal. At Deruta the pilgrims were welcomed by three confraternities—Della Morte, Rosary and Sacrament—who, after the Perugians had sung a motet, provided a substantial meal in the square of roast kid, sausages, hams, cheeses, omelettes, expensive vegetables and fountains of water (pp. 8–9). Three miles from Deruta, at Casalina, they were greeted by the Benedictine monks of S. Pietro of Perugia (who owned and intensively farmed this area) and offered another meal. All these kind and loving people are to be remembered in the confraternity's prayers, said the much impressed canon Masci (p. 10). At Todi they were welcomed by three confraternities, and led to the Cathedral to be greeted by organ music, bell-ringing and many people. They received supper from the Franciscans and accommodation from Todi gentlemen. The following night at Narni the Misericordia fraternity met them, and they were lodged in hostelries or by local gentlemen. On the third day they lunched at Borghetto and spent the night at Rignano (presumably without ceremony, and at their own cost). The following afternoon they were met by an emissary from Ascanio Della Corgna, Marchese of Castiglione del Lago (now one of the most important nobles in the Perugia region), who provided another feast in two carts—again described in loving detail. 'All the brothers were fully consoled by the magnificence and liberality of this Lord' (p. 12). Monsignor Cesare Della Corgna, who rivalled his brother in

[28] A.S. Pietro Mazzo XXXVI 'Descrittione del Peregrinaggio fatto dalla compagnia della Morte di Perugia a Roma a pigliare il santissimo Giubileo l'anno 1600. Alli 7 di maggio'. Anonymous unpaginated booklet of 36 pp. My own pagination will be cited in the text and notes for the rest of this section. A note on [p. 15] indicates that Marc'Antonio Masci, lieutenant to the Governor of the pilgrimage, is the author. Lacunae, interpolations and corrections suggest this is autograph. At least one page is missing at the end. On the Della Morte see: Crispolti, *Perugia Augusta*, pp. 175–6; Marinelli, *Le confraternite*, pp. 817–48; G.B. Crispolti, 'Memorie di Perugia dall'anno 1578 al 1586', *Cronache della Citta di Perugia*, ed. A. Fabretti (5 vols., Turin, 1887–94), vol. 4, p. 43, which mentions three choirs of musicians in 1581. On Masci: A. Oldoini, *Athenaeum Augustum in quo Perusinorum scripta publice exponentur* (Perugia, 1678). p. 235; G. Ermini, *Storia dell'Università di Perugia* (2 vols., rev. edn., Florence, 1971), vol. 1 p. 621.

[29] [p. 5]: '. . . con un bello dotto, et affettuoso ragionamento ci essorto et inanimi a quel santo peregrinaggio, con l'esempio di Giacobbe Patriarca e di Tobiolo, e fu tanto gustoso, e contanta pietà, e carità detto, che restammo tutti pienamente consolati . . .'; the bishop was N. Comitoli. Eubel, *Hierarchia*, vols. 3, p. 272, 4, p. 277; Black, 'Perugia and post-tridentine church reform', p. 435.

courtesy and love towards the Della Morte fraternity (of which the Marchese had once been a principal member), came personally to escort the governor of the pilgrimage, Marchese Alfonso da Este, in his carriage to the Villa Giulia. Representatives of the Roman archconfraternity Della Morte greeted the Perugians at Prima Porta and the Villa Giulia, and provided fifty large wax torches to enable them to make a noble and solemn entrance into Rome. The Della Corgna family provided food and money, continuing the generosity shown by Cardinal Fulvio Della Corgna (formerly bishop of Perugia) when the Morte company had made its pilgrimage in 1575.[30] The pilgrims were ordered to enter Rome with bare heads and feet, eyes lowered, modestly and devoutly, remembering that they were in Rome where they were observing similar fraternities coming for the holiest Jubilee, or more immediately out of curiosity; and they would have time to see the greatness of Rome.[31]

The Perugian company was met by 200 members of the Roman archconfraternity, whch included many leading prelates and Marchese Ascanio Della Corgna, who provided some extra musicians for the joint procession from Porta del Popolo. Behind the procession came forty carriages of Roman and Perugian gentlemen and nobles and a large crowd on foot. The company's demeanour, showing much humility and devotion, provoked many to tears, and it was reported that the Pope had received no greater satisfaction from the behaviour of any other company.[32] At the archconfraternity's Oratory they were welcomed by the most beautiful music on the organ, violins and with 'falsetti rarissimi'; from the bass Signor Paolo from the papal chapel, the lighter falsetto Signor Lodovico, and the violinist Signor Lorenzo, whose playing 'seized our souls from our bodies'.[33] After two motets the pilgrims had their feet washed with elaborate ceremony by their hosts, in imitation of Christ (pp. 22–3). They then ate in the hostel refectory, which was decorated with tapestries, while listening to readings (by a boy aged ten dressed as an angel) interspersed with organ music, and finally Lorenzo's violin. Canon Masci emphasises the noble impression made on the Perugian pilgrims by the archconfraternity's exemplary conduct.[34]

[30] On the Della Corgna: M.M. Donati-Guerrieri, *Lo stato di Castiglione del Lago e della Corgna* (Perugia, 1972); Black, 'Perugia and post-tridentine church reform', pp. 432–3 on Cardinal Bishop Fulvio della Corgna. He was responsible for Masci becoming a canon, and Masci delivered the funeral oration on him: BCP Ms 1221 Sotii, 'Annali', fol. 178r; A. Gabrijelcic, 'Alle origini del Seminario di Perugia (1559–1600)', *BSPU*, 68 (1971), p. 44.

[31] [pp. 16–17]: 'dando comandato espresso a tutti ch'andassero con la testa scoperta con gli occhi bassi, con modestia, e con ogni devotione, ricordevoli ch'erano in Roma dove osservavano simile fraternite si andavano per il santissimo Giubileo, o piu tosto per curiosità; che per veder le grandesse di roma havrebbero hauto tempo; e pero per la processione non guardassero nessuna cosa, ne meno parlassero, se non quanto era necessario, e per non usare mala creanza a chi havesse dimandata loro di qualche cosa.'

[32] [pp. 20–1]: 'che con tanta riverenza e somissione facessero questa entrata che fu detto che il Papa, non havea ancora hauta maggior sodisfattione che dall nostra compagnia, e che n'era restato molto consolato. sia il tutto a gloria di S.D.N.'.

[33] [p. 21]: 'v'era per Basso il S. Paolo Basso di Cappella cantore molto leggiadro per falsetto il S. Lodovico gratiosissimo che con gorga e passaggi mostrava quanto valesse in questa professione. il violino era sonato dal S. re Lorenzo discipolo del S. Giambattista detto dal Violino, e servente carissimo dell Ill.mo Vescovo di Padoua, il quale con tiratione et arcate dolcessime rapiva gli animi nostri fuor de' corpi, e ben facea conoscere, ch'era scolaro del primo huomo d'Italia in quella professione, e lasciava in dubio, qual di loro valesse piu il maestro o il discepolo'. The Bishop of Padua was Marco Cornaro. Eubel, *Hierarchia*, vols. 3, p. 267, 4, p. 275.

[34] [p. 25] 'Non poteano satiarsi i fratelli nostri di lodare magnificare, e esaltare la cortesia amorevolezza e gentilezza di tanto Signori che si degnassero far atti di tanta humilta, nel che bensi conosceva lo promesse lo zelo della religione cristiana, e che erano veramente imitatori di cristo nostro Signore che venne a servire, e non essere servito. e restammo tanto edificati di questi nobili esempi' [in margin: e tanto pieni di pietà] 'che piu d'una volta lagrimiammo di dolcessa, e di devotione'.

The next day, Ascension Day, the company celebrated in the archconfraternity church, with many receiving communion. They then went to Mass celebrated by Pope Clement VIII in the new (but incomplete) St Peter's.[35] A meal back in the hostel, prepared by their own servants, was accompanied by a reading from the whole book (unspecified) of Jean Gerson. It was announced that the Pope had conceded that these pilgrims could fulfil the Jubilee pilgrimage in one day, and still be eligible for the full indulgences; the company went back to St Peter's to kiss the Pope's feet in gratitude.[36] The next morning the company heard a beautiful discourse and received communion from Cardinal Gallo in the Cappella Gregoriana in St Peter's, and were shown the Lance and the *Volto Santo*.[37] They sang the *Jubilate*, and headed for the first of the four required churches, S. Paolo. On the way they were refreshed by wine and confections provided by some rich and noble Germans who had been students in Perugia. At S. Paolo they sang psalms, visited the four designated altars, then lunched, courtesy of the bishop of Padua, with a great variety of wine and fish on offer.[38] They moved towards S. Giovanni in Laterano, but first visited SS. Nereo e Achille, an early Christian church which had recently been restored by its titular cardinal, Cesare Baronio, who now greeted the pilgrims warmly and presented them with images of the saints.[39] At S. Giovanni in Laterano they were shown numerous relics, and climbed the holy stair. At S. Maria Maggiore they saw the reliquaries and visited the pilgrimage altars. They were invited to visit the church of S. Prassede to see its many relics. They then returned to the archconfraternity, on the way passing the new church of Madonna de' Monti (Giacomo Della Porta's influential design). They were welcomed with another feet-washing ritual, and a delicious supper, with the same musicians. The Perugian pilgrims remained in Rome for Sunday, and received crowns blessed for them by the Pope 'with very many beautiful indulgences' (p. 32).

On Monday, after Mass, the Perugians set off home, donating their standard to their host archconfraternity, as well as the torches that had not been fully used. Some of the Roman company saw them depart at Porta del Popolo, from where they retraced the outward journey via Prima Porta, Rignano, Borghetto and Narni. They then went to Terni, where they formed into orderly groups, and sang psalms. At Spoleto they were greeted by the local Della Morte company and made a solemn entrance, to be shown relics in the Cathedral, and in another church whose name the reporter forgot. There was good hospitality from local gentlemen, and some were presented with very good

---

[35] [pp. 25–6]: 'poi ci trovammo tutti a S. Pietro alla messa che celebrar sopra l'altar di S. Pietro, nella Chiesa nuova il sommo Pontefice Clemente viii e fummo presenti alla solenne benedittione che S.S. ta diede dalle logge come e solito.' On the Roman churches visited, and their condition at the time, Blunt, *Guide*, under relevant churches, and bibliography cited by him.

[36] [pp. 26–7]. It helped that a papal *Camoriero* was a Perugian, V. Vincioli.

[37] Cardinal Gallo; presumably meaning A.M.Galli/Gallo, former bishop of Perugia, rather than T. Galli, the more famous 'Cardinal Como', see Black, 'Perugia and post-tridentine church reform', p. 435. The Lance of St Longinus and the Veil of St Veronica were two of the relics around which G.L. Bernini was to design the Crossing of St Peter's and its sculptures: I. Lavin, *Bernini and the Crossing of St Peter's* (New York, 1968); Blunt, *Guide*, p. 133.

[38] [p. 29]: 'i vini furono delicatissimi Pusillipi, lagrima, montepulciani et altri esquisiti, che si lasciano per brevita, pesci buonissimi Cestali sturioni linguatti, triglia sarde, spigoli, e simili, pastici di sturioni formaggi ricotti, et altri latticesij, con scafi carcioffi mandorlini et altri frutti di quel tempo'.

[39] Masci seemed to think that Nereo and Achille were one saint, [p. 30]: 'e trovammo che SS. Ill.ma v'era presente e vi volea far cantare vespro, ci accolse con gran cortesia, e con molta domesticchezza; e ci fece dono d'alcune imagini di S. Nereo Archileo, e domitilla in Rome'.

wine. They trooped through Foligno to Assisi where, as there was not enough accommodation for all, some squads lodged below in S. Maria degli Angeli. They dined in S. Francesco, and saw relics in its sacristy. The next day the fraternity's priests celebrated in S. Maria degli Angeli, and many took communion. On they moved to Ponte S. Giovanni, to be welcomed by terrible rains but a good meal from the rector and others, and so to the monastery of S Pietro at one of the gates into Perugia. There they made arrangements for a solemn entrance. They were greeted by members of the three federated confraternities, and those of their own company who had remained behind; they processed to the Cathedral to greet the bishop and hear a final, very beautiful, sermon. The report ends, incomplete, at this final stage of the great pilgrimage.

The report on this Jubilee pilgrimage has been summarised at length to illustrate various points about confraternities and their activities. The participating pilgrims were probably mainly high-born; servants accompanied them and shared in some of the lavish hospitality. They did well from noble connections. The company made a major impression as it travelled and in Rome. The journey of one fraternity involved many others en route—in religious singing and ceremonies, as well as hospitality. The Perugians" took their own singing seriously; canon Masci—and by implication many confratelli—greatly appreciated the musical reception in Rome. The company was very interested in relics—or was assumed to be. The pilgrimage involved frequent communion. The indulgences to which they earned the right of access by their efforts were much prized—especially as the Pope allowed them to perform the pilgrimage to the great basilicas all in one day, not three. Canon Masci was notably impressed by the food and wine provided in great quantity, and quality. The generosity was beyond all expectations, even by comparison with that received by the company in 1575. The Perugian fraternity must have been spared much anticipated expenditure, even if some encounters with other confraternities had been planned in advance. Given the length of the report, and the details on food and music, it is somewhat surprising that Canon Masci offered no comments on ceremonial ritual, even at the pontifical Mass, nor on the churches visited, beyond noting that St Peter's and S. Maria de' Monti were new. Did they fulfil throughout the injunction, issued on entering Rome, to keep eyes lowered, sensing only with ears and mouths? This detailed account also indicates the effort expended by leading church dignitaries and noblemen in the Roman archconfraternity during a Jubilee celebration, humbling themselves to wash the feet of pilgrims and serve them at table—even if these pilgrims were mostly from the upper strata of society.

The public display of confraternities in processions and pilgrimages, which have been exemplified by a few lengthy illustrations, could be elaborate and costly. It could represent some of the deepest devotion of fraternal societies and have a profound impact on the outside world, encouraging outsiders to participate in religious devotion, join confraternities, and contribute funds. But the public ceremonies could equally cause tensions and improper behaviour, by members or outsiders; the pursuit of honour and precedence could come to predominate; a money-earning, philanthropic, activity turn into a costly extravanganza. However, one suspects that most contemporaries praised the external devotions of the confraternities, including their social aspects, long after a few worried puritanical bishops like Angelo Cesi or Carlo Borromeo—and modern historians concerned about cost-effectiveness—judged them irreligious.

6

CONFRATERNITIES AND FINANCES

Confraternities needed some money, intermittently at least, for their religious life even if they did not embark on major displays or philanthropic work. Money was required for maintaining, if not originally building, their chapel or oratory; for hiring priests and chaplains if clerical members or monastic hosts did not provide their services free; for robes, for crosses, decorations and processional banners; and even if all the rest was given by individuals, the institution would almost invariably have had to fund the supply of candles and torches for major occasions. Most confraternities probably lived a hand-to-mouth existence, soliciting alms and fraternal contributions as needed; some guaranteed a comparatively stable income through entrance fees, annual levies, and rents from properties which had been bequeathed to the fraternity or bought as investments. A few accumulated much wealth from donations and testamentary dispositions, becoming substantial property owners, or holders of investment bonds, and so being able to finance major philanthropic enterprises or lavish public processions.

Little is known about the financial working of confraternities and their philanthropic institutions. The subject has not proved popular with the historians concerned with confraternities, understandably so, since financial records are hard to find, and where available are patchy and ill-preserved, as I have discovered for Perugia. Few confraternities were systematic record keepers (as bishops and the Venetian Council of Ten complained), and most officials probably only considered it worth preserving documents proving entitlement to property and incomes. Recent studies however have indicated that a certain amount can be discovered at least about the larger philanthropic institutions in Rome or Venice from their own records. A few investigations have shown that the long and tedious search through the kilometres of surviving notarial registers of wills and property deals can bear fruit. But the study of testamentary dispositions generally has not proved enticing to Italian research students.

The discussion below indicates some of the resources available to confraternities, and on what it might be spent. Certain sources of income, notably specific legacies, could change the activities and priorities of the brotherhood. The selected examples show the considerable diversity in resources, and in the priorities involved in spending. It is hoped that these samples of what has been discovered for a few societies will stimulate some historians to pay more attention to confraternity finances.

Most confraternities would not have had, nor expected to have, a regular income based on property or legacies. The 1573 apostolic visitation to Assisi indicated that nine of the eleven city confraternities investigated did have a regular income, in money, grain or wine, but it might be as little as a barrel of wine a year. In the rest of the diocese only ten of twenty-nine confraternities had a recognised income, sometimes very meagre. In the similar visitation of the Foligno diocese none of the confraternities reported a regular income; all lived off alms—and all indulged in some charitable activity on that basis.[1] Many societies expected or wanted this situation. The SS. Annunziata of Lecce stated it had no regular income, and to fulfil its main duty of clothing the naked poor, it organised suitable mature members to solicit alms outside the Jesuit church to which they were attached. Soliciting alms for other people (rather than oneself) was felt by many to be a high and noble form of philanthropy, though by the seventeenth century some nobles seem to have found it a little ignoble and tried to leave alms-seeking to others.[2]

The Bologna S. Maria della Vita in its fifteenth-century statutes implied that it relied primarily on members' legacies, and ruled that those who did not leave something to the confraternity hospital in their will would not have fraternal participation at their funeral. In 1554–5 the confraternity agreed to have, like other confraternities, a collection box beside the altar for the poor—called 'la cassa di poveri infermi dell'oratorio della compagnia di S. Maria della Vita'—so that anybody could help 'per charita'. Such funding was clearly inadequate because the record book shows that when the society needed to help a particular person a special levy was imposed on members; for example, in 1557 Lucio Forbesini was declared incurably ill and unable to work, so brothers were asked to commit themselves to paying a monthly contribution for him.[3]

Most confraternity funding was by means of a haphazard mixture of resources. The Venetian Scuola della Beata Vergine della Concezione (in S. Francesco della Vigna) received its chapel in 1582 from Federico Curelli, who also provided a legacy to fund dowries for poor girls. The funds were increased by alms paid in the chapel from those coming to benefit from the indulgences which had been associated with devotions made there, and by what officially appointed alms-collectors could garner around the city. These alms-seekers were paid half their takings (at least from 1646), though paid alms-collecting was normally illegal in Venice.[4] Similarly in Rome the Pietà dei Carcerati gained some of the resources to help prisoners from paid alms-collectors (cercanti). This confraternity was privileged to have two fixed, licensed, alms boxes, one in the Campidoglio, the other in the Borgo. Its income from these sources was satisfactory, but as its reputation grew it received a fixed annual income from Pope Sixtus V of 2,050 scudi, later augmented by Clement VIII. Then there were major legacies from leading clerical supporters like Cardinal Antonio Barberini, as well as smaller donations. By the later seventeenth century there was a substantial accumulation of rentable shops, houses, gardens and rooms, to ensure a reasonably regular income and make the society less dependent on the vagaries of alms-collecting.[5] More unusually the

[1] Proietti Pedetta, 'Alcune note', pp. 461–2, 471–2; eadem 'Le visite', pp. 533–4.
[2] Lopez, 'Le confraternite laicali', pp. 213–16. On alms-giving and seeking see below chapter 9.
[3] BCB F.O.6 fol. 10r; F.O.14 fols. 7r–v, 12v–13r. Later on the brethren were making regular contributions for the saying of Offices and Masses.
[4] ASVen Scuole piccole, Busta 125/126, esp. fols. 100r and 8r, 9v.
[5] Paglia, 'La Pietà dei Carcerati' pp. 121, 135, 192–4, 208, 217–18.

national confraternity of S. Giovanni dei Genovesi in Rome relied almost entirely for its funding on a set levy of sixty *baiocchi* on each Genoese ship (or ship with a Genoese crew) entering the port of Ripa Grande. In 1624 this meant about 9,200 *baiocchi* (or 100 ducats) from 153 ships.[6]

Confraternities with financial resources could face problems in making effective use of their potential. The records for SS. Trinità, Venice, reveal difficulties in securing payments of legacies in the first place, in maintaining regular incomes from old donations, in keeping property in good repair to maximise rents that would have provided the fund from which to pay dowries for poor girls.[7]

My own researches into the haphazard and incomplete records of Perugian confraternities indicate the muddled situation of small and medium-sized companies. The society of Buon Gesù, with twenty-three members in 1545 largely concerned with their own affairs, relied on irregular donations and fines imposed on members for misdemeanors, such as swearing or playing immoral games. In S. Pietro Martire the constitutions and the council meetings both indicate that rents from shops and houses covered normal expenditure, most notably from property in the second most important square of the city, donated in 1441. This income was more significant than the twenty *soldi* entrance fee. The brothers could sometimes afford to provide dowries, but not when rebuilding or decorating their premises.[8] S. Pietro Apostolo's mediocre income also came largely from rents, especially of a granary. To build a new oratory after 1577 it was decided to sell property and raise loans, which were still seemingly being repaid up to the 1640s with donations from, and fines on, brothers. In 1601 they agreed to sell a 1471 printed Missal to one of the brothers for 2.50 *scudi*, to pay for a new cover (*benda*) for their Crucifix. The inventories suggest that this confraternity had an adequate supply of books and equipment. But it was operating close to the financial margins, and had to be very selective over what it could undertake at any given point.[9]

The three confederated Perugian confraternities were in a more solid position. They derived income from shops and houses in the city, and from lands in the countryside; they raised loans to buy land, or sold houses to liquidate outstanding loans. In 1579 between them they borrowed 1,500 *scudi* to buy grain to give to the poor during a food crisis. By the 1650s S. Francesco was using printed forms for basic contracts in renting farms and shops; the forms were probably provided by the papal financial department, the Camera Apostolica, but they still suggest a regular and business-like approach to confraternity funding. A number of legacies led to the establishment of specific trusts; that of 100 florins from Virginia, widow of Giapeco Grasso, in 1573 became a trust fund for providing dowries for poor girls. It should be stressed that these confraternities were

---

[6] G. Mira, 'Aspetti economici delle confraternite romane', *RSRR*, 5 (1984), 232–3; Serra, 'Funzioni e finanze', p. 273 n. 32.

[7] ASVen Scuole piccole, Busta 766, 'Libro Primo 1531–59' and 'Libro Secondo 1560–76' *passim*.

[8] BCP Ms 948 'Libro dei conti e ricordi della confraternita del Buon Gesù, 1545–1588', e.g. fols. 2r, 6v, 11r, 19r; *Constitutioni . . . S. Pietro Martire, Perugia*, chapter 17; ASP S. Pietro Martire, vol. 1, 'Adunanze' fols. 4r, 5r–6r; BCP Ms 3139 'Regola et Constitutioni' chapter 1 mentions 20 *soldi* entrance fee.

[9] ASP S. Pietro Apostolo, vol. 20, 'Adunanze' esp. fols. 2r, 3v, 9v–10r (Missal), 14r, 15r; vol. 6, 'Depositario 1531–1552'; vol. 7, 'Depositario 1552–7'; vol. 1, 'Miscellanea. Entrata e Uscita. Varia 1478–1647', esp. fols. 161v–3r, and [changing to pagination numbering] pp. 164–5, 171–2, 176, 183, 191, 200, 209–10, 236, 244–5.

not receiving the extensive legacies that went to the old dominant monasteries, the Dominican S. Domenico and Benedictine S. Pietro.[10]

In the overall context of testamentary dispositions it is likely that confraternities did not feature prominently, but much more work could profitably, if tediously, be undertaken in this area. While French pamphlets of the period might emphasise that generosity in the last will and testament could readily open the gates of Paradise, Italian donors may not have been generous outside the family. Studies of Bologna wills during the plague crisis of 1630–1 show that confraternities had a low priority, even those considered most relevant because dedicated to the plague saints, Rocco and Sebastiano. The Opera dei Mendicanti for confined poor (to be studied in chapter 10.1.) did receive some gifts, but the traditional ecclesiastical institutions benefited more. Sacrament confraternities tended to receive liturgical equipment. When the mason Giacomo Toppi, dying of plague in June 1630, made his parochial Sacrament company his residual heir, and left only five *soldi* to his family of two brothers, it may have been designed as a disinheriting snub.[11]

An indication of the kinds of donations that might come to confraternities is provided by A. Noto's chronological survey of donations to the poor he found in Milanese archives. By no means all the contributions he catalogued and summarised were channelled through confraternities. A rather limited number of societies seem to benefit, though there is an expansion from the later sixteenth century onwards. The donations were in land as well as money values. Often the donor specified how the legacy should be spent—on dowries for poor girls, on food for the poor, on helping prisoners; and the confraternity might well be limited in the choice of recipients by stipulations that preference should be given to relatives of the donor, or to noble or respectable poor girls when providing dowries.[12]

Legacies and donations to confraternities obviously could affect their devotions, and their philanthropic activities, especially if the amount was disproportionately large. It was easiest when a donor specified that Masses and prayers should be said in return for his gift, but imposed no other specific duties or allocations. Andrea Santacroce in 1471

---

[10] SBF S. Domenico, no. 427, 'Adunanze' fols. 94v, 104r; S. Francesco no. 511 (a) various documents relating to land and rents from 1590s to 1650s; nos. 511 (c) and (d) contain certificates of land measurements; no. 457 'Verbali' fols. 103r–4v, on dowry fund. Cf. on the monastery of S. Domenico: ASP Corporazioni Soppresse, 5. S. Domenico, vol. 8 'Ricordanze–Memoriali del Convento 1566–1720', esp. fols. 33r–8r listing lands, woods, houses, etc. held in 1577, when their value amounted to about 9,470 florins for 94 pieces; this volume notes a number of legal battles over substantial legacies when challenged by others in the family, notably of Francesco Herculani in the 1570s. In 1580 the monastery received a residual legacy of 5,000 florins from Captain Seracino Montemellini and his wife, which helped finance a major building programme. On S. Pietro see Black, 'Perugia and post-tridentine church reform', pp. 447–9 with sources.

[11] A. Pastore, 'Testamenti in tempo di peste; la pratica notarile a Bologna nel 1630', *Società e Storia*, 16 (1982), 263–97; *idem*, 'Rapporti familiari e pratica testamentaria nella Bologna del Seicento', *Studi Storici*, 25, no. 1 (January-March 1984), 153–68, which studies 470 wills, 320 of males, 150 of females, made in 1630; (G. Toppi discussed p. 165); cf. C.C. Fairchilds, *Poverty and Charity in Aix-en-Provence 1640–1789* (Baltimore and London, 1976), pp. 27, 55.

[12] Noto, *Gli amici dei poveri*. For the period 1501–1600 he named, quoted or summarised 741 benefactions (pp. 135–154); for 1601–1700 525 benefactions (pp. 255–344), and summarised the yield in terms of land measurements, housing, monetary or food values where these were specified. I was not able to consult this work long enough to work out how much went to confraternities. Some significant entries will be cited in chapter 9 below.

left fifty florins to the Roman Società del S. Salvatore ad Sancta Sanctorum to commemorate anniversaries. Most of this family through the century seem to have entrusted the minding of their anniversaries to this confraternity, and to the Società di S. Maria delle Grazie e della Consolazione, to which they also belonged. One assumes that such obligations could be fulfilled, with profit from the donation. The considerable increase during the fifteenth century in the number of anniversary masses to be said in some major churches—without adequate funding for priests—alarmed the delegates at the Council of Trent, who urged bishops and abbots to limit the commitments. It is not evident that the burden of masses affected Italian confraternities excessively.[13]

A large donation could turn a confraternity into a major philanthropic organisation. The Roman SS. Annunziata alla Minerva, well funded by Pius V in 1566 with 5,000 scudi, was left heir to Urban VII's patrimony of 30,000 scudi, and thereby became the city's leading provider of dowries for poor girls. The archconfraternity Stimmate could similarly provide assistance, when the notorious Beatrice Cenci on the eve of her execution allocated it her own rich dowry.[14]

In Naples the noble society of SS. Crocefisso dei Cavalieri was launched in 1553 under Theatine influence, primarily to look after prisoners. In 1587 a legacy from Costanza del Carretto enabled assistance to be given to those condemned to the galleys. In 1620–1 various legacies, such as those of Scipione de Curtis and the princess of Avellino (worth 3,000 ducats), led the company to provide dowries systematically. When Giovanna Morra added her legacy for such a purpose, she also committed the oratory to celebrating 500 Masses a year, and spending fifty ducats on candles and music for the sacrament to be exhibited every Monday in the Theatine church of S. Paolo. With this confraternity the well-organised saying of Masses for the dead may have become the inducement for donors to leave more money also for charitable purposes, so that the burden of Masses was still not economically counter-productive.[15] One of the largest private donations to assistance work came from the Netherlands merchant and art collector in Naples, Gaspare Roomer, who allegedly left 30,000 ducats; from this the Pio Monte della Misericordia became a major philanthropic assistance organisation (as well as art patron).[16]

Studies of the income and expenditure of Venetian confraternities, great and small, have proved revealing for an understanding of priorities as well as funding. R. Mackenney's detailed analysis of the goldsmith's scuola from 1540 to 1553 shows that 67 per cent of the income came from members' fees: as candle-money (luminaria of ten soldi per member a year, which more than covered the actual costs of candles), entrance fees, fines, and levies from the Ascension Day market. About 25 per cent of the income

[13] A. Esposito Aliano, 'Famiglia, mercanzia e libri nel testamento di Andrea Santacroce (1471)', Aspetti della vita economica a culturale a Roma nel Quattrocento, ed. P. Brezzi (Rome, 1981), pp. 207–8 and n. 48, 217. On the wider problem of anniversary masses: R. Gaston, 'Liturgy and patronage in San Lorenzo, Florence, 1350–1650', Patronage, Art and Society in Renaissance Italy, eds. F.W. Kent and P. Simons (Canberra and Oxford, 1987), pp. 129–31.

[14] Monachino, p. 251; Maroni Lumbroso and Martini, Le confraternite romane, pp. 51–3.

[15] M.G. Rienzo, 'Nobili e attività caritativa a Napoli nell'età moderna. L'esempio dell'Oratorio dei Cavalieri in S. Paolo Maggiore', Per la storia sociale e religiosa del Mezzogiorno d'Italia, vol. 2, eds. L. Galasso and C. Russo (Naples, 1982), pp. 262–3, 266–7, 280–6.

[16] S. Musella, 'Il Pio Monte della Misericordia e l'assistenza ai "poveri vergognosi" (1665–1724)' in Galasso and Russo (eds.), vol. 2, p. 296; Painting in Naples, pp. 16, 63–4, 227, 239–40.

in this period came from past investments, especially in the *monti*. In expenditure 21.85 per cent went on oil and wax (for lighting lamps before a devotional image, and processional candles), 19.88 per cent on alms, 8.76 per cent on priests, 8.28 per cent on facilities for the market, 3.56 per cent on musicians. As a percentage the alms contribution was reasonable; but the actual sums were small, since the amount spent in direct alms in a year, which might be divided between eighteen poor persons, was about what a master builder was paid for four days' work. Or, the average payment to a *povero* in alms a year (just under $3\frac{1}{2}$ *lire*) was a little more than a *lavorante*, journeyman, received as three days' wages. While the modern reader might judge the amount spent on candles as disproportionately high—'a guild might spend as much on burying two dead members as for sixteen who were still alive'—'in a sense candles lighted the way through the vale of tears and showed the path to eternal life'.[17] In the contemporary view the commemoration in the form of burning candles might have been better appreciated than a few *lire* spent prolonging a sick or miserable life by a few days.

The Venetian *Scuole Grandi* had a complex financial organisation. By the end of the sixteenth century they had large incomes from many sources; but they had considerable outlays, not all of which were strictly devotional or philanthropic. They were not immune from government impositions of taxation or forced contributions for example, to the galleys, that drained resources. These *Scuole* had graduated entrances fees, and annual payments from some. They were inclined to open their books to new members, above the legal limits on enrolments, in order to raise extra funds for specific purposes—with or without the prior permission of the Council of Ten. This move can also be found in the *scuola piccola* of S. Maria dei Mercanti. This *scuola* had an annual minimum *luminaria* fee of one ducat and, one deduces, an entrance payment. It considerably expanded its membership in the 1540s. On 19 December 1546 the official record stated that to help pay for new building they would allow 100 new members; half the money so raised would be for building work.[18]

The *Scuole Grandi* accumulated legacies and invested heavily in land and property; as lay institutions and not 'pious places' in the eyes of the Republic they escaped the republican laws against mortmain, though periodically some officials tried to include them. When they had the necessary control over their investments they tended to rely on renting out city property on short leases, the better to cover against inflation. Much was invested in government bonds, *monti*, which returned 3 per cent to 7 per cent annually. S. Marco derived about 70 per cent of its income in 1590 from *monti*, and only 30 per cent of its income came from real property. When subsequently it had to liquidate its *monti* and move more capital into property its income dropped considerably. These *Scuole Grandi* also administered major trusts. S. Rocco was involved, directly or indirectly, in about sixty trusts between 1509 and 1610. The leading ones

[17] Mackenney, 'Trade Guilds', pp. 149–92, esp. pp. 153 and 180 (value of alms), 186 and 191 (quotes). Figures and analysis now in his *Tradesmen and Traders*, pp. 171–3, with Fig. 5.1 and Table 5.1 (where the income from legal action should be 1.22 per cent no 11.22 per cent).

[18] Pullan, *Rich and Poor*, esp. pp. 88–94, 140–56 on membership fees and numbers, taxation and galleys. Wurthmann's 'The Council of Ten' will deal with similar policies and actions by the Ten in the fifteenth century; ASVen Scuole piccole, Busta 420 fol. 45v (when officials agreed to the increase and allocation of fees by 18–3), and cf. fols. 40r–1r for the addition of 100 members in November 1545, fol. 61v for 39 elected in April 1550.

were those bequeathed by Maffeo Dona (1528) for funding hospital and prison work; by Nicolo Moro (1552) for providing dowries; by Piero Zucca (1563) which enabled the distribution of about 1,000 ducats a year to the poor; by Pietro Cornovi 'della Vecchia' (1585) also for alms-giving; and in 1609 by Maria Marucini, who provided 6,000 ducats for funding dowries. Some of these trusts were predictably subject to qualifications, notably that relatives of donors should receive preference; sometimes they were liable to taxation; the administration might be shared with outside bodies or individuals. But such trusts were the means to much philanthropic activity. They were one of the factors that explained the considerable variations between the *Scuole Grandi* in how they apportioned their charitable expenditure between types of assistance—dowries (favoured by S. Giovanni Evangelista), general alms-giving (about half of S. Rocco's charity), hospitals and so forth. Aspects of these expenditures will be discussed again in chapters 9 and 10.[19]

It is almost impossible to judge how far confraternities responded to crises, and changes in charitable needs—issues which will be discussed in the following chapters—because we lack records concerning the state of confraternity finances over many years. However, in the case of Venice's San Rocco, B. Pullan was able to produce usable figures of expenditure for the period 1551 to 1620. His tables suggest a major jump in charitable expenditure in the 1580s and 1590s, and particularly for hospitals, which might be interpreted as a response to crises and new needs. On the other hand it might be more a question of slumps in the 1570s and between 1611 and 1620 caused by income problems (particularly through the liquidation of the *monti*), and the high taxation imposed by the state on the confraternities to pay for wars. The *scuole* were involved in an acute conflict of duty towards the poor and towards the state. The *Scuole Grandi* seem to have at least kept up with charitable contributions, despite state pressures and drops in existing incomes, by attracting new donations and trusts. The pressures may also have encouraged more careful and discriminating distributions from the funds.[20] Apart from the Venice case we have so far little idea how well Italian confraternities responded financially to short- or long-term crises, nor can we prove that they became noticeably more—or less—generous, however much more aware they were of growing problems and needs.

Recently excursions have been made into the financial records of some Roman confraternities. Though only covering short periods, they elucidate some other issues. The SS. Trinità had a more complicated problem than most since in normal years it assisted pilgrims and convalescents, but during Jubilee years (1550, 1575, 1600, 1625) it was the main helper of the extraordinary influx of Jubilee pilgrims. In 1575 it spent about 24,000 *scudi* assisting about 170,000 pilgrims; in normal years previously its cost had been about 7,500 *scudi*. During the 1570s most income (45–65 per cent in normal years) came from various forms of alms-collecting—including small donations from members, larger ones from the pope or cardinals. Little came from rents (4–7 per cent), or investments (1–2 per cent); while legacies varied considerably from one year to another (10–35 per cent). For the 1575 Jubilee there was a heavier reliance on alms-giving. *Confratelli* were themselves generous with money as well as their services, and

[19] Pullan, *Rich and Poor*, esp. pp. 81–5, 135–56, 159–62, 170–8.
[20] *Ibid.* esp. pp. 163–81, including Tables.

kept salaried staff to a minimum.[21] By 1624 SS. Trinità's income was 11, 554 *scudi*; 23 per cent came from immovables (rents, leases, etc.), 38 per cent from loans, investments and legacies, and 39 per cent from oblations and other sources. Of the recorded expenditure in that year of 7,673 *scudi*, 43 per cent went on assistance, 20 per cent on expenses in worship, 26 per cent on administration and organising the patrimony, and 8 per cent miscellaneously.[22]

Evidence for some other Roman confraternities in 1624 shows considerable variations in the kinds of income and expenditure involved. For some a high proportion of their income came from immovables, rents and leases: S. Angelo in Borgo (95 per cent), S. Anna dei Palafrenieri (88 per cent), Madonna del Pianto (74 per cent). For others land was of negligible importance: SS. Sacramento in S. Agostino (3 per cent), S. Maria dell'Orazione e Morte (7 per cent)—instead they obtained income more from oblations and special incomes (47 per cent and 63 per cent respectively). Several relied heavily on credits from loans, investments and legacies: S. Girolamo della Carità (70 per cent), S. Giovanni Battista dei Fiorentini (90 per cent). The same sources suggest for S. Stanislao dei Polacchi that 94 per cent of the expenditure (of only 206 *scudi*) was on worship, and 6 per cent on administration; but the cost of assistance to Polish co-nationals—part of fraternal duty—may have been recorded separately. In the case of Madonna del Pianto 89 per cent of expenditure went on administration, and only 10 per cent on charity; only 521 *scudi* was involved. At the other end of the scale the archconfraternity hospital of S. Spirito had the largest income reported: 133,134 *scudi*. This was over double that of the next largest institution recorded: the 61,951 *scudi* of the Basilica of St Peter's. The work that this hospital confraternity undertook on this basis will be outlined in chapter 9.[23]

The above figures suggest the variety in income and expenditure of the confraternities. Many confraternities could exist with very limited funding, provided they confined themselves to devotional activities of an undemonstrative nature. Even those that had an avowed philanthropic duty to members and their families, like the Venetian goldsmiths, might be distributing meagre sums. But a few complex confraternities in the great cities had considerable incomes, were major property holders, and could dispense a significant quantity of charitable assistance. It now needs to be considered further what attitudes governed the selection of those who should be helped, and then the sorts of philanthropy that were involved.

[21] M. Borzacchini, 'Il patrimonio della Trinità dei Pellegrini alla fine del Cinquecento', *RSRR*, 5 (1984), 237–60, esp. Tables pp. 242, 252.
[22] Serra, 'Funzioni e finanze', p. 275, Table 2. The figures referring to 1624 were included in an apostolic visitation report of 1656.
[23] *Ibid.*, p. 284, Table 5.

7

ATTITUDES TO POVERTY

In a significant proportion of confraternities some money and much time was spent in philanthropic actions towards less fortunate 'neighbours', whether they were connected with the fraternity, or were members of the wider community. As already indicated (chapter 1), confraternity members were encouraged to use the Seven Acts of Mercy as a guide to their conduct towards neighbours; examples of the way these were implemented will be given in chapters 9 and 10. Before embarking on these charities it might help to contextualise them in various ways. It has already been stressed (chapter 1.3) that in pursuing 'good works' the salvation of the soul was more important than the body, and the soul of the donor could be of more concern than of the recipient. However, there was a concern for 'neighbours'. What I want to consider now are the contexts in which 'neighbours' were selected for assistance, how their needs were perceived, and how as historians we should judge the priorities and efficacy of this early modern philanthropy.

Those receiving assistance from confraternities were physically and spiritually poor. This immediately raises questions about who were considered poor at the time, and why; what kind of assistance was being offered, and with what priorities; whether the definitions and priorities current at the time have been properly understood since then, and so whether some of the judgements about confraternities and their charitable activities have been valid. This chapter and the next will explain some of the problems of interpretation, and suggest some answers.

This chapter will concentrate on present and past attitudes towards the poor and poverty. It will involve some consideration of the mentalities of the age as well as known confraternity attitudes. Confraternity records are not very explicit about how they decided on priorities. We do not know whether they were more influenced by street squalor or by Jesuit manuals and personal advice. But there was a European-wide debate about poverty and how to treat the deserving poor and punishable vagabonds, and it is unlikely that officials in the major urban confraternities were immune from the effects of this debate. I have therefore spent a little time on the wider debate as a probable, if not provable, context for confraternity action. Modern historians seem increasingly interested in 'the poverty problem' of the early modern period, and the terms of their debates are profitably changing in part through changing attitudes to our own world poverty problems and possible solutions or ameliorations. Some ideas offered by modern writers on poverty and need, such as P. Townsend and M. Ignatieff, can help eradicate old prejudices and bring historians back to a better appreciation of the ideas that lay behind confraternity philanthropy, and of the strengths and limitations of brotherly charity. Historians of the early modern period see a hardening attitude towards the poor in Europe, and stress attempts by authorities to impose greater discipline and social control. A study of confraternities in their Italian context suggests some qualifications to be made in this debate, particularly that such institutions might have eroded a real willingness or intent by authorities to impose much discipline or efficient state control over the poor.

Chapter 8 will look at the physical world; the incidence of poverty, the measures that were taken by governments to assist in some areas, and the context in which confraternities could operate philanthropically. I will also attempt to give some guidance on what the physical assistance might have meant to the recipients in terms of food and purchasing power.

I SOME MODERN ATTITUDES

Both commentators at the time and modern historians are in general agreement that the number of poor people increased in the sixteenth and seventeenth centuries. There is, however, less agreement as to what this means, and even less as to whether an increase in the number of poor required an expansion of philanthropic help. Complex problems are involved in attempting a definition of 'poverty' and 'the poor', and then in establishing the numbers involved. Attitudes to poverty also varied considerably. Some poor might be deemed unworthy of benefiting from charity; some writers argued that works of corporal mercy were undesirable for spiritual reasons, while others have argued that philanthropic gestures impeded the development of more efficacious means of dealing with the problem of poverty.

Since my focus is on the confraternities — and institutions like hospitals or orphanages at least marginally connected with them — I am concerned with the confraternities' perceptions of the poor to be helped, not with an assessment of the numbers of the poor, and the causes of any increase such as a modern social scientist might attempt. This is not to say that there were not attempts by confraternities and parish priests to quantify those needing help in their locality.

Before looking at sixteenth-century attitudes it is worth commenting on modern definitions and prejudices. We cannot ourselves avoid subjective values in our approach to the poverty problem, which may affect our understanding of confraternities and their roles. Historical verdicts on these brotherhoods and their functions have been coloured, especially since the Enlightenment, by an evolving idea of poverty and changing notions on how to treat it. The work of confraternities may be condemned for impeding economic developments that could have eliminated some of the causes of poverty. Scepticism about modern theories of political economy and their ability to cure poverty may lead to a less hostile view of past philanthropy. Recent ideas about satisfying physical and spiritual 'needs' may also bring us back closer to some early modern attitudes, and help us appreciate better what a brotherly donation or action might have meant to a recipient, or the donor.

The difficulty of reaching an objective definition of poverty is commonly recognised. 'Poverty, like beauty, lies in the eye of the beholder. Poverty is a value judgement; it is not something one can verify or demonstrate, except by inference and suggestion, even with a measure of error.'¹ This view, coming from somebody who was involved in American welfare programmes which sought to establish some objective criteria in providing assistance for those in need, reflects the viewpoint of early modern commentators. It worries other modern poverty experts like P. Townsend and A. Sen, who argue for a degree of objectivity in definitions and assessments. Sen is primarily concerned to avoid famines and to establish food entitlements and rationing to ensure that food supplies move from areas of surplus to areas of dire want. This is a concern with a section of the poor, those in the direst physical need, whom all would agree are poor in the modern sense of the term.² In the early modern period some governments sought to ensure food supplies to cater for this category, as we shall see below. Townsend while pursuing objectivity in definition and assessment aims at a more pluralistic approach — as might be expected, since he is concerned with a Britain that is not at starvation level — which goes beyond cash income, or food entitlement, and seeks to encompass style of living. In this argument 'necessities' will vary historically and geographically, which leads Townsend to endorse Adam Smith: 'By necessaries I understand, not only the commodities which are indispensably necessary for the support of life, but whatever the custom of the country renders it indecent for creditable persons, even of the lowest order, to be without.' These authors take the context to be that of a country, but it is not a far step to using the 'style of life' in the context of social order, and to link this with the sixteenth-century attitudes that poverty should be alleviated, needs satisfied, according to the individual's or family's social style. Townsend recommends that modern commentators should produce evidence on (1) objective deprivation, (2) conventionally acknowledged or normative deprivation; representing a dominant or majority view in society, and (3) individual subjective or group deprivation, when we can admit that 'some individuals may feel poor, especially by reference to their previous situation in life, even when they are neither demonstrably poor nor acknowledged to be poor by society'. This attitude brings us closer to both sixteenth-century attitudes and to the viewpoint of historians studying this period.³

In linking modern commentators on poverty and need with our particular concerns we can draw on some of M. Ignatieff's ideas.⁴ He avoids 'poverty', but deals with different levels of 'need' within the modern welfare state, indicating the deficiencies, anomalies and ironies involved in the development of the concept 'welfare state'. Need is more than what is required for physical survival; we have other needs in order to live a human life. Individuals have different needs; the differences are what make them human, and humanly different. In the human species needs have a history and change historically; some needs, if not articulated over a period, may disappear in silence, as spiritual needs have nearly done, he argues. One need that he sees as not having been articulated properly is that for 'fraternity, social solidarity for civic belonging' (p. 138). This connects with one of the ironies he finds in the welfare state: 'One might have

¹ Quoted in P. Townsend, *Poverty in the United Kingdom* (Harmondsworth, 1979), p. 37 quoting from Miss M. Orshanky's 'How poverty is measured', *Monthly Labour Review*, February 1969; cf. S.J. Woolf, *The Poor in Western Europe in the Eighteenth and Nineteenth Centuries* (London and New York, 1986), p. 2.
² A. Sen, *Poverty and Famines* (Oxford, 1981), which starts with concepts of poverty.
³ Townsend, p. 49.
⁴ M. Ignatieff, *The Needs of Strangers* (London, 1984).

expected that the enactment of a vision of the shared good in the welfare state would have brought us closer together. The welfare state has tried to enact fraternity by giving each individual a claim of right to common resources. Yet meeting everyone's basic needs does not necessarily meet their needs for social solidarity' (p. 137).

While some of Ignatieff's concepts of 'need' go beyond definitions of 'poverty', most definitions of, or attitudes to, poverty that move beyond starvation-level physical needs, do include some of the non-physical aspects he invokes. In looking at early modern confraternities we can see such societies, at their best, as trying to fulfil the needs of the poor and deprived — physical needs for food and shelter, but also social and emotional needs, in alleviating loneliness, dishonour, spiritual deprivation or ignorance. On the other hand confraternities, when they were associated with the more repressive aspects of policies towards the poor — the social control through institutionalisation or hospitalisation and confinement, to which we shall return — may also have contributed to dehumanisation, as Ignatieff recognises. Another irony might be that both 'the old charity' and the welfare state that was designed to replace it leave the recipients spiritually poor and needy.

Moving to the historians writing about the sixteenth century, and their views on European and Italian poverty, we can start by noting some areas of consensus. The verdict that the number of the poor increased over the period can be based on the tentative evidence that the population overall increased, though with major variations, and that basic food resources did not expand enough to meet the new demand. The numbers of 'the poor' would therefore have increased numerically, and almost certainly as a percentage of the whole population. Italy was part of this general pattern. Within Italy many smaller towns or cities remained static or declined; certain rural areas were depopulated, while a few cities grew considerably: notably Naples, Venice, Rome, and Milan. The growth derived from increased bureaucratic centralisation, conspicuous consumption and building by the elites requiring large service populations, more elaborate church building and decorative projects. Venice had to absorb colonists as the Turks overran Mediterranean islands and parts of the Dalmatian coast. The better land-management of Venetian patricians drove surplus peasantry to the towns. Rome attracted more pilgrims, more clerics and artisans to serve the revived Church, and peasants who fled from landowners changing from arable to pasture, or from brigandage in the Papal State. In the Viceroyalty of Naples, refeudalism (when under exploiting lords, and not when requested by communities who preferred local nobles to royal tax collectors), or improved estate management at times drove peasants to the capital.[5]

Certain positive urban economic developments aided some incomers, but it has been assumed that the net result was an increase in urban 'poor', or at least poor who might

---

[5] M.W. Flinn, *The European Demographic System* 1500–1800 (London, 1981), is a valuable short general guide, and has a reasonable bibliographical section for Italy; see above chapter 1, nn. 18, 24–5; for a class-exploitation theory of the links between demographic growth, agricultural change and increased poverty see C. Lis and H. Soly, *Poverty and Capitalism in Pre-Industrial Europe* (Brighton 1979; and 1982 paperback edn). For developments in some cities and their causes: J. Delumeau, *Vie économique*; T. Magnuson, *Rome in the Age of Bernini* (Stockholm and New Jersey), vol. 1 (1982), esp. pp. 8–12, 115–21, 325–7; Villari, *La rivolta antispagnola*; Black, 'Perugia and papal absolutism', pp. 520–1, 537–8, with references to the Venetian state; also; A.D. Wright, 'Venetian law and order: a myth?', *Bulletin of the Institute of Historical Research*, 52 (1980), 192–202. For examples of urban populations see below, Appendix I.

need attention. In the small villages and towns extended family solidarity might cushion blows to individuals, or encourage mutual aid in a general crisis. Urban immigrants could lose this group and family solidarity, at least until they were fully accepted into a guild or confraternity; the 'national' confraternities (chapter 2.2 (d)), could be of some assistance. There is an argument that the move to the big city led to rising expectations, thereby causing changes in the individual's concept of need when faced with a food or family crisis. Since, as we shall see, most governments concentrated on facing the problem of the poor in the main cities — whether the measures were positive (bringing in food supplies) or negative (driving out recent immigrants and vagabonds) — they may have made the situation worse everywhere else, by creating more poor peasants. This in turn encouraged more movement to the city, and attempts to remain where assistance was concentrated. During the food crises of the 1590s the Roman government was partially organised to obtain food supplies from afar and distribute them with the aid of confraternities and hospitals. As Oratorian Father Pateri testified, this led people from all over the Papal State, and other parts of Italy, to seek food in Rome, but still they died of starvation in thousands.[6] Historians generally agree that the 'problem of poverty' increased as contemporaries alleged.

Historians also largely agree that attitudes towards the poor became more oppressive.[7] Many argue that the trend in state and church policies throughout Europe was towards greater social control over the population as a whole, and the poor in particular. It is fashionable to discuss religious and political history from the early sixteenth century in terms of social control and social discipline, affecting all levels of society. Various factors are stressed according to the predilections of leading historians. There was an increased fear (first evident in the Netherlands and Rhineland cities from the late fifteenth century) that the urban poor were becoming uncontrollable and new measures were required. Certain humanists, some of whose ideas were notably published by L. Vives (to be discussed below), stressed self-discipline and hard work, and provided a code that might be imposed on others to discourage idleness. Following this the Lutheran Reformation and the subsequent divisions led the different institutionalised churches to tighten control over their faithful through more effective parochial organisation and teaching, while at the same time becoming less tolerant of the unfaithful and deviant. Intolerance and the desire for conformity in theological and liturgical matters could readily spread to wider social and moral behaviour. For some commentators the supposed shift from feudalism to capitalism, no longer seen as confined to

---

[6] Paglia, 'La Pietà dei carcerati', p. 50; Delumeau, Vie économique, vol. 2, pp. 116–24, on the food crises of the 1590s, starving inhabitants, and attempts to secure grain supplies.

[7] For arguments about the growing oppression of the poor and debates about social control see generally: Lis and Soly; H. Kamen, The Iron Century. Social Change in Europe 1550–1600 (London, 1971), esp. chapter 11; J-P. Gutton, La Société et les pauvres en Europe (XVI–XVIII–siècles) (Paris, 1974); Pullan, 'Catholics and the poor'; M. Foucault, Discipline and Punish. The Birth of the Prison, trans. A. Sheridan (Harmondsworth, 1977); A.L. Beier, The Problem of the Poor in Tudor and early Stuart England (Lancaster Pamphlets, London and New York, 1983); G. Oestreich, Neo-stoicism and the Early Modern State (Cambridge, 1982); von Greyerz (ed.), Religion and Society, esp. articles by R. Muchembled, J. Wirth, B. Lenman, M. Ingram, which take up various arguments about social control. On Italy more specifically Bressan, L'hospitale' e i poveri, esp. chapter 2, which deals with the Italian literature on attitudes to poverty; Geremek, 'Il pauperismo'; Woolf, The Poor, chapter 1 deals briefly and effectively with the period from the fifteenth to eighteenth centuries. Specialist Italian articles will be cited below.

Protestant areas, fostered the movement towards greater social discipline, especially over the able-bodied idle. While enthusiasm for neo-Stoicism from the later sixteenth century may have added intellectual arguments in favour of social discipline, the growth of state bureaucracies — with or without the aid of military forces which the bureaucracies were largely developed to finance — made social control or engineering easier to contemplate, if not effect. Worsening weather conditions from the 1590s, an apparent increase in the incidence of food crises in most parts of Europe, the impact of war — notably the Thirty Years War, affecting areas far beyond the fields of battle — and plague, all encouraged states and established powers to attempt greater control particularly over the lower orders. In consequence, it is generally argued, the poor increased, and at the same time received more systematic and (by most modern criteria or prejudices) more adverse treatment. As R. Po-Chia Hsia comments in his discussion of Catholic Muenster when it was recovering from the Anabaptist disaster: 'Thus while society came to deal with poverty in a more systematic manner, the poor rapidly lost any dignity they had in the economy of salvation.'[8]

Historians are generally agreed that from the early sixteenth century the poor were increasingly divided systematically into two categories, the deserving and the undeserving; the deserving would receive help from philanthropic individuals and church institutions; the undeserving would be subject to greater secular control and discipline. If they were not driven away from the place where they were being idle and troublesome, they would be regulated, put in institutions and 'hospitals' and made to work if possible in return for food and shelter. The churches and religious bodies might be recruited to assist in the latter policy, though some governments and magistrates increasingly secularised the treatment of the poor and 'charitable' activity. In the fifteenth century municipal authorities in places like Lisbon and Turin considered ecclesiastical institutions offering charity to be inefficient, corrupt or inadequately funded, and so led the way in the municipalisation of hospital and related services. This policy was accelerated through the sixteenth century (chapter 9.4).

Much recent historical work has focused on vagrancy as the key to the adverse treatment of the poor. Contemporaries were aware of a mass of poor people, most of whom were feared as potential vagrants and criminals.[9] For Italy P. Camporesi most emphatically argues that the upper classes detested the poor, feared their multiplication and used the assistance systems to keep the vagabond problem under control until pestilence in a Malthusian way reduced the problem. He argues that the social discipline of the 'hospital' system successfully kept pre-industrial pauperism in balance in the sixteenth and seventeenth centuries, but that — in Italy — there was a real fear and crisis in the early eighteenth century during another major population increase, especially in the south. The upper, disciplining classes, rarely understood the real misery of the poor, whose voices were and are seldom heard—except when one reads the writings of the

---

[8] R. Po Chia-Hsia, 'Civic Wills as sources for the study of piety in Muenster, 1530–1618', *Sixteenth Century Journal*, 14, no. 3 (1983), 321–48, at p. 335.

[9] R. Jütte, 'Poor relief and social discipline in sixteenth-century Europe', *European Studies Review*, 11 (1981), 25–52: 'Poverty and its concomitant vagrancy were a perennial problem throughout the sixteenth century', (p. 25); Woolf, *The Poor*, pp. 28–9.

popular Bologna poet, G.C. Croce, who at the turn of the sixteenth century acted as an inter-class mediator in his realistic, moving, or witty verses dealing with the miseries and joys of 'ordinary' lives in town and country.[10]

By the seventeenth century there was a body of popular literature dealing with vagabonds and their lives, which was coupled with 'evidence' from the 1590s that in Rome at least there were organised gangs of thieves, tricksters and people intent on misusing charitable institutions and the generosity of donors. These alleged gangs included *Baroni*, who feigned unemployment, *Farfogli*, who pretended to be pilgrims, *Brisci* going about naked, or partly so, to elicit help, and *Ballarini*, who claimed to be cursed by God because their parents had refused to kneel before the Sacrament. The extent to which the organisation was exaggerated, and the vagabond world fictionalised by court witnesses or writers is debatable. Whether the literature was produced by elite or popular writers, whether it was realistic or romantic in its treatment, it was likely to encourage the fears of the upper orders that vagabonds, or the poor generally, were organised, criminal and dangerous. While some historians may doubt the reality of a subculture of criminal poor behind the literary evidence, the allegations about vagabond poor cannot be dismissed. Both myths and realities could foster a repressive response.[11]

For Italy one might argue that especially from the late sixteenth century there were increasing moves towards a harsher disciplining of the poor, and a castigation of the undeserving vagabonds. But we should be wary of seeing this as the product of a clear ideology, or a consistent policy, though once some institutionalisation of charitable activities was started the system was likely to become more rigid and harsher.[12] As will become clearer there were many variations in attitude, policy and institutions within Italy. The extent to which pieces fit into the 'social control' model can depend on the strength of small institutions, especially confraternities, guilds and hospitals, helping the poor and needy; on the strength of the local state's governmental institutions, the extent of a regional economy's structural crisis or temporary dislocation by war, plague or dearth. The reluctance or slowness of governments in Florence or Naples to move towards state-centralised social control and confinement policies may reflect the strength of older attitudes of existing confraternities or hospitals that determined the ability of both old ideas and old institutions to adapt to new purposes.[13] The history of fluctuating

---

[10] P. Camporesi, 'Cultura popolare e cultura d'élite fra medioevo ed età moderna', *Storia d'Italia. Annali* 4, pp. 107, 116–33; idem, *Il pane selvaggio* (Bologna, 1980), pp. 15, 45–6; M. Rouch (ed.), *Storie di vita popolare nelle canzoni di piazza di G.C. Croce. Fame fatica e mascherate nel '500* (Bologna, 1982) contains a selection of Croce's poems; see below chapter 8.1.

[11] P. Camporesi (ed.), *Il libro dei vagabondi* (Turin, 1973), with relevant texts and commentary. Now discussed by P. Burke, 'Perceiving a counter-culture' in his *The Historical Anthropology of Early Modern Italy* (Cambridge, 1987), pp. 62–75, 247–9 (notes): he argues that the 'documents' in certain law suits and the literature have some validity, and are valuable for understanding the perceptions of the time.

[12] See E. Grendi, 'Ideologia della carità e società indisciplinata: la costruzione del sistema assistenziale genovese (1470–1670)', *Timore e Carità, I Poveri nell'Italia Moderna. Atti del Convegno. Cremona 1980*, eds. G. Politi, M. Rosa and F. Della Peruta (Cremona, 1982), pp. 59–75, esp. pp. 59, 75, where he warns against accepting too readily a modern sociological approach, such as M. Foucault's, so concentrating too much on social control; E. Grendi, 'Pauperismo e Albergo dei Poveri nella Genova del Seicento', *RSI*, 87 (1975), p. 621: 'Every society at heart defines poverty differently and that definition which operates in the selection of individuals and groups of individuals, becomes more rigid the more it is consolidated in a structure for assistance, the more this evolves towards an "institutional consolidation" which tends to overcome the plurality of helping agencies.'

[13] D. Lombardi, 'Poveri a Firenze: programmi e realizzazioni della politica assistenziale dei Medici tra cinque e seicento', *Timore e Carità*, pp. 165–84; G. Muto, 'Forme e contenuti economici dell'assistenza nel Mezzogiorno moderno. Il caso di Napoli', *ibid.*, pp. 237–58; A. Musi, 'Pauperismo e pensiero giuridico a Napoli nella prima metà del secolo XVII', *ibid.*, pp. 259–73.

papal policies reflects the battle between old and new ideas within a religious–ethical framework. The confrontation took place in the context of a 'modern' absolutist state, which, however, had a weak fiscal structure, and of a capital city which had developed powerful, and 'independent', confraternity and hospital institutions (see chapter 9).

Some final qualifications that derive from consideration of *modern* attitudes to the poor and poverty, and affect my discussion, are highlighted by S.J. Woolf, though his article was primarily concerned with the late eighteenth and early nineteenth centuries. He accepts, in line with some French historians, that the history of poverty needs to be studied over a long period, and the history of the poor related to long-term structural changes, as well as short-term, conjunctural, crises. But there are dangers in not distinguishing between 'the process of pauperisation' and the world of the poor, and in treating poverty as 'normal' for the great majority of the population. It can lead to an explanation of poverty which: 'reduces the poor to an indeterminate passive mass, denying the possibility (perhaps even the validity) of exploring the internal differentiations among the pauperised, the mechanisms of survival employed by their various segments or groups, the practical and ideological significance of the relationships between these groups and the society which enveloped them'.[14]

To undertake a major study of Italian poverty requires an economic analysis over a long period; this is beyond the scope of this book, which is concerned with the history of confraternities in their many dimensions over a very long century. But it can be noted that the preoccupations with structures and long durations can lead to the imposition of a model, or modern scheme such as 'social discipline', which encourages the historian to treat the poor as a large mass, undifferentiated and inhuman. My discussion of confraternities and related institutions dealing with the poor, in this context of poverty, is designed to be a contribution to discussions of 'the world of the poor and society's response to their presence'. It should highlight 'the internal differentiation', and the variety of responses of those dealing with the poor.

2 CONTEMPORARY ATTITUDES

Commentators on the poor, or administrators of institutions and the law had various ways of classifying the poor, and put them in different categories; there were sub-divisions in terms of physical needs and deprivation, or in terms of deserving and undeserving; there were those who had a favourable view of most 'poor', those who distrusted or despised most of them.

A number of older attitudes, taking a favourable view of poverty and some poor, were inherited and hard to eradicate. Gospel teaching saw the poor as blessed, and the rich as having difficulties in entering heaven. Voluntary poverty and asceticism adopted for spiritual and penitential motives was laudable, and those undertaking this way of life were traditionally allowed to rely on begging to cover their necessities, which made a blanket condemnation of begging difficult to sustain. Of course this kind of poverty was expected to be undertaken in the context of vows and ecclesiastical control — and so was subject to discipline and licensing. Canon lawyers had condemned those whose poverty derived from idleness and other sinful motives. When dealing with the poor in secular society, whether the poverty was wholly the result of external factors, or partially self-induced, canon lawyers did not provide a clear policy on who should be

[14] S. J. Woolf, 'Problems in the history of pauperism in Italy, 1800–1815', *Timore e Carità*, p. 317.

helped. Medieval commentators could derive from Gratian both a doctrine of indiscriminate charity (which could be backed by a quotation from St John Chrysostom—one of the Greek Fathers whose teaching was to be revived in France and Italy in the sixteenth century) or a doctrine of discrimination in the distribution of charity. The latter attitude could rely on St Ambrose and his *De Officiis* whose list of deserving recipients was headed by faithful Christians and those unable to work through age or sickness. Texts could be used to argue that *hospitalitas* (hospitality, and by later extension, any indoor relief) should be extended to all who sought it; but that *liberalitas* (liberality, alms-giving, later interpreted as all outdoor relief) should be restricted and controlled by certain views about the recipients.[15] It is not clear how much attention sixteenth-century confraternities or private philanthropists paid to canon law, but it should be remembered that Italy was full of well-trained canon lawyers —even if Italian universities were deficient in theology, as Cardinal Roberto Bellarmino lamented in the 1590s.[16]

A distinction made in the past, and which remained, was that between those in dire physical need and the less needy, though poor; between those suffering from *egestas* and those from *povertas*; between the *miserabili* and the *poveri*; those in extremity and those in lesser states of need or poverty. One of the most influential Italian preachers and reformers in the fifteenth century, St Bernardino of Siena, frequently concerned himself with the poor, and with the causes of poverty, which he saw as the result of usury. In one analysis he identified three kinds of poor: those who rebel against their miserable condition; those rich who voluntarily cede their wealth; those who are voluntarily poor for Christ.[17] Among the impatient involuntary poor St Bernardino, in a vernacular sermon, indicated three levels: the *bisognosi* who can live without help; the *necessitosi* who can live, but badly; and those in *istremità* who cannot survive without help. Here, he tells his listeners, you have no excuse, you must help those in the state of *istremità*.[18] Those who reduced the poor to a state of *miseria*, (equated with the extreme position of poverty) through usurious practices are killers of the poor. Poverty means great tribulation and suffering; if undertaken voluntarily, it is meritorious like martydom. And there can be tranquillity and peace in poverty, since the poor can save himself, the rich man never (or not when remaining selfishly rich). Riches have their uses if honestly acquired and benevolently employed to benefit society for social purposes through the virtuous giving of alms. In this the rich fulfil a social function: 'The rich are necessary for republics; and the poor are necessary for the rich.'[19] For him the order of priority in giving alms is as follows: the donor's family, saints, the honest, friends, Christians (as

---

[15] B. Tierney, 'The Decretists and the "deserving poor"', *Comparative Studies in Society and History*, 1 (1958), 361–73.

[16] G. Pelliccia, *La preparazione ed ammissione dei chierici ai santi Ordini nella Roma del secolo XVI* (Rome, 1946), pp. 296–8.

[17] 'Tria tamen sunt pauperum genera: quidam mundo et non Deo, ut fures et pauperes impatientes; quidam Deo et non mundo, ut David et ceteri divites sancti, tam in Novo quam in veteri testamento; quidam Deo et mundo, sicut quolibet voluntarius pauper propter Christum'. San Bernardino da Siena, *Omnia Opera* (Florence, 1950–65), vol. 5, 247; cited by A. Spicciani in 'La povertà involuntaria', *Atti del simposio internazionale Cateriniano–Bernardiniano . . . 1980* eds. D. Maffei and P. Nardi (Siena, 1982), p. 814.

[18] *Omnia Opera*, vol. 8, 67, 'De eleemosynae descriptione'; cited *ibid.*, p. 824.

[19] *Omnia Opera*, vol. 3, 64; cited *ibid.*, pp. 828–9; cf. on the interdependence of rich and poor, A. Sperelli, *Della pretiosita della limosina* (Venice, 1666), p. 239: it was part of divine providence to have rich and poor in each city to help each other; the rich assist the poor, and the poor pray for the rich–so inequality is equalled (p. 243); see below, n. 43.

opposed to infidels), nobles whose poverty is not their fault and who are ashamed to be poor, and finally other poor. Among the last, other things being equal, preference can be given to the imprisoned, those afflicted by age, sickness, disability or blindness, and girls of marriageable age whose honesty is in imminent danger unless they are coupled in marriage — and similarly young wives.[20] The worst condition is the poverty of nobles who have lost their riches, and can no longer keep up their social status, so to help them secretly is a major work of charity. These attitudes and subdivisions were to be repeated throughout our period.

The category of poor, *poveri*, does not necessarily refer to the poorest members of society. The most deprived were sometimes called the *miserabili*. In the Tuscan tax registers of the fifteenth century, the *Catasti*, the category *miserabile* was for the person who was too poor to be registered for tax; while *povero* designated a person worth less than 50 florins. It should be noted that this latter category covered about half the Pisan population in the fifteenth century, and three-quarters of the inhabitants of areas like Chiusi and Vergheretto, or 65 per cent of Firenzuola, while the *miserabili* were 5–10 per cent. These are of course classifications for long-term conditions of dearth. Herlihy and Klapisch-Zuber, in their major study of the Florentine *catasto* commented on the *miserabili*: 'This category gathered in the infirm, the aged, minor orphans, and, above all, widows. The *miserabili* of the city were usually totally destitute, while those in the countryside often possessed some modest belongings. Common to miserable households everywhere was the absence of an adult male member.'[21]

The word 'poor' was used in various contexts, and could include a person with possessions, resources and employment. For example, we find *poveri* used in Venetian guild records as a classification of members. While R.T. Rapp assumes this to mean that they were unemployed, R. Mackenney in analysing the books of the mercers' guild, and a list of 'poor' for 1586, reckons that about 38 per cent of those so described owned their own business, and many others had full-time, independent occupations, especially in haberdashery; only 20 out of 285 of the listed *poveri* had no specific occupation. In this particular classification system we have *capomaestri, zoveni, poveri, donne; zoveni,* rather than being a category of youths or apprentices, indicated an earning bracket, those earning less than 50 ducats in the shops, as salary, living expenses or as a share of the turnover. In these circumstances deciding on the need of guild members through this classification poses difficulties.[22]

From the above it should be clear that where an individual or fraternity was helping the poor (*povero*), the recipient could turn out to be somebody clearly not in the lowest category of physical need, and with some means of support. Some officials came to think that helping the *povero* as opposed to the *miserabile* might be undesirable.

In 1500 the Genoese hospital for Incurables talked of *pauperes* and *miserabiles*. The city's Office for the Poor in its 1540 rules distinguished the poor who were handicapped and could not work, and those healthy but in misery and placed in extreme necessity— 'sani ma miserabili e posti in estrema necessità'. By 1593 the Office was ruling that only the category of *miserabili* should be given bread to help them. This category was then

---

[20] San Bernardino, *Omnia Opera*, vol. 8, 86–8; cited by Spicciani, p. 829.

[21] D. Herlihy and C. Klapisch-Zuber, *Tuscans and Their Families* (New Haven and London, 1985), p. 19.

[22] R.T. Rapp, *Industry and Economic Decline in Seventeenth-Century Venice* (Cambridge, Mass. and London, 1976), p. 30; Mackenney, 'Trade Guilds', esp. pp. 277–86, and *Tradesmen and Traders*, pp. 103–7. Cf. Woolf, *The Poor*, pp. 17–18 on different meanings of *paupertas*.

defined as those who had nothing of their own and were incapable of earning a living because they were old, children, or infirm in body or mind, or those burdened with a large family which their work efforts could not sustain. Bread should be given to the large family in misery to save it from dying of starvation, but not enough to encourage the worker to become idle because needs were satisfied. Here we see combined a classification in terms of dire need, but also the moral argument that assistance might encourage idleness. In Florence in the 1620s the deputies of the wool guild argued that workers were abandoning their work to beg, because they could gain more money that way than through the curtailed production of cloth during the slump; alms encouraged sloth.[23]

The concern about the idleness of the poor seems to have developed from the early sixteenth century, and was reflected both in the legislation of European cities and states that reformed or extended their laws dealing with the poor, and in related literary works. The person who was idle, but capable of work, who wandered about city or countryside seeking alms and other assistance, was increasingly cast as the dangerous, evil vagrant who might threaten the property of the possessors, but also, importantly, threaten the lives of the genuine poor — by limiting the availability of alms for those incapable of earning a livelihood. Magistrates like those in Ypres who, in 1525, aimed to curb idle beggars, notably and controversially banning all public begging, claimed support from canon law and the biblical text 'thou shalt eat thy bread in the sweat of thy brow'.[24]

The most influential book in this context has been seen as Juan Luis Vives' *De subventione pauperum*, first published in 1526. It was aimed at the magistrates of Bruges, where the Spanish author was living, and reflected attitudes behind recent legislation in Nuremberg and Ypres.[25] Vives feared most poor and saw them as dangerous, but argued that poverty was largely eradicable if the able were made to work, or provided with work opportunities within municipal hospitals or similar institutions; some idle hands in Bruges might be sent to other towns needing labour in textiles; foreign vagabonds should be driven away; and public works created to employ the native idle, who would receive a moral reeducation beneficial to their ultimate salvation, and thus save the city from riot. Those receiving help must be made to spend it wisely, not immorally — or be punished. Foundling children should be educated in a Christian way in city-controlled institutions, so that eventually they could live and work profitably (II.ii–iv especially). Vives was not helpful on how to assist the deserving poor, who remained ill-defined, nor on the financing of these policies, though he encouraged people to believe that existing hospitals had extensive funds, ill-employed in most cases, and that ecclesiastical resources should largely pay for the hospitals. He dared to suggest some

[23] Grendi, 'Ideologia', pp. 66, 68; and his 'Pauperismo', p. 629; Lombardi, 'Poveri', p. 175: 'elemosina . . . rende questa plebe infingarda et la desvia dall'escercizio'. On this basis the deputies erecting the hospital for confined poor argued: 'il mendicare non solamente era ridotto in forma di un particolar mestiero, a segno che molti abbandonavano l'Arti per accattare, e i padri richiesti di metter i loro figli con salario competente a bottega ricusavano di farlo, havendo da loro maggior guadagno nell'allevarli accattando . . .'

[24] Pullan, 'Catholics and the poor', pp. 17–18, with fuller references; Martz, *Poverty and Welfare*, p. 13; Woolf, *The Poor*, pp. 20–3.

[25] Edn. used: L. Vives, *De subventione pauperum*, ed. A. Saitta, with introduction (Florence, 1973). (He can be called Ludovico by Italians, rather than Juan Luis de Vives).

redistribution of wealth from rich to poor, through tax policies. On the positive side there was a strong defence of giving to benefit others, as a natural action, and as a beautiful and excellent one done in imitation of God.[26] But it might be argued that in the event Vives' benefactor lacked kindness and was more discriminating than God in raining down charity on the just and unjust. However, his book received wide publicity, through many editions in Latin and the vernacular, through city legislation and edicts from the Emperor Charles V which are seen as derived from the book and resulting discussions of it.

The attack on begging did not find favour everywhere; the Mendicants especially challenged this — notably in submitting Ypres' laws to the theologians of the Sorbonne in Paris — on the grounds that such a ban, and the expulsion of foreign beggars was contrary to divine law. They also argued that the laity could not claim jurisdiction over charitable revenues. The Sorbonne theologians in 1531 upheld the Ypres laws as generally 'pious and salutary', but ruled that begging could not be totally banned if there was not enough money in city funds to help the poor, that Mendicanst should be allowed to beg, that church revenues should not be commandeered by lay authorities, and that people could not be prevented from giving alms privately.[27] Such qualifications could effectively undermine any municipal or other lay attempt at strict controls against the idle poor.

There was a major debate in Spain on the Vives and Ypres attitudes, and related Castilian laws, culminating in 1545 in books by Juan de Robles (alias Juan de Medina) and Domingo de Soto, as has been outlined by L. Martz. The Benedictine Robles defended discrimination in alms-giving, and the tighter control of the poor. He was more aware than Vives of the variety of poor, and therefore of the different kinds of provision needed for them.[28] The Dominican de Soto attacked virtually all of the new attitudes, finding no justification for the expulsion of foreign beggars or depriving them of charity, instead he argued for a comparative freedom of movement for the poor, and for the voluntary principle behind alms-giving, which rules out restraints on whom the donor should help. As governments could not assure help for all the poor — not having the right or power to tax for this purpose — they could not deprive the poor of the right to beg or otherwise seek charity. De Soto opposed compulsory confinement of the poor, but he did encourage the idea of using 'hospitals' to help the poor voluntarily, claiming this as a major contribution of the early Christian church.[29]

In the year of this debate, 1545, an Italian edition of Vives' book was published in Venice. It is not clear how influential his book was in Italy. While its publication coincided with Venice's reiteration of its 'poor laws', these — enacted in the crisis of 1529 — were, according to B. Pullan, based on German city legislation. Pullan however argues that Girolamo Miani, one of the main promoters of confraternity philanthropy in northern Italy, had some principles that could have been based on Vives' work, especially his opposition to begging and his condemnation of idleness. But Miani had

---

[26] I.iv: 'Quam secundum naturam sit benefacere'. I. viii: 'Nullas causas debere impedire nos a beneficiendo . . . At vero pulchra res et excellens in primis, benefacere in qua decet homines aemulatores esse parentis sui Dei, cuius benignitatem ingratitudo nostra non exhaurit; pluit iustos et iniustos'. (pp. 15, 27).
[27] Martz, Poverty and Welfare, p. 13.
[28] Jütte, 'Poor relief', p. 26.
[29] Martz, Poverty and Welfare, pp. 22–30.

a greater concern or love for the poor than Vives. Those in his charitable institutions would pray and work constructively, and receive a wholesome Christian education.[30] The acceptability of Vives' book was likely to be influenced by the fact that in the 1520s he had been accused of heresy, as an Erasmian; added to which his Italian translator, Giandomenico Tarsia, was a friend of Pietro Paulo Vergerio who had turned Lutheran, and the edition was dedicated to Pietro Carnesecchi, who was finally executed for heresy in 1568.[31] De Soto, as a Spanish theologian dominating various discussions at the Council of Trent, was to antagonise many Italians. But his 'conservative' views on poverty and charity were likely to find much support in Italy from those who had vested interests in defending mendicancy, ecclesiastical control over pious institutions and their funds, and who would, like the Spaniard, resent the inflow of northern European ideas and institutions. Where, in Italy, some secular government officials (as in Venice) might have been happiest undermining ecclesiastical revenues or controls and on those grounds preferred Vives to de Soto, there were lay confraternities ready to continue some of the older charitable attitudes, and these the officials were not prepared to undermine. The main centres controlled by Spain — Naples and Milan — also had strong confraternities and private charitable institutions which would not encourage them to move towards a particularly forceful municipalisation or anti-pauper policy.

To exemplify the last point, and to demonstrate the complexity of theoretical attitudes in Italy, we can move to the early seventeenth century and the work of a Neapolitan jurist, Giovanni Maria Novario. In his *Tractatus de miserabilium personarum privilegiis* (1623) he argued that the church, rather than the state had the prime duty to assist the poor; the opposite attitude to Vives'. The church is the mother of the miserable, church possessions belong to the poor, and matters dealing with the poor should appear before ecclesiastical courts — though protection of the poor is also within the competence of the Prince, i.e. the secular state. Notably he argued, as a lawyer, that in the face of conflicting views for and against miserable persons, the decision should *favour* the miserable. He treated the *miserabilis* as a privileged person among the poor, somebody weak within the power structure of society, who needed legal protection, and charity. When it came to defining his privileged *miserabiles personae* he provided a long and interesting list, starting with children, widows and those exhausted and weak from daily illness. To these he added: 'Orphanus, Pauper et Inops, Captivus, Carceratus, Peregrinus, Advena Meretrix, Expositus, Libertus, Penitens, Nuper ad fidem conversus, Senex Virgo, Scholaris, Agricola, Mercator qui in itinere pro gabellis gravatur Ecclesia et Ecclesiasticus Amore Captus damnatus ad Triremes, Nauta Relegatus, Deportatus, Demoniacus, Decactus, [for Decoctus?] Ebriosus, Furiosus, Fatuus, Lunaticus.' [Orphan, pauper without work, captive, prisoner, pilgrim, novice prostitute, abandoned child, freed slave, penitent, recent convert to Christianity, old spinster, scholar, peasant, merchant who on his journey is burdened with taxes by the Church and an ecclesiastic possessed by love who is condemned to the galleys, dismissed

---

[30] B.S. Pullan, 'The famine in Venice and the new Poor Law 1527–1529', *Bollettino dell'Istituto della Società e dello Stato Veneziano*, 5–6 (1963–4), 141–3, 170–1; cf. AA.VV. *San Girolamo Miani a Venezia* (Venice, 1986).

[31] P. Simoncelli, 'Note sul sistema assistenziale a Roma nel XVI secolo', *Timore e Carità*, pp. 138–9; Saitta's introduction to *De subventione pauperum*, p. lxxxii; M. Fatica, 'Il "De subventione pauperum" di J.L. Vives: suggestioni luterane o mutamento di una mentalità collettiva', *Società e Storia*, 15 (1982), 1–30, esp. p. 26.

sailor, deportee, demoniac, bankrupt(?), drunkard, madman, simpleton, lunatic.] And *miserabiles* includes those also who fall into misery by their own fault ('quae culpa sua in miseria inciderunt').[32] While some of the categories of miserable poor given by Novario meet the criteria of others we have mentioned, several are precisely the kinds of undeserving and dangerous poor whom the magistrates of Ypres and Bruges, Venice and Rome were more likely to expel, imprison or discipline. But also many of these were to receive help, with or without loving care, from confraternities.

Poverty, like two of its causes, plague and famine, could be seen as an expression of the wrath of God, to be taken as a punishment or as a challenge to right-doing. Archbishop Gabriele Paleotti instructed preachers to remind their listeners constantly of the flails that God prepared for people on earth; to comfort or instruct the poor that God came to save souls not to provide goods; and to argue that poverty was often an easier and securer vehicle on the road to heaven — just as too big a shoe or garment impedes a journey. During a major plague year Marco Gonzaga, bishop of Mantua, secured the publication in Macerata, of a pamphlet — *Cause et rimedi della peste et di qualsivoglia altra infermità . . .* — which argued that plague, as the usual accompaniment of war and famine, was caused by pride and arrogance, and then heresy; so Jesus Christ inflicted plague on the people as a sign that the Antichrist would soon come. The pamphlet also contained a strong attack on the incidence of theft, rape, usury, carnality, indecent familiarity, infamous songs and madrigals, the reading of impure books, the use of nude pictures, etc., which were all things to be punished. Little could — or possibly should — be done except that people should return to God, the Virgin and the heavenly company.[33] Earlier Tullio Crispoldi from Rieti had published in Venice his *Orationi da far nel tempo della Carestia e d'altro Flagello* (1551), which had argued that it 'is just that we have been for long afflicted by hunger and need in all things' for disobeying God's commandments, but Crispoldi had taken a more positive approach in seeing this as a challenge for the faithful to do good. He was earlier part of the entourage of G.M. Giberti, often seen as a model Catholic Reform bishop in Verona.[34] In 1591 the Barnabite Giovanni Bellarini (*Instruttione spirituale per pigliar frutto dalla carestia* (Rome)) used the food and poverty crisis to warn not only the suffering poor, but also the rich. Famine and poverty, the flails of God, would remain as long as the world was so sinful, but the rich could play a part in remedying the situation, by fasting and by increasing alms-giving:

this [alms-giving] must now more than ever occupy the rich, because as the needs of the poor grow, so the help from those who have must be multiplied; so each day he who is rich should increase his alms-giving, and give with a generous hand to Christ's poor [*alli poverelli di Christo*] . . . So I remind them that now the poor are in extreme necessity and they [the rich] under pain of God's displeasure are held to give them the excess of their superabundance.[35]

[32] Musi, 'Pauperismo', pp. 264–70 on Novario, with quotation p. 265.
[33] G. Paleotti, *Instruttione . . . Per tutti quelli, che hauranno licenza di Predicare nelle ville, & altri luoghi della Diocese di sua Sig. Illustriss.*, Bologna, 1586, pp. 15r, 9r–10r; Simoncelli, 'Note', pp. 144–5. R. Palmer, 'The Church, leprosy and plague in medieval and early modern Europe', *The Church and Healing*, ed. W.J. Sheils, Studies in Church History, vol. 19 (Oxford, 1982), pp. 79–99, esp. pp. 83, 95 on plague and epidemics as flails of God; charity was one remedy.
[34] Simoncelli, pp. 141–2; cf. Prosperi, *Tra evangelismo e controriforma*, on Giberti.
[35] Simoncelli, 'Note', p. 151, n. 74.

Later in the seventeenth century the Jesuit Paolo Segneri, an influential adviser to the Grand Duke of Tuscany, adopted the attitude that the poor was especially sinful and this justified his being confined, in order to be educated for a better way of life. This attitude influenced another attempt in Florence to adopt a social discipline and confinement policy—as happened in France.[36]

In Italy there were many signs of hostility towards, and fear of, sections of the poor, whatever the terminology employed, from at least the later fifteenth century. Cities set about identifying the undesirable and desirable poor, often seeing the former as people who should be expelled. During the fifteenth century Genoese authorities expelled beggars from the city. In 1498 in Florence the *Uffiziali del Morbo* scoured the city seeking peasants who had come into the city during the food and health crisis, to drive out those who did not belong.[37] In the 1560s the Bologna authorities rounded up and expelled 'foreign vagrants', after flogging and briefly imprisoning them; the native poor were then placed in hospitals. The papal policy for Rome itself was, at moments of perceived crisis, to round up and expel undesirable beggars (as opposed to alms-seeking pilgrims) and prostitutes, as happened under Pius IV in 1561.[38]

In Mantua in the 1590s during food shortages, when large numbers of poor were begging in the city ('infiniti poveri andar mendicando per la città'), a special magistracy was created to ensure the expulsion to the borders of foreigners without gainful employment, and particularly the beggars ('i guidoni e mendicanti'); native poor ('i poveri terrieri') were placed in different hospitals according to status, or confined and controlled in rooms in the parishes; those who could be, were put to work. Officials recognised that they needed to protect artisans, especially knitters or weavers (members of the *arte dell'aguccheria*), who were temporarily unemployed because the very high prices for food meant people could not afford cloth. But charlatans and professional vagabonds, as well as prostitutes, faced beatings and imprisonment. The useless — but not dangerous — could be allowed to beg to give the rich an opportunity to demonstrate their piety.[39] These strategies of expelling aliens and confining sections of the native poor to prevent trouble from mendicants were described by P. Vizani in his account of the Bologna crisis in the 1590s. His contemporaries were seeking to prevent the insolence of a rabble of mendicants that only eats and shits ('insolenza di tanta canaglia', 'canaglia che sol mangia e caca'). Vizani noted the largesse of the rich, but that this was inadequate for the huge problem of dearth for his estimated 10,000 poor in the city and 30,000 in the countryside.[40]

[36] Lombardi, 'Poveri', p. 182; Pullan, 'Poveri, mendicanti', pp. 1017–18.

[37] B. Geremek, 'Renfermement des pauvres en Italie (XIV–XVII–siècles). Remarques préliminaires', *Histoire économique du monde mediterranée 1450–1650. Mélanges en honneur de F. Braudel* (Toulouse, 1973), pp. 205–17, esp. pp. 207–8; M. Livi Bacci, *La Société italienne devant les crises de mortalité* (Florence, 1978), p. 106.

[38] See below, chapter 10.1, on confining the poor or banishing them.

[39] R. Navarrini and C.M. Belfanti, 'Il problema della povertà nel Ducato di Mantova: aspetti istituzionali e problemi sociali (secoli XIV–XVI)', *Timore e Carità*, pp. 130–3; *Guidoni* were defined by A. Spinola in Genoa as 'a certain type of scroungers who, as enemies of work and resolved to live at others' expense, go about demanding alms under various forms and pretexts'; he saw the mountain people, especially from the Varese region, as the experts in this art, made rich by it. Their activity and its success was to him proof that indiscriminate charity was mistaken; Grendi, 'Pauperismo', p. 629.

[40] P. Vizani, *I due ultimi libri delle historie della sua patria* (Bologna, 1608), p. 138; Camporesi, *Il pane selvaggio*, pp. 75–6, 101.

Mendicants were regarded as criminals by some officials. The Venetian Savi alle Acque in 1600 defended the 'recovery' of mendicants in a new building: 'by these means the opportunity will be removed for these unfaithful to continue in the usual thefts and plunderings, which are committed by many youths and children'.[41] In Florence in the early seventeenth century officials were referring to the licentious and beastly lives of vagabonds ('vivendo vita licentiosissima e da bestie senza alcun altro indirizzo che dell'inclinazioni naturali'), abandoning children, stealing killing and disturbing church services. Begging was illegal so beggars were criminals. This justified expulsion or confinement. Government officials had to face the attitude of some beggars that their activity was a job like others, and justified. According to L. Branca this only encouraged the administrators to treat the mendicants as rebellious recidivists, deserving of harsher treatment.

But there was also some official recognition of the sanctity of the *pauper Christi*, and that it was necessary to request that Christian charity be given to the really needy who could only live through alms, which could of course be organised other than through street and church begging. The officials noted that many Florentines preferred to help the poor directly, rather than through the social control mechanism of the Opera dei Mendicanti set up in 1621; that they were not agreed that beggars should all be confined; that if there were beggars or other poor to be helped outside, the Florentines would contribute there rather than to the Opera; and that a full institutionalisation policy would only work properly with funding from direct applications of taxes, such as a salt tax, but that most Florentines would not accept such a solution. One committee report to the Grand Duke, arguing for confinement of the poor claimed that an early seclusion of them would save them from dying of hunger and cold in the streets, would prevent major disorders, and would stop many from becoming lazy and leaving their jobs to beg on the streets. The result of these attitudes was a muddled, and only partially effective mixture of state and private remedies for the ills of poverty.[42]

A persistence of some medieval attitudes, mixed with Catholic Reform emotions, and a hostility to modern ideas about discriminating against vagabonds and other less favoured poor, found eloquent expression in Alessandro Sperelli's *Della pretiosita della limosina* (1666). Sperelli had been a Curial lawyer and *Consultor* to the Roman Inquisition before becoming bishop of Gubbio (1644–72). He argued that if the rich did not distribute to the poor they could not save themselves (p. 382). But they should not give alms just to escape the pains of Hell (p. 116). Giving to the poor brings the giver closer to God, is a gift of God and is done in imitation of Him — for which there will be spiritual rewards, as St Gregory Nazianzen had argued (pp. 16, 107–13). Giving became a pleasure for both donor and recipient, and would be applauded in heaven (p. 76). If preference was to be shown in giving to the poor it should be for those in extreme necessity (whatever their quality), because, as St Ambrose argued, a failure to help such

---

[41] G. Ellero, 'Un ospedale della Riforma Cattolica veneziana. I Derelitte a SS. Giovanni e Paolo', (degree thesis, Università degli Studi di Venezia, 1980–1), p. 59: 'per questa via sarà levata la occasione agli infedeli per continuare nelle soliti furti, et rapine, che fanno di molti fanciulli e putti'.

[42] L. Branca, 'Pauperismo, assistenza e controllo sociale a Firenze (1621–1632): materiali e ricerche', *ASI*, 141 (1983), 427–8, 445–7, 457–62; Lombardi, 'Poveri', pp. 175 [and see quotation above, note 21], and 177: the mendicant's life was seen by officials as one of 'sfrenata libertà et abominevole licenza', full of 'scandoli e vitij enormi'.

persons was a kind of homicide (p. 308). But he insisted that it was wrong for men to distinguish between true and false poor — that was God's prerogative:

He is very badly advised who, in giving alms, wishes to investigate the quality of the poor, whether they are in such misery through their own fault, whether they are vagabonds, whether they go begging from the desire to escape effort, and to give themselves to idleness, whether they pretend to be maimed, whether they are of good habits; these are sophistries totally contrary to the loving hearts of mercy, and to the purity and simplicity which alms-giving prizes: God would have imposed too great a weight on our shoulders if, besides commanding us to distribute to the poor part of our substance, he had obliged us to make such examinations and inquisitions. (p. 297)[43]

In sixteenth- and seventeenth-century Italy there were mixed attitudes to the begging poor. While they might be increasingly categorised as criminal vagabonds, and charity towards them might evaporate, just as it did towards the gypsies who came into Italy, there were countervailing attitudes. While some historians see the period as a transitional phase between old style, indiscriminate charity with limited discipline, and a modern controlled, discriminating and often punitive policy, I prefer to see the Italian scene as more haphazard or irregular in its development. Harshness and control ebbed and flowed according to particular crises as we shall see in further consideration of places like Rome and Bologna. While the confinement policies were largely based on the attitude that those poor concerned were sinful and likely to be dangerous, there were — as Pullan has argued — those who did not see beggars as criminals, who supported confinement policies on the grounds that this would protect the vulnerable from serious sins and the insidious world. An enclosed environment could change habits and be a 'staging post on the road to virtue and salvation'. This might be particularly so with women, who were a major concern of philanthropists and confraternities, as will be discussed later. And confraternities were to maintain campaigns for private, non-governmental and specialist approaches to helping the poor — deserving or, sometimes, undeserving.[44]

It can also be noted here that in 1651 the Genoese Magistrato dei poveri admitted that because of numerous deaths amongst the poor in the *lazzaretto* used for confining the poor and sick, 'it has rendered the very name of the *lazzaretto* odious to the most miserable, and has almost declared charity to be harmful and deadly'. This led to institutional reform and a return to Christian traditions of charity, largely under the inspiration and work of Emanuele Brignole.[45]

[43] A. Sperelli, *Della Pretiosita della limosina*, which was dedicated to the Vice-chancellor of the Church, Cardinal [F.] Barberini. Cf. Fiorani, 'Religione e Povertà', pp. 66–9, who cites this last passage, but does not deal with the other points covered here. For the importance of St Gregory Nazianzen's writings, and his Byzantine teaching on philanthropy, in the early modern period see: N.Z. Davis, 'Gregory Nazianzen in the service of humanist social reform', *Renaissance Quarterly*, 20 (1967), 455–64; Ball, 'Poverty, charity and the Greek community', p. 135.

[44] B.S. Pullan, 'The old Catholicism, the new Catholicism and the poor', *Timore e Carità*, pp. 17–18; on attitudes to a 'transitional period' cf. B. Geremek, 'L'arrivée des Tsiganes en Italie; de l'assistance à la repression', *ibid.*, pp. 27–44; *idem*, 'Criminalité, vagabondage, paupérisme: la marginalité a l'aube des temps modernes', *Revue d'histoire moderne et contemporaine*, 21 (1974), 364–5; Branca, 'Pauperismo', p. 428. For the view that in the sixteenth–seventeenth centuries there was an overlay of older attitudes, even if the movement for control and seclusion is strong, see D. Zardin's review article on V. Paglia's books in *RSCI*, 39 (1985), 203–9. The founders of the Roman Pietà dei Carcerati are to be seen as humanitarian and culturally motivated.

[45] Grendi, 'Pauperismo', pp. 638, and 657 for codicil to Brignole's will in 1666, expressing his attitudes and priorities.

The conflicting views on poverty and who should be helped by alms-giving are reflected in Abbot De Angelis' *Della Limosina*. This large and tedious work is replete with biblical texts, and with the arguments and commentaries (especially from the Fathers) that interpret them. Though in Italian it is an indexed guide for the professionals, likely to influence public policy especially in the Papal State, rather than a lay philanthropist or confraternity. It is not always clear where De Angelis stood on certain controversies, as he summarised rival points. However, he sides with those who interpret the Bible as meaning that one should give charity even to bad people who request it, even to one's enemies, as Aquinas argued. But for somebody to request alms who does not really need it is gravely sinful, and it is not true *misericordia* to give them something, since it is depriving another, though again to help the evil and impious poor may do good by leading such persons through charity to a conversion.[46]

3 THE PREFERRED POOR

There was one category of poor, deemed to be deserving of support, which received increasing attention in our period: the *poveri vergognosi*, the 'ashamed poor'. This discussion connects with P. Townsend's third sector of poverty mentioned at the beginning of this chapter: 'individual or group subjective deprivation'. There was, and is, no agreement on who should be included among the 'ashamed poor'. Since shame encouraged secrecy it is difficult to find records that show who actually was helped, for example, by the confraternities that specialised in this category, or included it in their remit; they often went to great trouble to hide the identity of recipients. The secrecy and discretion of a Modena confraternity for helping *poveri vergognosi* was recognised in 1530 when the Spanish governor of the city, in trying to get citizens to denounce blasphemers, said they could use the confraternity's secret information box for recording their accusation without betraying their own identity.[47]

While the category of *poveri vergognosi* did include poor nobles, it cannot be assumed that they were the only members of the class, and it can be shown that at least in some areas this classification could include lowly artisans and unskilled low-born women in dire poverty.[48] *Poveri vergognosi* can refer to all persons in need, according to their own standards, who feel ashamed of asking for help. The assumption that this would indicate nobility was based on canon law concepts 'of shame which betrays the well-born', as R. Trexler has argued. He sees the confraternities that helped the *poveri vergognosi* as protecting the urban elite—noble men, women and children who had fallen on hard times. A preference for helping poor nobles was argued for by a leading Venetian reformer in the early sixteenth century, Gasparo Contarini, in advising bishops:

[the bishop should prefer] those for whom, because of their noble origins, poverty was ignominy; without calumny they cannot take a salaried position. One must contribute to them before anyone else. Since it is not to be expected that they will seek alms, one must give them without

---

[46] De Angelis, *Della limosina*, pp. 37–8: 'A qualunque li domanda dà, mali cattivi, ancorche siano tale, & immeritevole di quella, abbattendosi a chiedere la limosina al ricco, si le deue. Il medesimo douemo ancora fare con in nostri nimici, poiche è debito d'amarli, come nostri fratelli, e ciò apertamente ci comanda Christo Salvator nostro per il medesimo Evangelista.' and pp. 40, 45. See above, chapter 1, at nn. 47–8.

[47] G. Ricci, 'Povertà, vergogna e povertà vergognosa', *Società e Storia* 5 (1979), 305; this confraternity supposedly dated from 1258, and was prosperous by the early sixteenth century.

[48] Grendi, 'Ideologia', p. 61; see below chapter 9.2.

being asked, sometimes even to the anonymous. After these have been cared for, [the bishop] should tend to other poor persons.[49]

A Franciscan bishop, Francesco Gonzaga, who established the Mantuan Congregatione de'Poveri in 1594, indicated that preference should be given to nobles fallen on hard times, over those not ashamed to beg.[50]

Caution is needed about the rigidity of the labels of both nobility and *poveri vergognosi*. In 1585 Clemenza Grassi, widow of Gerolamo Castiglioni established a fund (Monte Angelico) to be administered by the Milanese Casa della Carità; it was to provide seven dowries of 100 *scudi* each to *fanciulle nobili*, who were suited to a religious life. In 1594 she explained the qualification about being 'noble'; this did not mean they had to be of noble birth but referred to their way of life—so the fund could accept daughters of artisans, merchants or similar people, provided they were not vagabonds or mendicants.[51]

An argument for preferential treatment of the high-born poor, and for the relative allocation of resources came from a lawyer, Cornelio Benincasa in his *De Paupertate, ac eius privilegiis* (1562); it has some links with modern attitudes to relative deprivation mentioned earlier in this chapter. The worst condition was *egestas*, indigence, being without food and goods. *Paupertas* was 'a necessity of those things required to live rightly' or 'deprivation in respect of riches and goods'; even if the person had food and basic needs, he could be poor in this sense. In judging the condition of the poor Benincasa argued that one should judge the person's position in terms of his deprivation of power in relation to the rich, and his lack of goods in relation to his past and his social expectations. Philanthropic remedies would be based on such relative qualities. The indigent should receive a great deal less than the poor nobleman; to give delicacies to the indigent from a poor sector of society would be sinful of the giver, becaue it would encourage excessive behaviour among the poor. The corollary was that a person used to having servants, but no longer able to afford them, should be treated as poor, should be considered deserving of charitable aid—for himself, and possibly in consideration of servants who would otherwise be dismissed and thus end up among the indigent.[52] This argument was likely to appeal to well-heeled members of confraternities dispensing charity; prefer your own kind, and do not overindulge those not used to indulgence.

Benincasa, however, went on to point out that in common parlance the distinction between *paupertas, egestas* and *inopia* was of little worth (p. 16r). He also argued that a girl who did not lack the necessities of life, but who—as a noble—lacked the amount considered necessary for her dowry, could not be counted as a pauper (p. 15r). Relative

---

[49] G. Contarini, *De Officio Episcopi*, cited by R.C. Trexler, 'Charity and defense of urban elites in the Italian Communes', *The Rich and Well Born and the Powerful. Elites and Upper Classes in History*, ed. F.C. Jaher (Urbana, Chicago and London, 1973), p. 74, and he discusses the canon law, p. 75.

[50] Navarrini and Belfanti, pp. 134-5.

[51] Noto, *Gli amici dei poveri*, p. 235: 'artefici o di mercatanti e simili persone purché non sieno vagabonde o mendicanti'.

[52] Cornelio Benincasa, *Tractatus de paupertate ac eius privilegiis uberrimus* (Perugia, 1562) p. 15. This part was discussed by Trexler, 'Charity', p. 69, though he used the later reprint in the *Tractatus universi iuris* (Venice, 1584) [citing vol. 18 fol. 146 va]; he did not discuss some other passages I have outlined below, which give a different impression of Benincasa's thinking. Benincasa dedicated his first edition to cardinal Archbishop Fulvio Della Corgna of Perugia.

deprivation requiring assistance did not extend this far. Benincasa discussed at length the legal treatment of the poor, and argued that the pauper should receive the benefit of doubt, and help (pp. 33v, 39v, 50v); that in legal cases poverty could be cited in mitigation in various circumstances (without excusing malefaction) (pp. 33v–6r, 104v), and that in contested wills preference should be given to the one that treats a poor man favourably–for the sake of the testator's soul (p. 184v). Benincasa also stressed that doctors and lawyers should serve the poor without charge (pp. 65r–7v), and that the clergy had an obligation to give to the poor out of ecclesiastical property (p. 130v). While Benincasa argued for the preferential treatment of respectable poor, he was basically an advocate of assistance for the poor, whether in alms or in action by professionals.

The secrecy of dealing with the ashamed poor encouraged fraud and deception, and ambiguity about who should be counted as ashamed and deserving compounded the problems. The Bologna authorities in 1548 publicly condemned frauds perpetrated by people claiming to be *poveri vergognosi*, whether poor but not 'ashamed', or noble but not genuinely poor. By 1567 the Bologna confraternity for the ashamed poor, which also ran the S. Marta *conservatorio* for orphaned and vulnerable girls, thought it should define the true ashamed poor:

true ashamed . . . are, and are understood to be, the gentlemen, citizens, merchants, and also good artisans [who have always] lived civilly [and who] may have fallen, and come into poverty, and misery, and to these one should give suitable alms . . . as to those who are ashamed to ask for alms or help from others. [Only secondarily should one help] those for whom, being in the middle between the true ashamed and mendicants, there is not much shame in asking for alms or help from others, and who must be content with what little help these people [in the confraternity] can give them.

By 1641 the confraternity had further defined *poveri vergognosi* to mean gentlemen, citizens, rich merchants, artisans with capital resources from honoured, not vile or abject, *arti*, who were born in Bologna, who have lived well and honoured in the city, but who had now fallen into poverty, and who at present were truly poor and needy. Later qualifications specified that shopworkers and servants were excluded, as well as those heading lowly enterprises, *botteghe*, without capital, but this was not intended to exclude sculptors, painters, surgeons, or similar people who had standing and credit in the city. In the case of widows, the condition of their late husbands should be assessed, and the dowry should not have been less than 2,000 *lire*.[53]

The concern for the ashamed poor, which is evident in the work of confraternities, is to be seen as part of the battle for status in a society of orders. While there was some bias towards nobles and gentlemen within this category it would be unwise to go too far in interpreting the defence of the *poveri vergognosi* as that of an old feudal class resisting the advance of a new bourgeois ethic and a class system based on economic values. There was too broad a spread of social groups included by some in this category to fit this interpretation. Old-fashioned moral attitudes as much as social position were involved in the definitions; a medieval usage of *pauper verecundus* as 'good poor' persisted. But there was clearly a feeling that it was difficult for those in menial jobs,

---

[53] Ricci, 'Povertà', pp. 326–32, quotation pp. 326–7.

irregularly employed and with no funds, to be 'good' or to feel shame. While the ashamed poor generally were less in need physically, while their poverty was relative, while they could be as fraudulent as their inferiors, it is clear that some poor ashamed nobles were in dire conditions at times. Grendi considers that by the seventeenth century about 5 per cent of Genoese nobles could be counted as truly poor.[54]

Another category of poor deemed worthy of preferential support was that of converts to Christianity, *catecumeni*. Their privileged status as poor was recognised in medieval canon law, and among seventeenth-century Neapolitan jurists. In various cities there were confraternities or funds designed to help Jews and Moors who converted. The financial incentives for converts led to many cases of fraud, as individuals 'converted' many times in order to collect donations. This did not, however, end the policy of preferring this category of poor over others, and including them among the licensed beggars in various cities. One generous benefactor for Venetian *catecumeni* persisted though aware that the money might be taken for the wrong reasons: 'I wish them to come to the faith not for the benefit of the legacy, but to save their souls and to become worthy of paradise.'[55]

B.S. Pullan has advanced the argument that a characteristic of the 'new philanthropy' of the early modern period was a preference for 'redeeming' the souls of Jews and prostitutes; they were sinners most in need of saving, and at the same time they presented the hardest task for the philanthropist, so that a successful conversion might be judged most meritorious.[56]

The discussion above has exemplified some of the problems of dealing with poverty, given the variable concepts used by both modern commentators and people in the early modern period. There is and was no clear-cut idea as to all the kinds of people who might be included as 'poor' and, within that classification, whether they were deemed worthy of philanthropy. Using some modern arguments about relative deprivation and about needs we may be better able to appreciate some sixteenth-century attitudes on who was to be helped and how. A perception at least by the end of the century that the poverty problem was worsening, and becoming more dangerous, did evoke some harsher, 'disciplining' approaches towards the poor. But for Italy we should be wary of accepting the modern theory that there was a consistent trend towards 'social control' under state and church authority.

Whatever their attitudes all contemporaries would have agreed that there were moments when people were in need, and when action was necessary from governments or private persons and institutions. It is to events and actions that we now turn.

[54] Grendi, 'Pauperismo', p. 61; G. Assereto, 'Pauperismo e assistenza. Messa a punto di studi recenti', *ASI*, 141 (1983), 265–6, 268; G. Ricci, 'Naissance du pauvre honteux: entre l'histoire des idées et l'histoire sociale', *Annales ESC*, 38 (1983), 158–77.

[55] Pullan, 'The old Catholicism', pp. 13–25, quoting p. 15; *idem, The Jews of Europe*, pp. 243–312, extensively on the *catecumeni*, and esp. pp. 294–312 on cases where fraud and materialism were suspected; Musi, 'Pauperismo', p. 265; Camporesi, *Il libro dei vagabondi*, pp. XCII–XCIII, 31–3, 44–5, 117–22.

[56] Professor Pullan presented these points in two talks given to the Glasgow Branch of the Historical Association and the Department of Modern History, Glasgow University, in November 1987: 'The conversion of the Jews: Italian style', and '"Support and Redeem": charity in Italian cities in the Renaissance and Counter-Reformation'. A version of the former talk has now appeared in the *Bulletin of the John Rylands Library*, 70, no. 1 (Spring 1988), 53–70.

8

POVERTY: NEEDS AND GENERAL RESPONSES

There were several kinds of crisis, public or private, that could cause many people to be in need and 'poor', though in 'normal' years they might not be so classified. The concatenation of various public crises — as in the 1520s–1540s or in the 1590s — probably affected long-term attitudes, as well as immediate responses, to poverty and charity. Contemporaries were aware of the needs of many people; governments responded in particular to food crises, but their remedies could be highly defective and counter-productive; so this left room for private assistance from individuals or from confraternities and hospitals. Some of the physical responses to needs offered by confraternities were obviously inadequate in terms of the population at large. But section 3 seeks to give guidance on what the sums of money donated to individuals or families might have meant to those lucky or foresighted enough to obtain allocations.

I THE NEED FOR HELP

There were moments in the lives of individuals, families and communities when they were afflicted by a disaster or crisis which necessitated some form of assistance from others, at governmental or private level. These crises could affect people whether they were normally classified as poor or not. In the case of individuals the crisis might come from illness or old age when others of the family could not, or would not, help; from temporary unemployment; from the death of a relative who was their main support. The need might be perceived by others, and philanthropic help be forthcoming. The kinds of personal crises that led to confraternity donations in such circumstances will be illustrated by individual examples in chapters 9 and 10.

There were general crises, caused by food shortages, plague and epidemic, that affected the bulk of the community and rendered most people 'needy', so then help might be hardest to find. Governments in the sixteenth century were expected to provide some general remedies, or limit the effects of the disasters, at least for the major cities; and possibly to coordinate help for the worst afflicted individuals.

There were many years in the sixteenth and early seventeenth century when large parts of Italy were afflicted by diseases, serious food shortages and war damage; often all three went together. Armies destroyed or seized food stocks, or prevented sowing; they spread plague, syphilis and other diseases; panics over plague, flight from the area, the death of farmers meant less farming the following season, with production probably falling more than the number of surviving mouths to feed. Italy was a major war theatre from the 1490s until 1559, with the inflow of French, Spanish, German and Swiss troops. The dislocation and disasters of these wars stimulated a number of the philanthropic developments outlined later. The worst years were probably the 1520s, with widespread repercussions from the great events such as the Sack of Rome in 1527, or the siege of Florence in 1530, but also from less famous sackings, pillaging and destruction. The major threat of war as such returned to northern Italy from the late 1620s, though one can argue that the repercussions of Spanish involvement in the Netherlands, and the German 'Thirty Years War' had already had a major impact on taxation and the economy, adding to the numbers of the needy, especially in southern Italy.

Plague was a persistent threat throughout the period — as of course it had been during the previous 150 years; but the most devastating epidemics were from 1522–8 for nearly all of Italy, from 1575–7 for Sicily, Lombardy and Venetia, from 1629–33 in northern Italy (with only parts of Friuli and Romagna escaping), and in 1656 in Rome and Naples. Venice can provide detailed figures to illustrate the impact. For example between 1 July 1575 and 28 February 1577 (the main plague period) 46,721 people died in Venice. The city's population recovered fairly quickly with a high birth rate. During the next visitation, between July 1630 and October 1631 about 46,490 persons died in the city and *lazzaretti*, and it was reported that at the height of the panic, on 14 and 15 August 1630, about 24,000 fled the city. It has been estimated that about a third of the people of Venice and Bologna died from plague, or half from cities like Milan, Mantua or Padua, and that the population of Tuscany fell 17 per cent between the 1622–8 census and 1632.[1]

Such deaths, coupled with government restrictions on trade and movement designed to reduce the chances of spreading the epidemic, caused major economic dislocation. Food distribution was an immediate problem, and the next season's sowing, pruning and harvesting were likely to be affected. Though there were fewer mouths to feed there was also less food, especially in an afflicted city. In a less severe crisis in 1598 the dependent city of Cividale was isolated for eight months, surrounded by Venetian troops ready to shoot escapees, as the Republic's officials tried (fairly successfully) to contain the epidemic.[2] Philanthropic help would be needed, but its organisation was disrupted, and sources of wealth contributing to it reduced.

In addition there were other disease epidemics, such as typhus, most especially in 1505, 1528, 1590–1, 1628–9 and (notably in Florence) 1648–9. Their effects have been less studied than those of plague. Livi Bacci argues that from the sixteenth century there

[1] Livi Bacci, *La Société Italienne*, pp. 35–60. For the previous century he deduced the main plague years to be: 1400, 1411–12, 1416–17, 1424–5, 1430–1, 1437, 1448–9, 1457, 1478–9 (p. 40). For Venice: AA.VV. *Venezia e la Peste 1348/1797* (Venice, 2nd edn., 1980), esp. articles by R.C. Mueller, 'Peste e demografia. Medioevo e Rinascimento', pp. 93–4; by P. Preto, 'Peste e demografia. L'età moderna. Le due peste del 1575–77 e 1630–31', pp. 96–8; cf; cf. G.M. Weiner, 'The demographic effects of the Venetian plagues of 1575–77 and 1630–31', *Genus*, 26 (1970), 41–57, esp. Table III. The city's population seems to have fallen from 168, 672 in 1563 to 134,871 in 1581, and risen to 148,637 by 1586. On other cities: Livi Bacci, p. 49.

[2] R.J. Palmer, 'L'azione della Repubblica di Venezia nel controllo della peste' in AA.VV. *Venezia e la Peste*, pp. 103–10.

was an increase in typhus, but that there was a decline in the number of crisis years of plague — in relation to 'normal' years.[3] Typhus was less lethal than plague — with 20–40 per cent of victims dying from it, as opposed to 70–80 per cent of those who caught plague.[4] In some ways this may have been more important for the problem of the needy; people survived, but in a very unfit state; families were more patchily affected leaving more to be looked after as needy, whereas plague killed — or spared — whole families. The dead also challenged the philanthropy of those who felt all should be given a decent burial — even though in practice this was hardly feasible in the great plague epidemics such as 1629–33.

The problem of famine or dearth is more important for our concerns. With food shortages more people were more regularly in need. It was considered that government actions and/or philanthropy could be beneficial. Chroniclers and diarists provide evidence on contemporaries' awareness of the food shortages. They also, along with some government records, show how prices for basic foods — grains, bread, wine — fluctuated wildly and rapidly. Such figures show how many people could rapidly be in need of relief — whether or not they received it.

Diplomatic dispatches and diaries reported the incidence of famine conditions in Italy and other parts of Europe. The famous Venetian diarist Marino Sanuto collected much of this information for the first half of the sixteenth century. For example he and the Republic's ambassador Antonio Giustiniani reported dire conditions in Rome during the winter of 1504–5, with Romans dying in the streets in January despite some papal largesse by Julius II. Giustiniani thought papal policy as harsh as nature — though his views may have been coloured by the political difficulties of his mission.[5] Another Venetian diarist, Priuli, noted *la grande charestia* throughout much of Italy in the same season — in Florence, Naples, Milan, Bologna, Mantua and Ferrara especially — *veramente incredibile*.[6] Sanuto reported on the famine and pestilence that afflicted Rome and the Papal States at the time of the 1527 Sack of Rome by imperial troops, but that also menaced other parts of Italy, including his own Venice, with poor men and women dying in the streets as a result.[7]

The regularity of urban food crises can be illustrated from Perugia's experience. On the evidence of chroniclers and of the government edicts (from communual officials and/or papal governors who tried to control food supplies, to ensure sufficiency at controlled prices), we can identify the following crisis years for grain between 1480 and 1540: 1484, 1489, 1491, 1496, 1505, 1509, 1511, 1517, 1519, every year from 1523 to 1534, 1536, 1538–9. In addition to nature's attack on the harvests, there was war damage

[3] Livi Bacci, pp. 16, 48–52.
[4] C.M. Cipolla, *I pidocchi e il granduca: crisi economica e problemi sanitari nella Firenze del 1600* (Bologna, 1979), pp. 9, 12.
[5] Sanuto, *I Diarii*, vol. 6, cols. 91, 93, 125, 134, 165; Setton, *The papacy and the Levant* (1204–1571), vols. 3–4 (Philadelphia, 1984), vol. 3, pp. 34, 36; cf. Pullan, *Rich and Poor*, pp. 239 n. 47, 245–7, 249–50.
[6] Cited by Setton, vol. 3, p. 36. He provides lavish quotations from Sanuto and other diarists, from ambassadors and envoys of the period.
[7] Sanuto, *I Diarii*, vol. 46, col. 400, 20 December 1527: 'È grandissima carestia et si crida per le strade. Poveri e povere muorono di fame ch'è una compassion; et niuna provision si fa, che par un purgatorio la piaza di San Marco, per la strada di la Marzaria, et per chiesie, et per tutto'. The Council of Ten provided some remedies to ensure flour for the poor, and to control prices, cols. 409–10, 417, 423–4.

as Perugia was caught up in Italian-wide politics, or was affected by faction fights within the oligarchy, and struggles over whether Perugia should be effectively ruled from Rome. Locusts added to the damage in 1491 and 1495, and plague in 1482, 1486–7, 1487–9, 1493, 1496, 1504–5 and 1522–9.[8]

While in the later sixteenth century war in Italy ceased to be a major cause of dislocation, misery and poverty, there was a deterioration of living conditions in the 1580s and more especially in the 1590s caused by climatic changes leading to wetter and colder growing seasons, a shift from arable to pasturage by leading landowners in various parts of Italy — especially in the Papal States and Kingdom of Naples — and an increase in brigandage and other social troubles. Food supplies were short and prices high throughout most of the 1590s, with limited compensation from rising wages even for those in work. It is generally agreed that the 1590s did not mark a major demographic turning point — just as overall population levels could recover quickly from the major plague disasters of 1575. The general population increase up to the 1590s, the failure to augment grain supplies within Italy to match the decline in the Sicilian wheat supplies, which for centuries had been an abundant source for other states in Italy, the need to rely on supplies from further afield, especially the Baltic, which were most likely to be carried by alien merchants and ships from the Netherlands and England — all meant that basic food costs rose in real terms, as did taxes. Some wages over the decades did rise to help cover prices, but the general verdict is that from the late sixteenth century the real cost of living rose, hence more people were potentially vulnerable, and likely to be in need at times. At the end of the sixteenth century Rome was one of the best-fed cities in Europe, as contemporaries were aware; from then on this privileged position was eroded.[9]

The general crises over plague, typhus and food supplies would have considerably increased the proportionate numbers in need among the survivors, but reduced the resources and opportunities for effective assistance. We shall see in section 2 some attempts by government to respond; their inadequacies left room for confraternity action (chapters 9 and 10). Here it is worth suggesting some general effects of the concatenation of certain crises. The death and dearth crises of the early sixteenth century, particularly in the 1520s and 1530s, in conjunction with a religious crisis, may have forcefully stimulated charitable responses, leading to heightened lay confraternity philanthropy, as well as that of religious Orders. The troubles of the 1590s had a less positive effect; in the short term they seem to have encouraged a hardening of attitude

---

[8] ASP Editti e Bandi, vols. 2–3; BCP Ms 1151, T. Bottonio, 'Annali', vol. 2, fols. 92v, 96v; Pietro Angelo di Giovanni, 'Cronaca Perugina inedita', *BSPU*, 9 (1903), 33–380; Giulio di Constantino, 'Cronaca', *Cronache della Città di Perugia*, ed. A. Fabretti (5 vols., Turin, 1887–94), vol. 4, pp. 145–287. These problems were outlined in my Oxford B.Litt Thesis, 1967, 'Politics and society in Perugia 1488–1540'; see also my 'The Baglioni as tyrants' on the conflicts that affected the city; Grohmann, *Città e territorio . . . Perugia* (2 vols., Perugia, 1981), esp. chapter 4 including Table 6, pp. 84–5, 'Pestilenze e carestie documentate a Perugia, 1300–1591', no. 7, pp. 86–7, 'Dati climatici documentati per Perugia. 1309–1492', and no. 8, pp. 91–2, 'Prezzi di derrate alimentari a Perugia, 1300–1493'. Cf. Genoa, which had crises of *carestia* 1539, 1542, 1546, 1555–7, 1561–2, 1568, 1577, 1589–91, 1596: Grendi, 'Pauperismo', pp. 625–6.

[9] See esp. P. Clark (ed.), *The European Crisis*, notably: N.S. Davidson, 'Northern Italy in the 1590s', pp. 157–76; P. Burke, 'Southern Italy in the 1590s: hard times or crisis?', pp. 177–90; B.S. Pullan, 'The roles of the state and the town in the general crisis of the 1590s', pp. 285–300, all of which provide valuable references to the literature and evidence on this period. See also Livi Bacci for the general demographic argument; J. Revel, 'Les privilèges d'une capitale: l'approvisionnement de Rome à l'époque moderne', *Annales ESC*, 30 (1975), 563–74.

towards the dangerous poor, and an extension of social discipline policies — however ineffective (see chapter 10). Confraternities were partly caught up in this, but may also have undermined the policy by offering alternative remedies. The third group of crises — in the late 1620s and 1630s — seem to have had a much greater structural impact in Italy; population, economic vitality and possibly morale failed to recover, leaving more needy people but less physical assistance. Among confraternities an increased concern with death and souls in Purgatory may have been a connected outcome.

In the context of need and assistance it is however the short term food crises, rather than overall trends that are of prime concern. During a *carestia* the basic prices of grain and bread changed dramatically. This made vulnerable those who were not rich, or who did not control their own food production. Wages or licit incomes from other sources would never adjust to cover higher market prices for food. In Venice during 1527–30, when the city was affected by food shortages and plague the price of wheat per bushel (*staio/staro*) varied from 4 *lire* to 15½ *lire*; wheat flour from 8 to 18 *lire*, coarse flour from 10 to 16 *lire*.[10] In a later crisis in Venice the average grain price for the period 1589–98 was 24 *lire* a *staio*, but in February 1591 it reached 40.[11] In Perugia in 1528 the most informative chronicler records the grain price as varying between 4 and 7 florins per *mina*.[12] In Rome a *rubbio* of wheat cost 5.30 *scudi* in early 1582, 8 *scudi* in October, and 13.14 in early 1583.[13] In Naples during the period 1573–9 the official grain buying price was 9.8 or 9.9 *carlini* a *tomolo*, but in December 1586 it was 16 *carlini*, by which time there had been food riots. The price fell to 8.5 by July 1587.[14] For the longer term a major statistical study suggests that grain prices in the second half of the sixteenth century were generally about double those of the first half, and this worsened in the 1590s, that incomes for agricultural or urban workers (manual, masons or washer-women), despite some compensatory rises, lagged behind the price increases.[15]

For Modena figures are available for the whole of the sixteenth and seventeenth centuries to show both long- and short-term changes in food prices, salaries and the availability of food. Taking yearly averages one can find the following fluctuations in the average cost in *soldi* of a *staro* of wheat:

| 1525: | 32.75 | 1526: | 47.25 | 1527: | 133.35 |
| 1528: | 150.00 | 1529: | 158.65 | 1530: | 53.75 |

or

| 1588: | 150.05 | 1589: | 169.50 | 1590: | 276.75 |
| 1591: | 390.00 | 1592: | 380.15 | 1593: | 328.20 |

But if one looks at monthly averages there are even more dramatic shifts:

[10] Pullan, 'The famine in Venice', Appendix I, pp. 196–9, using figures given by Sanuto, who has fewer quotations for coarse flour.

[11] Davidson, 'Northern Italy', p. 159.

[12] Giulio di Constantino, 'Cronaca', *Cronache della Città di Perugia*, ed. Fabretti, p. 154.

[13] Simoncelli, 'Note', p. 146; Delumeau, *Vie économique*, vol. 2, pp. 609–10.

[14] G. Coniglio, *Aspetti della società meridionale nel secolo XVI* (Naples, 1978), pp. 125–30.

[15] G. Coniglio, 'La rivoluzione dei prezzi nella città di Napoli nei secoli XVI e XVI', *Società Italiana di Statistica. Atti della ix riunione scientifica* (Spoleto, 1952), pp. 205–40, esp. pp. 232–7.

1590	February	167.0	June	208.6		July	254.0
	August	389.5	September	390.0		October	381.0
	November	392.0	December	414.0	1591	January	396.7
	February	350.0	March	432.0		April	488.0
	May	469.0					

A mason might have received a 25 per cent or so increase in piece-work rates from the mid-1570s to 1590, possibly covering general inflation; but increases in the 1590s did not cover high food costs; and presumably the amount of work available would have declined as food prices affected investment in new work from employers. G.L. Basini calculates, for the quinquennium 1590–4 a wages increase of 10 per cent for masons, 10 per cent for manual workers, 10.5 per cent for a carpenter (*falegname*), while his price index rose 79 per cent.[16] Under these circumstances respectable hardworking families could soon face serious poverty or destitution; those already poor faced disaster and death, unless help was forthcoming.

Officials and establishment leaders, as well as chroniclers were aware of famine conditions and dire poverty under such circumstances. Again to take Modena, in the 1540s a chronicler reported that poverty afflicted all classes, as a result of which the poor were billeted on the rich and on ecclesiastics; citizens might just survive, but the *contadini* in the countryside might not. Alms were totally inadequate for this crisis.[17] In 1592 Modenese officials calculated that 2,952 had died from *carestia* during 1591 in the city (some coming from outside looking for alms), and 1,411 in the district; the city's population was then 16,695, the district's 19,619.[18] In another crisis in 1620 city officials drew up a list of the extremely poor in each parish, *poveri posti in estrema necessità*, and enumerated 2,360 (for a population of 20,505 recorded in 1620).[19]

In the same year in Florence the health officials reported on living conditions of the poor, especially in the context of the typhus epidemic which coincided with high food prices and an industrial depression: the poor suffered from cold because they opened the windows to let out the infection; the basements of the houses were full of stinking, fetid water where all the waste was thrown; drinking water in their wells was mixed with fetid water and sewage. The rounding up of some of the poor inhabitants to put into a hospital for beggars, and the expulsion of others from the city was a partly efficacious remedy in the short term, even if a proper supply and drainage construction might have been better.[20] In 1630 the Florentine Compagnia di S. Michele was entrusted with investigating the sanitary conditions of the poor; after visiting about a third of the city its members warned government officials of the grim conditions and pointed out, for example, that they had discovered 'many houses where because of misery (*meschinità*)

---

[16] G.L. Basini, *L'uomo e il pane* (Milan, 1970), esp. Tables on pp. 155, 156, 158 and graphs after p. 96 for figures and trends; *idem, Sul mercato di Modena tra Cinque e Seicento. Prezzi e salari* (Milan, 1974), esp. Table on p. 127 for the 1590–4 comparisons; cf. price fluctuations in Pisa, Livi Bacci, *La Société italienne*, p. 50, which was based on figures from P. Malanima, 'Aspetti di mercato e prezzi del grano e delle segale a Pisa dal 1548 al 1818', AA.VV. *Ricerche Storiche* (Pisa, 1976), pp. 321–7.

[17] Basini, *Sul mercato*, p. 54.

[18] Basini, *L'uomo e il pane*, pp. 17–18.

[19] *Ibid.*, p. 81.

[20] Cipolla, *I pidocchi*, p. 12; Branca, 'Pauperismo'.

there is not even the comfort of a bed, people sleeping on a little uncovered and filthy straw, and some others have foul and fetid straw mattresses'.[21]

Throughout our period there were reports of starvation conditions in the city and Kingdom of Naples, though knowledge of this by the Viceroy and his officials often led to amelioration through the government organisation of supplies — at least for the Naples city and area — and rationing for rich and poor alike as in 1547, 1591 and 1595. Jesuits on their missions in the South reported on the dire conditions of peasants, living like animals; they sometimes argued that the poor should be allowed to work on feast-days for themselves, since they were required by their lords on virtually all working days.[22] A Jesuit preaching before the Duke of Ferrara in the 1590s declared that parents fled rather than see their children die from starvation because they could not feed them. Chroniclers at the time reported that many were very sick, mad or dying in Ferrara and Modena, as the bread that the poor could obtain was bad, being made of beans or wheat adulterated heavily with tares or darnel. In 1592 a Modena baker was arrested for such an act of adulteration.[23] In 1601 another Jesuit upbraided the Duke of Modena in the Cathedral that not enough was being done to help and protect the poor.[24]

Awareness of the plight of the poor also came from published books for those able and willing to read them. G.B. Segni for example reported on both past and current famines in books produced at the end of the sixteenth century. In his *Trattato sopra la carestia e fame* (1602), wishing to highlight the grotesque physical transformations that occurred in starving people, he referred back to the crisis in Padua in 1529 when 'every morning in the city twenty-five and thirty people were found dead from hunger on the dung of the streets. The poor did not have human features.'[25] Segni, in his *Discorso sopra la carestia e fame* (1591) reported that the peasants had eaten the seed, had abandoned the fields, seized animals and consumed them. He went on to attack all sectors of society for this plight, and the absence of true Christianity:

The worship of God, both external and internal, is reduced almost to nothing. Religion has become just a story for the people . . . The rich are avaricious, the poor without faith . . . Justice is administered only against the poor, and the powerful, who deserve a thousand fires and a thousand chains, escape unpunished . . . Nevertheless, O Italy, Christ has his scythe in his hand, has not yet lowered it, and your hunger is not yet over.[26]

---

[21] Cipolla, *I pidocchi*, p. 14.

[22] G. Coniglio, *Il viceregno di Napoli nel sec. XVII* (Rome, 1955), p. 32; *idem, Aspetti*, pp. 75–6, 290–2; *idem*, 'Annona e Calmieri a Napoli durante la dominazione spagnuola. Osservazioni e rilievi', *Archivio Storico per le Provincie Napoletane*, 65 (1940), 134–6.

[23] Camporesi, 'Cultura popolare', p. 107; Vizani, *Historie*, pp. 134–5, 138, also complained about the adulteration of food supplies to Bologna in 1589–90.

[24] Basini, *L'uomo e il pane*, p. 76.

[25] Camporesi, *Il pane selvaggio*, p. 5; Segni, *Trattato*, p. 53: 'in Padoa del 1529 ogni mattina si ritrovavano per la città vinticinque e trenta morte di fame sopra i lettami nelle strade. Gli poveri non avevano effigie umana.' He tended to use historical examples when illustrating the evils of bad government or the consequences of immorality. Segni was a Canon Regular from the Congregation of San Salvatore. On him see M. Rosa, 'Chiesa, idee sui poteri e assistenza in Italia dal Cinque al Settecento', *Società e Storia*, n. 10 (1980), 787–8.

[26] Segni, *Discorso*, pp. 22–4, esp. p. 23v: '. . . Gli ricchi avari. Gli poveri, senza fede . . . La Giustizia si aministra solo contra gli poveri, e gli potenti, che meritano mille fuoche, e mille cepipi, se ne passano impuniti'; partly used by Camporesi, *Il pane selvaggio*, pp. 188–9; cf. Segni, *Trattato*, pp. 55–6 for similar comments: 'la fame apunto è flagello appropriato alli peccati, che hoggidi sono in colmo, e dominano questo clima nostro'.

Segni also argued that people varied in their ability to cope with hunger; children and the old could resist hunger least, but phlegmatic people could resist hunger longer than the choleric — like a Scotsman (in Rome), who normally ate three times as much as others but, being phlegmatic, could withstand famine.[27]

In the same period G.C. Croce, as a man from a poverty-stricken background who had learned to read and write, wrote many poems describing the plight of the poor, their lives, joys and miseries. His *Lamento della povertà sopra l'estremo freddo di questa primavera del anno 1586* went through various editions, as did his *Lamento de'poveretti i quali stanno a piggione* and others. Faced with five months of cold, the poor burn everything they can, pawn what they possess, shoeless little children go begging, shivering under arcades:

> Oimè Dio, che freddo è questo!
> Quanti abrugian le lettiere
> le carieghe e le banchette
> e le sporte e le paniere
> le scaranne e le cassette!
> Quante donne, poverette,
> per ostare nel crudo giaccio,
> con il pegno sotto il braccio
> vanno a tor denari impresto
>
> Oimè Dio, che freddo è questo!
> Quanti son che vendut'hanno
> fin la penna de'suoi letti!
> Quanti ancor cercando vanno
> alle porte, a gl'altrui tetti!
> Quanti scalzi fanciulletti
> vanno atorno mendicando
> sotto i portici tremando,
> per sto freddo disonesto.[28]

In his lament for those who have to rent their accommodation he mentions those who are without clothing, wood, bread or wine and who receive no compassion from their landlords; rent takes up all the money, the dowry sends them off to the Monte pawn-broking institution, the only secure roof might be that of the prison.[29] Croce treated hunger as a potent drug, he saw the paralysing and narcotic effects of adulterated bread, the possible connection between witchcraft and plants eaten in the countryside to stave off hunger.[30]

Through official reports, the preaching of missionaries or the writings of polemicists and literary figures an awareness of need and poverty was created, images of the poor

---

[27] Segni, *Trattato*, pp. 6–7. His view was based on the story of a Scotsman in Rome who claimed to be able to survive for twenty to thirty days without food; his feat was tested by Clement VII who had him locked up in a closed room.

[28] *Lamento della povertà*, lines 54–62, 63–71, from modern edn. in Rouch (ed.) *Storie di vita popolare*, pp. 135–42, quoting from p. 137.

[29] *Ibid.*, pp. 151–8.

[30] *Ibid.*, pp. 125–70.

- in short-term or more permanent misery — were made known, and increasingly so. How governments and officials responded is our next concern, so that we can better understand the roles that confraternities, and the institutions they sponsored, could perform.

2 GOVERNMENT RESPONSES TO CRISES AND NEEDS

The government responses to crises created by, and causing poverty, took various forms: the expulsion of undesirable persons such as beggars, prostitutes, or alms-seeking foreigners from the major cities; the banning of begging in the city, or limiting it to licensed persons; confinement of the native poor in hospitals or asylums; accumulation of food supplies from the surrounding countryside or from other areas to be issued free or at controlled prices; the provision of new work for the able-bodied, in the 'hospitals', or through grants, tax concessions or protective legislation to reinvigorate industries.

Official responses showed a mixture of panic, confusion, helplessness, and the occasional misplaced confidence in one or two specific remedies, which often meant passing on the problems, preferably to another state. The small Republic of Lucca, among other states, faced a crisis in the 1520s. The city council tried to ensure food supplies for the city; to reduce the number of mouths to feed in 1527 it expelled undesirable aliens and beggars. When plague threatened in 1528 it considered confining the mendicants left in the city, but this policy seems to have lasted only for a limited period. In later crises, especially in 1539–40, the Lucca government expanded its control over the poor to be helped, and those to be expelled, and created an Office of the Poor as its main agency. The evidence on supplmentary private assistance is limited.[31]

Some policies can be exemplified by quoting reactions in Parma in 1591. On 8 February Cardinal Odoardo Farnese, then responsible for the Duchy at home, wrote to Duke Ranuccio:

I have called before me the deputies for the poor, who say they have made their visits and already distributed 500 *scudi* in alms and that the number of poor is very large and is on the increase everywhere, with people coming in from the *contado*, and it is cruel to chase them away since provisions are not made for them there either. However, it is said that they should not be allowed to spend the night in the city, but that they should be given a little alms and be threatened with punishment if they return, so that others do not follow their example and madly rush to the city, as might happen if word got around that they were certain to be given alms.

Following a distribution of grain supplies the Governor of Parma wrote to the Duke on the 12th:

This provision had been judged necessary because of the continual complaints and pleas made by the poor *contadini* coming here, not knowing how to sustain themselves, though we have kept the sum as low as possible.[32]

---

[31] S. Russo, 'Potere pubblico e carità privata. L'assistenza ai poveri a Lucca tra xvi secolo', *Società e Storia*, 23 (1984), 52–5.

[32] G. Papagno and M.A. Romani, 'Una cittadella e una città', *Annali dell'Istituto storico italo-germanico in Trento*, 8 (1982) [1984], 180 n. 65. On the problem of outsiders flocking to a city if help seemed on offer, see comments of contemporary writers like L. Da Porto for Vicenza in 1528 and G. Priuli for Venice in 1505, cited by Pullan in 'The famine in Venice', pp. 145 n. 17, 153.

The rulers felt impelled to act, but the alms and grain supplies reluctantly given were inadequate, partly because it was felt that more generous provision in the city would simply attract more petitioners from outside. In the event the refortification of the city, in providing more jobs for about 3,000 workers, was the most beneficial government contribution to the poor. Duke Alessandro Farnese also supplied grain from Antwerp to give bread to workers on the citadel site, though there were accusations in 1592 that adulteration of the bread with darnel was causing diarrhoea. Protests from the citizens led in December 1591 to the dismissal of about 500 aliens in that workforce, mainly from the other leading Farnese city of Piacenza, and the restriction of this employment to the Parmegiani. Neighbourliness, even in a small state, could be very localised. The notion of putting the destitute poor to work, of having job-creation schemes, was unusual here, though the Luccan Republic in 1630 put its able-bodied vagabonds to work on the fortifications. As we shall indicate later some of the institutions created for confined poor had work schemes within them.[33]

The problems of ensuring basic food and income could be beyond the competence of both private philanthropy and government efforts. This might be recognised even in the comparatively well-regulated city of Genoa, when state institutions (such as the Office for the Poor and the Magistrato della Misericordia) and the philanthropy of rich patricians cooperated to control poverty, and maintain social peace. In the 1590s it was admitted that this peace was threatened by the inadequacies of state and private resources. The Bologna chronicler-historian P. Vizani praised the charity of the rich in his city, but noted that this was totally inadequate to deal with the food crises faced from 1589 onwards. In 1590 he indicated that there were about 10,000 poor in the city, according to official lists, and about 30,000 in the contado seeking help. The government could not secure adequate supplies from abroad. Government deputies dispersed four once of rice per person in the contado to stave off starvation there. Possibly the most successful example of official action was in Prato, where the Pia Casa dei Ceppi Riuniti, under government control, was a considerable distributor of food assistance to the city's poor. There seems to have been a well-regulated licensing system for those who should be helped. In the 1621–2 crisis 801 persons, out of a population of about 3,000, were licensed to receive assistance. The officials of the Ceppi were able clearly to distinguish 55 heads of families (27 of them women) as poveri vergognosi, and grant them special help. There were some more private institutions also ready to assist. Prato may be a rare case where government and private philanthropy managed to respond adequately to serious long-term and short-term crises throughout the early modern period.[34]

In the face of food shortages governments in the sixteenth century took positive action by collecting supplies of grain (and sometimes other foods) to be released at set prices supposedly below the highest market prices, or for some to be distributed free

[33] Ibid., pp. 178–80, 184; Russo, 'Potere pubblico', p. 69 and n. 104; see below chapter 10.1, for confined poor.

[34] Savelli, pp. 175–7, and on the work of the Genoese Office of the Poor, and the State's attempt to guarantee grain supplies, pp. 199–206; Vizani, Historie, pp. 138–9; Fasano Guarini (ed.), Prato, esp. pp. 430, 434–7, 440, 451. The Pia Casa dei Ceppi was the result of Duke Cosimo I de' Medici's reorganisation in 1545 of the older Ceppi, assistance institutions of considerable wealth (derived for example from the famous 'Merchant of Prato', Francesco Datini); it was a lay rather than an ecclesisastical institution, with government-appointed officials, and does not seem to have had a confraternity element, (ibid., pp. 286, 330, 430 and 337 n. 12).

to deserving cases. There might be rulings on the size and price of bread loaves, and price controls on a wide front, and even (as in Naples) rationing.[35]

These procedures entailed a number of complications and disadvantages that may have made more people poor, or rendered the situation worse for some categories of poor. Priority was given to the main governmental cities. If a state was securing supplies from within its territory it meant that stocks were sent to central repositories by the producers. Peasant farmers would almost certainly not be able to keep enough for themselves; in a serious crisis they were likely to have to go to the city, and pay there, even at officially controlled prices, much more than they had received when selling. The better quality grains, especially wheat, went to the city, the inferior ones being left to the peasantry. City dwellers might be protected, the *contadini* not. The knowledge that produce might be commandeered by city officials probably led to lower production.[36] A policy designed to help a metropolis like Rome, which may thereby have become one of the best provisioned and fed cities in Europe (though the calculation of average wheat, meat and wine consumptions disguises the great contrasts between rich and poor) was to the detriment not only of the immediate countryside and its rural population, but to that of the many other cities in the Papal State. To some extent this was recognised at the time, as happened after the 1586 food riot in Perugia, though it did not lead to any dramatic change in policy. The policy was not seriously reconsidered until the Enlightenment.[37] The concentration of considerable expenditure and administrative effort on Rome could not prevent trouble there either. In 1591 major food shortages coincided with carnival; Pope Gregory XIII spent 100,000 *scudi* seeking foreign grain, and cancelled the usual carnival celebrations (including banquets which were a notable feature of the Roman season) except for a few carefully licensed spectacles. But there was still a riot on 6 February against bread prices which was reported in other states. However, one might argue that without government action, and confraternity work, there would have been more than a riot.[38]

There were some cities, such as Bergamo, that did seek to defend the interests of the *contado* as well as the city, but generally policies designed to help the urban community would have depleted the resources of the other areas.[39]

The policy of having official prices set by bureaucracies that stored and controlled supplies also had drawbacks. Detailed studies of such official prices, *calmieri*, especially for Naples and Modena, indicate that the official levels were not much below market ones. However, the Neapolitan government did have a policy that was better thought out than most, and worked on long-term calculations, rather than simply reacting to the worst crises. Calculating what was needed globally (using a basic figure of one *rotolo*, 0.89 kilos, per person a day), it regularly secured large quantities of grains, especially wheat. Its officials made strenuous efforts to regulate the issue of standard loaves of

[35] Coniglio, *Aspetti*, pp. 75–6; more generally see *idem* 'L'Annona' in AA.VV. *Storia di Napoli* (10 vols., Bari, 1975–81), vol. 3, pp. 247–71.

[36] Coniglio, *Aspetti*.

[37] Black, 'Perugia and papal absolutism'; M. Petrocchi, *Aspirazioni dei contadini della Perugia dell'ultimo trentennio del Cinquecento ed altri scritti* (Rome, 1972), pp. 11–64; M. Tosti, 'Poveri, carestia e strutture assistenziali nello stato della chiesa: il caso di Perugia (1764–1767)', *RSCI*, 37 (1983), 143–72; Delumeau, *Vie économique*, esp. pp. 122–34, 521–649; M. Caravale and A. Caracciolo, *Lo Stato Pontificio da Martino V a Pio IX* (Turin, 1978), pp. 375–83, 391–6.

[38] Clementi, *Il Carnevale*, pp. 339–40.

[39] Tosti, 'Poveri', pp. 158–9; Pullan, 'Poveri, mendicanti', p. 994.

bread. Attempts to foster increased production within the Kingdom, so as not to rely on long–distance supplies, were inadequate to meet the needs of a rising population. So the situation deteriorated for the population at large. A study of Pavia suggests that the government secured wheat for the city to the detriment of the countryside, and that within the city the food supply was very unevenly distributed. A policy of commandeering and redistributing may have created more needy families, rather than fewer, though such a policy might have saved some of the families most at risk.[40]

Government policies on food supply were defective, as one might expect. They left plenty of room for non-governmental initiatives, or additional programmes that combined government and, for example, confraternity activities, as we shall see later in discussions of places like Rome, Venice and Perugia. In Verona and Salò Compagnie della Carità were founded (under the influence of Miani and his friends, 1539–42) as organisations for clergy and laymen to fill the gaps left by other charitable organisations; they were to work in cooperation with civic authorities to identify and assist the poor.[41] The combination of private and public action would still be inadequate to satisfy the needs in a major crisis, as P. Vizani noted, but there were incentives for confraternities to attempt assistance. Furthermore governments were not generally concerned with the problems of the long-term or structural poor, nor with those who were poor through difficulties in their own lives and families, outside periods of general dearth. Individuals might join confraternities so that in personal crises they might receive help from within the brotherhood. Some confraternities were ready to provide assistance to outsiders in many different ways, physical and spiritual. This will be illustrated in the following chapters.

3 THE VALUE OF THE ASSISTANCE OFFERED

Before reviewing the kinds of philanthropic help offered by the confraternities, some indication of the value of help in monetary terms for the recipients may illuminate the situation. All that is intended here is a rough guide to how far a confraternity grant went towards the partial satisfaction of needs, when — especially in the next chapter — figures are given for the award of a dowry, or for a grant of alms to a poor widow. It is not feasible to assess the wider financial contributions of confraternities, even the disbursements of those in one city for a given crises year; the data does not exist. Only rarely can one tell how much a single confraternity paid out in a year or two. It is difficult to be accurate about the real value of a grant to a recipient; there are problems over the relationship between money of account, and coinage actually used;[42] not to

---

[40] Basini, 'Sul mercato'; Coniglio, 'Annona', and *Aspetti*, esp. pp. 75–6, 129–30, 276–85. The Neapolitan (or Spanish) policy was more circumspect and foresighted after the serious food riots and murders of 1585 (*Aspetti*, pp. 87–9); D. Zanetti, 'L'approvisionnement de Pavie au XVI-siècle', *Annales ESC*, 18 (1963), 44–62.

[41] Pullan, *Rich and Poor*, pp. 273–7.

[42] *Scudo* or *ducato* could be used in notional monies of account (and could be treated as similar), but then have different values when interpreted in the coinage of the state concerned. The records sometimes indicate the rate of exchange intended; but a paper *scudo* or ducat does not in this period necessarily signify the gold coins of those names; e.g. after 1596 the papal *ducato di camera*, which had been a real coin, became increasingly a theoretical unit of account, and in the next few years was generally disbursed in *scudi d'oro*, at the rate of 100:109. See especially Delumeau, *Vie économique*, pp. 636–8.

mention the difficulties of matching information on dowry or alms payments, with reliable series of prices for what that money could buy — in the same city or area, and in the same years. The value of a dowry award in particular could vary enormously, depending when it was collected; as we shall see later, there could be a long interval between the original allocation, and its final payment. Given the dramatic variations in the price of basic foods — especially grains and bread — between one year and another, or within a year (as has been indicated above) the dowry paid in a year of good harvests and employment would have a very different value from one paid in a bad season. The allocation of a dowry, or even of alms to a poor blind man, was likely to follow a long-term formula for suitable payments, and not take account of short-term real values.

Given these uncertainties I have considered it expedient to restrict the discussion to an approximate estimate of values under certain circumstances in four cities (or their neighbourhood) for which I give examples of particular donations in the next chapters: Perugia, Venice, Naples and Rome. The main comparative test will be the relationship between the nominal dowry sums offered to poor girls, and their purchasing power in grain.

In the late sixteenth century the Perugian confraternity of S. Francesco normally offered dowries to poor girls of 10 florins, or 6 *scudi* 25 *baiocchi*, each, though with a special vote the sum might go up to 20 florins. A dowry from S. Domenico after 1565, and into the seventeenth century, varied between 6 and 11 florins. During the bread riot of 1586 it was stated that a *mina* (about 60 kg) of grain had reached the excessively high price of 25 *paoli* (2 *scudi* 50 *baiocchi*), when 'normally' in recent years it had been 13 or 14 *paoli*.[43] Within the Papal State it was more or less officially calculated that there should be a *rubbio* ($\simeq$ 200 kg) of grain per mouth a year — though in other parts of Italy the allowance for a mature working, or fighting, adult was taken to be nearer 300 kg.[44] So a Perugian in the 1586 crisis would have needed about 8.33 *scudi* to buy a year's supply of 200 kg of grain, and 12.50 *scudi* for 300 kg; while in a more normal year he would have needed 4.33 or 6.50 *scudi*. The couple awarded a poor girl's dowry from S. Francesco in 1586 would have had about three months' basic grain supply for the two of them; in better years they could have stocked up for half a year. In the 1590s the S. Francesco confraternity was charging annual rents of 4 florins for a room above a shop, 5 florins for a house out by a city gate, or 9 *scudi* for a house near the confraternity hospital.[45]

The dowry allocation from S. Francesco is similar to what seem to be the average annual earnings of a Perugian wood-worker and minor painter, who happened to work for some confraternities. By chance the record book of Tisco di Federigo survives among the main hospital archival records. In it he records what he is owed for his work; minor repair work, carpentry in shops, making tables, beds, picture frames, and painting

[43] For Perugian dowries see below chapter 9.3; for 1586, the values of measures and money, Black, 'Perugia and papal absolutism', esp. pp. 532 n. 6, 533–4.
[44] Partner, *Renaissance Rome*, p. 73; M. Aymard and H. Bresc. 'Nourritures et consommations en Sicile entre XVe et XVIIe siècle', *Annales ESC*, 30 (1975), 592–9; cf. B. Bennasar and J. Goy, 'Contribution à l'histoire de la consommation du XIVe au XIXe siècle', *Ibid.*, pp. 402–30.
[45] SBF S. Francesco no. 511 (a): esp. documents dated 19 December 1594 with Gio. Belardino della Verdi; 3 November 1595 with Aurora d'Arcangelo de Menaco and her daughter Bernardina; 21 August 1598 with Conte di Gostino di Berto perugino 'al presente venditore di pane': — 9 ducats for a confraternity house in Porta S. Susanna district, parish of S. Nicolo, next to the oven and hospital of the confraternity.

small religious scenes. For the period from June 1580 until the end of 1605 he claims he is owed for this work 168 *scudi* 62 *baiocchi*, or 6.49 *scudi* a year. Thereafter the record becomes less clear and he repeats some entries, when he was still to be paid, but it looks as if the total until 1620 (the end of the book, and possibly his working life) would have been 243.11 *scudi*, or 5.93 a year. His best year appears to have been 1595 when he recorded work worth 23.65 *scudi*, but in some years less than 2 *scudi* worth of work was recorded. He sometimes shows how he was paid and when, but one cannot deduce that when he fails to do this he is unpaid. We do not know whether this was all his work or income, or whether he had simultaneous records for other contracts; one hopes so (given the grain prices in some years), but there is no cross-reference to another record book.[46] The explanation of his survival is presumably the unrecorded cash payments for other routine maintenance work — a great imponderable! Such a low-earning artisan could have found a confraternity dowry sum significant if he chose to marry a poor girl sponsored by a confraternity. Tisco worked for several confraternities in Perugia and district — providing a *credezone* for holding wax for the Sacrament confraternity in S. Fortunato, or a wooden table or board listing the names of the brothers in the company at Madonna del Pianto, or painting Sts Sebastian and Rocco for the fraternity of Madonna de la Pace.[47]

As other indicators of value in Perugia there are the annual salaries of officials in the hospital Della Misericordia, where Tisco's account book came to rest. In 1622 the carpenter was to be paid 32 *scudi*, the factor 30, the mason 24, the chaplain, shoemaker, dispenser of food and medicines all 18 *scudi*; the muleteer was salaried at 12, the infirmary cook at 9.60 and a female servant at 3 *scudi*. All of these, however, also had food provided in the Casa or were given a food distribution — of $2\frac{1}{2}$ to 3 *libbre* of bread a day for male workers, or under 2 *libbre* for female servants working with the children. Meat was provided three times a week and wine daily. The school-master was paid 48 *scudi* a year without expenses, or 18 *scudi* and expenses. These rates of pay had probably not changed recently — just as the standard S. Francesco dowry was still 6.25 *scudi* in 1617, at the close of a surviving record book.[48] Finally it can be recorded that rural workers outside Perugia in the 1590s were paid between 10 and 20 *baiocchi* a day, though some day wages of 5.30 to 7 *baiocchi* were recorded in the early 1570s. Should the worker manage to work for 250 days a year, an annual income of 25 to 50 *scudi* would have been a happy result.[49]

[46] ASP Ospedale della Misericordia, Miscellanea 18 'Ricordi vari 1580–1620': fols. 8r in 1590 painted in oil a Madonna with frame for 1 sc. 30 baiocchi; 10r, in 1591 50 b. for a counting table; 11v, in 1592 30 b. for a day (*giornata*) spent painting certain marzipans for a feast held by the Cambio guild; 12r, in 1594 15 b. for sign-painting a shop. 14v, 1595 8 sc. 50 b. for painting a whole shop with ceiling, and 2 sc. 50 b. for painting the heraldic arms of Cardinal Montalto in gold and silver; 30v, in 1605 2 sc. 50 b. for a 'chuchietta de letto'.

[47] *Ibid.*, fols. 17v, work for S. Fortunato 1 sc. 24 b.; 19v, May 1598 25 b. for two *tavolette* for Madonna de la Pace; 47r, December 1620 3 sc. for the table with names for Madonna del Pianto; and 45v, October 1617 1 sc. 20 b. for making a table for the Sacrament confraternity at Compignano. This last place was close to the Perugia–Orvieto border: Grohmann, *Città e territorio*, vol. 2, pp. 961–2.

[48] ASP Ospedale della Misericordia, Miscellanea 15, esp. fols. 15v–16r, 17r–v, 19r; SBF S. Francesco no. 442 'Libro delle Dote 1590–1617'.

[49] Petrocchi, *Aspirazioni*, pp. 57–8. He cites some other prices: a pair of shoes cost 20 baiocchi in 1571, between 22 and 30 in 1586; cheese 3 to 6 b. a *libbra* in 1572, 2 b. in 1579, 8 b. in 1599. These prices are admittedly based on limited evidence in records of the nunnery of S. Giuliana.

In Venice it has already been noted that when the *scuola dell'arte* of the goldsmiths (*oresi/Orefici*) paid a *povero* alms of 3 *lire* (70 *soldi*) a year, it was the equivalent of what a journeyman would earn in just over three days, in the mid-sixteenth century.[50] In the same period a worker in the Arsenal was paid 20 *soldi* a day in winter, 24 in summer; a skilled caulker was paid 30 and 40 *soldi*. Boys who kept watch at the Zecca (mint) earned 20 ducats a year. Among building workers employed by the Scuola di S. Rocco during the 1550s the masters were paid about 30 *soldi* a day, the *lavoranti* 20; by 1605 these had risen to about 63 and 38 *soldi*, which B. Pullan calculates adequately compensated for a period of inflation, especially when recently there had been a marginal decline in the cost of living. Similarly the charitable payments of the *Scuole Grandi* largely maintained their purchasing power (in terms of grain), from the late 1560s to 1615. Dowry payments made by some confraternities in the 1530s to 1550s (discussed below, chapter 9.3), ranged from 10 to 25 ducats (at 124 *soldi* a ducat). Even in the 1590s the lowest award would have purchased a year's supply of wheat for the couple. In juxtaposing these awards against the wages of artisans and skilled workers who might receive such a dowry for a bride, there are problems of knowing how many days a year individuals had paid employment, and how much food went with the job in addition, as sometimes happened. However, it might be argued that a skilled worker on 30 *soldi* a day could work up to 250 days a year, and so earn about 60 ducats a year, which is what a *partidor* (an official at the Mint dealing with the separation of gold and silver) earned. Secretaries working for the Council of Ten had a salary of 100 ducats a year. When in 1605 the Scuola of S. Maria dei Mercanti met Nicolo Marin's petition for help and awarded him 25 *scudi*, they were giving him what a healthy master builder might have gained in fifty working days.[51] As another rough guide to value and need we have the claim from the cashier of the hospital of S. Lazzaro in 1599 that forty to fifty poor girls or women could be maintained in the dependent house of S. Lorenzo for 1,2000 ducats a year: 24 ducats each.[52]

In Naples the confraternity of SS. Crocefisso in the seventeenth century was providing dowries at the rate of 50 to 60 ducats each for poor girls. If my interlocking calculations and the given dimensions of containers are correct, this could be a more generous dowry contribution than the examples in the other cities, when expressed in terms of grain purchases. The above ducats equalled approximately 650 and 780 silver *carlini* (of varying silver quantity through the period). From 1600 to 1646 the price of the standard *tomolo* of grain varied from 9 *carlini* 8 *centesimi* (in 1639) to 22.29 (in 1607). To reach the low requirement of 200 kg of grain for a year (as above), 4.18 *tomoli* would seem to be required; to purchase this at the worst price would have cost 93.17 *carlini*.

---

[50] See above chapter 6 at note 17.

[51] See below chapter 9.2 and 9.3, for alms and dowries, and chapter 9 n. 23 for N. Marin's petition; Braudel, *The Mediterranean*, pp. 455–8; B.S. Pullan, 'Wage-earners and the Venetian economy 1550–1630', in his *Crisis and Change*, pp. 146–74; Rapp, pp. 131–7, esp. Tables 4.6 and 4.7; Mackenney, *Tradesmen and Traders*, pp. 97–9 and Fig. 3.3 'Real wages in Venice, 1567–1599', plotting how many days masters and workers might need to work to achieve subsistence. Pullan, *Rich and Poor*, pp. 178–80 on food requirements, costs of wheat, and monetary value of donations.

[52] Ellero, 'Un ospedale', p. 59; cf. in Florence in 1625 Francesco de'Medici, *provveditore* of the Ospedale della Misericordia, reckoned food and clothing for 520 *reclusi* would cost 10,400 *scudi*, or 20 *scudi* per head a year: Branca, 'Pauperismo', p. 441.

So this particular dowry payment is well above those given in the other cities mentioned, using this rather crude evaluation.[53]

Turning to Rome for some final examples, we find that the S. Annunziata, one of the largest donors of dowries in the city, valued them at 50 *scudi* through the late sixteenth century. At that stage masters in the construction business were earning 40 to 45 *baiocchi* a day, and assistants (*garzoni*) 25 to 30, in a boom building period. (In money of account there were 100 *baiocchi* to the *scudo*). So the dowry could be seen as the equivalent of 100 to 200 days work. In the 1590s the cost of a *rubbio* of grain (the low level requirement per person a year, as indicated above) ranged from 50 to 110 *giulii* or 500 to 1110 *baiocchi*.[54] In these terms the Roman dowry recipients could fare better in the crisis decade than their Perugian equivalent.

Some large sums, quoted in connection with philanthropy or the size of confraternity budgets, also need a context. In 1586, during the food crises in Perugia, the relevant city council authorised the raising of a loan of 12,000 ducats to secure wheat supplies for the city. This can be seen in the perspective of a communal budget of about 20,000 ducats income in 1574. If all this loan money had been spent on giving wheat to the poor, 1,445 persons could have been provided with a year's requirement (at the lower level) at the top purchase price in the city. The loan was designed to secure grains at lower prices from abroad, and to subsidise the selling price in the city, rather than give away supplies, except in rare circumstances, and it was hoped that confraternities would make free distributions of grain.[55]

Large sums of money are cited in the context of philanthropy in Rome. We can read that the S. Annunziata confraternity was heir to a patrimony of Urban VII of 30,000 ducats; or that the confraternity–hospital of S. Spirito had an annual income of over 130,000 *scudi*; or that Cardinal Ottavio Acquaviva (d. 1612) spent at least 90,000 *scudi* on charity during his life-time.[56] In 1592 the papal expenditure on direct alms was 13,482 *scudi di moneta*, in 1619 it was 84,187, but these sums were only about 0.8 per cent and 4.5 per cent of known papal income. As P. Partner points out the record might look marginally more philanthropic if one could include under alms the subsidies of food prices for the poor. In the same years the expenditures on the papal palaces were 132,840 and 175,100 *scudi di moneta*.[57] Again for an indication of value one can cite the estimated costs of some major building projects in Rome, whether or not financed by the popes and their families. The Jesuit Collegio Romano (1581–8) cost about 165,000 *scudi*; Sixtus V's Lateran Palace 172,884; the Palazzo Borghese 275,000; the Oratorian Chiesa Nuova 170,000, with another 30,000 for the facade — and then over 800,000

[53] See below chapter 9.3; Coniglio, *Aspetti*, p. 264; *idem*, 'La rivoluzione dei prezzi', esp. p. 212; Delumeau, *Vie économique*, p. 535.

[54] *Ibid.*, p. 695; P. Partner, 'Papal financial policy in the Renaissance and Counter-Reformation', *Past and Present*, no. 88 (August 1980), 45 esp. n. 72; P. Scavizzi, 'Considerazioni sull'attività edilizia a Roma nella prima metà del Seicento', *Studi Storici*, 9 (1968), 173–92, esp. pp. 183–5.

[55] Black, 'Perugia and papal absolutism', pp. 533–4.

[56] Above chapter 6 at notes 14 and 22; below chapter 9.3 at n. 82; Clementi, *Il Carnevale*, p. 350 n. 1. A cardinal of parts: Acquaviva was credited with the conversion of Henri IV of France when Legate; and was Archbishop of Naples. He sponsored and took part in a comedy which was one of the major entertainments for the 1597 Roman Carnival.

[57] Partner, 'Papal financial policy', esp. pp. 50–1 with Tables 6–7, and p. 57.

scudi for the extra living and working buildings and oratory for the Fathers and their guests, when the architect Borromini became extravagant with his revolutionary sculptural architecture and decoration.[58]

In the light of the above, readers will find that the monetary contributions offered by confraternities to alleviate needs were often meagre or mean, even if some Neapolitan dowries appear adequate. Small sums, providing a few months' worth of food supplies, would, however, be important for those close to the margins of existence. Also there were many other dimensions to confraternity philanthropy, both physical and intangible, which contemporaries found significant. The next two chapters will finally concentrate on the different types of philanthropy on offer.

[58] J. Connors, *Borromini and the Roman Oratory. Style and Society* (New York, Cambridge Mass., and London, 1980), pp. 59–60 summarising accounts and studies of variable quality.

9

CONFRATERNITY PHILANTHROPY.
1: HUNGRY, THIRSTY, A STRANGER,
NAKED AND ILL

The subtitles of chapters 9 and 10 derive from the Seven Acts of Mercy (based on Matthew 25) which — as already indicated — were at the time cited as a guide to philanthropic activity. The Seven Acts together may have inspired confraternities, but in the sixteenth century we increasingly find fraternities specialising in one or two acts, such as prison visiting or burying the dead. Some philanthropic activities, such as religious education (discussed in chapter 10.3), may be better viewed as offspring of the seven spiritual acts, but in Italy, unlike Spain, the spiritual acts do not appear to have been emphasised collectively as a guiding policy.

This chapter will concentrate on activities that stem from the corporate acts of providing food, drink, clothing and hospitality to the poor and to strangers. However, the discussion is not organised in terms of these separate acts; they are better seen as linked aspects of 'alms-giving', and physical welfare.

'Indiscriminate alms-giving' was attacked by humanists and Reformers. The confraternities often sought to ensure that their provision of assistance was discriminating, both by establishing priority categories, and by selecting the worthiest individuals within those categories. The paucity of most fraternities' funds dictated the need for priorities as much as moral values. Children, vulnerable females, whether young or old, and the sick were notably preferred; they dominate the discussion here.

Throughout it should be remembered that as well as looking at physical needs, philanthropists were concerned about the salvation of souls, which could dictate the nature of the assistance offered or imposed, as will become clearer in chapter 10.

I PRIORITIES

All confraternity members would have recognised an obligation to help their neighbour — *il prossimo* — and that this might be a condition of their own salvation. But there was no more agreement than now on who should be included as a neighbour, what help should be given, and with what order of priorities when resources were limited. Previous discussion has indicated that there were differing views on how far the body should be helped as well as the soul, on the discrimination to be used in selecting those to help, on who to treat as deserving. It is not clear how far some of the debates about poverty and philanthropy influenced confraternities generally, but some openly indicated their priorities and preferences in their statutes, or in their practical application, where evidence of this can be found. The problem of priorities varied according to the type of confraternity. Many had no resources to distribute, and restricted themselves to spiritual philanthropy. The majority confined their neighbourliness to the fraternity and relatives; here the problem was choosing between deserving cases. Some outward-looking confraternities immediately limited the problems of priorities by specialising in a particular type of philanthropy. A few were constitutionally open to all manner of philanthropic activity, and thus posed themselves the worst dilemmas over who to assist.

In the wider world charity might first go to the clergy and monks, on the precept of canon law that where need was equal, distribution should choose the more virtuous — and by definition the clergy were virtuous. The virtue came from the office and was not necessarily observed in the moral conduct of individuals. These recipients might also be most effective in praying for the souls of donors. So people writing their wills were more likely to donate to the Orders than to confraternities, and donations made in the street and in church might favour friars over lay questors, though importuning friars could cause irritation, for example in Venice.[1] Carlo Borromeo put poor priests and monks at the top of his list of those who should be assisted by charity, then hospital buildings within the donor's parish.[2] One deduces that once money was in the hands of confraternities there was no evident preference for clerical needy.

The general preferences were firstly for members of the fraternity, and their immediate dependents, especially marriageable daughters and widows. Secondly would come the ashamed poor from outside, again notably women and children who were least able to help themselves. Poor sick clergy, or poor nuns, might come in this category as well. Thirdly there were the deserving indigent, those who could not work through illness and disabilities, and those who were unemployed through no fault of their own. Awareness of this last category may have increased in the later sixteenth century, especially in Rome, and hence the schemes to release imprisoned debtors to enable them to become breadwinners again. Last came the remaining indigent, who might be 'helped' though deemed undeserving, partly because otherwise they might endanger society through criminal behaviour. They could also be helped because it would be to the benefit of the donor's salvation if he helped simply according to need and not merit, which was God's prerogative to assess not man's.

Church leaders encouraged confraternities to look outside their own brotherhood. A friend of Carlo Borromeo, the Observant Minor Antonio Pagani (d. 1589) promoted a number of confraternities and Third Orders around Vicenza. In one of his instructions he argued that the company should exercise charity not only towards the sick of the fraternity, but to the poor sick of the city, to hospitals visited by them, and those needing corporal and spiritual help. Brothers should not only love their friends (as neighbours), but enemies and persecutors, and show them spiritual and corporal benefits. The *gastaldo* of the fraternity of S. Bernardino in Vicenza in distributing bread and wine to the poor gave first to the poor of the confraternity, then to prisoners, then to the poor of the land and hospitals.[3]

Priority in various cases was expressly given to *poveri vergognosi*, the ashamed poor. In Modena there was a confraternity, dating from 1248, that concentrated on helping

[1] Trexler, 'Charity', pp. 65–7, 75; Pullan 'Catholics and the poor', pp. 18, 25–30; *idem, Rich and Poor*, pp. 303–5.

[2] *AEM*, vol. 2, col. 601, the 5th Provincial Council: 'In eleemosynae autem erogatione, habitu ratio, cum in primis inopiae, paupertatisque sacerdotium, et Monasteriorum cuiusvis generis, et Ordines, tum hospitalium aedium, locorumve, quae intra Parochialis viciniae fines sita sunt'.

[3] Giacomuzzi, pp. 110–11, and 73 n. 11.

those who could not publicly implore pity. In 1498 an Augustinian friar founded S. Martino in Lucca for this purpose, and in 1495 Dominican inspiration led to one in Bologna (in which the brothers wore a striking red cloak), though this became more notable as the organiser of the 'conservatory' of S. Marta for vulnerable girls.[4] When Bishop F. Gonzaga founded the Mantuan Congregatione dei Poveri for all classes, he indicated that preference should be given to *poveri vergognosi* in the distribution of alms, procuresses and prostitutes should be excluded from assistance, and beggars strictly licensed. The Roman S. Girolamo della Carità, to which St Filippo Neri belonged, stated in 1536 that those neighbours to be helped came in four categories: the *poveri vergognosi*, the imprisoned, the sick, and the dead who could not be buried properly. Preference among those in equal need should be towards the higher born.[5]

When confraternities became involved in helping the least favoured category, the undeserving or unashamedly begging indigent, they were likely to be part of a government policy of social control and discipline (as will be discussed in chapter 10.1); they would provide food and clothing, but the beneficiaries would be institutionalised.

2 ALMS-GIVING: DISCRIMINATION AND SELECTION

Indiscriminate and haphazard alms-giving was seen as characteristic of the old Catholic church in attacks by Luther and later Protestants; in particular the ineffective and corrupting work of monasteries was criticised. Protestant philanthropy had to be selective and discriminatory. Modern secular commentators from the Enlightenment onwards have similarly attacked general alms-giving, as merely a sop to the conscience of the guilty rich as donors, and they have argued that it did the poor little good beyond immediate and temporary relief in dire conditions, and could worsen problems by encouraging idleness, criminality and the fraudulent misuse of charitable funds. Some such charges could be levelled against organised, programmed philanthropy, but the main target was the casual donation of alms.

In the case of confraternities it is difficult to tell how indiscriminate alms-giving was, before or after Luther; monies collected on the streets and at church doors, and then disbursed to callers at the oratory could easily escape entry into record books. In Venice officials operating trust funds for the Scuola di S. Rocco between the 1560s and 1590s moved away from giving at the Scuola, and developed a system of distributing in the *sestieri* to properly recorded poor. Riotous crowd behaviour had prevented discriminating distribution at the confraternity's door.[6] A few confraternity account books or other

---

[4] Ricci, 'Povertà, vergogna', esp. pp. 305, 316–24. According to an eighteenth-century source the Modena confraternity was to help 'quelli, a quali la lor condizione non consente l'implorare publicamente la pietà'. Cf. Trexler, 'Charity', p. 86 for fraternities in the fourteenth and early fifteenth centuries defending declining gentility; Zardin, 'Le confraternite in Italia settentrionale', p. 12 and n. 50.

[5] Navarrini and Belfanti, pp. 121–36, esp. 134–5: 'Secondo, preferiscano alli altri poveri da sovenirsi li nobili et civili ridotti in calamità alli plebei et rustici, ai quali non è cosi vergogna l'andar mendicando'; they must not 'ammettere all'elemosina ruffiane, meretrici et simili persone, quale vivono in notorio peccato morale'. Di Mattia Spirito, 'Assistenza e carità', pp. 152, 154, Proemio and chapter 7 of 1536 statutes. Cf. a Venetian confraternity to help *poveri vergognosi* was inspired by Capuchins in 1537, Pullan, *Rich and Poor*, pp. 267–8.

[6] Pullan, *Rich and Poor*, p. 182. On alms-giving generally: Jordan, *Philanthropy in England*, pp. 17–18, 163, 191, 229–30; A. Forrest, *The French Revolution and the Poor* (Oxford, 1981), chapter 2 'The Revolution and the idea of social obligation'; Pullan, *The Jews of Europe*, pp. 294–312, and 'The old Catholicism', pp. 19–21 on the fraudulent misuse of charity. Cf. Woolf, *The Poor*, p. 18.

records have been investigated to enlighten us on the distribution of confraternity funds. There could be considerable thought and scrutiny in the confraternities before anything but a minimal sum was donated. There were priorities and selected targets. Alms-giving may have been merely palliative, and not addressed to abolishing 'the causes of poverty' as charged, but it was not necessarily indiscriminate.

An impassioned plea for, and defence of, alms-giving by confraternity brothers was made by Giulio Folco in the 1570s. He was a member of the Roman Compagnia delle Vergini Miserabili di Santa Caterina della Rosa. When appointed as the deputy responsible for funding the charitable work of helping poor girls and providing dowries, he found the society's income limited and the alms-giving of the brothers meagre. He decided to write a book putting forward the many arguments in favour of alms-giving based on the Bible and the Fathers — though, as he apologetically noted, he was himself a layman involved in secular business and not a writer of religious works.[7] He thought some were reluctant to give alms because this was a work little rewarded by God; others feared that if they gave generously they would be reduced to begging themselves; others loved their own children and family so much that they put their own salvation at risk. But if he advanced the arguments in favour of alms-giving, a man would have to be of stone to reject them. In particular his own company was saving souls as well as bodies, while other confraternities will present bodies made healthy, this one will present souls preserved from innumerable sins and from the mouth of hell. In undertaking the work the *confratelli* should remember their own souls also; *elemosina* was an easy way to salvation; our treasures can be placed in heaven through the hands of the poor, and we can leave to our children a great patrimony — the piety and merit of the alms-giving. Folco then provided arguments and quotations in support of charitable donations, notably from the writings of Sts John Chrysostom (pp. 176–202) and Gregory Nazianzen (pp. 202–19), the teaching of Innocent III (p. 94), or from the biographies of charitable leaders of the past — with stories such as that of Pope Gregory who, having given alms to the poor, was told by Heaven that for his excellent alms he would be made pope (pp. 29–31). Folco's book was both a plea for general alms-giving, for the good of the donors' souls in particular — as De Angelis or Bellarmino also stressed — and for special support for poor girls who needed dowries. Neither Folco nor other commentators on alms-giving that I have noted distinguish between the individual and the corporate body as potential givers, or argue that the institution should be discriminating when the individual was not. The institution was a collection of individual souls, without a separate institutional moral code.

Confraternity record books show conscious policy-making and selectivity in the

---

[7] G. Folco, *Effetti mirabili de la Limosina et sentenze degne di memoria, appartenenti ad essa. Raccolte per opera di Giulio Folco* (Rome, 1581). The prefatory letter on his motivation addressed to his *confratelli* is dated 24 December 1573, pp. [a2–a5v]. [a3]: 'Il che stimai, che procedesse per essere alcuni, i quali si terano à dietro nel far limosina; stimando, che cio sia opera di poca mercede appresso Dio. O vero perche alcuni altri temono, che col far limosina largamente, sia un ridursi ad essere poi essi sforzati à gir accatando; overo essere altri i quali tanto discordinamente amano i figliuoli, & la famiglia loro, che quasi si scordano de la propria salute.' [a5]: 'Altre compagnie, & veramente con gran merito di pieta, presenteranno nel cospetto de gli Angeli d'Iddio i corpi degli uomini fatti sani, ma la nostra presenterà l'anime, che sono di miglior conditione di essi corpi; l'anime dico liberate, & preseruate da innumerabili peccati, & dalla bocca dell'inferno.' [a5v]: 'Accresciamo le nostre ricchezze & li nostri beni, con porgere del nostro in queste si fatte opere pie. Riponiamo le nostri thesori in cielo per le man de poveretti.'

charitable enterprises. The council meetings of Perugian confraternities record decisions on specific donations, and on a policy of unselective help to the needy during crises. For example in April 1596, during a major Italian food crisis, the company of S. Pietro Martire (which had a few resources, and which seldom indulged in external philanthropy) voted to donate alms to buy bread for distribution to the poor who came to the door of the oratory, a deliberate decision made during a crisis.[8] The confraternity of S. Domenico more frequently supplied help to outsiders; in the 1564–5 period, for example, meetings voted to distribute grain or bread to the poor generally, but there were also specific grants to two convents, a Franciscan monastery and to girls in the house of Charity. They also voted to spend five *grossi* and a *libbra* of wax on the funeral of a Giovanni Batista from Cremona who had died while in the confraternity hospital.[9]

Sampling S. Francesco's records for the year 1573 we discover that this society, and the whole confederation, were under pressure from the papal Governor to provide grain as charity to poor monasteries and nunneries. One recorded vote of 21–5 shows opposition to the proposal, whether against the method of distribution or the principle being unclear. Voluntarily this confraternity voted extra grain supplies to the Governor's cause, in addition to money for the Capuchins, beans for abandoned girls in the district of S. Pietro, wine to the sisters of the S. Clara convent and to the confraternity of 'S. Justitie' (presumably S. Bernardino della Giustizia, which succoured prisoners), and grain to the monastery of S. Salvatore in Assisi. They could still vote money or grain for individuals.[10] Such records suggest that confraternities did consider who to help, according to priorities, from general funds, and that the decision to offer assistance was carefully deliberated.

Some confraternities were founded to give general aid to the poor, or to devote a large proportion of resources and time towards this end. General aid meant providing food, drink, clothing or money for those found to be poor. In Perugia the S. Martino company was created in 1574, following the preaching of a Servite friar, to help the miserable poor and sick in the city and suburbs, by giving money, clothes and medicines, and by securing the assistance of a doctor, and to assist *poveri vergognosi* with alms.[11] In 1576 a general congregation discussed the company's name, and whether the term 'de vergognosi' was suitable, rather than 'de miserabili', because the former might be too general, and because the company might not have enough resources to help the *vergognosi*. The members voted 22–13 to call it 'La compagna de' Visitatori de Poveri Vergognosi et infermi'. This implied that there were more ashamed poor who could be helped than there were extreme poor ready to declare their need. However, in 1578 it was recorded that a new book was being started, entitled 'Memoriale della Compagnia de Poveri infermi e miserabili'.[12] In 1578 it was decided that blankets could be

[8] ASP S. Pietro Martire, vol. 1, fol. 40v.
[9] SBF S. Domenico, no. 427 fols. 12r, 23r–v. On the House of Charity and similar institutions for girls see below section 6.
[10] SBF S. Francesco, no. 457, esp. fols. 99r–109r, for 1573.
[11] Crispolti, *Perugia Augusta*, pp. 176–7; Marinelli, *Le Confraternite*, pp. 771–817, esp. pp. 771, 812–13; ASP S. Martino, Div. II. Cl. IV Pl. III, no. 1 Verbali: 'Libro I. delle Congregazioni' 1576–1643.
[12] *Ibid.*, fols. 5v–6r: 'che la compagnia si chiamasse de' Vergognosi, ma piutosto de miserabili, o con altro nome, parendo loro, che questo nome de'Vergognosi fosse troppo generale; et altro curasse (?) troppo, et che per poter souvenir a i vergognosi non bastassero le forze della Compagna', and fol. 16r.

supplied to the poor sick by visitors only in the presence of the district's councillor, and after checks on true need. The secretary recorded that there was a long discussion on the problems of deciding on the quality and quantity of poor sick to be assisted; the visitors must use diligence and charity in exercising their duty. At times the society obtained and preserved elaborate attestations of poverty and respectability.[13]

A contemporary historian claimed the fraternity spent 100 *scudi* a month on such activities. Patchy records suggest this might be true. Perugia's major historian Pompeo Pellini was a founder member, acting as counsellor and visitor to the poor in his turn, but his History does not publicise it.[14] For a later period, 1645–50, a booklet survives indicating the activities of visitors to one of the five districts of the city, Porta S. Angelo. During the year April 1645–March 1646 they distributed 228 *scudi* 75 *baiocchi* (at 100 *baiocchi* per *scudo*) in 1,582 payments. Donations of between 10 and 30 *baiocchi* were made weekly; if one excludes the 20 *baiocchi* a week paid throughout to the curate of Pilonico (presumably under some permanent arrangement) an average of twenty-nine 'poor' received 14 *baiocchi* a week. The great majority (about 74 per cent) of the handouts went to women. The names on the list change gradually, with some people receiving grants over weeks or months, and three women in a 'hospital' were helped throughout the year sampled. Occasionally the cause of poverty is noted: Menico was an injured muleteer, Donna Francesca di Severe blind and bedridden.[15] Two visitors operated for each district, serving for two months, but with one changing each month to ensure continuity of knowledge of those helped. The 1645–50 list is for those who could be openly registered as poor.[16] According to an order in December 1576, 10 *scudi* was to be distributed 'ad arbitrio dei visitatori' to 'i poveri vergognosi oltre a l'ordinario'; there was another category of ashamed poor being helped secretly at the visitor's discretion. No records for this survive, and may never have been kept. During the food crisis of 1576 members of the sodality went out collecting grain to supply to the poor; they had their own oven for baking bread, which needed renewal in 1579.[17]

Members of leading families were brothers in S. Martino, and from them eventually the company received properties and income, though not without legal squabbles.[18] They were ready to act as visitors to the poor and sick, but were less willing to act as

---

[13] *Ibid.* fol. 17r; ASP S. Martino, Div. I Cl. V Filza II.I, for attestations, e.g. no. 36 3 April 1615 when a parish priest and six laymen confirmed the poverty of a household of six youngsters, aged 26 or under.

[14] Crispolti, *Perugia Augusta*, pp. 176–7; ASP S. Martino, Verbali 'Libro I.', fols. 3v–4v, 18r–v on Pellini's involvement. Pompeo Pellini's *Dell'Historia di Perugia* (vols. 1–2, Venice, 1664; vol. 3, with Introduction by L. Faina, Perugia, 1970, photo reprint of surviving sheets), in its surviving form ends in 1572 before the foundation of this fraternity. Most of Pellini's text was written by 1585, and ready for the printer by his death in 1594; preliminary printed copies circulated in the 1620's, but bickering with the Venetian printer R. Meietto prevented a proper edition. G.G. Hertz in 1664 published surviving or new copies of the first two volumes (for the period up to 1490). Though Pellini's work is very valuable on political and administrative history, it is unfortunately not so for confraternities, despite the author's own membership of one.

[15] ASP S. Martino, Div. II Cl. IX Reg. I 'Elemosine fatte dai visitatori 1645–1650'; see above chapter 8.3 for rough values, though for an earlier period.

[16] ASP M. Martino, Verbali I, fols. 3v–4r.

[17] *Ibid.*, fols. 3v, 5r, 21v.

[18] Dominant families that had active members of the fraternity included: Della Corgna, Baglioni, Oddi, Bigazzini, Crispolti, Pellini, Montemellini and Scotti. On the oligarchy see my 'Perugia and papal absolutism'. Legal squabbles about legacies and land-holdings in e.g. ASP S. Martino Div. I Cl. VI Lettere, Filza I for 1511–1620, and Cl. V Filza II.I Miscellaneous.

alms-collectors on Saturdays; as early as 1579 there was a warning that those appointed should collect alms personally and not employ substitutes unless good reason were shown.[19]

One of the most famous confraternities designed to assist the poor was the Roman SS. Dodici Apostoli, founded in 1553 as a *sodalizio* on the initiative of Fra Felice di Montalto — better known as Sixtus V, who could himself claim humble origins. This was a group of gentlemen inspired by Ignatius Loyola, who collected alms after Jesuit sermons for distribution to the poor; they became recognised as a formal confraternity in 1564 and archconfraternity in 1586, under Sixtus' patronage. The 1573 statutes clarified who should be helped: (1) *famiglie vergognose*, ashamed families; (2) single men and old widows unable to work; (3) wives abandoned by their husbands, provided that they were of good reputation and were burdened with two or three children, that they were not begging or working, and that they were not being 'accompanied' [i.e. by another male supporter]; (4) families where the husband or wife worked, but could not earn enough for subsistence. The Apostoli excluded from help 'children sick with *moriviglioni*, German measles, scabies and similar, or those sick with gout, blind, crippled or having an incurable disease or of little moment' ('o di poco momento'). Presumably they considered most of these were cases for the hospitals. Instructions later in the seventeeth century clarified some definitions. People should not be given *elemosina* 'unless they are needy persons and cannot go to hospital'. 'By *persone bisognose e vergognose* are meant artisans, who have a shop, or who stay in their houses with wives, children and similar. Excluded are those persons who live in rooms, inns or hostelries, when it is not possible to visit them through any door other than the crowded public one.'[20]

The Instructions specified some sums of money to be given: 4 *giulii* for sick priests; 3 for heads of families and women with children (*infantate*) and 2 *giulii* for able-bodied sick. There were alms given publicly, fully in conformity with rules, but also alms given to *persone civile*, who had fallen into poverty. These instructions illustrate the gradations of poverty thought to exist, and the various meanings attached to 'ashamed poor'. Those selected by the Apostoli could receive help, given six times a year, for life or until the need ceased. By the seventeenth century the fraternity had income from property and bonds to supplement that collected at Jesuit sermons. Giuseppe Calasanzio (José de Calasanz) was an Apostle between 1596 and 1601, during which time he made 157 visits to eleven of the thirteen districts of Rome to check on the needy poor, and to distribute about 539 *scudi*; much effort spent on limited alms-giving. He progressed to the more famous philanthropy of educating the poor illiterate, and launching the Scolopians.[21]

That confraternity members might feel shame in asking for help from their own confraternity is indicated in Zuan Francesco Corbelli's petiton in 1556 to the brothers

---

[19] ASP S. Martino, Verbali, fols. 19r–20r.

[20] Monachino, pp. 216–17; Maroni Lumbroso and Martini, pp. 130–1; Paglia, 'La Pietà dei Carcerati', p. 153 quoting *Instruttione a Signori visitatori dell'arciconfraternita de SS. XII Apostoli* (Rome, 1677, 6 pages); Fiorani, 'Religione e Povertà' pp. 111–12. The phrase 'o di poco momento' is ambiguous: it might indicate that the disease or the person was of little consequence; or that the person had only a little time to live?

[21] See above chapter 8.3 on values of money, 1 *giulio* = 10 *baiocchi* = 0.1 *ducato*; Fiorani 'L'esperienza religiosa', p. 181.

of S. Maria dei Mercanti, Venice. But his *vergogna* had to be overcome in the face of great misery and hunger for his family of eight.[22]

The poor might submit an elaborate petition for help, presumably with the assistance of priest, lawyer or literate member of the confraternity. For example Nicolo Marin petitioned for help from the Scuola di S. Maria e S. Cristoforo dei Mercanti on 29 August 1605 on the grounds of his sickness and infirmity, being confined to bed and unable to walk most of the time; though brought up with some property and fortune, and with a notable father, he now needed help. The Banca e Zonta committee awarded him 25 *scudi* as *elemosina*. On the same day they similarly favoured two other petitioners. G.B. Udizzotti, a brother in the confraternity, had one night lost his hearing in both ears and, unable to recover it, could no longer perform his job in the palace. Another brother, B. Frazer, aged 65, was suffering from an incurable illness, which meant he could no longer serve the *scuola* as *massaro* — as he had done for four years; so he was 'in etretissima fortuna, anzi in grandissima povertà', having a wife and six children, with the eldest of four daughters born deaf and dumb.[23]

The records of the *scuola* show its meetings scrutinising these petitions, and voting on the allocation of dowries (usually of 10 to 15 ducats) to poor daughters of members, so that they do not take an evil road, of grants to secure the release of brothers from the debtor's prison, or for help in burying the dead. The decision on dowries or on a major petition for alms was voted upon by the officials (usually the full twenty-four) and details of the petitions are often recorded to show that the case was well deserving. In July 1557 having decided to award dowries to five girls, they had to ballot on thirty-four listed applicants. In November 1541 the committee decided on the case of Simon de' Mariani': his daughter's husband had died leaving her with two little girls, following years of financial disaster in his enterprises on land and at sea. Simon had taken them all in to prevent them coming to a bad end, to add to his other poor children and family (not specified); now he found himself in great necessity, misery and burdened with debt. He was awarded 10 ducats.[24] The Guardian of the *scuola* was, however,

---

[22] ASVen Scuole piccole, Busta 420 fol. 99r: 'con le continue spesi io sû rimasto nudo et con pocho piu di niente', so appeal for help to satisfy debts 'ma Idio e sia con quanta vergogna et respito lo fazo et questo per esser respitoso et vergognoso alliornor mio ma la fame enza il lupo del boscho sapiano le sig.ri vostri che mai haueuei pensato avenire davanti le signore vostre per mendichato suffragio ma patientia dio mandi tutti le nostri citadini da simil acidenti,' He had been a brother for nineteen years. He was awarded 5 ducats, by a 23–1 vote.

[23] ASVen Scuole piccole, Busta 413, filza 'Secolo XVII': N. Marin — 'Fratutte l'opere pie, e meritorie a sua Divina Mestà è il sovenir a quei Bisognosi, e quei veramente che sono da dovero pieno di meserie, e tanto piu quanto sono stati civilmente nasciati, e con qualche poco de beni di fortuna arleuati. Io credarò dunque M. ci e prudentissimi Signori ch'ogn'uno delle M. cie V. mi conosca, e sappia ch'io son Nicolò Marin figlio del M. Domenego Marin cittadino originario di questa città Serenessima huano veramente tanto conosciuto da tutti di bonta e di vita exemplisissima. Io dunque suo figlio colmo d'ogni miseria, e pieno di tutte quelle maggior infirmità, ch'ogn'uno delle M.V. molto bene me può vedere, ch'io non posso ne camminar, ne star fermo ne star sopra il letto, e questo per la grandissima repugnantia c'hanno l'infirmita, che continuamente contrastano, e mi lasano cosi oppresso e mal composto: non potendo io pure pararmi co'[?] una minima di esse per la grandissima povertà mia, che con il dolor continuo da esse, non me lassa procurare di qualche amico mio. Dormo come posso, mangio quando ne ho, camino quando la tregua mi da qualche poco di scanso, et alla conclusione quando il Sig. Iddio vole cosi.' The record is partly damaged by damp. The committee voted 21–0 in favour of his petition, and 19–2 to award him 25 *scudi*. The votes for G.B. Udizzotti were 19–2 and 18–3; for B. Frazer 21–1 and 20–1.

[24] Ibid., Busta 420 'Notariato, 1533–57, e.g. fol. 7v awarding 4 ducats to 'trazer de prejon' Alvise Scarpa, or fol. 29v on awarding dowries to poor girls 'non andasino per mala strada'.

allowed to distribute small sums, according to his conscience, to the sick, the poor and those in bad housing conditions; in 1545 the sum was limited to 20 *scudi* a month, and 6½ *scudi* in any one instance.[25]

Another Venetian fraternity, SS. Trinità, similarly shows elaborate consideration of its alms-giving. There were ballots to select who should be helped with a dowry, with houses or rooms for the poor ('Case di Dio'), and elections of who should be the 'poor of the month'. There could be strong competition for the houses; in December 1575 there were twenty-four applications (two men and the rest women) for three houses in the S. Gregorio district. Individual petitions were dealt with by the committees when people wanted alms for emergencies. But there were sums available, largely from money left by Bishop Piero Contarini in 1563, for less scrutinised distribution, 'Amore Dio'.[26]

When confraternities were helping the poor outside their immediate circle they sometimes tried to ensure a fair distribution to the 'right' people by having registers of the poor, as we have noted for the Scuola di S. Rocco in Venice. By the 1570s the Misericordia of Bergamo (and probably other such fraternities in northern Italy) had developed a highly organised census of the genuinely needy poor in the city, and then assisted in house to house visits, thus taking charity off the streets.[27] The Roman S. Girolamo della Carità, founded early in the sixteenth century, developed by the end of the century a register system that allowed members to distribute bread every Sunday to poor needy families — on a district by district rota system. By 1602 the Papacy, under Clement VIII, undertook a systematisation of charity. Each parish was to elect two gentlemen who would provide the parish and a central office of Elemosineria Apostolica with details of the deserving poor to be helped. Parishes gradually organised themselves to distribute aid, often assisted by a Congregazione del Soccorso. How far confraternities generally coordinated their activities with the parochial system is unclear. Popes, cardinals and others had intermittently been generous with handouts of food and money; now there was a more scrutinised allocation as well. By the seventeenth century the needy in Rome could, and should, have received stamped licences to collect food supplies, or to sanction their own alms-collecting. In Italy there appears not to have been any major resistance to such centralised and rationalised systems for assisting the needy, in contrast to some Spanish cities like Zamora, Salamanca and Valladolid where such procedures were opposed by both citizens and theologians like Domingo de Soto.[28]

Certain types of needy people could be officially licensed to collect alms for themselves instead of, or as well as, receiving aid from a regulated distribution network. In 1613 Pius V founded the confraternity of S. Elisabetta or Della Vergine, for blind and crippled men and women, designed to defend their legitimate rights of begging,

---

[25] *Ibid.*, fols. 44v–5r.

[26] *Ibid.*, Busta 706, 'Libro Primo 1531–59' and 'Libro Secondo 1560–76'; the latter. fol. 18v, mentions the money left by Bishop Contarini; it raises a problem on the date of the bishop's death, and suggests a minor correction to the entry on him in the *Diz. Bio. Ital.*, vol. 28 pp. 265–7. During the plague epidemic of 1574–5 their chaplain was taken to the Lazzaretto; he lost his goods worth four ducats, and having survived his 'longa et pericolosa malattia' he asks to be paid his full salary, although he had been unable to serve the fraternity; he was awarded three ducats 'per conto del limosina et non per supplimento al salario', (fol. 131r).

[27] Pullan, *Rich and Poor*, pp. 182, 311–14.

[28] Monachino, pp. 214–15 on papal donations on feast-days; and on licences to collect bread handouts. For resistance against a coordinated approach to charity in Spain: Flynn, 'Charitable ritual', pp. 344–7.

and encourage their own piety. They were exempted from the vagrancy laws and normal restrictions on begging. On Sundays they organised begging sessions around the hostelries and tobacco shops, accompanied by musicians and a poet singing sacred prayers. They distributed part of their funds to those members too sick to be active beggars. Membership may have risen to 400 or 500. This S. Elisabetta fraternity was connected with the hospital of S. Sisto, and used the Rosary chapel there. It may have been founded as a separate organisation when the hospital was in difficulties coping with the sick and needy. The new society could both control self-help, and add piety to the lives of its members.[29]

There were similar fraternities for licensed beggars elsewhere. Milan from 1471 had the Scuola di S. Cristoforo for the blind and other invalids, based on the church of S. Salvatore in Xenodochio. Archbishop Carlo Borromeo revised its statutes in 1569, and heightened its religious activity. In Venice the blind and invalid were officially recognised in their own Scuole, the Scuola degli Orbi and Scuola degli Zotti, the latter dating from 1392. It helped foreign beggars coming to the city, and so partly frustrated state policies to exclude such incomers, so in 1542 the Provveditori alla Sanità increased their control over the scuola.[30]

The main Venetian scuole devoted large proportions of their expenditure to the distribution of general alms; they were the main agencies acting for the relief of the poor, subject to important government controls and interventions. In 1527 (amidst famine conditions here as elsewhere in Italy) the Council of Ten undertook to provide 6,000 ducats worth of coarse bread for the poor in the parishes; the Scuole Grandi were ordered to contribute 300 ducats each towards this. In 1570, facing another famine, the Ten declared that the Scuole Grandi, other scuole and the officials of St Mark's should redirect all money scheduled to be spent on charitable purposes to the single cause of aiding the 'miserable poor' of the whole city, whether they were confraternity members or not. Most Scuole Grandi spent between 35 per cent and 50 per cent of their income on general alms to the poor. S. Rocco spent well over 50 per cent in this way both in the 1550s and 1600s. S. Giovanni Evangelista used less than 10 per cent thus, preferring to specialise in dowries for poor girls, with 75 per cent of their expenditure devoted to this purpose. However, much of this alms-giving was internal: S. Rocco in the 1550s spent two-thirds of its alms on its own poor members rather than outsiders. The situation was complicated by an alleged tendency of many people to join these large confraternities with the express purpose of securing alms (or a place in an almshouse) after a brief period of membership. The scuole tried to curb this mercenary procedure — or utilise it — by insisting that recipients of charity should reciprocate by attending funerals as mourners. In meeting the requests of petitioners officials might well reward those who demonstrated a long-term loyalty to the fraternity, or a willingness to pray for the donors.[31]

[29] Monachino, p. 220; Maroni Lumbroso and Martini, pp. 143–4; L. Cajani, 'Gli statuti della Compagnia dei Ciechi, Zoppi e Stroppiati della Visitazione (1698)', RSRR, 3 (1979), 281–313, with pp. 281–90 on foundation and background.

[30] Cajani, p. 297; Pullan, 'Poveri, mendicanti', p. 990.

[31] Pullan, Rich and Poor, pp. 77–9, 86, 163–84; idem, 'Le Scuole Grandi', pp. 96–8; idem, 'The famine in Venice', pp. 174, 187–8; idem, 'Due organizzazioni per il controllo sociale', La Memoria della Salute. Venezia e il suo ospedale dal XVI al XX secolo, ed. N-E. Vanzan Marchini (Venice, 1985), p. 20. In 1550 Nicolò Sovero, a member of S. Marco since 1524, not only had his debts to his landlord of 3 ducats paid — as requested — but also received an unsolicited 1 ducat for himself. He had offered to pray for his potential benefactors.

The general philanthropic alms-giving of the confraternities — whether in terms of money, food or clothes (Lecce's S. Annunziazione specifically undertaking to clothe the naked) — was under most pressure during times of dearth. Then governments, like the Venetian or Perugian, or bishops pressurised them to help if it was not their normal role to assist outsiders. The poor might come knocking at the door, as they did to Perugia's S. Pietro Martire. In the dearth of the 1560s the Neapolitan hospice of S. Gennaro extra moenia found itself feeding 1,000 mouths a day at times. But it is impossible to assess the overall numbers assisted during crises, given the mixture of systems involved, and the lack of records in most cases. Some poor were part of a continuous support system, others received in response to *ad hoc* petitions, others were helped through the hospitals, to which we will come later.[32]

It is clear from confraternity record books that such societies in the sixteenth century and later had procedures for discriminating and selecting before they awarded benefits. They had to select the more needy cases from their own poor members and relatives; they registered the deserving poor in the community, or worked on the basis of parochial registers of the poor. There were funds for immediate alms-giving at the discretion of officials, but within low limits. Most giving was discriminating and considered. Much of the philanthropy became specialised — and here there was even more room for careful deliberation by members.

3 DOWRIES FOR POOR GIRLS

It should already be clear that confraternities were often concerned with supplying dowries for poor girls, whether related to members of the fraternity, or outsiders. It might be considered one of the commonest forms of confraternity philanthropy for the living. The evidence is inadequate for a judgement on the extent to which confraternities resolved what was clearly seen as a pressing problem in society. But from documentation available it is evident that there was considerable competition for confraternity dowries; there were restrictions on who could be awarded them, and fairly careful scrutiny was applied in the process of selecting the girls or women.

To achieve a respectable marriage a girl or woman needed an appropriate dowry according to her family's station in life. By the fifteenth century the female dowry was felt to be a major burden for families, while the husband's equivalent donation had declined or disappeared. Communal authorities had sometimes tried to limit dowry excesses by sumptuary legislation, but usually to no avail. For want of a suitable dowry many girls were condemned by fathers or brothers to nunneries. The inability to provide a suitable dowry through relative impoverishment might bring shame on a family, reflecting on the social incompetence of its male leaders. Discreet philanthropy might save the situation, so might a strategic entrance into a nunnery. It is often forgotten that many nunneries themselves required an entrance 'dowry' and annual

---

[32] Lopez, 'Le confraternite laicali', pp. 213, 220; G. Doria, *Storia di una capitale. Napoli dalle origini al 1860* (Milan and Naples, 6th edn, 1975), p. 135.

contributions towards maintenance, but these contributions were considerably less than the marriage dowry.[33] When Tridentine legislation, and subsequent activity, strenuously sought to impose strict enclosure on nuns, and an enforcement of religious poverty, there was lay resistance. Male relatives sometimes wished to retain some contact with the women they had banished to the nunnery; some noblemen at least were anxious to preserve certain nunneries as high-class brothels, and were ready to battle against Neapolitan archbishops or Venetian Patriarchs in such a cause. But most nunneries probably became stricter, and less acceptable for those without religious dedication. Many females themselves were thus likely to be more anxious to marry than enter a nunnery.[34]

Spinsterhood in the outside world was not considered by many as a suitable alternative. A study of the Florentine patriciate in the sixteenth century suggests that in the upper classes more women remained unmarried, and were not nuns, than was usually thought; in this case over a quarter of girls living to twenty and not becoming nuns remained unmarried at fifty.[35] The result would have been a significant number of women at risk, as *povere vergognose*, vulnerable to the death or whims of father or brothers. While some from this class would in fact remain happily protected as spinsters, their equivalents from lower orders would be more insecure. The unmarried girl outside a nunnery was likely to become a servant at an early age, and be subject to the dangers of sexual abuse.[36] As already indicated various philanthropists considered that a charitable dowry would save girls from an evil road to prostitution. Giulio Folco, already encountered as an advocate of alms-seeking, was also concerned with dowries as an official of the Roman Compagnia delle Vergini Miserabili di Santa Caterina della Rosa. He was upset that his society was not providing enough money to marry the girls who needed help; he did not want them to fall into brutish ways, nor to remain in cloistered

---

[33] On marriage and dowries generally see C. Klapisch-Zuber, *Women, Family, and Ritual in Renaissance Italy*, transl. L.G. Cochrane (Chicago and London, 1985), esp. articles 6, 8–11; D.O. Hughes, 'From brideprice to dowry in Mediterranean Europe', *Journal of Family History*, 3 (1978), 262–96, and in M.A. Kaplan (ed.), *The Marriage Bargain. Women and Dowries in European History*, (New York, 1985), pp. 13–58, and see esp. pp. 34, 38–9; E.S. Riemer, 'Women, dowries, and capital investment in thirteenth-century Siena', *ibid.*, pp. 59–79, esp. pp. 64–71 on the dowry as a necessity of life, and on its value to women. M.D. Taylor, 'Gentile da Fabriano, St Nicholas and an iconography of shame', *Journal of Family History*, 7 (1982), 321–32, comments on the painter's *St Nicholas providing dowries for three daughters* (Vatican Gallery, 1525), which he sees as highlighting parental shame.

[34] O.M.T. Logan, 'Studies in the religious life of Venice in the sixteenth and early seventeenth centuries. The Venetian clergy and religious Orders 1520–1630', (Cambridge PhD thesis, 1964), chapter 6, pp. 340–92. I am most grateful to Dr Logan for letting me see a microfilm of this thesis, and some unpublished papers updating part of this work; A.D. Wright, 'The Venetian view of church and state: Catholic Erastianism?' *Studi Seicenteschi*, 19 (1979) [1979], 96–8, which also refers to Naples; Lopez, *Riforma Cattolica*, p. 40. See generally on post-tridentine attempts at control and reforms: G. Zarri, 'Monasteri femminili e città (secoli XV–XVIII)', *Storia d'Italia. Annali*, vol. 9 (1986), esp. pp. 398–420.

[35] C.A. Corsini in *Genus*, 30 (1974), p. 328 n. 1, reviewing D'Addario's *Aspetti* but commenting on an article by R.B. Litchfield, 'Caratteristiche demografiche delle famiglie patrizie fiorentine', *Saggio di demografia storica* (Florence, 1969).

[36] Ruggiero, *The Boundaries of Eros*, pp. 150–3.

conditions in the confraternity conservatory once of marriageable age, because places were needed for more vulnerable younger children.[37]

The Florentine government in the fifteenth century took an unusual initiative by establishing a special fund in 1425, the Monte delli Doti, in which parents could invest at the birth of a daughter to provide an adequate dowry later. While assisting some girls, this solution was discredited by subseqent misuse of the fund by state officials. Its partial success did not much reduce the need for a confraternity like that of the Buonomini di San Martino, founded in 1441, to provide charitable dowries as well. The Florentine state initiative may have had an impact on private ventures. In the sixteenth century there were some pious institutions called Monte di maritaggio in the poorest southern dioceses of the Abruzzi, Molise and Basilicata regions which would have provided cheap loans, or an investment system, to enable dowries to be paid. But the nature of these institutions, and the extent of confraternity and philanthropic involvement in funding them, are unclear.[38]

It had been traditional for some confraternities to assist member families with dowries for their poor respectable daughters. This was continued and possibly expanded during the sixteenth century; and additionally confraternities were formed to provide dowries for girls unconnected with their membership.

Confraternities might be constrained by the terms of a donation in deciding how to award dowries. When Paolo Forrario left money to the Milanese Scuola di S. Maria di S. Satiro in 1515 for awarding dowries to poor girls, he required preference to be shown for girls of his agnation and affinity. In 1576 G.A. Seroni left money to the confraternity of S. Maria della Pietà (based in S. Barnaba, Milan) for dowries, and stipulated that a third of the amount should be for penitent sinners, and so this fraternity, unlike most others was able, and willing, to help those not of good reputation.[39]

Even when the dowries were confined to relatives of the donor or of confraternity members, the competition could be intense. When in 1535 the Venetian SS. Trinità issued dowries it balloted ninety-three *donzelle* to select six. An earlier record suggests these were valued at twenty-five *scudi* each. Dowry provision here was not a regular occurrence, which might explain the competition. Because of the numbers competing for dowries from S. Rocco's trusts, selection involved both ballots and scrutiny. In 1546 214 girls competed for 20 dowries of 15 ducats each. Scrutiny and voting reduced the list to 59 deemed worthy; the winners were then selected by lottery. In 1573 when 2,000 competed for dowries from another fund, lots were drawn to reduce the number by three-quarters before the officials undertook the still lengthy process of scrutiny.[40]

---

[37] Folco, *Effetti mirabili de la limosina*, p. [a2v]: as an official he had dealt with many young girls coming of age to marry, and many other 'li quali non voler cadere in cose brutte, demandavano con grande instanza d'essere riceute, li quali cose mi premeuano sin à l'anima, & io mi affligeua grandamente, perche io vedeua da una parte, che il ritenere piu in chiusura quelle, ch'erano gia nubili, era cosa brutta, & disdiceuole: & ributtare queste, che chiedeuano d'entrare, era di molto periocolo, & lontano dal santo instituto della nostra Compagnia.'

[38] A. Molho and J. Kirshner, 'The Dowry Fund and the marriage in early Quattrocento Florence', *Journal of Modern History*, 50 (1978), 403–38; J. Kirshner, *Pursuing Honor while Avoiding Sin: The Monte dell Doti of Florence* (Milan, 1978); Klapisch-Zuber, *Women, Family*, esp. pp. 214–17; Herlihy and Klapisch-Zuber, *Tuscans and their Families*, pp. 225–6; Donvito and Pellegrino, *L'Organizzazione Ecclesiastica*, esp. Tables pp. 61–106.

[39] Noto, *Gli Amici dei Poveri*, pp. 158–9, 227.

[40] ASVen Scuole piccole, Busta 706, 'Notariato, Libro Primo', fols. 10v–11r, and 2r; Pullan, *Rich and Poor*, pp. 185–6.

Petitions, and votes upon them, survive from several confraternity records to indicate the background or attitude to some applications, as for example in the Venetian Scuola di S. Maria dei Mercanti. In December 1553 Francesco Bonaventura, a *fratello* whose luck had belied his name, was awarded 25 *scudi* towards a dowry for his daughter Cecilia, after he had lost a *carvela* at sea, with half the cargo belonging to him, and he had returned with plague and in *miseria*. In 1556 Domingo Biancho petitioned for help; he had eleven children (six female), a wife about to deliver another, and a poor helpless old woman to support. He requested 50 *ducati* to clothe them, pay rent and marry off two daughters. He was awarded ten ducats. In December 1613 Michiela, widow of Pelegrin Ficini, who had been inscribed in many *scuole*, requested a dowry of 25 *scudi* for one of her daughters to marry or become a nun. She had been advised to apply to this *scuola* by her godfather who would speak to one of the officials. This makes clear that applications could appear well ahead of any consideration of a suitor, or a decision between the secular or religious life.[41] To the Scuola di S. Marcilian on 13 December 1613 Chiara Galletti, widow of a confraternity member, addressed a request for a dowry for a daughter; she had other children to feed, was in great need and faced calamity. She was granted 25 *scudi* by a 68–14 vote. This was a more contested award than most, but the nature of the opposition is never clear.[42] A more unusual petition came in 1550 from Anzola Bagno to SS. Trinità, again in Venice. She was the widow of a poor butcher of S. Marco, with two daughters to marry and 'in grandemissima miseria'; she requested dowries in return for her help in securing for the *scuola* its share of a legacy that had been usurped, and for which it had long been in pursuit as a fund for dowries. Six years later she reported that she had found some written evidence to help the cause, but the final result is not recorded. Obtaining a dowry from a confraternity was no easy matter. How much the lesser *scuole* spent on dowries is unclear, but B.S. Pullan has calculated that the *Scuole Grandi* spent between 30 per cent and 75 per cent (in the case of S. Giovanni Evangelista) of their extensive income on dowries.[43]

The extent of confraternity dowry support is impossible to assess. It has been suggested that all Roman confraternities, whatever their main purpose, had funds for providing some dowries, for relatives of members if not outsiders. Even so, many would have made only a minimal contribution in terms of overall 'need', whatever the value to the individual. There were, however, significant contributions from several fraternities who wished to assist poor girls in the wider community. Two new ones were specially founded for this purpose in the first half of the sixteenth century: SS. Crocefisso (1522) and S. Maria del Pianto (1546).[44] But they were outstripped in importance (according to available information) by the SS. Annunziata alla Minerva. This had been fostered in the fifteenth century by Cardinal Torquemada, to provide dowries for poor

---

[41] *Ibid.*, Busta 420 'Notariato', fols. 77r–8r (voted by 16–6), fol. 98v (by 23–1); Busta 413 filza 'Secolo XVII', 8 December 1613 folder. The document is damaged by damp, and the exact verdict is not decipherable, but was presumably favourable in some way.

[42] *Ibid.*, Busta 296, no. 13 31 December 1603: 'molto bisogno mio', facing 'miseria et profonda calamita'.

[43] *Ibid.*, Busta 706, fol. 92v. The sum of 200 ducats was involved; to be shared between the Scuole of SS. Trinita, Spirito Santo, and Madonna S. Maria Maggiore. The officials agreed by 16–0 to accept her offer of help. In 1556 she reported she had a writing 'della commissaria' of the late Lucretia Zaccaria, the benefactor (fol. 130v). The Scuola in 1548 had attempted to secure this potential dowry fund (fol. 80v). On the *Scuole Grandi*, Pullan, *Rich and Poor*, pp. 183–7, 190, 192; *idem*, 'Le Scuole Grandi', p. 99.

[44] Monachino, p. 251; Partner, *Renaissance Rome*, p. 105; Delumeau, *Vie économique*, pp. 430–2.

girls on the feast of the Annuciation. His patronage was celebrated in a painting commissioned from Antoniazzo Romano in 1500, showing the Cardinal in the *Annunciation* distributing dowries.[45] Weighty investments in the fraternity by Pius V in 1566, and then by Urban VII in 1590 made this the most significant contributor of dowries, at least publicly. To be eligible the girls had to be virgins, poor and honest, legitimate and Roman by birth. Among those excluded from consideration were servants (unless by special dispensation of the company), and those who did certain kinds of manual work — such as gathering chicory or hoeing. The usual dowry payment was 50 *scudi*. A processional ceremony to the church was organised for the chosen girls, as was witnessed by Montaigne in 1581.[46] The 1565 statutes for the SS. Crocefisso in S. Marcello had similar rules about concentrating on respectable Roman virgins, who could use the dowry to enter a convent if desired.[47]

It is probable that most dowry-giving organisations stringently excluded many girls who might have been helped to remain, or become, 'respectable' married ladies. However, some of the poorest, most vulnerable, or even contaminated could be 'rescued' through the conservatories — discussed below, in section 6. An account in 1698 suggests that 150,000 *scudi* a year was expended by Roman confraternities or hospitals on dowries for the poor; a conservative estimate would indicate this meant 3,000 dowries a year. The value to the girl (or effectively the husband) might be the equivalent of from 100 to 400 days work by a mason.[48]

Perugian records are again revealing on aspects of this philanthropic activity, even if the contribution was proportionally less than in the large cities. (The 'need' for subsidised dowries may have been less). Providing dowries on a small scale was a regular concern. Some fraternities minimally allocated a fixed number each year, others were always haphazard. Allocations went to girls from the dependent *contado* villages as well as the city, and they were only rarely used for entry into a convent. Many offers were not taken up, others only after many years. According to the records of S. Domenico 316 dowries were offered during the period from 1536 to 1598, only 262 were paid out by the closing date of this record. Up to 1565 the dowries were worth between three and six florins, thereafter from six to eleven florins. From S. Francesco, between 1590 and 1617, there were 217 offers, with only 160 collected. These were usually worth ten florins (6.25 ducats). Payment might not be made for nine, or even twelve years. We can contrast the case of Caterina of Perugia who was declared eligible for a dowry on 23 December 1590 and was paid it on 14 March 1602, with that of Clarina who was allocated hers on 25 August 1596 and received in on 3 September. In the latter case the confraternity brethren could feel that philanthropy had led successfully and rapidly to the desired marriage. One girl allocated a dowry in 1598 later declared she would not marry, and requested that the money should go to her sister; this was approved in 1611.

[45] Cavallaro, 'Antoniazzo Romano', pp. 351–2 and Fig. 6.
[46] *The Oxford Dictionary of Popes*, ed. J.N.D. Kelly (Oxford, 1986), p. 273; *Montaigne: Travel Journal*, p. 97; see above chapter 6 n. 14, and chapter 8.3.
[47] *Statuti et Ordini della Venerabile Arcicompagnia di Santiss. Crocefisso in santo Marcello di Roma con l'origini d'essa* (Rome, 1565), chapters 49–51 (on eligibility), 47 (on procession); Delumeau, 'Une confrérie romaine'.
[48] Monachino. p. 251; Delumeau, *Vie économique*, pp. 431–2; he condemns such policies of helping the poor on the grounds that the only true solution was to help the poor by providing productive employment. He calculates that a 100 ducat dowry would have been worth up to 400 days of earnings for a mason.

We do not know in the Perugian cases how many of the non-payments are explained by death soon after the allocation.[49]

The delays noted here have various possible implications. Perugian girls of marriage-able age may have had particular difficulty securing suitable partners. In the Venetian Scuola of S. Maria dei Mercanti officials voted on whether to keep the award of a dowry open for a number of years, the implication being that they expected the dowry to be taken up soon after it was offered.[50] The Perugian donation, and its presumed accolade of respectability, if not attractiveness, might not have been enough to persuade men to come forward. There may be implications here for historians of the family in assessing how many mature, unmarried women there were in society. It is possible that girls married sooner, but delayed collecting the dowry payment, for example, until they had a viable family, or had dire need of the actual money. In higher levels of society, according to C. Klapisch-Zuber, the 'honour' of an agreed dowry sum might be as important as the actual payment; provided a portion was paid before the exchange of rings, the rest might be sent in instalments over many years. So even for the poorer sectors the grace of a confraternity dowry might have been adequate to secure a suitor, with the girl's respectability and honour attested. Money might follow a long time later, as and when sickness or other need dictated.[51] This possibility is partially suggested by another Venetian case. In June 1609 Zuanna Canagia presented a notarised receipt to the Scuola of S. Maria dei Mercanti, for the *remainder* of an award of 25 *scudi*, which had been made in December 1597; there is no indication when she married, or when the first payment(s) were made. She may have recently married, after a long hunt for a husband. But alternatively was she cashing what amounted to an insurance policy? Was it because she now had a male heir? Was she now in real need?[52]

A recent study of a Neapolitan confraternity, SS. Crocefisso dei Cavalieri in S. Paolo Maggiore, for the seventeenth century and later, also shows long delays before some dowries were collected — twenty-two years in one case. The amounts granted depended on the particular fund being administered, but they were usually between 50 and 60 ducats. Officials had to check on the girls' honesty and legitimacy. Dowries could be awarded from the age of twelve; most recipients were aged from thirteen to thirty, but one woman (in 1717), was forty-eight when she was awarded hers. In 1646 Grazia Bolcana petitioned for a dowry; she found herself 'in such misery that she had nowhere to sleep, having been in the house of a woman through charity in Arinella but the said woman can no longer maintain her'; she was 'fearful of falling into a bad life (*malavia*) and having found a person who wishes to marry her . . . begs their illustrious Lords to give her a dowry from the Monte de Curtis as a work of charity'. Most recipients were orphans, very poor, or from large families. The officials investigating the cases made personal comments: 'has the requisites and is, moreover, beautiful'; 'an ugly girl

[49] SBF S. Domenico, no. 450, 'Libro delle Dote, 1536–1598'; S. Francesco, no. 442, 'Libro delle Dote, 1590–1617', e.g. p. 3 for *donna* Caterina, and p. 14 for *donna* Clarina. Cf. on other Perugian confraternities giving dowries, Marinelli, *La Compagnia*, p. 29; Crispolti, *Perugia Augusta*, p. 127. See above chapter 8.3 on values.

[50] ASVen Scuole piccole, Busta 420, e.g. fols. 7v, 23r.

[51] Klapisch-Zuber, *Women, Family* pp. 124, 218–19, 224. She also argues for the importance of the husband's gifts, and especially the clothing of the bride in return for the dowry.

[52] ASVen Scuole piccole, Busta 413, 16 June 1609.

of 16, poor enough, honourable, and does not look her age'; 'of mediocre appearance, aged 17, honourable and an orphan'. This confraternity was helping the deserving genuine poor, though not in great numbers — from one to ten a year; the nobles providing the dowries sought prayers for the repose of their souls in return.[53]

4 HOSPICES, HOUSING AND HOSPITALS

Offering *hospitalitas* was one of the main charitable tasks required of a loving Christian, traditionally the act of charity to be offered to the seeker without question. For De Angelis writing in the early seventeenth century the virtue of hospitality is demonstrated when we receive strangers spontaneously, guided by a meek soul and not by self-interest.[54] The *ospedale* was in part the institutional extension of private hospitality, though obviously there were other motivations and concepts involved as well. The hospice, or *xenon* for strangers, foreigners, travellers and pilgrims, was part of the life of the church from the earliest centuries, particularly in the Byzantine Empire. They were organised by bishops and monasteries; equivalents are found in the West. But in urban Italy monastic hospitality was supplemented by hospices, *ospedali*, provided by guilds and confraternities.[55]

The word *ospedale* was used loosely in our period, signifying anything from a small room set aside for a pilgrim or sick traveller, to a general hospital. The *ad limina* visitation reports and other usable records often fail to indicate the size or type of institution involved. The medieval attitude still prevailed whereby the hospital was a place for hospitality and care, not cure; it was ecclesiastical not medical. It was intended for those too poor to stay in inns when travelling, or without housing in their own community. It was for those too young, too old, or too poor and sick, when they were without wider family support to enable them to live in the community. C. Benincasa treated residence in a hospital as a proof of poverty.[56]

The connections between confraternities and hospitals were variable, and they are often difficult to interpret from the limited records. A confraternity might provide the building for the hospice/hospital, raise funds for it and for a paid staff. Some of the brothers and sisters might act as visitors to their hospital, ideally checking that the administration was not fraudulent, and that the needs of the patients and residents were reasonably satisfied. In other cases the hospital was a civic institution, or was run by an Order, but members of confraternities assisted as part-time voluntary nurses, comforters and fund-raisers. They then worked alongside paid staff, and members of religious Orders. Records for the sixteenth and seventeenth century are rarely clear on who did

---

[53] Rienzo, pp. 263–77, quoting p. 269.

[54] De Angelis, *Della limosina*, p. 219: 'L'hospitalità è quando spontaneamente, & indotti dalla mansuetudine dell'animo, non allettati da alcuno nostro interesse, riceuiamo i forastieri'; cf. Vives, *De subventione pauperum*, p. 57.

[55] D.J. Constantelos, *Byzantine Philanthropy and Social Welfare* (New Brunswick and New Jersey, 1968), chapter 12; Ball, 'Poverty, charity'; Monti, *Le confraternite*, vol. 2, pp. 72–3; Marinelli, *Le Confraternite*, p. 375.

[56] Benincasa, *De paupertate*, p. 56; on the medieval hospital as ecclesiastical more than medical — Pullan, *Rich and Poor*, p. 205. Cf. the argument that Reformation hospitals were Protestant monasteries: H.C.E. Midelfort, 'Protestant monastery? A reformation hospital in Hesse', *Reformation Principle and Practice: Essays in Honour of Arthur Geoffrey Dickens*, ed. P.N. Brooks (London, 1980), pp. 71–93, and Review by S. Ozment in *Catholic Historical Review*, 65 (1982), 345–6.

what in the hospitals. What follows is designed to give as broad an idea as possible of the different kinds of hospital that existed in Italy — and the various possible contributions of confraternity members. Some of what follows may be tangential to confraternity life, but it is hoped that information on a hospital with only a marginal — or conjectural — connection will help us understand others which are stated to be confraternity hospitals, but for which there is virtually no other information.

There seem to be several trends in the history of Italian hospitals in the early modern period. There was probably an increased concern for physical aspects of hospitality, for nursing care, if not always medicinal treatment. The institutions came under increased control from state or church, with a general policy to amalgamate the smaller hospices to create larger, ideally more efficient, institutions. A secularisation policy reduced the confraternity role in hospital work in many cases, but in certain areas, as in Rome, or in poorer southern regions, the confraternity contribution seems to have increased in quality and quantity. There was a growing notion that hospitals would take the needy off the streets, control them and — if they were young and able-bodied enough — prepare them physically and morally for a more profitable role in the outside world. Sometimes confraternities assisted in this control policy, as will be discussed in chapter 10.1; sometimes they provided the alternative way, that undermined rigid state policies.

A hospice/hospital might be intended primarily for the pilgrim or traveller, but have its uses extended as needed; and in accordance with developing philanthropic ideas. The hospitals run by Perugia's three confederated confraternities seem to be fairly elementary hospices; but they were used, as already noted, as centres for food distribution to the poor. When hospitals are mentioned in diocesan reports, especially in the poorer southern areas, the term would almost certainly mean small hospices for travellers, but they could be used for other poor as well. It has been argued that where such hospitals existed in rural areas, giving alms and shelter, there was a recognised reduction of figures for the 'poor' — at least at the eighteenth century.[57] A small hospital might be like the one in Castel del Piano (in Sienese territory) which gave priority to pilgrims and travelling Capuchins and other poor religious, but which — if there was spare room — would help the poor sick. It was also to concern itself with *poveri vergognosi*, pregnant women, and girls unable to find husbands.[58]

Small confraternity hospitals appeared in unexpected places; in 1531 Clement VII approved the foundation of a hospital by a discipline confraternity on Isola Maggiore in Lake Trasimeno. This was presumably a refuge primarily for fishermen and others threatened by the storms that can suddenly whip up on this placid-seeming lake.[59]

The confraternity hospital of S. Spirito in Ferentino still fulfilled the traditional role of the *xenodochio* in the sixteenth century, giving hospitality to pilgrims and other travellers to Rome, including confraternity groups. It gave alms to clergy and laity in some quantity, fed the sick, and provided a doctor in the hospital. However, it sent abandoned babies on to Rome's famous S. Spirito in Sassia hospital complex.[60]

[57] Tosti, 'Poveri', p. 657.
[58] I. Imberciadori, 'Spedale, Scuola e Chiesa in popolazioni rurali dei secc. XVI–XVII', *Economia e Storia*, 1959 no. 3, 423–49, at pp. 427–30.
[59] Meloni, 'Topografia', p. 6.
[60] B. Valeri, *La Confraternita dello Spirito Santo di Ferentino* (Perugia, 1981), esp. pp. 19–27; its statutes (p. 51) stated that its principal obligation was hospitality. See below at note 82 on S. Spirito in Sassia, and section 5, on abandoned babies.

Developments of the smaller confraternity hospice can be seen in the case of Bologna's S. Maria della Vita. Early statutes (probably of 1408) allowed alms to be taken out from the obviously adequately funded hospital and given to the poor at home, preferably to the deserving *poveri vergognosi* of the congregation.[61] In 1535 there were further developments; the creation of a granary and a permanent stock of 250 *corbe* of grain to be ready for emergencies, and the construction of a room above the infirmary with three well-furnished beds, for the discreet use of *poveri vergognosi*.[62] This confraternity's leading rival, S. Maria della Morte, had been founded (in 1336 it claimed) as a confraternity that would operate a hospital. Though it developed a greater claim to fame in comforting the condemned, it maintained its hospital in the sixteenth century. The 1562 statutes ordered that there should always be both a physician and a surgeon attached to the hospital, and that the brothers appointed as visitors to it should ensure that their medical orders were fulfilled, as well as check on sanitary conditions, food supplies and the comfort of the sick. A medical student was paid as assistant within the hospital. The rules made clear that this was a hospital for the sick, and only such should be admitted. Those with contagious or incurable diseases could only be accepted with the approval of the major confraternity officials.[63] These rival Bologna institutions are good examples of two kinds of 'hospital' — the medical and the 'general philanthropic'.

The poor and old could sometimes receive long-term hospitality in a room within a hospital, or in rooms or almshouses owned by the confraternity and hospital. Almshouses and rooms are particularly associated with Venice, or at least best known there. The hospital of S. Giobbe in 1574 was composed of 120 separate almshouses, a dispensary and a church. Some Venetian *Scuole Grandi* ran large complexes of almshouses; houses and rooms to be occupied freely by approved respectable poor. S. Giovanni Evangelista had 42 of them in 1490, and 76 in 1581, when S. Rocco had 44 and the Misericordia 60. Confraternities received houses and individual rooms in bequests, some they could rent out, and use the income for different purposes, but others were specifically to be used to house the poor *pro Amore Dio*.[64] S. Rocco also had a conscious policy of developing a complex of housing facilities for the poor near its great confraternity building. At the end of the century it was under pressure to expand this sort of philanthropy. When in 1590 a barber Francesco Dalfo died, having had the free occupation of no. 33 Corte San Rocco on two floors, the property was divided into

[61] BCB F.O.6 fol. 14v: 'debiamo fare a quelli che le meritarano, e piu tosto a li poveri vergognoxi della detta congregatione, che a quelli dela ditta congregatione che non sono vergognoxe'. This would seem to be part of the early statute (1408 according to a marginal comment), copied out and approved in 1488.

[62] *Ibid.*, fol. 24r: 'una stancia assai grande sopra la Infermaria deli homini, cum tre letti bene ornati, in li quali per li tempi futuri se li possano, e debiansi mettere, e acceptare nel modo, e ordine infrascripto. E' non Altramente li poveri vergognosi, e, honesti di bone caxe, e nomi, che capitaranno in lo ditto hospitale, e li honestamente in occulto governansi secondo la conveniente e qualita dele persone'.

[63] BCB F.O.42 esp. pp. 4–5, 17–18, and 23–4, where the contagious are given as: 'leprosi, etici, infranzosato, rognosi, et piagati, et altro simili', and the incurable: 'infermi di cancero inveterato, di flusso epatico, di fiatiche, podagre, dogliose di giunture, hidropici, et altri simili'. Such persons could be admitted for 20–30 days to encourage some improvement and purgation, except if oppressed by 'mal francese' (syphilis) or 'lebra'.

[64] B.S. Pullan, 'Abitazione al servizio dei poveri nella Republica di Venezia', *Dietro i Palazzi. Tre secoli di architettura minore a Venezia 1492–1803*, eds. G. Gianighian and P. Pavanini (Venice, 1984), pp. 39–44; *idem, Rich and Poor*, pp. 64–5, 77, 149, 185 (figures), 337–55, 428 (S. Giobbe). On Venetian hospices and hospitals, catalogued, mapped, and photographed where they survive: F. Semi, *Gli 'Ospizi' di Venezia* (Venice, 1983); S. Giobbe is discussed pp. 189–97, as incorporated into a larger complex.

two lodgings 'to house as many poor as possible, especially in these very calamitous times, and finding these poor in greater numbers than ever before'.[65] The system was open to abuse and fraud, both by officials who allocated houses to friends and relatives who were not in the greatest need, and by people who joined the Scuola primarily to obtain free accommodation, and pretended they were poor without real justification. Those who did receive free housing might be bound by contract to pray for their benefactors, and participate in confraternity processions.[66]

Venetian guilds and the *scuole piccole* also had some rooms or houses for the poor. The SS. Trinità's records show that it made reasonable efforts to ensure its housing was used by respectable persons for proper purposes. In 1536 it deprived widow Luchina of her house for her *malavita*, and for not fearing God, and Gerardo Masser for having a wife with evil habits whom he would not send away. On another occasion it tried to ensure that those granted free houses did not sneak in extra children. The competition for the housing was strong: in 1540 sixty-two people were balloted, for three vacant houses.[67]

There were problems, besides fraud, in running such a philanthropic system. In 1318 Giovanni Polini left money jointly to the Scuole of S. Maria dei Mercanti and of Madonna S. Orsola to purchase houses for the use of six poor. Sixteenth-century records show that there were many problems in maintaining the houses in good repair (especially when the full membership would not accept proposals by officials to sanction major expenditure, as in 1535), and in securing agreement between the two *scuole*, especially over the supervising Prior for the houses, which had become categorised as a 'hospital'.[68]

A profusion of small *ospedali* was unlikely to be an efficient way of helping those in need. Many would be under-used or ill-equipped, as Bishop Della Corgna of Perugia complained, while those that had major endowments were vulnerable to fraudulent manipulation. From the fifteenth century there were two tendencies in remedial action. First, a process of amalgamation under municipal authority or supervision, to create large hospital complexes, serving many functions and different kinds of people. The best example of this was the great hospital complex of the Ca' Granda, or Ospedale Maggiore, in Milan — for which Filarete between about 1456 and 1465, designed and

---

[65] Pullan, 'Abitazione', p. 41: 'de loggar quel maggior numero de poveri che sia posibile, massime in questi tempi tanto calamitosi, et atrovandosi essi poveri nel maggior numero che mai siano stati'.

[66] *Ibid.*, pp. 41–2, where he illustrates the fraud of Hieronimo Laner attempted in 1583 against S. Rocco, parading six apparently destitute children when only two were his.

[67] ASVen Scuole piccole, Busta 706 'Libro Primo' fols. 15r–16r: 24 September 1536 'questa Luchina non havendo timore di Iddio, ne neancho al proximo, ne al honor di questa sanctissima Trinidatte, de la qual habuto tenuto beneficio, per la male vita che lei ha tenutto, et tiene, come per el processo apar, con grandissimo scandolo di ogniuno: Sia Privado, et casa di beneficio che lei ha dela Cassa, nella qual lei habita dela scuola dela Sanctissima Trinitade'; her deprivation was agreed by 18–5. G. Masser's case was dealt with on the same day; he declined to dissolve his marriage, or dismiss his wife; he also had to forfeit a salaried office (unspecified) in the *scuola*. He appeared before the officials, thanked them for their decision, and begged them to allow him to stay in the house until he found other accommodation. Fols. 46v–7r on the ballot for houses in 1540.

[68] *Ibid.*, S. Maria dei Mercanti, Busta 420 fols. 6r–v (1535, when the meeting rejected the proposal to make major repairs by 32–33), 9v–11r (1539), 15v (1540); Busta 413, 14 December 1585 agreement between S. Maria and S. Orsola over the Prior of the 'hospital'. See Semi, pp. 101–2, with photos of the building, now a private house. It had three rooms. She quotes Polini's (or Pollini's) will.

initially constructed a magnificent central building.[69] Secondly, there could be an extension of ecclesiastical control over lay societies. The first policy mainly affected the large cities, the second the smaller towns and rural hospices. Inevitably the controls were muddled and contentious. Despite the Council of Trent ruling that all hospitals and pious places should be under episcopal supervision, divided control (or none) persisted as before.

Successive popes ruled that hospitals could not escape visitation on the grounds that they were lay institutions. Since many in hospitals were close to death, the church was concerned about their testamentary dispositions, and the salvation of their souls. Archbishop G. Paleotti was also concerned about the quality of religious life generally in hospitals and hospices, and that the inmates should live as well as die good Christians.[70] But bishops had to accept they could not control all such places. There were jurisdictional battles in Naples; in the end the secular power stood firm in resisting any intervention with hospitals and pious places under royal patronage, but gave way a little to bishops over less significant institutions. Venice in particular resisted ecclesiastical supervision, and had the hospitals and confraternities (as well as nunneries) excluded from the 1581 apostolic visitation of the city. On the Terraferma, hospitals in places like Bergamo and Brescia claimed historical precedents for immunity from ecclesiastical jurisdiction; and resisted Carlo Borromeo's visitations; his archiepiscopal province overlapped the Republic's secular territory. In Milan itself the Ca' Granda's history suggests in practice a reasonable cooperation between municipal authorities, secular sovereigns (Dukes of Milan and then Kings of Spain), popes and archbishops. Borromeo made the hospital his universal heir; though he left little, it provided a good example.[71]

The threat of ecclesiastical intervention could encourage state and city authorities to supervise the institutions better, and so remove the excuse for involvement. Jurisdictional battles could well serve the interests of philanthropic efficiency. In many cases bishops and local secular powers cooperated in the amalgamation of small hospitals into larger municipal complexes, for example, in Bergamo and Brescia as well as Milan in the fifteenth century, or Como and Florence in the 1540s. The Italian centralisers and reformers of hospital systems seem to have had an easier task than their Spanish counterparts, when the Dominican De Soto led the resistance.[72]

---

[69] AA.VV. *La Ca' Granda. Cinque secoli di storia e d'arte dell'Ospedale Maggiore di Milano* (Milan, 1981), an exhibition catalogue of major importance, which well illustrates the building developments.

[70] Paleotti, *Arciepiscopale Bononiensis*, pp. 467–72.

[71] Muto, p. 251; De Maio, 'L'Ospedale dell'Annunziata' in his *Riforme e miti*, p. 252; M. Bettoni (ed.) *Nunziature di Napoli, volume terzo (11 luglio 1587–21 settembre 1591)* (Rome, 1970) pp. 130–3, no. 87 Marcantonio Bizzoni to Alessandro Peretti, 16 September 1588, indicating Viceroy Juan de Zúñiga's partial concessions); Tramontin, 'La visita apostolica'; Cairns, *Domenico Bollani*, pp. 155–9, 215–16, 228 nn. 98 and 100; AA.VV. *La Ca' Granda*, esp. p. 103 for Borromeo's will. When Borromeo had a dispute over a private hospital in Treviglio, Rome ruled that he should restrict investigations, in the case of private hospitals, to ensuring that testators' wishes were being fulfilled: A.M. Rinaldi, 'S. Carlo e la magnifica comunità di Treviglio', *Archivio Storico Lombardo*, 10 (1960), 28–40.

[72] Pullan, *Rich and Poor*, pp. 202–6; M. Dubini, '"Padrone di niente". Povertà e assistenza a Como tra medioevo ed età moderna', *Timore e Carità*, pp. 103–20. The incurably sick became permanent residents of the hospitals, and there were major problems with the 'army' of women and children needing assistance. On Florence see below. On the general background of hospital reform, including earlier crises, see M. Mollat, *Les Pauvres au moyen Age. Etude sociale* [Paris], 1978), pp. 324–35, 338–44. On jurisdictional battles over confraternities and their hospitals, see above chapter 3.1. On Spain, Flynn, 'Charitable ritual', pp. 344–5.

State reorganisation of hospital activities had varied effects on confraternity involvement. When the Modena hospitals were amalgamated in 1541 into a single system, the Santa Unione, the confraternities were specifically excluded. A number protested vigorously to Duke Ercole D'Este of Ferrara, who ruled Modena, but to no avail. There had been many abuses among the confraternities, as the reforming bishop, Giovanni Morone, recognised. He probably felt that their form of assistance was inefficient and outdated. When he returned to the city in 1542 he briefly excommunicated the Unione, in order to bring about some organisational changes, and assert the right to be consulted. The reformed statutes gave a few places on the Unione's governing body to representatives from the confraternities and guilds.[73]

The contemporaneous reform of the Florentine hospital system was a little different. Since the early fifteenth century Florence and Siena had set precedents for reforming confraternities and their hospital activities, and had influenced Venetian attitudes. In 1527 ambassador Marco Foscari was still praising Florence's forty-odd hospitals, making it a most devout and religious city.[74] But from time to time there had been worries about fraud, lack of enthusiasm and paucity of funds. Under Duke Cosimo I, as part of his bid for efficiency and absolutist control, the hospital institutions were subjected to a government supervisory committee, the Buonomini del Bigallo. Cosimo's 1542 reforms not only received episcopal support, but were granted a papal Bull in July 1543. State supervision was imposed, but room was left for archiepiscopal involvement as well. Also powerful confraternities remained as philanthropic practitioners, notably the Compagnia Maggiore di Santa Maria del Bigallo (probably founded by St Peter Martyr in 1244), which had managed many hospices from an early date, and the Compagnia Maggiore di Santa Maria della Misericordia (of less certain origin), which had undertaken to transport the sick to hospitals, to succour orphans, and bury the dead fittingly. Previous government action had amalgamated these companies in 1425, only to put them asunder in 1525. Cosimo's concern over the increased number of abandoned poor, especially young children, had led him to increase the activity of the Bigallo to foster such children, and then led him to create the committee to supervise hospitals and assorted confraternities. It should be stressed that in the crisis of 1621 it was the brethren of the Compagnia di S. Martino who produced the most thorough investigation of the conditions of the poor, and supplied the state officials with its shocked reactions. It did not favour multi-occupancy hospitals for the poor, because they helped spread contagious diseases; it preferred to help people at home if possible (though this attitude in turn was challenged for leading to the spread of infection in the family).[75]

[73] S. Peyronnel Rambaldi, *Speranze e crisi nel Cinquecento Modenese* (Milan, 1979), pp. 147–61; Basini, *Sul mercato*, pp. 19–20; Rusconi, 'Confraternite', p. 483.

[74] Pullan, *Rich and Poor*, pp. 205–6; E. Alberi (ed.), *Relazioni degli Ambasciatori Veneti al Senato*, series II (Florence, 1857), vol. 1, p. 25; or in A. Ventura (ed.), *Relazioni degli Ambasciatori Veneti al Senato*, (Bari, Universale Laterza edn, 1980), p. 109: 'concludo adunque che la città di Ferenze è una devota, cristiana e religiosa città'.

[75] D'Addario, *Aspetti*, pp. 89–92, 464–71; M.A. Mannelli, 'Istituzione e soppressione degli ospedali minori in Firenze', *Studi di Storia Ospitaliera*, 3 (1965), 171–82: she notes among the smaller hospitals the Ospedale del Piccioni, with twelve beds, administered by the confraternity of Madonna S. Maria, which survived until 1752; H. Saalman, *The Bigallo. The Oratory and Residence of the Compagnia del Bigallo e della Misericordia in Florence* (New York, 1969), pp. 5–7, 26; Lombardi, 'Poveri', pp. 165–84, which stresses the morality behind the Bigallo's help to the needy. The disabled were given lodging and food, the able-bodied lodging only. The compagnia of Or San Michele provided alms on the basis of *polizze* attesting legitimate need; Cipolla, *I Pidocchi*, pp. 53–67 on S. Martino.

The republican government of Lucca amalgamated hospitals in the early sixteenth century. But from 1535 this still left room for a hospital for incurables, for the syphilitic and chronically ill sponsored by the Compagnia dello Spirito, the Compagnia della Rosa, and the Confraternita dei Genovesi. In 1540 the Compagnia dei Poveri was started primarily to bury the poor decently, but also to help needy families with money. This was at a time when the government office for the poor was pursuing policies of rigid control. In 1580 the Compagnia del Crocefisso founded the Ospedale della Trinità for pilgrims and convalescents. The Dello Spirito ran an orphanage for girls, and the Compagnia della Zecca refuges for widows, as well as for children. The state systematisation had not eradicated confraternity involvement in hospital work.[76]

Elsewhere one finds contrasting policies and developments. In Turin from 1562 the municipality took over the problem of abandoned babies, *esposti*, and the relevant charities; whereas in Pavia the hospital Degli Esposti, which had been founded under full lay administration in 1479, was by 1576 under the control of a congregation of laymen and clerics appointed by the bishop. The experienced apostolic visitor, Angelo Peruzzi, in that year reported favourably on the hospital, praising the foster mothers' teaching of Christian Doctrine to the children, and the clean kitchens. An adverse visitation report could lead to hospital reforms, as happened at Piacenza's Ospedale Maggiore, after Bishop Sega's 1585 criticisms.[77]

Ecclesiastical legislation tried to ensure that the patients' spiritual as well as physical needs were satisfied, that priests would be summoned to the sick by doctors. The Ravenna provincial council of 1568 claimed control over all doctors, as assistants in spiritual welfare; it also demanded strict Christian practices in hospitals, with the exclusion of beggars seeking refuge, unless they fulfilled the precepts about regular communion. G. Paleotti in Bologna wanted religious readings, confession and consolation provided in hospitals, which could be facilitated by having old poor priests resident in their own rooms there.[78] One of the roles of confraternity members visiting or administering hospitals was to ensure religious philanthropy and orderliness.

Hospital work as a philanthropic activity was encouraged by many sixteenth-century reformers, by the leaders of the Capuchins, Jesuits and Theatines, and by individuals such as Filippo Neri, Cesare Baronio, Luigi Gonzaga, Carlo Borromeo, Bartolomeo Stella and Camillo de Lellis. The last two had a particular impact on hospital work, through both confraternities and religious orders or congregations. Stella, from Brescia, had been a member of the Roman Company of Divine Love. In 1521 he launched a hospital for incurables in Brescia, with a society of friends, Amicizia. His influence spread across northern Italy, aided by his friend Girolamo Miani, inspiring many institutions and companies.[79] De Lellis, a soldier, came to Rome to have a foot cured. He stayed to become a leading administrator in the confraternity hospital of S. Giacomo

---

[76] Russo, 'Potere pubblico', pp. 60–2.

[77] E. Nasalli Rocca, Review of T.M. Caffarato, *Storia del'assistenza degli esposti a Torino* (1963), *Studi di Storia Ospitaliera*, 3 (1965), 211–12; C. Biglieri, 'L'ospedale degli esposti di Pavia', *ibid.*, pp. 139–55, esp. pp. 154–5, Appendix; S. Maggi, 'Il vescovo Filippo Sega e gli "Ordini" dell'Ospedale Grande di Piacenza (1585)', *Studi Storici in onore di Emilio Nasalli Rocca* (Piacenza, 1971), pp. 303–13.

[78] Mansi, vol. 35, cols. 620, 639–41; Prodi, 'Lineamenti', pp. 355–6.

[79] Pullan, *Rich and Poor*, pp. 234–5, 258–63; AA.VV. *Storia di Brescia*, vol. 2, pp. 453–4; Lopez, 'Le confraternite laicali', pp. 178–9.

degli Incurabili from 1580. He established a hospital-visiting group, which in 1586 was approved as a full Order, the Ministri degli Infermi, which remained at the centre of nursing activities, including ministrations on the battle-field, until the nineteenth century.

Hospital care was also undertaken by the Ospedalieri di S. Giovanni di Dio; this association's status fluctuated between that of a confraternity and an Order. It was founded in Spain, but became prominent in Italy under the better known name of Fatebenefratelli, a name deriving from their standard half-sung greeting when collecting alms: 'Fate bene fratelli, per l'amor di Dio', 'Do good, brothers, for the love of God'. Camillo Fanucci in 1601 noted that most of the Fatebenefratelli were laymen, but behaved as regulars, without the rules of a formal confraternity. He admired their ability to collect alms for hospital activities. These brothers ran hospitals all over Italy, notably in Florence and Naples as well as Rome, but also in smaller, poorer places such as Ortona, Lanciano, Melfi and Montepeloso. In Perugia's major city hospital they worked alongside confraternity members and salaried officials. Before this begins to sound like a eulogy, it should be noted that their hospital in Penne was taken from them in the 1590s, when the bishop accused them of maladministration.[80]

By the late sixteenth century Rome was seen as the model city for hospital philanthropy. If the model developments in the earlier period — in Milan, Florence, Piacenza or Venice — had resulted largely from civic influence and some central consolidation, Roman prestige came from the impact of religious philanthropy, including confraternity enthusiasm, and diversification. Rome benefited from the influx of dedicated reformers from all over Europe, from being the headquarters of the dominant Orders, and from the papal award of attractive indulgences. Diversity was perpetuated by the enthusiasm of individual popes for particular projects: Gregory XIII fostered the Fatebenefratelli's own hospital of S. Giovanni di Dio, Paul V backed S. Spirito in Sassia, Clement VIII was generous to a number of hospitals, without being tempted to consolidate or centralise. The favourable position of Roman hospitals also owed much to Cardinal Antonio Maria Salviati, a leading benefactor who became official Protector of the Hospitals in 1583. Most notably he promoted the redevelopment of S. Giacomo degli Incurabili, which included the elliptical church designed by Francesco da Volterra; the hospital and confraternity complex was heir to about 100,000 scudi in money and property when he died in 1604. Under the influence of the hierarchy, and many lowly supporters, old hospitals were renewed and expanded in scope, and new ones created. When Camillo Fanucci published his guide to 'pious works' in 1601 he could describe or mention some forty hospitals: 17 general-specialist hospitals, 19 'national' ones and 4 guild hospitals. Various in the first category had started as guild hospices and had expanded their coverage. In addition there would have been small hospices and confraternity rooms for simple hospitality.[81]

The functional relationships between Roman hospitals and confraternities were

[80] Monachino, pp. 197–8, who uses: G. Russotto, L'origine dei Fatebenefratelli in Roma (Rome, 1966); Barletta, Aspetti della Riforma, pp. 36–42; N. Del Re (ed.) Roma centro mondiale di vita religiosa e missionaria (Bologna, 1968), pp. 133–4; De Angelis, San Giacomo, p. 17; C. Fanucci, Trattato, pp. 68–71; Donvito and Pellegrino, L'Organizzazione Ecclesiastica, pp. 17–18, 91–2, 101 (Montepeloso; now called Irsina, p. 43).

[81] Monachino, pp. 191–210; Fanucci, Trattato. For particular hospitals see notes below. On S. Giacomo degli Incurabili: De Angelis, San Giacomo; Blunt, Guide, p. 48.

varied and fluctuating, and they are often frustratingly unclear to the historian. One of the leading hospitals was S. Spirito in Sassia. It was in operation for some time before its canonical approval in 1201; it was considerably expanded in the fifteenth century, and again in the sixteenth, when new buildings were designed by Ottaviano Mascarino. In 1601 it could normally accommodate the wounded and fevered in 150 beds, but could take 400 patients during summer epidemics. By the eighteenth century it had 840 beds — all individual, as the dangers of patients sharing beds had finally been appreciated. According to Fanucci patients had to confess and receive communion before admission. The church, built (1538–45) by Antonio Sangallo, celebrated many masses daily, and there was much organ music. The hospital looked after abandoned babies and children; up to 500 were deposited there annually, or fished out of the Tiber in nets. Those that survived were educated in the hospital.

The confraternity contribution fluctuated. In the 1550s the confraternity had full administrative responsibility but, after an adverse report from Bernardino Cirillo in 1556, Paul IV returned administration to a full-time Preceptor and his staff. However, the dark-blue habited brethren visited the hospital daily, especially to help with meals; they assisted in the church at major feasts, carried the sacrament to the sick in the neighbouring parish, and helped with fund-raising. By 1624 the hospital had an income of about 133,000 *scudi* a year, the largest of the religious institutions, and over double that of St Peter's basilica. The complicated financing of its operations was aided from 1605 by the creating of the Banco di Santo Spirito, which developed into one of Italy's most notable banks. Its international reputation was indicated by the aggregation of 170 confraternities to this archconfraternity by the end of the sixteenth century, with another 164 added in the seventeenth.[82]

S. Giacomo degli Incurabili owed its development in the early sixteenth century to the Company of Divine Love; there was major building work from 1520, and a female wing was started in 1537. Under Cardinal Salviati there was a complete redevelopment between 1580 and 1593, so that it could normally accommodate about 120 patients. It was staffed by a doctor, a surgeon with his assistant, a chemist and assistant, eight *infermieri* and six or seven female assistants. Various confraternities provided visitors for the hospital inmates. The Capuchins were also involved as priests, money-raisers, and environmental hygiene specialists — burning aromatic herbs in the long corridors along which most beds were arranged. Fewer women than men recovered in this hospital, possibly because they entered in a worse condion. The hospital produced a famous potion — boiled 'legno santo', holy wood — to alleviate venereal diseases; to Fanucci 'opera di somma carità e rara', a work of great and unusual charity.[83]

A third notable Roman hospital, S. Maria della Consolazione, was the result by 1506 of the amalgamation of three old confraternities and their hospitals, possibly under

[82] Monachino, pp. 201–4; Maroni Lumbroso and Martini, pp. 407–14; Fanucci, *Trattato*, pp. 15–17; De Angelis, *S. Spirito*, esp. Appendix III on aggregations; Blunt, *Guide*, p. 147; G. Martin, *Roma Sancta* (1581). *Now revised from the manuscript by George Bruner Parks* (Rome, 1969), pp. 185–6; Serra, 'Funzione e finanze', p. 267; Trevor, p. 62 on B. Cirillo's investigation; R. Grégoire, '"Servizio dell'anima quanto del corpo" nell'ospedale romano di Santo Spirito (1623)', *RSRR*, 3 (1979), 221–54.

[83] De Angelis, *San Giacomo*; Monachino, pp. 193–6; Fanucci, *Trattato*, pp. 42–9; Martin, *Roma Sancta*, p. 187; M.C. Giuntella, L. Proietti Pedetta and M. Tosti, 'Modelli di povero e tipologia di assistenza', *RSCI*, no. 2 (1984), 494, reporting on a conference paper by A. Cavaterra on S. Giacomo and its patients.

pressure from the local Trastevere artisans and manual workers whom they had served. After 1506 it had beds for twenty-two women and for eighty to a hundred men. The hospital came to specialise in surgery in cases of industrial accidents, or the results of violent attacks and by the early seventeenth century they were doing significant anatomical research. After 1650 there was a major building development, and its work had a wide impact and reputation. Though there were some leading benefactors, the bulk of the income came from the local *popolo minuto*. Various confraternities assisted the hospital, especially the Nobili del Gesù and the companies Della Communione Generale and Delle Stimmate. By statute the archconfraternities of SS Annunziata at the Jesuit Collegio Romano and of the Immacolata Concezione at the Gesù organised Sunday visits, when they offered the sick 'things delicate and suitable for their condition, such as Spanish bread, sweetmeats, oranges, plums, cooked apples'. Various saintly persons proved their vocation in this hospital, including St Luigi Gonzaga who died helping in the 1591 plague epidemic. Overall responsibility for the hospital after 1506 seems to have fallen to the confraternity of S. Maria in Portico della Consolazione e delle Grazie (with its oratory across the river), but their precise role is obscure. Fanucci in 1601 himself complained of the lack of written documentation.[84]

The Trastevere district also had the hospital of S. Maria dell'Orto with (in 1598) fifty beds, primarily for members of thirteen local guilds, and their male relatives. The guilds formed a confraternity to run it, which was canonically approved in 1492, and elevated into an archconfraternity in 1588. It reputedly had the best-stocked pharmacy in Rome. The local gardeners, fruiterers, poulterers, millers, vermicelli makers, river-bank traders who joined as brothers made it one of the richest confraternities in Rome, though more money went on the church, its guild-linked chapels, worship and festivals than on the hospital. The hospital, rebuilt in 1739, remained under the confraternity until the mid-nineteenth century, and the fraternity survives for worship.[85]

The inn-keepers and boatmen of the Ripetta port area created their own confraternity hospital of S. Rocco in 1500. During major expansion under Cardinal Salviati a female section was added to specialise in the care of expectant mothers, poor sick girls, and 'fallen' noble women. It was situated in an area favoured by prostitutes. The male section cared primarily for members of the associated guilds, who paid dues both for the confraternity and hospital. After a period of administrative chaos the male section was closed in 1770, but the female part thrived, to have a school of obstetrics opened there by Pius VI in 1786.[86]

The archconfraternity of SS. Salvatore (based on the basilica of S. Giovanni in Laterano) ran a general hospital; in 1592 it had eighty beds in the female and a hundred in the male section, with fifty more beds in secluded corners for the more reputable patients. The archconfraternity owned a third of the Colosseum, and could sell pieces of the ruins to fund the hospital. Income also derived from ownership of the source of

---

[84] Monachino, pp. 205–6; Maroni Lumbroso and Martini, pp. 282–5; Barletta (ed.), *Aspetti della Riforma*, pp. 46–50; Fanucci, *Trattato*, pp. 38–42; Paglia '*La Pietà dei Carcerati*', no. 28 on map of sixteenth-century creations; Blunt, *Guide*, p. 86.

[85] Monachino, p. 207; Maroni Lumbroso and Martini, pp. 261–71; Martin, *Roma Sancta*, p. 186; Blunt, *Guide*, pp. 102–3.

[86] Monachino, pp. 198–9, 207; Maroni Lumbroso and Martini, pp. 343–5; Fanucci, *Trattato*, pp. 52–3; Blunt, *Guide*, pp. 140–1.

the Acqua Santa water supply, feeding into the aqueduct system. Brothers from the confraternity Nobili del Gesù (from 1593), as well as Oratorians sent by Filippo Neri, also assisted as visitors. Fanucci praised this as a spacious hospital, suitable for the fevered and wounded.[87]

Finally in Rome it is worth mentioning S. Maria della Pietà dei Pazzarelli, as a confraternity hospital that showed unusual philanthropic spirit. In 1548 Ferrante Ruiz, a Spanish chaplain in Rome, and two Navarre noblemen, Diego Bruno and his son Angelo, founded a Compagnia dei Poveri Forestieri to help the mad or abnormal people they had noticed wandering about Rome; they collected these wanderers and succoured them in Ruiz' house. By 1561 they received official approval as a confraternity, entitled S. Maria della Pietà. The statutes approved in 1563 specifically ruled that the mad were not to be restrained by chains or strait-jackets. From 1575 the confraternity was exclusively concerned with the insane. The Jesuit leader Diego Lainez secured them a hospital home near the Piazza Colonna; other support came from Filippo Neri and Carlo Borromeo, who sometimes stayed in the institution when in Rome. But all too soon there were signs of a decline, as indicated in a visitation report of 1592, when twenty-four men and twenty-two women were being treated (inadequately) by fifteen paid attendants. The hospital was heavily in debt and could not cope with the crisis prices of the 1590s, though the basic facilities were judged to be adequate. In 1599 a Cardinal Protector and outside deputies were appointed to bolster the hospital. When Cardinal Protector Francesco Barberini had the statutes revised in 1635, he sanctioned a return to methods of fear and force in dealing with the mad, though a minimum use was urged. It is unclear whether this represented a generally harsher attitude towards the poor and insane, or the intractable problems of dealing with the criminally violent. This confraternity hospital was never well-endowed and partly for this reason in the eighteenth century it was linked to S. Spirito, took in paying patients, and received direct government subsidies for helping violent madmen sent from the city prisons.[88]

By the early seventeenth century Rome had an international reputation for hospitality. Some hospitality was readily offered by the obscurer national hospitals mentioned by Fanucci and the Englishman Gregory Martin — such as those for the English, Scots, Lombards, Genoese, Flemings and others. They were little more than hospices and almshouses for foreign travellers, whether businessmen, lawyers, students or pilgrims and sometimes for poor foreign residents. They would have helped and impressed the foreign visitor. The more recognisable hospitals, whether specialist or general, would have impressed those staying longer, however deficient they might be by modern standards. But the institution with the widest impact and propaganda value was the archconfraternity of SS. Trinità dei Pellegrini e dei Convalescenti.

The SS. Trinità had been started in the 1540s by Filippo Neri (then a layman),

---

[87] Monachino, pp. 204–5; Maroni Lumbroso and Martini, pp. 394–7; Fanucci, *Trattato* pp. 34–7; Martin, *Roma Sancta*, p. 204.

[88] Monachino, pp. 196–7; Maroni Lumbroso and Martini, pp. 276–7; Martin, *Roma Sancta*, p. 132; Fanucci, *Trattato*, pp. 56–8; R. Lefevre, 'Don Ferrante Ruiz e la Compagnia dei Poveri Forestieri e Pazzi', *Studi Romani*, 17 (1969), 147–159; M.G. Ruggiero Pastora, 'Una "visita" del 1592 al Ospedale dei "Pazzarelli" di Roma', *Rassegna degli Archivi di Stato*, 1972, 47–67. Cf. H.C.E. Midelfort, 'Madness and civilisation in early modern Europe: a reappraisal of Michel Foucault', *After the Reformation. Essays in honor of J.H. Hexter*, ed. B.C. Malamant (Manchester, 1980), pp. 247–65.

Persiano Rosa (his spiritual adviser) and others to assist poor Romans; they then faced the challenge of the influx of pilgrims for the 1550 Holy Year. Thereafter they specialised in organising help for pilgrims for the Jubilees, held normally every twenty-five years. In between the gentlemen brothers of SS. Trinità used their facilities to look after the normal traffic of pilgrims, and succour convalescents from other hospitals. In this way they assisted about 20,000 persons a year. They also organised *Quarantore* celebrations and major processions to encourage devotions and spiritual welfare, for visitors or Roman residents.[89]

Gregory Martin, an English Jesuit translator of the Bible, spent eighteen months in Rome in 1576–8, and prepared a major account of religious activities and institutions in his *Roma Sancta*, though it was not published until modern times. He was much impressed by the work of the SS. Trinità, known among the companies as 'la gloriosa' for its activities during the 1575 Jubilee. He reported on their regular religious services, their help for sick members, their dowry provisions, their succour of convalescents, and their weekly preaching to the Jews, who were offered practical assistance in compensation for hearing Christian sermons. In the 1575 Jubilee the archconfraternity looked after 169,000 to 170,000 pilgrims, as well as convalescents (possibly 175,000 in all). In 1600 it was over 200,000 with sometimes 5,000 to 6,000 persons catered for in one day. Pilgrims were given lodging and food for up to three days, their feet were washed, they were entertained with music, and they were guided on pilgrimage processions to the basilicas. Foreigners coming from a great distance, such as from Bohemia or Portugal, could stay longer or be given financial assistance. According to Martin there was some instruction in Christian Doctrine for pilgrims; priests were provided with breviaries, some lay visitors sent away with Catechisms, the Office of the Virgin, and sacred tokens.[90]

A mule-keeper from Viterbo left a record of his fraternity of Buon Gesù's pilgrimage to Rome in 1575, and its reception by the SS. Trinità. As with the 1600 Perugian pilgrimage already described (chapter 5.3), there is much praise for the hospitality received, for the music and prayers. Lay gentlemen were clearly dominant in this confraternity work. The Viterbo fraternity affiliated to the SS. Trinità archconfraternity after their favourable treatment there — without changing its name. Other confraternities welcomed and maintained pilgrims, notably the Gonfalone and the Morte archconfraternities. The latter catered primarily for the more prestigious visitors, as the Perugian pilgrimage indicates. It similarly welcomed the equivalent Bologna archconfraternity in 1575: 'exemplary in its piety as in its sumptuousness', with its treasures and a select group of musicians, including Daniele Reni, father of the famous painter Guido Reni, who was born during his father's absence on this pilgrimage.[91] However, it was probably the SS. Trinità, with its wider ranging work for more socially diverse groups of pilgrims, and for the convalescents year by year, that was the best example of Roman

---

[89] Monachino, pp. 360–5; Maroni Lumbroso and Martini, pp. 425–8; Martin, *Roma Sancta*, pp. 188, 205, 232, 236–7; Fanucci, *Trattato*, pp. 54–6; Barletta, *Aspetti della Riforma*, pp. 194–205; P. Brezzi, *Storia degli Anni Santi*, pp. 91–126; Delumeau, *Vie économique*, pp. 167–88; Simoncelli, 'Note', p. 143–7.

[90] Martin, *Roma Sancta*, as in note 90; Borzacchini, pp. 237–60, esp. p. 240. From June to August 1573 the confraternity lodged 1,222 pilgrims and 4,489 convalescents.

[91] Martin, *Roma Sancta*, Appendix pp. 267–72 gives the account of the Viterbo pilgrimage; C.C. Malvasia, *The Life of Guido Reni*, trans. by C. and R. Enggass (University Park and London, 1980), p. 36.

philanthropy, as sponsored and practised by the Roman elite, and the best propaganda for Catholic charity.

Stress has been placed here on hospitals in Rome because they were seen as models by other Italians and Europeans, and because they were more closely linked with confraternities than were general hospitals in most other cities. It can be argued that the Roman systems were slow to develop, and reacted rather late and inadequately — particularly to the poverty side of 'hospital' work, as opposed to the medical or pilgrim aspects.[92]

Information about hospitals outside Rome is even more patchy. The largest city, Naples, was probably inadequately served by general hospital institutions, though it had some notable specialist 'conservatories', such as the Conservatorio dello Spirito Santo, run by a section of the city's largest confraternity, for vulnerable children. From the early fourteenth century a congregation administered the S. Casa dell'Annuziata as a hospital and church. By 1600 there were 388 beds, with separate sections for fever cases, the wounded and incurables. There was an excellent pharmacy. In summer the hospital could accommodate 500, and under severe pressures of epidemics, or galleys arriving in port, 1,500 might be treated. Bishop Gilbert Burnet in 1686 judged this 'the greatest hospital in the world'. From the late fifteenth century this hospital congregation ran a thriving pawn-broking and deposit bank (the Monte di Pietà), supposedly to help poorer borrowers. Much of Neapolitan philanthropy was in the hands of Orders such as the Theatines, Oratorians and Scolopians. Though they had their own institutions, such as the Somaschi orphanage which was opened by 1607, or worked in confraternity institutions and other pious places, their assistance was frequently offered in the street and houses. It might be argued that, given hygiene problems and medical ignorance, these were better places to treat many kinds of poor and sick who elsewhere were institutionalised.[93]

In the rest of the Kingdom of Naples our limited knowledge suggests that there was a haphazard spread of hospices and hospitals. Where we know of them, it is often difficult to tell whether confraternities were involved or not. The Catanzaro diocesan records mention a number of hospices, usually stated to be for pilgrims, but occasionally for the poor; dedication of some hospitals to S. Nicola suggest they might have helped poor girls with dowries. While many hospices were parochial, confraternity involvement is specifically mentioned in some cases. In Catanzaro itself the Nome di Dio confraternity had a hospital that supposedly attracted many sick, and the S. Corpo di Cristo in the Cathedral (aggregated to a Roman archconfraternity) took care of abandoned children.[94] Reggio Calabria seems to have had only one hospital in the

---

[92] Simoncelli, 'Note', esp. pp. 137–41, 156 is more sceptical about Roman successes and responses. See below chapter 10.1 on the confined poor.

[93] J. Mazzoleni (ed.), *Aspetti della Riforma Cattolica e del Concilio di Trento a Napoli. Mostra documentaria* (Naples, 1966), pp. 18–26; Lopez, *Riforma Cattolica*, pp. 65–76, 93, 97 101–4; G. Burnet, *Some Letters containing an Account of what seemed most remarkable in Switzerland, Italy &c* (Rotterdam, 1686; Scolar reprint, 1972), p. 193: 'The riches of the Annunciata are prodigious. It is the greatest Hospital in the world, the Revenue is said to be four hundred thousand crowns a year; the number of sick is not so great as in Milan', but he noted the convenience of the sick in the galleries, each bed in an alcove, with walls separating it from the bed on either side; he was surprised by the number of children being maintained in the hospital complex.

[94] A. De Girolamo, *Catanzaro*, pp. 97, 112–16, 184–5, 194–5, 202–5.

sixteenth century, that run by the Carmelites; burnt down during the disastrous Turkish raid on the city in 1594, it was reconstructed by the reforming archbishop A. D'Afflitto (1594–1638), who also from 1612 organised a conservatory for twelve poor girls. There is no evidence of confraternity involvement here. There were some hospices for pilgrims and the poor in other parts of the diocese, the responsibility for which is again unclear.[95] Despite similar problems of poverty and neglect the regions of the Basilicata, Molise and Abruzzi seem to have been better provided with hospitals and philanthropic confraternities than Calabria. The diocese of Isernia claimed a hospital in each of its fourteen communities; Boiano had 34 hospitals in 27 out of 28 places. While most would have catered primarily for travellers, they would probably have helped a few local poor and aged as well. In the diocese of Marsico the main town had two hospitals for both poor and sick, and a single hospital in most other places, according to its 1594 visitation report, but again whose responsibility they were is not clear.[96]

Hospitals in remoter areas might be run by a board of management that was not formally a confraternity, but whose actions and policies were similar, as far as the hospital was concerned, in that religious and moral concerns accompanied the physical. The proper confraternity hospital would have a regularly constituted religious life for the managers. In a Lombard example, the small hospital of S. Erasmo in S. Magno housed old paupers, provided dowries, and distributed alms; abandoned babies were sent to the Ospedale Maggiore (Ca' Granda) in Milan. In 1566 it coped with 16 *ospiti* (i.e. resident poor or sick), 18 in 1580, 14 in 1594, but only 4 in 1628. Many 'hospitals', whoever managed them, would have been of this size.[97]

The qualitative ebb and flow of a general hospital on the larger scale, and its mixed organisation, can be illustrated from Perugia's S. Maria della Misericordia. This was an old communal hospital, with an attached confraternity. The latter, of fixed numbers, and with some *ex officio* members, acted as a board of management, while the hospital was operated by paid staff. The extent of confraternity religious life remains obscure.[98] Through the sixteenth-century commune and church, confraternities and bishops, secured the expansion of the hospital in response to new socio-religious demands. Under communal law notaries were obliged to press those making wills to donate something to the hospital. By the early seventeenth century there were 800 beds for both sexes in the medical wards. The S. Martino confraternity operated an additional convalescent section. There was an orphanage that kept boys until aged eighteen or twenty, girls until marriage or the profession of vows; some literary and practical education was provided, while several boys were led to the priesthood.

[95] F. Russo, *Storia dell' Archidiocesi di Reggio Calabria*, pp. 162–7; Misefari, pp. 241–2; Sposato, pp. 67–8, 183, 191–2, 212. Squillace had hospices for pilgrims and miserable poor; Troppea one for sick and pilgrims; reports for Cariati for 1608–16 mention a new hospital for the poor, sick and pilgrims.

[96] Donvito and Pellegrino, *L'Organizzazione Ecclesiastica*, esp. Tables on pp. 61–106. Larino, Marsia and Chieti were also well served, though in Marsia there was a decline in the number of hospitals from twenty-eight in 1631 to seventeen in the 1680s, which is probably not explained by rationalisation or concentration of resources. This work is a good example of the strength — and limitations — of *ad limina* visitation reports as evidence. On Marsico: G.A. Colangelo, *La diocesi di Marsico nei secoli XVI–XVIII* (Rome, 1978), p. 23.

[97] Zardin, *Confraternite e vita di pietá*, pp. 124–5, 145–62.

[98] L. Stroppiana. *Storia dell'Ospedale di S. Maria della Misericordia e S. Nicolo degli Incurabili a Perugia* (Perugia, 1968), disappointingly brief and erratic; Valeri, but he is primarily concerned with the origins, and with the membership lists; Marinelli, *Le Confraternite*, pp. 692–3, 700–1.

In 1622–3 Bishop Napoleone Comitoli faced opposition to his jurisdiction over the hospital and its administration, and resorted to printed declarations of his authority. The battle which involved the Holy See and communal officials, may have been occasioned by an adverse report the bishop had made on the complex. He had been worried about administrative inefficiencies; he wanted wetnurses to nurse not more than two babies at a time, and wanted children in the hospital schools taught Christian Doctrine, grammar and *belle lettere*.[99] The hospital authorities accepted some of the criticisms, and published a decree in 1628 to prevent fraudulent behaviour by wetnurses outside the hospital: to prevent substitutions each baby was to be marked with a special sign on one foot; wetnurses could not draw their monthly stipend unless the suitably marked child was presented to officials or to the local parish priest if resident outside Perugia. Within a few decades the hospital was in decline again, facing major financial difficulties. Abbot Verduccioli, who arrived as a reforming administrator in 1669, outlined in print the problems and defects, while claiming some remedial successes. Maladministration and the general economic decline, with the negligent culture of the land, the poverty of workers, and the failure of debtors in Umbria had depleted income from properties. A greater number of abandoned babies had to be accepted daily. The buildings were in a poor state, and two infirmaries that had been found unhealthy because of poor air circulation in 1622 were uncorrected (and remained so until the nineteenth century). Verduccioli found the spiritual state of the hospital and its institutions better than the physical, which may have owed something to attendant confraternities and religious orders. But the education of the orphans was considered inadequate, with the boys leaving too early (at about 16) before properly literate or skilled. Few had recently been attracted to the priesthood through the seminary section. Since the 1590s the main confraternity had helped teach the seminarians (up to 40 of them) alongside a paid schoolmaster. Under Verduccioli an income of about 3,000 *scudi* had to support about 212 permanent residents (staff, orphan girls and boys), and 200 patients in the medical sections. Verduccioli described his hospital complex as: 'the unique exchequer of the poor, the shelter of the miserable, refuge of the abandoned, the house of God, the house of piety and of mercy, no less for strangers than for natives and for all a house truly worthy among the most beautiful and worthy splendours of Perugia and Umbria'. But despite the Abbot, difficulties increased. Umbrian economic problems and possibly a lessening of the philanthropic spirit took their toll.[100]

Complaints about hospitals, whether involving confraternities or not, were regular. They came from secular reports on Venetian hospitals, or from reforming archbishops like Giulio della Rovere in Ravenna (1566–7), Gabriele Paleotti in Bologna (as late as 1584, despite years of effort), or Marc'Antonio Del Tufo in Mileto from 1588. Maladministration, fraud, inadequate resources, desultory philanthropy were all

[99] ASP Ospedale S. Maria della Misericordia, Misc. 15 fols. 13r–9v, copy made in 1803 of the 1622 visitation reports; Marinelli cites some of the bishop's printed notices, esp. *Ragionamento di Monsig. Napoleon Vescovo di Perugia letto per suo ordine nella generale Adunanza dell' Hospitale della Misericordia* (Perugia, 1623), six sheets.

[100] F. Verduccioli, *Lo Spedale Grande di S.M. della Misericordia di Perugia* (Orvieto, 1672), esp. pp. 39–46, 51–68, 84, 98, with p. 68 quoted.

blamed. Attempts to amalgamate small hospices often failed.[101] These complaints have to be offset against the more favourable reports on the Roman hospitals (which Martin Luther could praise before his onslaught against Roman monsters), or Thomas Coryat's enthusiasm (during his 1608–9 Italian visit) for Milan's great hospital, with its 122 chambers in which 'foure thousand poore people are relieved'.[102] The modern study of Florence's hospital of S. Paolo (supervised by Franciscans, with the help of secular women, then nuns) suggests that in 1567–8 it was a successful hospital, medically and otherwise. But only a few years before it had been found inadequate, and by 1599 it was reduced to a convalescent home. Standards could change rapidly.[103]

The hospitals, as indicated in the course of the above discussion, contained many who were not considered medically sick: abandoned children, women in need of protection, the 'poor' unable to support themselves and without a protective family. The numbers involved could be sizable. A Roman census in February 1591 recorded 3,666 as in hospital, out of a population of 116,695, or 3.14 per cent. B. Pullan has calculated that Venice had about 4,000 'perpetual poor' in hospitals — the old, widows, orphans, Franciscan female tertiaries — or 2.67 per cent of the population of about 150,000. Florence in the mid-seventeenth century had approximately 2,500 persons, or 4 per cent institutionalised, orphans or mendicants. In Naples in 1606 out of a population of supposedly 280,746 there were about 2,500 sick in hospital, with about 3,000 boys, girls, old men and women in 'conservatories', or about 2 per cent placed in hospitals. Bologna in 1570 from a population of 61,742 registered 990 persons in hospitals, and a further 133 orphans placed elsewhere, (1.18 per cent). Out of Ferrara's population of 32,860 in 1601 there were 442 people recorded as resident in conservatories and hospitals (1.3 per cent).[104] These figures may mislead, since many of those in hospitals would have come from the surrounding villages or smaller towns to the main city, whether initially seeking jobs or charity, and are therefore part of a larger population. Some confrater-

[101] Pullan, *Rich and Poor*, pp. 211, 330–5, 344–51; Prodi, *Paleotti*, vol. 2, p. 192; Samaritani, 'Fonti inedite', *Ravennatensia*, vol. 2, p. 475; E. Nasalli Rocca, review in *Studi di storia Ospedaliera*, 3 (1969), 211–12; AA.VV. *Storia di Milano*, vol. 10 (Milan, 1957), p. 242; F. Santucci, pp. 157–9 shows how attempts to amalgamate five Assisi hospitals/hospices in the interests of efficiency proved unsuccessful from 1573 until the 1750s, despite efforts of successive bishops, visitors and Sacred Congregations. Sposato, pp. 67–8 quotes Del Tufo's blunt statement of the problems first made in an edict of 1588 and repeated in his 1591 synodal legislation: 'For three years in various ways we have greatly striven to take from the hands of the Devil some Masters and administrators of certain hospitals, who in disregard of the Blessed God, and of the Sacred Canons, have dared to dissipate the incomes of pious places, which are the blood of the poor and the patrimony of Christ, by converting part shamelessly to their own sometimes sordid uses, and by distributing part to uses, illicit, scandalous or at least remote from the institution, against the intentions of the founders and of the Holy Church. [The income must no more be used] to marry more witches, servants, prostitutes or concubines of the deputed masters, or other relatives or friends.'
[102] T. Coryat, *Coryats Crudities* (London, 1611; Scolar Press reprint, London, 1978 used), p. 102; Simoncelli, 'Note', p. 137. For other praise of Italian hospitals and philanthropy by English visitors, see E.P. de G. Chaney, 'Giudizi inglesi su ospedali italiani, 1545–1789', *Timore e Carità*, pp. 77–101.
[103] B.J. Trexler, 'Hospital Patients in Florence: San Paolo 1567–68', *Bulletin of the History of Medicine*, 48 (1974), 41–59; cf. D'Addario, *Aspetti*, pp. 76–7, 95.
[104] Pullan, 'Poveri, mendicanti', pp. 990–9; *idem, Rich and Poor*, pp. 207, 423–8; K.J. Beloch, *Bevölkerungsgeschichte Italiens* (3 vols., Berlin, 1937, 1939, 1961), vol. 1, p. 176: for Naples there are two different sets of figures for 1606: 2,506 or 2,256 sick in hospital, 762 or 680 boys, 1,580 or 2,390 girls, 20 men and 528 women (according to one source) or 103 of both sexes (the other) in conservatories. For Bologna and Ferrara, Beloch, vol. 2, pp. 93, 109.

nities had a particular concern for two groups within the 'hospitalised' population: abandoned children and females at risk. These are the subject of the next sections of this chapter.

5 ABANDONED CHILDREN

The problems of abandoned or unprotected children, especially female, have already been mentioned. In some cities and towns confraternities became involved through their hospitals, or through special homes or conservatories, even if it was the municipal hospitals like the Innocenti in Florence or Ca' Granda in Milan that experienced the major problems. There were two major categories of children involved: those abandoned at birth, and older ones found at a later age to be in need of help and protection. The former were largely unsolicited; most babies were deliberately abandoned — exposed — on the threshold of a confraternity, hospital or nunnery. The older children, and a few babies, might arrive through positive philanthropic efforts, as from members of the Neapolitan company Dei Bianchi dello Spirito Santo, which ruled that some should seek out the needy children on the streets.[105] The abandoned newborn might be a temporary, if for ever repeated, problem because of the high mortality rate; the older abandoned child required a deeper commitment as each individual child was more likely to survive to adulthood, demanding longer care and education. By the sixteenth century Italian reformers realised that the problem of abandoned babies and children was a serious one for philanthropists to deal with; the solutions they attempted may have aggravated the situation, or changed its dimensions.

The subject of exposed babies, *esposti*, or foundlings is highly emotive. It has been made more so by the statistics and myths about foundlings and the related wetnursing systems from late eighteenth-century France, which have dominated and distorted discussions until recently.[106]

In Italy the best recent research has been on the Florentine situation, in particular on the foundling hospital of the Innocenti. While the Florentine institutions were not the particular concern of confraternities, evidence about them is worth considering first. It is not clear when the 'problem' of exposed babies began or became serious; but R.C. Trexler argues that for a long time infanticide had been tolerated; when church and civic authorities finally campaigned against its incidence, there was pressure to save babies, and commit them to institutions — though this might turn out to be only a delayed form of infanticide. The greater the facilities, the more babies would arrive. If the

---

[105] Miele, 'L'assistenza sociale', p. 855.

[106] Cf. O.H. Hufton, *The Poor of Eighteenth-Century France 1750–89* (Oxford, 1979, paperback edn), esp. pp. 318–51; A. Forrest, *The French Revolution and the Poor* (Oxford, 1981), pp. 136–7; C. Delaselle, 'Les enfants abandonnés a Paris au XVIIIᵉ- siècle', *Annales ESC* 30 (1975), 187–218; Flinn, pp. 39–43; S. Wilson, 'The myth of motherhood myth: the historical view of European child-rearing', *Social History*, vol. 9, no. 2 (May 1984), pp. 181–198, esp. p. 195. The French, particularly the Parisians, may have been normally more inclined than Italians to put children out to wetnurses; and have been served by a more organised system for supplying nurses, or for sending foundlings to city hospitals. But Italian cities, like the French, could suck children in from great distances, with little chance of survival. Studies in both areas show that legitimate children were to be found among the foundlings. Cf. L. Tittarelli, 'Gli esposti all'Ospedale di S. Maria della Misericordia in Perugia nei secoli XVIII e XIX', *BSPU*, 82 (1985) [1987], 23–130; he also digests findings on other parts of Italy and France, though only for the early eighteenth century onwards.

institutions were perceived to be life-saving, then the influx would be greater. There were varying reasons for babies being 'unwanted' and so 'exposed'. Many were unwanted because they were the bastard children of slaves and servants who could not be socially integrated into the main family, especially if female. Bastardy governed the fate of many others, though not all bastards were rejected by both families and so exposed. C. Klapisch–Zuber argues that there were pressures on servants to abandon their own children to nurse the legitimate children of the master, and on poor mothers to abandon their own offspring to be paid as wetnurses to the rich. But it is clear from Trexler's sampling in Florence that other babies, and older children, legitimate and illegitimate, were handed over to the hospitals when parents faced devastation through war or famine, or when they felt they could not manage to feed an extra mouth. The babies or young children might be 'wanted' emotionally, and be abandoned as a possibly temporary measure; remorse was expressed in accompanying notes, or enough evidence of identification might be left so a parent could recover the child if conditions improved. While sometimes these partial identifications may merely have been intended to ease the parental conscience, C.A. Corsini's evidence shows that some children were later reclaimed.[107]

Florence had hospitals looking after foundlings from the thirteenth century at least; the S. Maria di San Gallo, and the S. Maria della Scala (from 1316). From about this time the brethren of S. Maria della Misericordia took in lost or abandoned children to care for them until claimed or sent to a foundling home. In 1419 the commune and silk guild decided to launch a home specially for foundlings, which finally opened in 1445. This hospital of the Innocenti soon became central to Florence, a model for hospitals elsewhere, whether civic or confraternity, and famous to this day for its architecture (by Brunelleschi), if not its philanthropy. The new foundling hospital looked attractive, being spacious and airy. It was inundated with children. What started as a hope for parents soon became a death sentence for too many babies. The death rate went up either because overcrowding increased the risks of infections, or because the supply of enough caring wetnurses was inadequate, especially when government authorities failed to allocate the requisite funds.

Florence influenced other Italian areas, especially Venice and its dependent cities. In major cities there were the same problems in the later fifteenth and sixteenth century; facilities for looking after the *esposti* were expanded, the numbers deposited increased, the funding failed to keep pace. This seems to be the pattern whether in civic hospitals like Milan's Ca' Granda with its dependencies, and Parma's Ospedale Maggiore, or confraternity institutions like Venice's Pietà and Rome's S. Spirito in Sassia. Possibly one of the more successful developments was that of the Casa Santa della SS. Annunziata in Naples, administered by the Compagnia dei Bianchi dello Spirito Santo, which

[107] R.C. Trexler, 'Infanticide in Florence: new sources and first results' and 'The foundlings of Florence, 1395–1455', *History of Childhood Quarterly*, 1, no. 2 (1973), 98–116 and 259–84; C.A. Corsini, 'Materiali per lo studio della famiglia in Toscana nei secoli XVII–XIX; gli esposti', *Quaderni Storici*, 33 (1976), 998–1052; Klapisch-Zuber, *Women, Family*, esp. chapter 7 'Blood parents and milk parents: wet nursing in Florence, 1300–1530', esp. pp. 140–4, and see also pp. 104–5. Professor Pullan, during a seminar on foundlings and abandoned children at Edinburgh University in March 1987, indicated that there was other evidence, as for Brescia, of children being reclaimed by parents, and of bishops pressurising parents to do so when institutions became overcrowded; Tittarelli, 'Gli esposti', pp. 69–70.

had the chief responsibility for abandoned babies in its foundling nursery (*brefotrofio*), as well as for educating older orphans and vulnerable youths, and operating proper medical facilities. It has recently been described as constituting a 'feudal state' within the city, a major business enterprise of considerable wealth by the seventeenth century, dominated by the middle-class *popolo*, rather than the nobles. It was essentially an independent enterprise, not reliant on, or controlled by, the government.[108]

Venetian hospitals by the mid-fifteenth century considered that there was a crisis over abandoned children. They expressed concern about the growing number of babies deposited, and about the rumours concerning high death rates. They appealed to the government for money. The Senate contributed and put pressure on the popes to allocate more benefices to the pious institutions concerned. The main hospital handling abandoned infants was the Pietà, which was run by two confraternities, male and female, though it was closely supervised by the Council of Ten. In 1466 it claimed it had had 460 infants abandoned on its doorstep. In 1472 it cited the deaths of 600 foundlings in that year as a reason for receiving more money to cope. In the 1520s it was again, or still, severely overstretched. In 1525 the wetnurses working for the Pietà were expected to feed as many as four babies at a time, and they were well in arrears for pay. In the 1550s this hospital had between 800 and 1,200 inmates — obviously including staff and some older orphans. Conditions and procedures have not yet been clarified.[109]

As one might expect Rome was another city where confraternities were involved in the problem of *esposti*. Chiefly concerned was the confraternity hospital of S. Spirito in Sassia. Foundlings were cared for in its *brefotrofio*, which in the early seventeenth century employed between forty and fifty wetnurses able to feed two or three children each. In-house nursing was designed to avoid the extra dangers of transporting babies into the countryside, and of having virtually no supervision over the nurses. The intake was a mixture of bastard foundlings and those sent in by poor honest women who could not afford to maintain them. There were links with confraternities and hospitals outside Rome. The confraternity of Spirito Santo in Ferentino in the seventeenth century gathered in abandoned children from its locality, had them baptised in the Cathedral, and then sent them to S. Spirito in Rome. An official report indicates a bleak record for initial survival: 'from the beginning of 1580 until the end of November 1584 of the 3,503 babies abandoned in the hospital 2,672 died'. A mid-seventeenth-century report firmly blamed numerous deaths on the long travels of many babies brought half-alive from fifty or sixty miles away, a problem repeated in eighteenth-century France. By that century many of the S. Spirito foundlings were being sent back to wetnurses in the

[108] AA.VV. *La Ca' Granda*; V. Benassi, *Storia di Parma* (Bologna, 1971 reprint of 1899–1906 edn), vol. 5 pp. 247–9; Musi, pp. 259–62; De Maio, 'L'Ospedale dell'Annunziata' in his *Riforme e miti*, pp. 245–53; Miele, 'L'assistenza sociale', pp. 833–5; Bishop C. Musso of Bitonto called the Annunziata and Incurabili hospitals 'le due occhi di Napoli'; Villari, *La rivolta antispagnola*, pp. 235–6 notes that two nobles killed a *popolare* governor of the hospital when the *popolari* dared to hold a meeting without the participation of a noble representative. See below on Venice and Rome. London's Coram Hospital had similar problems in the eighteenth century, though there may have been greater care over nursing, R.M. McClure, *Coram's Children. The London Foundling Hospital in the Eighteenth Century* (New Haven and London, 1981).

[109] Pullan, *Rich and Poor*, pp. 207, 259–60, 375, 413, 416–17, 424; Ruggiero, *The Boundaries of Eros*, p. 29 and p. 172 n. 31, p. 172 n. 33; Semi, pp. 70–1, 103–5, though mainly dealing with the later building; another volume in the series may deal with some of the work of such hospital institutions.

country, suggesting that in-house nursing was incapable of satisfying the need. For the survivors there were hospices for boys and girls, which became primary schools. Some boys were trained for crafts, others sent to an agricultural colony on Monte Romano owned by the confraternity-hospital.[110]

In Bologna a number of confraternities in the fifteenth century took in *esposti*, and S. Maria della Misericordia (or della Carità) maintained this role in the sixteenth. However, between 1567 and 1570 some lesser confraternities and hospitals were amalgamated to form the hospital of SS. Pietro e Procolo for the exposed babies and older abandoned children; it became commonly known as the Ospedale dei (poveri) Bastardini — though not only bastards were involved. The preamble to the statutes argued that reorganisation was necessary because the number of abandoned babies was rising, and that alms to support them were falling. Responsibility for the new work was shared between the Cathedral canons, a Senator as perpetual proconsul for hospitals, a board of twenty-four governors (aristocrats and lawyers), and members of a fraternal company for the hospital. The last seemingly provided the visitors in the city and country to check on the conditions of the babies being nursed. For the confraternity and hospital there was a strong emphasis on the moral and devotional life — at least theoretically.[111]

For most of the above institutions little is known about the procedures and treatment of the abandoned babies. Some were brought direct to a recognised institution by a relative; often grilles or revolving windows were provided where a child could be safely but anonymously deposited, especially at night. Other nunneries and confraternities had similar arrangements; these might send them on to the big hospitals or arrange for wetnursing. Other babies were found on the streets or in the fields, and eventually brought half-dead to a supposedly competent institution. Sometimes parents brought their babies to a parish priest who then arranged for assistance, bound by the secrecy of the confessional. Some points are exemplified and clarified by Perugian information.

The Perugian city hospital of S. Maria della Misericordia (with its fraternal management board) dealt with most *esposti*. Interesting points emerge from a sample of the year 1584 — the first for which records on the foundlings survive. In that year the hospital nursery, or Casa, dealt with 223 exposed or abandoned children — 123 male and 100 female — from city and *contado*.[112] In 135 cases the records note some form of

---

[110] Monachino, p. 234; S. Pagano, 'Gli esposti dell'ospedale di S. Spirito nel primo Ottocento,' *RSRR*, 3 (1979), 353–92, esp. pp. 356, 357 n. 11, 359; B. Valeri, pp. 36 (Statute Cap. II no. II), and 14–27. The nineteenth century could produce some horrifying mortality figures; in Cosenza 1865–74 about 99 per cent of the babies left in the *brefotrofio* dies, but only 26.7 per cent of those sent out to nurses; for Como 1876–81 the figures were 72.9 per cent and 26.3 per cent, see M. Gorni and L. Pellegrini, *Un problema di storia sociale, l'infanzia abbandonata in Italia nel secolo XIX* (Florence, 1974), esp. pp. 54–5. Cf. also L. Dodi Osnaghi, 'Ruota e infanzia abbandonata a Milano nella prima metà dell'Ottocento', *Timore e Carità*, pp. 427–35. The shortage of wetnurses was a fundamental problem, especially in summer when country women were required for harvesting.

[111] Fanti, *Ospedale . . . Carità*, pp. 21–36; *idem, San Procolo*, pp. 154–231; BCP F.O.81 'Statuti dell'Ospedale dei Santi Pietro e Procolo' (1570, with additions). Note fol. 1v: 'et per il contrario essere molto diminuite le consuete elemosine, et carità, cosi per li tempi penuriosi, come per altre cause'.

[112] ASP Ospedale di S. Maria della Misericordia. Movimento degli Esposti I (1584–90), fols. 1r–29v. The sex distribution figures are approximate, since the writing is not always clear between Domenico and Domenica, Giovanne and Giovanna; the assumption has been that Felice is always female, as it clearly is in some cases. All children were given a name even if they died almost immediately. Cf. the period 1700–19: 2,747 were abandoned (1,357 male, 1,389 female, 1 sex unknown); or on average 137 a year, ranging from 96 in 1709 to 190 in 1719; Tittarelli, 'Gli esposti', pp. 25, 32, 77.

identification, varying from a written notification (*polizza*) from a parent, parish priest or finder giving some details, or indicating knowledge about the child to a very marginal identification by threads, strings, medals or coins; since the last were not usually current Perugian coinage they could be treated as indicators, rather than conscience money, if the parent(s) later wanted to reclaim the child, or to be covered against an accusation of infanticide, if neighbours queried the outcome of an obvious pregnancy. Some of the objects may have been provided as good-luck talismans.[113] In 116 cases the child seems to have been baptised in the Casa; it is either so stated, or it can be fairly safely inferred from the record. For most it was necessary because of the unknown origin of the child, but occasionally information arriving with the child indicated that it was not yet baptised. The age is given — known or estimated — for 129 children: 71 were less than a month old when registered (including six born in the Casa); 50 were between a month and a year; 8 were over a year old.[114] In all 153 died in the Casa (68.6 per cent) — in one case after being sent out to nurse, and being returned as ill; 26 were sent to nurses in the city, 34 in the *contado*, while 8 appear to have stayed and lived on in the Casa, or the record does not make their fate clear. (In two other cases the record is too damaged to decipher the outcome). The date of death, or of the transfer to an outside nurse is not necessarily recorded, but from examples where it is given, it is clear that a child could remain for months in the Casa.[115] This volume was only very rarely concerned with the fate of the child once it was allocated to an outside nurse. Other volumes, but from a much later period, deal with wetnurses. In the 1670s they were paid to keep children for many years, and some became foster parents for older children. The contractor for the nursing or fostering could be male or female. A cursory look at this later record does not suggest that the death rate with

---

[113] *Ibid.* e.g. fol. 26r, 19 November, a *polizza* saying the child is called Julio Cesare and 'Che sara reconosciuto che bono padre si pigliera con filo d.o rese bianco'; he went to a *balia* in the city. Fol. 22v, 12 October, Chiara, just born ('nata alora') — 'con segnale di un corallo in filzato in una bandella de seta in carnationi, e una poliza che la racommendata ai padri priori che diceva che era nata di nobil padre, e chi laueria arecognosciuta al tempo del maritagio e che si batisasse e gli se paresse nome chiara'. She died in the Casa, 10 November 1584. In the period 1700–19 less than 8 per cent were abandoned with a recognition sign, Tittarelli, 'Gli esposti', p. 71. On good-luck talismans, Fasano Guarini (ed.), *Prato*, p. 103.

[114] *Ibid.*, fol. 8v: Nestisia was brought to the Casa, aged about three; she died in the Casa (date not given). Fol. 9r: Menico was brought to the hospital aged about two, with a *fede* from a priest at Monte L'Abbate to say he had been abandoned by everybody. In the 1700–19 period 1.5 per cent of abandoned children were aged over a year, 1.9 per cent aged 1–11 months; Tittarelli, 'Gli esposti', p. 62.

[115] *Ibid.*, fol. 6v: Benedetta, newly born, placed naked and without any identification in the *buca* (receptacle to facilitate anonymous deposit of babies); she stayed in the Casa for eleven months before being sent to a wetnurse in the *contado*. Fol. 29v: 30 December, a mother came with her son of two days, and said she would like to stay in the Casa and act as wetnurse as well. Her son, Innocentio, died 28 March 1585. Cf. Giuntella et al. 'Modelli', p. 494 on mothers staying on in hospital as *balie*, though this seems to be for a later period. Tittarelli, 'Gli esposti', pp. 95–7, 10; by the eighteenth century there was greater pressure to send the babies out quickly because of the shortage of in-house wetnurses; in 1700–19 53.9 per cent died before they could be sent out. In Ferrara the foundlings were looked after by the confraternity of S. Cristoforo; in 1574 it reported it had 140, with 26 of them being brought up in private houses, so it presumably had a good supply of in-house nurses: Peverada, 'Note', pp. 326–7, 330–5. The high proportion of children sent to wetnurses within the city caused surprise when I cited it at the Edinburgh seminar (see n. 107 above); Professor Pullan, who is currently studying poverty and children, in particular considered this unusual.

wetnurses was particularly high, especially if the new arrival survived the initial weeks.[116]

The 1622 visitation reported seven wetnurses, *balie*, living in the hospital, and that there were about 270 *esposti* being tended by hospital wetnurses in the hospital or outside at the time of the report. It is difficult to tell from this record how many orphans, those that survived the wetnursing stage and outside fostering, were based in the hospital for education. In the main dormitories there seem to have been 35 girls and 25 boys; others were placed elsewhere in the hospital or housed in the city, but were fed, schooled and trained under hospital supervision. This possibly meant about 70 girls and 60 boys were under hospital tutelage. Girls were provided with a blue serge dress or tunic every four years, and hose twice a year; boys were allocated clothes each year according to need.[117]

The main hospitals looking after abandoned babies also had sections within the complex, or orphanages, for those that survived the early period, as in Perugia. There were in addition children who were later taken into institutions as orphans or in need. For Naples the work of the Spirito Santo brethren has already been mentioned. In 1587 their male conservatory, and others such as that of S. Maria di Loreto, housed about 680 boys or youths. Genoese orphans were succoured, educated and trained in a hospital orphanage organised by a branch of the Divino Amore confraternity, with assistance from Somaschi fathers.[118]

In Rome during the bitterly cold winter of 1582 Leonardo Cerusi, a lay schoolmaster and groom to Cardinal Ferdinando de' Medici, started gathering up vagabond children and giving them shelter at night. Eventually, encouraged by Filippo Neri (his confessor), Cardinals Cesare Baronio and Federico Borromeo he established a residence for such children near the Piazza del Popolo; Romans started calling it the Spedale de'fanciulli spersi, or Spedale del letterato. Cerusi became a well-known figure collecting alms for it, until his death in 1595. Baronio took over responsibility, and then entrusted it to a sodality of deputies. Clement VIII transferred this hostel, then housing about 150 boys, to a new site on the Via Flaminia. From earlier in the century the archconfraternity of S. Maria della Visitazione degli Orfani had operated hospices for orphan or vulnerable boys and girls. This orphanage could maintain about 200 children. The brighter boys could move on to a college, promoted by Cardinal Salviati and later expanded by Cardinal Edoardo Farnese. Such orphanages had a mixture of those who had been in care since birth, and those added later by confraternity members and priests when they found them on the streets, and were informed that they were at risk.[119]

Philanthropic concern for needy children was shown by these Roman, Genoese and

[116] ASP Ospedale di S. Maria della Misericordia, Baliatrice degli Esposti, vol. 5 (1670–75), e.g. p. 8: in July 1670 Don Angelo di Pietro of Agello was to be paid at 6 *paoli* a month to take 'a balia' an abandoned girl, Agostina; she died, and in July he took Alessio, and was paid in grain and bread for him until July 1677; p. 1: Donna Lucretia of S. Cristoforo di Piscelle in June 1671 took on Marta Felice, reputedly legitimate, aged eight; to teach her 'leggere e calzette'. Cf. on the organisation of wetnursing by men, Klapisch-Zuber, *Women, Family* pp. 143–4. For a reasonably optimistic view of the death rates among those babies put out to Italian wetnurses: C.A. Corsini, 'La fecondité naturelle de la femme mariée. Le cas des nourrices', *Genus*, 30 (1974), pp. 243–59.
[117] ASP Ospedale di S. Maria della Misericordia, Miscellanea vol. 15, esp. fols. 13v, 15v, 17r–19r.
[118] Miele, 'L'assistenza sociale', pp. 853–7, 860–1; Savelli, pp. 189–90; see above n. 93, and chapter 2.2.
[119] Monachino, pp. 234, 240–2.

Neapolitan institutions, by the various general hospitals like those in Perugia or Piacenza that had orphanage sections, and by other orphanages started by Miani and his friends in northern Italy. Some of Miani's friends created the Somaschi Order which soon developed a major reputation for educating the neglected and poor.[120] The children were educated and trained, sometimes to a reasonable standard, so that boys could become priests or artisans, girls well-domesticated wives, servants or textile workers. A study of a Venetian hospital of SS. Giovanni e Paolo and its abandoned children, called I Derelitti, suggests that the boys and girls from there eventually did quite well, with honourable marriages, or careers in the church after receiving an education comparable to that of boys from the middle classes in the city. Some of the girls were noted as singers. In Perugia tax incentives were offered to persuade respectable people to marry orphan girls from the Misericordia.[121] Some orphans could receive unusual attention. When the notable seventeenth-century sculptor, Alessandro Algardi, drew up his will he left as residual heir a male orphan from the orphanage of S. Bartolomeo di Reno in Bologna (to be chosen by the archbishop or his vicar general), provided the young man took the name and arms of the Algardi family. The procedure was to be repeated if this heir died childless.[122] Different kinds of philanthropic concern, enticing or restrictive, for orphan girls will be evident in the next section, which considers vulnerable females more particularly.

6 GIRLS AND WOMEN AT RISK

Girls and women were clearly the target of much philanthropy; this has been demonstrated in the concern to provide dowries to poor and deserving girls, and in cases where old women were given some priority in the distribution of alms, or the allocation of alms-houses. The concern is also seen in the increasing provision of conservatories, refuges and orphanages. These institutions were not only for the surviving foundlings, and older abandoned children already mentioned above, but for other females considered at risk: prostitutes' daughters, repentant prostitutes, widows lacking family support, deserted wives or those in danger of attack from husbands and relatives. Such institutions were mainly in the largest cities (though some of these females at risk elsewhere would have received assistance in smaller 'hospitals'), where the fluidity of the population and the separation of more people from protective extended families made the problems worse, or more obvious. Also the resources to maintain such specialist establishments would have been more readily available. The institutions were run by nuns, by independent confraternities, or by general hospitals to which nuns and confraternities might provide additional support.

---

[120] AA.VV. *San Girolamo Miani e Venezia*, esp. articles by C. Pellegrini and G. Ellero; Pullan, *Rich and Poor*, pp. 259–63.

[121] Ellero, 'Un ospedale', pp. 38–9; ASP Ospedale di S. Maria della Misericordia, Miscellanea, vol. 5 fol. 107r–v, vol. 6 fols. 188v–92v: 'propterea aliquod erga dictus hospitale, et illius puellarum charitatis, et pietatis opus amore Dei, in quantam Magnifici Communis Perusiae paupertas patitur. exercer volentis, ut praesertim homines ad eiusdem Hospitalis puellas sibi uxores accipiendum eo facilius inducantur, quo se nouerint alicuius exemptionis adiuvarj . . .'. For the view that Venetian orphan girls were adopted with a view to sexual exploitation, though they might eventually be married off 'respectably' with a dowry, Ruggiero, *The Boundaries of Eros*, pp. 150–1.

[122] J. Montagu, *Alessandro Algardi*, pp. 208, 232.

A prevalent male attitude was that female virginity and chastity must be protected and this was likely to lead to a restrictive and, to in modern eyes, uncharitable regime for those females being helped. In Bologna G.B. Segni warned that poor girls facing dearth would kill their virginity, trade their honesty for life, while married or unmarried women, unable to do a menial job like hoeing would sell their marital honesty or virginity for bread, though ashamed to beg, and mothers, rather than die from hunger with their daughters, would help them lose their honesty and live infamously. Hence the need for alms, dowries and safe institutions, of which Bologna had a number, including the Casa del Soccorso di S. Paolo, founded in 1589, and run by a congregation, which took in girls and women who had already sinned or been dishonoured. It received about 600 girls between 1589 and 1667, some of whom had been prostitutes. The difficult girls were sent for harsher treatment in the Opera dei Mendicanti (discussed in chapter 10.1), but most were expected to marry or become nuns, through the support of patrons, or to return to their families (husband, mother, siblings, etc.). In addition the conservatory of S. Maria del Baraccano existed mainly for young girls from poor, but so far respectable families, who could be housed away from temptations and dangers — 'un conserva dell' onore' — until a dowry was available for a respectable marriage. Enclosed in such a conservatory temptation and the evils noted by Segni could be avoided. A dowry could be paid for by investments from the girl's family over several years, by investments in the conservatory, or by outside donations, including occasional confraternity gifts.[123] The attitude to 'risk' is indicated by the rule that the Florentine home of S. Caterina for abandoned girls would not accept those who were blind, deaf, dumb or otherwise seriously handicapped, because apparently they ran a limited risk of falling into sin.[124]

Conservatories for younger girls, of varying backgrounds, were developed through the sixteenth century. The main challenge came from the effects of the Italian wars. Of considerable influence was the Conservatorio delle Convertite della Carità, in Brescia — promoted by Countess Laura Gambara, sister of the Blessed Paola Gambara. This was initially designed to protect young girls who had been the victims of rampaging soldiers after the sack of the city in 1512, but subsequently also assisted a variety of vulnerable girls and women. This set in motion other philanthropic enterprises in the city, such as the confraternity of SS. Trinità's hospital for incurables, and an orphanage started in 1532 by G. Miani. He and his friend Bartolomeo Stella spread ideas about conservatories and orphanages across northern Italy.[125]

In Rome in the early sixteenth century abandoned girls were given refuge in S.

[123] Segni, *Trattato*, p. 53: 'Quante povere Donzelle, miserabili verginelle, per farsi schermo contra la fame, che lo combatte per uccidere in loro le loro verginità, vanno mendiche, procacciandosi con l'honestia il vivere? E quante sono quell'altre infelici cosi maritate, come nò, che non potendo sustenere l'essercitio della zappa, e vergognandosi di mendicare, possano sostenere il peso dell'infamia, & del peccato, e non si vergognano di vendere per prezzo di pane l'honesta maritale, & l'honor virginale a scellerate persone, che à questo attendono con molto studio, & con offesa infinita della divina pietà?'. L. Ferrante, 'L'onore ritrovato. Donne nella Casa del Soccorso di S. Paolo a Bologna (sec. XVI–XVII)', *Quaderni Storici*, 18 (1983), 499–527; L. Ciammitti, 'Quanto costa essere normale. La dote nel conservatorio femminile di Santa Maria del Baraccano (1630–1680)', *ibid.* pp. 469–97.
[124] Lombardi, 'Poveri', p. 168: not accept an abandoned girl who was 'Cieca, sorda, muta, stroppiata, et questo perché simile non sono cosi pericolose a capitar male'.
[125] AA.VV. *Storia di Brescia*, vol. 2, pp. 451–4.

Spirito in Sassia. Then the archconfraternity of S. Maria della Visitazione degli Orfani
more systematically faced the problem of abandoned boys and girls. By 1542 they had
a separate hospice for young girls, who were expected to be aged seven to ten, and
legitimate. They were given a refuge, and spiritual guidance, with the assistance later
of Somaschi fathers and female Augustinian Tertiaries. They remained until they left
to get married or entered a nunnery. The Compagnia delle Vergini Miserabili di S.
Caterina dei Funari (or della Rosa) was founded in 1536, with the support of Loyola,
Neri, Gaetano da Thiene and Cardinal G.P. Carafa (later Paul IV), to protect daughters
of prostitutes, or persons in extreme poverty. The conservatory was operational from
1543, and by the early seventeenth century could house about 160 girls — though some
were fee-paying by then. It was for this institution that G. Folco wrote his previously
cited book on alms-giving. The girls left to become domestic servants, to marry or to
enter a nunnery. Up until 1610 there was a procession of the girls on St Catherine's day;
this was resumed from 1640 onwards because not enough men were coming to ask for
the girls as brides, and publicity was deemed necessary.[126]

Naples had several major conservatories for protecting the young, male or female.
By 1608 there were 1,890 females recorded in conservatories, mainly in those of the SS.
Annunziata operated by the Compagnia dei Bianchi dello Spirito Santo (which had had
400 girls in 1587) and of the S. Spirito hospital.[127] These institutions emerged from a
broader confraternity-hospital context. But the previously mentioned Bologna hospital
of S. Maria del Baraccano for poor girls, administered by a confraternity, was a planned
result of a complex series of amalgamations and reorganisations in the hospital system
in the 1550s, involving civic and episcopal authorities. In Ferrara the confraternity of
S. Agnese operated a female orphanage from 1554; in 1574 it contained forty-seven
girls, of whom seventeen were of communion age. Here three older women, *professe*,
who were attached to the Somaschi Congregation, assisted the confraternity members
in educating the girls.[128] Poorer parts of Italy had few resources to support organised
institutions for vulnerable girls. For the dioceses in the regions of the Abruzzi, Molise
and Basilicata the assiduous researchers could find two conservatories — in Lanciano
and Barisciano, in the diocese of L'Aquila.[129]

In Perugia there were two confraternity institutions helping vulnerable females for
which I have found some more revealing information. In 1539 the confraternity of S.
Tommaso d'Aquino, inspired by the preaching of the Capuchin Bernardino Ochino,
just before he was publicly denounced as a heretic and fled from Italy, inaugurated the
Pia Casa delle Derelitte. By 1544 it had forty girls in care. The 1577 visitation found
it satisfactory and rich in Christian fervour, but by 1622 Bishop Comitoli had completed

---

[126] Monachino, pp. 240–2; Trevor, p. 95 notes that a woman penitent in about 1559 went to visit a Roman
orphanage, in the Piazza Capranica, and found the conditions grim, and lice-ridden; Simoncelli, 'Note',
pp. 154–5; Blunt, *Guide*, p. 26. On Folco see above section 2.

[127] See above n. 118; AA.VV. *Storia di Napoli*, vol. 3 (1976), p. 227 n. 7. In 1606 two separate sources record
1,680 and 2,390 girls in Neapolitan conservatories, and the first source recorded 528 older women, Beloch,
vol. 1, p. 176.

[128] *Statuti ed Ordini sopra il governo della Compagnia, o dell'Opera, chiamata gia lo Spedale di S.M. Del Baracano.
E delle Povere Donzelle di detto luogo, e di S. Gregorio in esso raccolte* (Bologna, 1740). It included the first
statutes printed in 1554 and revised in 1647. The hospital is normally called Baraccano not Baracano;
Peverada, p. 335.

[129] Donvito and Pellegrino, *L'Organizzazione Ecclesiastica*, Tables.

the transference of the Derelitte to the Barnabites, whom he considered would be better educationalists than the confraternity brethren.[130] In the early years five members of the confraternity were responsible for the conservatory; they collected alms, sought out benefactors, kept the accounts and administrative documents. The company provided the necessary food for the girls and the officials of the home, provided dowries annually, and took the girls on an annual pilgrimage to S. Maria degli Angeli (near Assisi). In 1544 the prior of S. Tommaso organised the move to a new site near S. Stefano, also buying a house with a garden and well there for the institution. The wider confraternity contributed towards dowries, and secured further funding from benefactors. It superintended the collection of alms, particularly through a special box (marked 'Elemosina per le Derelitte') installed in the Cathedral of S. Lorenzo; also there were special collections on major feast-days, as in the churches of S. Domenico and S. Maria della Misericordia (the hospital church). Benefactions in the period came from members of the leading patrician families, like the Della Corgna, Baglioni, Oddi and Montemelini, from the silk merchant Pietro di Lattanzio, the eminent librarian and bibliophile G.B. Pontani, and also from lesser artisans.[131]

By 1620 the confraternity had enrolled at least 278 girls in the Casa delle Derelitte, from Perugia and its *contado*. The confraternity members usually voted on who should be admitted, though in 1582 on the orders of the bishop they had to admit Maddalena, found in the city and of unknown background.[132] For the others the surviving contemporary record book does not always indicate the background or reasons for entry, and an early nineteenth-century summary of lost documentation is not always helpful. Most girls had probably lost both parents, but some were admitted when the mother was still alive, and when she or the daughter was considered vulnerable. Most of the *derelitte* were considered poor, but they were not necessarily without money and property, or they might come into it when they came of age or married. These resources were taken into account when later making awards of dowries to the girls.[133] The impression is that the numbers having possessions, and their value, increased over the period. This factor could

[130] Marinelli, *La Compagnia*, p. 38 n. 66; Crispolti, *Perugia Augusta*, p. 174; ASP Compagnia delle Derelitte, Miscellanea vols. 16 'Movimento delle Zitelle Derelitte 1579–1625' (original documents), 21 (E. Agostini's digest in 1805 of old records), and 20 (random collection of orginal documents and copies from 1539 to 1796, compiled by Agostini). Misc. 20 pp. 145, 149–64 deal with the transfer of the Derelitte to Barnabite control, and the new rules.

[131] *Ibid.*, Misc. 21 esp. fols. 24r–26v, 28r on key administrative points; fols. 47r–51r list some benefactors, but Misc. 20 contains original documents indicating additional donations.

[132] Based on Agostini's figures in Misc. 21, which clearly used Misc. 16, but not fully, and at times misleadingly. But he also used documents that have since been lost. Misc. 16, p. 30: 'Maddalena di —— la quale trovata per la cita e non sapendo che se fusse'.

[133] *Ibid.*, Misc. 16 p. 31: daughter (Ginsionna?) of Sepio, proposed to the company in May 1582 'per essere pupilla di padre e madre ne nessuno per essa, di eta di anni 5 in circa', and was accepted in June. They found she had 90 florins above a house in the district of Porta S. Pietro, which was later sold for 100 florins. She died in July 1591 and was buried in S. Domenico (where most were buried if they died in the Casa); p. 33: Agostina di Masso was accepted in September 1585 'per essere pupilla di padre e madre e povera', but was found to have fifty florins which was handed over to the depositor. In October 1587 she was elected to a dowry of sixty florins, but when she married Costantino di Francesco of Santo Marco in 1598 or 1599, the dowry was 100 florins, including her own original fifty; from this she bought some land; she was not to sell it again without permission from confraternity officials. In 1602 eight ducats of her dowry was taken to assist her when very ill in bed. This implied that dowries might be awarded, but all or part be held in trust rather than given in total control to the couple on marriage.

readily have affected the confraternity decisions on whom to admit. The socio-economic quality of the orphans rose; the lower-order destitute were less likely to be granted a place, especially in the 1590s. It is significant that when the Barnabites took over the bishop ruled that to be considered for admission the child should have lost both parents, and that they should have been respectable — onorati. In the competition for assistance, the respectable disadvantaged were preferred over the most miserable needy.[134]

The initial intake of 1539, and those girls admitted soon after in the 1540s, included a number of troublesome cases. Some were clearly incorrigible, and dismissed or returned to their mothers. Others left without permission. Equivalent examples of delinquency were not found in the later period. During the period of confraternity control twenty derelitte became nuns, though one left the nunnery again after fourteen years, with the permission of the superiors.[135] Dowries were provided for a fair number of other girls; but they were not necessarily taken up. Clemenza, who entered in 1580, was awarded a dowry in 1587, but was still in the Casa in 1626. In other cases it was years before they married. Susanna arrived in 1584, was allocated a dowry of 60 florins in 1587, but did not marry until 1607, when the dowry was 100 florins.[136] Some girls were requested by outsiders or relatives to be servants or companions; as such they were released on condition that eventually they should be provided with a suitable dowry. In a few cases marriage and dowry were more closely timed. Artimitia was admitted to the Casa in 1590, in 1609 she was allocated a dowry of 100 florins from the bishop, and in 1611, on marrying, this money was used by the couple for buying a house in the city. A worthwhile sum was put to good use.[137]

Two other cases might be cited for significant indications of attitudes. In 1606 two sisters Camilla and Scolastica di Constantino of Passignano were admitted; they had houses to their name in both Passignano and Perugia. Scolastica died in the Casa in 1607, but in 1622 Camilla was allowed by the superiors to leave, without marrying or entering a nunnery. The transference of control to the Barnabites may have affected the situation on either side; but presumably she was now considered to have the resources of the houses to support herself, without becoming morally vulnerable. On 24 May 1587 the confraternity accepted Eufrosina di Tomasso 'il lainola' of Monte del Lago, on condition that her brother Marco paid 85 florins as her share of the inherited land and house. Eufrosina died unmarried in 1622, but on that same May day in 1587 it had been agreed that Marco should marry another girl already in the Casa, Aura of Cibbotola, who had arrived in 1579 and been promised a dowry in 1583 worth 100 florins. Marco gained a wife, and netted 15 florins; and relinquished responsibility for his sister.[138]

There was another Perugian conservatory for needy and abandoned girls, the Pia

---

[134] Ibid., Misc. 20, p. 147. The child should be aged seven to ten, be in good health, and her status properly authenticated by testimonials (fedi).

[135] Ibid., Misc. 21, p. xxv; Misc. 16, p. 35: sister Catterina, born Chiara, entered Casa in 1583, poor and with nothing; she was vested in 1606 and left the nunnery in January 1620, (the reason not given).

[136] Ibid., Misc. 16, pp. 20, 39. Susanna died childless, and without making a will; two-thirds of the dowry returned to the Casa. Cf. the Bologna Casa del Soccorso, where similarly the award of a dowry by the institution was no guarantee of an early marriage, Ferrante, 'L'onore ritrovato', p. 525 n. 84.

[137] Ibid., Misc. 20, p. 138; Misc. 16, pp. 16, 18: in 1588 the sister of Cardinal Bishop Gallo took one girl as a camoriera, on condition she was married off within ten years; in fact she was soon married with a dowry provided from various sources, and she died in 1591 (in child-birth?); p. 46 (for Artimitia).

[138] Ibid., Misc. 16, p. 58 (Camilla and Scolastica), p. 44 (Eufrosina), p. 12 (Aura).

Casa della Carità, administered by the confraternity of S. Girolamo. The impetus for the creation of the Casa came primarily from the Capuchin friar Stefano da Ferrara, preaching in November 1562; the city council agreed to entrust it to the confraternity of S. Girolamo, and inaugurated it in 1563. Franciscan Tertiary sisters helped with the education of the girls. The confraternity brothers supervised the administration and seem to have made most of the decisions about who to admit, about the allocation of dowries, or whether a girl should enter a nunnery.[139] In September 1619 it was agreed that Flavia should be allowed to remain in the Casa as a servant, as she did not want to live in the secular world. It led to a general policy decision that girls should not be forced to marry against their will, nor be sent to a nunnery; it was better to serve God in this house. Earlier there had been a somewhat violent confrontation. In 1616 the confraternity had voted to accept Lavinia, seemingly with a vow to become a nun eventually; then two officials had seized her in the public square, because her mother had not wanted to surrender her. She was placed in a private house; the confraternity proceeded to vote to overrule the statutes and admit her into the Casa presumably to override the oppostion of a parent. It is unclear who initiated the original application for Lavinia's entry, or how the affair ended. The S. Girolamo confraternity, on the evidence of its book of religious Office, had a strong devotion to the Virgin, but the Trinity is also cited as guarding the city and company against scandal and danger. The guard lapsed sometimes. Also in 1616 the confraternity dismissed the Casa's gatekeeper, for stealing money, and frightening the girls. Perhaps the divine guard was watching again in 1617 when a confraternity meeting allowed Innocentia, daughter of a weaver, to enter aged 11, because of dangers to her from her mother, and for other unstated reasons.[140]

This institution was partly financed through renting city properties and farmland bequeathed by benefactors; as share-cropping, *mezzadria* contracts were involved, a certain amount of supervision was required by the brothers. From 1657 printed forms were used for standardising contract terms. A significant number of the city properties were rented to women. Confraternity supervision of such an institution would have been time-consuming and worrying for those who became responsible officials.[141]

A third Perugian confraternity, the Annunziata, was responsible through the period from 1558 to 1645 for succouring converted dishonest women; this philanthropic work was inspired by a Dominican preacher, and received the approval of the communual magistracy and the papal governor. Detailed documentation about its operation has not been found.[142]

---

[139] Nessi, pp. 75–115; Urbanelli, *Storia dei Cappuccini delle Marche*, vol. 2, pp. 568–9, vol. 3/I, pp. 174–5, 229–32: the Council of Priori and Camerlenghi of the guilds, in approving the statutes expressed the desire to receive good girls who had bad parents: 'Vogliamo che questa S.ta Casa sia ordinata per lo scampo e ricovero di quelle povere zitelle virgini di buona vita e fama, le quali sono nate da Padre e Madre cattivi e di mala vita, acciò esse fanciulle non seguitino il loro esempio nel mal fare'. ASP Conservatorio della Carità, 'Adunanze' vol. 1 (1615–26). Here records of meetings survive, but not an equivalent volume on the girls received. We do not know how many were admitted, or the capacity of the Casa.

[140] *Ibid.*, fols. 26r–27r (Flavia case and aftermath), 8r–9r (Lavinia), 23r–5r (Innocentia); Misc. 15/13 'Offizio della Compagnia di S. Girolamo', with Office of the Madonna and extensive prayers with Ave Marias. Four miniatures show Sts Jerome, Francis, Bernardino as well as the Virgin. Fo. 25v on the Trinity.

[141] *Ibid.*, 'Istromenti' vol. 1 (1555–1779). One of the more important legacies was from Monsignor Arciprete Alessio with land in Ripa (p. 17, 22 November 1614).

[142] Pizzoni, pp. 146–55.

Philanthropy towards former prostitutes or 'fallen women' was a major concern of Catholic reformers. Frequently the converted had to submit to very strict discipline and seclusion, in case they were tempted by the world into renewed sin. Houses for the Convertite, as they were often called, frequently became formal nunneries. Ignatius Loyola and Cardinal Rusticuccio Farnese founded the refuge of S. Marta in Rome in the 1540s, where former prostitutes (and, later, rejected wives needing refuge) took the veil, and occupied themselves in penitential prayer, sewing and weaving. It eventually became a house of Augustinian sisters. So did the house for former Roman prostitutes founded by Carlo Borromeo in 1563, eventually called the Casa Pia of S. Girolamo alla Lungara. In 1552 a layman founded a Retiro Ospizio di S. Valera for the protection of Milan's syphilitic prostitutes seeking to reform or retire. It was called a convent, and its inhabitants, wearing black habits, were under strict confinement. The Senate in 1561 threatened that those who broke this confinement would be branded. In this institution there lived for thirteen years, in a cell 1.80 × 3 metres a Sister Virginia Maria (née Mariana) de Leyva, daughter of the Count of Monza, otherwise known as the nun of Monza, or Gertrude in Manzoni's *I Promessi Sposi (The Betrothed)*. The degree of strictness, however unphilanthropic it might seem to modern readers, derived from the view that the salvation of the soul had preeminence over physical well-being.[143]

The above institutions in Milan and Rome were not the concern of confraternities, but a few others were, in Rome as in Perugia. In 1520 Leo X had founded a pioneer institution Delle Convertite, to be administered by the confraternity Della Carità. Within the house the women were subject to the Augustinian Rule. Filippo Neri was at one stage concerned with their spiritual welfare. The 1536 statutes made it clear that the confraternity should accept only genuine converts, not the sick, the brutish, or those entering old age who could no longer exercise the art of sinning. The refuge was for converts, not retired professionals. Other recovered girls or women were looked after in the confraternity hospital of S. Spirito in Sassia. Its officials expressed doubts about the harsh discipline of enclosure imposed on such women. In this they were at one with Veronica Franco in Venice, a reformed courtesan who had moved in high literary circles, and who sought to rescue prostitutes. She argued that it was too difficult for many women to move from such a life to strict enclosure, and a more liberal institution, where they could also keep their children, was preferable. The Venetian Casa del Soccorso, founded in 1577 — whether or not with her assistance — was more in tune with her attitude.[144]

An immoral past did not necessarily lead to perpetual confinement and dishonour. A recent study of the Casa del Soccorso in Bologna shows that girls of marriageable age or married women coming from a dishonourable background could be redeemed

---

[143]   Monachino, p. 257; Blunt, *Guide*, p. 49. The Casa Pia was rebuilt in the early seventeenth century and became the largest Roman refuge for reformed prostitutes. Urban VIII, Cardinal Francesco Barberini, and Ippolito Merenda (who was rewarded with a tomb by G.L. Bernini), were leading patrons of the institution; G. Crispolti, 'Il Ritiro Ospizio di Santa Valeria a Milano Ospedale d'Isolamento per meretrici sifilitiche', *Studi di Storia Ospitaliera*, 2 (1964), 77–82. Olivieri Baldissarri, *I 'poveri prigioni'*, pp. 80, 93 n. 46, where it is noted that the nun of Monza had been tortured when under investigation. On Convertite and social control generally, Lombardi, 'Poveri', p. 168.

[144]   Barletta, *Aspetti della Riforma*, p. 56; Pullan, *Rich and Poor*, pp. 378, 391–3; cf. for similar more liberal attitudes in Vicenza, Mantese, *Memorie*, vol. 4, pp. 526–31, 552–6, 761–4; A. Canezza, *Gli arcispedali di Roma nella vita cittadina, nella storia e nell'arte. I: Santo Spirito in Sassia* (Rome, 1933), p. 54.

by a stay in the Casa, and be 'honourably' reintroduced into society, marital or conventual, under the patronage of the honourable, or the forgiveness of a husband. The chief function of the members of the congregation was to find suitable husbands for the unmarried, and secure adequate dowries. Here is evidence of a paternal philanthropy that was far from being punitive.[145]

Finally it is worth turning away from institutions to the philanthropic assistance on offer to individual women within their own environment. The noble Neapolitan confraternity of Pio Monte della Misericordia has recently been shown as not only assisting with dowry funds, but as secretly as possible offering help to vulnerable single women. Despite the secrecy some documentation on whom they helped has survived. Some were poor nobles, others were well down the social scale. Single women, often widows abandoned by other male relatives, were given money for lodging, clothing or food. Many had dependent children or other helpless relatives, such as Giuseppa Guttierez, a widow, disabled or demoralised (cionca), who lived with two daughters, one blind, the other herself a widow, with a grand-daughter (or niece) of marriageable age.[146] Such a study gives a too rare glimpse of how individuals in serious need were helped.

This long chapter has demonstrated confraternity involvement in the wider world of philanthropy, when seeking primarily to satisfy physical needs. This work could be time-consuming for the officials involved. Discrimination, scrutiny and debate took place, as internal records make clear. Preference was given to close neighbours, likely to be known: members of the fraternity and their relatives. Given the limited resources available in most confraternities, these recipients were genuinely in need, and deserving by both contemporary and modern standards. However, there was a willingness to look outside, especially in crisis situations, to cooperate with parish and government organisations in providing dowries, food or hospital services to a wider range of needy — even the undeserving. There was also prejudice, fraud and meanness and, by many modern standards, repressive social control, as when dealing with 'fallen women'. But always we need to remember the priority given to salvation of the soul rather than the body.

[145] Ferrante, 'L'onore ritrovato', esp. pp. 510–11.
[146] Musella, 'Il Pio Monte', esp. pp. 303–5, 314–16.

10

CONFRATERNITY PHILANTHROPY. 2: THE IMPRISONED, IGNORANT AND DEAD

The main elements in this chapter as suggested by the subtitle are not as disconnected or perversely associated as they might seem. Two are traditional corporate acts of mercy: helping the imprisoned and burying the dead. A third is one of the seven spiritual acts: teaching the ignorant. While discussion of 'the confined poor' may seem to present an uncharitable antithesis to helping the imprisoned, it has its place on the philanthropic stage. Granted the mentalities of the age, social control and 'liberation' could be involved in the same action. Loving one's neighbour meant liberating him from ignorance and from the many temptations of the world where his soul might be in dire jeopardy. People might be liberated from prison and debt to live honestly again. The undeserving might be confined to liberate them from the temptations of serious crime, and thereby to free the deserving from competition from the undeserving in the pursuit of charity. Ultimately the priority was to liberate the soul from Purgatory, having already tried to ensure a minimal period there through beneficial activities and attitudes in this world. Confinement of the poor provides a link between one form of philanthropy towards women, which was discussed in the last chapter, and charity for the traditional prisoner in need of assistance.

I THE CONFINED POOR

Hostility towards some of the poor and the fear of vagabonds led to the institutionalisation of beggars and the dangerous poor in 'hospitals', especially during periods of dearth and high unemployment. Enforced confinement in a kind of penal monastery does not sound philanthropic now, but at the time it was defended by some as beneficial for the soul of those confined, especially if it led to moral rehabilitation. At the very least it was defended as protective custody to avoid further sinning. For some the physical conditions were also an improvement on conditions outside, except possibly for the skilled beggars and con-men. The policy of confinement was very largely a matter of state, but there is a marginal relevance to the history of confraternities, since occasionally such companies were involved within the institutions or as money-raisers, and the confinement of some poor was deemed to help the other poor who were the preferred targets of fraternal philanthropy.

When in 1594 the officials of the Sanità office in Venice finally adopted a policy of confining the mendicants in hospitals, it was argued that unless this was done hospitals which relied on legacies to help the poor would suffer; paying for mendicants they would not be able to assist other (more deserving) poor. These officials were impressed by what had happened in Bologna. In this papal city once the confinement policy had been established it was claimed that the true poor were no longer deprived of alms.[1]

Bologna's Opera dei Mendicanti was a prime example of a hospital for confining the poor, and it involved confraternity assistance. Civic and social protectionism combined with philanthropic zeal to launch this enterprise. The idea arose about 1548 when papal and civic authorities attempted an accurate assessment of the many poor in Bologna, but the institution was only formally launched by papal brief in 1560, and not till 1563 was enough money raised to allow the beggars to be rounded up and enclosed in the ex-convent of S. Gregorio (which had already served as a leper hospital, and later as a refuge for orphan girls). The project was supported by the municipal authorities, and by Legate Carlo Borromeo. Though the financial situation was made more difficult by the starvation conditions of 1558–61 (which a chronicler claimed took 10,000 lives out of a population of over 60,000), they may have stimulated official help for the surviving beggars — assisted by the Lenten preaching of Father Teofilo of Treviso. Initially about 800 persons, two-thirds female, were escorted to the Opera dei Mendicanti hospital. It only catered for citizens of Bologna; the foreign beggars were expelled from the city, after brief periods of imprisonment and floggings. Begging was then banned in the city, with citizens facing imprisonment for contraventions.[2]

The Opera was governed by elected civic officials, and there were a few paid full-time workers in the complex, but the major activity came from unpaid members of a congregation which was created, with Borromeo's support, to replace the old Compagnia dei Poveri Mendicanti that had hitherto more informally assisted the poor. The alms-collectors and benefactors of the Opera joined this Congregation, and received the benefits of indulgences. There was also a Congregation delle Gentildonne to assist the mendicants. By 1574 doctors were formally attached to the Opera. Somaschi fathers acted as spiritual advisers, at least in the early years.[3] Bishop G. Paleotti used his own money to institute a *bottega di agocchiera*, where a hundred inmates could be employed in needle-work. The Opera expanded its buildings and scope; the S. Gregorio site became a female section, and a new site was developed with the church of the Pietà for males. In 1592 the old hospital of S. Orsola was added to the complex, and became the medical centre. By the turn of the century the Opera was a hospital that took the begging poor, the indigent, off the streets for shelter, food and clothing. It provided some work for a portion of the able-bodied, medical assistance for the sick, with facilities for the incurables, protection for girls whose 'honour' was in danger, and a prison for the troublesome. Entry was regulated by vetting and passes — mostly to ensure that citizens, and not outsiders, were being helped. Procedures for release other than by death are unclear, presumably an indication of job prospects or family support was needed, since inmates were not to return to begging.

[1] Ellero, 'Un ospedale', p. 58; *Statuti dell'Opera de Poveri Mendicanti della Citta di Bologna. Nuovamente riformati et ampliati* (Bologna, 1574; reprinted 1603), esp. [p. 6]: 'non piu restano spogliati di elemosina i veri poveri'.
[2] G. Calori, *Una iniziativa sociale nella Bologna del '500. L'Opera Mendicanti* (Bologna, 1972), on which the following paragraphs are based unless otherwise stated; A. Bellettini, *La popolazione di Bologna dal secolo xv all'unificazione italiana* (Bologna, 1961), p. 9 n. 9: in 1570 the population was estimated at 61,742 persons with about 990 in hospitals, and 133 housed elsewhere as orphans.
[3] *Statuti dell'Opera*.

The numbers in the Opera fluctuated considerably, according to rough estimates: 500 in 1567, 600 in 1589, 1,400 in 1590, 900 in 1591, 1,000 in 1596, 800 in 1610. By the early nineteenth century the members were down to about 300, nearly half of them in the medical section. The financial position was always unstable; monasteries had levies imposed upon them; there were some legacies and donated funds, but the main providers were seemingly the official alms-seekers from the fraternal congregation.[4]

Other cities had civic projects for the forcible enclosure of indigent beggars — Turin in 1583, Modena 1592, Venice 1594, Florence 1621, Naples 1667. But it is Rome's experiment under Sixtus V that is best known — for its failure. In part it was attempted because of deficiencies in the provision by confraternities. During the sixteenth century there had been muddled policies for handling the beggars and poor; periodic expulsions of the least desirable, and encouragement of confraternities to help the deserving. In 1581 Gregory XIII called on the SS. Trinità archconfraternity to assemble the Roman beggars at S. Sisto, and care for them in an abandoned nunnery there. The site was unhealthy, and remote from potential philanthropists. The SS. Trinità developed financial problems. Faced with this failure, and the food shortages of 1585–6, Sixtus V undertook to create a new S. Sisto hospital (designed by Domenico Fontana, for about 400 inmates) on the banks of the Tiber, where the beggars would be forcibly enclosed. When it opened in 1587 some poor were reluctant to accept enforced shelter, and ignored the harsh edicts. Though Sixtus provided much money, the institution encountered financial difficulties soon after his death. In the worsening economic climate of the 1590s the hospital faced the problem of keeping the poor out of an asylum, and applicants were carefully vetted. Begging on the streets had to be permitted, under licence. According to C. Fanucci in 1601 there were only 150 inmates, including the staff. By then Clement VIII had redirected funds away from this hospital to the SS. Trinità archconfraternity. S. Sisto was left to house the blind, maimed widows, and poor girls. It had some medical facilities. Rome returned to a mixed, decentralised philanthropic world, where the confraternities predominated, and beggars had their freedom.[5]

The policy of confining the dangerous or idle poor became more prevalent in Europe through the seventeenth century, and was given a major impetus with the *hôpitaux généraux* of Paris, Lyons and other French cities. Influenced by this the papacy under Innocent XII in 1692 again attempted the enforced seclusion of the beggars; it was resisted by some philanthropists as well as beggars, and again failed. The old piecemeal solutions persisted. Similarly in Genoa and Turin policies of confinement and social control were undermined or modified by the activity and attitudes of powerful confraternities and their independent approach to philanthropy.[6]

---

[4] Pastore, 'Testamenti', esp. p. 283. Donations to the Opera seem to have come from donors of higher social status in the group studied; Vizani, *Historie*, pp. 63–4 eulogising the enterprise, and the charitable donations.
[5] Pullan, 'Poveri, mendicanti', p. 1018; Fanucci, *Trattato*, pp. 54–6. 58–67; P. Simoncelli, 'Origini e primi anni di vita dell'Ospedale romano dei poveri mendicanti', *Annuario dell'istituto storico italiano per l'età moderna e contemporanea*, 25–26 (1976), 121–72; Monachino, pp. 218–20. By 1596 it had been ruled that: 'In the Hospital of Ponte Sisto there should be retained only those miserable poor who are deprived of all help and who, either through age, blindness, or severe crippling of limbs cannot obtain food for themselves by begging or in any other way', (Simoncelli, p. 147). Cf. similar problems for a hospital for the confined poor in Toledo in the 1580s and 1590s, and the unsatisfactory role of confraternities: Martz, pp. 141–50.
[6] Lis and Soly, pp. 116–29 on 'the great confinement'; Fairchilds, pp. 29–37; Gutton, *La Société et les pauvres*, 122–57; Geremek, 'Renfermement des pauvres', pp. 205–17; M. Fatica, 'La reclusione dei poveri a Roma

2 THE IMPRISONED AND CONDEMNED

Several confraternities specialised in helping prisoners, sometimes with more fellow-feeling and liberality than was offered to the begging poor. The paradox is explained by the prevalence of debtors among the imprisoned, many of whom might be deemed worthy of assistance and liberation. There were two main dimensions to prisoner relief: those condemned to death should be assisted in passing from this life with compassion, and prepared for eternal judgement; other prisoners should receive compassionate treatment, and be released if in some way deserving.

Historians have recently shown an increasing interest in confraternities that special-ised in assisting those condemned to death, in their motives and procedures, and how they reflect changing attitudes to death. Specialist confraternities emerge from the fourteenth century, with the S. Maria della Morte in Bologna (1336), and the Florentine Compagnia di Santa Maria della Croce al Tempio (1343) being probably the earliest and most influential. They were followed over the next century by similar fraternities in cities like Padua, Verona, Vicenza, Siena and Perugia. In Rome (in 1488) the fraternity of S. Giovanni Decollato, also called Della Misericordia, was founded by some Floren-tines, and this became a model society.[7] These early confraternities are seen as products of the discipline confraternity movement. Their roles in escorting the condemned to execution had as much to do with the living as with comforting the victim. A processional involvement, with the blessings of priests, has been interpreted as a ritual through which the living, seeing justice done, were protected against the revenge of the condemned from the next world. The spilling of blood through violence, the shaming of the body, would be seen to be controllable, and lead to reconciliation. The contrition of the condemned, and his chance of salvation, would be an inspiration to the observers. In this spirit S. Bernardino da Siena encouraged his fellow citizens to support the comforting, escorting roles of the company of S. Giovanni Decollato, or Della Morte.[8]

Throughout the sixteenth century, and especially in the seventeenth, increasing emphasis was placed on the tasks of comforting the condemned, and seeking his soul's salvation. The role of comforter became an honourable, but intense, philanthropic one. Manuals were produced to ensure that those brethren undertaking this work secured the

durante il Pontificato di Innocenzo XII (1692–1700)', *RSRR*, 3 (1979), 133–79; M.T. Bonadonna Russo, 'I problemi dell'assistenza pubblica nel Seicento e il tentativo di Mariano Sozzini', *Ibid.*, pp. 255–80; A. Erba, 'Pauperismo e assistenza in Piemonte nel secolo xvii', *Timore e Carità*, p. 224: in Turin the *confratelli* of S. Paolo administered a whole range of institutions: a Monte di Pietà, Albergo di virtù (essentially a school for boys), Opera del soccorso delle vergine, Opera del deposito delle convertite, Opera del retiro delle forzate, Ufficio pio or Ufficio generale di assistenza. From 1628 it shared in the policy of confinement of certain poor with its Ospedale della Carità. Unfortunately little seems to be known of these institutions at present; but Erba cites M. Abrate, *L'Istituto bancario San Paolo di Torino* (Turin, 1963), which I have not yet seen. Grendi, 'Ideologia', and 'Pauperismo' on such institutions generally and the Genoese Albergo dei Poveri in particular, with reaction to its unphilanthropic rigidity.

[7] On early societies: A. Prosperi, 'Il sangue e l'anima. Ricerche sulle Compagnie di Giustizia in Italia', *Quaderni Storici*, 51 (1982), 964–6; M. Fanti, 'La confraternita di S. Maria della Morte e la conforteria dei condannati in Bologna nei secoli XIV e XV', *Quaderni di Centro di Ricerca e di Studio sul Movimento dei Disciplinati (Perugia)*, 20 (1978), 3–101; Edgerton, 'A little-known "Purpose of Art"', pp. 46–7 foundations, pp. 57–8 nn. 9 and 12 on links with other fraternities; an expanded version of his article, with better illustrations, is now chapter 5, 'Pictures of Redemption' in his *Pictures and Punishment. Art and Criminal Prosecution during the Florentine Renaissance* (Ithaca and London, 1985); V. Paglia, *La morte confortata. Riti della paura e mentalità religiosa a Roma nell'età moderna* (Rome, 1982), pp. 31–6; cf. a valuable review of Paglia's book by D. Zardin, *RSCI*, 39 (1985), 209–12.

[8] Prosperi, 'Il sangue e l'anima', pp. 960–4.

most efficacious confession, and deepest contrition. The condemned was helped to face his ordeal resolutely, even happily, as a good Christian — with the thought that his genuine contrition might lead his soul immediately to heaven. A Jew sentenced to death in Bologna in 1593, having accepted baptism, allegedly showed great happiness that he would soon be in Paradise.[9] This confidence that a grim execution for a fully contrite criminal could mean the avoidance of Purgatory was based on the treatment of the repentant thief executed with Christ. The message is suggested in Jacopino del Conte's altarpiece in the oratory of the main Roman comforting confraternity of S. Giovanni Decollato: *The Descent from the Cross*, where the repentant thief looks yearningly towards Christ.[10] The art of securing contrition from the condemned was also connected with the wider concern with the art of dying well on the part of those who might die less violently. By the seventeenth century these confraternities were also concerned in society at large with preparing for death, and burying the dead.[11]

The confraternity brethren visited the condemned person in prison as soon as they learned of his sentence. In Bologna by the mid-seventeenth century there was a very specialised confraternity of comforters, who arranged for members to be on stand-by duty week by week in case there was a capital sentence and they were needed for the execution. In prison the comforters, possibly alongside a priest, encouraged confession and repentance; they offered spiritual consolation to the contrite, and exerted great pressure on recalcitrant prisoners to confess — alternately persuading and threatening. If the condemned was cooperative the brethren would keep a vigil and pray through the last night. The Perugian brothers from the confraternity Della Giustizia were obliged to provide good wine and sweetmeats for a last meal.[12] The prisoner was escorted to his place of execution by the brothers and a priest; other members of the confraternity might join in to make a fuller procession, and protect the prisoner from the crowd. According to the statutes of the Naples confraternity Dei Bianchi della Giustizia (or S. Maria Succurre Miseris), the brethren were to recite the seven penitential psalms, litanies, orations and prayers as they progressed to the scaffold. On returning

---

[9] BCB F.O.43 fol. 33r: 'fu fatto morire Alegro Ebreo qual essendo in conforteria domando con gran dolore di venire alla Acqua del S. to Batesimo la qual contanta alegrezza accetò che dopo la morte sua fu iudicato andar in paradisso che cosi dio nostro Signore lo voglia'. On comforters and manuals see Paglia, *La morte confortata*, pp. 12–17. The expanded nature of this comforting task by the eighteenth century can be judged by the 200-page *Direttorio de' Confortatori nel quale si insegna la pratica di confortare i Condannati alla Morte . . . compilato per uso . . . della Scuola di Conforteria della Ven. Arciconfraternita della Morte di Ferrara* (Bologna, 1729); a simpler, shorter manual by the Capuchin Mattia Bellintani, *Utili ricordi e remedj per quelle che dalla Giustizia sono condannati alla Morte* ([Salò, 1614?]) did not indicate precisely that there was a direct path to Paradise, but he stressed (p. 53) that the comforter should very strongly emphasise the delights of Paradise when seeking confession and contrition. The condemned man had the great advantage over those who died suddenly in that he had time to repent and die fully cleansed (p. 12), and he was like the repentant thief with Christ in having an honoured death (pp. 23, 26).

[10] J. von Henneberg, *L'oratorio*, pp. 4–5, citing the tract for comforters by Zanobi de Medici; Luke 24: 43: 'And Jesus said unto him, Verily I say unto thee, Today shalt thou be with me in paradise'; J.S. Weisz, *Pittura e Misericordia; the Oratory of S. Giovanni Decollato in Rome* (Harvard PhD thesis, 1982; University Microfilms International, Ann Arbor, 1983), pp. 119–35, esp. 131–2 and Fig. 32.

[11] On connections with the art of dying: Paglia, *La morte confortata*, pp. 37–41; Edgerton, *Pictures and Punishment*, p. 176.

[12] *Constitutioni della Congregatione, o Scuola de' Confortatori della Città di Bologna* (Bologna, 1640). It is not clear when this society took over from the Morte fraternity in this role. C. Cutini, 'I condannati a morte e l'attività assistenziale della Confraternita della Giustizia di Perugia', *BSPU*, 82 (1985) [1987], pp. 175 (the meal, and spiritual help), 183–4 (persuasion).

with the body, or its pieces, they were to sing or recite more psalms, and end with the *Requiem aeternam.*[13]

Some confraternities like Florence's Tempio, Rome's S. Giovanni Decollato, Ferrara's Buona Morte, Perugia's Della Giustizia, and Bologna's S. Maria della Morte had painted pictures, *tavolette*, to hold before the prisoner as they processed and until the moment of execution. The frontispiece of the 1562 revised statutes of the Bologna fraternity shows two white-hooded brethren holding such *tavolette* (see Frontispiece).[14] These pictures would remind the condemned of crimes committed, encourage penance and remorse, hold out the hope of salvation for the repentant, and possibly shield him from seeing the crowd or the scaffold and instruments of execution. The confraternities were often then responsible for the burial of the body, and with fulfilling his last wishes with reference to his family.

In Bologna the S. Maria della Morte was mainly responsible for assisting the condemned. It also arranged sumptuous funerals for the more respectable, as well as administering a medically equipped hospital. Sampling one of its burial books, we find that in 1540 the Morte officials were involved in 135 burials, 34 of them after executions. In two cases they could not comfort the man; one was hanged in the middle of the night before they could confess or comfort him; the other died of his wounds too soon — and was hanged dead.[15]

Capuchins and Jesuits were the priests most involved in comforting work. They were considered specialists, and confraternal intervention was not always welcome. When in 1586 a Ferrarese doctor was due to be hanged in Bologna, Cardinal Salviati tried to ban the brothers of the Morte company, and only have the Capuchins present. The archconfraternity protested and was eventually allowed to come in the morning and be at the execution place.[16]

Some prisoners were saved from execution by 'privileges' periodically granted to confraternities, with the right to release somebody condemned to death or to a major penalty such as the galleys for life. For some fraternities this was a regular element in Easter or Christmas celebrations, for others a more occasional privilege. Confraternities especially connected with prison work, like Rome's S. Giovanni Decollato, the Gonfalone or the Pietà dei Carcerati were most likely to have such privileges, but others could be similarly rewarded, as when in 1635 the Compagnia della Concezione della Madonna was able to include a liberated prisoner in its procession (along with forty-

[13] Mascia, *La Confraternita dei Bianchi della Giustizia*, pp. 24, 105–6, 109 — the 1525 statutes are printed, pp. 77–115; the psalms were: *Miserere (50)*, *De Profundis (129)*, *Ad Dominum cum tribuales (119)*, *In Convertendo (125)*, *Laetatus sum (121)*, *Ad te levavi oculos meos (122)*.

[14] BCB F.O.42, frontispiece; on the *tavolette* see article and book by Edgerton cited in note 7 above. The two most accessible examples are from the Buona Morte, Ferrara now in the Pinacoteca Comunale, Ravenna, which show 'Torture of St Euphemia' and 'Torture of [?] St Hadrian', (Edgerton, *Pictures and Punishment*, Figs. 50, 51, and see p. 173 n. 6); Cutini, p. 176.

[15] BCB F.O.53 fols. 1v–6r: of the executions 21 were hangings, 5 decapitations, 5 quarterings, 2 strangulations and one burning. One was a woman — decapitated for killing her husband. Cf. Edgerton, *Pictures and Punishment*, pp. 234–8 for Florentine executions from 1420 to 1574 as recorded by the Tempio confraternity.

[16] BCB F.O.43 fol. 27v. But cf. the Capuchin encouragement, under Bonaventura da Reggio, of a confraternity to help the condemned at Fermo in 1564; this became aggregated to S. Giovanni Decollato, Rome; Capuchins remained involved as well: Urbanelli, *Storia dei Cappuccini della Marche*, vol. 2, pp. 564–7, vol. 3/I, pp. 216–17.

three dowered poor girls) to celebrate the decoration of its chapel in S. Lorenzo in Damaso.[17] In the Pietà the confraternity congregation discussed the prisoners who might be saved, selected one and petitioned the pope for his release; if accepted, the nominee was induced to seek salvation. On the first Monday in Lent he would be escorted to the confraternity church, join in confession and communion, and be freed.

In Perugia the confraternity of S. Bernardino della Giustizia (or SS. Andrea e Bernardino) — whose membership was officially limited to seventy brothers over 25 years old — looked after prisoners, escorted the condemned and, after 1592, administered the city's prison. Surviving records indicate those the fraternity escorted to execution (from 1525), and those they had the privilege of saving (from 1548). The reprieves were exercised at Easter, and sometimes at Christmas; there was not in practice a uniform rate of one per occasion, though this seems to have been the terms of the privilege. Between 1561 and 1580 there were 88 executions, and 46 were saved from execution or the galleys; from 1581 to 1600, 250 were executed and 54 saved. The rise in the number of capital sentences, peaking in the 1590s, seems partly connected with rising banditry in a period of dearth. Most cited offenders were homicides, and most of those saved were so categorised, though Pius V in 1568 had ruled that homicides should not be included in the reprieve system. Sodomites and those assisting bandits were also among the saved. Infanticides were common. There was one witchcraft case, and she was not reprieved. All social classes, male and female, from city and *contado*, were involved. The record sometimes notes that people died with contrition, and occasionally that they refused to confess, which was clearly seen as a failure by the brothers. For those reprieved there was often, but not invariably, a public ceremony of thanks in the Cathedral or in the Benedictine church of S. Pietro. Books of prayers and Offices suggest that the brethren had an active religious life. They took part in other public processions and celebrations.[18]

The choice of prisoners to be saved by a Milanese confraternity was subject to financial considerations. The confraternity of S. Croce e della Pietà received from the city Governor the privilege of releasing one condemned man a year, and in 1605 Philip III of Spain granted an extra privilege of releasing a person condemned to the galleys. The policy was adopted of selecting prisoners who could pay compensation in exchange for life and liberty, though the confraternity officials were also wary of the possible adverse reaction of public opinion if this meant releasing a notorious criminal. The mercenary attitude to this selection was justified on the grounds that, being a relatively ill-endowed brotherhood, money so gained could be used to assist indebted prisoners

[17] G. Gigli, *Diario Romano (1608–1670)* ed. G. Ricciotti (Rome, 1958), pp. 157–60; on releasing prisoners, *Statuti . . . S. Crocefisso*, chapter 43; Maroni Lumbroso and Martini, pp. 407–14, 421–4; Paglia, 'La Pietà dei Carcerati', pp. 201–3, 297–300.
[18] ASP Confraternita SS. Andrea Bernardino Della Giustizia, Miscellanea 3 'Libro delli Giustitiali'; Marinelli, *Le Confraternite*, pp. 86–131; Meloni, 'Topografia', pp. 47–8; Cutini, pp. 173–86, esp. pp. 183–4, where she quotes at length the account of a long struggle by confraternity members, Capuchins and a Jesuit to secure the confessions and conversion to God of a couple in 1597; and of the failure to break a prisoner's silence in 1642; U. Ranieri, *La Bella in mano al boia. Una storia inedita di Perugia nel seicento* (Milan, 1965), pp. 112–29 discusses a case where somebody refused to confess to infanticide, though this is not Ranieri's main story. Cf. on Roman executions and the work of S. Giovanni Decollato: L. Firpo, 'Esecuzioni capitali in Roma (1567–1671)', AA.VV. *Eresia e Riforma nell'Italia del Cinquecento. Miscellanea*, 1 (Florence and Chicago, 1974), pp. 307–42.

The choice of prisoner was not always acceptable to the punishing authority, and the Milan company had to accept a veto from the Governor or Senate. Elsewhere a similar confraternity might win the day. In 1596 the Auditors of Bologna did not want the confraternity of S. Maria della Morte to release Giulio Guidetti and his son. In the event Cardinal Legate Montalto sanctioned the choice and, because the company had not exercised the privilege for two years, the father and two sons were pardoned.[19]

More confraternities were concerned with assisting prisoners not facing a capital charge, often alongside other philanthropic work. Lecce's S. Annunciazione required some brothers to visit the prisons once a week, to bring spiritual comfort, to distribute a booklet on Christian Doctrine, to reconcile disputes, settle matters between debtors and creditors, having sought alms to enable poor debtors to be released, and to encourage officials to expedite processes. This society was not, however, to interfere with the work of the Gonfalone fraternity which, like many homonymous societies in other cities linked to the Roman archconfraternity, served the condemned. The Neapolitan Confraternita Della Croce after 1600 had a fund to assist the release of debtors; it was already providing free burials for prisoners and other poor. Florence's S. Bonaventura congregation, founded for thirty-three gentlemen in 1582, was a prisoners' aid society similar to Lecce's, but showing a more modern concern it continued assisting prisoners after release so they could start afresh in an honest occupation.[20]

Prisons in the sixteenth century were not designed to hold people for long. People were there awaiting trial, or the fulfilment of a sentence of execution, banishment, the galleys, or the payment of fines. Many were in prison for debt, with their release soon expected. Under canon law imprisonment was custodial, not punitive, though it developed the idea of prison as a punishment for priests who could not be executed. Imprisonment was private, not an exemplary punishment for public edification. Under particular circumstances political prisoners might suffer lengthy terms of protective custody, and others might be long-term prisoners of the Inquisition. But the Inquisition's own prisons were probably more salubrious than those of other ecclesiastical or civic establishments. It should be remembered that even if a life sentence was imposed by the Inquisition most offenders would be released after about three years, if they showed contrition, or be sent into more tolerable monastic surroundings, or placed under house arrest. The idea of the prison as a set-term punishment was slowly developed in tracts of the seventeenth century.[21]

Though imprisonment was assumed to be a short-term problem, Italian philanthropists of the sixteenth century — like contemporaries in Spain and Latin America — increasingly concerned themselves with prisoner welfare and release. Given that most

[19] Olivieri Baldissarri, I 'Poveri prigioni', pp. 171–84; BCB F.O.43 fols. 43r–v, 44v, 45r; the crimes would appear to have been evading arrest under suspicion of another (unspecified) crime, and aiding such evasion.
[20] Lopez, 'Le confraternite laicali', pp. 221–2; S. Musella, 'Dimensione sociale e prassi associativa di una confraternita napoletana nell'età della Controriforma' in Galasso and Russo (eds.), vol. 1 p. 375; D'Addario, Aspetti, pp. 96–7.
[21] On prison theory and attitudes, and Roman prisons generally: Paglia, 'La Pietà dei Carcerati', pp. 1–14, 39–41, 72, 95–8, 132–3, 162–72; Monachino, pp. 267–74, where other Roman confraternities involved in prison visiting are mentioned: Congregazione della visita, Congregazione delle Carceri (1612). Cf. on theories about social discipline and the increased use of prisons: D. Melossi and M. Pavarini, The Prison and the factory (London, 1981); M. Foucault, Discipline and Punish.

were in prison for debt and begging, the population was highly mobile. V. Paglia has estimated that from 1600 to 1739 the six Roman prisons held about 300 persons between them at any one time, but about 6,000 persons passed through these prisons in a year. It is likely that this was the pattern from the mid-sixteenth century. The Jesuits were among the first to show concern for these prisoners, and encouraged confraternities like Rome's Pietà, Milan's S. Croce e della Pietà, and Lecce's SS. Annunziata to assist. Their involvement stemmed from the awareness that many indebted prisoners came form rural backgrounds deprived of adequate religious knowledge; their spiritual needs were as great as their physical. Religious help would raise the Christian consciousness in society generally. Rapid release from prison would lessen the impact on debtors of the hardened criminal element. There was also the simple comment of Matthew 25: 36: 'when in prison you visited me'.[22]

Confraternity involvement in prisons was most prominent in the Papal State. The Jesuits became the official confessors in the Roman prisons, and drew in their associated confraternities, which then became the official administrators. The S. Girolamo della Carità controlled the Tor di Nona prison from about 1563; the Pietà dei Carcerati did much of the practical work in other prisons like those of the Campidoglio, Curia Savella, Ripa and the Borgo. The confraternities, especially the Pietà, collected alms for bread for the prisoners; they checked on prison conditions, and handled complaints; they assisted the priests with services, with encouraging confessions, in providing religious books for those prisoners able to read or read to them; and they catechised prisoners on the basis of books and sermons. They provided similar missionary services to those sentenced to the galleys, based at Civitavecchia. They secured the release of debtors, utilising funds donated by the popes, and raising other monies. Some debts were paid off entirely, with some they persuaded creditors to cancel, ameliorate or postpone the debt, and with others they paid the debt, and asked for repayment from the debtor when he had an income. There were also confraternity funds available to help the ex-prisoner to feed and clothe himself and his family until he was again earning.[23]

The effect of the spiritual assistance cannot be gauged, but there is little doubt that the release of indebted prisoners was a major contribution to philanthropic assistance to the poor of Rome (and possibly other cities which have not been similarly investigated). In 1652 S. Girolamo brothers released 501 prisoners, 290 of them from the Tor di Nona prison.[24] This confraternity in 1624 spent 3,965 scudi on assistance (about 66 per cent of its total expenditure); of this, roughly 2,000 scudi was on bread as alms to prisoners and to the poor of the district; 500 more on secret help to prisoners; and 250 variously for the sick or poor prisoners.[25]

In 1592 Clement VIII abolished the office of General Prefect for Prisons in the Papal State (which had been unsatisfactorily farmed out to contractors) and handed over the guardianship of the prisons to those confraternities (lay, clerical or mixed) that in each

[22] Paglia, 'La Pietà dei Carcerati', pp. 39–41, 146; on Spain and Latin America, Flynn, 'Charitable ritual', pp. 341–2.

[23] Ibid., pp. 162–211. and Appendix pp. 253–315; Serra, 'Funzioni e finanze', p. 270.

[24] Monachino, pp. 270–1.

[25] Serra, 'Funzioni e finanze', p. 285 n. 3. It spent 600 scudi on the Conservatorio della Convertite or its girls, 250 on dowries for poor girls, 100 on poor widows and girls. The funds and categories are difficult to disentangle. Cf. Delumeau, Vie économique, pp. 497–501 on debtor prisoners and assistance for them.

city had exercised charity towards prisoners. They were to continue such charitable work, including the free feeding of poor prisoners. In Bologna this duty fell on the S. Maria della Morte, already noted for assisting the condemned. In 1595 under Archbishop Alfonso Paleotti's orders, a sub-section of the confraternity was created to administer the prisons — to be called the Compagnia della Carità dei Carcerati di Bologna. Its members would control the paid prison officials and act as prison visitors, securing food and medicines for the poor inmates.[26]

In Milan also confraternities were involved in prison-relief work, though without such an administrative role as in the Papal States. However, the brothers and sisters of S. Croce e della Pietà seem to have been more forthcoming with physical assistance, employing doctors and barbers, and supporting a trusted prisoner as an in-house nurse ('infermiere di dentro'). Their somewhat limited resources went on assisting indebted prisoners — but precise details of this philanthropic contribution have not been traced. The confraternity also undertook to ensure that creditors who had persons sent to prison for debt contributed to the upkeep of such prisoners.[27]

More specialised and less local aid went to those imprisoned and enslaved by the Turks when Christians were captured in naval wars and piratic encounters in the Mediterranean. Rome's Pietà and Gonfalone confraternities, Genoa's Della Carità di Gesù Maria, Chioggia's SS. Crocefisso, and Naples' Pio Monte della Misericordia were involved in ransoming such prisoners. Reversing the coin the Pietà also helped slaves in Rome, essentially people captured from North Africa who could legally be held by Christians (as confirmed by Paul III in 1548), by paying their owners to release them, or encouraging their baptism — and so release.[28]

A. Prosperi and S.Y. Edgerton have suggested that confraternity involvement in comforting and escorting in procession the condemned, and in ensuring that they accepted the verdict of the courts, prolonged the barbarous practices of torture and public executions. This may be to accept too readily the influene of confraternities on public ideas about punishment and retribution, and to repeat misleadingly the prejudices of enlightenment reformers against confraternities. Some of the work for other prisoners can be seen as a continuation or revival of humanitarian philanthropy, running counter to the harsh disciplining policy prevalent in some other areas.[29]

3 RELIGIOUS EDUCATION

Arguments about the nature of confraternity philanthropy, about whether it was liberating or repressive, can also emerge from a discussion of religious education. Especially after the Council of Trent there was an expansion of teaching of Christian

---

[26] *Statuti della Compagnia della Carità de' poveri carcerati della città di Bologna fatti . . . 1595* (Bologna n.d. [after 1635]), pp. 29–37. Bull of Clement VIII 'Inter multiplices' pp. 3–21 for the original seventeen chapters establishing the new company and its duties. Reforms in 1611, confirmed in 1635, allowed for a smaller committee of management as it was difficult to assemble the full company for quick decisions (pp. 22–8).

[27] Olivieri Baldissarri, *I 'Poveri prigioni'*, pp. 84, 96 n. 60, 165–70.

[28] Monachino, p. 266; Paglia, '*La Pietà dei Carcerati*', p. 71; Arsenio D'Ascoli, *La Predicazione dei Cappuccini*, pp. 216–18; Savelli, p. 180; on Naples see below chapter 11, nn. 60 and 63.

[29] Prosperi, 'Il sangue e l'anima', esp. pp. 992–3; Edgerton, *Pictures and Punishment*, p. 220 n. 56; Zardin, in reviewing Paglia's *La morte confortata*, in *RSCI*, 39 (1985), pp. 208–9 supports my stress on the humanitarian aspect of prisoner aid.

Doctrine in Sunday schools, primarily under the parish priest, but with the assistance of members of religious Orders and confraternities. These schools can be seen as standardising the teaching of religious belief in the community, eradicating heresy, and also marginal 'popular' religious practices and beliefs, and as imposing a stricter morality on the laity. This could be an exercise in social control and standardisation. Alternatively, or in addition, one can stress that this exercise in mass education liberated many from superstitions and profound ignorance, and in many cases led to greater literacy, and even debate about religious belief.

It should be noted at the outset that there were different kinds of Christian Doctrine schools. Some were run by parish priests and chaplains; others by members of Orders. In some areas of Italy there were many lay helpers who were organised into confraternities, but the amount of fraternal activity this involved for the teachers outside the schools was seemingly very variable.

The Christian Doctrine schools, teaching on Sundays and feast-days, have been primarily seen as a post-tridentine and Counter-Reformation development, especially associated with Borromean pastoral reform and control. But there were important pre-tridentine precedents. In about 1417 a schoolmaster in Bologna, Matteo dal Gesso started teaching Christian Doctrine in various churches on feast-days; Bishop Albergati welcomed this work and encouraged him to form a confraternity of S. Girolamo with twenty-four men to develop this teaching. It was formally constituted in 1433 when its own oratory was ready; it split into youth and adult societies, and both survived until the eighteenth century.[30] Of wider significance was the work of a Como priest Castellino da Castello who, aided by a Milanese nobleman Angelo Porro, started catechistic teaching of children in Milan in 1536, with clerical and lay supporters. In 1539 the Compagnia della Dottrina Cristiana was formed, and approved by the Milan church in 1540. Apparently the original proposal to call the fraternity a 'Compagnia della reformatione christiana in carità' was vetoed as having dangerous implications. The founders had to agree to ecclesiastical supervision. Soon companies following its rules were established in many cities. Their existence stimulated the Tridentine decree of 11 November 1563, under which parish priests were to organise the teaching of the faith to children on Sundays and other feast-days. In October 1567 Pius V issued a Brief exhorting all ordinaries to assign churches to lay confraternities in each diocese in which they could teach Christian Doctrine.[31]

The schools were not developed uniformly. Most were based on the parish church, with or without the assistance of, or organisation by confraternities; others were in confraternity buildings, or those of religious Orders. The extent of teaching also varied. Basically the schooling involved the learning of the Credo, Pater Noster, Ave Maria and Commandments with elementary explanations, and elucidation of the meaning of

---

[30] Fanti, *San Procolo*, pp. 139–41.

[31] Turrini, pp. 407–89 is the crucial study of the Christian Doctrine schools, and guide to the literature; pp. 411–12 give pre-tridentine schools and companies, spreading under Milan's influence, in Pavia (1538), Genoa, Vigevano, Verona, and Piacenza (1541), Mantua and Parma (1542), Lodi (1545), Cremona (1547), Varese (1550), Novara (1553), Bergamo and Brescia (1554), Rome (1560), Monza and Ascoli (1562), Savona, Turin and Ferrara (1563); P.F. Grendler, 'The schools of Christian Doctrine in sixteenth-century Italy', *Church History*, 53 (1984), 319–31; A. Prosperi, 'Intellettuali', p. 245 on Castellino; Tacchi Venturi, *Storia*, vol. 1.i, pp. 340–53; G. Franza, *Il Catechismo a Roma dal Concilio di Trento a Pio VI* (Rome, 1958), pp. 59–67 on Trent; *COD*, p. 763, Canon IV; Barletta (ed.), *Aspetti*, p. 174, Doc. 212 on 1567 Brief.

the Sacraments and fundamental tenets of Christian Doctrine. Much was rote learning, with the aid of singing. Boys and girls were separated, and in the larger schools at least there were a number of different classes according to age and understanding. Some schools taught reading: particularly the Jesuit and some Capuchin ones, and schools operated by confraternities in Milan, Como and other areas of Lombardy, and in Turin, Venice and Rome. But confraternities in other major areas like Bologna, Parma and Ferrara, seem not to have included reading in their schools. Few taught writing. In various schools, such as those associated with the Roman archconfraternity of Christian Doctrine and the Bologna schools, there were organised disputations, including competitions for the senior classes of boys. There were many different catechisms and manuals in use. Most were for the teachers, but some were for the pupils to use, and even keep. Some catechisms were lengthy and tediously produced guides for priests, others were simple question and answer manuals such as various forms of an *Interrogatorio*. Adults were sometimes required to attend the schools, especially when in preparation for marriage they were found to be deficient in elementary Christian knowledge.[32]

The schooling involved some moral and social teaching: instructions about regular prayer, good conduct in church, how to greet people and show hospitality, and about self-control. The *Interrogatorio* emphasised the importance of good works to prove that the person was a good Christian, and to follow the Gospel injunctions to help the poor. Discipline could be strongly enforced; corporal punishment was sometimes used for correcting misbehaviour, though it was banned in some schools. There were prizes for good conduct, as in Rimini, and several instruction books stressed that the schools should by joyful, with singing, processions and competitions. Some parents, in Bologna for example, were apparently reluctant to send girls to the schools, because they would be too free and nobles disliked their children mixing with the plebeians. Sometimes the schools were only for boys — as in the Christian Doctrine school in Strongoli Cathedral (Calabria). In Bologna, and elsewhere, children were rounded up and compelled to attend. In Rome there were cases of some children trying to prevent others attending. It has been argued that most Roman girls had some access to education precisely because of the confraternity schools. Social and religious conformity and uniformity should have been the long-term result. The occupation of older children for many hours in church and school on feast-days was likely to diminish the juvenile playfulness and the misconduct previously found in festive games and dances.[33]

---

[32] Turrini, pp. 428–30 on reading in schools; pp. 468–89, Appendix on rule books, and vernacular catechisms for these schools in the sixteenth century; Grendler, 'The schools of Christian Doctrine', esp. pp. 323–7, takes a more optimistic view of how much reading and writing was intended, and even practised. He describes the typical catechism, *Interrogatorio*, pp. 327–30. Franza, *Il Catechismo . . . Trento a Pio VI*, esp. pp. 25–58, 219–32 on manuals and catechisms; *Decreta Dioecesanae Synodi Ravennatis primae a Pietro Aldobrandino . . .* (Venice, 1607), fols. 8v–10v 'De Doctrina Christiana', required sodalities to be established where they did not exist within four months; children had to attend if they were receiving private education as well; adults could not contract a marriage until they knew their doctrine.

[33] Turrini, pp. 446–7 on girls being too free. Cf. Posperi, 'Intellettuali', pp. 246–7: the girls at such schools would be 'troppo libere, et audace'. The reply to the point about mixing with plebeians was 'che la Chiesa non fa distinzione tra nobili e ignobili, et perciò, sicome è comune a tutti, cosi deve essere frequentata da tutti'; Prodi, *Paleotti*, vol. 2, p. 187; Sposato, p. 215 on Strongoli; Franza, *Il Catechismo . . . Trento a Pio VI*, p. 142 on frustrating attendance; G. Pelliccia, 'Nuove note sulla educazione femminile popolare a Roma nei secoli XVI–XVII', *Istituto di Scienze Storico-Politiche Facoltà di Magistero — Università degli Studi Bari. Quaderni* 1 (1980), 293–346; G. Lercaro, 'La riforma catechista post-tridentina a Bologna', *Ravennatensia*, vol. 2, pp. 11–23, esp. n. 79 on compulsion; Turchini, *Rimini*, pp. 116–17.

The involvement of confraternities in the Christian Doctrine schools varied across the peninsula. It was extensive in Lombardy, Bologna and Rome. Carlo Borromeo wanted such a teaching fraternity or sodality created in every parish, and he imposed common rules on them. In 1584 it was claimed that the Milan archdiocese had 740 schools with 40,000 members; in 1599 that Milan city had 20,504 children enrolled in Christian Doctrine schools — for a population of about 200,000.[34] Borromeo recommended in 1576 that his friend Paleotti should follow suit in the Bologna archdiocese. Paleotti had already started producing suitable texts to be used in the existing schools. He later outlined the basic questions on Christian Doctrine that should be asked and answered in the schools. Paleotti at first started using parochial schools, but found them inadequate; by 1583 he had organised a special Congregatione della Dottrina Christiana to consolidate a fraternal network for the city and diocese, but where branches of such specialist confraternities could not be created, he asked the existing Sacrament companies to assist the parish priest. For the city about forty schools, with 600 adults teaching three or four thousand children, became operational.[35]

Some doubts have been expressed about the genuine success of the Borromean programme in Lombardy, especially outside the largest cities; the attempt at rigorous control over the institutions and teaching brothers and sisters may have soon diminished enthusiasm. However, the enthusiasm and vitality of the initial propagation of the schools shines forth in the diary of a Milanese carpenter, Giambattista Casale (or Ioan Batista Caxal as he called himself). Seeing himself as a 'spiritual son of Father Castellano', and a fervent admirer of Carlo Borromeo, he taught in Christian Doctrine schools, helped found new ones, and became an inspector by 1575. As subprior of the company of S. Jacobo in Porta Nova he was ready to teach writing 'gratis et amore Dei, for the honour of God and the salvation of souls and the common good'.[36]

In Rome the archconfraternity of Christian Doctrine was launched in 1560, by a Milanese layman, Marco de' Scali Cusani, to teach and catechise children in Roman churches. By 1585 he was ordained priest, and started a congregation of Regular Clerks for Christian Doctrine to work alongside the lay confraternity. Both were based in S. Agata in Trastevere, until 1600 when the archconfraternity moved to S. Martino alla Regola. By then all parish priests were members *ex officio*. Roberto Bellarmino's catechism, the *Dottrina Cristiana Breve* (1597), became the main teaching instrument. The archconfraternity organised the production and distribution of many editions to be

---

[34] *AEM*, II col. 170, 2nd Provincial Council (1569), cols. 234–5, 3rd Provincial Council (1573), orders to observe common rules now issued; AA.VV. *Storia di Milano*, vol. 10, pp. 174–5; Tacchi Venturi, *Storia*, vol. 1.i, pp. 340–53; Prodi, *Paleotti*, vol. 2, pp. 15–16; Wright, 'Post-tridentine reform', chapter 5, pp. 13–14; Pelliccia, 'Educazione femminile', pp. 313 n. 30, and 325–6. The city population was almost certainly not 200,000 as claimed for 1599; it was probably nearer 120,000. The higher figure may include surrounding villages in the diocese dependant on Milan.

[35] Paleotti, *Archiepiscopale Bononiense*, pp. 7–23; Prodi, *Paleotti*, vol. 2, pp. 182–9; idem 'Lineamenti', pp. 358–9; Prosperi, 'Intellettuali', pp. 245–6; *Statuti per la Congregatione Christiana nella Città et Diocesi di Bologna* (Bologna, 1583): these schools were to have six classes for different ages of boys (aged 4–14) and girls (4–12), and the top level had disputations on doctrine. Cf. Grendler, 'The schools of Christian Doctrine', p. 321.

[36] Cf. doubts expressed by Zardin, *Confraternite e vita di pietà*, pp. 60–1, 106 n. 198. Translated extracts from Casale are printed in E. Cochrane and J. Kirshner (eds.), *Readings in Western Civilization. 5. The Renaissance* (Chicago, 1986), pp. 411–26 — quoting from p. 411. I have not yet seen the full text, edited by C. Manacorda in *Memorie storiche della diocese di Milano*, 12 (1969), 209–437.

sent around Italy, and even Dalmatia, for associated fraternities to use. Besides debating competitions, the archconfraternity periodically organised elaborate processions with sacred representations — for example the story of Esther in about 1600 — to stimulate the pupils' enthusiasm. By 1611 there were 78 schools, which in July 1612 had 529 confraternity brothers and 519 sisters teaching 5,800 boys and 5,090 girls, plus some adult students. But after about 1630 enthusiasm, and teaching, waned.[37]

Elsewhere confraternity involvement in Christian Doctrine teaching is patchy or less known. In Florence the new parochial fraternities took up the task of instructing the young, among other functions. Here the proselytising enthusiasm of Ippolito Galantini (1565–1619) was significant. In Ferrara Christian Doctrine fraternities were developed particularly after the 1574 visitation of G.B. Maremonti, though a master, Rinaldo Lanzi, had laid some foundations in the 1560s. From 1568 Ferrara parishes and confraternities had their own catechism in question and answer form. For Turin in 1590 a visitation report stated that pious men and women were forming congregations to help teach doctrine, and according to a similar report the diocese of Vercelli had 180 Christian Doctrine schools in 1603, compared with 253 discipline confraternities. In Naples the S. Maria della Purità, in the church of S. Nicola a Toledo might be judged successful and influential, by its provision of young ordinands for the church; and one leading brother who had spent time teaching Christian Doctrine sought, at the age of 54, to become a priest. Further off in the Neapolitan extra-urban communities a few Christian Doctrine confraternities (if not always under that name) were founded in the early seventeenth century, especially under the influence of the Jesuits. However, progress in religious education there was judged to be slow. It is probable that, as in the remoter parts of the diocese of Bologna, members of Sacrament fraternities also helped the parish priest in whatever instruction took place in communities that did not establish a specialist teaching fraternity.[38]

Confraternities were also involved in Christian education in non-parochial contexts, as in the orphanages and conservatories. If the orphan girls in the Roman hospice of S. Maria in Aquiro were taught by an associated confraternity, so also were the prisoners in gaols or attached to galleys, by members of the Pietà dei Carcerati.[39]

The above outline has been primarily concerned with the work of Christian Doctrine teaching. The extent to which the teachers who were formed into a confrater-

[37] G. Franza, Il Catechismo a Roma a l'Arciconfraternita della Dottrina Cristiana (Alba, 1958), esp. pp. 69–161; Maroni Lumbroso and Martini, pp. 132–5; Mira, 'Aspetti', pp. 29–30, calculates that at one point nineteen printers in twelve cities were involved in printing Bellarmino catechisms for the archconfraternity; Pelliccia, 'Educazione femminile', p. 300 n. 11 on sending the catechisms to Dalmatia; G. Garzya, 'Reclutamento e sacerdotalizzazione del clero secolare della diocesi di Napoli' in Galasso and Russo (eds.), vol. 2, pp. 113–22 on use of Bellarmino's work.

[38] D'Addario, Aspetti, pp. 45–7; Weissman, Ritual Brotherhood, pp. 213–14, 218, 223; Grosso and Mellano, vol. 1, pp. 247–50 for Cardinal della Rovere's visitation ad limina report. Earlier visitations in the diocese had noted the absence of such schools and fraternities, and sometimes encouraged their foundation, ibid., vol. 2, pp. 18–20, 145, 196–202, 209, 226–7; the Jesuits were reported to be good teachers in Turin cathedral in the 1570s, with many children attending, pp. 46–7. Erba, La Chiesa Sabauda tra Cinquecento e seicento (Rome, 1979), p. 423; Peverada, pp. 309–16, and in Ferrara the company of S. Orsola also helped with religious education (pp. 317–19); Garzya, 'Reclutamento', p. 120 n. 34; Russo, Chiesa e comunità, pp. 360–2 and Table xiv, pp. 333–4.

[39] Pelliccia, 'Educazione femminile', pp. 329–30; see above, section 2, on the Pietà's prison work, and chapter 9.6 on conservatories.

nity had their own fraternal religous life is largely undiscussed in the literature. They were required in some areas to meet after the school sessions, but primarily to discuss pedagogical problems. D. Zardin doubts whether the Christian Doctrine companies in rural Lombardy had a real corporate life, and considers them no more than parish assemblies of the catechism teachers; except that there were special indulgences to be earned by membership. In Rome, however, the confraternity members had weekly meetings for their own business and spiritual purposes; made pilgrimages to the main Roman churches, and visited the sick, poor and imprisoned. The statutes for the Bologna congregation required the teaching brothers to confess at least once a month, and on major feasts; they should, if literate, read the booklet on Christian Doctrine frequently, the better to assist in instructing the children. They were also to select a Saint of the Month, whose virtues were to be imitated. The Jesuit spiritual adviser would recommend suitable readings for the confraternity in connection with the chosen model. Probably in Bologna under Paleotti there would have been a more active confraternity life than in some other areas.[40]

In sharing in the teaching of Christian Doctrine the confraternities were participating in one of the most important developments in the post-tridentine Italian church. Through the catechism schools the knowledge of basic beliefs, rituals, prayers and commandments was spread, even if no precise idea of the extent and quality can be gained from available evidence. Given that the schools involved could be dominated by the parish priest, by one of various religious orders, or confraternities, that a variety of catechisms was used, and that some were compulsory but others voluntary, the amount of standardisation was more limited than a Borromeo would have liked, but that might now be considered beneficial and stimulating. Indirectly if not directly there should have been some impact on literacy, as some at least were encouraged to move on from rote learning. In terms of confraternity involvement this was an area of outward philanthropy that, at least in Milan, Rome and Bologna, must have involved more people than any other activity (except attending funerals?). It is also worth contemplating the likely impact on females in particular — whether they were involved in teaching, however rudimentary, or earlier as children in a school. Were they, as those Bologna parents complained, too liberated by such schools?

4 CHEAP LOANS

Some confraternities were involved in institutions designed to provide loans to the poor. The cynical might judge the topic, given the title of this chapter, as the product of ignorance, and of a policy likely to increase the imprisoned. But genuine philanthropy existed in so far as the institutions were designed to let the poor avoid high interest rates, or raise money economically to prepare for the next season.

The main institutions concerned were the Monti di Pietà, one of which has already been mentioned, when Todi confraternities used sacred representations to raise money for the pawn-broking institution (chapter 5.3). The Monti di Pietà or Monti dei Poveri had been developed in Perugia and other cities of Umbria in the 1460s, primarily under

---

[40] Zardin, 'Confraternite e comunità', pp. 715–16; Franza, *Il Catechismo . . . l'Arciconfraternita*, pp. 69–161; *Statuti per la congregazione Christiana*.

the influence of Franciscan preachers who wanted to take the poor out of the hands of professional money-lenders, especially the Jews. They planned to lend small sums of money to the poor, on the security of pledged goods, charging minimal interest (if any) to cover administrative costs. The idea spread through Italy, especially in the wake of antisemitic campaigning in central and northern areas by fra Bernardino da Feltre. Expansion continued through the sixteenth century, despite heated arguments about usury if interest was charged, and under-financing if it was not. Some key cities like Rome and Naples did not establish Monti until the 1530s; Venice preferred to use the Jews (under strict control) in the city, but many Monti were founded in dependent cities of the mainland. The Council of Trent ruled that these pious institutions should be subject to episcopal supervision along with hospitals and confraternities, though this rule was not always effectively enforced.[41]

Confraternities became involved with the Monti di Pietà as promoters or fund-raisers, and sometimes they contributed to the administration. In Venetian territory many were developed in the 1490s when confraternities raised the capital required to launch them. In Verona the existing Fraglia della Carità recognised that 'good works' included fostering these institutions for the poor. The preaching of Michele of Acqui led to the foundation in 1490 of a new confraternity of S. Bernardino, which supposedly enrolled 18,000 people at once, and eventually 70,000 — in the city and surrounding district. (It is difficult to treat this as a single large confraternity; even if the figures are accepted as indicating associated members, the organisation would have been fragmentary, and many would only have been names on a list — for indulgences? — and not participants.) The same preacher started similar confraternities in Brescia, Cremona and Genoa where brothers were committed to funding and maintaining Monti.[42]

In Bologna an Observant friar, Bartolomeo Milvio, promoted the reform of the city's Monte in 1504; a newly created confraternity (limited to 5,000, though husbands and wives counted as one) would provide financial and spiritual sponsorship, and elect officials to serve on the organising congregation, along with civic and church members. By the 1560s confraternity enthusiasm waned, financial contributions fluctuated considerably, and brothers proved reluctant to serve on the board of directors. The Bologna institution then came to rely heavily on professional administrators, and less on philanthropic volunteers.[43]

Confraternities played a major role in the creation and maintenance of two Neapolitan Monti. When Emperor Charles V ordered the expulsion of the Jews, the Monte di Carità confraternity started a Monte di Pietà in 1539. In 1563 some lawyers who wished to assist indebted prisoners formed what became the fraternity of S. Maria dei Poveri and created the Monte dei Poveri; in this they were joined in 1599 by the Nome

[41] For general literature see above chapter 1, note 15; M.G. Muzzarelli, 'Un bilancio storiografico sui Monti di Pietà: 1956–1976', *RSCI*, 33 (1979), 165–83; Rusconi, 'Confraternite', p. 499 and n. 51. For an indication of 'small loans', though from a communal institution not a confraternity one: the Perugian Monti in 1514 were lending *contadini* sums from 45 *soldi* to 5 florins 45s. The borrowers could redeem their pledges over five years, paying a fifth a year. The original 10 per cent interest rate was reduced to 6 per cent in 1468, and to 2 per cent in 1571: ASP Miscellanea di Computisteria, vol. 5, debtors of the Monti in 1514; Miscellanea vol. 65, no. 38, Monti di Pietà council records 1473–1539, fols. 80r–1r; Majarelli and Nicolini, p. 39.

[42] Pullan, *Rich and Poor*, pp. 473–4.

[43] M. Maragi, *I Cinquecento Anni del Monte di Bologna* (Bologna, 1973).

di Dio confraternity, whose initial campaigns had been to curb blasphemy and to reconcile social conflict. The Neapolitan Monti became major banking institutions. In mid-century popes had sanctioned the payment of interest by Monti to investors who were prepared to utilise their capital for this philanthropic project rather than in land investments, commerce, or government bonds. Hence these Monti, and others else-where, blossomed into full banking complexes (as the titles of various modern Italian banks demonstrate), possibly to the detriment of the 'poor' borrowers.[44] However, small Monti continued to be created, as in Piedmontese towns, or especially in southern-central areas: a number have been traced in the Abruzzi, Molise and Basilicata regions. In seventeenth-century Bitonto there was a Monte di Pietà that not only operated as a lending institution, but helped the sick, pilgrims, widows, orphans, the old, and dowered poor girls. And there are indications of Monti elsewhere in Puglia and one in association with a hospital in Moliterno (diocese of Marsico), though my sources do not clarify the extent of confraternity involvement.[45] At Lonigo in the diocese of Vicenza a hospital confraternity helped start a Monte in the later sixteenth century, along with the communal government, by donating 100 ducats. It faced various difficulties, with a crisis point about 1586; but in 1616 it claimed to the visiting bishop that the Monte was valued at 6,000 ducats.[46]

There were specialist Monti. The Monti di Maritaggio, for which there are some cryptic indications in certain southern areas, allowed savings to be made for dowries. Monti di Frumentari lent seed or capital to poor farmers at a modest rate (6 per cent or less) so that the new sowing could be started. This way one bad harvest might be prevented from harming the next. They were also sometimes involved in attempts to control grain prices. The Monti di Frumentari institution may have been inaugurated in Macerata in 1492, and been developed through encouragement from Franciscan Observants. A number of these Monti were run by confraternities in the Spoleto diocese in the later sixteenth century. Their popularity increased, especially when Paul V sanctioned one for the Rome area in 1611, and they may have reached their peak only in the late eighteenth or nineteenth century. It has been claimed that in eighteenth-century Umbria where such institutions existed, the numbers of poor needing alms as assistance was reduced.[47]

Frustratingly little is known about many of these Monti, their organisation, the degree of assistance they gave to the poor (or not so poor) borrowers, and the involvement of confraternities with their organisation and development.

[44] Mazzoleni (ed.), pp. 14–17.

[45] Erba, *La Chiesa Sabauda*, pp. 250–1 and notes; Donvito and Pellegrino, *L'Organizzazione Ecclesiastica*, Tables; S. Mililo, 'Società civile e religiosa a Bitonto nella seconda metà del secolo '600' in Garofolo (ed.), p. 42; V. Gallotta, 'Le diocesi pugliesi fra '500 e '600', *ibid.*, pp. 58–9; Colangelo, p. 23.

[46] Mantese, *Memorie*, vol. 4–2, p. 720.

[47] Gallotta, pp. 58–9; Donvito and Pellegrino, *L'Organizzazione Ecclesiastica*, Tables; G. Caneva, 'Contributo allo studio dei Monti frumentari come forma assistenziale e nei rapporti ospedalieri', *Studi di storia Ospitaliera*, 3 (1965), 199–209, but disappointingly thin in material; Cairns, pp. 67–9; C. Penuti, 'Carestie ed epidemie', *Storia della Emilia Romagna*, ed. A. Berselli, vol. 2 (Bologna, 1977), p. 203; Casagrande, 'Ricerche', pp. 45, 61 n. 101; Giuntella et al., pp. 494–5; Tosti, p. 165; Mollat, *Les Pauvres au Moyen Age*, pp. 335–8. Capuchin preachers promoted Monti Frumentari, though it is not clear whether associated confraternities were also involved: Arsenio D'Ascoli, *La Predicazione dei Cappuccini*, pp. 227–9.

5 BURYING THE DEAD

As already indicated (chapter 4.8), nearly all confraternities were deeply concerned with preparation for death and the afterlife, primarily for themselves and their immediate associates. This might be extended to attending funerals of parishioners who were not members of the fraternity or of eminent citizens.

Here we return to the subject in connection with external philanthropy and concern for the poor. Some confraternities became specialists in caring for the dead bodies of the poor and neglected. It was felt that a person, even if neglected in life, should have a decent burial. The rejected body implied a rejected soul, like an unrepentant criminal or heretic destined for hell-fire. Old confraternities such as Florence's Misericordia and Rome's S. Girolamo had included among their philanthropic activities the seventh act of mercy of burying the poor dead. But the ravages of the Italian wars in the early sixteenth century, and their economic consequences, leaving dead bodies scattered about streets and countryside, shocked reformers. By 1538 some formed a sodality to collect abandoned corpses in the Roman countryside and give them a decent burial. This became a formal confraternity and from 1560 the archconfraternity of S. Maria dell'Orazione e Morte, to which Carlo Borromeo belonged when in Rome. From 1552 to 1896 it averaged twenty-five such burials a year, though in the Jubilee year 1625 it buried fifty poor persons from Rome, as well as (more sumptuously) sixty-six company members and their relatives. By the end of the sixteenth century a number of other Roman confraternities had joined in the work of burying the poor and neglected, and so lessened (according to C. Fanucci) the Orazione e Morte's activity in this area. Similar confraternities, often linked to the Roman archconfraternity, emerged through north and central Italy, and occasionally in the south, as in Marsico.[48] Other old confraternities also took on this philanthropy. In the 1565 Naples synod the city's confraternity Della Croce (founded by 1321) was praised for burying many poor dead, who would otherwise have gone without burial because of the rapacity of local priests. Its revised statutes gave prominence to this act of mercy, which it saw as stemming from carrying the standard of the Cross through the world.[49]

Perugia's Della Morte e Orazione, founded in 1570, was one of the offshoots of the Roman archconfraternity. Originally it was concerned only with the poor abandoned dead, but soon it began to provide processions for wealthier deceased, visited the sick in hospital, assisted the living poor, and contributed with some splendour to general processions in the city. Leading patricians joined, and helped finance an impressive oratory near the city centre. According to one patrician member they met some

---

[48] Monachino, pp. 275–6; Fanucci, *Trattato*, pp. 272–8; Maroni Lumbroso and Martini, pp. 256–8; Paglia, 'Le confraternite e i problemi della morte', pp. 198–201; Colangelo, p. 37; Urbanelli, *Storia dei Cappuccini delle Marche*, vol. 2, pp. 558–9, and vol. 3/I, pp. 290–1 on the Compagnia di S. Girolamo della Carità erected in Tolentino (c. 1554), by P. Marco da Mercato, who had been shocked at seeing dead bodies of poor people and foreigners lying about; and on a similar society at Corridonia (1568); P. Paschini, 'Il primo soggiorno di S. Carlo Borromeo a Roma 1560–1565', in his *Cinquecento romano e Riforma Cattolica* (Rome, 1958), pp. 95–181, at p. 169.

[49] Musella, 'Dimensioni', pp. 374, 395: 'essendo questa nostra compagnia coadunata sotto il vexillo della Santissima Croce per operare l'opere di misericordia, come seppellire i morti per amor d'Iddio', and p. 432 (chapter 21). Poor prisoners were buried by this confraternity. In 1576 there seem to have been 321 brothers in the fraternity, 165 of them nobles; leading bureaucrats joined in the next century (pp. 359–61).

opposition to their activities in venturing forth in black robes to collect poor dead from the countryside, and returning with the corpse behind a black standard: 'they had some disputes with many churches where they took the dead for interment; some of these (perhaps avaricious and envious) religious opposed them, not wishing to support them, alleging very strongly (but vainly) that this act would prove prejudicial to the churches'.[50] Another patrician member, and chronicler, was particularly upset by one funeral the fraternity conducted: that of young Virginia Bufalena, a sufferer from venereal disease (*mal francese*), who had died unconfessed while her husband was away in Rome.[51]

A possibly happier outcome — in worldly terms — for one such morbid expedition was reported by a Roman chronicler. In September 1618 members of the Orazione e Morte archconfraternity set out to bury a poor man who had been killed by a falling beam outside the Porta del Popolo; on returning they heard a baby's cry, and eventually found five naked abandoned babies — four males with names on a label, and an anonymous female. These children were taken to the S. Spirito hospital to be brought up at the Morte's expense, with orders that they should not be sent out of Rome for fostering.[52]

How widespread this burial philanthropy was in unclear, but that many might have been involved to solve a considerable problem is suggested by the information that the comparatively small town of Borgo San Sepolcro had three confraternities concerned with burial of the dead — though they also assisted the abandoned poor before death, plague victims, and condemned persons.[53]

The last two sections in this chapter in particular have ended with doubts about the extent and quality of confraternity involvement in the philanthropic activities discussed. They reflect our inadequate knowledge about Italian social history in general, and the work of confraternities in particular. It is hoped that other local researchers will investigate more deeply the quantity and quality of this philanthropy. Some assessments are probably impossible; we are not to know how much real comfort the condemned and other prisoners received form their fraternal comforters and assistants. The evidence on the hospitals for the poor is ambiguous — sometimes the officials record problems in keeping the inmates in, at others in keeping some poor out. The teaching of Christian Doctrine clearly involved large numbers in certain areas; those happen also to be the regions of highest literacy (comparable to that of Protestant countries which supposedly put a higher premium on education) in the nineteenth century. But too little is known about the wider educational context and literacy before and after the sixteenth-century campaign to judge fully the extent of any causal relationships involved. More could

[50] BCP Ms 1221 R. Sotii, 'Annali', fol. 62r–v; Marinelli, *Le Confraternite*, pp. 817–48; G. Cernicchi, *Confraternita della Misericordia* (Perugia, 1900) [BCP Misc.II.E.1]; in 1872 the Della Morte e Orazione confraternity changed its name to Confraternita della Misericordia; this booklet was written as a defence and explanation of its work, by its then Governor.

[51] G.B. Crispolti, 'Memorie di Perugia dall'anno 1578 al 1586', *Cronache*, ed. Fabretti, vol. 4, pp. 119–20.

[52] Gigli, *Diario Romano*, p. 42.

[53] Meloni, 'Topografia', pp. 45–6.

probably be discovered form surviving records about the impact of the Monti, and the degree of assistance through loans to different categories of borrowers.

The aim here has been to demonstrate the range of confraternity involvement in the wider community. In some places the contact was with the mass of ordinary people — at least when they were children and in need of rudimentary religious instruction. Fraternal philanthropy also extended to the criminal and destitute, in life and in death. The assistance could be both repressive and liberating, helping to impose protective custody on some (though in order to liberate the soul later), but offering to others the chance of starting a new life on a more secure financial foundation.

CONFRATERNITY BUILDINGS AND
THEIR DECORATION

The physical and visual environment within which confraternity members operated is
relevant in various ways to their worship and social activities. Where confraternities had
their own separate buildings, independent of a parish church or monastery, they were
most likely to be able to preserve lay initiative. There also we should expect to find the
most meaningful corporate life, within an environment which, through instructive
decorations, could foster devotion, encourage philanthropic activity and express the
pride or social esteem of the brotherhood.

The following discussion is primarily concerned with the significance of chapels,
oratories and paintings for the confraternities, rather than the importance of confraternities for the history of architecture and painting. A full-length study from the latter
viewpoint would be valuable, clarifying what they commissioned, or what was ordered
on their behalf, their impact on building design, on the financing of large churches
within which some confraternities operated, the selection and popularity of certain
images and subject matter in paintings. Some of these latter aspects will be touched
upon, but the main purpose here is to use selected examples — for the most part ones
I have personally visited — to discuss the significance of environmental spaces for the
brethren, and the value of buildings and decoration as evidence of the beliefs and way
of life of confraternity members.

I CONFRATERNITY BUILDINGS

Confraternities worked in various physical environments. By the sixteenth century all
were attached to a particular church, chapel or cloister. Earlier, at least the Genoese
discipline confraternities, *casacce*, operated largely in the open, without being associated
with a particular building, but this had been discouraged by civic authorities, and by
our period they all had a headquarters.[1] Most confraternities would have been associated
with a chapel within a parish or monastic church. Others had larger spaces available,
where they had their own oratories or chapels, separate meeting rooms, and possibly
rooms for hospices. A few confraternities like Rome's S. Spirito in Sassia or S. Giacomo
degli Incurabili controlled large hospital complexes with churches attached, as well as
having their own confraternity rooms. A few, such as Venice's Scuola di S. Rocco and
Rome's S. Giovanni Decollato have left us major architectural treasures, reflecting their

[1] Grendi, 'Morfologia', pp. 244–5, 249, 292–8.

taste and power. The size and nature of a confraternity's physical environment can indicate the autonomy, or dependence, of that company, the sense of cohesion and brotherhood, the social and political power of the group, or occasionally that of a few important members and patrons. The buildings and internal decorations can also reflect the company's range of activities, and its use of the arts for religious education, philanthropic activity and social propaganda.

Those confraternities attached to chapels within a church or cloister were likely to sacrifice some lay autonomy, and have to succumb to clerical influence from the parent church. It is not usually clear where the business meetings of such confraternities were held; in the body of the church, the sacristy, other rooms off the church, or (least likely), in the home of a leading official. It is unlikely that many Sacrament or Rosary confraternities had their own rooms outside the church to guarantee some autonomy, though several in Lombardy and Genoa sought and achieved this position by the eighteenth century; those in the Neapolitan extra-urban communities that tried to secure this may have been less successful.[2] The chapel-based devotional confraternities were dependent on the parish priest, or chaplain of the sponsoring church, not only for conducting their services but for permitting meetings and fraternal celebrations.

On the other hand the clergy could be beholden to confraternities, and have to mollify them. As indicated in chapter 3.4, a confraternity might constitute the vestry committee. It was often responsible for the maintenance and lighting of its chapel within the main church, but also contributed to the overall decoration of the church for major festivals. A confraternity might provide an altar-piece or other painting which became the best-known feature of the church down to the present time — for example some Sacrament confraternity commissions from Tintoretto to which we shall return. The priest might have to plead with his confraternities for assistance, as when priests appealed to the Venetian Convicinato Scuola of S. Marcilian for financial help for organ repairs in 1575, and the decoration and furnishing of the sacristy in 1603 and 1642. The Venetian Scuola d'arte dei Pittori at different stages funded the churches and priests of S. Sofia and S. Luca, and contributed to their maintenance, decorations and music in return for services from their priests. The fraternity also retained its own separate premises for business and religious purposes. If a confraternity paid for the patronage rights over a chapel, then it could have a major say in the financial position of the church and its incumbents, though, especially in the larger churches, confraternities were unlikely to be able to outbid the influence of patrician families who controlled other chapels. The operational funding of churches is a neglected topic, but it would be revealing to know the relative importance of finances derived from the patrons of chapels, and the relative contribution of families or confraternities. Patrician and confraternity control could be combined. In late fifteenth-century Florence the confraternity of St Peter Martyr (dei Laudesi) had a dominant influence over the high altar area of S. Maria Novella. In 1486–7 Giovanni Tornabuoni used his wealth and his position as a confraternity official to secure from the Dominicans patronage rights for his family clan (the Tornaquinci *consorteria*) over the chapel and altar. Giovanni's

---

[2] Zardin, *Le confraternite e vita di pietà*, pp. 54–7; Russo, *Chiesa e comunità*, pp. 315–20. For fraternity meetings sometimes being held in a private house, Olivieri Baldissarri, *I 'poveri prigioni'*, p. 124 n. 12. See chapter 3.4 on parish churches and confraternities.

donations allowed for lavish celebrations in the chapel and funded both the confraternity and church. The Dominicans could hardly resist his blandishments, and the confraternity had to associate its rights with his. He was then in a position to influence the completion of the fresco cycle by Ghirlandaio — to the honour of his family as well as the Virgin.[3]

Some problems that could arise when a confraternity was based in a chapel attached to, or within, a larger church can be exemplified by Venice's S. Francesco della Vigna. In 1582, after negotiations that had been going on since 1579, a Scuola della Beata Vergine della Concezione was created, which took over a chapel (in the complex of buildings attached to the new church designed by J. Sansovino) from Federico Curelli — a Milanese merchant who had come to Venice. Under the terms of the transfer only Curelli, his wife and sons could be buried there, and no alterations to the chapel structure were permissible. The confraternity inherited the Bulls and privileges associated with the chapel, as well as some money to create a dowry fund for poor girls. By 1584 there were serious conflicts with the Franciscan Fathers of S. Francesco, who were accused of *malignità* against the *scuola*, whose brothers then took steps to transfer themselves to the chapel of S. Giovanni Battista in the church of S. Stefano. Bitter words were said on many sides, and the friars of S. Stefano were accused of being rebels — 'ribelle della sede apostolica'. Among other things the fraternity had tried to take with them the indulgences and privileges inherited from Curelli, which was impermissible. The Franciscans had earlier opposed the fraternity's plans to get certain indulgences moved from the main altar to their own. They had objected to the way the *scuola* collected alms (for the dowry fund) from those coming to their chapel for the indulgences; presumably they were particularly upset that the confraternity had a paid official, *nonzolo*, in daily attendance at the chapel to control it, and the alms. In return the fraternity complained about the lack of security in their chapel (against theft of their alms by Franciscans?). After much negotiating and arguing the papal Nunzio in Venice imposed a settlement, ratified by the pope in 1586, whereby the *scuola* stayed in S. Francesco. Among later developments it is notable that the *scuola* took legal action against the Franciscans in 1613 for destroying an epitaph on the altar during building work, and that in 1642 the Fathers allowed the *confratelli* (illegally, given the Curelli will) to build a new altar. The attachment of many popular indulgences to this chapel, and the difficulty of relocating them, would have inhibited further attempts by the *scuola* to move to another church, or create their own independent oratory.[4]

---

[3] ASVen Scuole piccole, Busta 296, no. 2 28 December 1575, no. 17 31 December 1603, and miscellaneous sheets for 1542; no. 23, undated but c. 1599, is another petition to help repair the organ (40 ducats requested), at the request of the *gastaldo* of the church's Sacrament confraternity. By 1704 the Convicinato members (who primarily were concerned with helping the poor) were required to join the Sacrament confraternity as well. The church, in the Cannaregio district, was also known as S. Marcillian or S. Marziale. Cf. Zardin, *Le confraternite e vita di pietà*, pp. 126–8. See below at n. 67 on the contribution of a Sacrament confraternity to the church of S. Cassiano. On the Scuola d'arte dei Pittori: Favaro, pp. 112–14. On S. Maria Novella: P. Simons, 'Patronage in the Tornaquinci Chapel, Santa Maria Novella, Florence' in Kent and Simons (eds.), pp. 221–50, esp. pp. 233–7.

[4] ASVen Scuole piccole, Busta 125–126: (i) Catastico, fols. 4r, 40r–v (agreements about the chapel), 42r ('malignità' of Franciscans), 42r–3v (attempts to transfer to S. Stefano), 44v (1613 and 1642 issues); (ii) Miscellanea, esp. 18 March 1586 Patriarch G. Trevisan to the Scuola; 24 March 1586 Zambattista Bembo in Rome to Scuola; and copy of undated document outlining the Scuola's case to an unnamed cardinal. It is not clear how often the confraternity paid the annual obligation of 20 ducats to the church (as under

The frustrations of finding an independent home for a confraternity can be seen in the experience of the Perugian 'Venerabile congregatione de' Visitatori de' poveri vergognosi', or the Sodalizio di S. Martino as it became known. This society, led — as already noted — by leading patricians desirous of assisting the poor, was inaugurated in 1574 and fully operational by 1576. Initially it met in the church of S. Arrigo, in the Cathedral or in the hospital of S. Maria della Misericordia. By 1578 there were discussions about finding suitable rooms of their own, in or near a church, but 'free' from the priest of that church. In initially choosing between the short-listed sites of S. Lucia and S. Martino they selected the latter where they could build above the church for less than at S. Lucia, and be free from the priest. They could have a room for grain and for the fraternity's property. St Martin was already their 'advocate' and patron saint. The clergy of S. Lucia then pressed the fraternity to think again — while the neighbours of S. Martino objected to any new building there. Finally in 1581 the brothers resolved to buy a hospital near S. Maria Novella that had previously belonged to the Capuchins, deemed suitable for their charitable activities, for processions, for visiting the sick, and for the creation of their own chapel (for monthly celebrations at least), for which they would have their own priest, who would also be the custodian. The then Prior of the fraternity bought the site and *amore Dio* presented it to his co-brothers. His reward was to have the benefits of the fraternity for life, without any expenses or duties. Not until April 1585 was the company finally settled into its new oratory. It was finally independent and self-contained.[5]

A less successful pursuit of independence is found in the history of the Milanese fraternity of S. Croce e della Pietà. This company became increasingly unhappy with the canons of the parish church of S. Babila in which they had a chapel. They argued about who controlled suitable altars. After various attempts to rent separate rooms, or to move to another church (S. Cipriano) the officials found a site for a church and meeting rooms, and by 1619 had constructed an oratory. This was almost immediately declared to be illegal, because they lacked building permission from the archbishop. Their argument that they were only providing an oratory, not a proper church, was found to be false, and they had to demolish part of their building. The fraternity (or the S. Pietà section of it) possessed a partially built and unusable home, and had to remain in S. Babila until about 1692, when the reintegrated fraternity could move openly to a completed building.[6]

Curelli), or whether this was also part of the contentious relationships. The main church of S. Francesco had been constructed by Jacopo Sansovino (from c. 1534), with a facade designed by Palladio (1568–72). Indulgences had been allocated to this chapel to help earn money for the new church; it had held a Virgin and Child painted by Giovanni Bellini (1507); Curelli had his own portrait substituted for that of the original donor, Giacomo Dolfin, when he took over the chapel. The painting is not mentioned in the above documents on confraternity–church controversies. G. Lorenzetti, *Venezia e il suo estuario. Guida storico-artistica* (Trieste, LINT 1985 reprint edition), pp. 371–5 (S. Francesco), 502–6 (S. Stefano); D. Howard, *Jacopo Sansovino. Architecture and Patronage in Renaissance Venice* (New Haven and London, 1975), pp. 66–74.

[5] ASP Sodalizio di S. Martino, 'Libro I°- delle Congregazioni', esp. fols. 2v, and 15v; at S. Lucia 'bisogna fabricarci e nondimeno non se può haver libera, ma comune con il clero; et san Martino chi è advocato della Compagnia, bisogna fabricar sopra la chiesa, sendo che al sito sopra la chiesa, quale offerisce il Prete, bisogna de spendersi manco, che in S. Lucia, e ce se offerisce libero dal Prete' (and the recommendation was accepted by 24–11); fols. 17r, 19r–21v, 26r–v (42–o agreed to buy the hosptial site), 27r, 39r (168 people present for the inaugural *adunanza* in the completed oratory, when Alessandro Baglioni was elected the new prior).

[6] Olivieri Baldissarri, *I 'poveri prigioni'*, pp. 199–216, 223–31.

Several problems encountered by confraternities which had to use a chapel within a major church they did not control are revealed by an account of the reconstruction of the great Florentine churches of S. Croce and S. Maria Novella after 1565. Duke Cosimo I de' Medici, with the assistance of Giorgio Vasari as architect and designer, sought to support the Tridentine reform spirit by clearing the interiors of the churches so that the congregation could see the high altar and hear sermons clearly. The naves were cleared of tombs, screens, and the famous *tramezzi* that had separated the laity from the choir and high altar area, and from where sermons had been preached. But the whole system of side altars, and some cloister chapels, was altered, and under Vasari's new scheme various confraternities lost their chapels, while a few powerful families gained them despite intense competition. Eventually in S. Croce (c. 1575–80) the Compagnia della SS. Concezione managed to displace the Machiavelli family in control of a chapel on the left of the nave; the confraternity offered to build an altar similar to, but more lavish than, the Cavalcanti one opposite. However, its plans to wall up the door, presumably to contain and control the chapel better, as well as to position the altar more effectively, were vetoed by the church's office of works. The Compagnia di Gesù Pellegrino had had a number of chapels in the cloisters of old S. Maria Novella, a major one of which was due for demolition by Vasari; it sought a replacement within the new nave. But it had to be content with sharing a chapel, in the first bay of the left aisle, with the Compagnia della Croce al Tempio, as joint patrons of the tomb of Beata Villana. The latter company selected the theme for the altar-piece by Santi di Tito, *The Raising of Lazarus*, relevant to the company's role in comforting the condemned. The alternative theme of the Resurrection had already been chosen for a different altar. A Rosary confraternity soon controlled another chapel in S. Maria Novella, designed by Vasari, with a *Madonna of the Rosary* altarpiece painted by Jacopo Zucchi. However, the work had been paid for through the will (in 1568) of Camilla Capponi and it seems that the fraternity had no say in the nature of the chapel over which it became patron. In famous churches such as this it was desirable to have a confraternity altar, but the fraternities had limited control and little space. It is not clear what facilities in particular the SS. Concezione and Rosary fraternities had elsewhere for meetings or worship. The confraternities had public prestige, but limited privacy or control.[7]

In contrast some confraternities had a church and associated buildings, to which the public — or sections of it — might be admitted on the confraternty's terms. In the sixteenth century several Roman confraternities, such as those connected with hospitals, were in this position — and recruited the best architects. S. Spirito in Sassia built a new church between 1538 and 1545, to the designs of Antonio Sangallo the Younger; the facade was completed by Ottaviano Mascarino in the 1580s. Some paintings, such as those by Livio Agresti have suitably encouraging or propagandist subjects — such as *The curing of the paralytic* or *The curing of the blind man*.[8] The similar hospital confrater-

---

[7] Hall, *Renovation*, esp. pp. 103–4, 114–17, 140–2 for specific chapels discussed, plates 105 (*The Raising of Lazarus*), 33 (*Madonna of the Rosary*); M. Wackernagel, *The World of the Florentine Renaissance Artist*, trans. A. Luchs (Princeton, 1981), pp. 48–9; Weissman, *Ritual Brotherhood*, pp. 220–1, where he suggests that the Concezione confraternity was not founded until 1579. There was also a clerical company called Concezione dei Preti in a church of that name — see D'Addario, *Aspetti*, pp. 191 and 585 (index).

[8] M.J. Lewine, *The Roman Church Interior, 1527–1580* (Columbia University PhD thesis, 1960; University Microfilms International, Ann Arbor, 1963), pp. 451–84; Blunt, *Guide*, p. 147; *Guida d'Italia. 16. Roma e Dintorni* (6th edn., Milan, 1965), p. 459.

nity of S. Giacomo degli Incurabili had a new church designed by Francesco da Volterra in about 1590, though Cardinal A.M. Salviati contributed more to financing it than the confraternity members. The church, with its oval plan, was architecturally significant and impressive, and is prominently positioned on the major thoroughfare of the Corso.[9] Another significant oval church was produced by the confraternity of papal grooms, S. Anna dei Palafrenieri, designed by Jacopo Barozzi da Vignola, and completed by his son Giacinto. The church served as the confraternity chapel, and as a pilgrims' church on the road into the Vatican.[10] The Jesuit-sponsored confraternity of the Vergini Miserabili Pericolanti took over an old medieval church, which they then rebuilt as S. Caterina dei Funari, to the designs of Guidetto Guidetti, from 1560 to 1564. It served the confraternity, the girls under its protection, and the public. Now not readily accessible, it apparently maintains the basic simplicity of sixteenth-century interior design, without later more grandiose embellishments. Finally in this context it is worth mentioning S. Maria dell'Orto, for the hospital confraternity of fruitsellers. Built slowly between the 1490s and 1563 (and fully consecrated only in 1583), it served various guilds and families in the Trastevere area. An oratory was also attached for the private devotions of the founding guild-confraternity. In these confraternity complexes the company largely controlled its environment and design; it could open the church to the public for some services and so earn prestige, but it could ensure private worship, and facilities for business or social meetings.[11]

The independent confraternity buildings and rooms used for the more private celebrations and meetings are the most significant for understanding the aims and roles of confraternities through visual evidence. The independent structures were likely to be rectangular blocks, with one main room on each of two levels, with the actual size varying considerably according to the numbers and wealth of the members. Venice provides surviving examples, great and small. There are the most spectacular *Scuole Grandi* buildings such as those of S. Rocco (still a confraternity) and S. Marco, the facade of which serves as a main entrance to the city hospital. The lavish external decorating was done in a competitive spirit, a fact we will return to later.[12] Somewhat more modest is the Scuola di S. Maria dei Mercanti (next to the church of Madonna dell'Orto) (Plate 1). This has the two floors of the standard model, well-proportioned with restrained classical decoration externally, to the design of Andrea Palladio in 1570. Over the side-door is a low-relief carving showing the Virgin and Child, with Saints, protecting the *confratelli* under the canopy of her cloak — a traditional Madonna della

[9] L. H. Heydenreich and W. Lotz, *Architecture in Italy 1400–1600* (Harmondsworth, 1974), pp. 282–3, 384 n. 42; R. Wittkower, *Art and Architecture in Italy 1600–1750* (rev. paperback edn., Harmondsworth, 1973), pp. 103–4; Blunt, *Guide*, p. 48; *Guida — Roma*, p. 180.

[10] M.J. Lewine, 'Vignola's church of Sant'Anna de' Palafrenieri in Rome', *The Art Bulletin*, 47 (1965), 199–209; Blunt, *Guide*, pp. 14–15; *Guida — Roma*, pp. 562–3.

[11] Lewine, *Interior*, p. 29, 38–40, 56, 62, 178–91; Blunt, *Guide*, pp. 26, 102; *Guida — Roma*, pp. 440–1. Guidetti may also have helped design this church.

[12] On confraternity rooms: Rosand, p. 89; Howard, pp. 98, 110; J. Schulz, *Venetian Painted Ceilings of the Renaissance* (Berkeley and Los Angeles, 1968), pp. 81–91. See generally on the building of the *Scuole Grandi*: Logan, *Culture and Society in Venice 1470–1790* (London, 1972), pp. 204–71; Howard, pp. 96–112; AA.VV. *Scuole di Arti Mestieri*, pp. 74–9 (S. Rocco), 103–8 (S. Marco); Lorenzetti, pp. 336–8 (S. Marco), 593–600 (S. Rocco); Pullan, *Rich and Poor*, pp. 96, 118–19, 125–6, 129; N-E. Vanzan Marchini (ed.), *La Memoria della Salute. Venezia e il suo ospedale dal XVI secolo al XIX secolo* (Venice, 1985), esp. pp. 112–13, illustrations on p. 15 (facade entrance), pp. 22–3 (main hall), pp. 114–15 (entrance hall), pp. 118–37 (decorations).

1 Scuola di S. Maria e S. Cristoforo dei Mercanti, Venice (see pp. 90, 239). Designed by Andrea Palladio for the confraternity of S. Cristoforo, 1570, before amalgamation with the brothers of S. Maria in 1576.

Misericordia image.[13] Smaller still is the Scuola di Sant'Alvise's rectangular building (near the church of that name), which was built in 1402 and restored in 1608, and is now somewhat dilapidated. Its dimensions and limited pretensions suited the select group of *cittadini originari*, worthy middle-class brethren, who belonged to the fraternity.[14]

In the larger confraternities there might be two major meeting rooms, one for assemblies of the whole fraternity, and a smaller one for council meetings or lesser religious occasions. There were altars in both main rooms, there being no strict division between religious and business functions. The Venetian *Scuole Grandi* had a large *salone* (or *sala grande*), and a smaller *albergo*. The Scuole Grandi of S. Rocco and Della Misericordia had these above a lower hall, *androne*, for more informal meetings, and for the distribution of alms and food for the poor. In Perugia the Oratory of S. Francesco (now the Sodalizio Braccio Fortebraccio) is an independent building with a very modest and inconspicuous outward appearance. Within there is a large and elegant hallway, the rectangular oratory with a major series of paintings and a small sacristy with another altar; there are some other minor rooms tucked in at the back.[15] Many confraternities, however, relied on one main room, which served for all religious, business and social purposes. It might be large, as is the case of the Oratory of S. Giovanni Decollato in Rome, built 1534–5, which set a pattern for sixteenth-century developments. It is a single rectangular room, with an altar at one end opposite the entrance; it has a flat wooden ceiling, with banks of seats along the side and pictorial decoration above. This was for the confraternity members meeting in private. They also had a church for more public celebrations, and ceremonies of thanksgiving for the release of condemned men.[16]

The main confraternity rooms were used for many purposes — for saying and singing prayers, receiving communion, flagellating, or mourning the dead; for general assembly meetings, for scrutinising new applicants, deciding on the distribution of charity, or occasionally for public events such as receiving honoured visitors, and (in the cases of the Venetian Scuola Grande di S. Rocco or Roman SS. Crocefisso) giving concerts of high musical quality.[17] In the sixteenth century confraternity meeting rooms were often well decorated with frescoes or canvases along the walls, as well as with altar paintings or sculptures. It is in this environment that religious art was to be potentially most effective, rather than in most churches. It is often forgotten by the modern church visitor (who may have his own complaints about visibility) how ill-lit many works of art would have been in the sixteenth century — or have been obscured by huge candles and their smoke. Fixed seats did not exist in the nave or most chapels (except round the edge of larger ones), and there were probably few movable benches; worshippers, when not kneeling were probably inattentively ambulatory. Some preachers would draw attention to narrative paintings to illustrate biblical passages. Certain paintings of the Virgin or a saint were the object of intense devotion and veneration, though also

---

[13] AA.VV. *Scuole di Arti Mestieri*, no. 71, pp. 118–19; Pignatti (ed.), *Le Scuole di Venezia* (Milan, 1981), pp. 219–20.

[14] AA.VV. *Scuole di Arti Mestieri*, no. 76, p. 123.

[15] *Guida d'Italia. 14. Umbria* (5th edn, 1966), pp. 93–4. Personal knowledge of the interior from studying archives there. See below on interior at n. 21.

[16] Blunt, *Guide*, p. 50; see below, n. 27.

[17] D. Arnold, 'Music at the Scuola di San Rocco', *Music and Letters*, 40 (1959), 229–41; Henneberg, *L'oratorio*, pp. 49, 58–9.

occasional blame and even damage when the saintly image failed to fulfil the aspirations
of the pleader — but these were iconic, and not pedagogical in their impact.[18] Much
church art was difficult to assimilate under the prevailing conditions, especially before
the seventeenth century produced grandiose illusionistic nave decorations, or large-scale
narrative cycles (in apses or on the ceiling) more readily visible from a distance.[19]

However, in the context of the sixteenth century (and later) confraternity room the
situation was different. There was a smaller, 'controlled' space; the brothers and sisters
could be seated for some time around the sides of the room on benches or carved seats.
At times the room would be well lit, given the confraternal predilection for candles and
the use of elaborate lamp standards. In this environment frescoes or paintings around
the walls, or altar-pieces (some of which might occasionally be taken as banners in
public processions), could be seen and appreciated as stimuli for devotion and charitable
activity, or instructive in the faith. The pictorial content of such confraternity decorations may give us some insights into religious, philanthropic and social attitudes.

2 CONFRATERNITY ART: PEDAGOGY AND PROPAGANDA

The pedagogical aspect of confraternity art, potentially most effective in the more
private confraternity rooms, is best seen in the series of canvases, or frescoes, that were
commissioned to adorn the walls of these rooms; especially series dealing with fundamental Old and New Testament stories, and the lives of saints who were patrons of the
particular confraternity. These were visual Bibles and Golden Legends, instructors in
religious belief and philanthropic commitment, both for the illiterate and for the
well-educated brethren; style and content could be elementary or erudite.

Several series were simply illustrations of the lives of the Virgin and Christ. In Padua
members of the Scuola del Carmine had their room decorated in the first half of the
sixteenth century by various artists, including Domenico and Giulio Campagnola, who
served various local confraternities. They produced a set of paintings around the
meeting room on the life of the Virgin and Christ (in his early life) that combined clarity
and stimulating brightness; an exemplary narrative cycle.[20] A thematically similar series
was commissioned by Perugia's S. Francesco in 1611 from Giovanni Antonio Scaramuccia; eight huge canvases fill the side walls of the oratory above the benches. When last
seen they were grimy and in need of repair, but they would once have been fairly
successful didactic pictures, and hard to ignore. In the painting of Christ disputing with

[18] R. Trexler, 'Florentine religious experience: the sacred image', *Studies in the Renaissance*, 19 (1972), 7–41.
[19] For example, the apse decorations on the life of St Andrew by Mattia Preti in S. Andrea della Valle, Rome,
or Pietro da Cortona's nave ceiling in S. Maria in Vallicella (Chiesa Nuova), Rome. For a complaint that
people in church were too inattentive and ambulatory see the remarks of the Florentine archbishop's vicar to
a Medici prince in 1564: AA.VV. *La Comunità cristiana fiorentina e toscana nella dialettica religiosa del Cinquecento*
(Florence, 1980), p. 53.
[20] *Guida d'Italia. 5. Veneto* (5th edn., 1969), pp. 388–9, and personal visit. The building dates from 1377. On
the theoretical arguments about the need for clarity in religious art, and the recapitulation of Gregory the
Great's arguments about using painting as the Bible for the illiterate: G. Paleotti, *Discorso intorno alle
imagine*, reproduced in P. Barocchi (ed.), *Trattati d'Arte del Cinquecento* (3 vols., Bari, 1960–2), vol. 2, pp.
117–509, esp. pp. 148, 178, 208, 216, 221, 500; R. Alberti, *Trattato della Nobiltà della Pittura*, in ibid., vol.
3, esp. pp. 212–13, 218–19; P. Prodi, 'Ricerche sulla teorica delle arti figurative nella Riforma Cattolica',
Archivio Italiano per la Storia della Pietà, 4 (1965), 123–212, esp. p. 163; M. Baxandall, *Painting and Experience
in Fifteenth-Century Italy* (Oxford and London, 1974 paperback edn.), pp. 40–56.

the Doctors some of the latter appear as gnarled peasants; an intentional comment on their calibre and background? There was a long battle between Scaramuccia and the confraternity over the amount and method of payment, and in 1627 the painter was made to redo one work which seemed to be deteriorating, before he received a 200 *scudi* payment. This is some evidence that the brothers cared for the quality of work produced.[21]

Confraternities often illustrated their specialist concerns or dedications. The Paduan Scuola del Santo (or di S. Antonio), having extended its buildings (1504–5), commissioned various artists to tell the story of St. Antony in fresco; the most famous contribution was an early work by Titian, *The newborn proclaims the innocence of his mother*. In the same city the Scuola di S. Rocco from about 1537 had its room frescoed by the Campagnola family with stories of their plague saint's life and work.[22] In Ferrara the confraternity Della Morte in the mid-sixteenth century had its meeting room above the church. It was adorned with a mixed collection of illustrative, didactic paintings; linked to the Resurrection were several stories about the Cross, and about the Emperor Constantine who was associated with the rediscovery of the True Cross.[23]

In Venice the Scuola di S. Giovanni Evangelista made an early impression with a series of paintings on the Miracles of the True Cross, by Gentile Bellini and V. Carpaccio especially, which gave publicity to the relic that was the confraternity's main pride and devotion. Gentile Bellini's *Procession in Piazza S. Marco* (now in the Accademia Gallery, Venice) depicts the relic carried under a canopy, escorted by brothers with candles.[24] The Scuola di S. Orsola in the 1490s obtained from Vittore Carpaccio eight paintings illustrating her life, though modern critics may find them more interesting as evidence on Venetian social life than of devotion.[25] Carpaccio also provided a set of paintings on the life of St George for the Scuola di S. Giorgio degli Schiavoni, the fraternity for the Slavs; they adorn the lower room of its beautiful

[21] SBF S. Francesco no. 598 (a), 'Carte varie relative ai lavori d'arte esequite nell'Oratorio' 1573–1849, esp. nos. 3 (1573 addition of a sacristy), 4 (a) and (b), and 7–9 dealing with ceiling construction and painting 1577–99, nos. 15, 16, 18, 21, 27–38, 46, 50 which in various ways deal with Scaramuccia's affairs, both his work on and conflict over the paintings, and some land deals in which he was also involved. No. 458 fols. 257r (1618 decision to employ), 259r, (to pay him partly through land income), 267v, 292v, 300v, 315v–6r, 319r, 322v on financial disputes and calls for more money. It might be noted that in 1589 the rank and file members had refused to stop decorating the ceiling as requested by the superiors, and the bishop's vicar had relented in allowing them to continue; the confraternity agreed not to spend money beyond what was already allocated: no. 457 fols. 291v, 293v, 294v.

[22] *Guida — Veneto*, pp. 368., 387; C. Cagli and F. Valcanover, *L'Opera completa di Tiziano* (Milan, 1969), plates I–III, and no. 30 p. 93. H.E. Wethey, *The Paintings of Titian. I. The Religious Paintings* (London, 1969), pp. 9–10, Cat. nos. 93–5 (pp. 128–9), plates 139–43 on the Scuola del Santo works; pp. 173–4 confirm the attribution of the Scuola di San Rocco paintings to the Campagnola, without any involvement by Titian.

[23] G. Medri, *Ferrara* (Ferrara, 1952) lent to me as a guide there, with details of paintings, but not found subsequently. The room is now the Oratorio dell'Annunziata or di S. Apollinare.

[24] Logan, *Culture and Society in Venice*, p. 206; Marconi, *Gallerie . . . secoli XIV e XV*, no. 94 pp. 96–7; S.M. Marconi, *Gallerie dell'Accademia di Venezia. Opere del secolo XVI* (Rome, 1962), nos. 62–4, pp. 61–4; AA.VV. *Scuole di Arti Mestieri*, no. 47. pp. 94–9; Pignatti (ed.), *Le Scuole*, pp. 41–66, and esp. Fig. 47. The *Scuola* was later expanded, and Palma the Younger's story of the Apocalypse became the main pictorial attraction. On Bellini's paintings see chapter 1, n. 5.

[25] Rosand, pp. 41–3, Figs. 25–7 on 'the chatty realism' of Carpaccio's work, and 'the narrative continuity' of his and other Venetian series. Cf. Logan, *Culture and Society in Venice*, p. 206; Marconi, *Gallerie . . . secoli XIV e XV*, nos. 95–103, pp. 97–103; Pignatti (ed.), *Le Scuole*, pp. 68–88, and Figs. 77–90.

2 Scuola di S. Giorgio degli Schiavoni, Venice. Confraternity for the Slavs in Venice, lower room, showing paintings by V. Carpaccio on the life of St George and other Dalmatian saints (see pp. 243, 245)

confraternity building, still used for regular worship. These paintings of the saint's life are an ideal example of illustrative didactic art. (Plate 2) They were commissioned as part of the commemoration of the relic of St George received by the fraternity in 1502. There were also paintings to illustrate the lives of other saints to whom the Slav community owed allegiance, Sts Trifone and Gerolamo (once Bishop of Spalato in Dalmatia). From the sixteenth to eighteenth centuries paintings were provided for the staircase and the *Albergo* on the upper floor; there some space was given over to commemorating the patronage of confraternity officials — sometimes out of proportion to the religious scenes also painted in the room.[26]

Two leading Roman confraternities, the SS. Crocefisso di S. Marcello and S. Giovanni Decollato, had more elaborate intellectual approaches in their narrative cycles — as befitted their more erudite memberships. (Aesthetically they are less appealing than Carpaccio's works). In the Oratory of S. Giovanni Decollato the frescoed narrative cycle (painted by various artists from 1536 to the 1550s) not unnaturally tells the life story of the Baptist. There is a strong didactic emphasis on the importance and impact of preaching (as in Jacopino del Conte's *Preaching*), an art which was used by the comforters to secure the confession and repentance of the imprisoned and condemned. Battista Franco's uncommon subject, *Arrest of the Baptist*, is interpreted by J. Weisz as a visual statement of the relationship between the sacraments of Baptism and Eucharist. This painting, like others in the oratory, has visual and theological allusions to Michelangelo's work, which should have been appreciated by the members of this particular confraternity.[27] The Oratory of SS. Crocefisso is decorated with scenes from the medieval *Legenda Aurea* account of the story of the wood from which the Cross was made. Von Henneberg considers that the narrative cycles found here and in S. Giovanni Decollato are based upon Sacred Representations, a notable feature of fifteenth-century Florentine drama. The didactic purpose is common to both. The Florentine influence is explained by the fact that these two confraternities were dominated by Florentines living in Rome. In the SS. Crocefisso narrative each scene is introduced by a Prophet or Sybil, whose postures stress the educational function of the scenes depicted. The structure of the building and its narrative decorations intensify the sense of collective participation in an educational religious experience.[28]

Some chapels within large churches could come close to the conditions of the independent oratory. The Capranica family possessed a chapel in S. Maria sopra

[26] Lorenzetti, pp. 366–9; AA.VV. *Scuole di Arti Mestieri*, no. 5, pp. 38–9, with illustration of lower room and St George slaying the dragon; Pignatti (ed.), *Le Scuole*, pp. 99–118, esp. pp. 108–17 and figs. 116–30 for Carpaccio's works. Upstairs there are inscriptions such as: 'Vettor Tromba Guardian e Compagni MDLXXXV. ADIXV MAZO', or (all in capitals):' Giorgius Pallavicinus e Perastus Novarchus cum esset collegii huius scriba tempore pestilentiae ex voto anno MDCXXXI Guardiano Iacobo e Petro De Sebenico Vicario Nicolao Gallio Iustiza Protho Ingeni', next to a painting of the Virgin and child with Sts Sebastian and Rocco.

[27] J.S. Weisz, *Pittura e misericordia; the Oratory of S. Giovanni Decollato in Rome*, esp. pp. 79–86 and Fig. 22 (J. Del Conte's *Preaching*), pp. 95–8 and Fig. 25 (Franco's *Arrest*); R.E. Keller, *Das Oratorium von San Giovanni Decollato in Rom* (Rome, 1976) has better reproductions of the same, Figs. 12 and 19; Blunt, *Guide*, p. 50. The oratory is open for worship and readily visible.

[28] Henneberg *L'oratorio*, esp. pp. 52–7 on the impact of drama, and the sense of belonging. The painters involved in the 1570s–1580s: Giovanni de' Vecchi, Niccolò Circignani (Il Pomarancio), Cesare Nebbia, Paris Nogari, Cristoforo Roncalli; Vannugli, pp. 429–43; Blunt, *Guide*, p. 33. This oratory is now sometimes used for concerts, but otherwise difficult to see inside.

Minerva which was for the use of a Rosary confraternity. Giovanni De' Vecchi here painted scenes from the life of Catherine of Siena (whose body lay in the chapel) and Marcello Venusti painted the mysteries of the Rosary on the vault. Though the chapel is not completely autonomous there was sufficient containment of the worshippers to give a sense of corporate solidarity as in an oratory. So the learned members of this confraternity could have concentrated upon the didactic narrative art which is in a complicated mannerist style — assisted by some explanatory inscriptions (now covered over).[29]

The best-known illustrative series of paintings produced for a sixteenth-century confraternity are probably those in Venice's Scuola Grande di S. Rocco. S. Rocco is a monument to the talents of Tintoretto (Jacopo Robusti), who worked there from 1564 to 1587, the artist who contributed most to confraternity art.[30] In 1564 the ceiling of the upper *albergo* room was prepared to receive paintings; various artists submitted designs, but Tintoretto showed his determination to win the contract by installing a full painting in a prepared oval frame, and offered it as a gift. The whole Scuola was summoned to decide whether this was acceptable; despite some opposition, the majority accepted the gift and awarded Tintoretto the contract. Thereafter the artist used various gambits, including offers to paint some portions in return for expenses only, to ensure he was able to paint each successive stage; he filled the ceiling and walls of the *albergo* (1564–6), the upper *sala grande* (1575–81), and finally the lower hall (1583–7). The confraternity received a vast set of illustrations of the lives of Mary and Jesus, and a commemoration of the patron saint, St Roch/Rocco. Tintoretto's ambitious programme involved linking many New Testament stories with analogies or prefigurations from the Old. It is unclear how much advice Tintoretto received from the fraternity in developing the programme, and how much was Tintoretto's interpretation. Some of the linkages are commonplace, but others are not. The Rock of Horeb is seen as a type for the baptism of Christ; the Rain of Manna, Elijah and Elisha, the Paschal Feast were visually and typologically close to the Last Supper; the Brazen Serpent is positioned above the Resurrection and Ascension of Christ.

The Tintoretto paintings, especially in the upper hall, strongly emphasise the cleansing and life-giving powers of baptism and the eucharist. In the *albergo* there are personifications of Charity, Felicity, Liberality and Truth. The *Great Crucifixion* scene, which occupies a whole wall of the *albergo* (Plate 3), with its powerful emphasis on the raising of the three crosses, appears to overflow into the room, the crowd in the painting absorbing those in the room. Portraits of the Scuola's leading officials and brethren were probably included in the crowd. Finally it is worth noting the *Last Supper* painted for this series. It includes two beggars waiting for charity, positioned below steps that place them outside the historical scene, and are by implication connected with the viewers of the painting. For a philanthropic confraternity feeding the spirit — their own and

---

[29] C. Strinati, 'Espressione figurativa e committenza confraternale nella Cappella Capranica alla Minerva (1573)', *RSRR*, 5 (1984), 395–428.

[30] For what follows see esp.: R. Pallucchini, *Tintoretto a San Rocco* (Venice, 1937); Logan, *Culture and Society in Venice*, pp. 206–10; Schulz, pp. 86–93; Rosand, pp. 182–218; Pignatti (ed.), *Le Scuole*, pp. 151–86 and Figs. 171–219. For Tintoretto's work for lesser confraternities see P. Humphrey and R. Mackenney, 'The Venetian trade guilds as patrons of art in the renaissance', *The Burlington Magazine*, 128 (1986), 317–30, with Fig. 4 illustrating one of them, *The Baptism of Christ*, for the Scuola dei peateri, bargemen.

3 Scuola Grande di S. Rocco, Venice. Sala dell'Albergo, upstairs, showing Jacopo Tintoretto's vast Crucifixion painting, 1565 (see p. 246).

others' — and feeding the hungry poor are inseparable. D. Rosand has concluded that with Tintoretto and his work in the Scuola di S. Rocco in particular: 'The act of painting has become a gesture of piety' and 'in every respect, Tintoretto's is the voice of the Venetian *scuole* and the society they represent'. In 1577 Tintoretto had declared his dedication to S. Roch (San Rocco) and the Scuola:

> Now wishing to demonstrate the great love that I bear towards the said revered Scuola through the devotion that I feel for the glorious *messer* San Rocho, from my desire to see this scuola finished and adorned with pictures wherever they may be needed, I am content and undertake to dedicate the remainder of my life to his service, promising to carry out, besides the aforesaid ceiling, all the other pictures in the Scuola . . . and I promise each year for the feast of San Rocho to install three large paintings . . .[31]

There were doubts from some brethren about his monopoly of the decoration (as indicated by various votes in council meetings), but in the event the confraternity secured a vast array of paintings that should have given assembled members ample stimuli for piety, for thought about the Bible, the sacraments, and charitable dispositions, as well as aesthetic pleasure. These paintings also helped this Scuola win the battle for prestige that had been waged between the *Scuole Grandi* for over a century.

The motivation behind confraternity art patronage was obviously mixed, though we have limited direct testimony of their attitudes. Educational and devotional motivations were coupled with a competitive spirit between confraternities, with a desire to have the donors or officials remembered by their successors for their benefit in this world or the next. Philanthropy and vainglory were intertwined. When the Venetian Scuola of SS. Trinità opined in 1550 that it still had insufficient pictures, the Guardian was authorised to spend a small sum on paintings — to honour the Trinity, adorn the Scuola, and encourage devotion in the people.[32] When the Perugian confraternity of S. Agostino decided on new decorations for its Oratory in 1616 a paper outlining motivations and attitudes was prepared and read to the assembly. It argued that three main considerations entered into the ornamentation of divine temples for the worship of God. The first was beauty linked to magnificence, making the work rich and delightful, and equally praiseworthy on both grounds; secondly it should induce in the onlookers piety and devotion, and by the representation of virtuous examples inspire the desire for good, from which Christian perfection should grow; thirdly the paintings should be durable, so that the work could be maintained and receive praise in future centuries, and earn credit through longevity. The document elaborated on various aspects of the three conditions. Arguing that the soul was nourished through the eyes, both for good and ill, paintings were most suitable in sacred places to encourage the imbibing of goodness. Painting was preferred to tapestries and silks in decorating because though a less rich medium, it was physically less susceptible to damage, and closer to perfection. So the confraternity was recommended to decorate with paintings of the lives of their protectors and advocates, St Philip and St James. Then G.C. Angeli was commissioned to execute twelve large canvases, subject to the scrutiny of the

---

[31] Rosand, p. 216 for both quotations; my translation of the Tintoretto text. The full text of two letters from him in 1577: Pallucchini, *Tintoretto*, pp. 14–17.

[32] ASVen Scuole piccole, Busta 706, 'Libro Primo' fol. 87r: 'ad honor et laudi della Sant. ma trinita et per adornamento de detta nostra Schuola, necnon per indur le persone a devotion'.

brethren.[33]

A factor not stated in this document, but one that should not be forgotten, was the element of competition between Perugian confraternities, particularly with another of the confederated trio, S. Francesco, busy redecorating with paintings since 1611, as noted above. There seems little doubt that in the early sixteenth century the Paduan *scuole* mentioned for their narrative cycles were emulating each other. In Rome when the SS. Crocefisso was planning a new oratory and having difficulties over a site in about 1561, it secured the measurements of the oratory of the Gonfalone confraternity, to make sure its own would be bigger.[34]

The competitive factor was most blatant in Venice. An official of the Scuola di S. Giovanni Evangelista back in 1441 clearly stated this when he argued that it was necessary:

to consider the provision of the things that are most necessary, acting always in praise of God and for the glory of our Evangelist, St John, and for the honour and increase of our confraternity in respect of all other flagellant confraternities in this land. On [this] day, from the purses of its brothers, the Scuola di San Marco is constructing its rooms and meeting house and an [ornate] ceiling at great expense near SS. Giovanni e Paolo. And even the Scuola della Misericordia is increasing and enlarging [its] meeting house with other additions and expenditures opportune for that purpose . . . [It is therefore important that] for the honour of God and *messer* St John . . . our confraternity have a commodious meeting place according to God and reason.

In 1506 the Scuola della Carità prefaced a lesser commission: 'Because it is necessary first to honour God and then to be equal to the other confraternities, it is necessary to have a painted banner.'[35]

So the Venetian *Scuole Grandi* indulged in a considerable programme of competitive building and decoration, employing the best architects and painters. Some of the finished results can be admired today, but many projects, notably the new Scuola della Misericordia remained incomplete — 'a depressing monument to the absurd competitiveness of the Venetian Scuole Grandi'.[36] It was absurd in that it created considerable financial problems. Instead of attracting new wealth that might have funded other projects, those philanthropic funds were sacrificed. There were desperate attempts to be allowed by the Council of Ten to enrol new members to raise cash in the short term, but many of these new members might become a burden later. The unseemly

---

[33] V. Tiberia, 'L'Oratorio di S. Agostino a Perugia. Appunti per una storia dal XVI al XIX secolo', *Storia dell'Arte*, 38–40 (1980), 291–310, with plates in a second volume, esp. pp. 302–3: 'La prima è vaghezza congiunta a magnificenza, che faccia l'opera ricca e dilettevole e per l'uno e per l'altro rispetto non men lodata, che ammirabile. La seconda conditione è che apporti à gli animi de' riguardanti un non so che di pietà, e di devotione, le quale per gli esempi delle virtù rappresentate ravvivi i sopiti desiderij al bene, e sparga per la volontà, e gli affeti i semi delle computationi e de' santi e buoni propositi; onde poscia germogli la vera perfettione Christiana. La terza e l'ultima è una certa durabilità . . . La seconda conditione . . . cioè addurre à gli Animi de' riguardanti una certa pietà e devotione, la quale gli stimola al bene operare . . . '. G.C. Angeli was a Perugian, much influenced by various Bolognese artists. The cycle of paintings is not stylistically or thematically coherent — unlike the rival S. Francesco's — and it was not completed until the 1680s, with the successive employment of B. Gagliardi and M. Battini.

[34] Henneberg, *L'oratorio*, p. 16. The oratory was designed by G. Della Porta, and built with the assistance of G. Guidetti and Tommaso dei Cavalieri, Michelangelo's friend.

[35] W.B. Wurthmann, 'The *Scuole Grandi* and Venetian Art, c. 1260–c. 1500', (PhD Thesis, Chicago University, 1975), pp. 150, 194; adapted from his translations, for the use of which I am most grateful. On the Scuola di S. Giovanni Evangelista see above, note 24; on the Carità, below n. 45.

[36] Howard, p. 112.

competition led to a satirical poem, *Il Sogno di Caravia*, probably written by a jeweller called Alessandro Caravia, which particularly attacked the extravagance of the Misericordia, its pride and folly in trying to compete with S. Rocco, leading to the starvation of the poor. Prestige, at least outside the competing companies, was thus diminished, not increased. To some extent the lesser *scuole*, such as the *scuole delle arti*, imitated their seniors in altar-pieces and decorations, though with less damage to their financial and spiritual health.[37] When the *scuola piccola* of SS. Trinità decorated its premises in 1535, and needed 400 ducats to pay for a decorated ceiling, it was made clear that this must not involve taking money from the poor.[38] It showed some awareness of the possible criticisms.

Officials and donors desired to perpetuate the record of good deeds through confraternity art — allying themselves to the company's reputation. When in 1519 the officials of the guild-confraternity of shoemakers in Udine commissioned an *Annunciation* from Pellegrino da San Daniele, their names were recorded at the bottom of the parapet running between two figures, in the centre of the painting (Accademia, Venice). The painting cost 32 ducats. Similarly when Veronese and his assistants painted a *Madonna of the Rosary* (Accademia) in 1573 for the Rosary confraternity in S. Pietro Martire, Murano, they recorded the officials' names on the steps of the throne. Probably more frequently officials and others sought to ensure that their portraits were included among adoring crowds, as almost certainly in this Rosary picture — though specific identifications are usually hard to prove.[39] To take other Venetian examples — Titian's famous *Presentation of the Virgin in the Temple* painted between 1534 and 1538 for the Scuola Grande of S. Maria della Carità (and now incorporated into the Accademia gallery) portrayed *confratelli* as witnesses.[40] Paris Bordone's *Giving of the Ring to the Doge* (Accademia) recorded, in the lower left, some officials of the Scuola of S. Marco, for whose *albergo* it was painted in the early 1530s. Paris Bordone himself became a brother in 1534.[41] Members of the Scuola di S. Maria e S. Cristoforo dei Mercanti were more ostentatious in having two group portraits, with eighteen figures in each, painted by Domenico Tintoretto in 1591–2; they were placed beside the altar, and completed a series of decorations by Jacopo and/or Domenico Tintoretto, and Antonio Aliense for the *sala*. Jacopo was a member of the confraternity.[42]

[37] *Ibid.*, pp. 105–6; Logan, *Culture and Society in Venice*, pp. 204–5; on imitation and emulation by the *scuole delle arti*, Humphrey and Mackenney, esp. pp. 318–321; on Caravia, and some trouble with the Inquisition for his criticisms and for possible Lutheran interests, Mackenney, *Traders and Tradesmen*, pp. 176–8; Martin, 'Popular culture', p. 117.

[38] ASVen Scuole piccole, Busta 706, 'Libro Primo', fols. 12r–13r.

[39] Marconi, *Gallerie . . . secolo XVI*, no. 276 pp. 168–9 (Pellegrino, alias Martino da Udine, 1467–1547), nos. 143 and 144, pp. 90–2 (Veronese, alias Paolo Cagliari), For examples of officials from the *scuole delle arti* being portrayed in paintings, Humphrey and Mackenney, p. 323.

[40] Marconi, *Gallerie . . . secolo XVI*, no. 451 pp. 258–9; Rosand, pp. 85–144 esp. pp. 123–4 on confraternity officials; Cagli and Valcanover, p. 109 no. 184; Pignatti (ed.), *Le Scuole*, p. 34 and Fig. 27 for Titian's *Presentation*: the leading *confratello*, dressed in red, has been identified as Senator Andrea dei Franceschi, who was also a friend of the painter.

[41] Marconi, *Gallerie . . . secolo XVI*, no. 117 pp. 70–2.

[42] *Ibid.*, nos. 379–80 p. 215; A. Clarke and P. Rylands, *Restoring Venice. The Church of the Madonna dell'Orto* (London, 1977), p. 14 and plates 6 and 8, on Scuola's attitude to the neighbouring church [beautifully restored by the British Venice in Peril fund]; ASVen Scuole piccole, Busta 413, esp. unnumbered folder of 18 sheets, 1574–91 (starting 'Fu presentato, letto e porta parte . . .'), fols. 17r–18v; AA.VV. *Scuole Arti Mestieri*, no. 71 pp. 118–19 with Fig. XI for left hand panel of portraits.

That vanity affected the commissioning of works, with the desire to commemorate individuals, is clear; there were irate protests from some brothers of the same Scuola dei Mercanti when Veronese's *Annunciation* (Accademia) was installed above the door of the *albergo*, because it obscured a stone commemorating a former governor responsible for earlier building expansion. It was eventually agreed to have a differently placed inscription above the *albergo* door briefly noting the said governor's contribution. Stones could be more lasting memorials than portraits incorporated into paintings — as the critical arguments over portrait identifications demonstrate.[43]

But it is too simple to dismiss the commemorations in paintings as manifestations of vainglory. The inclusion of brethren in a scene as adorers of the Virgin, or as witnesses to an event such as her Presentation implied an association of those individuals and of that confraternity with the adoration, and with the contemplation of great events. The picture was proof of belief, worship and participation. In return there was the hope that blessings and benefits offered in the pictorial world would accrue to the brethren in reality and earn favourable intercessions for a quicker passage to heaven. Paris Bordone and Tintoretto portrayed brothers and neighbours in their adoring crowds, and so gave individuals additional satisfaction. When Federico Barocci painted the *Madonna del Popolo* for an Arezzo confraternity (to be discussed below) without visiting the city, his depiction of *confratelli* symbolised corporate participation. But irrespective of individual portraiture, all fraternity members in agreeing to pay for, and house, devotional paintings were implying their participation in the events depicted, or in the acts of charity, and were all seeking recognition in return — for the group as well as for individuals.

These points about participation and commitment are best illustrated in Mirabello Cavalori's painting for the Florentine company of S. Tommaso in 1568: *Father Cini as St Thomas and the fellows of the confraternity* (still in the Oratory). Santi Cini founded the sodality in that year, or just before, for priests and laymen. The painting shows St Thomas Aquinas, apparently looking like Cini, surrounded by brothers, while above is the Trinity surrounded by *putti*. The names of kneeling brothers are written on their cloaks, a chain links them to their founder/saint, and flowers of spiritual grace fall on them from heaven. Ribbons of explanatory writing allude to the society's intended philanthropy, with one saying: 'charitatem habete quod est vinculum perfectionis', 'you have charity which is the chain of perfection'. A ribbon linking the saint's gesturing right hand with the Trinity: 'sic currite ut comprehendatis', 'so run that you may grasp'. From Christ's hand a third ribbon runs down warning: 'non coronabitur nisi qui legittime certabitur', 'there will be no crowning unless it be legitimately striven for'. This painting demonstrates the interlocking of individuals within the group, their beliefs and functions in this world and the connections with the next world and its rewards. It is a testament to fraternal dedication, and witnesses to the belief in a hard-earned reward. The recording of names is an act of commitment, not vanity.[44]

Confraternity paintings, though vainglorious in some cases, were acts of worship, of belief, and part of an educational process. Motivations were interlocking, but seldom

---

[43] ASVen Scuole piccole, Busta 413, folder (as in n. 42), fol. 11r–v, 29 October 1581, agreed by 18–4 to have a new incription: 'Fù fatto questo Albergo l'anno 1573 essendo Gov.° il Mag.° M. Valentin Cesaro'.

[44] AA.VV. *La Comunità cristiana*, pp. 209–10, Fig. 10; D'Addario, *Aspetti*, pp. 53, 55, 424–5, 429. Santi Cini died in 1570; his society was impressive enough for Carlo Borromeo to visit it in 1574.

articulated. In 1538 the Venetian Scuola della Carità, having received Titian's *Presentation of the Virgin*, decided to proceed with further decoration of their rooms:

How necessary and appropriate to mortal men are the adornments of the tabernacle of omnipotent God and the most glorious protectress, mother of charity, our Holy Lady Mary, cannot be expressed with words . . . As a result, they [the adornments] not only increase devotion but kindle the souls of many, who, all the more willingly and with good heart, may hasten to enrol in the aforesaid confraternities and congregations.[45]

3 PAINTINGS: PROCESSIONAL AND PHILANTHROPIC

It is worth considering more particularly the message-making of confraternity art in two outward-looking aspects. Firstly, some works were designed to communicate publicly with the outside community, and secondly, certain commissions were intended to encourage the brotherhood to act outwardly in philanthropic ways.

Some confraternity art was used in procession and so exhibited to non-members. Confraternities when they formed public processions took large and small crosses, reliquaries often protected by canopies, and candles and tapers — as well as banners or *gonfaloni*. These could be painted cloths with confraternity emblems, or simple pictures of Christ, the Virgin or a saint. But sometimes large and elaborate paintings were involved. The use of the word *gonfalone* (or *palio*) can ambiguously cover the whole range. The processional use of paintings and standards seems to have been popular in the fifteenth century at least in Umbria, Tuscany and Rome. Their survival rate was obviously limited, especially if they were often paraded; some soon became prized enough to be kept permanently indoors as altar-pieces. A *Beheading of St John the Baptist* (in the Opera del Duomo museum in Florence) on cloth has just been attributed to Antonio Veneziano, and identified as an early *gonfalone* from the first decade of the fifteenth century, though it is not clear who used it. In Umbria in the fifteenth century banners might also be commisioned by civic councils and guilds, but entrusted to a favoured confraternity for safe keeping and suitable veneration when not being paraded.[46]

In Rome in the later fifteenth century a painter called Antoniazzo specialised in producing banners for confraternities, such as that for the SS. Annunziata at S. Maria sopra Minerva. In 1505 he was commissioned by the company of S. Antonio di Padova in Rieti to paint their saint on a silk standard with gold and ornaments — for which they paid 100 ducats, two quarts of grain, and free hospitality in Rieti while he worked on it. It would advertise the devotion, and wealth, of the parading confraternity.[47]

[45] Rosand, pp. 89 and 234 Doc. 19, combining his and my translations; pp. 85–144 discuss this masterpiece at length, with plate 5 and Fig. 56; and see above n. 35. For an early example of a confraternity debate about ordering an altar-piece, and what should be included cf. H. Glasser, *Artists Contracts*, pp. 62–4; the Compagnia della Trinità, Pistoia, in 1455 commissioned a work from Francesco Pesello as the absence of an altar-piece was detrimental to the Company. There was some debate on what should be spent, and which saints should be included.

[46] A. Ladis, 'Antonio Veneziano and the representation of emotions', *Apollo*, CXXIV, no. 295 (September 1986), 154–61, Fig. 3; on *gonfaloni* generally: Wackernagel, pp. 138–41. Michael Bury (Edinburgh University) is currently writing a major book on Umbrian banners, based on archival materials and surviving banners. He sees the confraternities as the chief custodians of *gonfaloni*, even if civic councils or guilds commissioned and paid for them.

[47] Cavallaro, 'Antoniazzo Romano', pp. 354–6.

During the fifteenth century Perugia, and Umbria generally, produced a number of elaborate standards, that continued in use and survived the centuries, often as fixed altar-pieces. In 1465, or later, Benedetto Bonfigli of Perugia produced the *Gonfalone di S. Bernardino* (now in the National Gallery or Pinacoteca, Perugia), which showed St Bernardino of Siena and Christ surrounded by a choir of angels with below, on a disproportionately small scale, officials of the city and the bishop offering candles to help the construction of the confraternity Oratory which commemorated the saint and his work. This painting became the pride of the confraternity and city and was periodically paraded. From 1473 it was kept in the Oratory, set into a niche which depicted the miracles of the saint.[48] In 1466 the newly founded S. Annunziata based in S. Maria dei Servi (and after 1540 in S. Maria Nuova) commissioned its *Gonfalone dell'Annunziata* — probably from Nicolo di Liberatore called L'Alunno. Below the Annunciation scene is a group of the confraternal lawyers who founded this devotional confraternity, dressed in red legal togas, or confraternity garb, and seeking intercessions (Pinacoteca, Perugia) (Plate 4). The confraternity still used this standard in the seventeenth century.[49]

In 1501 a greater artist, Pietro Perugino, painted the *Gonfalone della Giustizia* (Pinacoteca, Perugia) for the confraternity of S. Andrea (or Della Giustizia) which escorted the condemned to execution. It shows the Madonna in glory, with Sts Francis and Bernardino. The depiction of the crowd, including women and children, behind the saints was designed to encourage corporate involvement in intercessional prayers and processions. Some on the left are white-garbed and hooded confraternity brethren; two on the right act as escorts for the women.[50] Perugino also painted a small *gonfalone* on silk in 1499 for the confraternity of S. Francesco; it shows four brothers of the discipline confraternity kneeling in prayer behind the saint. The picture clearly shows the hoods that could be pulled forward during public ceremonies to ensure anonymity (Pinacoteca, Perugia).[51]

It is not clear how often in the sixteenth and seventeenth centuries major paintings — as opposed to simpler banners — were used during public processions. In the mid-sixteenth century in Arezzo the S. Maria della Misericordia annually on 2 June paraded on a stand its painting of *The Virgin protecting the people of Arezzo, with Sts Lorentinus and Pergentinus*, by Parri Spinelli (1435; Pinacoteca, Arezzo).[52] In 1631–2

[48] F. Santi, *Gonfaloni Umbri del Rinascimento* (Perugia, 1976), p. 16, Plate II. Measures 392 × 213 cms. The Oratory dates from 1461; the painting puts '1465' on the Oratory which might indicate the picture's date. In 1463 the confraternity had ordered another banner of the Saint, on red silk; Santi, *Galleria Nazionale*, pp. 41–2 and plate 28; Santi, *La Galleria*, p. 27 and plate 32, p. 76; Crispolti, *Perugia Augusta*, pp. 125–7; Marinelli, *Le Confraternite*, p. 209 for Bonfigli work, and for other standards pp. 61, 69, 163–82, 194, 514, 622, 658, 976; E. Hutton, 'The father of Perugian painting', *The Burlington Magazine* 7 (1905) 133–8 on Bonfigli and his banners.

[49] Santi, *Galleria Nazionale*, pp. 36–7 and plate 22; Santi, *Gonfaloni*, p. 18, plate II. L'Alunno also produced a two-sided banner for the company of S. Antonio Abbate, Deruta which on one side (plate VI) shows white-robed *confratelli*, some hooded. On the reverse side is a flagellation scene, witnessed by Sts Egidio and Bernardino.

[50] Santi, *Galleria Nazionale*, pp. 104–6 and plate 89; Santi, *Gonfaloni*, p. 34 plate XXIII; AA.VV. *Pittura in Umbria*, p. 76 (ill.); C. Castellaneta and E. Camesasca, *L'Opera completa del Perugino* (Milan, 1969), p. 105 no. 80; P. Scarpellini, *Perugino* (Milan, 1984), p. 105, Fig. 207, Cat. no. 122. The confraternity amalgamated with S. Bernardino in 1534. The painting includes a view of Perugia. It has suffered from various repaintings.

[51] Santi, *Galleria Nazionale*, pp. 102–3 and plate 87; Santi, *La Galleria*, p. 30 no. 349; AA.VV. *Pittura in Umbria*, p. 79 (ill.); Scarpellini, p. 99, Fig. 176, Cat. no. 176. It is on silk. Perugino, first paid in April 1499, was assisted by Francesco Ciambella, called Il Fantasia, 'suo charzone'. The main figure has been repainted.

[52] T.S.R. Boase, *Giorgio Vasari*, (Princeton, 1979) pp. 181–2, Fig. 117.

4 Nicolo di Liberatore, called L'Alunno, *Gonfalone dell'Annunziata* (Pinacoteca, Perugia). Standard produced for the S. Annunziata confraternity for lawyers, Perugia, 1466. (See p. 253.) The adoring brothers wear legal or fraternal garments.

Guido Reni painted a *Madonna and Child in Glory* (Pinacoteca, Bologna), with various protector saints of Bologna; this was a votive standard ordered by the city officials, to be carried annually in procession, to prevent further devastations by plague. Over the previous two centuries confraternities, churches and communal authorities in Perugia and elsewhere had similarly organised anti-plague standards and processions.[53]

There were probably many simpler standards used in processions. The Venetian Scuola of SS. Trinità in 1541 agreed to renew its processional standard — as part of the battle against heresy. It argued that the poor condition of artefacts dedicated to divine worship caused heretics and infidels to despise the Catholic faith, and worse, caused people to suspect that money given as alms or *luminarie* would be misused. The processional standard had become torn, and no picture could be seen — a matter of great shame and vituperation, said the Guardian. This was especially worrying for a fraternity founded under the Trinity standard, so that it could no longer compare with the least of the fraternities — that of the blind and lame mendicants. So a new standard with a glorious Trinity painted on it was ordered.[54]

Paintings and banners were prophylactics; they were also testimonies to the status, taste and pride of the brotherhood; they might act as incentives to the general public to worship, and possibly to join the confraternity.

As an emblematic illustration of the devotional art of the discipline confraternity we can consider another Perugino painting, the recently cleaned *Madonna della Consolazione*, or *Madonna dei Battuti* (Pinacoteca, Perugia) (Plate 5). It was commissioned by the discipline confraternity of S. Maria Novella in April 1496, but not completed until 1498. It was probably not a *gonfalone*, though sometimes so described, but an altar-piece intended for private contemplation by members of the fraternity. Six robed brothers are kneeling in prayer to the Virgin and child, sharing the adoration of two angels. Two of the brothers wear badges of the Virgin and child — now revealed to close inspection since cleaning.[55] This was devotional art for the inward-looking confraternity; a timeless invitation to the contemplation of salvation through prayer and penitence.

Confraternity art was also used to encourage outward-looking philanthropy, and this appears to be more significant from the mid-sixteenth century. A few works can be discussed here, to be seen both as messages to the brethren, and as possible evidence to the historian of attitudes to philanthropy and salvation, as demonstrated by the confraternity or an influential artist, like Barocci.

Towards the end of his life Giorgio Vasari (d. 1574) was responsible for modernising his home parish church in Arezzo, S. Maria della Pieve (or Pieve di S. Maria). The leading confraternity of S. Maria della Misericordia was based there and asked Vasari to paint the altar-piece in their new chapel, but he died before it could be produced. The confraternity consulted the Arezzo ambassador to the Florentine court, who

[53] C. Garboli, *L'Opera completa di Guido Reni* (Milan, 1971). p. 149, plates XLV–VI. Cf. Perugia's Cathedral *Gonfalone del Duomo* paraded to ward off plague – Santi, *Gonfaloni*, p. 39, plate XXXI; the Virgin implores Christ to spare the Perugians.

[54] ASVen Scuole piccole, Busta 706, 'Libro Primo', fol. 53r, 6 October 1541.

[55] Santi, *Galleria Nazionale*, pp. 101–2 and plate 86; AA.VV. *Pittura in Umbria*, pp. 74–5 (ill.); Santi, *La Galleria*, p. 28 no. 270; Scarpellini, p. 95: he thinks the picture was used in parades. The communal government largely paid when the confraternity claimed it could not afford sixty florins for it; Gallery note, 1986. An exhibition close-up photograph showed the badge well.

5 Pietro Perugino, *Madonna della Consolazione* (Pinacoteca, Perugia) (see p. 255), 1496–8, for the
flagellant confraternity of S. Maria Novella, Perugia. Two brothers show insignia indicating their
special devotion to the Virgin.

recommended Federico Barocci. This artist was developing a reputation for providing
the new kind of religious art required in the Tridentine mood — combining clarity of
interpretation with an emotional commitment and involvement that would win over
onlookers.[56] Barocci was, however, a difficult artist, and a slow worker — partly
because of real or imaginary illnesses allegedly caused by poison. He lived most of his
long life (1535–1612) in his home city of Urbino, jealously and caringly protected by
its Dukes from outside harassment and hurry. The officials of the Arezzo fraternity
suggested to Barocci a painting 'with figures that would represent the mystery of the
misericordia or another mystery and stories of the most glorious Virgin'. Barocci
expressed his willingness to paint for them, but argued that a traditional *Misericordia*
(Virgin of Mercy) subject would not produce a beautiful painting, and he asked for
further suggestions. After various designs and cartoons had been discussed Barocci
produced the highly innovative *Madonna del Popolo* (the *Madonna of the People*, now in
the Uffizi gallery, Florence). There were many delays and complications before it was
delivered in 1579; the confraternity indicated its displeasure over this, and complained
that the finished work was not of the quality expected. Barocci never produced a
separate round painting of God the Father which was to have been placed above the
main picture. It was not unusual for confraternities to complain about delays or the
work submitted — as has been noted with Perugia's S. Francesco. The Arezzo
confraternity's grounds for complaint about quality are not clear form the surviving
documentation. An explanation may be found in comparing the painting with an earlier
sketch; in the latter a gentleman is shown prominently giving alms to a cripple, while
in the finished version the gesture of giving is more discreetly and indirectly shown,
with the relevant gentleman at the edge of the painting, and a child becomes a giver.
The confraternity priors may have been displeased at this reduction in the role of the
donor.[57]

However, Barocci had provided the Arezzo confraternity with a striking painting
in a public church that to most observers then and since must have been excellent
testimony to the members' devotion and philanthropy. In the heavenly scene at the top
the Virgin's intercession leads Christ to bless the activities of the people below, while
through look and gesture, an angel entices observers of the painting to share in similar
charitable work, leading to the desired blessing. On the earthly plane of the painting
women are inviting overdressed children to pray and to observe the blessings from
heaven. However, the children are distracted by a blind musician and by a begging
cripple, but these 'poor', and a mother with basket and child (the group which replaced
the alms-giving gentleman in the earlier sketch) receive philanthropy on earth and
blessings from heaven. Various men in the central areas of the painting are presumably

[56] A. Emiliani, ed. *Mostra di Federico Barocci (Urbino, 1535–1612). Catalogo critico* (Bologna, 1975), is richly
documented, and illustrated. Barocci's new religious art had already been demonstrated in his *Deposition
from the Cross* for Perugia Cathedral, 1568, no. 50, pp. 77–81; with nos. 38–49, pp. 74–8 dealing with earlier
designs; there is a colour plate opposite p. xlviii.

[57] *Ibid.*, no. 106, pp. 112–18. G.R. Walters, *Federico Barocci: Anima Naturaliter* (Ann Arbor and London,
University Microfilms International, 1981), pp. 94–102, interprets the changes as implying that one needs
to become like a little child to enter heaven — cf. Matthew 18: 3. Walters stresses the Franciscan influence
on Barocci, who became a Capuchin Tertiary in 1566 (p. 23). Illustrations of this work in, e.g. C.
McCorquodale, *The Baroque Painters of Italy* (Oxford, 1979), plate 4; S.J. Freedberg, *Paintings in Italy
1500–1600* (Harmondsworth, rev. paperback edn. 1975), plate 257.

intended to represent the charitable confraternity brothers, who divide their attention between earthly problems and celestial salvation. The helix structure of the painting's composition, the interconnections of gestures, looks and colour tones, all emphasise the harmonious interlocking of this world and the next within the painting, while gestures and looks seek to involve the spectator and encourage emulation. Barocci has provided an ideal visual exhortation for a philanthropic confraternity of Marian devotion.

Barocci worked for a number of confraternities and provided them with innovatory interpretations to suit their devotions. For the Urbino Compagnia della Concezione he painted an *Immaculate Conception* in the 1570s (well publicised by a print based on it in 1591), which is notable for its sense of immediacy and involvement of the spectator. He painted for two competing confraternities in Senigallia: the *Burial of Christ* for the Compagnia Della Croce e Sacramento (1578–82), which was immediately popular, copied and damaged, and the *Madonna del Rosario* (completed 1592) for the Confraternita Dell'Assunta e del Rosario, which adeptly combined elements from both the Assumption and Rosary traditions, while remaining simple and emotive. Barocci was providing the confraternities with devotional inspiration, and prestige — even if he was a difficult and costly artist.[58]

Pictorial incentives to exercise philanthropy, based on the Seven Acts of Mercy, came in various forms. Santi di Tito provided inspiration on a small scale for the Florentine confraternity Della Misericordia. In 1579 the brothers commissioned him to decorate the high altar of their oratory. He painted the protecting saints Tobias and Sebastian beside an existing painting of the Virgin, and a *predella* of seven small scenes representing the seven acts. Only three survive (still held by the archconfraternity), following the dismantling of the altar in the eighteenth century: the *Last Supper* (measuring only 19.5 × 85.5 cms) with *Visiting the sick* and *Burying the dead* (both 20 × 86 cms). The Last Supper scene was used to illustrate the feeding of the hungry, with two confraternity members in their black robes present at the institution of the Eucharist, one of them casting an eye towards observers in the oratory to encourage participation. *Burying the dead* has a body being escorted by three priests and nine *confratelli*, wearing black hoods with a red cross emblem, carrying a cross and four lighted torches. In *Visiting the sick* two brothers are visiting Christ — for the sick man has a halo. Here we have a visual reminder of St Matthew 25: 36, 'I was sick and ye visited me'. The simple depictions of, and incitements to, philanthropic actions came from a committed painter — a member of the austere fraternity of St Thomas Aquinas to which he had donated a painting.[59]

A better known depiction of the *Seven Acts of Mercy* is the painting of the whole theme by Caravaggio. It was commissioned by the noble Neapolitan confraternity, Pio Monte della Misericordia. This institution had been started by seven nobles in 1601, who had decided to assist the poor and needy, and had initially based themselves on the

---

[58] Emiliani, ed. *Barocci*: no. 86 pp. 105–6, *Immaculate Conception*; no. 118 pp. 123–5, *Burial of Christ*, for which Barocci wanted 600 *scudi*, but settled for 300, and he was paid 150 *scudi* when he repaired the damage and altered it in 1607–8; no. 198 pp. 168–70, *Madonna del Rosario*, for 500 *scudi*.

[59] AA.VV. *La Comunità Cristiana*, pp. 211–12, Figs. 13–14, and colour plate of the Visiting and Burying scenes opposite p. 241; Santi di Tito, when he became a member of the fraternity, presented it with a work on the Vision or Ecstasy of St Thomas Aquinas as part of his devotion: AA.VV. *Il Primato del Disegno* (Florence, 1980), pp. 35, 204–8, no. 494.

hospital for Incurables. This noble venture expanded, prospered and became in the course of the seventeenth century one of the most significant philanthropic enterprises, involved in virtually all types of good works.[60] Caravaggio's painting was ordered soon after the confraternity had received from Paul V in 1606 a second brief conceding privileges for the high altar in the oratory they were constructing. Caravaggio had recently arrived in Naples, having fled Rome to escape a murder charge and, according to a January 1607 document, he was to be paid 400 ducats — four times the average payment for other paintings the officials were commissioning. Though the documentation on Caravaggio's activities is by no means clear, it is probable that the artist had already painted one other work in Naples, and that the Neapolitan brothers could have received favourable reports on Caravaggio's painting, if not demeanour, from contacts in Rome. The commissioned work was originally entitled *Nostra Signora della Misericordia*.[61]

The Seven Acts of Mercy were traditionally depicted separately, as by Santi di Tito, but Caravaggio's painting incorporates all the charitable actions in one, somewhat confusing, work.[62] They are acted out by twelve persons, who are difficult to distinguish as their bodies are crowded together or are only partially included within the frame. Their activities are observed and blessed by the Virgin (added at a late stage in recognition of the confraternity's dedication to the Virgin), with two swooping angels, conveying mercy. The welcoming of strangers is represented by a stout host on the left (possibly greeting Christ on the way to Emmaus, in H. Hibbard's interpretation); while Samson quenching his thirst from a jaw-bone in the desert suggests the second act. Clothing the naked is indicated by St Martin with a plumed hat offering his cloak to a bare-backed man prominent at the bottom of the scene; a figure hardly visible at bottom left is a reclining sick man waiting to be healed. A second group of figures on the right illustrate the acts of burying the dead (where only the corpse's feet are shown, escorted off by candlelight) and of visiting the imprisoned and feeding the hungry. These last acts are illustrated by one episode where Caravaggio has borrowed from the *Caritas Romana* of Valerius Maximus, with Pero breast-feeding her starving father in prison. Caravaggio's composition, complicated both visually and thematically, hardly conformed to the Tridentine pleas for clarity, but it had, and has, a powerful emotional appeal, as those who managed to see it in the Naples oratory, or London's Royal Academy exhibition (1982), can testify.

The immediate reactions of the confraternity and others to this work were highly favourable, in contrast to the reception of some other Caravaggio works. In 1613 leading noble officials, including those in charge of philanthropy for captives, the sick, and the *poveri vergognosi*, testified that Caravaggio had succeeded absolutely:

---

[60] R. Causa, *Opere d'Arte nel Pio Monte della Misericordia a Napoli* (Cava dei Terreni and Naples, 1970); V. Pacelli, *Caravaggio. Le Sette Opere di Misericordia* (Salerno, 1984), esp. pp. 12–24 on foundation and early history. The oratory suffered in the recent earthquake; the Caravaggio painting was thus released for public exhibition.

[61] On Caravaggio's Madonna painted for Nicolò Radolovich in Naples, and the Pio Monte's Roman contacts, Pacelli, pp. 8–11.

[62] For discussion of the painting and detailed illustrations see esp. Pacelli; H. Hibard, *Caravaggio* (London, 1983), pp. 282–319, Figs. 138–43; *Painting in Naples*, no. 16 pp. 125–8, colour plate p. 65; *Guida d'Italia. 19 Napoli e Dintorni* (5th edn. 1976), pp. 244–5.

Such that it has been made with such excellent artifice to correspond with the greatness of the Good Works of God there represented, and has reached such perfection that more than once 2,000 *scudi* has been offered for it. The said nobles have, however, concluded that it could not be sold for any price, but must always be retained in the [said] church.[63]

They did allow a copy to be made for the Viceroy, the Count of Villamedina, on condition that the original was not removed from the altar — just in case the covetous Viceroy had other ideas. The Pio Monte had an emotional appeal for philanthropic activity, and a highly prestigious work of art.

The Pio Monte brothers did not confine themselves to the Caravaggio in their pursuit of art as a stimulus to their activities, devotions and reputations. In their original oratory they wanted to have seven altars showing seven acts of philanthropy as conducted by the fraternity.[64] They obtained (much more cheaply, at only 120 *scudi*) a *Burial of Christ*, sent from Rome, by G.B. Baglione — Caravaggio's former friend, now enemy, and later an influential art critic. Individual brothers paid for three more works. Fabrizio Santafede's *St Peter reviving Tabitha* may well portray some brothers as witnesses of the joyful scene. Battistello Caracciolo's *Liberation of St Peter from prison* (produced later after various problems and alterations to the contract) was closely related to a major aspect of the confraternity's philanthropy; as was the *St Paolino redeeming a slave*, attributed to Giovan Bernardino Siciliano, called Azzolino, or to Carlo Sellitto. The confraternity raised money to release local indebted prisoners, and Christians enslaved by Turks. Here as the saint looks after the slave newly released from chains, women and children rejoice; from above the Trinity, the Virgin and saints observe and bless the scene below. Santafede's first success led to the commissioning of another work, matching the first in size; this is normally called *Jesus and the Samaritan woman*, but V. Pacelli has recently argued that it is better seen, on biblical grounds (Luke 10: 38–42) as *Jesus received as a pilgrim in the house of Martha and Mary*; there is no well, normally included in the former episode and two observers below the scene seem to be carrying pilgrim batons; it is a colourful, if not very well constructed scene. In 1608 G.V. Forli had been commissioned to paint *The Good Samaritan*; here again the Virgin and angels bless such charity. As one might expect from a confraternity of nobles, the Samaritan had a servant to help him.

The governors appear to have had some misgivings about this last painting, but they were generally proud of their artistic possessions. When a new oratory was planned in the 1650s they considered all the above works precious and irreplaceable, except Baglione's (which was smaller than the others), and the new building was planned to some extent around these treasures. The Baglione painting went into the sacristy, and was replaced by Luca Giordano's *Pietà* to maintain a balanced decoration.

The illustration of two other aspects of confraternity philanthropy is worth exempli-

---

[63] Causa, pp. 28–9. Those expressing this view were Don Carlo Caracciolo (confraternity official for captives), Duca di Cilenza (official for the sick), Marchese di Bracigliano (official for the *poveri vergognosi*).

[64] Causa, pp. 31–4; Pacelli, pp. 71–4 on the plan for seven altars, and the reidentification of the second Santafede painting (Fig. 63). The commission price for this was 150 *scudi*, that for the Forli work 100; three nobles (Carlo Caracciolo di Vico, Duchessa Vittoria Caracciolo di Castro, and Duca di Vietri) paid 300 *scudi* for the first three works by Santafede, Caracciolo and Azzolino. For the Caracciolo *Liberation* see also *Painting in Naples*, no. 7 p. 120; for the Azzolino/Sellitto attribution, W. Prohaska, 'Carlo Sellitto', *The Burlington Magazine*, 117 (1975) 3–12.

fying here. The confraternity of S. Prospero in Reggio Emilia commissioned in 1587–8 a *St Roch distributing alms*, from Annibale Carracci, though it was not completed until 1595. This large canvas (331 × 477 cms, now in Dresden) shows a crowded scene that is well controlled and structured. The crowd is full of mothers and children, though there is also a sick man in a barrow; the painting thus emphasises the poor who should be helped — and the numbers of ordinary people who can be involved in the distribution of alms.[65]

Philanthropy involved praying for the release of souls from Purgatory. A Venetian *scuola* was dedicated to this task: S. Fantin (or Della Giustizia, or di Santa Maria e di S. Girolamo, or other variations). Confraternities meeting in the church of S. Fantin had amalgamated in the mid-fifteenth century; they expanded their buildings at various stages. Following reconstruction after a fire in 1562 and the creation of an imposing facade (1592–1600) Jacopo Palma the Younger was employed to decorate their meeting house (now the Ateneo Veneto) near the church, and most notably the ceiling of the *sala terrena* (1600–3). The confraternity was primarily concerned with comforting condemned men; developing their philanthropy from this the brethren spent much time praying for the expiation of sins, offering masses and good works to secure the release of souls from Purgatory. In this ceiling Jacopo Palma provided thirteen panels depicting help for souls in Purgatory, and the leading Doctors of the Church who had written best about related doctrines. The main scenes, which have received varied titles, stress the value of masses, papal indulgences and alms in helping release souls from the pains of Purgatory. In one panel alms offered to a begging pilgrim lead to the escape of souls (Plate 6). In another this result is achieved by imploring papal intervention (Plate 7). Within their room the brothers had a constant reminder of the object of their prayers, the release of souls from dire torment (shown in two long panels), with the reassurance that the Church's great minds supported their work. S. Fantin provided a full, visual, Counter-Reformation defence of the doctrine of Purgatory.[66]

The above examples show how paintings were used to encourage various types of philanthropic activity; the approach could be very direct, an obvious advocacy of alms-giving or helping the sick, or by analogy to an historical event. A more indirect approach can be found in some paintings by Tintoretto in Venice, especially eucharistic ones. The link between the Last Supper and charity has already been noted in Tintoretto's work for the Scuola Grande di S. Rocco. Tintoretto also found time, with or without the assistance of family and pupils, to paint for the Scuola Grande di S. Marco (the great series on St Mark's life), for *scuole delle arti*, and Sacrament confraternities. Some of the work for the last type is most significant in our context.

[65] D. Posner, *Annibale Carracci. A Study in the Reform of Italian Painting around 1590* (2 vols., London, 1971) no. 86, vol. 2, pp. 35–7, with plate 86, and discussed vol. 1, pp. 51–2.

[66] Lorenzetti, pp. 508–10; Schulz, no. 24 pp. 82–3, plates 142–6; Pignatti (ed.). *Le Scuole*, pp. 187–200 and Figs. 227–9. The saints and teachers involved were, on the left: Athanasius and Basil; Gregory and Jerome; John Chrysostom and Gregory Nazianzen; on the right: Bernard and Bede (not yet recognised as a Doctor of the Church); Augustine and Ambrose. On the late appearance of an iconography for Purgatory see Ariès, *Images of Man and Death*, pp. 160–70, where he stresses that the general image was now (in contrast to rare medieval depictions) of a place run by angels, and where the physical pains were not great. This is born out by Palma's paintings here, and by the influential Guercino *St Gregory and the souls in Purgatory* (S. Paolo, Bologna), where the arising souls are placid and delicate. Cf. Male, *L'Art religieux après le Concile de Trente*, p. 62 and Fig. 29; see above, chapter 4 n. 92.

6 Palma il Giovane, *Offering of Alms for Souls in Purgatory*; panel in the ceiling of lower room in Scuola of S. Fantin, Venice. 1600–3 (see p. 261).

7 Palma il Giovane, *Gaining of Indulgences for Souls in Purgatory*: panel in the ceiling of the lower room in Scuola of S. Fantin, Venice, 1600–3 (see p. 261).

Though few Sacrament confraternities in Venice had their own separate premises like that of S. Giovanni Bragora, a number had control of large-sized chapels within parish churches, and could dominate church affairs. In Tintoretto's original parish of S. Cassiano the Sacrament confraternity paid for vestments, for the Lenten preacher, for altar furnishings; from 1527 it helped elect the organist, and had a major role in planning services and ceremonies. It had special prayers for the release of souls from the pains of Purgatory; the church unusually had its own cemetery. Tintoretto painted the *Resurrection of Sts Cassiano and Cecilia* for the altar of this church, and a *Crucifixion* and *Christ's descent into limbo* for the side-walls of the chapel.

Other Sacrament confraternities commissioned sets of paintings to comment on the eucharist. Because altars were increasingly dominated by elaborate tabernacles for the Host, altar paintings were often omitted, and paintings were set at the sides instead, as *laterali*. Despite previous remarks about the general darkness of many chapels, it should be said that a number of the Venetian chapels are spacious and light enough to allow such *laterali* to be effective. Apparently benches often ran under the *laterali* for confraternity officials who might remain in the chapel to conduct business. Again vanity was sometimes satisfied by having the portraits of officials included, or names recorded on inscriptions.[67]

The visual messages of these paintings could be powerful. Tintoretto's work, possibly influenced by Ignatius Loyola or the Franciscans (especially Capuchins), stressed the link between the eucharist and charity.[68] In the *Last Supper* in S. Polo (Plate 8), Christ thrusts out his arms to feed two disciples, while another gives bread to a beggar on the pavement, and a fourth feeds a child.[69] In the original *Last Supper* in S. Marcuola (Plate 9) one servant comes in on the left with the chalice, to be matched by another on the right with a dish which is being grabbed at by the child she carries; a second child is naked at her feet, pointing out the supper scene. This group traditionally personifies Charity. It shows that spiritual food, and food for the poor and needy cannot be divorced. This last figure, the servant as charity, implies an exchange process whereby charity brings back spiritual food comparable with the eucharist sacrament.[70]

The visual messages are that Christ made the sacrifice for us; we must make physical sacrifices to help the needy, and the body of Christ is present in that physical assistance. This will bring a return in spiritual food for the donor leading to the fulfilment of Christ's sacrifice in salvation.

[67] P. Hills, 'Piety and patronage in Cinquecento Venice: Tintoretto and the Scuole del Sacramento', *Art History*, 6, no. 1 (March 1983), 30–43, and for the S. Cassiano pictures, plates 29–30; Rosand, pp. 206–13 on 'Prandium Caritatis' and Tintoretto's Last Suppers; *Guida d'Italia. 6. Venezia e Dintorni* (2nd edn, 1969), pp. 244–5, 288–9, 305–6; Lorenzetti, pp. 414, 469, 573.

[68] Niero, 'Riforma cattolica', pp. 86–7, 92–6. St Roch was a Franciscan Tertiary. In commenting on the links between eucharist devotion and assistance Niero also points to Tintoretto's S. Giorgio Maggiore *Last Supper*, where Christ's role is that of a poor servant, rather than the master dominating the table.

[69] Hills, plates 24–5; Rosand, fig. 149, and p. 303 n. 71 speculates that Judas' giving a piece of fruit to the child may be interpreted as passing on original sin to the innocent; M. Levey. 'Tintoretto and the theme of the miraculous intervention', *Journal of the Royal Society of Arts*, 113 (1965), 707–25, and Figs. 11–12 for S. Polo. In Venetian S. Polo = S. Paolo. Cf. Zardin, *Confraternite e vita di pietà*, pp. 122–3 on Sacrament confraternities that also looked after the (deserving) poor of the parish.

[70] Hills, plate 23; Rosand, Fig. 147. The original Last Supper is on the left wall; a copy of a *Last Supper* now in Madrid, emphasising the washing of feet, is on the right wall. According to the current (1986) parish priest there is an active confraternity of S. Crocefisso in the church, which in the past has been responsible for burying unidentified corpses found in the canals.

8 Jacopo Tintoretto, *Last Supper*, for the Sacrament confraternity in the church of S. Polo, Venice (see p. 264).

9 Jacopo Tintoretto, *Last Supper*, for the Sacrament confraternity in the church of S. Marcuola, Venice. 1547? (see p. 264).

Confraternities had varied physical environments, which were the product of different confraternal orientations, and which affected the member's behaviour and life. Many brotherhoods were not interested in art, and could not afford to be. But for some, especially those in self-contained environments, paintings in particular made a significant contribution to confraternity life. Some companies spent too lavishly. A major altar-piece from a leading artist could cost as much as fifty dowries or a hundred donations to the poor. But for very mixed reasons brothers cared about their environment and its decoration.

Confraternity art could satisfy the vanity of individual members or the corporate body; it could involve expensive and unseemly competition. But for many, paintings must have been visual reminders of the purposes of the confraternity, devotional and philanthropic. They stressed the need to pray for the souls of the departed, or distribute alms, the requirements to serve the sick or venerate the Host, or the efficacy of invoking the help of the Virgin or a patron saint. The pictures might more simply be used as visual Bibles and saintly stories.

Above all the visual evidence should have emphasised that for some commissioning confraternities, and their committed painters (like Tintoretto and Santi di Tito), the spiritual, the devotional and the philanthropic were all intermingled.

CONCLUSIONS AND SUGGESTIONS

In 1570 an old man called Gaspar Ribeiro moved to a different Venetian parish, S. Maria Formosa; his wife had died the previous year. He was soon a member of the parish Sacrament confraternity, and not long after its *gastaldo*. While he held this office the confraternity commissioned an expensive tabernacle for the Host and redecorated the chapel, where an inscription apparently read: 'Gaspar Ribeiro has had this done'. He lent hangings to the church when it needed special decorations, he gave alms to friars who called at his door, he carried a candle or torch behind the Host on Good Friday, and he occasionally took communion himself. This account might be typical of stalwart old middle-class Venetian men. But Gaspar was not a typical *cittadino*, but a member of a *marrano* family of merchants, Portuguese Jews who had been converted to Christianity.[1]

Gaspar had been born in or near Lisbon in 1493–4, had travelled and traded with many parts of the world before arriving in Venice, from Ratisbon, in about 1560. He and his son João from there traded in jewels, spices, meat and money. The family first faced the Inquisition in 1569 when a daughter Violante publicly and noisily protested that her brother was trying to beat her into marrying a Jew. The Inquisition dropped the investigations when it was agreed that she should marry a good Christian; three years later she married into a noble family from Vicenza. Gaspar himself took a good Christian from Venice as his second wife in 1574. But in 1580 the Inquisition again investigated Gaspar and his family; he died in 1581 while the case was proceeding. Three years later the investigation ruled that he had been an apostate and judaizer, and his body was ordered to be buried at night among the Jews. B.S. Pullan concluded that Gaspar may have been trying to find a synthesis of Christianity and Judaism, without understanding either. His son, João, was with the Jews; his daughter, Violante, with the Christians and anti-Jewish.

For us the significance of the story is that Gaspar joined a Sacrament confraternity in his last decade, and after intimations of trouble. It could have been a cover to help a devious man, who was certainly disliked by many Jews in Venice, but the close proximity to the Host required of such a brother would have been hard for somebody sympathetic to Judaism to accept. The case demonstrates the tolerance — or in the eyes of some Catholics elsewhere, the laxity — of Venetian society, that such a person could

---

[1] Pullan, *The Jews of Europe*, pp. 230–40. Cf. on the difficulties of alien nationalities and businessmen in Venice, and inquisitorial investigations of their confraternities; and for the possible defence against charges on the grounds of membership of a Sacrament confraternity, above chapter 3.1, at nn. 11–13; Davidson, 'The Inquisition and the Italian Jews', on general attitudes and procedures.

join a Sacrament confraternity, especially within a few months of an inquisitorial investigation. Very soon he was a pillar of that mixed society, and succeeded a dyer as its top official; he was no passenger, but an active brother who was prominent in devotions and philanthropy. His money may have helped, but he had a reputation for meanness. Most likely he was seeking a kind of salvation for himself, in what many Christians at the time would have considered the most appropriate fashion; as such in Venice at least he was accepted. There were fraternities among the Jewish communities in Italy, so the concept of such a society need not have been alien.[2]

This account of Gaspar's position should not appear surprising in the light of my earlier comments, and it emphasises a number of aspects of confraternity life and attitudes. Most confraternities would have theoretically required better credentials of Christian birth and belief than Gaspar possessed as an applicant. But the past could be forgiven, for Jew as well as prostitute; repentance was all. And there was much merit in converting or confirming the conversion of a Jew (chapter 7.3). Enrolling Gaspar in a Sacrament confraternity and trusting him as an official might be a prized salvation-earning act of philanthropy. The varieties of confraternities and their numbers, especially in major cities, could allow many kinds of people to find a place in a suitable brotherhood. The growth of parochial confraternities made it easier for persons of dubious social or moral backgrounds to join; a commitment to the parish in some way, and a willingness to respect the Host — given the magical concepts associated with it — might be enough. Once a member a person was not easily expelled (chapter 4.3).

Lay confraternities were joined by all conditions of men, women and children (chapter 2.1). Princes of the church and state, nobles, lawyers, goldsmiths and dyers, peasants and blind mendicants, respectable dames and reformed prostitutes could all enter. There were exclusive societies based on criteria of sex or status, but there were also those which helped people cross the barriers of sex, age, social or ecclesiastical status, and occupational or territorial demarcations. There were confraternities that were intensely inward-looking and puritanical, requiring lengthy commitments to frequent periods of flagellation and night vigils. Others were open societies, where members could alternate between minimal attendance at an annual communion and assembly, and extended periods of alms-seeking or hospital visiting. The choices between types of confraternities were greatest in the large cities, like Rome, Venice, Naples, Milan, Genoa and Florence, though considerable varieties could be found in less likely places such as Perugia, Bergamo or Lecce. At present it has to be concluded that in the poor, remoter regions such as the Abruzzi, Basilicata or Reggio Calabria only a Rosary or Sacrament confraternity was available — limited in scope and numbers, though philanthropic enterprises are associated with some of them.

Quantifying the numbers of confraternities and those involved is only possible in scattered cases, certainly not regionally or for all Italy. Far too many confraternities exist as names only, with no evidence of the numbers involved. New names, in remote areas and in quite well-studied cities still emerge, but the types of records that supply these names and places rarely give the number of persons involved (chapters 1.4 and 2.3). There seems little doubt that the numbers of new confraternities founded in the later

---

[2] *Ibid.*, p. 27 and n. 52 for a Jewish *scuola* in Ferrara from 1481; Horowitz, 'A Jewish youth confraternity', esp. p. 38 on Jewish confraternities in Verona at the time.

sixteenth century, together with those clearly rejuvenated, outnumbered those that had petered out or were lost in amalgamations. By the late sixteenth century the majority of larger villages would have had a confraternity. In a very small community the formation of a confraternity was unlikely; the parish would have been a fraternal community itself, or have been so beset by divisions that it would have been hard to form a coherent sodality. If a Sacrament fraternity was imposed by episcopal fiat it might then be a meaningless institution.

Where we do know membership numbers we find that some had only a handful of brothers or sisters, while a few had thousands. It is difficult to establish a mean or average. I can make a very rough estimate that the city of Perugia, with 19,000 persons, had about 2,000 full adult members of fraternities at the end of the century. But we are totally in the dark when it comes to numbers for the whole dependent *contado* area. Given the discrepancies between active and passive members, and the fluctuations in enthusiasm within an individual's period of membership — as shown in one sound study of a fifteenth-century Florentine fraternity[3] — there may be little point agonising about crude membership numbers. Additionally there is a problem that some in-dividuals joined several confraternities, and presumably varied their level of activity between them; but we have little idea how common this was (chapter 2.3, n. 96).

In evaluating the social and religious importance of confraternities it might be suggested that a quarter or a third of the adult male population in significant urban areas were confraternity members at some time in their lives. In smaller towns and rural areas fewer would have joined. Others in the population, as adolescents or wives, were partially involved in some confraternity activities and spiritual benefits, as dependent relatives. One major contact in a life-time with confraternal activity — as by a pilgrimage to Rome, Assisi or Loreto — might be statistically insignificant, but for the individual concerned — in his or her estimation — a life-enhancing or soul-saving experience of great value.

What was the value of confraternity membership to the individual? In the absence of surviving testimony by brothers, other than a few indirect or partial comments such as the pilgrimage reports (chapter 5.3), Tintoretto's dedication of himself and his work to S. Rocco (chapter 11.2), or the carpenter Giambattista Casale's diary mentioning his teaching of Doctrine (chapter 10.3), we have to deduce the answers from constitutional declarations, evidence from activities, the expenditure of money and time. The con-fraternity was a protective society, religiously and socially. It reinforced belief through the saying of offices, the singing of lauds and the more frequent taking of communion; it encouraged atonement for sins committed in deed or thought, and so protected against eternal damnation, by the exercise of the discipline or by good works, both of which were fostered by corporate solidarity. Most important, the fraternal association persisting from generation to generation was a preferred protection against eternal damnation and a better hope for the eventual repose of the soul. Families could be very fickle and forgetful of past members, mass priests might have no commitment in their prayers, beyond their fees, and might be praying for too many souls, so dissipating the

---

[3] Weissman, *Ritual Brotherhood*, chapter 3, pp. 107–61, on active membership in S. Paolo, Florence. See above chapter 4.3.

effect.[4] But a confraternity of small or medium size could better perpetuate the memory of past members, and take the prayers for souls more seriously. The attention paid to offices for the dead, the commemoration of past members, the lighted processions of the Host to the dying, and the body to the grave, all emphasised the benefits expected. With these activities the living prepared a path to salvation, which successors could help complete by continuing the prayers (chapter 4, especially section 4 at n. 62, and section 8).

Socially, confraternities were protective societies. Those that were socially exclusive could constitute an extended family, a way of cementing relationships and fostering peace between groups of families, much like godparenthood associations. The secrecy and codes of honour ordered or implied by the statutes sought to exclude the socially or politically unwelcome. Other confraternities aimed at social protection by cutting across family and status divisions to intermingle social groups; these can be seen as creating clientele networks and being part of a wider patronage system, as in Florence. The confraternity office-holder could 'play the patron' and distribute assistance to suitably recommended people, who would respond with public gratitude towards the patron. Social tension might be dissipated in major cities by making rich and poor, master craftsmen and journeymen, mutually dependent. To add a rural example, the Benedictine monastery of S. Giustina in Padua joined with a dependent parish priest to promote a S. Rocco confraternity in Villa Del Bosco in 1478. They hoped to bring social cohesion to the area during a period of economic expansion under Benedictine management, and bring 'new' families together to foster the new agricultural system.[5]

Social protection was most in evidence in the provision of philanthropic assistance. Confraternity members might expect to receive some help, however meagre, if they faced dire circumstances through old age or illness, if daughters needed help for a dowry, or if bereft widows had no other support from the family. Guild-confraternities and some discipline companies looked after the members and their relatives in this way on a small scale, though some also provided almshouses and hospitals. Exclusive noble confraternities could provide more lavishly for members who became relatively poor. Scrutiny and means-testing was involved, and the pursuit of assistance might be embarrassing (chapter 9.2–3). Philanthropic provisions could become too attractive and cause scandal (as in Venice) because people seemingly joined to gain financial benefits. But for many brothers and sisters the social security aspect would legitimately affect membership, even if spiritual security was the chief consideration.

A less obvious motivation for joining confraternities was the entertainment or 'play'

---

[4] Cf. J.T. Rosenthal, *The Purchase of Paradise. Gift Giving and the Aristocracy, 1307–1485* (London, 1972), pp. 11–30, and p. 14: 'many nobles [in England] implicitly held the view that the fewer people one massed, the greater the impact of prayers (and the safer the political repercussions). Emphasis and comprehensiveness were mutually contradictory', On prayers for the dead, P. Ariès, 'Richesse et pauvreté devant la mort', *Etudes sur l'histoire de la pauvreté*, ed. M. Mollat (2 vols., Paris, 1974), vol. 2, pp. 519–33, esp. p. 531. R. Gascon has recently argued that in Italy the saying of special Masses was an increasing burden in parish and collegiate churches through the fifteenth century, though somewhat lessened in the later sixteenth: 'Liturgy and patronage in San Lorenzo, Florence, 1350–1650' in Kent and Simons (eds.), pp. 129–31.

[5] R. Weissman, 'Taking patronage seriously: Mediterranean values and Renaissance society' in Kent and Simons (eds.), pp. 15–45, and quoting p. 31; G. De Sandre Gasparini, *Contadini, Chiesa, Confraternita in un paese Veneto di Bonifica. Villa Del Bosco nel Quattrocento* (Padua, 1979), pp. 112–23. See above chapter 2.2 (c) and (e).

element, it being understood that this is not divorced from high seriousness, and that one can extend J. Huizinga's phrase to 'homo religiosus ludens'.[6] This motivation is deduced from the amount of time, effort and money that many confraternities expended on the decoration of churches and chapels (whether as permanent features, or ephemerally for a feast-day), on candle- and torch-lit processions, on parading relics, crosses and banners, on hiring musicians to accompany their singing, on feasts and plays (chapters 4.4, 5 and 11). Attention to the last two activities almost certainly declined in the later sixteenth century as Counter-Reformation puritanism attacked what had given scandal before. But the records suggest that confraternity meals and sacred representations were not entirely eliminated. Losses in play here were balanced by more elaborate and expensive decoration, whether in terms of paintings for confraternity rooms and altars, or in tabernacles for the Host, or in theatrical scenery for the Forty-Hour Eucharist displays (chapter 4.5).

By the seventeenth century the Forty-Hour devotions were high points in the religious and cultural life of Rome in particular, with elaborate scenery built in Il Gesù or in the Pauline chapel in the Vatican. Gian Lorenzo Bernini designed for the latter in 1628, as possibly the first of the front-rank artists to be involved, and Pietro da Cortona contributed to the celebrations in S. Lorenzo in Damaso in 1633. In 1610 the *apparato* in Il Gesù had been lit by 2,300 lamps and 500 candles. Hidden lights illuminated the scene of heavenly glory in Cortona's apparatus, with light seeming to emanate from the monstrance holding the Host. Such designs were partly derived from scenic ideas in the sacred representations staged by confraternities from the late fifteenth century onwards. But the Forty-Hour devotions, organised by the Orders with the assistance of confraternities were more controlled, with a better supervised congregation or audience. This should not, however, contradict the argument that the elaborate scenery and lighting effects, to the accompaniment of music and sermons, constituted serious devotion and entertainment. On a reduced scale such devotions were a regular part of the religious play in other cities like Perugia and Bologna.[7]

I have argued (chapter 11), that for some confraternity members the visual contributions to their environment were of considerable significance; paintings stimulated devotion and philanthropy, provided religious education through biblical or saintly narratives, or contributed to competitive propaganda.

How far music also constituted a play element attracting people to confraternities, or encouraging their participation is hard to deduce. The singing of psalms, hymns and vernacular religious songs was clearly important in the devotions of many confraternities, and not just those designated as *laudesi*; but most of the singing would have been plainchant. In one Bologna confraternity at least the music was proudly praised by officials along with paintings and scenic decoration (chapter 4.5). This S. Maria della Morte company had, by statute, a paid organist, and was proud of its singing of vespers and other music. In 1597 there was a patrician wedding, with beautiful music, in its hospital church (highly decorated and lit), to the great glory of the Virgin — and

---

[6] J. Huizinga, *Homo Ludens: A Study of the Play-Element in Culture* (Boston, 1950).

[7] M.S. Weil, 'The Devotion of the Forty Hours and Roman Baroque illusions, *Journal of the Warburg and Courtauld Institutes*, 37 (1974), 218–48, esp. plate 53a reproducing Cortona's drawing for the apparatus in S. Lorenzo, and pp. 226–7, 230 on lighting effects and Cortona's works. See above chapter 4.5.

doubtless of the boastful prior. In the late sixteenth century priors quite often paid personally for extra musical contributions to festivities.[8] In Rome the Oratory of SS. Crocefisso di S. Marcello was provided with a musicians' gallery. This has been seen as an important environment for musical developments that culminated in Emilio dei Cavalieri's pioneering sacred opera, *Rappresentazione di Anima e Corpo*, (first performed in the Oratorian Chiesa Nuova in 1600); the Cavalieri family had long been associated with the SS. Crocefisso and had produced music for its devotions.[9] The musical contribution of the Roman Della Morte company much impressed the Perugian pilgrims (chapter 5.3) and it implied a long-standing commitment to music.

It was the Venetian *Scuole Grandi* that provided the most notable musical entertainment. S. Giovanni Evangelista employed professional musicians in the fifteenth century to accompany the procession of relics and from 1430 it had its own organ. The *Scuole* then competed to employ the best singers and instrumentalists; the competitive extravagance in music, as in building and painting, alarmed state officials by the midsixteenth century. S. Rocco could afford the services of the organist-composer Giovanni Gabrieli and some eminent singers; in the 1590s S. Giovanni Evangelista employed another important organist-composer, Francesco Sponga. Foreign visitors like Thomas Coryat, who attended S. Rocco, were made aware of the musical devotion and entertainment offered in the leading *scuole*, and confraternal reputations were enhanced. But under adverse conditions in the seventeenth century confraternity music was the first target for financial cuts, as the most ephemeral of play elements.[10]

How did the broader church appreciate and use the confraternities in the changing environment of the sixteenth century? Different leaders saw advantages and disadvantages in powerful and active confraternities. The lay autonomy that had developed in the middle ages was suspect to many in the hierarchy, whether because axiomatically the clergy distrusted unprofessional lay involvement in church government, or because it was feared that the laity might concentrate too much on worldly matters like banquets rather than on devotion. As a result after the Council of Trent episcopal supervision increased, leading to some standardisation of confraternity regulations, if not necessarily of behaviour. There was some lay opposition to this interference as a Perugian group prominently showed, but generally lay autonomy and inititative diminished (chapter 3.1). Bishops feared that confraternities might frustrate the new parish organisation which reformers were intent on fostering after Trent. In practice many bishops became promoters of confraternities, but favoured those that would foster parochial loyalties rather than cut across parish boundaries. The Sacrament confraternities particularly, but also Marian companies, became important buttresses of the parish, both financially and devotionally; sometimes dominating the priest, sometimes being under his control (chapters 3.4 and 11.1). In some areas, notably Lombardy, Bologna and Rome, confraternities of Christian Doctrine were used to improve religious education among

---

[8] BCB F.O.43 fol. 46r; and fol. 30r: prior Camillo Fava 'fece cantare in musica li offici della Maria a sue spese' (1590); fols. 32r–33r: prior Taddeo Ghelli paid for 'una superbissima Musica' on Holy Monday, for the special Forty-Hour celebrations in 1593.

[9] Henneberg, *L'oratorio*, pp. 49, 58–9; Lewine, *Interior*, pp. 18–19, 49–50, 210–19.

[10] D. Arnold, 'Music at a Venetian Confraternity in the Renaissance', *Acta Musicologica*, 37 (1965), 62–72; *idem* 'Music at the Scuola di San Rocco'; *idem Giovanni Gabrieli and the Music of the Venetian High Renaissance* (London, New York and Melbourne), 1979, pp. 188–210; Coryat, pp. 251–3.

the population at large, even if much was mechanical learning; a standardisation of moral and social behaviour was also attempted (chapter 10.3).

The religious Orders clearly favoured confraternities as notable adjuncts to their work; this could again alarm bishops, since diocesan bishops and Orders were jurisdictionally at loggerheads over reform policies and procedures. Jesuits promoted all varieties of confraternity, stressing both devotional practices and philanthropic works, and made their presence felt as spiritual advisers. Dominicans and Franciscans concentrated more on devotional confraternities, and appear to have been less forceful leaders (chapter 3.2, and *passim*).

Confraternities can be profitably studied in the context of debates about Catholic Reform and Counter-Reformation — as suggested in chapter 1.2. The lay confraternities contributed to both 'movements'; they affected and were affected by the changing emphasis from the one to the other during the sixteenth century. Revitalisation, and diversification, of confraternity life and devotion from the late fifteenth and early sixteenth century is part of the Italian (and wider European) Catholic Reform. This is most evident in the societies directly or indirectly linked to the oratories of Divine Love, and to the circle of Girolamo Miani's friends and contacts. Under their influences philanthropy was extended to a wider range of 'needy', outside the families of fraternity members. As part of Catholic Reform there were the campaigns for more frequent confession and communion on the part of the laity and the early spread of the Rosary cult, possibly under German influence. The apparent increase in the involvement of women within confraternities, including those dedicated to the Rosary (chapters 2.2 (b), and 4.7), may be interpreted at least in the early phases as part of a Catholic Reform movement designed to foster greater religious participation by all sectors of lay society.

Lay initiatives and older confraternity practices came under threat as the clerical authoritarianism associated with Counter-Reformation increased. Greater episcopal supervision became evident, with the authorisation of statutes and investigations through visitations. The enhanced role of the parish church, the more obvious presence and power of the parish priest led to greater parochial control over existing and newly created fraternities. These societies were not immune to theological debate and the threat of heresy; they were therefore exposed to more investigation and control (chapter 3). Lay sermons probably disappeared (chapter 4.4) to be replaced by clerical sermons and spiritual advice. Confraternity feasting and entertainment went into decline, or at least was more circumspect (chapter 4.4). More positively one can see the confraternities promoting the Counter-Reformation by encouraging eucharistic devotions, the cult of the Virgin, and prayers for souls in Purgatory. The contribution to the teaching of Christian Doctrine can be interpreted as counter-reformationary in character much of the time, since it largely involved instruction in the basic tenets of the faith, based on approved catechisms. However, a Catholic Reform element may be detected when such schools went on to teach reading and to encourage some measure of debate (chapter 10.3).

The philanthropic aspects of confraternity activity may be judged to have been ambivalently affected by a transition from Catholic Reform to Counter-Reformation outlooks, especially with the development of new and reformed religious Orders. On the one hand the growing impact of Jesuits and Capuchins in particular increased the number of confraternities, and often encouraged philanthropy alongside devotions (chapter 3.2). However, the clerical supervision and spiritual advising that was involved possibly discouraged lay initiative. Additionally it seems likely that the growing popularity of religious Orders which operated in public with good works would have attracted leading philanthropists away from lay confraternities and into clerical congregations and Orders, or encouraged others to commit themselves to the latter rather than to lay fraternities. The extent of this kind of movement might be tested if more fraternity membership lists, which might indicate whether brothers (or sisters) left to take vows, could be traced; or if more biographical information was accumulated on the early careers of Theatines, Jesuits, Ursulines or Oratorians. Lay members of the oratories of Divine Love moved on to become Theatines and associates of Girolamo Miani became religiously and philanthropically committed as founders of the Somaschi Order. Filippo Neri and the Oratorians developed an Order from confraternity associations. The Fatebenefratelli moved in and out of the borderlands between confraternity, congregation and Order. Symptomatically De Lellis moved from a group working in a confraternity hospital to found a full Order — the Ministri degli Infermi (chapter 9.4). Refuges or conservatories for vulnerable girls and women became more convent-like, even if they were not turned into nunneries. There seems to have been an increased influence over some of them by the Orders, sometimes replacing lay confraternity administrators; a major Perugian example is discussed in chapter 9.6.

Italian confraternities obviously contributed to the Counter-Reformation by promoting various tenets that had been attacked by Protestants, most notably the doctrines of Transubstantiation and the Eucharist, the cult of the Virgin, including subsidiary doctrines such as the Immaculate Conception, the cult of saints and the miraculous power of relics, which they paraded in their processions, and the efficacy of prayer for the salvation of souls in Purgatory. The affirmation of this last belief was incorporated into prayer and the work of confraternities; praying for souls may be seen as the most consistent and persistent purpose of confraternities. But usually the concern was for the souls of a select group of people who had been known and named. The Venetian Scuola of S. Fantin was possibly exceptional — in the sixteenth century — in its very overt concern for a host of Souls in Purgatory (chapters 4.7, and 11.3). The Italian situation contrasts with Spain where, as in Toledo, most parishes apparently had a confraternity almost exclusively dedicated to the Souls in Purgatory. By the late seventeenth century Italy had many more societies with this specialist preoccupation.[11]

In the debates about the degree of 'social control' that developed from both Reformation and Counter-Reformation institutions, as well as from political absolutism, the history of confraternities can again be interpreted in two ways. In France a case can be made for confraternities being major agents of social control; Sacrament and other societies became stalwart and vindictive upholders of strict puritanical behaviour, as well as pursuers of Huguenots, other heretics, and vagabonds. In Italy, while there is some indication that confraternities linked with Saint Peter Martyr or the Crocesegnati had a theoretical obligation to pursue heretics, this does not appear to have been

---

[11] W.A. Christian, *Local Religion in Sixteenth-century Spain* (Princeton, 1981), p. 143. Cf. Martz, p. 164, where this type of confraternity is noted as the fastest expanding in Toledo between 1550 and 1576, with twelve new ones.

a particularly prominent activity, even when and where there was a 'Lutheran' heresy problem in the mid-sixteenth century (chapter 3.4). Freer access to central Inquisition files may reveal more collaboration from fraternity delators. The prevalence or effectiveness of Nome di Dio companies in curbing blaspheming and swearing (potentially a heresy matter) has not been much considered by historians; to elucidate this would require research in ecclesiastical court records. Social control and orthodoxy were promoted by Christian Doctrine confraternities when disciplining children, regularising church attendance and beliefs, or introducing moral teaching. A counter argument is that such schools could also have a liberating effect, through encouraging wider social intercourse (especially for girls) or — more rarely — through stimulating literacy and debates (chapter 10.3). Philanthropy was to some extent a moral crusade, to make the recipients as good as the donors supposedly were, to regulate and control the deviants. In selecting 'deserving' needy and practising discriminatory assistance, confraternity officials were trying to impose a stricter moral-religious code on the poor (chapters 7.2–3, 9 and 10.1).

The argument that social control was increasingly exercised through the parish is reinforced when one notes the growth of Rosary and Sacrament fraternities based on the parish church and presided over by the parish priest. However, one can point to confraternities that had some control over the parish church, its fabric and finances, and fraternities might move out of the parish church into their own premises. Competition also persisted between parishes and monastic institutions as hosts to sodalities (chapters 3.4 and 11.1).

Examples of secular elitist control, through upper class confraternity officials dominating the rest in a socially mixed brotherhood, can be counter-balanced by cases of more equitable office-holding in other fraternities, or by the persistence of fraternities that catered for the middle orders rather than the elites (chapter 2.2 (c) and (e)).

Balancing the evidence of contradictory trends in the course of the early modern period it would appear that by the later sixteenth century Italian confraternities were often agents of social control and of the clerical authoritarianism of the Counter-Reformation. But controls and authority could be evaded, and lay catholicism be pursued independently — especially in self-contained oratories and chapels. At least in the larger communities individuals would have some choice in the role they wanted to play; people might willingly accept clerical leadership, and flock to join Nome di Dio or Rosary fraternities designed to control them. It was not easy to discipline those who subsequently wished to evade leadership and control (chapter 4.3). The pressure to conform and to accept discipline was on those desirous of assistance in their need; the donors of charity might require recompense in prayer and accepting the moral code (chapter 9).

State authorities, like the bishops, had mixed views about confraternities, but tended to see them as beneficial, provided they were properly controlled (chapter 3.1). Fraternities were potential centres of opposition to the regime, though — despite episodes in Florence, Siena, Bologna and Naples — the fear was probably greater than the reality. The major states ensured some supervision, and then utilised the confraternities' initiatives for the states' benefit, most notably in Venice. The confraternities could become agents for state propaganda in Venice and Naples, especially by means of processions (chapter 5.1). Confraternity activity was likely to promote social security through philanthropy. Socially mixed societies could reduce tension, enable the rich to help the poor, and allow the upper classes to influence the lower orders in a more subtle way than through overt political domination (chapters 2.2, and 9). In the case of hospitals some governments preferred to create large civic complexes under bureaucratic control and curtail inefficient confraternity or guild hospitals and hospices; but elsewhere, as in Perugia, Naples and Rome, confraternity involvement was welcomed (chapters 9.4, 10.1–2). Governments clearly found confraternities suitable agencies for the relief of the poor through alms-giving and food supplying. In times of dearth they would command them to act, with or without supporting state action (chapters 9.2). Through confraternity philanthropy, governments in Venice, Naples, Bologna, Rome, Perugia and Modena sought to avoid bread riots and other popular disturbances — though they were not always successful.

In assessing the roles and social value of confraternities it has been important to clarify the priorities of their members. The predominant concern was with the eventual salvation of the souls of brothers and sisters. This could be achieved by devotions, through prayers and penances, praising God and invoking the intercession of the Virgin and saints, sharing in and venerating the Body of Christ. Salvation could also be sought by efficacious works for others. These could include physical assistance to the needy, but also acts that brought others towards their own salvation — by encouraging their belief, devotion, penance, confession and communion (chapter 1.3). In earlier centuries confraternal devotion and philanthropy were predominantly confined to the closed society of the group; good works were for the neighbour sitting along the bench in the oratory or chapel. Through the sixteenth century there was a tendency to broaden the term 'neighbour' to include unknown poor in the outside world, or anonymous souls in Purgatory. Contemporaries perceived social conditions in Italy to be worsening, the poor however defined to be becoming more numerous, and the religious ignorance of many to be more obvious (chapter 8.1). So the pursuit of personal salvation encompassed concern for others; spiritual self-interest was combined with compassion. The concern was prompted by evidence of the disasters of war and plagues, and also by literature on poverty and the poor, written and read by spiritual advisers like Possevino and Loarte, who then influenced confraternity statutes — even if the original treatises were not read by lay confraternity brothers, (chapters 7.2, 8.1, and 9.1). Additionally the increased emphasis on the Eucharist reinforced the attitude, expressed visually in some paintings (chapter 11.2–3), that as Christ offered his Body, so the faithful should pass on physical and spiritual bread to the less fortunate, as charity.

Confraternity priorities can be judged partly by their expenditure, though there are great difficulties in assessing confraternity budgets, especially since the sums involved in casual alms-collecting and giving were unlikely to be registered. The existence of a priority group of ashamed poor, *poveri vergognosi*, to whom assistance must be most secret, discouraged some record-keeping. The rich Scuola Grande of S. Rocco spent about the same amount — 5,000 ducats a year — on processions and ceremonials as on various forms of alms-giving; the goldsmiths' guild-confraternity spent a little more on lighting than on alms.[12] In Perugia the confraternity of S. Francesco in the 1590s spent over 600 ducats on gilding the ceiling of its oratory (having already paid for

---

[12] Pullan, *Rich and Poor*, pp. 165–6; see chapter 6, n. 17 on goldsmiths' finances.

paintings within the ceiling frame). This can be contrasted with the handful of dowries — at about 6¼ ducats each — it provided annually, or the 17 ducats on the Feast of the Ascension celebrations in 1603, with at least 9 ducats being paid to the painter Gioseph Manueli for what was presumably ephemeral decorative work.[13] Ceremonials and aids to devotion (including paintings) were given high priority; they were connected with the pursuit of salvation for confraternity members.

The confraternities' financial contributions should not, however, be used as the major yard-stick in assessing the extent of philanthropy. For the givers as well as for many recipients of spiritual philanthropy, aids to ultimate salvation were more important than alleviating temporary physical needs. Their concepts of need (cf. chapter 7.1 and 2), encompassed spiritual and psychological needs and deprivations as much as physical. Even in terms of terrestrial assistance the financial contributions were often, anyway, means to higher ends, not the end itself; dowry payments were to create Christian marriages and moral families, debtors were released from prison so they could avoid worse sins, escape criminality, and reestablish a stable family through new employment.

The major success stories (as exemplified in chapters 10 and 11), though not uniformly recorded across Italy, were apparently in the teaching of Christian Doctrine; in bringing spiritual comfort and some nursing care to those in hospitals; in expanding several hospitals into more effective medical centres; in operating prisons and helping the inmates; in providing conservatories and refuges for the vulnerable, especially women and orphans. Modern commentators may judge the institutional conditions primitive and condemn the philanthropists for trying to fashion the recipients to fit their own narrow Christian, puritanical moulds.[14] Not all recipients appreciated the philanthropic ministrations, as the flight of some beggars from confined quarters, or the complaints about monastic conditions for reformed prostitutes, indicate (chapters 10.1, and 9.6). But one suspects that the majority of recipients, fearing death and their fate in the afterlife, appreciated the value and priorities of the philanthropists.

Nobody would claim that confraternity philanthropy solved the problems of poverty, or provided ideal solutions for poor relief. There were times of great need, through harvest failures and war, when many were in absolute need (chapter 8.1); unless provided with food, they soon died. It was reckoned in the later sixteenth century (especially in Venice, Naples and Rome) that the state should and could organise food supplies from a distance and regulate grain prices. With the cooperation of state officials, parish priests, monasteries and confraternities there could be some alleviation of the misery. Even so thousands died of starvation in and around Rome in the 1590s. Confraternities, like other institutions, could only make a minor contribution.

It was also increasingly realised that in more 'normal' times there were many — believed to be increased in numbers — who were close to dire need and worthy of support: foundlings, young and old women without full family protection, the chronically sick and crippled, those close to death and also without family support. Here confraternities responded better both with supplies of food, clothes and money, and

---

[13] SBF S. Francesco No. 508 (a), 'Carte varie' nos. 4 (a) and (b), 7, 8, 9, 12 and 13; see above chapter 11.2, n. 19.

[14] Lis and Soly, pp. 121–2.

with new hospitals and similar institutions. Solutions at this level were complicated by assumptions about relative poverty (as noted by C. Benincasa at the time) and by conflicting views about *poveri vergognosi*. This category, while normally meaning nobles and distressed gentlefolk, could include humble women of low birth but good moral standing. The better born 'poor' would appear to have had a greater chance of receiving assistance and quantitively more of it than those of lower class. But by the end of the sixteenth century there were greater opportunities for more varied help than a century earlier for any person who claimed to be poor. The available evidence suggests that confraternities scrutinised applicants with some care and that those that received dowries, rooms or housing, and even financial donations, had a strong case for receiving support (chapter 9.2).

As the provisions for philanthropy increased, so did the demand; the existence of institutions or supplies attracted people from afar — disastrously so in the case of foundling hospitals (chapter 9.5). From the 1590s confraternity assistance could not keep pace, as the number in 'real need' also rose more than the overall population. In Rome average bread consumption may have declined about 30 per cent during the seventeenth century, meat consumption by about 25 per cent; whatever the qualifications, this evidence of declining conditions is as good as one is likely to find.[15] It has been argued that because private and church philanthropy failed in the early seventeenth century to meet the problems of the poor, and especially when this endangered state security, many parts of Catholic and Protestant Europe produced the Great Confinement. This theme has been particularly popularised by C. Lis and H. Soly — though they were not concerned with Italy in this context.[16] Earlier Sixtus V had attempted to confine Roman beggars and had failed (chapter 10.1), and thereafter Italians did not pursue the policy with the rigour and ruthlessness attempted in Amsterdam or France. Italy being a more divided area, with a more diverse society, with a stronger history of confraternity philanthropy, preferred the piecemeal approach. It meant that vagabondage continued (as it did in France) and few Italians were forced into workhouses or *hopitaux généraux* as in England and France. The muddled and conflicting priorities of confraternities and their advisers helped ensure the persistence of mixed and confused approaches to philanthropy. Whether this is seen as detrimental, because economically and socially inefficient or desirably libertarian, depends on the philosophy of the critic.

One suspects that the quantity and quality of physical philanthropy diminished through the seventeenth century, under the impact of economic decline, increased warfare, plagues and spiritual malaise. The spiritual concern for others' souls may have been a counter-development of uncertain merit. That is beyond the scope of this book; though it can be said that for their members eighteenth-century confraternities were of considerable importance. O. Chadwick sees them as the focal point of religious life, sometimes almost totally displacing the parish and priests — as some sixteenth-century bishops had feared they would.[17]

This book is an interim report on confraternities. So often guesses and suppositions have had to be offered, deductions made on the basis of very limited case studies, or

---

[15] Lis and Soly, p. 113; see above chapter 8.1, n. 9.
[16] Lis and Soly, pp. 116–29.
[17] Chadwick, p. 40.

dubious reporting past and present. Limitations in the available evidence were indicated at the outset (chapter 1.4). The book has been designed to show a variety of dimensions to confraternity life and activity in the long sixteenth century and to point to the kinds of studies that have been made. It is hoped that the exemplification of what is now known will stimulate further enquiries.

It might help to suggest overtly some lines for future studies. It would be beneficial if the process of mapping ecclesiastical and social institutions was renewed to produce a better quantification of the confraternities and their dependent institutions like hospitals and Monti di Pietà. Crude figures and names are of limited value; we need a fuller count of the numbers within individual societies. We require assessments of the kinds of people who were members, of the differences between active and passive members (as R. Weissman and M. Olivieri Baldissarri attempted with single confraternities in, respectively, Florence and Milan), between rich/giving and poor/receiving members (as B. Pullan and R. Mackenney have done for some Venetian *scuole*). This would mean the close scrutiny of record books of individual confraternities, for the activities of individuals. Names need to be taken from confraternity lists and traced through other records to establish their careers and roles in society more widely, as Olivieri Baldissarri has partially managed for the Milanese fraternity of S. Croce e della Pietà. One may readily spot the domination of some confraternities by leading patricians from a city like Perugia or Bologna, or Roman ones by noted curial families, but what of the majority of societies? Were confraternity officials dominant bourgeois, or frustrated local politicians? How socially mixed were the fraternities that obviously did combine patricians with others who are less identifiable? What was the normal economic life of those males who sought and received philanthropic support? What happened to the recipients of dowries? Though in many cases when a name is given it is difficult to identify the recipients in the absence of family names, there may be some cases where marriage records could prove valuable.

We have an adequate idea of what should have constituted confraternity life, from printed and manuscript statutes, but these sources have featured too prominently in many local studies. Visitation records provide important, but limited evidence on official views concerning confraternities. What we need above all else are more studies of archival material produced by the fraternities and hospitals themselves. I am aware of the difficulties and frustrations involved in such studies from samplings first in Perugia, and more recently also in Bologna and Venice; the task is especially difficult given the random survival of material. But more could be done by local historians ready to penetrate new archival series, and most profit could be gained from doing so outside the comparatively well-favoured cities of Venice and Florence. Only rarely, one suspects, will sufficient amounts of coherent interlocking material be found to provide statistically analysable data, but the use of narrative material on individuals or groups will still enhance the historical appreciation of confraternity life and beliefs and provide deeper insights than those provided by officially approved statutes.

Chapter 1 commenced with visual images; this will conclude with another: Tintoretto's *S. Rocco healing the plague-stricken*, in the church of S. Rocco, near the Venetian Scuola Grande (Plate 10). Tintoretto painted a number of canvases about S. Rocco/St Roch; this may have been the work that secured his membership of the Scuola in 1549.

10 Jacopo Tintoretto, *S. Rocco among the plague-stricken*, in church of S. Rocco, Venice. *c.* 1549 (see pp. 280, 282).

As we have noted earlier, Tintoretto dedicated much of his life and work to S. Rocco, and the confraternity that took the saint's name. The scene is a hospital, with many sick men and women, who show their sores and wounds to the helpers and to the saint in the centre. He casts light, and hope, from his halo into a gloomy atmosphere; he appears close to a patient as a charitable doctor offering physical and spiritual comfort, rather than as a distant miracle-worker. Members of the rich Scuola di S. Rocco in prosperous times could enjoy spiritual uplift from religious painting and music in their elaborately decorated meeting rooms a few yards away from the church; they could join spectacular processions admired by the outside world. There was prestige for the rich members, and financial assistance or housing for the needy, relative to their status and expectations. But there was also group solidarity when fearing the uncertainties of this life and the next. Invocations of S. Rocco as patron saint might bring alleviation. S. Rocco in this picture is shown as the ideal confraternity hospital visitor, even if an imitator was not to have miraculous powers. He could inspire confraternity members in his name to offer comfort, if not cure, in hospital. Then the fear of death could be overcome; hope offered in this world and for the next; the salvation of both comforter and patient brought nearer.[18]

The brethren joined fraternities to gain spiritual benefits, and these could be achieved through their charities. To judge the confraternities as precursors of the welfare state in satisfying physical needs is unhistorical. In this context money spent on candles is as well spent as on dowries or hospital facilities. Unlike the modern welfare state, as depicted by M. Ignatieff, involvement with confraternities satisfied more than basic physical needs (chapter 7.1). For donors and recipients, for those praying and those being prayed for, for comforters and patients, the confraternities could satisfy the needs for fraternity, social solidarity and spiritual comfort in this world as they contemplated the possibilities of joining the ultimate fraternity of Christ and his saints.

[18] M. Levey, p. 717 and Fig. 8; E. Newton, *Tintoretto* (London, 1952), pp. 77, 140–4; S. Mason Rinaldi, 'Le imagini della peste nella cultura figurativa veneziana', AA.VV. *Venezia e la Peste*, pp. 209–24. esp. p. 243. The painting measures 307 × 673 cms. See above chapter 11.2, at n. 31.

APPENDIX I

POPULATION

The following table is designed to give rough estimates of the population within Italy and for the major cities and towns that feature in my discussion of confraternities. For most places the figures are given as approximates at half-century intervals. But for certain cities precise figures for specific years are also recorded, where it is judged that these are reasonably reliable.

The following table is designed to give rough estimates of the population within Italy and for the major cities and towns that feature in my discussion of confraternities. For most places the figures are given as approximates at half-century intervals. But for certain cities precise figures for specific years are also recorded, where it is judged that these are reasonably reliable.

Area/City	c. 1500	c. 1550	c. 1600	c. 1650	c. 1700
Italy	10 m	11.0 m	12 m	11 m	13.0 m
Piedmont		0.6 m			0.9 m
Lombardy		0.5 m			1.0 m
Veneto		1.6 m			
Liguria		0.4 m			0.4 m
Tuscany		0.8 m			0.9 m
Papal State		1.6 m			2.0 m
Naples and Sicily		3.6 m			4.0 m
Bergamo		18,000	27,000		
Bologna	55,000	[1570] [1581] 61,742 70,661	62,844 [1624] 61,691	58,000	63,000
Brescia	65,000	42,000	36,000	[1630] [1642] 43,235 25,063	63,000
Catanzaro		11,500	12,000		
Cosenza		8,700	12,000		
Ferrara		42,000	[1601] 32,860	25,000	27,000
Florence	70,000	60,000	70,000	[1622] [1642] 76,023 69,495	
Genoa	60,000	65,000	[1597] 62,396	[1660] [1662] 38,360 47,668	

City					
Lecce	26,000	32,000	16,000		
Lucca	24,000	24,000	25,000	23,000 [1688]	
Milan	100,000	70,000	120,000	100,000	125,829
Modena	18,000	16,000	[1590] [1591] [1620] 19,911 16,695 20,505	15,000	19,000
Naples	150,000	212,000	[1596] [1606] 237,784 280,746	300,000	315,000
Padua	27,000	[1557] 35,852	36,000	[1648] 32,714	
Perugia	25,000	[1551] [1582] 19,876 19,581	[1618] 19,722	[1656] 17,385	[1701] 16,045
Perugia contado			33,129	35,097	
Prato	6,800	[1562] 5,996		5,600	[1672] 6,623
Reggio Calabria	12,000		17,000		
Rome	55,000	45,000	[1591] [1602] 116,695 99,312	118,047	[1701] 138,568
Turin	14,000		24,000	37,000	42,000
Venice	100,000	[1563] 168,627	[1581] [1624] [1633] 134,877 142,804 98,244 (or) 141,600 102,250		132,000

The above figures came mainly from: Beloch, *Bevölkerungsgeschichte*, esp. vol. 1, pp. 46, 173–6, vol. 2, pp.13–14, 71–4, 92–4, 102, 109, 141–6, 170, 263, 276, and vol. 3, pp. 15, 70–1, 122–5, 143, 181–9, 250, 288–9, 356–61; C.M. Cipolla, 'Four centuries of Italian demographic development', *Population in History*, eds. D.V. Glass and D.E.C. Eversley (London, 1974 paperback edn), pp. 570–87; J. De Vries, *European Urbanization 1500–1800* (London, 1984), esp. Appendix 1. For some particular cities: Basini, *L'uomo e il pane*, p. 17; Bellettini, *La popolazione di Bologna*, esp. pp. 24–7, 40; Black, 'Perugia and papal absolutism', p. 511 n. 1, with sources; Grohmann, *Città e territorio*, esp. pp. 69–79, 114–23; G. Felloni, 'Per la storia della popolazione di Genova nei secoli XVI e XVII', *Archivio Storico Italiano*, 110 (1952), 236–53; G. Galasso, *Economia e società nella Calabria del Cinquecento* (Naples, [c. 1967]), p. 110; C. Petraccone, *Napoli dal Cinquecento all'Ottocento* (Naples, 1974), pp. 4–5, 13, 51, 131–2. See above chapter 8, nn. 1 (on Venice), 18–19 (Modena), 34 (Prato).

APPENDIX II

CURRENCIES

1 Rome, Bologna and Perugia:

As money of account: 1 ducato = 100 baiocchi
1 baiocco = 4 quattrini = 16 denari
1 paolo = 1 giulio = 10 baiocchi
10 florini = 6 scudi 25 baiocchi

In relating these to actual coins, or relating coins with each other there were many variations over the period. As a very rough guide, for when some figures are mentioned in the text:

1 ducato di camera = 1.09 scudi d'oro in oro
1 scudo d'oro in oro = 1.2 scudi di moneta (silver) di 10 giulii in 1592
= 1.3 scudi di moneta (silver) di 10 giulii in 1619
1 giulio = 9.5 baiocchi in 1504
= 10 baiocchi from 1519
1 grosso = ½ giulio, from 1540s
A gold scudo expressed in terms of baiocchi might vary from 80 to 110 baiocchi

2 Venice:

As money of account: 1 ducato = 124 soldi
1 lira = 20 soldi

3 Milan:

As money of account: 1 lira (imperiale) = 20 soldi = 240 denari
a ducatone = 5 lire 17 soldi in 1605
= 8 lire 17 soldi in 1700

4 Naples:

As money of account: 1 carlino = 10 grani = 100 centesimi

For some rough indications of what some amounts of money might mean in terms of food, dowries, salaries, see chapter 8.3.

BIBLIOGRAPHY

A MANUSCRIPT SOURCES

(Titles or descriptions given below in quotations are those that appear on the cover or at the beginning of the volume/folder. Other Italian descriptions are those that appear in inventories to the archives.)

Perugia. Archivio di Stato [ASP]

Confraternita SS. Andrea e Bernardino Della Giustizia. Miscellanea 3: 'Libro delli Giustiziali'.
'Nel presente libro si noteranno tutti quei meseri, che finiranno la vita loro per ordine della Giustizia . . . 1525'
Corporazioni Religiose Soppresse:
No. 5, S. Domenico: vol. 8, Ricordanze — Memoriali del Convento 1566–1720. Miscellanea 77, 'Nomi dei Fratelli e delle Sorelle del SS. Nome di Dio 1601-'
No. 20, S. Pietro Apostolo: vol. 1 Miscellanea. Entrata e Uscita, Varia 1478–1647; vol. 6 Depositario, 1531–52; vol. 7 Depositario, 1552–7; vol. 20 Adunanze, 1575–1688; vol. 23 Miscellanea, 'Inventario delle robbe della Confraternita che si danno in consegna al sagrestano', 1571–1830
Ex Congregatione di Carità, No. 30, Confraternita di S. Pietro Martire: vol. 1, Adunanze e ricordi vari, 1548–1601
Sodalizio di S. Martino:
Div. II C1.IV P1.III, no. 1 Verbali di Adunanze, 'Libro I°- delle congregazioni 1576–1643'
Div. II C1. IX Reg. 1, Elemosine fatte dai visitatori, 1645–50
Div. I C1.VI, Lettere Filza 1 1511–1620 (Letters pre-date the Sodalizio's foundation (1574) presumably because they were colleced as relevant to various properties and families of concern to the fraternity.)
Div. I C1.V Filza II.1 Miscellaneous: includes attestations of births, marriages, confessions of poverty. The relevance to the sodality is not always clear.
Ospedale di S. Maria della Misericordia:
Misc. 5, Nomi di confratelli, ordinanze e regolamenti, 1305–1787. Copies and originals.
Misc. 6, mainly copy of above, eighteenth century.
Misc. 15, collection of documents, old and new copies, made in 1803 for an apostolic visitation, covering the period from 1558.
Misc. 18, Ricordi Vari 1580–1620. An account book of Tisco di Federigo, woodcarver and minor painter.

Movimento degli Esposti, I: 1584–90

Baliatrici degli Esposti, 5: 1670–75

Conservatorio della Carità:

Istromenti, I: 1555–1779

Adunanze, I: 1615–26

Miscellanea, 15/13 (latter is the new numbering). Offizio della Compagnia di S. Girolamo

Conservatorio delle Derelitte:

Misc. 16, Movimento delle Zitelle Derelitte, 1579–1625. Original.

Misc. 20, Diverse Memorie, 1539–1796. Random collection of material, possibly made by Don E. Agostini in 1805.

Misc. 21, 'Derelitte Pia Casa Eretta 1539'. Compilation made by Don E. Agostini in 1805 from old records (including Misc. 16).

Miscellanea di Computisteria, vol. 5. Debtors of the Monti di Pietà, 1514

Miscellanea, vol. 65, no. 38. Monti di Pietà, council records 1477–1539

Editti e Bandi, vols. 2 and 3: 1484–1540. Copies of edicts and orders emanating from papal officials and communal councils.

Perugia. Archivio di San Pietro [A.S. Pietro]

(The archive is administered by a Benedictine archivist, though the old monastic buildings around it are secularised as part of an agricultural Foundation.)

Diverse 38, Libro di Ricordi da 1527 al 1610. Annals kept by successive Cellarers of the Abbey.

Mazzo XXXVI: 'Descrizione del Peregrinaggio fatto dalla Compagnia della Morte di Perugia a Roma per pigliare il santissimo Giubileo l'anno 1600. Alli 7 di maggio.'

Perugia. Archivio del Pio Sodalizio Braccio Fortebraccio [SBF]

(The Archive is housed in a room attached to the Oratory of S. Francesco. The records of the three confraternities to which this sodality is heir are kept in separate bookcases, Scaffole, which are the basis of the classification. Scaffola A = S. Agostino B = S. Francesco C = S. Domenico.)

A. S. Agostino, no. 489. *Constitutioni et Capitoli . . . Perugia, 1565.* See Printed works.

B S. Francesco. No. 151. An account book for 1609.

no. 442 Libro delle Dote, 1590–1617

no. 456 Libro dei Verbali, 1438–1510

no. 457 Libro dei Verbali, 1566–90

no. 458 Libro dei Verbali, 1591–1629

no. 508 (a) no. 1 'Sacrestie Fraternit. S. Franc.i Inventarij'.

no. 508 (a) 'Carte varie relative ai lavori d'arte eseguite nell'Oratorio', 1573–1849

no. 509 1260–1628. Documents from episcopal visitations, including: '1564, Visitatio Epi. cornei' '1566 Aprile 8/1610 Ott. 9' '1628, Verbali di esami testimoniali sulla questione della pretesa giurisdizione del Vescovo sulle Fraternite'

no. 511 (a) Various documents relating to land and rents, 1590s–1650s

no. 511 (c) and (d) Certificates of land measurements.

C. S. Domenico, no. 427 Adunanze, 1488–1514; no. 430 Adunanze, 1564–1607; no. 450 Libro delle Dote, 1536–98.

Perugia. Biblioteca Comunale [Biblioteca Augusta] [BCP]

Ms. 135 'Lettere del rev. mons. F.V. Herculani perugino.' Letters copied and annotated by the bishop's nephew, Timoteo Bottonio, 1570s–1580s. Includes correspondence with B. Cacciaguerra. Most letters were from the bishop, but some are letters to him.

Ms. 479 'Lettere di mon. V. Erculani.' 1546–69. Similar to above.

Ms. 948 'Libro di conti e ricordi della confraternita del Buon Gesù. 1545– '

Ms. 1151 T. Bottonio, 'Annali', vol. II: 1401–1591

Ms. 1186 Libro dell'entrata ed uscita della ven. Confraternita degli Oltramontani, 1579–1615

Ms. 1198 Anon. 'Descritio de Perusia.' 1590s

Ms. 1221 R. Sotii, 'Annali, Memorie et Ricordi, scritte de Raffaello Sotii cominciando l'anno MDXL.' Autograph.

Ms. 1301 Libro dei partiti che fanno nella confraternita dei SS. Rocco e Sebastiano di Perugia. 1653–1743.

Ms. 3121 'Visite dei Spedale e delle Chiese delle Arti della Città di Perugia fatte da Lodovico Vescovo Lodigiano Visitatore Apostolico Confermate dal Breve di Clemente Ottavo.' Eighteenth-century hand. Brief is dated 18 June 1601.

Ms. 3139 'Regola et Constitutioni de la devota Compagnia del Corpo de Christo et de Sancto Pietro Martyre.' Rules of 1531 (fols. 2r–9v); 1548 reforms (fols. 10r–11v); reforms of 1561, 1564, and 1590 (fols. 2r–15r); some names of members (fols. 15v–17r); Litany of the Rosary (fols. 19v–20v).

Ms. 3140 'Officio, regole e matricole della Compagnia del Corpo di Cristo e di San Pietro Martyre di Perugia.' Sixteenth-century hand, written after indulgences were granted in 1545.

Ms. 3288 Anon. 'Istoria di Perugia.' From p. 81 the author is keeping a contemporary record for 1600–31

Venice. Archivio di Stato [ASVen]

Scuole piccole e suffragi:

Busta 31 Anime del Purgatorio. Scuola in Chioggia, at S. Giacomo: 'Libro de Ballottati, 1666–c1718.'

Busta 125/126 Beata Vergine della Concezione. Scuola in S. Francesco della Vigna. (i) Catastico delle Scritture . . . MDCXCIII. Well-bound book, with copies of earlier documents from 1582. (ii) loose-leaf collection of documents.

Busta 296 Convicinato Scuola di S. Marcilian. Riduzione e Parti.

Busta 413 S. Maria e S. Cristoforo dei Mercanti. Parti della Scuola.

Busta 420 S. Maria e S. Cristoforo dei Mercanti. Notariato 1533–57.

Busta 599 S. Orsola. Miscellaneous folders.

Busta 706 SS. Trinità. Notariato. Bound volumes. Libro Primo, 1531–59. Secondo Libro 1560–76.

Santo Uffizio: Processi, Buste 61 and 66.

Provveditore di Comun. Busta 47: Leggi, Testimonianze, 1508–1764. Collection of printed booklets.

Bologna. Biblioteca Comunale [L'Archiginnasio] [BCB]

Fondo Ospedale [F.O.]:

Vol. 6, Statuti e matricole della Compagnia dei Devoti Battuti di S. Maria de la Vita. fourteenth–sixteenth centuries.

vol. 14, 'Libro di partiti della Compagnia di S. Maria della Vita 1554–67' (with later additions until 1589.

vol. 42, 'Statuti ordinationi et provisioni della Compagnia dell' Hospitale de S. M² della Morte nouellamente corette et ampliate et riformate . . . ' 1562, with additions in 1626 and 1725. Contains miniatures.

vol. 43, Memorie riguardanti l'uffizio di Priore dell' Archiconfraternita dell'Ospedale di S. Maria della Morte, vol. i: 1572–1604.

vol. 53, Libro de Morte del anno 1540 al 1563, or Libro dei morti dell'Arciconfraternita di S. Maria della Morte e dei giustiziati da essa assistata. 'Mors omnia vincit', with skull and bones on cover.

vol. 81, Statuti dell'ospedale dei Santi Pietro e Procolo. 1570, with additions.

B PRINTED WORKS

The bibliography lists those works that have been cited in the notes more than once, and those works cited once which have some major importance in that citation, or have had a wider influence on my attitude or approach, even if not cited again for specific information or ideas. In the case of some of the more obscure early printed works that have been hard to trace the library location of the copy used has been indicated to assist other searchers; the following abbreviations have been used:

ASP. Archivio di Stato, Perugia

A.S. Pietro. Archivio di S. Pietro, Perugia

BCB. Biblioteca Comunale, Bologna (L'Archiginnasio)

Bibl. Vat. Biblioteca Vaticana

Bol. Ist. Istituto per le Scienze Religiose, Bologna

Bol. Ist., BAB. Biblioteca Arcivescovile di Bologna; the old section now held by the Istituto

SBF. Archivio del Sodalizio Braccio Fortebraccio, Perugia

AA.VV. (Autori Varii/Various Authors. Using the Italian system, for multi-author works where the editor is not clearly identified.)

'Barocco' Leccese. Arte e ambiente nel Salento da Lepanto a Masaniello, n.p., 1979.

[La] Comunità cristiana fiorentina e toscana nella dialettica religiosa del Cinquecento, Florence, 1980 (Catalogue for an exhibition in the series Firenze e la Toscana dei Medici nell'Europa del Cinquecento)

La Ca' Granda. Cinque secoli di storia e d'arte dell'Ospedale Maggiore di Milano, Milan, 1981

[La] Liguria delle Casacce. Devozione, arte, storia delle confraternite Liguri. Genova, 8 maggio–27 giugno 1982, 2 vols., Genoa, 1982

[Il] Movimento dei Disciplinati nel Settimo Centenario dal suo inizio (Perugia–1260). Convegno internazionale (Perugia 25–28 settembre 1960), Perugia, 1962

Pieve e Parrocchie in Italia nel Basso Medioevo (sec. XII–XV), 2 vols., Rome, 1984

Pittura in Umbria tra il 1480 e il 1540. Premesse e sviluppi nei tempi di Perugino e Raffaello, Milan, 1983

[Il] Primato del Disegno Florence, 1980 (Catalogue for an exhibition in the series Firenze e la Toscana dei Medici nell'Europa del Cinquecento)

Risultati e Prospettive della Ricerca sul Movimento dei Disciplinati. Atti del Convegno Internazionale di Studio, Perugia 5–7 dicembre 1969, Perugia, 1972

San Girolamo Miani a Venezia. Nel V° centenario della nascita, Venice, 1986

Scuole di Arti Mestieri e Devozione a Venezia, Venice, 1981

Storia di Brescia (Treccani degli Alfieri), n.p., vol. 2, 1961: 'Il dominio Veneto 1426–1575'

Storia d'Italia. See below under Storia d'Italia

Storia di Milano (Treccani degli Alfieri), n.p. vol. 10, 1957: 'L'età della Riforma Cattolica (1559–1630)'

Storia di Napoli, 10 vols., Bari, 1975–81; esp. vols. 3 (1976) and 6.1 (1970)

Venezia e la Peste 1348–1797, Venice, 1979; 2nd edn, 1980, used.

Acta Ecclesia Mediolanensis ab eius initiis usque ad nostram aetatem. Opera et studio Presb. Achillis Ratti. Volumen secundum, Milan 1890 (Cited as *AEM*)

Alberigo, G. 'Contributi alla storia delle confraternite dei disciplinati e della spiritualità laicale nei secoli XV e XVI' in AA.VV. *Movimento dei Disciplinati*, pp. 156–256

Angelozzi, G. *Le confraternite laicali. Un'esperienza cristiana tra medioevo e età moderna*, Brescia, 1978

[*Gli*] *Archivi dell' Umbria*, Ministero dell' Interno, Pubblicazioni degli Archivi di Stato, vol. 20, Rome, 1957

Ardu, E. 'Lo statuto cinquecentesco dell'Arciconfraternita dei disciplinati di S. Francesco e di S. Bernardino in Cavaglia' in *Quaderno 5*, Centro di Documentazione sul Movimento dei Disciplinati, Perugia, pp. 37–79

'Risultate e prospettive della ricerca sul movimento dei disciplinati', *Rivista di storia e letteratura religiosa*, 5 (1969), 765–8

Ariès, P. *The Hour of Our Death*, London, 1981

Images of Man and Death, trans. J. Lloyd, Cambridge, Mass., and London, 1985

'Richesse et pauvreté devant la mort' in M. Mollat (ed.), *Etudes sur l'histoire de la pauvreté*, Paris, 1974, vol. 2, pp. 519–33

Arnold, D. *Giovanni Gabrieli and the Music of the Venetian High Renaissance*, London, New York and Melbourne, 1979

'Music at a Venetian Confraternity in the Renaissance', *Acta Musicologica*, 37 (1965), 62–72

'Music at the Scuola di San Rocco', *Music and Letters*, 40 (1959), 229–41

Arsenio D'Ascoli [Padre Cappuccino] *La predicazione dei Cappuccini nel Cinquecento in Italia*, Loreto (Ancona), 1956

Assereto, G. 'Pauperismo e assistenza. Messa a punto di studi recenti', *Archivio Storico Italiano*, 141 (1983), 253–71

Ball. J. 'Poverty, charity and the Greek community', *Studi Veneziani*, 6 (1982), 129–45

Barletta, E.A. (ed.) *Aspetti della Riforma Cattolica e del Concilio di Trento. Mostra documentaria*, Ministero del Interno, Pubblicazioni degli Archivi di Stato, vol. 55, Rome, 1964

Barocchi, P. (ed.) *Trattati d'Arte del Cinquecento*, 3 vols., Bari, 1960–2

Barron, C.M. 'The parish fraternities of medieval London' in C.M. Barron and C. Harper-Bill (eds.), *The Church in Pre-Reformation Society. Essays in Honour of F.R.H. Du Boulay*, Woodbridge, Suffolk and Dover, New Hampshire, 1985, pp. 13–37

Basini, G.L. *L'uomo e il pane. Resorse, consumi e carenze alimentari della popolazione modenese nel cinque e seicento*, Milan, 1970

Sul mercato di Modena tra Cinque e Seicento. Prezzi e salari, Milan, 1974

Baxandall, M. *Painting and Experience in Fifteenth-Century Italy*, London, Oxford and New York, 1972; 1974 paperback edn., used

Becker, M.B. 'Aspects of lay piety in early Renaissance Florence' in C. Trinkaus with H.A. Oberman (eds.), *The Pursuit of Holiness in Late Medieval and Renaissance Religion*, Leiden, 1974, pp. 177–99

Bellarmino, R. *Dell'Arte di Ben Morire*, translated from the Latin, Florence, 1927

Bellettini, A. *La popolazione di Bologna dal secolo xv all'unificazione italiana*, Bologna, 1961

Bellintani, M. *Utili ricordi e remedj per quelle che dalla Giustizia sono condannati alla Morte* [Salò, 1614?] [Bol.Ist., BAB]

Beloch, K.J. *Bevölkerungsgeschichte Italiens*, 3 vols., Berlin, 1937, 1939, 1961

Benassi, V. *Storia di Parma*, vol. 5, '1523–1534', Bologna, 1971 reprint of 1899–1906 edn

Bendiscioli, M. and Marcocchi, M. (eds.) *Riforma Cattolica. Antologia di Documenti*, Rome, 1963

Benincasa, C. *Tractatus de paupertate ac eius privilegiis uberrimus*, Perugia, 1562 [BCP]

Biglieri, C. 'L'ospedale degli esposti di Pavia', *Studi di Storia Ospitaliera*, 3 (1965), 139–55

Black, A. *Guilds and Civil Society in European Political Thought from the Twelfth Century to the Present*, London, 1984

Black C.F. 'The Baglioni as tyrants of Perugia, 1488–1540', *English Historical Review*, 85 (1970), 245–81

'Perugia and papal absolutism in the sixteenth century', *English Historical Review*, 96 (1981), 509–39

'Perugia and post-tridentine church reform', *Journal of Ecclesiastical History*, 35 (1984), 429–51

Blunt, A. *Guide to Baroque Rome*, London, 1982

Boase, T.S.R. *Giorgio Vasari. The Man and the Book*, Bollingen series xxxv 20, Princeton, 1979

Bonadonna Russo, M.T. 'I problemi dell'assistenza pubblica nel Seicento e il tentativo di Mariano Sozzini', *Ricerche per la Storia Religiosa di Roma*, 3 (1979), 255–80

Bonazzi, G. *Storia di Perugia dalle origini al 1860*, 2nd edn, 2 vols., Città di Castello, 1959–60

Borromeo, C. *Instructionum Fabricae et Supellectilis Ecclesiasticae libri duo*, 1577; reprinted in P. Barocchi (ed.), *Trattati d'Arte*, vol. 3, pp. 3–113

Borzacchini, M. 'Il patrimonio della Trinità dei Pellegrini alla fine del Cinquecento', *Ricerche per la Storia Religiosa di Roma*, 5 (1984), 237–60

Bossy, J. *Christianity in the West 1400–1700*, Oxford, 1985

'The Mass as a social institution 1200–1700', *Past and Present*, no. 100 (August 1983), 29–61

Branca, L. 'Pauperismo, assistenza e controllo sociale a Firenze (1621–1632): materiali e ricerche', *Archivio Storico Italiano*, 141 (1983), 421–62

Branca, V. and Ossola, C. *Cultura e società nel Rinascimento tra riforme e manierismi*, Florence, 1984

Braudel, F. *The Mediterranean and the Mediterranean World in the Age of Philip II*, trans. S. Reynolds, from 2nd edn, 2 vols., London and New York, 1972–3

Bressan, E. *L''hospitale' e i poveri. La storiographia sull'assistenza: l'Italia e il 'caso lombardo'*, Milan, 1981 [1982]

Brezzi, P. *Storia degli Anni Santi. Da Bonifacio VIII ai giorni nostri*, Milan, 1975

Brigden, S. 'Religion and social obligation in early sixteenth-century London', *Past and Present*, no. 193 (May 1984), 67–112

Cacciaguerra, B. *Trattato della SS. Comunione*, Venice, 1575 [BCB]

Cagli, C. and Valcanover, F. *L'opera completa di Tiziano*, Milan, 1969

Cairns, C. *Domenico Bollani. Bishop of Brescia. Devotion to Church and State in the Republic of Venice in the Sixteenth Century*, Nieuwkoop, 1976

Cajani, L. 'Gli statuti della Compagnia dei Ciechi, Zoppi e Stroppiati della Visitazione (1698)', *Ricerche per la Storia Religiosa di Roma*, 3 (1979), 281–313

Calace, M. 'Vita religiosa e francescanesimo a Bari nel secolo xvii'; as yet unpublished conference paper, kindly made available to me by the author

Calori, G. *Una iniziativa sociale nella Bologna del '500. L'Opera Mendicanti*, Bologna, 1972

Camporesi, P. 'Cultura popolare e cultura d'élite fra medioevo ed età moderna' in *Storia d'Italia. Annali 4* (1981), pp. 81–157

Il pane selvaggio, Bologna, 1980

Camporesi, P. (ed.) *Il libro dei vagabondi*, Turin, 1973

Caneva, G. 'Contributo allo studio dei Monti frumentari come forma assistenziale e nei rapporti ospedalieri', *Studi di Storia Ospitaliera*, 3 (1965), 199–209

'L'Ospedale della Darsena in Genova', *Studi di Storia Ospitaliera*, 1 (1963), 9–28

Canezza, G. *Gli arcispedali di Roma nella vita cittadina, nella storia e nell'arte. 1: Santo Spirito in Sassia*, Rome, 1933

Canons and Decrees of the Council of Trent, trans. H.J. Schroeder, Rockford, Ill., 1978

Capitoli che devono li Confratelli della compagnia della Santissima Croce di Bologna, ampliate e riformati nuovamente MDCXXXVII, Bologna, 1637 [Bol.Ist., BAB Opp.1215]

Capitula . . . corporis Christi, Rome: Capitula Statuta et Ordinationes, Piae ac Venerabilis Confraternitatis, Sacratissimi Corporis Christi in Ecclesia Minervae Alma Urbis Romae. Romae. Apud Antonium Bladium Impressorum Cameralem. MD.LXI. [BCP: I–I. 1255 (17)]

Caravale, M. and Caracciolo, A. *Lo Stato Pontificio da Martino V a Pio IX, Storia d'Italia*, directed by G. Galasso, vol. 14, Turin, 1978

Casagrande, G. 'Ricerche sulle confraternite delle diocesi di Spoleto e Perugia da "visitationes" cinquecentesche', *Bollettino della Deputazione di Storia Patria per l'Umbria*, 75 (1978), 31–61

Castellaneta, C. and Camesasca, E. *L'opera completa del Perugino*, Milan, 1969

Causa, R. *Opera d'Arte nel Pio Monte della Misericordia a Napoli*, Cava dei Terreni and Naples, 1970

Cavallaro, A. 'Antoniazzo Romano e le confraternite del Quattrocento a Roma', *Ricerche per la Storia Religiosa di Roma*, 5 (1984), 356–60

Cecchini, G. 'La vertenza fra una Confraternita di Disciplinati a Crema e il visitatore apostolico', *Bollettino della Deputazione di Storia Patria per l'Umbria*, 67 (1970), 155–78; and *Quaderni* 10 (1970), Centro di Documentazione sul Movimento dei Disciplinati, Perugia, pp. 3–26

Cerasoli, F. 'Diario di cose romane degli anni 1614, 1615, 1616', *Studi e documenti di storia e diritto*, 15 (1896), 263–301

Chadwick, O. *The Popes and European Revolution*, Oxford, 1981

Chambers, D.S. *The Imperial Age of Venice 1380–1580*, London, 1970

Chaney, E.P. de G. 'Giudizi inglesi su ospedali italiani, 1545–1789' in *Timore e Carità*, pp. 77–101

Chastel, R. *The Sack of Rome, 1527*, trans. B. Archer, Bollingen series xxxv. 26, Princeton, 1983

Cherubini, G. 'Parocco, parrocchiale e popolo nella campagne dell'Italia centro-settentrionale alla fine del Medioevo' in AA.VV. *Pievi e parrocchie*, vol. 1, pp. 351–414

Chiacchella, R. 'Per una storia della parrocchia in Umbria nei secoli XVII e XVIII', *Bollettino della Deputazione di Storia Patria per l'Umbria*, 74 (1977), 54–79

Chiaretti, G. 'Di alcune fraternite laicali di disciplinati dei secoli XV–XVII regolate dalla spiritualità cappuccina', *Bollettino della Deputazione di Storia Patria per l'Umbria*, 65 (1968), 229–60; and published separately, Perugia, 1968

Christian, W.A., jr. *Local Religion in Sixteenth-century Spain*, Princeton, 1981

Ciammitti, L. 'Quanto costa essere normale. La dote nel conservatorio femminile di Santa Maria del Baraccano (1630–1680)', *Quaderni Storici*, 18 (1982), 469–97

Cipolla, C.M. *I pidocchi e il granduca: crisi economica e problemi sanitari nella Firenze del 1600*, Bologna, 1979

Clark, P. (ed.) *The European Crisis of the 1590s*, London, 1985

Clarke, A. and Rylands, P. *Restoring Venice. The Church of the Madonna dell'Orto*, London, 1977

Clementi, F. *Il Carnevale romano nelle cronache contemporanee. 1: Dalle origini al secolo xviii*, 2nd rev. edn, [Rome], 1939

Cochrane, E. (ed.) *The Late Italian Renaissance 1525–1630*, London, 1970

Colangelo, G.A. *La Diocesi di Marsico nei secoli XVI–XVIII*, Rome, 1978

Colombi Ferretti, A. *Dipinti d'altare in età di Controriforma in Romagna 1560–1650. Opere restaurate dalle diocesi di Faenza, Forlì, Cesena e Rimini*, Bologna, 1982

Conciliorum Oecumenicorum Decreta, ed. J. Alberigo et al., 3rd edn, Bologna, 1973 [cited as COD]

Concilium Tridentinum: diariorum, actorum, epistolarum, tractatum nova collectio, 13 vols., Freiburg, 1901–38 [cited as CT]

Coniglio, G. 'Annona e Calmieri a Napoli durante la Dominazione spagnuola. Osservazioni e rilievi', *Archivio Storico per le Provincie Napoletane*, 65 (1940), 105–94
    Aspetti della società meridionale nel secolo XVI, Naples, 1978
    Il viceregno di Napoli nel sec. xvii, Rome, 1955
    'La rivoluzione dei prezzi nella città di Napoli nei secoli XVI e XVII', *Società Italiana di Statistica. Atti della ix riunione scientifica*, Spoleto, 1952, pp. 205–40
Conoscere L'Italia. Enciclopedia dell'Italia antica e moderna, Novara: vol. 18 Umbria, 1982; vol. 21 *Abruzzi-Molise*, 1983
Constantelos, D.J. *Byzantine Philanthropy and Social Welfare*, New Brunswick and New Jersey,1968
Constitutioni della Congregatione o Scuola de' Confortatori della Città di Bologna, Bologna, 1640 [Bol.Ist., BAB]
Constitutioni . . . Madonna della Consolatione, Perugia. Constitutioni et Capitoli Della Venerabile Confraternita della Madonna della Consolatione di Perugia P.S.A. Reformati nell'Anno MDCXII. Perugia. 1613. Nella Stampa Augusta, Appresso Marco Naccarini [ASP: Perugia I.36]
Constitutioni . . . S. Pietro Martire, Perugia: Constitutioni della Ven. Confraternita del Sacratissimo Corpo di Christo et di S. Pietro Martire di Perugia. Reformati. Perugia 1601. [BCP: II–I 108 (4)]
Corsini, C.A. 'Materiali per lo studio della famiglia in Toscana nei secoli XVII–XIX: gli esposti', *Quaderni Storici*, 33 (1976), 998–1052
Coryat, T. *Coryats Crudities*, London, 1611; Scolar Press reprint, London 1978, with an introduction by W.M. Schutte
Costitutioni . . . SS. Agostino, Domenico, Francesco. Perugia. Costitutioni et Capitoli Generali delle Fraternite de S. Agostino, S. Domenico, et S. Francesco di Perugia, reformati dell'Anno 1520 con le Aggiunte et reformatione fatte dell'Anno 1565. Perugia. Andrea Bresciano. 1565. [SBF: S.Agostino no. 489]
Crisci, G. *Il Cammino della Chiesa Salernitana nell'opera dei suoi vescovi (Sec. V–XX)*, 3 vols., Naples and Rome, 1976–80
Crispoldo, T. *Orationi volgari per la confessione et Communione, et per lo tempo della morte, & anco per le Anime de Morti Utili ad essercitar la Fede, & ad impetrare gratia perse, & per altri. Raccolte per M. Tulio Crispoldo da Riete. In Brescia. MDLXVI.* [Bol.Ist., photocopy]
Crispolti, C. *Perugia Augusta descritta da Cesare Crispolti Perugino*, Perugia, 1648; and photographic reprint, Bologna, 1974
Crispolti, G. 'Il Ritiro Ospizio di Santa Valeria a Milano Ospedale d'Isolamento per meretrici sifilitiche', *Studi di Storia Ospitaliera*, 2 (1964), 77–82
Crispolti, G.B. 'Memorie di Perugia dall'anno 1578 al 1586' in A. Fabretti (ed.), *Cronache della Città di Perugia*, 4 (1892), pp. 3–141
Cross, F.L. (ed.) *The Oxford Dictionary of the Christian Church*, Oxford, 1963 edn used
Cutini, C. 'I condannati a morte e l'attività assistenziale della Confraternita della Giustizia di Perugia', *Bollettino della Deputazione di Storia Patria per l'Umbria*, 82 (1985) [1987], 173–86

D'Addario, A. *Aspetti della Controriforma a Firenze*, Ministro del'Interno, Pubblicazioni degli Archivi di Stato, 77, Rome, 1972
D'Ancona, A. (ed.) *Sacre rappresentazioni dei secoli XIV, XV, e XVI*, 3 vols., Florence, 1872
D'Ascoli, Arsenio. See Arsenio D'Ascoli
Davidson, N.S. 'Northern Italy in the 1590s' in P. Clark (ed.), *The European Crisis of the 1590s*, pp. 157–76
    'The Inquisition and the Italian Jews' in S. Haliczer (ed.), *Inquisition and Society in Early Modern Europe*, London and Sydney, 1987, pp. 19–46
Davis, H. 'A Rosary Confraternity Charter of 1579 and the Cardinal of Santa Susanna', *Catholic Historical Review*. 48 (1062). 221–41

Davis, N.Z. 'City women and religious change' in her *Society and Culture in Early Modern France*, London 1975, pp. 65–95 and 321–41 (notes)

    'Gregory Nazianzen in the service of humanist social reform', *Renaissance Quarterly*, 20 (1967), 455–64

    'Some tasks and themes in the study of popular religion' in Trinkaus with Oberman (eds.), *The Pursuit of Holiness*, pp. 307–36

D'Avray, D.L. *The Preaching of the Friars. Sermons diffused from Paris before 1300*, Oxford, 1985

De Angelis, P. [Paolo] *Della limosina overo opere che ci assicurano nel giorno del final giudizio*. Autore L'Abbate Paolo de Angelis. Libri x. Per Giacomo Mascardi. MDCXV. [BCB: 2 CC I 15]

De Angelis, P. [Pietro] *L'Arciconfraternita ospitaliera di Santo Spirito in Saxia*, Rome, 1950

    L'arcispedale di San Giacomo in Augusta, Rome, 1955

De Bartholomeis, V. (ed.) *Laude drammatiche e rappresentazioni sacre*, 3 vols., Florence, 1943

Decreta Dioecesanae Synodi Ravennatis primae a Pietro Aldobrandino . . . Archiepiscopo celebratae Anno MDCVIII. Venetiis, apud Juntas, 1607. [Bol.Ist., BAB]

De Girolamo, A. *Catanzaro e la Riforma Tridentina. Niccolo Orazi (1582–1607)*, Reggio Calabria, 1975

Delaselle, C. 'Les enfants abandonnés à Paris au XVIIIe siècle', *Annales ESC*, 30 (1975), 187–218

Del Re, N. et al. *Roma centro mondiale di vita religiosa e missionaria*, Roma Cristiana, vol. 9, Bologna, 1968

Del Tufo, G.B. *Historia Della Religione de' Padri Chierici Regolari*, Rome, 1609 [BCP: I.D. 1088]

Delumeau, J. *Catholicism between Luther and Voltaire: a new view of the Counter-Reformation*, trans. London, 1977

    L'Italie de Botticelli à Bonaparte, Paris, 1974

    'Une confrérie romaine au xvi siècle. "L'arciconfraternita del SS.mo Crocefisso in S. Marcello"', *Mélanges d'archéologie et d'histoire, 68 (1951), 281–306*

    Vie économique et sociale de Rome dans la seconde moitié du XVIe siècle 2 vols., Paris, 1957–9

De Maio, R. *Bonsignore Cacciaguerra un mistico senese nella Napoli del Cinquecento*, Milan and Naples, 1965

    Riforme e miti nella Chiesa del Cinquecento, Naples, 1973

De Sandre Gasparini, G. 'La confraternita di S. Giovanni Evangelista della Morte in Padova e una "riforma" ispirata dal vescovo Pietro Barozzi (1502)' in *Miscellanea G.-G. Meersseman*, vol. 2, Padua, 1970, pp. 765–815

    Contadini, Chiesa, Confraternita in un paese Veneto di Bonifica. Villa Del Bosco nel Quattrocento, Padua, 1979

Dickens, A.G. *The Counter-Reformation*, London, 1968

Di Mattia Spirito, S. 'Assistenza e carità ai poveri in alcuni statuti di confraternita nei secoli XV–XVI', *Ricerche per la Storia Religiosa di Roma*, 5 (1984), 137–546

Direttorio de' Confortatori nel quale si insegna la pratica di confortare i Condannati alla Morte . . . compilato per uso della Scuola di Conforteria della Ven. Arciconfraternita della Morte di Ferrara, Bologna, 1729 [Bol.Ist. BAB]

Donvito, L. 'Chiesa e società nelle diocesi di Terra di Lavoro a nord del Volturno in età postridentina (1585–1630)', *Archivio Storico di Terra di Lavoro* (Caserta), 6 (1978–9) [1979], 137–260

Donvito, L. and Pellegrino, B. 'L'organisation ecclésiastique au lendemain du Concile de Trente en deux régions du royaume de Naples', *Miscellanea Historiae Ecclesiasticae*, vol. 5, Louvain, 1974: 'Colloque de Varsovie', pp. 213–18

    L'Organizzazione Ecclesiastica degli Abruzzi e Molise e della Basilicata nell'età Postridentina, Archivio dell'Atlante storico Italiano dell'età moderna, Quaderno 2, [Florence], 1973

Doria, G. *Storia di una capitale. Napoli dalle origini al 1860*, Milan and Naples, 1975

Dubini, M. "'Padrone di Niente". Povertà e assistenza a Como tra medioevo ed età moderna' in *Timore e Carità*, pp. 103–20

Duhr, J. 'Confréries', *Dictionnaire du Spiritualité*, vol. 2 (1953), cols. 1469–79

'La confrérie dans la vie d'Eglise', *Revue d'Histoire Ecclésiastique*, 35 (1939), 437–78

Edgerton, S.Y. jnr. 'A little-known "Purpose of Art" in the Italian Renaissance', *Art History*, 2, no. 1 (March 1979), 45–61

Pictures and Punishment. Art and Criminal Prosecution during the Florentine Renaissance, Ithaca and London, 1985

Ellero, G. 'Un ospedale della Riforma Cattolica veneziana. I Derelitti a SS. Giovanni e Paolo', degree thesis, Università degli Studi di Venezia, Facoltà di Lettere e Filosofia, Istituto di Studi Storici, 1980–1

Emiliani, A. (ed.) *Mostra di Federico Barocci (Urbino, 1535–1612). Catalogo critico*, Bologna, 1975

Erba, A. *La Chiesa Sabauda tra Cinquecento e Seicento. Ortodossia tridentina, gallicanesimo savoiardo e assolutismo ducale (1580–1630)*, Rome, 1979

Ermini, G. *Storia dell'Università di Perugia*, rev. edn. 2 vols., Florence, 1971

Esposito Aliano, A. 'Famiglia, mercanzia e libri nel testamento di Andrea Santacroce (1471)' in P. Brezzi (ed.), *Aspetti della vita economica e culturale a Roma nel Quattrocento*, Rome, 1981, pp. 197–227

Eubel, K. et al. *Hierarchia Catholica*, Regensburg, vol. 3 (1910)

Evennett, H.O. *The Spirit of the Counter-Reformation*, Cambridge, 1968

Fabretti, A. (ed.) *Cronache della Città di Perugia*, 5 vols., Turin, 1887–94

Fairchilds, C.C. *Poverty and Charity in Aix-en-Provence 1640–1789*, Baltimore and London, 1976

Fanti, M. *La chiesa e la compagnia dei Poveri in Bologna. Una associazione di mutuo soccorso nella società bolognese fra il cinquecento e seicento*, Bologna, 1977

'La confraternita di S. Maria della Morte e la conforteria dei condannati in Bologna nei secoli xiv e xv', Centro di ricerca e di studio sul Movimento dei Disciplinati, *Quaderni*; 20 (1978), 3–101

'Il "Fondo Ospedali" nella Biblioteca Comunale dell' Archiginnasio. Inventario', *L'Archiginnasio*, 58 (1963), 1–45

L'Ospedale e la Chiesa di S. Maria della Carità, Bologna, 1981

San Procolo. Una parrochia di Bologna, dal Medioevo al età contemporanea, [Bologna], 1983

Fanucci, C. *Trattato di tutte le opere pie dell'alma citta di Roma . . .* , Rome, 1601 [Bibl.Vat.: R.G. Storia V. 3068]

Faralli, G. 'Le missioni dei Gesuiti in Italia (sec. XVI–XVII): problemi di una ricerca in corso', *Bollettino della Società di Studi Valdesi (Société d'Histoire Vaudoise)*, 138 (1975), 97–116

Fasano Guarini, E. (ed.) *Potere e società negli stati regionali italiani fra '500 e '600*, Bologna, 1978

Fasano Guarini, E. (ed.) *Prato storia di una città* (directed by F. Braudel), vol. 2: *Un Microcosmo in movimento (1494–1815)* [Prato], 1986

Fatica, M. 'La reclusione dei poveri a Roma durante il Pontificato di Innocenzo XII (1692–1700)', *Ricerche per la Storia Religiosa di Roma*, 3 (1979), 133–79

Favaro, E. *L'Arte dei pittori in Venezia e i suoi statuti*, Florence, 1975

Febvre, L. *The Problem of Unbelief in the Sixteenth Century. The Religion of Rabelais*, trans. B. Gottlieb, Cambridge, Mass., and London, 1983

Febvre, L. 'The origins of the French Reformation: a badly put question?' in P. Burke (ed.), *A New Kind of History from the Writings of Febvre*, London, 1973, pp. 44–107

Fenlon, D. *Heresy and Obedience in Tridentine Italy. Cardinal Pole and the Counter Reformation*, Cambridge, 1972

Ferrante, L. 'L'onore ritrovato. Donne nella Casa del Socorso di S. Paolo a Bologna (sec. xvi–xvii)', *Quaderni Storici*, 18 (1983), 499–527

Fino, A. 'Chiesa e società nelle diocesi di Terra di Lavoro a sud del Volturno in età postridentina (1585–1630)', *Rivista di Storia della Chiesa in Italia*, 35 (1981), 388–449

Fiorani, L. 'L'esperienza religiosa nelle confraternite romane tra cinque e seicento', *Ricerche per la Storia Religiosa di Roma*, 5 (1984), 155–96

   'Religione e Povertà. Il dibattito sul pauperismo a Roma tra cinque e seicento', *Ricerche per la Storia Religiosa di Roma*, 3 (1979), 43–131

Fiordelisi, A. 'La processione e il carro di Battaglino', *Napoli Nobilissima*, 13 (1904), 33–7, 54–7, 75–8

Fiori, A. 'L'archivio dell' Arciconfraternita della Dottrina Cristiana presso l'Archivio Storico del Vicariato. Inventario', *Ricerche per la Storia Religiosa di Roma*, 2 (1978), 363–423

Firpo, L. 'Esecuzioni capitali in Roma (1567–1671)', AA.VV. *Eresia e Riforma nell'Italia del Cinquecento. Miscellanea*, 1, Florence and Chicago, 1974, pp. 307–42

Flinn, M. *The European Demographic System 1500–1800*, London, 1981

Flynn, M.M. 'Charitable ritual in later medieval and early modern Spain', *Sixteenth Century Journal*, 16, no. 3 (1985), 335–48

Folco, G. *Effetti mirabili de la Limosina et sentenze degne di memoria appartenenti ad essa. Roma, appresso F. Zanetti. 1581* [Bol.Ist., BAB]

Foucault, M. *Discipline and Punish. The Birth of the Prison*, trans. A. Sheridan, Harmondsworth, 1977

Frame, D.M. (ed.) *The Complete Works of Montaigne*, n.p., 1958

Franza, G. *Il Catechismo a Roma dal Concilio di Trento a Pio VI*, Rome, 1958

   Il Catechismo a Roma e l'Arciconfraternita della Dottrina Cristiana, Alba (Cuneo), 1958

Galasso, G. and Russo, C. (eds.) *Per la storia sociale e religiosa del Mezzogiorno d'Italia*, Naples, vol. 1 (1980) and 2 (1982)

Gallotta, V. 'La diocese pugliese fra '500 e '600 ' in V. Garofolo (ed.), *Cultura e Società a Bitonto*, pp. 46–61

Garboli, C. *L'opera completa di Guido Reni*, Milan, 1971

Garofalo, F. *L'ospedale della SS. Trinità dei Pellegrini e dei Convalescenti*, Rome, 1950

Garofalo, V. (ed.) *Cultura e Società a Bitonto nel sec. XVII. Atti del Seminario di Studi. Bitonto, dicembre 1978–maggio 1979. Centro Ricerche di Storia e Arte Bitontina*, Bitonto, 1980

Garzya, G. 'Reclutamento e sacerdotalizzazione del clero secolare della diocesi di Napoli' in Galasso and Russo (eds.), *Per la Storia Sociale e Religiosa*, vol. 2, pp. 81–157

Geremek, B. 'Criminalité, vagabondage, paupérisme: la marginalité à l'aube des temps modernes', *Revue d'histoire moderne et contemporaine*, 21 (1974) 337–75

   'Il pauperismo nell'età preindustriale (sec. XIV–XVIII)' in *Storia d'Italia*, vol. 5 (1): *I Documenti*, (1973), pp. 669–98

   'Renfermement des pauvres en Italie (XIV–XVIIIᵉ siècles). Remarques préliminaires' in *Histoire économique du monde mediterranée 1450–1650. Mélanges en honneur de F. Braudel*, Toulouse, 1973, pp. 205–17

Giacomuzzi, L. *Vita cristiana e pensiero spirituale a Vicenza dal 1400 al 1600*, Rome and Vicenza, 1972

Gigli, G. *Diario Romano (1608–1670)*, ed. G. Ricciotti, Rome, 1958

Giovio, A. *Descrittione de sei Apparati et pompe fatte in Perugia nella Translatione del Corpo di S. Ercolano Vescovo, et Martire, di S. Pietro Abbate, et di S. Bevignate Confessore Perugini: Alli 17 di Maggio 1609. Perugia 1610* [BCP: S.C.R. 38 (1)] [BCP Ms 3288, Anon., 'Storia di Perugia', contains, pp. 116–153, a version of this account, which may be an original draft]

Giulio di Constantino, 'Cronaca' in A. Fabretti (ed.), *Cronache della Città di Perugia*, vol. 4, pp. 145–287

Giuntella, M.C., Proietta Pedetta, L., and Tosti, M. 'Modelli di povero e tipologia di assistenza nell'età moderna in Italia centrale', *Rivista di Storia della Chiesa in Italia*, 38 (1984), 486–98

Glasser, H. *Artists' Contracts of the Early Renaissance*, (DPhil, Columbia University, 1965), New York and London, 1977

Gombrich, E.H. 'Celebrations in Venice of the Holy League and of the Victory of Lepanto' in J. Coutauld (ed.), *Studies in Renaissance and Baroque Art*, London, 1967, pp. 62–8

Gordini, G.D. 'Sinodi diocesani emiliani dal 1563 al 1648 ed il Concilio provinciale di Ravenna del 1568', *Ravennatensia*, vol. 2, pp. 235–73

Gorni, M. and Pellegrini, L. *Un problema di storia sociale, l'infanzia abbandonata in Italia nel secolo XIX*, Florence, 1974

Grégoire, R. '"Servizio dell'anima quanto del corpo" nell'ospedale romano di Santo Spirito (1623)', *Ricerche per la Storia Religiosa di Roma*, 3 (1979), 221–54

Grendi, E. 'Ideologia della carità e società indisciplinata: la costruzione del sistema assistenziale genovese (1470–1670)' in *Timore e Carità*, pp. 59–75

'Morfologia e dinamica della vita associativa urbana. Le confraternite a Genova fra i secoli XVI e XVIII', *Atti della Società Ligure di Storia Patria* 79 (1965), fasc. 2, pp. 239–311

'Pauperismo e albergo dei poveri nella Genova del Seicento', *Rivista Storica Italiana*, 87 (1975), 621–65

Grendler, P.F. 'The schools of Christian Doctrine in sixteenth-century Italy', *Church History*, 53 (1984), 319–31

Greyerz, K. von (ed.) *Religion and Society in Early Modern Europe 1500–1800*, London, 1984

Grohmann, A. *Città e territorio tra medioevo ed età moderna. (Perugia, secc. XIII–XVI)*, 2 vols., plus folder of maps, Perugia, 1981

Perugia, Series: Le Città nella storia d'Italia, Rome and Bari, 1981

Grosso, M. and Mellano, M.F. *La Controriforma nella Arcidiocesi di Torino (1558–1610)*, 3 vols., Vatican City, n.d. [c. 1957]

Guerrini, P. *Atti della visita pastorale del vescovo Domenico Bollani alla Diocesi di Brescia*, 3 vols.: 1 Brescia, 1915; 2 Toscolano, 1936; 3 Brescia, 1940

Guèze, R. 'Confraternite di S. Agostino, S. Francesco e S. Domenico a Perugia' in AA.VV. *Movimento dei Disciplinati*, pp. 597–623

Guida d'Italia del Touring Club Italiano, Milan. Volumes used:
5. *Veneto*, 5th edn. 1969; 6. *Venezia e Dintorni*, 2nd edn, 1969; 10. *Emilia-Romagna*, 5th edn, 1971; 14. *Umbria*, 5th edn. 1966; 16. *Roma e Dintorni*, 6th edn, 1965; 19. *Napoli e Dintorni*, 5th edn, 1976

Gundersheimer, W.L. *Ferrara. The Style of a Renaissance Despotism*, Princeton, 1973

Gutton, J-P. 'Confraternities, *Curés* and Communities in rural areas of the diocese of Lyons under the Ancien Régime' in von Greyerz (ed.), *Religion and Society*, pp. 202–21

Gutton, J-P. *La Société et les pauvres en Europe (XVI siècles)*, [Paris], 1974

Haliczer, S. (ed.) *Inquisition and Society in Early Modern Europe*, London and Sydney, 1987

Hall, M.B. *Renovation and Counter-Reformation. Vasari and Duke Cosimo in Sta Maria Novella and Sta Croce 1565–1577*, Oxford, 1979

Hatfield, R. 'The Compagnia de' Magi', *Journal of the Warburg and Courtauld Institutes*, 33 (1970), 107–61

Hay, D. *The Church in Italy in the Fifteenth Century*, Cambridge, 1977

'The Church in Italy', *Historical Studies*, Papers read before the Irish Conference of Historians, 9 (1974), 99–118

Henderson, J. 'Confraternities and the church in late medieval Florence' in W.J. Sheils and D. Wood (eds.), *Voluntary Religion*, pp. 69–83

'The flagellant movement and flagellant confraternities in central Italy, 1260–1400' in D. Baker (ed.), *Religious Motivation*, Studies in Church History, vol. 15, Oxford, 1978, pp. 147–60

Henneberg, J. von. *L'oratorio dell' Arciconfraternita del Santissimo Crocefisso di San Marcello*, Rome, 1974

Herlihy, D. and Klapisch-Zuber, C. *Tuscans and Their Families. A study of the Florentine Catasto of 1427*, New Haven and London, 1985. (An abridged translation from *Les Toscans et leurs familles*, Paris, 1978)

Heydenreich, L.H. and Lotz, W. *Architecture in Italy 1400–1600*, The Pelican History of Art, Harmondsworth, 1974

Hibbard, H. *Caravaggio*, London, 1983

Hills, P. 'Piety and patronage in Cinquecento Venice: Tintoretto and the Scuole del Sacramento', *Art History*, 6, no. 1 (March 1983), 30–43

Hoffman, P.T. *Church and Community in the Diocese of Lyon, 1500–1789*, New Haven and London, 1984

Horowitz, E. 'A Jewish youth confraternity in seventeenth-century Italy', *Italia. Studi e ricerche sulla storia, la cultura e la letteratura degli Ebrei d'Italia*, (Jerusalem), 5 (nos. 1–2) (1985) 36–74

Housley, N.J. 'Politics and heresy in Italy: anti-heretical crusades, orders and fraternities, 1200–1500', *Journal of Ecclesiastical History*, 33 (1982), 193–208

Howard, D. *Jacopo Sansovino. Architecture and Patronage in Renaissance Venice*, New Haven and London, 1975

Hufton, O.H. *The Poor of Eighteenth-Century France 1750–1789*, paperback edn Oxford, 1979

Huizinga, J. *Homo Ludens: A Study of the Play-Element in Culture*, Boston, 1950

Humphrey, P. and Mackenney, R. 'The Venetian trade guilds as patrons of art in the renaissance', *The Burlington Magazine*, 128 (1986), 317–30

Hutton, E. 'The father of Perugian painting', *The Burlington Magazine*, 7 (1905), 133–8

Ignatieff, M. *The Needs of Strangers*, London, 1984

Jedin, H. and Dolan, J. (eds.) *History of the Church*, vol. 5: *Reformation and Counter Reformation*, by I. Iserloh, J. Clark and H. Jedin, London, 1980

Jordan, W.K. *Philanthropy in England 1480–1660*, London, 1959

Jütte, R. 'Poor relief and social discipline in sixteenth-century Europe', *European Studies Review*, 11 (1981), 25–52

Kelly, J.N.D. *The Oxford Dictionary of the Popes*, Oxford, 1986

Kent, F.W. and Simons, P., with J.C. Eade. (eds.) *Patronage, Art and Society in Renaissance Italy*, Canberra and Oxford, 1987

Kirshner, J. *Pursuing Honor while Avoiding Sin. The Monte delle Doti of Florence*, Milan, 1978; originally in *Studi Senesi*, 89 (1977), 177–258

Klapisch-Zuber, C. *Women, Family, and Ritual in Renaissance Italy*, trans. L.G. Cochrane, Chicago and London, 1985

Ladis, A. 'Antonio Veneziano and the representation of emotions', *Apollo*, 124, no. 295 (September 1986), 154–61

Larner, J. *Italy in the Age of Dante and Petrarch 1216–1380*, London and New York, 1980

La Sorsa, S. *Religiosità popolare pugliese*, Florence. 1962

Laven, P. *Renaissance Italy 1464–1534*, London 1966 and 1971 paperback edn

Le Bras, G. 'Les confréries chrétiennes' in his *Etudes de sociologie religieuse*, vol. 2, Paris, 1956, pp. 423–62

Lefevre, R. 'Don Ferrante Ruiz e la Compagnia dei Poveri Forestieri e Pazzi', *Studi Romani*, 17 (1969), 147–59

Lercaro, G. 'La riforma catechista post-tridentina a Bologna', *Ravennatensia* vol. 2, pp. 11–23

Levey, M. 'Tintoretto and the theme of the miraculous intervention', *Journal of the Royal Society of Arts*, 113 (1965), 707–25

Lewine, M.J. *The Roman Church Interior, 1527–1580*, Columbia University PhD thesis, 1960; University Microfilm International, Ann Arbor, 1963
  'Vignola's church of Sant'Anna de' Palafrenieri in Rome', *The Art Bulletin*, 47 (1965), 199–209

Lis, C. and Soly, H. *Poverty and Capitalism in Pre-Industrial Europe*, Brighton, 1979; paperback edn 1982 used

Livi Bacci, M. *La Société italienne devant les crises de mortalité*, Florence, 1978

Logan, O. *Culture and Society in Venice 1470–1790. The Renaissance and its heritage*, London, 1972

Lombardi, D. 'Poveri a Firenze: programmi e realizzazioni della politica assistenziale dei Medici tra cinque e seicento' in *Timore e Carità*, pp. 165–84

Lopez, P. *Inquisizione Stampa e Censura nel Regno di Napoli tra '500 e '600* [Naples, 1974]
  'Le confraternite laicali in Italia e la Riforma Cattolica', *Rivista di studi salernitani*, 2 (1969), 153–238
    Riforma Cattolica e vita religiosa e culturale a Napoli. Dalla fine del Cinquecento ai primi anni del Settecento, Naples and Rome, n.d. [c. 1965]

Lorenzetti, G. *Venezia e il suo estuario. Guida storico-artistica*, ed. N. Vianello, Trieste, 1985, LINT reprint edn

Lucertini, P. 'La compagnia dei SS. Antonino e Jacopo di Anghiari', *Bollettino della Deputazione di Storia Patria per l'Umbria*, 70, ii (1973), 235–64

Lumbroso, M. and Martini, A. *See under* Maroni Lumbroso, M.

Luther, M. *Luther's Works*, eds. J. Pelikan and H.T. Lehman, 55 vols., published variously Saint-Louis and Philadelphia 1955–75:
  vol. 35 (Philadelphia, 1960), pp. 47–73: 'The Blessed Sacrament of the Holy and true Body of Christ, and the Brotherhoods, 1519'; vol. 44 (Philadelphia, 1962), pp. 21–125: 'Treatise on Good Works, 1520s'; pp. 123–217: 'To the Christian Nobility of the German Nation concerning the reform of the Christian Estate'

Maas, C.W. *The German Community in Renaissance Rome, 1378–1523*, ed. P. Herde, Freiburg, 1981

McClure, R.M. *Coram's Children. The London Foundling Hospital in the Eighteenth Century*, New Haven and London, 1981

Mackenney, R. 'Devotional Confraternities in Renaissance Venice' in Sheils and Wood (eds.), *Voluntary Religion*, pp. 85–96
  'Guilds and guildsmen in sixteenth-century Venice', *Bulletin of the Society for Renaissance Studies*, 2, no. 2 (October 1984), 7–12
  'Trade Guilds and devotional confraternities in the state and society of Venice to 1620', PhD thesis, Cambridge, 1981
    Tradesmen and Traders. The World of the Guilds in Venice and Europe, c. 1250–c. 1650, London and Sydney, 1987

Maggi, S. 'Il vescovo Filippo Sega e gli "Ordini" dell'Ospedale Grande di Piacenza (1585)' in *Studi storici in onore di Emilio Nasalli Rocca*, Piacenza, 1971, pp. 303–13

Magnuson, T. *Rome in the Age of Bernini*, vol. 1: *From the election of Sixtus V to the death of Urban VIII*, Stockholm and New Jersey, 1982

Majarelli, S. and Nicolini, U. *Il Monte dei Poveri di Perugia. Periodo delle origini (1462–1474)*, Perugia, 1962

Male, E. *L'Art religieux après le Concile de Trente*, Paris, 1932

Malvasia, C.C. *The Life of Guido Reni*, translated and introduced C. and R. Enggass, University Park and London, 1980

Mannelli, M.A. 'Istituzione e soppressione degli ospedali minori in Firenze', *Studi di Storia Ospitaliera*, 3 (1965), 171–92

Mansi, J.D. *Sacrorum Conciliorum Nova et Amplissima Collectio . . .*, reprinted Paris and Leipzig, 1901–13, vols. 0–47

Mantese, G. *Memorie storiche della Chiesa Vicentina. Volume Quarto. (Dal 1563 al 1700)*, Vicenza, 1974. [In 2 vols., continuous pagination; vol. 2 has pp. 632–1557]

Maragi, M. *I Cinquecento Anni del Monte di Bologna*, Bologna, 1973 [Limited edn issued by the Banca del Monte di Bologna e Ravenna]

Marchetti, V. *Gruppi ereticali senesi del Cinquecento*, Florence, 1975

Marcocchi, M. *La Riforma Cattolica. Documenti e Testimonianze*, 2 vols., Brescia, 1967–70

Marconi, S.M. *Gallerie dell'Accademia di Venezia. Opere d'Arte dei Secoli XIV e XV*, Rome, 1955
    Gallerie dell'Accademia di Venezia. Opere d'Arte del Secolo XVI, Rome, 1962

Marinelli, O. *La Compagnia di San Tommaso d'Aquino di Perugia*, Rome, 1960
    Le Confraternite di Perugia dalle origini al sec. XIX. Bibliografia delle opere a stampa, Perugia, 1965, with later index vol., n.d.

Maroni Lumbroso, M. and Martini, A. *Le confraternite romane nelle loro chiese*, Rome, 1963

Martin, G. *Roma Sancta (1581). Now revised from the manuscript by George Bruner Parks*, Rome, 1969

Martin, J. 'Popular culture and the shaping of popular heresy in Renaissance Venice' in Haliczer (ed.), *Inquisition and Society*, pp. 115–28

Martz, L. *Poverty and Welfare in Habsburg Spain*, Cambridge, 1983

Maschini Marconi, S. *See under* Marconi, S.M.

Mascia, G. *La Confraternita dei Bianchi della Giustizia a Napoli 'S. Maria Succurre Miseris'*, Naples, 1972

Mastalli, A. 'Parrocchie e chiese della Pieve di Lecco, ai primordi del 1600', *Memorie storiche della Diocesi di Milano*, 2 (1955), 72–125

Mazzoleni, J. (ed.) *Aspetti della Riforma Cattolica e del Concilio di Trento a Napoli. Mostra documentaria*, Naples, 1966

Mazzone, U. and Turchini, A. (eds.) *Le visite pastorali. Analisi di una fonte*, Annali dell'Istituto storico italo-germanico, Quaderno 18, Bologna, 1985

Medri, G. *Ferrara*, Ferrara, 1952

Meersseman, G.G. 'La riforma delle confraternite laicali in Italia prima del Concilio di Trento' in *Problemi di vita religiosa in Italia nel Cinquecento*, Padua, 1960, pp. 17–31
    Ordo Fraternitatis. Confraternite e Pietà dei laici nel medioevo, 3 vols., Rome, 1977

Meloni, P.L. 'Topografia, diffusione e aspetti delle Confraternite dei Disciplinati' in AA.VV. *Risultati e Prospettive*, pp. 15–98

Meneghin, V. 'Due compagnie sul modello di quelle del "Divino Amore" fondate da Francescani a Feltre e a Verona (1499, 1503)', *Archivum Franciscanum Historicum*, 62 (1969), 518–64
    Bernardino da Feltre e i Monti di Pietà, Vicenza, 1974

Midelfort, H.C.E. 'Madness and civilisation in early modern Europe: a reappraisal of Michel Foucault' in B.C. Malament (ed.), *After the Reformation. Essays in honor of J.H. Hexter*, Manchester, 1980, pp. 247–65

Miele, M. 'L'assistenza sociale à Napoli nel Cinquecento e i programmi della compagnia dei Bianchi dello Spirito Santo' in R. Creytens and P. Kunzle (eds.). *Xenia Medii Aevi Historiam Illustrantia Oblata Thomae Kaeppeli O.P.*, vol. 2 (Rome, 1978), pp. 833–62

Milillo, S. 'Società civile e religiosa a Bitonto nella seconda metà del secolo '600 ' in V. Garofolo (ed.), *Cultura e Società a Bitonto*, pp. 29–45

Mira, G. 'Aspetti economici delle confraternite romane', *Ricerche per la Storia Religiosa di Roma*, 5 (1984), 221–35

Miscellanea Historiae Ecclesiaticae, vol. 5, Louvain, 1974: 'Colloque de Varsovie 27–29 Octobre 1971 sur la cartographie et l'histoire socio-religieuse de l'Europe jusqu'à la fin du xviiᵉ siècle'

Misefari, E. *Storia sociale della Calabria*, Milan, 1976

Mode, R.L. 'Adolescent *Confratelli* and the *Cantoria* of Luca della Robbia,' *The Art Bulletin*, 68, no. 1 (March 1986), 67–71

Mollat, M. *Les Pauvres au Moyen Age. Etude sociale* [Paris], 1978; translated as *The Poor in the Middle Ages. An Essay in Social History*, trans. A. Goldhammer, New Haven and London, 1986

Mollat, M. (ed.) *Études sur l'histoire de la pauvreté*, 2 vols., Paris, 1974

Moltedo, D. 'Aspetti dell'applicazione della Controriforma in una diocesi dello Stato Pontificio: Macerata', *Quaderni Storici*, 5 (1970), 814–43

Monachino, V. (ed.) *La Carità cristiana in Roma*, Roma Cristiana vol. 10, Bologna, 1968

Montagu, J. *Alessandro Algardi* 2 vols., London, 1985

Montaigne, Michel Eyquem de. *Montaigne: Travel Journal*, translated with an introduction by D.M. Frame, San Francisco, 1983

Monti, G.M. *Le confraternite medievali dell'alta e media Italia*, 2 vols., Venice, 1927

Monticone, A. 'L'applicazione del Concilio di Trento a Roma, I "Riformatori" e l'Oratorio (1566–1572)', *Rivista di Storia della Chiesa in Italia*, 8 (1954), 23–48

Mostra di Federico Barocci. See Emiliani, A.

Muir, E. *Civic Ritual in Renaissance Venice*, Princeton, 1981

Musella, S. 'Dimensione sociale e prassi associativa di una confraternita napoletana nell'età della Controriforma' in Galasso and Russo (eds.), *Per la storia sociale e religiosa*, vol. 1, pp. 339–438
  'Il Pio Monte della Misericordia e l'assistenza ai 'poveri vergognosi' (1665–1724)' in Galasso and Russo (eds.), *Per la storia sociale e religiosa*, vol. 2, pp. 291–347

Musi, A. 'Pauperismo e pensiero giuridico a Napoli nella prima metà del secolo xvii' in *Timore e Carità*, pp. 259–73

Muto, G. 'Forme e contenuti dell'assistenza nel Mezzogiorno moderno. Il caso di Napoli' in *Timore e Carità*, pp. 237–58

Muzzarelli, M.G. 'Un bilancio storiografico sui Monti di Pietà: 1956–1976', *Rivista di Storia della Chiesa in Italia*, 33 (1979), 165–83

Navarrini, R. and Belfanti, C.M. 'Il problema della povertà nel Ducato di Mantova: aspetti istituzionali e problemi sociali (secoli XIV–XVI)' in *Timore e Carità*, pp. 121–36

Nessi, S. 'La confraternita di S. Girolamo in Perugia', *Miscellanea Francescana*, 67 (1967), 78–115

Newton, E. *Tintoretto*, London, 1952

Niero, A. 'Riforma cattolica e concilio di Trento a Venezia' in Branca and Ossola (eds.). *Cultura e Società*, pp. 77–96

Noto, A. *Gli amici dei poveri di Milano. Sei secoli di lasciati e donativi cronologicamente esposti*, Milan, 1953

Novi Chavarria, E. 'L'attività missionaria dei Gesuiti' in Galasso and Russo (eds.), *Per la storia sociale e religiosa*, vol. 2, pp. 159–85

Oldoini, A. *Athenaeum Augustum in quo Perusinorum scripta publice exponentur*, Perugia, 1678

Olivieri Baldissarri, M. *I 'poveri prigioni'. La confraternita della Santa Croce e della Pietà dei Carcerati a Milano nei secoli XVI–XVIII*, Milan, 1985

Pacelli, V. *Caravaggio: Le Sette Opere di Misericordia*, Salerno, 1984

Pagano, S. 'Gli esposti dell'ospedale di S. Spirito nel primo Ottocento', *Ricerche per la Storia Religiosa di Roma* 3 (1979) 353–92

Paglia, V. 'Le confraternite e i problemi della morte a Roma nel Sei–Settecento', *Ricerche per la Storia Religiosa di Roma*, 5 (1984), 197–220

    La morte confortata. Riti della paura e mentalità religiosa a Roma nell'età moderna, Rome, 1982

    '*La Pietà dei Carcerati': Confraternita e Società dei Carcerati a Roma nei secoli XVI–XVII*, Rome, 1980

    'Vita religiosa nella Confraternita della Pietà dei Carcerati (sec. xvi–xvii)', *Ricerche per la Storia Religiosa di Roma*, 2 (1978)·, 51–96

Painting in Naples 1606–1705 from Caravaggio to Giordano, eds. C. Whitfield and J. Martineau, Royal Academy of Arts Exhibition catalogue, London, 1982

Paleotti, G. *Archiepiscopale Bononiense, sive De Bononiensis Ecclesiae administratione . . . Romae* Zannettiis. *1594* [Bol.Ist., BAB]

    Instruttione . . . Per tutti quelli, che hauranno licenza di Predicare nelle ville, & altri luoghi della Diocese di sua Sig. Illustriss., Bologna, 1586; reprinted 1599 [Bibl.Vat. Ferr. IV.9833]

Pallucchini, R. *La pittura veneziana del Seicento*, 2 vols., Milan, 1981

    Tintoretto a San Rocco, con note storiche di Marco Brunetti, Venice, 1937

Papagno, G. and Romani, M.A. 'Una cittadella e una città (il Castello Nuovo farnesiano di Parma 1589–1597): tensioni sociali e strategie politiche attorno alla costruzione di una fortezza urbana', *Annali dell'Istituto storico italo-germanico in Trento/Jahrbuch des italienisch-deutschen historischen Instituts in Trient*, 8 (1984), 141–209

Papi, M. 'Confraternite ed ordini mendicanti a Firenze. Aspetti di una ricerca quantitativa', *Mélanges de l'Ecole Française de Rome. Temps Modernes*, 89 (1977), 723–32

Partner, P. 'Papal financial policy in the Renaissance and Counter-Reformation', *Past and Present*, no. 88 (August 1980), 18–62

    Renaissance Rome 1500–1559. A Portrait of a Society, Berkeley, Los Angeles and London, 1976

Paschini, P. *Tre ricerche sulla storia della Chiesa nel Cinquecento*, Rome, 1945

Pastor, L. von *History of the Popes*, English translation, 40 vols., London, 1898–1953; *Storia dei Papi*, Italian translation, eds. P. Cenci and A. Mercati, 16 vols., 1910–34, and later reprints

Pastore, A. 'Rapporti familiari e pratica testamentaria nella Bologna del Seicento', *Studi Storici*, 25 (1984), 153–68

    'Strutture assistenziali fra Chiesa e Stati nell'Italia della Controriforma' in *Storia d'Italia. Annali*, vol. 9, pp. 431–65

    'Testamenti in tempo di peste: la pratica notarile a Bologna nel 1630', *Società e Storia*, 16 (1982), 263–97

Pelliccia, G. *La preparazione ed ammissione dei chierici ai santi Ordini nella Roma del secolo xvi*, Rome, 1946

    'Nuove note sulla educazione femminile popolare a Roma nei secoli XVI–XVII', *Istituto di Scienze Storico-Politiche Facoltà di Magistero — Università degli Studi Bari. Quaderni* 1 (1980), 293–346

Pellini, P. *Dell'Historia di Perugia*, vols. 1–2, Venice, 1664; vol. 3, with Introduction by L. Faina, Fonti per la Storia dell'Umbria, Perugia, 1970

Penuti, C. 'Carestie ed epidemie' in A. Berselli, *Storia della Emilia Romagna*, vol. 2, Bologna, 1977, pp. 189–207

Pericoli, M. *Il trionfo della Passione e Resurrezione a Todi nella Pasqua 1563*, Todi, 1963

Petrocchi, M. *Aspirazioni dei contadini nella Perugia dell'ultimo trentennio del Cinquecento ed altri scritti*, Rome, 1972

Peverada, E. 'Note sulle confraternite e luoghi pii a Ferrara dal 1574 al 1611', *Ravennatensia*, 4 (1974), pp. 297–344

Peyronnel Rambaldi, S. *Speranze e crisi nel Cinquecento Modenese*, Milan, 1979

Pietro Angelo di Giovanni, 'Cronaca Perugina inedita', ed. O. Scalvanti, *Bollettino della Deputazione di Storia Patria per L'Umbria*, 9 (1903), 33–380

Pignatti, T. (ed.) *Le Scuole di Venezia*, Milan, 1981

Pignatti, T. and Romanelli, G. (eds.) *Drawings from Venice. Master works from the Museo Correr*, Venice, New York, 1985

Pizzoni, C. 'La Confraternita dell'Annunziata in Perugia' in AA.VV. *Movimento dei Disciplinati*, pp. 146–55

Po-Chia-Hsia, R. 'Civic wills as sources for the study of piety in Muenster, 1530–1618', *Sixteenth Century Journal*, 14, no. 3 (1983), 321–48

Politici, G. (ed.). *See Timore e Carità*

Ponnelle, L. and Bordet, L. *St. Philip Neri and the Roman Society of his Times*, translated and introduced R.F. Kerr, London, 1932; 1979 reprint used

Pontieri, E. 'Sulle origini della Compagnia dei Bianchi della Giustizia in Napoli e su suoi Statuti del 1525', *Campania Sacra*, 3 (1972), 1–60

Posner, D. *Annibale Carracci. A Study in the Reform of Italian Painting around 1590*, 2 vols., London, 1971

Prodi, P. *Il Cardinale Gabriele Paleotti (1522–1597)*, 2 vols., Rome, 1959–67

'Lineamenti dell'Organizzazione diocesana in Bologna durante l'episcopato del card. G. Paleotti (1566–1597)' in AA.VV. *Problemi di vita religiosa in Italia. Convegno di Storia della Chiesa in Italia*, Padua, 1960 pp. 323–94

'Ricerche sulla teorica delle arti figurative nella Riforma Cattolica', *Archivio Italiano per la Storia della Pietà*, 4 (1965), 123–212

Proietti Pedetta, L. 'Alcune note sulla situazione delle confraternite nel Assisi nel periodo post-tridentino (secc. xvi–xvii)' in AA.VV. *Chiesa e Società dal secolo IV ai Nostri Giorni. Studi storici in onore del P. Ilarino da Milano*, Rome, 1979, vol. 2., pp. 457–73

'Le visite apostoliche e pastorali nelle diocesi di Foligno, Assisi ed Orvieto' in AA.VV. *Orientamenti di una regione attraverso i secoli. Scambi, rapporti, influssi storici nella struttura dell'Umbria. Atti del X Convegno di Studi Umbri. Gubbio. 23–26 Maggio 1976*, Perugia, 1978, pp. 543–56

Prosperi, A. 'Il sangue e l'anima. Ricerche sulle Compagnie di Giustizia in Italia', *Quaderni Storici*, 51 (1982), 960–99

'Intellettuali e Chiesa all'inizio dell'età moderna', *Storia d'Italia. Annali*, 4 (1981), pp. 161–252

Tra evangelismo e controriforma: G.M. Giberti (1495–1543), Rome, 1969

Pullan, B.S. 'Abitazione al servizio dei poveri nella Repubblica di Venezia' in G. Gianighian and P. Pavanini, *Dietro i Palazzi. Tre secoli di architettura minore a Venezia 1492–1803*, Venice, 1984, pp. 39–44

'Catholics and the poor in early modern Europe', *Royal Historical Society Transactions*, 26 (1976), 15–34

'Due organizzazioni per il controllo sociale' in N.-E. Vanzan Marchini (ed.), *La Memoria della Salute. Venezia e il suo ospedale dal xvi al xx secolo*, Venice, 1985, pp. 13–24

'The famine in Venice and the new Poor Law 1527–1529', *Bollettino dell'Istituto di Storia della Società e dello Stato Veneziano*, 5–6 (1963–4), 141–202

The Jews of Europe and the Inquisition of Venice, 1550–1670, Oxford, 1983

'Natura e carattere delle Scuole' in T. Pignatti, *Le Scuole di Venezia*, Milan, 1981, pp. 9–26

'The old Catholicism, the new Catholicism and the poor' in *Timore e Carità*, pp. 13–25

'Poveri, mendicanti e vagabondi (secoli XIV–XVII)' in *Storia d'Italia. Annali*, 1 (1978), pp. 981–1047

Rich and Poor in Renaissance Venice. The Social Institutions of a Catholic State, to 1620, Oxford, 1971

'Le Scuole Grandi e la loro opera nel quadro della Controriforma', *Studi Veneziani*, 14 (1976), 83–109

'Wage-earners and the Venetian economy in the 16th and 17th centuries', *The Economic History Review*, 16 (1964); reproduced in his *Crisis and Change*, pp. 146–74

Pullan B.S. (ed.) *Crisis and Change in the Venetian Economy in the Sixteenth and Seventeenth Centuries*, London, 1968

Ranieri, U. *La bella in mano al boia. Una storia inedita di Perugia nel seicento*, Milan, 1965

Rapp, R.T. *Industry and Economic Decline in Seventeenth-Century Venice*, Cambridge, Mass., and London, 1976

Ravennatensia. Centro Studi e Ricerche sulla Antica Provincia Ecclesiastica Ravennate, Cesena: 1 Atti dei Convegni di Cesena e Ravenna (1966–7), 1969; 2 Atti del Convegno di Bologna (1968), 1971; 3 Atti dei Convegni di Piacenza e Modena (1969–70), 1972; 4 Atti del Convegno di Ferrara (1971), 1974; 6 Atti dei Convegni di Faenza e Rimini (1974–5), 1977

Reardon, B.M.G. *Religious Thought in the Reformation*, London and New York, 1981

Ricci, G. 'Naissance du pauvre honteux: entre l'histoire des idées et l'histoire sociale', *Annales ESC*, 38 (1983), 158–77

'Povertà, vergogna e povertà vergognosa', *Società e Storia*, 5 (1979), 305–37

Rienzo, M.G. 'Nobili e attività caritativa a Napoli nell'età moderna. L'esempio dell'Oratorio del SS. Crocefisso dei Cavalieri in S. Paolo Maggiore' in Galasso and Russo, *Per la storia sociale e religiosa*, vol. 2, pp. 251–89

Riis, T. 'I poveri nell'arte italiana (secoli XV–XVIII): in *Timore e Carità*, pp. 45–58

Rinaldi, A.M. 'S. Carlo e la magnifica comunità di Treviglio', *Archivio Storico Lombardo*, 10 (1960), 28–40

Rosa, M. 'Chiesa, idee sui poteri e assistenza in Italia dal Cinque al Settecento', *Società e Storia*, no. 10 (1980), 775–806

'Geografia e storia religiosa per l' "Atlante Storico Italiano"', *Nuova Rivista Storica*, 53 (1969), 1–43. Reprinted in his *Religione e Società nel Mezzogiorno*, pp. 17–74

'Pietà mariana e devozione del Rosario nell'Italia del Cinque e Seicento' in his *Religione e Società*, pp. 217–43

Religione e società nel Mezzogiorno tra Cinque e Seicento, Bari, 1976

'Vita religiosa e pietà eucaristica nella Napoli del Cinquecento' in his *Religione e Società*, pp. 193–216

'Travaux sur les cartes ecclesiastico-religieuses del l' "Atlante Storico Italiano" ' in *Miscellanea Historiae Ecclesiasticae*, vol. 5, 'Colloque de Varsovie', pp. 205–12

Rosa, M. (ed.) *Problemi e ricerche per le Carte Ecclesiastiche dell'Atlante Storico Italiano dell'età moderna. Atti del Convegno di Bari. 3–4 Novembre 1970*, Florence, 1972

Rosa, M. et al. 'Poveri ed emarginati. Un problema religiosa', *Ricerche per la Storia Religiosa di Roma*, 3 (1979), 11–41; text of a discussion

Rosand, M. *Painting in Cinquecento Venice. Titian, Veronese, Tintoretto*, New Haven and London, 1982

Rossi, S. 'La compagnia di San Luca nel Cinquecento e la sua evoluzione in Accademia', *Ricerche per la Storia Religiosa di Roma*, (1984), 367–94

Rouch, M. (ed.) *Storie di vita popolare nelle canzoni di piazza di G.C. Croce. Fame fatica e mascherate nel '500*, Bologna, 1982

Ruggiero, G. *The Boundaries of Eros. Sex Crime and Sexuality in Renaissance Venice*, New York and Oxford, 1985

Ruggiero Pastora, M.G. 'Una "visita" del 1592 al' Ospedale dei "Pazzarelli" di Roma', *Rassegna degli Archivi di Stato*, 1972, 47–67

Rusconi, R. 'Confraternite, compagnie e devozioni' in *Storia d'Italia. Annali*, vol. 9 (1986), pp 469–506

    'Dal pulpito alla confessione. Modelli di comportamento religioso in Italia tra 1470 circa e 1520 circa' in P. Prodi and P. Johanek (eds.), *Strutture ecclesiastiche in Italia e in Germania prima della Riforma*, Bologna, 1984

Russell-Wood, A.J.R. *Fidalgos and Philanthropists. The Santa Casa da Misericórdia of Bahia, 1550–1755*, London, 1968

Russo, C. 'Parrocchie, fabbricerie e comunità nell'area suburbana della diocesi di Napoli (XVI–XVIII secolo)' in Galasso and Russo (eds.), *Per la storia sociale e religiosa*, vol. 2, pp. 9–79

    Chiesa e comunità nella diocesi di Napoli tra Cinque e Settecento, Napoli, 1984

Russo, F. *Storia dell'Archidiocesi di Reggio Calabria*, vol. 2: *Dal Concilio di Trento al 1961*, Naples [1963]

Russo, S. 'Potere pubblico e carità privata. L'assistenza ai poveri a Lucca tra XVI e XVII secolo', *Società e Storia*, 23 (1984), 45–80

Saalman, H. *The Bigallo. The Oratory and Residence of the Compagnia del Bigallo e della Misericordia in Florence*, New York, 1969

Samaritani, A. 'Catechismo, Eucharistia e Tempio nella Comacchio postridentina' with documentary support in 'Fonti inedite sulla riforma cattolico-tridentina a Comacchio' in *Ravennatensia*, vol. 2, pp. 433–66 and 467–547

Santi, F. *Galleria Nazionale dell'Umbria. Dipinti, Sculturi e Oggetti dei secoli XV–XVI*, Rome, 1985

    La Galleria Nazionale dell'Umbria in Perugia, 6th edn, Rome, 1974

    Gonfaloni Umbri del Rinascimento, Perugia, 1976

Santucci, F. 'Gli statuti in volgare trecentesco della confraternita dei Disciplinati di S. Lorenzo in Assisi', *Bollettino della Deputazione di Storia Patria per l'Umbria*, 69, pt. i (1972)

Sanuto, M. *I Diarii*, 58 vols., Venice, 1879–1903

Savelli, R. 'Dalle confraternite allo stato: il sistema assistenziale genovese nel Cinquecento', *Atti della Società Ligure di Storia Patria*, n.s. 24 (1984), 171–216

Sbriziolo, L. *Le confraternite veneziane di devozione. Saggio bibliografico e premesse storiografiche*, Quaderni della Rivista di Storia della Chiesa in Italia, 1, Rome, 1968

    'Per la storia delle confraternite veneziane: dalle deliberazioni miste (1310–1476) del Consiglio dei Dieci. Le Scuole dei battuti' in *Miscellanea G.-G. Meersseman*, vol. 2, Padua, 1970, pp. 715–63

    'Per la storia delle confraternite veneziane: dalle deliberazione miste (1310–1476) del Consiglio dei Dieci. Scolae comunes, artigiane e nazionali', *Atti dell'Istituto Veneto di Scienze, Lettere ed arti*, Anno Accademico CXXX (1967–68), vol. 126, classe di scienze morali, lettere ed arti, Venice, 1968, pp. 405–42

Scaduto, M. 'Carestie in Roma e iniziative assistenziali nella seconda metà del Cinquecento', *Redenzione Umana*, (Rome), 8 (1970), 161–76

    'Iniziative di redenzione sociale nel Cinquecento', *Redenzione Umana*, 5 (1967), 267–82

Scaramucci, L. 'Considerazioni sui statuti e matricoli di Confraternite dei Disciplinati' in AA.VV. *Risultati e Pospettive*, pp. 134–94

Scarpellini, P. *Perugino*, Milan, 1984

Scavizzi, P. 'Considerazioni sull'attività edilizia a Roma nella prima metà del Seicento', *Studi Storici*, 9 (1968), 173–92

Schulz, J. *Venetian Painted Ceilings of the Renaissance*, Berkeley and Los Angeles, 1968

Segni, G.B. *Discorso sopra la carestia e fame*, Ferrara, 1591 [BCB]
[*Trattato sopra la carestia e fame*] Bologna, 1602 [BCB. 17.V.VII.22. Copy, so identified in the catalogue, had frontispiece missing, and is bound in with *Antidotario contro peste di Gio. Antonio Vignati Bolognese*, Bologna, 1630]

Sella, D. *Crisis and Continuity. The Economy of Spanish Lombardy in the Seventeenth Century*, Cambridge, Mass., and London, 1979

Semi, F. *Gli 'Ospizi' di Venezia, Carestia e Assistenza a Venezia*, 1, Venice, 1983

Sen, A. *Poverty and Famines*, Oxford, 1981

Sensi, M. 'Fraternite disciplinate e sacre rappresentazioni a Foligno nel secolo XV', *Bollettino della Deputazione di Storia Patria per l'Umbria*, 71 (1974), 139–217

Serra, A. 'Funzione e finanze delle confraternite romane tra il 1624 e il 1797', *Ricerche per la Storia Religiosa di Roma*, 5 (1984), 261–92

Setton, K.M. *The Papacy and the Levant (1204–1571)*, vols. 3–4: 'The sixteenth century', Memoirs of the American Philosophical Society, vols. 161–2, Philadelphia, 1984 [continuous pagination]

Sheils, W.J. and Wood, D. (eds.) *Voluntary Religion*, Studies in Church History, vol. 23, Oxford, 1986

Siepi, S. *Descrizione Topologico-Istorico della Città di Perugia esposta nell'anno 1822*, 3 vols., Perugia, 1822; and photographic reprint, Perugia, n.d. [1960s]

Simoncelli, P. 'Note sul sistema assistenziale a Roma nel XVI secolo' in *Timore e Carità*, pp. 137–56
'Origini e primi anni di vita dell'Ospedale romano dei poveri mendicanti', *Annuario dell'istituto storico italiano per l'età moderna e contemporanea*, 25–6 (1976), 121–72

Spedicato, M. 'Episcopato, istituzioni ecclesiastiche e vita religiosa a Bitonto nel XVII secolo attraverso le "Relationes ad limina" ' in V. Garofalo (ed.), *Cultura e Società a Bitonto*, pp. 62–94

Sperelli, A. *Della Pretiosita della Limosina. Di Monsignor Alessandro Sperelli Vescovo di Gubbio, E del Collegio de Vescovi assistenti alla Santita di N. Signore . . . In Venetia. Appresso Paolo Baglioni. MDCLXVI* [BCB]

Spicciani, A. 'La povertà involontaria', in D. Maffei and P Nardi (eds), *Atti del simposio internazionale Cateriniano–Bernardiniano . . . 1980*, Siena, 1982

Spini, G. (ed.) *Architettura e politica da Cosimo I a Ferdinando I*, Florence, 1976

Sposato, P. *Aspetti e figure della Riforma Cattolico-Tridentino in Calabria*, Naples, n.d. [c. 1965]

Statuti della Compagnia della Carità de' poveri carcerati Della città di Bologna fatti l'anno di nostra salute 1595 . . . Bologna, [1595] [Bol.Ist., BAB]

Statuti dell'Arciconfraternita di S. Gio. Evangelista della Natione di Bologna eretta in Roma l'anno MDLXXVI, Bologna, 1636 [BCB]

Statuti dell'Opera de Poveri Mendicanti della Città di Bologna. Nuovamente riformati, et ampliati in Bologna Per Alessandro Benacci. MD.LXXIIII. Et ristampati. Per Vittorio Benacci. MDCIII [BCB]

Statuti . . . S. Crocefisso, Roma. Statuti et Ordini della Venerabile Arcicompagnia dell' Santiss. Crocefisso in santo Marcello di Roma. Con l'origine d'essa . . . Romae apud Antonium Bladum Impres. Cam. MDLXV [BCP I–I 1255 (18)]

Statuti ed ordini sopra il governo della Compagnia, o dell'opera chiamata gia lo Spedale di S.M. Del Baracano. E delle Povere Donzelle di detto Luogo, e di S. Gregorio in esso raccolte. Dopo le Riforme degli Anni 1554 e 1647 nuovamente reveduti, e riformate nell'Anno 1739, Bologna, 1740 [BCB]

Statuti per la Congregatione Christiana nella Città et Diocesi di Bologna, Bologna, 1583 [BCB]

Storia d'Italia (Giulio Einaudi editore). Initially 5 vols., Turin, 1972–8, coordinated by R. Romano and C. Vivanti. Especially vols. ii 1–2 (1974), 'Dalla caduta dell'Impero romano al secolo XVIII'; vol. v 1–2 (1973), 'I Documenti'. Subsequent vols. of *Annali*, esp. *Annali*, 1 (1978) 'Dal feudalismo al capitalismo', eds. R. Romano and C. Vivanti; vol. 4 (1981)

'Intellettuali e potere', ed. C. Vivanti; vol. 6 (1983) 'Economia naturale, economia monetaria', eds. R. Romano and U. Tucci; vol. 9 (1986) 'La Chiesa e il potere politico dal Medioevo all'età contemporanea', eds. G. Chittolini and G. Miccoli

Stroppiana, L. *Storia dell'ospedale di S. Maria della Misericordia e S. Nicolo degli Incurabili in Perugia*, Perugia, 1968

Tacchi Venturi, P. 'Il Giubileo del 1575' in *Gli Anni Santi*, Rome, 1933, pp. 67–84

    Storia della Compagnia di Gesù in Italia, vols. 1–2, Rome, 1930–1

Terruggia, A.M. *Attività teatrale a Rieti nei secoli XV e XVI*, Perugia, 1966; reprinted, with index added, from *Bollettino della Deputazione di Storia Patria per l'Umbria*, 62 (1965), 307–55

Tiberio, V. 'L'Oratoria di S. Agostino a Perugia. Appunti per una storia dal XVI al XIX secolo', *Storia dell'Arte*, 38/40 (1980), 291–310, with the plates in a volume separate from the text

Tierney, B. 'The Decretists and the "deserving poor"', *Comparative Studies in Society and History*, 1 (1958), 361–73

Timore e Carità. I Poveri nell'Italia Moderna. Atti del Convegno. Cremona 1980, eds. G. Politi, M. Rosa and F. Della Peruta, Cremona, 1982

Tittarelli, L. 'Gli esposti all'ospedale di S. Maria della Misericordia in Perugia nei secoli XVIII e XIX', *Bollettino della Deputazione di Storia Patria per l'Umbria*, 82 (1985) [1987], 23–130

Tosti, M. 'Poveri, carestia e strutture assistenziali nello Stato della Chiesa: il caso di Perugia (1764–1767)', *Rivista di Storia della Chiesa in Italia*, 37 (1983), 143–72

Townsend, P. *Poverty in the United Kingdom*, Harmondsworth, 1979

Tramontin, S. 'La visita apostolica del 1581 a Venezia', *Studi Veneziani*, 9 (1967), 453–533

Trevor, M. *Apostle of Rome. A Life of Philip Neri 1515–1595*, London, 1966

Trexler, B.J. 'Hospital patients in Florence: San Paolo 1567–68', *Bulletin of the History of Medicine*, 48 (1974), 41–59

Trexler, R.C. 'Charity and defense of urban elites in the Italian Communes' in F.C. Jaher (ed.), *The Rich and Well Born and the Powerful. Elites and Upper Classes in History*, Urbana, Chicago and London, 1973, pp. 64–109

    'Florentine religious experience: the sacred image', *Studies in the Renaissance*, 19 (1972), 7–41

    Public Life in Renaissance Florence, New York and London, 1980

    'Ritual in Florence: adolescence and salvation in the Renaissance' in Trinkaus with Oberman (eds.), *The Pursuit of Holiness*, pp. 200–64

    'The foundlings of Florence, 1395–1455', *History of Childhood Quarterly*, 1 no. 2 (1973), 259–84

    The Spiritual Power. Republican Florence under Interdict, Leiden, 1974

Trinkaus, C. with H.A. Oberman (eds.) *The Pursuit of Holiness in Late Medieval and Renaissance Religion*, Leiden, 1974

Turchini, A. *Clero e fedeli a Rimini in età post-tridentina*, Rome, 1978

Turrini, M. '"Riformare il mondo a vera vita christiana": le scuole di catechismo nell'Italia del Cinquecento', *Annali dell'Istituto storico italo-germanico in Trento* 8 (1982), 407–89

Ughelli, F. *Italia Sacra, sive de episcopis Italiae . . . ed. secunda . . . cura N. Coleti*, Venice, 1717–22; anastatic reprint, 10 vols., Bologna, 1972–4

Urbanelli, C. *Storia dei Cappuccini delle Marche*, 3 vols. in 4, Ancona, 1978–84

Vaes, M. 'Les fondations hospitalières Flamandes à Rome du XVᵉ au XVIIᵉ siècles', *Bulletin de l'Institut historique belge de Rome*, 1 (1919), 161–371

Valeri, B. *La Confraternita dello Spirito Santo di Ferentino. Origine e caratteristiche*, Centro di Ricerca e di Studio sul Movimento dei Disciplinati, Perugia, Quaderno 21, Perugia, 1981

Valeri, E. *La Fraternita dell'Oratorio di S. Maria Della Misericordia in Perugia nei secoli XIII–XVII*, Perugia, 1972

Vannugli, A. 'L'arciconfraternita del SS. Crocefisso e la sua cappella in San Marcello,' *Ricerche per la Storia Religiosa di Roma*, 5 (1984), 429–43

Vanzan Marchini, N-E. (ed.), *La memoria della Salute. Venezia e il suo ospedale dal XVI al XX secolo*, Venice, 1985

Ventura, A. *Nobiltà e popolo nella società veneta del '400 e '500*, Bari, 1964

Ventura, A. (ed.) *Relazioni degli Ambasciatori Veneti al Senato*, Universale Laterza edn, Bari, 1980

Verduccioli, F. *Lo Spedale Grande di S.M. della Misericordia di Perugia. Relatione dell'Abbate Felice Verduccioli, in fine del suo Priorato* . . . Orvieto, 1672 [BCP I.N. 4768 (1)]

Vezza, A. 'Evoluzione socio-religiosa della parrocchia e dei benefici parrocchiali di Pescantina (Verona)', *Sociologia religiosa*, 8 (1964), 61–77

Villari R. *La rivolta antispagnola a Napoli. Le origini (1585–1647)*, Laterza edn. Rome, 1976

Vives, L. *De subventione pauperum*, ed. A. Saitta, Florence, 1973

Vizani, P. *I due ultimi libri delle historie della sua patria*, Bologna, 1608 [BCB. 17 G.V.56 op. 1, bound with P. Vizani, *Dieci Libri Delle Historie della sua Patria*, Bologna, 1602]

Wackernagel, M. *The World of the Florentine Renaissance Artist. Projects and Patrons, Workshop and Art Market*, trans. by A. Luchs, Princeton, 1981

Webb, D.M. 'Penitence and peace-making in city and contado: the "Bianchi" of 1399' in D. Baker (ed.), *The Church in Town and Countryside*, Studies in Church History, vol. 16, Oxford, 1979, pp. 243–56

Weil, M.S. 'The Devotion of the Forty Hours and Roman Baroque illusions', *Journal of the Warburg and Courtauld Institutes*, 37 (1974), 218–48

Weissman, R.F.E. *Ritual Brotherhood in Renaissance Florence*, New York and London, 1982

Weisz, J.S. *Pittura e Misericordia: the Oratory of S. Giovanni Decollato in Rome*, Harvard PhD thesis, 1982; University Microfilms International, Ann Arbor, 1983

Wittkower, R. *Art and Architecture in Italy 1600–1750*. The Pelican History of Art, rev. paperback edn., Harmondsworth, 1973

Woolf, S.J. *The Poor in Western Europe in the Eighteenth and Nineteenth Centuries*, London and New York, 1986

'Problems in the history of pauperism in Italy, 1800–1815' in *Timore e Carità*, pp. 317–29

Wright, A.D. 'Post-tridentine reform in the archdiocese of Milan under the successors of Saint Charles Borromeo, 1584–1631', Oxford DPhil thesis, 1974

The Counter-Reformation. Catholic Europe and the Non-Christian World, London, 1982

Wurthmann, W.B. 'The Scuole Grandi and Venetian Art, *c.* 1260–*c.* 1500', Chicago University PhD thesis, 1975

'The Council of Ten and the "Scuole Grandi" in Early Renaissance Venice', forthcoming in *Studi Veneziani*

Zanetti, D. 'L'approvisionnement de Pavie au XVIᵉ siècle', *Annales ESC, 18* (1963), 44–62

Zardin, D. *Confraternite e vita di pietà nelle campagne lombarde tra Cinquecento e Seicento. La pieve di Parabiago-Legnano*, Milan, 1981

'Confraternite e comunità nelle campagne milanesi fra Cinque e Seicento', *La Scuola Cattolica*, 112 (1984), 698–732

'Le confraternite in Italia settentrionale nell'età moderna e contemporanea. Bilancio storio-grafico e prospettive di ricerca', forthcoming in *Le confraternite in Italia nell'età moderna e contemporanea (secoli XV–XX). Grado 29 sett.–1 ott. 1983*, coordinated by F. Salimbeni

Zino, P.F. *L'Anno Santo MDLXXV* . . . [Venice, 1575]. [Bibl.Vat., Barberini v. xv.49]

INDEX

[Note. The entry for 'confraternities' indexes confraternities and archconfraternities under type or major preoccupation. Undifferentiated references under infrequently mentioned cities and regions include mention of fraternities. In the case of cities and regions frequently mentioned, there are sub-entries for confraternities and their preoccupations or dependent institutions. Individual confraternities and their hospitals or other institutions are only listed separately when there are frequent references to them, or when they provide a major example for a key point in the discussion.]

Printed in the United Kingdom
by Lightning Source UK Ltd.
121237UK00002B/84